RUSSIAN AVANT-GARDE

THEORIES OF ART, ARCHITECTURE AND THE CITY

Vladimir Tatlin, right, beside the newly completed model of his Monument to the Third International in the Mosaics Studio of the former Academy of Arts, Petrograd, 1920

RUSSIAN AVANT-GARDE

THEORIES OF ART, ARCHITECTURE AND THE CITY

CATHERINE COOKE

A.D. ACADEMY EDITIONS

FOREWORD

This is a book about ideas – ideas that came out of a specific period and from specific people, but which still have extraordinary relevance seventy years later.

With that emphasis I have had two simultaneous aims which I hope complement each other. The first has been to offer a readable account of the main features, ideas and individuals of this period in their cultural context for anyone interested in the historical Soviet Union, in Russia more generally, or in twentieth-century arts and architecture. The second has been to create what in both senses of the word is a 'text' book. In the original texts, be they the artists' and architects' own manifestos or descriptions of activities and buildings from the contemporary journals, the voices of the people and time speak with such clarity that they best of all communicate the life out of which the ideas came.

For students and schools in relevant fields, however, I hope this may also be a textbook in the sense of providing the raw material for lecture courses and the starting point for dissertations. By the grouping of pictures as well as the themes of the text I have sought in particular to spotlight some of the individuals here who deserve far more detailed study in their own right.

Whilst the book's organisation is generally chronological, different chapters cut through the material in different ways thematically, with extensive cross referencing to both pictures and text, so that any chapter could be an entry point into the story.

Rather than list further reading in a separate bibliography I have provided the maximum number of leads towards recent English-language literature within the footnotes, where they are closest to the relevant themes.

On the technical matter of transliterating the Cyrillic alphabet I have basically used the Library of Congress system, which is now the most widespread. As Fred Starr remarked in his book on Melnikov, who should be Mel'nikov, odd inverted commas only impede readability for non-Russian speakers. In the main text I too have therefore omitted them, whilst footnotes are accurately transliterated in full.

In publishing material that draws on many years' work it is an opportunity for some acknowledgements and thanks. First, to Lionel March, whose intellectual enthusiasms initially diverted me from architectural practice into these fields. Secondly, to the late Anatole Kopp in Paris and the late Oleg Shvidkovsky in Moscow, without whose coordinated support and personal hospitality in both cities I would then have got nowhere. As Kopp used often to remark, this was 'not a fashionable field' when I started. Thirdly, to my own contemporaries who made it always so pleasurable to penetrate that unlamented Curtain. I must warmly thank Irina Kokkinaki, Andrei Gozak and Leonid Seitkhalilov in Moscow and Boris Kirikov in Leningrad-Petersburg for all the walking and talking we did through some very dark political periods.

In production of the book I have been grateful to two colleagues in the Russian architectural field, Polly Walcot-Stewart and Victor Buchli, for very practical help at a moment when it was needed. And at Academy, to Andrea and Mario Bettella for the pleasure of working with them again.

Catherine Cooke

Published in Great Britain in 1995 by
ACADEMY EDITIONS
an imprint of

ACADEMY GROUP LTD
42 Leinster Gardens, London W2 3AN
Member of the VCH Publishing Group

ISBN: 1 85490 390 X

Printed and bound in the United Kingdom

Contents

Tatlin's assistants building the model of his monument

1: PRECURSORS: RATIONALISM, NATIONALISM AND THE SCHOOLS

Russian architecture of the nineteenth century, just like that of the twentieth, was directly affected by the character of each successive leader. Indeed the impact of tsars was often more direct, because they were culturally relatively sophisticated, and as individuals they were major clients for building. In cultural and philosophical issues, on the other hand, as well as political affairs, Imperial attitudes to Europe were selective and vacillating rather than simply being withdrawn behind ideological walls as in the USSR. Western architectural ideas however were used in a similar way under both regimes, as ammunition in internal debates not for their own content.

In the 1920s, the Western architect who polarised the Soviet profession was Le Corbusier. Fifty years earlier, as the debate between Historicism and Modernism hotted up in tsarist Russia, it was Viollet-le-Duc who played this role, first warmly invited by one professional group as a prestigious international endorsement for their stance, then demonised by others as proof that the outside world 'understands nothing about us'.

In the early eighteenth century, Peter the Great had opened up many aspects of Russia's lifestyle, technology and culture to Western influences In an orthodox Russia that had been entirely by-passed by the Renaissance, Classical architecture was as much one of Peter's conscious imports as European shipbuilding: he commissioned translations of Vignola alongside manuals of navigation. Under his successors, the urban environment across Russia was transformed by a series of Empire-wide programmes using standard patternbooks for a hierarchy of Classical buildings which formed the architectural manifestation of new local government and taxation regimes. Classicism became increasingly seen as 'the modern Russian style' as its symmetries and formality replaced the rambling functional plans and picturesque massing of traditional Russian timber architecture.

During the nineteenth century, as the shape of a future 'modern' Russia became an issue, questions of the proper relationship between traditional Russian culture and this European overlay became central elements of the wideranging philosphical, social and political debate. Under autocratic government, however, such issues could not be openly debated and became subverted into other media such as literature, the arts and architecture. Thus the general evolution of stylistic trends in nineteenth century Russian architecture roughly parallels the familiar European progress through Rationalism and Nationalism to Art Nouveau, but the intentions and content of Russian work were often far more urgently and explicitly political.

Classicism found its highpoint as a national language under Alexander I, with the great state ensembles of Zakharov's Admiralty and Rossi's General Staff Headquarters in St Petersburg reflecting the Imperial self-confidence of the nation that had defeated Napoleon. One dimension of the populist sentiment and realist aesthetics that developed as a reaction to the War was increasingly scholarly research, part anthropological, part aesthetic, into the traditions of Russia's half-forgotten cultural hinterland, exploring peasant artefacts and buildings as embodiments of what is called in Russian their *byt*.

This word *byt* can be roughly translated into English as 'way of life', but the inadequacy of that term reflects the absence of a similar synthetic concept in English culture or in general in Europe. The *byt* is the totality of inter-personal relationships, collective consciousness, spiritual values and their forms of material expression or manifestation. The notion that this holism is an identifiable and internally self-consistent system, and thus a system that could be 'made different' or 'reconstructed' into a *novyi byt* or 'new system for living', was a long-established constant of Russian culture. Issues of the *byt* became increasingly important as a category of debate during the mid-nineteenth century. In the present context, the concept is important because building the new *byt* was one of the central aims of the Bolshevik social programme of the 1920s, and hence of the avant-garde's architectural agenda. *Zhit' po drugomu* – to live in a different way; *perestroika byta* – reconstruction of the way of life; *novyi sotsialisticheskyi byt* – the new socialist lifestyle: these were recurrent phrases of the 1920s which comes straight out of the previous century. When the word *perestroika* became familiar even to Westerners in the late 1980s and early 1990s, it was again accompanied by the hope that some magic wand could effect the desired human and material transformations instantly and effortlessly. The subsequent disillusionment reflects that failure to accrue experience which results from suppressing the objective study of a society's own history.

Growing populism was one dimension of the insecurity felt by Alexander's successor Nicholas I. His court architect Konstantin Ton was commissioned to devise a style that would spread the message of cultural appeasement through a nationwide building programme. The result was the 'Russo-Byzantine' style, where the 'Russo-' element was the overall Classical compositional framework, and the 'Byzantine' element lay in populist, vernacular detailing. The grotesquely large Cathedral of Christ the Saviour just outside the Kremlin in Moscow, built as a belated monument to Russia's defeat of the 'impertinent Frenchman', was the central building of this programme. With exquisite irony it stood for only forty years after final completion before Stalin demolished it in 1931 to build his Palace of Soviets, an equally grotesque monument to the victory of Socialism over capitalism which never rose above foundations [p.205]. It was in the competition for that building that Le Corbusier, as another 'impertinent Frenchman', was finally discredited, along with his architecture and his Soviet supporters, in the final *dénouement* of avant-garde Modernism.

By the mid-ninteenth century, Russia's main centres of architectural theory were the schools. In general the Architecture School of the Imperial Academy of Arts in St Petersburg was a bastion of Classicism, but it had two more radical rivals, the architecture department of the St Petersburg Building College (the *Stroitel'noe uchilishche*, later the Institute of Civil Engineers, IGI), and the Royal College (*Dvortsovoe uchilishche*) down in Moscow. In the 1850s and '60s it was teachers in these two schools, Krasovsky in Petersburg and Bykovsky in Moscow, who laid the foundations in Russia for a Rationalist view of architecture rooted in new the technologies and social tasks.

What is 'rational' ?

As might be expected, the first major statement of opposition to Classicism emerged in Moscow. Mikhail Bykovsky joined the staff of the Royal College in 1831 and became responsible for its programmes and hence for the orientation of design work. Moving amongst free-thinking literary circles in Moscow, which was increasingly a centre of Romantic and populist thought, his contributions to the academic and aesthetic debates in the College became increasingly radical. Having refreshed the design teaching by setting projects not just for many new building types, but for their execution in a whole range of styles ('Gothic', 'English', 'Venetian' and so on) which established the equal validity of Classicism's rivals, he embarked on a parallel reorientation of theoretical debate. In May 1834 he delivered a public paper 'On the unsustainability (*neosnovatel'nost'*) of the view that Greek or Graeco-Roman architecture can be universal and that beauty in architecture is founded upon the five well known Order systems'.

Drawing on Plato, Kant and Hegel, Bykovsky demolished the view that 'being sanctified by time' is of itself any proof of 'truth'.

> *'Any sort of rule or principle that relates to art, regardless of how long it has existed or how fundamental it seems, must be investigable* (issledyvaemyi)*, and when found as a result to be found to be inappropriate or untrue* (nevernyi) *in its very foundations, it must be rejected.'* [1]

Any system of aesthetic rules and norms, he insisted, was historically and culturally conditioned and therefore transient, 'dependent on aims, time and place', on 'the moral force of a given people', rather than universal. 'The architecture of any given people is in the closest degree conjugate with the development of their own philosophy.' 'Christian and pagan, Greek and Scythian' could not possibly have 'identical conceptions of things', and 'the philosophy of one people cannot govern the actions of another.' Thus he demolished Academic authority with the assertion that an architecture of the Orders was 'applicable only to Greek temples.' Where then did the architect's proper territory lie? 'As Russian architects we must not imitate the forms of

A.Zakharov, Admiralty, St.Petersburg, 1806-23

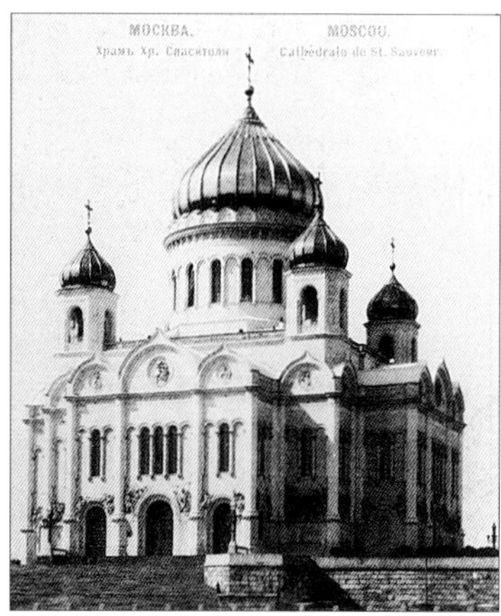

K.Ton, Cathedral of Christ, Moscow, 1832-89

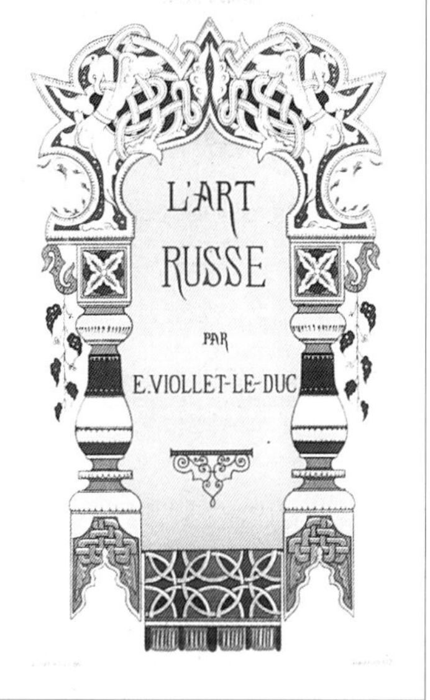

L'Art Russe, *1877: Title page and Viollet's concept of a modern Russian architecture using iron*

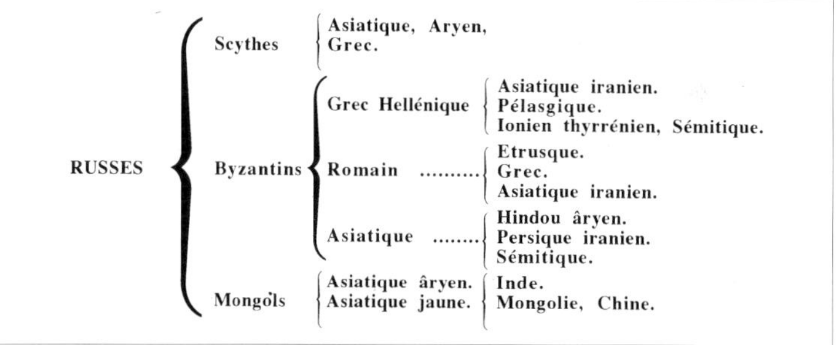

Viollet-le-Duc's diagram of the genealogical derivation of Russian architecture from L'Art Russe

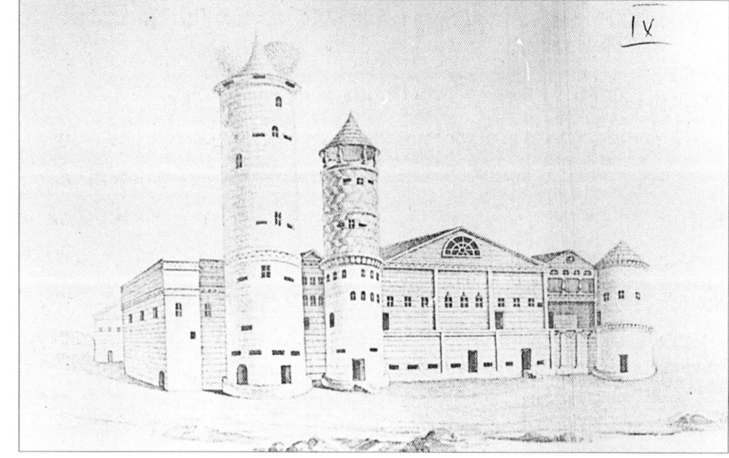

Count Sergei Stroganov, example of 'true Russian architecture', 1565, from his 'Russkoe iskusstvo' E.Violle-le-Diuk i arkhitektura v Rossii ot X-XVIII vek, *St.Petersburg, 1878*

the ancients, but follow their example: we too must have an architecture which is our own, which is national.'[2]

Two years after this radical paper Bykovsky became the school's Director. Whilst he consolidated his freethinking approach in Moscow, Apollinari Krasovsky was the first to produce a clearly argued theoretical position in relation to the new technologies, in the Introduction of his work on building construction called *Civil Architecture*, published in St Petersburg in 1851.

Krasovsky already saw the split inherent in the nature of a positivist or 'rational' approach to architecture. Was it to be based on a technological rationality and science of construction, or on an aesthetic rationality and science of 'form'? Precisely this duality would later lie behind the debates of the two main Modernist groups of the 1920s, with Constructivists adhering most closely to the former, and Rationalists (in their own specific use of the term), adhering to the latter. In 1851, conflict was already brewing:

'Designers of the historicist school offend their anti-historicist contemporaries by refusing to recognise any creativity in them. The anti-historicists accuse them of not understanding that art's purpose is to mirror the contemporaneity that surrounds it. Already those who do see and aspire to the new direction are separating into two camps: the "aesthetic rationalists" and the "technological rationalists". The slogan of the first is "form" and of the second, "construction". The "aesthetic rationalists" see architecture as an art of abstract form, to be composed according to rules that have been established a priori. *The "technological rationalists" approach the problem of form from the other side, and in designing they believe that everything in the parts and the whole must emerge purely in response to utility and construction.'*[3]

Krasovsky's own view of 'the path of architecture' and the designer's approach to creating it was a synthesis of these two. It is effectively the typical nineteenth century Rationalist position that would be taken further by the Constructivists in the 1920s. As he continued in typical voice:

'In our opinion, however, the path of architecture must lie not in the exclusive pursuit of either the beautiful or the utilitarian. The true path of architecture lies between these two. Our slogan is the transformation of one into the other: the transformation of what is functional into something beautiful.'[4]

Thus art followed technology in the design process in linear sequence.

'The main source of architectural form is technology, or construction. Art participates in the creation of this architectural form only by giving an aesthetic finality to the crude forms of technology. ... Observation of this principle gives that quality to the erection which is known as architectural truth.'[5]

This clear embracing of the role of technology as the generator rather than merely a facilitator of architecture became the hallmark of teaching in the Institute of Civil Engineers. It did not preclude engagement with the contextual or symbolising functions of decoration or particular forms, but established their role as secondary to the act of construction. It was not a radical position in either social or aesthetic respects, however. That was Bykovsky's contribution, and became increasingly characteristic of Moscow.

After consolidating a regime of free-thinking in his school, Bykovsky amalgamated it with the equally anti-academic College of Painting and Sculpture in 1865. The resulting Moscow College of Painting, Sculpture and Architecture, MUZhVZ would be a vehicle of free-thinking right through the turn-of-the-century and became part of the Vkhutemas in the 1920s.

In 1867, on the basis of discussion groups held in his own apartment, Bykovsky also founded Russia's first independent architectural association, Moscow Architectural Society, MAO. On its first anniversary he addressed the members with a clear statement of position. He recognised that 'for lack of a tradition of public discussion [in Russia] we know that we cannot operate on a level akin to that of architectural societies in other civilised countries.' Nonetheless, 'as builders for the public ... we cannot avoid our obligations to propagate a healthy understanding of our art.' He reminded them of the anti-canonical approach to design around which the Society had been created:

'Utilising the whole treasurehouse of contemporary civilisation and science, and all its newest inventions, respectfully studying the historical development of our art as manifested in its most glorious monuments, we shall be led by free analysis and our own experience. Our activity will be as far as possible independent of all the prejudices bequeathed to us by tradition. Thus we shall be enabled to work for the achievement of those benefits which architecture can bring to society through the erection of buildings which satisfy the contemporary requirements of life, and answer to local climatic conditions, with solidity, convenience, hygiene and economy.'[6]

'The study of architectural history shows', he said, how 'the original and truly national' is that which 'serves as a complete expression of the way of life (*byt*) and spirit (*dukh*) of its time.' Also, that 'a work of beauty is always characterised by the absence of any falsification or deception (*falsh*). ... This must be the direction of our aspirations.'[7]

Among MAO's many initatives it organised training courses for building foremen and exhibitions to raise the consciousness of architecture in the

A.F. Kokorinov & J-B. Vallen de la Mothe, Imperial St Petersburg Academy of Arts, on the Neva embankment, 1764-88

Mikhail Bykovsky (1801-1885), founder of MUZhVZ and MAO

Apollinari Krasovsky, Civil Architecture*, St. Petersburg, 1851: Title page to volume 2: 'The parts of the building: drawings'.*

general population. To stimulate experimentation in the profession itself the Society pioneered the use of architectural competitions. It was some years before Petersburg saw the formation of a comparable independent professional society. After the 1917 Revolution, when Moscow again became Russia's capital, MAO was inevitably spurned as a bastion of conservatism by the younger avant-garde. In fact, these activities and the public climate they created bequeathed the Soviet profession a radical and socially-oriented tradition.

Viollet-le-Duc: what is 'national'?

Alexander II who succeeded Alexander I in 1857 was a relative liberal. The Emancipation of Serfs over which he presided four years later was a prelude to optimism and considerable social progress. With it went further growth of Populist sentiment and a serious Populist movement. The 1870s were then the highpoint of the freedom movement and of relative free speech in nineteenth century Russia. With this liberty to debate new political agendas went a flowering of debate about 'the Russian style' in architecture that was both documentary and theoretical. Private ethnographic research done as far back as the 1830s finally entered the public domain in a flood of publishing. The year 1872 alone saw the emergence of three major works, including the last volume of *The History of Russian Ornament* by Viktor Butovsky of the Stroganov College of Drawing in Moscow, which trained young people for industry.[8] In the same year, Russia's first architectural journal, *The Architect* (*Zodchii*) was founded in St Petersburg with a strongly Slavophile editor. On the theoretical front, there was increasingly subtle debate over approaches to the generating of 'Russian' form and the epistemological legitimacy of various approaches. In this atmosphere, the complex reactions to Viollet-le-Duc's writing on Russia's own art and architecture are understandable.

Publication of his *Entretiens* was also completed in 1872, and in Russia, as a French-speaking country with close contacts to Paris, the earlier parts had already had significant influence. These substantial writings permeated deep into Rationalist professional traditions in Russia as they did in Europe. By comparison his *L'Art Russe* was trivial, but generated far more noise.

The work originated when Viollet's curiosity was aroused by Russian pavilions at Paris World's Fairs, and he got hold of Butovsky's partwork *Russian Ornament*. A sympathetic review led to Butovsky inviting the Frenchman to collaborate on a joint work. Instead, Viollet assembled albums and texts, put them together with 'some ancient documents on the Far East', and in 1877 he produced an independent text entitled *L'Art Russe. Ses origines, ses éléments constitutifs, son apogée* – and with typical presumption – *son avenir.*[9] His account of the *éléments* was superficial. His vision of the *avenir* was projected through advice to Russians on deriving an iron-based modern architecture from their 'uniquely suited' traditions. All this would have been passed by as charmingly foreign had it not come from an authority respected in Russia for his historical method, but whose account of *origines* was so innaccurate as to undermine his observations and hypotheses.

As a passionate Westerniser, Butovsky had invited Viollet's direct engagement in Russian debates for a purpose. He himself believed that Russia's revived interest in her national artistic traditions was a symptom of growing self-awareness associated with bourgeois progress. It therefore proved how integrally she belonged to the family of Europe. But she could not truly achieve the freedom promised by her technological advance whilst she lived by 'copying ... and borrowing alien forms', either in her products or her architecture.[10] Viollet was co-opted to show how application of his historical method could lead precisely to new indigenous forms.

By concocting a phoney 'genealogy' of Russian architecture out of Asiatic, Mohammedan and even Roman roots, however, Viollet had merely exposed himself to viscious critiques throughout the Russian profession. In the end his work served the cause of Slavophiles more than the Westernisers. To those smarting from Russia's treatment by the 1878 Congress of Berlin, after her victorious war against Turkey, this was further evidence that Europe knew nothing of Russia and should not be allowed to influence her fate. The most important voice was that of F.I. Buslaev who had founded serious art history in Russia on the principle that 'it is firm historical fact that gives basis to both artistic practice and theory.' 'It is small wonder that the French architect, immersed in his professional specialisms' does not understand the historical geography of Slavic culture, wrote Buslaev,

> *'when even the great diplomats of Western Europe, far more versed than him in geography and ethnography, equipped with the most vigilant binoculars, cannot see its boundaries in deciding its fate in Berlin.'*[11]

Viollet's choice of stylistic paradigms in Russia proper was equally contentious. Count Sergei Stroganov, founder of the eponymous College where Butovsky was Museum Director, published his own volume to

The Stroganov College of Applied Arts (formerly of Drawing), Rozhdestvenka St, Moscow, in 1910. Later, 1st Svomas, then part of Vkhutemas, now MArKhI.

Miasnitskaia Street, Moscow, looking south about 1905 from Garden Ring. MUZhVZ building, by Vasily Bazhenov, late 18th century, Classical with corner rotunda middle right. Later 2nd Svomas and then part of Vkhutemas.

'correct' Viollet's sequence with buildings of quite different type. In itself Viollet-le-Duc's intervention was lightweight, but coming from one of such international status, it served to reinforce the Russian profession's scepticism of foreign opinions on where their architecture should be going.

The *Moderne*: a democratic synthesis

After revolutionaries of the People's Will movement assassinated Alexander II in 1881, the reign of his hardline successor Alexander III was one of rigid political discipline and only small democratic concessions. Moscow however was developing a very distinctive social and cultural character. A whole new class of multi-millionaire industrial and banking dynasties had grown from liberated serfs. As a highly principled meritocracy themselves, many adhering to the Quaker-like Old Believer sect, most were virulently hostile to the entire system of rigid social ranks and financial privilege that propped up the autocracy. Those who were politically engaged had a vision of future Russia built essentially in their own image: morally principled at a level profoundly rooted in Russian peasant values, and democraticly based in a mercantile and industrial culture. The architecture which these people commissioned for their new homes and business headquarters in Moscow formed one of the most distinctive examples of a subversive political programme being proclaimed through architecture when its open propagation was thwarted by censorship.

Their main architect was Fedor Shekhtel, trained in MUZhVZ to the extent that he had trained at all, whose conception of a modern *Gesamtkunstwerk* drew on many arts and sources: from medieval Russian to the latest work in Paris, Brussels, Vienna, Glasgow, from Russian Symbolism and the theosophical ideas of Vladimir Solovev. His work was the fullest pre-Revolutionary manifestation of the radical Moscow tradition created by Bykovsky. He wrote no theory but his buildings offered mould-breaking pointers to theoretical ideas of a modern Russian architecture.

These features of it are characterised here through the illustrations. First was the typical Art Nouveau attitude to materials as having distinctive properties and 'ways of behaviour' that should be harnessed and expressed. For his clients, rich on the minerals of Russia, this celebration of material had an almost spiritual dimension. His second mould-breaking contribution was the free plan. Mansions of extreme individuality screamed their hostility to the statist hierarchies of the Classical box whilst also refering to the picturesque functional forms of Russian vernacular building before Classicism. Third, there was the celebration of manufacture and commerce as a cultured activity which Shekhtel projected equally dramatically in their new business headquarters. Fourth, there was a celebration of cleanness, efficient control through technology, that was entirely unlike the casual fatalism historically characteristic of Russia. The houses had advanced ventilation systems and every means to eliminate dust, to provide convenience. The functional planning reflected this in the pastel ceramic finishing of its free forms.

In designing the total art work as mood creator he used Symbolist painters, notably Mikhail Vrubel, and superb artist-craftsmen. After the Revolution his approach to a 'union of the arts' was famously pilloried by Tatlin [Doc.2], but it established that union as part of the Russian agenda.

Serious commentary on this architecture known as the *Moderne* blossomed after the anti-autocratic uprisings of 1905. The most explicit statement of this generation's conception of the function and process of a 'modern' architecture came in that year from a teacher at IGI, Vladimir Apyshkov, in his book *The Rational in the Latest Architecture*. Where Bykovsky's Rationalism had focussed on the topics that must be harnessed to design, Apyshkov returned to Krasovsky's concern with process, explicitly noting the similarities with Otto Wagner's approach in *Moderne Architektur* of 1895. Apyshkov's formulation of the two-stage design process aims for a quality he calls *konstruktivnost'*: constructiveness. Thus

> *'The basic cell of a rational architecture is a form, maybe still crude and unrefined, that satisfies its functional purpose. The architect has then to achieve a further perfection of that form from the aesthetic point of view, not destroying that level of functional suitability which the form already possesses, but merely bringing to it a more refined delineation or underlining its function. Observation of this rule leads to so-called constructiveness of forms and to architectural truth.'* [12]

In the wake of Symbolism, 'the radical basis of the new architecture' had become a dual one. It involved not just 'satisfying the material requirements of a civilised human being' but also satisfying *dukhovnye* ones: the needs of the spirit.' 'Originality' – *samobytnost'*, literally 'the possession of a life of its own' – derived from the design's success in achieving a synthesis of

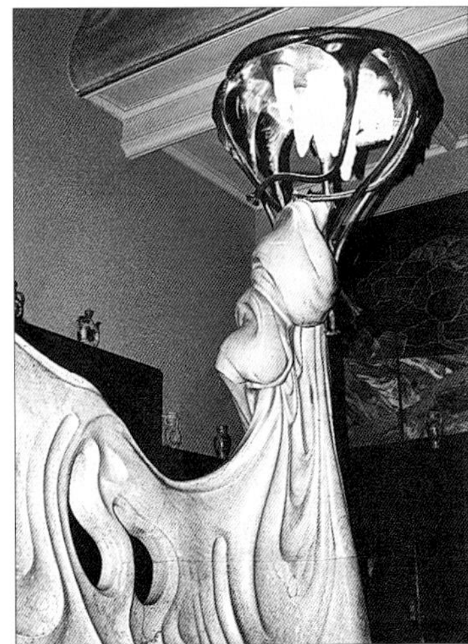

Fedor Shekhtel, Riabushinsky House, Moscow, 1900-2: stair balustrade and lamp

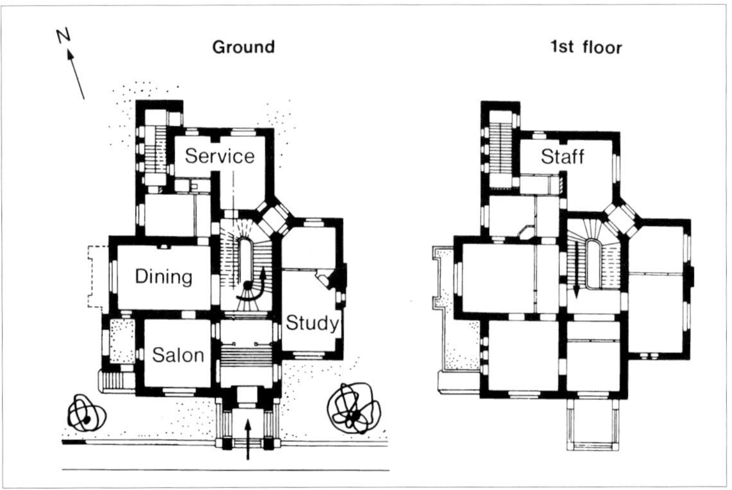

Shekhtel, Riabushinsky house, 1900-2: plans at ground and first floor levels, showing functional planning around central stair, informal relation to street and garden, free form of exterior.

Fedor Shekhtel (1859-1926): photograph of about 1902

the two. In the liberated atmosphere of that year Apyshkov explicitly identified this approach with a 'democratic' political attitude, and even more significantly with an 'aspiration to serve not only the limited circle of of rich people ... but also to serve the poor, bringing light, cheerfulness and warmth to their dwellings.'[13] Such strong social commitment had hitherto been characteristic among doctors and lawyers, but not among aesthetic theorists of architecture.

Models from science and engineering

In Russia's eclectic thought at this time of enormously rapid economic growth and a new liberation, bridges were thrown from one field to another in a manner that was as shocking to European intellectual orthodoxy as it was inherently creative. Between 1905 and the First World War some of the most radical theoretical ideas about architecture emerged from attempts to draw parallels with natural science and engineering.

The Role of Physical Principles in Architecture by Boris Nikolaev, also from IGI, came out in the same year. Influenced by new work in geometry and mechanics, and particularly by crystalographers' studies of relationships between morphology and materials, his was a radical appeal for free-form.

> *'It is time to throw out the dead idea that form can have a canon. Form must be as varied as the endless diversity of conditions that generate it. The only "style" that the designer must pursue is the style of nature, where nothing is superfluous, where everything has meaning and serves the underlying idea. ... Only these principles can create a new architecture that will be a step foward and not a mere marking time.'*[14]

Pavel Strakhov's book *Aesthetic Tasks of Technology* in 1906 ranged over all areas of culture and knowledge but most prescient of avant-garde ideas was his discussion of 'style' in machines which derived from Franz Reuleaux's *Uber den Maschinenbaustil* of 1862. Strakhov distinguished 'dynamic' aspects of a machine which 'adapt its external form to its requirements for movement', and those 'static', loadbearing aspects which constitute 'the machine-building architecture'. Where Reuleaux saw 'beauty' as residing in a machine's forms, Strakhov insisted, as Ginzburg would in 1924 [Chapter 5], that the essential new basis of 'beauty' in the machine is 'the clarity of movements executed by the machine and its parts.'[15]

In the country of Mendeleev, it was chemistry that provided the most powerful model of the factors involved in designing, from the Moscow philosopher and engineer Peter Engelmeier. In public lectures at home and philosophy congresses abroad he deplored the fact that while technology was becoming a central determinant of human life, no-one had yet formulated a philosophical structure to describe and guide the use of it. His book *A Philosophy of Technology* appeared as a popular part-work in Moscow in 1912. The task to which he applied a chemical analogy was essentially that described by Nikolaev, of analysing the 'endless diversity of conditions' that generate the form of an object – here all artefacts, not just buildings.

In Engelmeier's model there were four 'classes of impulse' underlying any 'technological act', or design, and their relationship could be described by analogy with 'that single formula, $C_mH_nO_pN_q$ ... by which the chemist describes any one of the infinite number and diversity of natural bodies.' Where the organic substance in nature comprised differing proportions of carbon, hydrogen, oxygen and nitrogen, the 'technological act' or 'intention' could be seen as comprising certain proportions of 'Truth, Beauty, Good and Utility' (*istina, krasota, dobro* and *pol'za*), and described by the general formula $I = T_mB_nG_pU_q$. 'Unlike in chemistry', as he observed, these components may have negative values, when they would stand for degrees of Falsehood, Ugliness, and moral or physical Harmfulness. When all coefficients m, n, p, q, have the value '+ infinity', the act is 'sublime', and when they have the value '- infinity', it is utterly pernicious. When three of the four coefficients are zero we have the discreet fields out of which design is synthesised, and which by most people, then as now, are far better understood than the synthetic act itself. 'Thus the relations $I = T_m$, $I = B_n$, $I = G_p$, and $I = U_q$', represent respectively 'pure science, pure art, pure ethics with religion, and pure technology in the utilitarian sense.' Another set of 'familiar' cases occurs when one coefficient is extremely large but the rest are still greater than zero. Then 'we have applied science, applied art, applied ethics' – which is effectively politics – 'and applied technologies'.[16] The infinite variety of relationships between these factors could be conceived on the model of chemical valency. This imaginative model meant that factors influencing the form of artefacts had been analysed with unusual breadth in Russia before the task got a political orientation.

In that same year a series of articles was published in the professional

Shekhtel, Offices and showrooms for companies of the Moscow Trading Society, Moscow, 1909: white glazed brick facing, bronze fittings, concrete frame.

Shekhtel, Derozhinskaia's mansion, Moscow, 1902: exterior of stair tower: eau-de-nil *glazed brick, cream stucco, for colour see: Cooke, 'Fedor Shekhtel', in M. Raeburn, ed.,* The Twilight of the Tsars, *London, 1991, pp.43-66.*

Ippolit Monigetti, Maritime Pavilion on Moscow River embankment, for the First Russian Polytechnical Exhibition, 1872: the first prefabricated iron and glass framed building in Russia, modelled on the Crystal Palace. Drawing by E.V. Beggrov, during unpacking of exhibition crates.

High-tech end of the Russian building industry: the Russo-Polish company, Artur Koppel Ltd advertises 'specialities from our factories: iron and steel structures, lift equipment, narrow guage and cable railways', with a photograph of its steel frame for a recent rolling mill. (1912)

Craft end of the industry: I.N. Veidt, St Petersburg, 'executes all types of artistic metalworking and blacksmithing: gates, railings, light-fittings, shop fronts, chapel fit-outs etc'. (1913)

weekly *The Architect* which propounded a similar universality and cultural relativism in specifically architectural terms under the title 'The Beauty of architectural forms: fundamental principles.' Pavel Sokolov's text typically refers backwards on some topics and is prescient of avant-garde discussions on others. Thus Krasovsky's two types of Rationalism are one of his reference points, whilst in discussions of visual 'heaviness' and 'lightness' in different kinds of 'constructive form' he is charting the territory that would be explored by the post-Revolutionary 'aesthetic Rationalists' of the Asnova group who were the Constructivists' main rivals. There are echoes of Apyshkov, but this is no longer the apologia for any particular style. By now Russian architecture was a pluralist battleground of many styles. In Sokolov's discussions the ground was cleared for all parameters of the design task to be assigned entirely new values, and for re-evaluating the connections between them.

> *'The ideal of architectural beauty is just as fluid as all ideals of the human spirit. It cannot be determined once and for all time. The only eternals are the connections between man and nature, and the eternal laws governing the world. It is only knowledge of these connections and these laws that can lead to the supreme results and the fullest success.'*[17]

Thus when building stopped in Russia for the First World War, the range of factors to be considered in design had been defined and the challenge of establishing a proper relationship between them had been clearly placed on the agenda of the Russian profession. The question of form was wide open.

Letting women build

Architectural education was also bubbling and fluid by the eve of the War. The last pre-war Congress of Russian Architects, held in Petersburg in January 1911, showed three issues under urgent debate.

The first was the need for far more specialised training courses for site supervisors and foremen. The craft traditions were superb, but engineering aspects of building were being held back by training '30-40 years out of date'.

The second, equally a symptom of technical progress, was the length and content of architectural training. The problems were those familiar again in the 1990s: when knowledge is exploding, how much should be taught in school and how much learned in practice? Doyen of the profession Ieronim Kitner violently opposed 'the German model' of ever longer formal training. It did not produce people who could learn, he said, but people mentally exhausted, with children and mortgages, who felt they had done enough study to last all their lives. Another speaker focussed on the proper balance between 'acquiring bodies of knowledge' and engagement with the synthetic processes of design itself in the studio. Lengthy discussions ensued.

The third educational issue aired was that of qualifications for women. One determined girl named Rakhel Bernstein who had qualified in Europe raised this issue many would like to ignore: why was full qualification from the best schools of Europe not recognised in Russia when its holder was female? Women who studied law or medicine abroad now had the right to sit Russian professional exams. Why not architects? Rather embarrassed, the session 'gave support to expedite the matter', but behind it lay a long history of women battling for training in this field, and an even longer one for the right of women to enter any form of higher education in Russia.[18]

Successive Russian Education Ministers had been plagued by this question, and women's access to universities had come and gone with the waves of repression and progress. Female students were so often radical supporters of workers' demands that their presence was not regarded as politically neutral when the universities were threatening anti-government unrest. Due to the requirement for talent, rather than just rank or money, the social profile of all art and architecture schools was much wider than for higher education as a whole. Hence the Academy in particular, under Imperial patronage and on the government's doorstep, was a constant and worrying troublespot – even when it only had boys in it. At best, as in the university, women were generally only admitted as *volnoslushately*: literally 'voluntary listeners' attending courses without getting qualifications. In art and architecture of the 1920s women are so pervasive that the novelty of their presence there is not immediately apparent.

Amongst five women at the 1911 Congress were in fact two, Elena Bagaeva and Liusi Molas, who ran their own women's architecture school. It had started in 1905-6 with eleven students, a practice office and hostel. By 1916-17 there were 160 students. They used the Academy curriculum and professors from IGI also taught here. It was recognised that most of the girls were better suited to be assistants than principals, but 'Bagaeva's' was highly praised for its seriousness and open critical atmosphere.

Moscow had pioneered here with architecture classes advertised in 1902 as 'Womens Construction Courses', run by young Ivan Fomin, William Walcot and others in Shekhtel's office premises, but their fate is not clear.

By 1917, women had their own polytechnics in both cities with full five year courses in architecture, structural engineering, chemistry and eletro-mechanics. Not until 1915 however, amidst the social changes brought by the war, had they got statutes from the Ministry and official recognition. That year, when the first three Petrograd architecture students graduated, their diploma examination was remarked upon as the first time Russian students defended their work on the walls for open jury, rather than handing in portfolios to a committee. The equivalent Women's Polytechnic in Moscow was formed in 1916. At last a government decree had permitted women the essential qualification of 'the right to erect buildings', but even as the February 1917 Revolution was under way they were protesting at 'the irregular situation' whereby even the Academy was failing to implement the decree. An end to this anomaly came, with many other practical and educational freedoms, through the Bolshevik Revolution that October.

■

1 M.D. Bykovsky, *Rech' o neosnovatel'nosti mneniia chto arkhitektura grecheskaia i greko-rimskaia ...*, Moscow, 1834, p.3 **2** ibid, pp.5, 10 **3** A.K. Krasovsky *Grazhdanskaia arkhitektura*, StP., 1851, vol.1, p.5 **4** ibid, p.12 **5** ibid, p.27 **6** M.D. Bykovsky, Speech to MAO, 24.11.1866, in *Ezhegodnik MAO*, no.5, 1928, p.9 **7** ibid **8** V.I. Butovsky, *Istoria russkogo ornameta s XI po XVI stol.*, Moscow, 1870-2 **9** Tr., Moscow, 1879, as *Russkoe iskusstvo*. **10** V. Butovsky, *O prilozhenii esteticheckogo obrazovaniia k promyshlennosti*, StP., 1870 **11** F.I. Buslaev, 'Russkoe iskusstvo v otsenke frantsuskogo uchenogo', *Kriticheskoe obozrenie*, 1879, no.2, pp.2-20 **12** V. Apyshkov, *Ratsional'noe v noveishchei arkhitekture*, StP., 1905, p.59 **13** ibid, pp.55, 63 **14** B.N. Nikolaev, *Fizicheskie nachala arkhitekturnykh form*, StP., 1905 **15** P. Strakhov, *Esteticheskye zadachi tekhniki*, Moscow, 1906, pp.97-8 **16** P. Engelmeier, *Filosofiia tekhniki*, Moscow, 1912, vol.3, pp.92-4 **17** P. Sokolov, *Krasota arkhitekturnykh form*, StP., 1912, pp.25-6 **18** *Trudy IV s"ezda Russkikh arkhitektorov*, StP., 1911, pp.568-70; 551-68; 127-8.

Advertisement of January 1903 for the Women's Construction Courses organised by young assistants in Shekhtel's office on Tverskaia Street, Moscow, from catalogue of the exhibition 'Architecture and Design of the New Style'. Director of the Courses was Ivan Fomin [cf.p.80].

ЖЕНСКІЕ

АРХИТЕКТУРНЫЕ КУРСЫ

Е. Ф. БАГАЕВОЙ.

(С.-ПЕТЕРБУРГЪ, Ковенскій переулокъ, № 17).

Состоять въ вѣдѣніи Мин. Нар. Просвѣщ., курсъ 4-лѣтній. Для поступленія требуется аттестать средне-учебнаго заведенія; для лицъ домашн. образов. — экзам. по матем. (ариометикѣ, алгебрѣ и геометріи) въ объемѣ курса женск. гимназій. Прошеніе подается въ совѣтъ курсовъ. Плата на 1 и на 2 курсѣ по 150 р. въ годъ, а на 3 и 4 по 200 р. въ годъ, вносится по полугод. При курсахъ имѣется интернатъ и столовая.

КРАТКАЯ ПРОГРАММА.

Повторительный курсъ элементарной математики, высшая математика, физика, химія, анатомія, теоретическая и строительная механика, начертательная геометрія, теорія тѣней, перспектива, геодезія, строительные матеріалы и работы, строительное искусство, отопленіе и вентиляція, санитарное зодчество, строительное законовѣдѣніе и составленіе смѣтъ, сельскохозяйственная архитектура, исторія искусствъ, рисованіе орнаментовъ, масокъ, фигуръ и живой натуры, архитектурное черченіе (ордена, монументальная и деревянная архитектура), рисованіе образцовъ художественной архитектуры, акварельное рисованіе, композиція орнаментовъ, композиція предметовъ художественной промышленности и внутренняго убранства помѣщеній, композиція архитектурныхъ проектовъ, проекты и разсчеты желѣзныхъ фермъ и сводовъ.

Программы и подробныя свѣдѣнія за 2 семикоп. марки, которыя просять высылать заказнымъ письмомъ.

Advertisement of 1909 for E.F. Bagaeva's Women's Architectural Courses, 17, Kovesnky Lane, St. Petersburg, from the Ezhegodnik (Annual) of the Society of Architect-Artists, *for 1908. 'Four-year courses, approved by the Ministry of Education; middle-school certificate required, or by examination for persons educated at home. 1st and 2nd year fees, 150 rubles a year, 200 rubles for 3rd and 4th years. The school has a hostel and dining rooms. Classes include: maths, physics, anatomy, theoretical mechanics, design of steel girders, theory of perspective, history of art, building materials and site works, sanitary services, heating and ventilating, building law, etc. Prospectus on receipt of two 7-kopek stamps, which please send by registered mail.'*

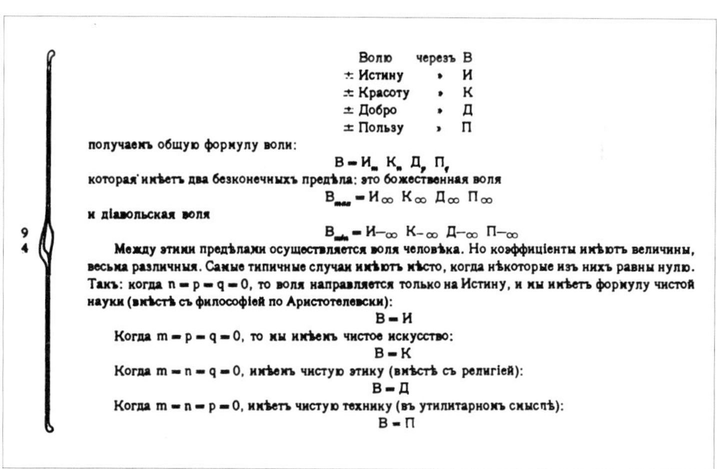

Волю через В
± Истину » И
± Красоту » К
± Добро » Д
± Пользу » П

получаемъ общую формулу воли:

$$В = И_m\ К_n\ Д_p\ П_q$$

которая имѣетъ два безконечныхъ предѣла: это божественная воля

$$В_{max} = И_\infty\ К_\infty\ Д_\infty\ П_\infty$$

и діавольская воля

$$В_{min} = И_{-\infty}\ К_{-\infty}\ Д_{-\infty}\ П_{-\infty}$$

Между этими предѣлами осуществляется воля человѣка. Но коэффиціенты имѣютъ величины, весьма различныя. Самые типичные случаи имѣютъ мѣсто, когда нѣкоторые изъ нихъ равны нулю. Такъ: когда $n = p = q = 0$, то воля направляется только на Истину, и мы имѣетъ формулу чистой науки (вмѣстѣ съ философіей по Аристотелевски):

$$В = И$$

Когда $m = p = q = 0$, то мы имѣемъ чистое искусство:

$$В = К$$

Когда $m = n = q = 0$, имѣемъ чистую этику (вмѣстѣ съ религіей):

$$В = Д$$

Когда $m = n = p = 0$, имѣетъ чистую технику (въ утилитарномъ смыслѣ):

$$В = П$$

Engelmeier's exposition of his analogy between the factors influencing design of an artefact and the structure of a complex organic molecule [see also p.127].

Peter Engelmeier, from frontispiece to his book A Philosophy of Technology, *Moscow 1912, and title page of Part 3: 'Our Life', which includes this discussion.*

2: NEW ARTISTIC FOUNDATIONS

Between 1900 and the outbreak of World War 1, St Petersburg and Moscow were almost as awash with art as Paris, indeed the mix was richer. Everything new from the West was shown or known in Russia as soon as it emerged, be it French and Belgian Symbolism, new work from Scandinavia, the new ideas of Matisse or Picasso in Paris, but it was intermingled with highly original indigenous work and painterly explorations of Russia's own tradition. These were a product of the national rediscovery mentioned in Chapter 1, and were fostered by the arts-and-crafts colonies, first at Abramtsevo near Moscow and later at Talashkino near Smolensk, of millionaire patrons inspired by William Morris. The result, in a generation of extraordinary inherent talent, was an explosion of creative work. Its earlier Symbolist phases in literature and art are known as the Russian Silver Age, and after 1911-12, as the first manifestations of the Modernist avant-garde.[1]

Journals combining artistic and literary ideas were one of the main motors to this explosion, the first of importance being *The World of Art* (*Mir iskusstva*) launched by the opinionated young Petersburg trio Alexander Benois, Sergei Diaghilev and Dmitri Filosofov in 1898.[2] It propagated an eclectic mix of aestheticist views and ran exhibitions. European and Scandinavian material alternated with new Russian work of their own languid kind, alongside such figures of intense originality as Mikhail Vrubel, already mentioned as collaborator of the architect Fedor Shekhtel in Moscow.

Meanwhile new Paris work was being bought and shown by collectors among the 'new rich' Moscow business tycoons, notably Ivan Morozov and Sergei Shchukin who travelled to Paris annually from the mid-1890s to buy from the artists.[3] By regularly opening their private galleries, these two made the new work of Matisse, Picasso, Gauguin more easily and rapidly accessible to young Russian painters than it was outside small circles in Paris.

The change that occurred around 1911-12, like all such sea-changes, came out of such a complex mix of cross-fertilisation and the accidents of individual's thought that it is not by nature a reconstructable narrative. What we see now as key moments of breakthrough are recorded only by the works of art that embody them. One feature of the avant-garde, with its pursuit of theoretical ideas, was a growth of written texts, by which the artists sought to mediate their intentions to colleagues and the public or to define the current problematics of 'art' as a whole. By 1911-12, as we can see looking back at their oeuvres, a number of artists who would emerge as key figures had been experimenting with the recent 'styles' one after another for several years. This is true in varying degrees of all the three artists who would be most important for the future, Vasili Kandinsky and in the younger generation Kazimir Malevich and Vladimir Tatlin. They had tried Impressionism, Cubism, Futurism, in Kandinsky's case various kinds of Expressionism, and in Malevich's, Neo-Primitivism.[4] But a distinct qualitative difference divides them generationally in formal terms.

If we accept the observation Kandinsky would make in his text of 1911, that painting has two resources at its disposal, colour and 'line' which is the boundaries of colour, then line is the repository of 'formal' aspects, i.e. the grammar of shapes.[5] Kandinsky's work of these years moved from one language of form to another to the extent that it is hard to identify it as from a single hand. By contrast the work of Malevich and Tatlin both have extraordinary constancy: Tatlin in intersecting curvilinear forms that become planes, and Malevich in the thrusting solidity of stable squarish forms of extraordinary presence. In both cases there is manifestly one single eye at work whatever the superficial 'style'. In formal terms, by contrast, Kandinsky seems to be floundering. It comes as entirely natural that he, as a lawyer and thus literate, should seek to define verbally what the essence of the current problematic was in those aspects other than form, i.e. of colour itself.

Around 1910 Kandinsky was a one of several Russian artists working in Munich with the Expressionist group Der Blaue Reiter. He contributed art criticism to a range of journals at home notably to one of *World of Art*'s successors, *Apollon*, and exhibited there both in purely Russian shows and as a foreigner. In 1909 he finished the text of a small book of his developing ideas. Though it was hardly more than an extended article he could not get a publisher to accept it in Germany ('obscure ideas' and 'written by an obviously non-native German speaker' were the reasons.)[6] In the interim as Valentine Marcadé has pointed out, some of the ideas in it were already coming out in his journalism, notably in one exhibition review for *Apollon* in 1910 where he asks, at the end, whether all this describing the 'things' of the world around us in so many different ways, in this style and that, is actually what 'art' is or ought to be about.[7] Is it not about something quite different: feelings that the images merely serve to arouse? And how exactly are those effects actually created and transmitted in painting? Can the tools be better analysed in order to use them more effectively?

Eventually a publisher took on the little book, and *Über das Geistige in der Kunst* appeared in December 1911, rapidly selling out three editions.

Kandinsky's Congress paper

The role of great professional congresses as catalysts and disseminators of ideas in late nineteenth and early twentieth centuries is hard to imagine now when other means of communication have supplanted them. To most artists even then they would have been anathema, but in Russia geography so divided the professional community that from late December 1911 to early January 1912, nearly a thousand people assembled in Petersburg for the All-Russian Congress of Artists held in the Academy, two hundred more than had come to the architects' congress a year earlier discussed in Chapter 1.

Among two hundred papers given at the Congress, Kandinsky's colleague Nikolai Kulbin gave a resumé of his book. It provoked such interest that a full reading and discussion was arranged for New Year's Eve. On 12 February another colleague, David Burliuk, gave a similar reading at the Polytechnical Museum in Moscow to coincide with an exhibition where Kandinsky was showing.[8] Only in 1914 was a text published, cut for Congress proceedings,[9] but long before that its content was well known in the artistic community.

It is a rambling paper largely devoted to concepts of colour 'polarity' and colour association, and to the synesthetic cross-stimulae or parallels between colour and musical sensations. This material has a certain interest as a document of its time, notably reflecting Kandinsky's interest in Schönberg, but most of its propositions were long ago overtaken by more sophisticated and scientific work. The parts on 'meanings' of specific hues, notably of black and white, and on whether form and colour are related or independent variables, served as important stimuli to young Malevich and Rodchenko. More important and I am sure more widely resonant at the time were the larger questions it threw up incidentally as challenges for next generation.

When 'the strong hand of Nietzsche' was legitimating fundamental probings it was inevitable that vocabulary was being stretched. Many of Kandinsky's discussions are also convoluted, even in his native language. This has led to two problems in the historical transmission of these ideas through translation.[10] Firstly, the texts have been much cut. Secondly, key words have been rendered by synonyms that are inexact (sometimes through semantic limitations of English), but are different from those used by other translators of other artists' texts. Continuity of the original discourse is thus broken.

Thus at the simplest semantic level, the key words 'spiritual' (*dukhovnyi*) and 'feeling' (*oshchushchenie*) are respectively less specifically religious and emotional terms than in English. For the latter I prefer 'sensation': a message received by one of the senses. Greater disruption comes from the more subtle problems. In the case of Malevich and Kandinsky, for example, once Kandinsky's terms *predmetnyi* ('having a subject matter') and *materialnyi* (relating to the material world), have both been rendered as 'material' in contrast to 'abstract', all connection with Malevich's *bezpredmetnyi* ('having no subject', always confusing rendered in English as 'non-objective') has got lost. Part of this results from an absence of conceptual vocabulary in English (cf. my discussion of *konstruktsiia* in Chapter 5). Other distortions occur in the pursuit of friendly, Western-sounding prose, as for example when the Dane on whom we gratefully depend for access to certain Malevich texts renders the often wild process of '*formobrazovanie*' (giving some 'shape' to that *bezobrazie* or 'imagelessness' which is chaos), by the homely 'design'.[11]

Tatlin, 1914: the work he saw as the purest embodiment of his 'counter-relief' concept. Cf.p.103.
Malevich's room at 'Zero-Ten' (0.10), December 1915, with Black Square *in the 'icon corner'.*

I stress this language issue to convey the cultural gulf across which some ideas from the avant-garde have to leap. And to indicate, optimistically, to future researchers how conceptually rich this material is in its own language.

With the artistic material of this date it would be another gross distortion to trace trains of thought too neatly from one to another across the ferment. However, in comparing Kandinsky's full Russian text with Sadler's English translation made in 1914, (from the German of someone 'obviously not at home in the language'!) it is clear that far more of the themes pursued by the younger avant-garde were there as problems and challenges thrown out, if unwittingly, in Kandinsky's text, than has previously appeared. In Document 1 I have translated three previously mangled or deleted passages which may have helped stimulate thought on the problematics, respectively, of whether there can be an abstract 'art' at all; restoring three-dimensionality to the 'picture'; the nature of the 'constructive' and of a 'construction'. Kandinsky treats these two throughout as attributes of and means to 'composition', where as Chapter 4 shows, the young artists of Inkhuk who inherited a programme from him in the early Twenties decided they were opposites.

Tatlin and Malevich

Activity never slackened on Russian exhibition circuits during the War. Two young artists, Malevich and Tatlin, took off from the general platform of late Cubist work in entirely new directions. Stimulae acknowledged by both included, in different ways, Moscow's vast icon exhibition of 1913. Tatlin recounted how the richly three-dimensional icon 'masks', or *oklady*, of precious metals and stones were what caused him 'to drill his boards, mount metal rings on them'.[12] His visit to Picasso in Paris was also crucial as he was now making reliefs, though they still had 'subjects', and Tatlin would soon move beyond that (as Kandinsky had asked: are 'subjects' what art is about?). Like Kandinsky, Malevich pursued Theosophy. His break into abstraction was a set for the Futurist opera *Victory over the Sun* in 1913.

By the first year of the War, 1914-15, these two artists who would dominate the whole avant-garde had both made that breakthrough in their formal language which would set the agenda for everything that followed. At a series of exhibitions during 1915 and 1916, their new work left colleagues stunned, sometimes favourably, sometimes in disgust. When Tatlin came to hang a board with some nails in it at a show of 'Moscow artists for the War wounded' in December 1914, instead of the theatre designs that had been invited, colleagues insisted it should stay.[13] To 'Zero-Ten' in Petrograd a year later, Malevich brought a black square and hung it in high across his corner of the room as the most sacred icon would be in the 'icon corner' of a Russian home, and Benois' accusation of 'blasphemy' was merely the most violent attack of many.[14] The work of these two became, as Vasili Rakitin has put it, 'the most important stimulae in the self-determination of the other avant-garde artists. ... In order to clarify their own tasks, it was important that artists define themselves in relation to these new concepts.'[15] Equally important was the independence they brought to Russian art as a whole. As Rakitin continues, 'Tatlin's reliefs and Malevich's Black Square introduced a new artistic yardstick. Competition with the Paris school, which had been the main engine in the evolution of new Russian art around 1910, had now lost its meaning.' Tatlin produced a pamphlet illustrating his reliefs in 1915.[16] Malevich gave a polemic legitimation of his work in a booklet called *From Cubism and Futurism to Suprematism: the New Painterly Realism*.[17] More graphically, he wrote in letters to his friend Mikhail Matiushin of how his painting had now 'abandoned the earth' to pursue an 'aspiration towards space that is deep in man's consciousness'.[18]

■

1 C. Gray, ***The Great Experiment***, London 1962 /*The Russian Experiment in Art*, London 1971; J. Bowlt, *The Silver Age*, Newtonville, 1979; I. Paperno & J. Grossman, *Creating Life*, Stanford, 1994 **2** N. Lapshina, *Mir Iskusstva*, Moscow, 1977; Bowlt, *Silver Age*. 3 B.W. Kean, *All the Empty Palaces*, London, 1983; N. Dumova, *Moskovskie metsenaty* (Moscow Patrons), Moscow, 1992 **3** H.K. Roethel, *Kandinsky*, NY 1979; C. Derouet & J. Boissel, eds., *Kandinsky*, Paris, 1985; L. Zhadova, *Malevich*, London, 1982; W. Beeren & J. Joosten, eds., *Malevich*, Amsterdam-Leningrad, 1988; L. Zhadova, ed., *Tatlin*, London, 1988; A. Strigalev & J. Harten, *Tatlin*, Cologne, 1994 **5** W. Kandinsky, M. Sadler, tr., *Concerning the Spiritual in Art*, NY, 1977, pp.28-9 **6** Derouet etc, *Kandinsky*, p.72 **7** V. Marcadé, *Le Renouveau de l'Art Pictural Russe*, Paris, 1971, pp.149-52 **8** Marcadé, *Renouveau*, p.153; Derouet etc, *Kandinsky*, p.72 **9** *Trudy Vserossiskogo s"ezda khudozhnikov*, Petrograd, 1914, vol.1, pp.47-76 **10** Originally, M. Sadler, tr., *The Art of Spiritual Harmony*, London, 1914, later as n.5; full Russian text, *O dukhovnom v iskusstve*, NY, 1967; Moscow, 1992 **11** T. Andersen, ed., *K.S. Malevich, Essays on Art*, Copenhagen-London, 1968-9 **12** M. Reading, P. Coe, *Lubetkin and Tecton*, London, 1993, p.126 **13** V. Rakitin, 'Artisan and Prophet', in A. Calnek, ed., *The Great Utopia*, NY, 1992, pp.25-37 **14** J. Sharp, 'Critical reception of 0.10', in ibid, pp.38-52 **15** Rakitin, 'Artisan', p.26 **16** *V.E. Tatlin*, Petrograd, 1915 **17** *Ot kubizma i futurizma k suprematizmu. Novyi zhivopis'nyi realizm*, Moscow, 1916 (three editions had slightly differing titles). Full text in J. Bowlt, ed., *Russian Art of the Avant-Garde*, NY, 1976, pp.116-35 **18** E. Kovtun, 'K.S. Malevich. Pis'ma k M.V. Matiushinu', *Ezhegodnik Pushkinskogo doma*, 1974, Leningrad, 1976, pp.177-94; cf. Zhadova, *Malevich*, p.122.

Doc. 1

VASILI KANDINSKY ON THE SPIRITUAL IN ART, Munich-St Petersburg, 1911

FROM CHAPTER VI: COLOUR AND FORM

For all the diversity which form may adopt, it can never break through two external limits: either it aims through the act of delimiting to distinguish a certain material subject from the plane, or the form remains abstract (*abstraktnoi*), in that it does not signify any real subject matter, but is a purely abstract being. The square, circle, triangle, rhombus, trapezium are such purely abstract beings which have their own life, their influence and their activity, as are countless other forms too complex for mathematical description. All these forms are citizens with equal rights in the kingdom of the abstract. ...

In our time the artist cannot manage just with purely abstract forms. They are too imprecise for him. To limit himself only to the imprecise would mean to exclude many possibilities, to exclude what is purely human and reduce his means of expression to poverty. **Abandonment of subject-matter** and exclusion of the third dimension ... were the first steps into the realm of the abstract in painting. Modelling was discarded. The real subject matter underwent a shift (*sdvig*) to the abstract. It was progress but soon brought a certain 'attachment' (*prikreplenie*) to the plane of the canvas itself which gave the painting a new materiality (*material'nyi prizvukh*) and then in turn limited possibilities.

The aspiration to get free of this limitedness, in connection with the aspiration to a new kind of composition, must naturally lead to rejecting the single plane. ... Thus from a composition with flat triangles arose a composition of triangles standing sculpturally [lit. plastically], triangles in three dimensions, that is pyramids, which is Cubism.

FROM CHAPTER VII: THEORY

Art stands higher than nature; that is no new discovery. What matters for us is to discover the state of this principle today, and where it will get us to tomorrow... Natural forms establish a boundary that often obstructs the manifestation. These boundaries are redrawn and replaced by the objective elements of form, by construction for the purpose of composition (*konstruktsii v tselakh kompozitsii*). This explains the aspiration already clear today, to discover the constructive forms of the epoch. Thus Cubism shows how often natural form finds itself subordinated to constructive purposes, and what obstacles such forms can create. Today in general we find naked construction applied. However if we think about the definition of modern harmony given in this book, then we shall find the spirit of the age in the field of constructions too. And finally this relationship can be expressed in mathematical form. ... Number is the ultimate abstract expression in every art.

3: AVANT-GARDE OR TRADITION? THE REVOLUTIONARY STREET FESTIVALS

In an era when live revolutions are fed to the world's breakfast tables by television, it requires a conscious act of mental refocusing to grasp what the Russian Revolution of 1917 actually felt like, in particular to grasp its speed, or rather its slowness. Even after power was seized and the new government was organised, it faced the real problems of persuading an illiterate population of its legitimacy, and winning their hearts and minds by a sympathetic social contract. In this wider consolidation of power, problems of communication quickly turned into opportunities for those who could make images, that is for artists.

Much later, when the economy had started to recover, architecture would also be co-opted to offer symbols and practical tokens of what the Soviet government was delivering. In the imaginative use of the arts, however, immediately after the revolution, some of the issues which would later determine the fate of Modernist architecture were already being formulated and tested: issues of cultural continuity and the use of tradition, or of appropriate languages for communicating to the mass population.

The immediate post-Revolutionary period was also a testbed for entirely new relationships between art, and a political party for most of whom art was a frippery of social parasites. By a mutually useful coalition immediately after the Revolution, when the new government was grateful for youthful and energetic help in its attempts to address the people by visual means, the first new contract was struck between the artistic avant-garde and the Soviet government. The wild young abstractionists whom Lenin liked to despise under the label of 'futurists' in fact first showed their serious potential as more than bohemians through responding to government appeals for artists to help, during 1917. Vladimir Tatlin, Kazimir Malevich and many others who never did anything but mock 'bureaucrats' suddenly themselves became heads of departments in the new government's cultural hierarchy. The love affair did not last long, but it brought issues of art theory and party policy to the fore, and in negative as well as positive senses it laid foundations for many avant-garde ideas in the next decade.

Taking power

A uniquely vivid insider's view of the October 1917 Revolution in Petrograd (as St. Petersburg was renamed in 1914) was left to us by Leon Trotsky. His ironic eye for the details brings its practical reality to life and reminds us of what Russia's technical level was at that time. He also shows how those revolutionaries in their turn, making historical comparisons backwards to the French Revolution, recognised that in the longer historical perspective their own times were characterised by 'a new tempo' made possible by new technologies of transport and communications. They were well aware of how much depended on control of such media as they had, and how much would depend on their success in using them to communicate revolutionary ideals to the larger Russian population that they claimed to represent.

Russia in 1917, like Britain, France and America, was deeply embroiled in the First World War against Germany. For Russia however, the chaos and impoverishment of war were being superimposed on what were already clearly the last gasps of a morally exhausted autocracy. In March of 1917, Tsar Nicholas II abdicated his powers as absolute ruler 'of all the Russias' in what was essentially an admission of non-comprehension at the problems surrounding him. Concessions had already been won from him twelve years before in the so-called First Revolution, in 1905, to permit the formation of an elected Parliament or State Duma. Uprisings in February 1917 had lead to Nicholas's dissolution of the last such Duma, and its replacement by a coalition Provisional Government. This had just enough control to continue the war effort, and it sent a delegation round Europe to reassure Russia's allies that the February Revolution did not alter Russia's determination to fight 'war till victory'. But it could not put bread into the shops, resolve industrial disputes, or answer the demands of a highly disaffected intelligentsia and industrial labour force. Far less could it build a dialogue with the growing network of socialist workers' councils, or soviets, who formed the Bolshevik Party and had groups in factories and slums throughout the big cities.

By the summer, when Alexander Kerensky took over leadership of the Provisional Government, all they could do against this growing force was ban its leader, Vladimir Lenin, from entering the capital city of Petrograd. But he did get in, and was there in hiding. The great Russian memoirist Konstantin Paustovsky wrote of his period between the two revolutions that:

'In the course of a few months, Russia spoke out everything she had kept to herself for centuries. Day and night, from February to the autumn of 1917, the country seethed from end to end like one continuous rowdy meeting.' [1]

Trotsky's account describes how the 'rowdy meeting' climaxed in the streets and buildings of central Petrograd, on the day of revolution, 25 October 1917. His story starts about 10am:

'The situation in the city was getting worse from hour to hour ... All the Winter

Palace telephones had been cut off. The close approaches to the Palace and the Headquarters were absolutely unguarded. If the Bolsheviks had not penetrated this far, it was only through lack of information. Kerensky rushed across an empty Palace Square to the headquarters building [where the phones were still working] and hastily summoned his ministers to come there. The majority of them had no motor-cars. These important instruments of locomotion, which impart a new tempo to modern insurrection, had either been seized by the Bolsheviks or got cut off from the ministers to whom they belonged by cordons of insurrectionists ... What should the head of the government do? ... Kerensky ordered his own "magnificent open touring car" to be got out. As he later wrote, "In a manner that I do not know, the news of my departure had reached the Allied embassies." The representatives of Great Britain and the United States had immediately expressed the desire that "an automobile carrying the American flag" should go with the head of government, in making his get-away from the capital. Kerensky ... was a little embarrassed, but accepted it as an expression of the solidarity of the Allies, and drove out of the city. Red [i.e. Bolshevik] Guards rushed into the road at the sight of the madly flying automobile, but did not venture to shoot: in general shootings were still being avoided.'

Kerensky said he was leaving the city to meet loyal troops. 'And what were those troops that were on their way?' Trotsky asks.

'The Third Bicycle Battalion, it seems. There were 200,000 soldiers in Petrograd and its environs, and things were going pretty badly with the regime if the head of the government had to fly off with an American flag at his back to meet a Bicycle Battalion.'[2]

In fact the Bicycle Battalion had diverted, being unsure of its orders, and Kerensky just kept going. A few days later he made a vain attempt to return with Cossacks from the Imperial estate at Tsarskoe Selo, and after failing, was helped out of Russia by Britain to end his days in the land that had lent him the protection of its flag.

At 6.30pm manoeuvres began on the river Neva, leading up to the firing of the famous blank shot by the battle cruiser *Aurora* at 9pm, to signal moves on the Winter Palace by a series of those motley 'cordons of insurrectionists'. Their *confrères* already on site moved into the corridors of the enormous Palace to find remnants of the government huddled more or less in the dark, leaderless without Kerensky. Thus the Military Revolutionary Committee's 'storming' of the Palace resulted in a few more occupants for the Peter and Paul Fortress across the river. The next day's papers had already been printed, but a hastily produced broadsheet stuck up around the city informed this small world of 'the arrest of the Provisional Government at ten-past-two this morning'.

Through that historic day and the next, 25 and 26 October, the Bolshevik Party was conducting its Second Congress of workers' councils or soviets down the road at the former girls' school, the Smolny Institute. Lenin, who had hidden for four months in a house over the river in the Vyborg district had emerged from hiding for the first time about 3pm that afternoon and made a speech. All evening, he, Leon Trotsky, Anatoli Lunacharsky and the other Bolshevik leaders in the city were ensconced in their Congress. In advance of the final *dénouement*, they had already that morning declared their 'takeover of power' as soon as Kerensky was known to have fled. Now they were formulating policy statements, most notably their 'Decree on Peace' which next day would take Russia out of the First World War, and their 'Decree on Land' which would lead to nationalisation of all real estate, creating whole new perspectives for architecture and city planning. As the good news from the Palace came through, they stuck at it till 6am. This was Russia's new government.

A cultural policy

That initial wresting of power is the easy bit of a Revolution, as events in Russia and Eastern Europe are reminding us again now. Its consolidation, both practically, into a functioning administration, and psychologically, to win recognition of its legitimacy amongst the whole of a factional population, is a far more extended and complex process, continuing even as economic reconstruction starts. In Russia, the consolidation was also a more bloody and destructive process than the takeover. The Tsarist forces resisted the Bolsheviks right across the continent in a civil war that lasted till 1921. The war-time Allies of the Imperial government remained allies of these so-called 'White' Tsarist forces, as the counter-revolutionary army against the Bolshevik 'Reds'. Thus troops of what was now called 'The Entente' entered Russia through the Arctic port of Murmansk in the following March, 1918, just as Lenin was moving his capital away from Petrograd down to the ancient Russian capital of Moscow.

The difference in intellectual calibre between old government and new was remarkable, and tends now to be forgotten. With characteristic asperity, Trotsky described the White General Denikin whom the British were reinforcing in the South as 'not without character, but for the rest a perfectly ordinary army general who had read five or six books.'[3] Thus spoke the supremely scholarly intellectual as well as an arch-organiser and politician. Indeed, this was the man who would create the Red Army out of nothing to defeat those Whites. But the general thrust of Trotsky's remark highlights a crucial difference between the shambling old regime and the new. The Bolsheviks were intellectuals who had been debating and writing for years about their programme, and formulating its ideological and philosophical bases. On many fronts, most notably the economic, their internal differences of interpretation, and the divergence between the Russian reality and what any theoretical model could have predicted, led to some strong oscillations of policy and the devising of operational principles 'on the run'. In cultural matters on the other hand, there were basically two viewpoints within the Bolshevik canon, and an identity of view amongst those at the top, who in this field were Lenin himself and Anatoli Lunacharsky.

Lunacharsky was a highly cultivated man, of middle-class intellectual origins rather than the working class, who had been long in and out of emigration like other Russian Marxists since the late 1890s. Since his encounter with Georgi Plekhanov, so-called 'father of Russian Marxism' during his period as a student philosopher under Richard Avenarius in Zurich in 1896, Lunacharsky had been engaged with sociological issues of art and cultural theory, as well as with the arts themselves. Later he had become an equally serious student of progressive educationalists' work in Europe.

This was the obvious candidate to whom Lenin gave the educational and propaganda portfolio in the new government. Under Lunacharsky this Narkompros, literally translated, the Commissariat of Enlightenment, was a body of extraordinary vision and extent. Of remarkable and still undervalued seriousness, it shaped a policy of public education within the near-illiterate Russian population.[4] As the Twenties progressed, however, amid the increasing political tensions and paranoia under Stalin, it was forced to become increasingly the arbiter of orthodoxy. In this, Lunacharsky would be the main formulator and mouthpiece of government policy on the arts, and crucially, in the late Twenties and early Thirties, on architecture.[5]

Unanimity at the very top did not mean total unanimity a little lower down, however, amongst almost equally central and old-established activists in the party. One of Lenin and Lunacharsky's closest colleagues amongst the previously emigré and exiled was Alexander Malinovsky, called Bogdanov, whose sister Lunacharsky had married. Bogdanov and Lunacharsky had spent years in agitational and cultural lecturing around Russian provinces, or amongst workers in audiences they found in Europe. They were colleagues in the little 'Party schools' for Russian worker leaders they ran with Maxim Gorky in Capri and Bologna in 1909-11, as they were through the Revolution back in Russia itself.[6]

Soon after 1917 there would be a divergence of view on the theoretical basis of Bolshevik cultural policy, and a split between these colleagues. The view of Lenin in which most of the Party followed him derived very directly from certain key statements of Marx. In this view, socialism would move forward with those elements of capitalism which that particular society had achieved which remained positive, either for a historical content that remained valid, or as a familiar vessel to fill with a new content.[7]

There was a counter-view, however, which increasingly came to be defended in the operational practice of cultural activity and curricula by Bogdanov. This asserted that whatever forms proletarian cultural activity would take, they would be new, generated *ab initio* by the proletariat themselves. The result of this would be entirely new 'socialist' genres that through this very provenance would be inherently international rather than nationally or locally specific. The battle between Bogdanov and the Leninist orthodoxy came to a head in 1920, with Bogdanov's powerbase lying in the new organisation for building this 'proletarian culture' known as Proletkult of which he was head. Proletkult's units were everywhere and highly active, but grew to be something of a parallel and competitive force to government line. Hence Bogdanov had to go, and the organisation was absorbed into Lunacharsky's Narkompros.[8] But the issue of the 'correct' path would remain central to the debates between modernism and traditionalism in the arts through the middle and late Twenties.

Here in 1918, though, the divergence within the Party was not yet substantial. Thus the principles of 'critical reworking' of past culture and 'a planned appropriation of the heritage of the old world' were being expounded in July 1918 by Bogdanov too.[9]

In its long gestation period in internal and foreign exile, and in preparatory work within the Russian working population, Bolshevik thinking on both sides of this debate was quite clear in its insistence that cultural aspects of the Revolution, in the broadest sense, were of central importance. They well understood that ingrained cultural expectations and behaviour patterns were as solid an obstacle to political transformation as the structures of the old economic system. Here we return to the question of available media and technologies of communication, and to the leap required now to grasp the extraordinary size of the country and the extremely low cultural level of its population. To spread the political message, Lunacharsky harnessed the arts as they had never been used by a government before, perhaps anywhere.

Harnessing art

Already on 6 November 1917, barely two weeks after they seized power, the new Central Committee of the Bolshevik Party called a meeting of leading representatives of Petrograd's progressive younger painters, writers and theatre designers at the new government headquarters in the Smolny, to discuss their potential collaboration with Soviet power. Amongst them were such poets as Vladimir Mayakovsky and Alexander Blok, the theatrical director Vsevolod Meyerkhold and painter Natan Altman.[10] These were circles with which Lunacharsky was familar, having written much serious art and theatrical criticism himself in recent years and being well able to hold his own on current ideas.

With equal speed the new Commissar harnessed support of the more establishment artists, in particular the members of the famous World of Art society, originally set up by Serge Diaghilev and Alexander Benois, who had published the eponymous artistic and critical journal and organised much exhibition activity in the city. He charged these more established figures with organising the preservation of art works in public buildings

'Lenin addressing workers at the Putilov Factory in Petrograd, May 1917' by Isaac Brodsky, 1929 (detail).

Anatoli Lunacharsky (1875-1933) Commissar of Enlightenment, 1920.

The traditional Orthodox procession of icons: detail of painting by Ilarion Prianshnikov, c.1890, depicting such a Krestnyi khod, *literally ' Procession of the Cross', in a country village.*

and with creating a preservation policy for historic buildings.[11] The main vehicle for harnessing support of artists, musicians and theatrical people was a network of specialised organisations which Lunacharsky established under his Commissariat, Narkompros. He gave charge of the fine-art section, Izo, to a World of Art painter whom he had met and admired when both were in Paris back in 1914, David Shterenberg, and charge of its Moscow operations to the young painter turned 'relief'-maker, Vladimir Tatlin.[12] In the same process Tatlin's old rival for leadership at the cutting edge of abstraction, Kazimir Malevich, who lately had some involvement with cultural organisations for soldiers in Moscow, found himself appointed Commissar for Preservation of Monuments and Antiquities under the Military-Revolutionary Committee there, with temporary personal responsibility for ensuring the safety of monuments and art works in the Kremlin.[13] Though not considering abstract avant-garde art as such to have great public relevance, Lunacharsky frequently expressed his appreciation of the energy which its adherents brought to the organisational tasks of his early Izo programmes.[14] Notable amongst them was the Lenin Plan of Monumental Propaganda which Narkompros launched in early 1918.[15] This was a typical example of their policy of harnessing established elements of the cultural environment to convey a new political message. Many sculptors got work replacing tsarist statues by images of the new revolutionary heroes, but it was as critique of the Plan's traditional conception of a 'monument' that Tatlin provocatively offered his Tower in 1919. The avant-gardists liked to spit at the more conservative of the World of Art brigade like Benois, for joining up with the very Bolshevism which a year before they had railed against. In the end, however, these different generations and social groups within the arts found common cause enough to work together in the new organisations.

In seeking compelling and attractive ways to involve and communicate to mass populations of workers in the cities, one medium that was immediately appropriate and available were the mass public festivals. These *prazdniki* were a central element of the Russian cultural heritage, both religious and civic, and deeply rooted in the experience and expectations of every Russian.[16] Festivals and 'mass actions' became the medium which the new regime used most actively for education and inspiration of its politically and functionally illiterate population, creating in the process something of a new artistic and cultural genre.

The new government's decree of April 1918 which launched the Monuments Programme also set in motion what became the bi-annual public festivals for May Day and the Revolutionary anniversary. Narkompros committees were instructed to 'organise decoration of the cities ... with emblems, inscriptions etc reflecting the ideas and mood of the revolutionary working Russia.'[17]

In the previous month, March, Moscow had become the capital again. The government had thus returned to Russia's historic heartland and its symbolic Kremlin, two hundred years after Peter the Great took it off to his new 'window on the West' of St Petersburg in 1703. The first meeting of the new Moscow City Soviet's Arts Board after the decree brought together Tatlin, as head of Narkompros operations in the city, and two established young architects, Alexei Shchusev and Viktor Vesnin. Vesnin's younger brother Alexander was an architect and painter who had shared a studio with Tatlin in the past. The meeting voted to bring in Alexander Rodchenko, another rising young avant-gardist who had been on the periphery of the Tatlin-Malevich exhibiting circle, to join Viktor Vesnin and one Korotkov on 'a board of three persons' which would create the overall plan for May Day decoration of the city centre, in particular for the area around the Kremlin and Red Square.[18] For some reason Rodchenko did not stick with it and was replaced by one F. F. Fedorovsky,[19] but the designs of red banners were produced by Viktor and Alexander Vesnin, executed and installed with the help of another young architect in the city, Nikolai Vinogradov, now head of architectural preservation in the Kremlin after Malevich's temporary tenure passed to civilian hands.[20] The new government paper *Izvestiia* for 3 May described the decorations of Shekhtel's Neo-Russian Iaroslavl Station as 'particularly splendid', with banners to the Third Communist International and a vast red sheet with other slogans draped around its south tower.[21]

Petrograd, still feeling itself the capital and psychologically ebullient as the hearth of the Revolution, was more ambitious in its decorations. Lunacharsky's diary for May Day 1918 revealed him thrilled at the fireworks and ecstatic at what the young artists had achieved in transforming Petrograd: 'Is it not intoxicating to think that the state, until recently our worst enemy, now belongs to us and has celebrated May 1 as its greatest festival?'[22] Some of the processions were very similar in their banners and style to those which had paraded a year before, when May Day was celebrated with demonstrations before the uprising, differing only in being rather more organised. Thus poet Alexander Blok could rather cynically describe the processions which converged on the memorial Field of Mars 'with neat little red posters' as an 'exemplary Nicholas II formation'.[23] The cosmopolitan World of Art man Mstislav Dobuzhinsky was highly critical of the 'futile' effect of it: how 'pathetically feeble' the flagpoles looked in competition with the Alexander Column on Palace Square; how inexperienced these young artists were at handling the monumental scale required for open air work.[24]

Can new art communicate?

Lunarcharsky too was already aware of other drawbacks to their language. He also confided to his diary that

> *'Of course, I am absolutely certain that the posters will be criticised. After all, it is so easy to criticise the "futurists". In essence all that remains of real Cubism and Futurism here is the precision and force of the general form and the brightness of colour so essential for paintings intended for the open air and for a giant audience with hundreds of thousands of heads.'*[25]

But it was a start, and given the socialist nationalisation of all land and real estate, it was seen by a few as the start of a larger opportunity to handle the aesthetic environment of the Soviet city with a new large-scale coherence. When Mayakovsky issued 'Marching orders to the army of art' in the first issue of Izo-Narkompros's newspaper *Art of the Commune* on 7 December that year it was a call to come out of studios and into the public domain. In the famous lines 'The streets are our brushes. The squares our pallettes',[26] he proclaimed the artistic possession of the city. Now a far less radical voice, from the critic P. M. Kerzhentsev reviewing the achievements of

May in the July issue of *Creative Work* (*Tvorchestvo*) reflected a wider recognition that this was indeed happening, and considered its implications from a less avant-garde position.

> *'Now we have the chance to concern ourselves with the city's aesthetic integrity; we can create a harmony of the parts and districts of the city; we can work to ensure restraint in the style of individual corners and squares; we can think about the visual effect of building colour, put aesthetic controls on new buildings and reconstruction work, and concern ourselves with achieving an integrated overall look for the city. Some things will have to be destroyed, others skilfully disguised, and yet others highlighted. A broad field of activity is opening up for architects and artists.'*[27]

Six months later the First Anniversary of the Revolution gave a chance to further develop their technique in this new genre.

In Petrograd this became an enormous festival involving a total of eighty-five separate design projects across the length and breadth of the city, and almost as many artists and architects as designers. Coloured drawings that have been preserved recreate the effect very graphically.[28] In scale its closest precedent was the decoration of the city for the Tercentenary of the Romanov dynasty back in 1913, which had been Imperial Russia's last great self-congratulatory civic party before the war, or before that, for St Petersburg's Bicentennial in 1903.[29] The results were as diverse as the contributors' artistic origins. Some of the architects like Iosif Langbard, Alexander Klein or young Vladimir Shchuko [p.83], had done festival decoration for pre-Revolutionary events including the Tercentenary.[30] The painters ranged from leading abstractionists like Natan Altman or Ivan Puni to well-established realists of the World of Art group like Dobuzhinsky, Boris Kustodiev and Kuzma Petrov-Vodkin, with variants in between such as David Shterenberg or Vladimir Lebedev. The latter was almost the only painter represented without a Paris sojourn behind him, but most were now teaching in the Svomas, or Free Studios, that had been formed out of the old Imperial St Petersburg Academy of Arts schools (see Chapter 10).

Some of their schemes were merely essays in decorative colour and playfulness, like the ships and flags that decorated many bridges and celebrated Petrograd's character as a great seaport. Elsewhere realistic figurative images were establishing a new iconography of worker-heroes in parallel with the more permanent *dramatis personae* of the new monuments. Everywhere these were reinforced by boldly heroic political slogans. They celebrated the very fact of revolution and the workers' role in achieving it, and catchy phrases reminded them of its goals.

The set piece in Petrograd on this occasion was Natan Altman's relatively abstract treatment of the former Palace Square, now renamed Uritsky after an early Revolutionary casualty, which stretched from the rear of the Rastrelli's Winter Palace to the great semi-circle of Karl Rossi's classical General Staff headquarters. Here was a textbook example of putting new content into the established habits of the old culture. This space had been the regular focus of pre-Revolutionary gatherings for major church festivals. Divine service would be held there for thanksgivings and commemorations with the Alexander Column as their backdrop. Altman 'set myself the task of ... transforming this into a place where a revolutionary populace would

Crowds gathered in Palace Square , St Petersburg, during a celebratory divine service around the Alexander Column, c.1900: looking north towards Rastrelli's Winter Palace.

Altman, design for decoration of Palace Square for the 1st anniversary of the Revolution, 1918.

Children in fancy dress and various uniforms pose with banners of the 'Peterhof Children's Commune' round the Alexander Column beneath Altman's abstract flames, November 1918.

come to celebrate its victory.'[31] But in seeking 'to change the historical image of the square' he created for the first time in these events a genuinely new abstract architecture on an urban scale.

Rather than merely 'decorate', when 'the creations of Rastrelli and Rossi require no decoration' he set out to build a contrasting set of freestanding forms between the buildings and in adjoining spaces that created a whole new ensemble. At that time the buildings were painted a deep red-brown all over, not picked out in light classical colours as now, and hence formed a strong if gloomy structure against which to play a new abstract urban composition. Three vast bold paintings peopled the space at heroic scale with one figure and a banner each declaring Land, Factories and Art 'to the workers'. All the rest was abstract and three-dimensional. Around the Alexander Column and its four lamp-posts he erected a cluster of cubist flames in blazing red, orange and yellow to consume this symbol of the old order.[32] (He later recalled having to 'put up quite a fight' to use anything but ideologically approved Red.)[33] Workers' groups came to be photographed by this new symbol.

Even more extraordinarily, Altman made a cage of pale green cloth over the whole row of trees that screens the Square from the adjoining urban space behind Zakharov's Admiralty. 'It was late autumn and all the leaves had fallen. I erected constructions ... and once again the trees became green.' On the vast and strangely shaped 'building' thus created were oddly neat little letters spelling the classic slogan 'Proletariat of the world unite.'[34]

In a more radical way than Kerzhentsev conceived, but with that same sense that the whole city was not to be composed as an entity, Altman had shown that there was a compositional medium between 'architecture' and 'art' in the old senses, that could be employed in this new genre. In *Art of the Commune* , soon after this autumn festival work, he reflected on what it meant for art to be 'proletarian'. That large-scale compositional venture, half a choreography of people through city spaces and half an 'object', had plainly had an impact.

Art, he wrote, is not proletarian because it is 'a sketch done by a worker or a poster on which a worker is depicted'. It is proletarian if it is in some deep sense 'collective'. That does not mean it has been created by many artists together, but that 'each part of it acquires meaning only through its interaction with all other parts.' To look for 'meaning' or a clear representation of an individual object in a particular part, 'is like trying to distinguish an individual face in a proletarian procession', Altman said. Just as you might if they were simply 'an accidental assembly of people going their own ways down Nevsky Prospect'. 'Such a procession is meaningless if you try to understand it as individual people. It is only as in conjunction that they acquire strength or meaning.' This is the key principle distinguishing 'all the new left art', meaning effectively all the new abstraction – for which 'in the everyday parlance' as he says, he too uses the word 'futurist'. Thus the key ingredient is a force or organisation which makes a whole greater than its parts. This is the sense, he says, in which 'futurist (i.e. left or abstract) art is 'collective'. It is itself a 'collective' of parts which only have meaning as a linked entity with common purpose.[35]

This may partly have been a subtly devised argument to construct their own legitimacy, but it was already an emphasis on structuring principle, on how parts come together rather than simply what they are, which would become fundamental to such later avant-garde theories as Constructivism.

These first festivals were thus seminal not only for their scale of action and level of political engagement. They stimulated a discussion of what that political engagement actually meant for the structure of a work of art.

Altman and his colleagues might rest on the argument of their deep political relevance, but as ever the general public's reading of the specific forms they produced was not necessarily sympathetic. This inner structural congruence was too subtle a quality to be recognised even by most of the conventional art critics. As Lev Pumpiansky put it in the Petrograd journal *The Flame*, there were deep shortcomings here 'that resulted from a disparity between the spiritual make-up and rhythm of modern art, and the rhythm, experiences and feelings of the revolutionary popular masses.'[36] Questions were soon being asked about 'the apparently preferential "patronage" given by Soviet power to left-wing artistic trends'. That was the critic A. A. Sidorov, writing like Kerzhentsev in *Creative Work*, the journal of the new Artists' Union. Down in Moscow on the Revolutionary anniversary in 1918, he said, Ilia Mashkov had done 'Garlands of fruit, workers and sailors powerfully and cheerfully drawn' on the front of 'the former painting school on Miasnitskaia Street' (old MUZhVZ). These were 'truly worthy of the

'Fornicators of Russia: Unite!' by cartoonist Perun, mocking the Duma elections on cover of satirical magazine Octopus *(Sprut), January 1906.*

Cut-out figures of Lloyd George, Millerand, Kerensky, caricatured as 'The Heroes of the Entente' in Red Square, 17 June 1921, during parades marking the 3rd Congress of the Third Communist International, Comintern, then meeting in Moscow.

language in which the art of a proletarian country must speak'. But 'decoration of the city exclusively by "left art"' such as Moscow had experienced on Red Army Day 'was not a success.' 'Suprematists, Futurists and all of them, have made it their sacred goal to "revolutionise" people's sight, just as the revolution must change their consciousness', but how could this be useful if the art was not actually 'intended for the people'? [37]

The questions that would later hit Modernist architecture were already being raised by these first 'new environments' created for the festivals. At root it was the simplest question of linguistics. Can a language that is unfamiliar be the medium for communciating an unfamiliar message? Altman's rather Cubist flames were still recognisably a bonfire. His green covered fruitcages were manifestly the trees people knew to be inside them. Even these had been very successfully combined (as critical reaction confirmed) with realistic monumental figures. But one stage further to real abstraction of the kind Altman was theorising about in *Art of the Commune*, and all communication was lost.

Old and new conceptions of 'festival'

Despite the raging Civil War and current invasions of anti-Bolshevik troops from the Entente powers, the bold satire and caricature of 'class enemies' which soon became characteristic of these bi-annual festivals are still embryonic at this date, though that genre had already built a rich tradition in Russia during the brief political liberations of 1905 and some of the same artists had been involved, notably Dobuzhinsky and Kustodiev.[38] Still less is there any hint here of the overt propagandising for the national industrial effort that would characterise these anniversaries by the mid-Twenties.[39]

In 1918 and 1919 the economy was still on the downward spiral of profiteering and chronic shortage which began in 1914 with the war. The aim in these years was a further injection of revolutionary enthusiasm into a nation where Civil War and industrial collapse were daily increasing the vicissitudes of existence to the point of threatening public morale. There was no television through which to address the cold, illiterate and increasingly hungry population. Instead, the Bolsheviks' political message was carried continuously through street newspapers in cartoon form, and taken to the provinces by carts and trains full of colourful slogans.[40] Those things, like so much else to which the masses were now exposed, were novel. These great street festivals, on the other hand, though new in content, had a reassuring familiarity.

Still intensely religious, both town and country in Russia had deeply rooted traditions of celebratory processions carrying sacred images and banners, whether in the *Krestnyi khod*, (Procession of the Cross) in the country village, or in the celebration of church services in great spaces of the city like Palace Square. On the annual feast of Shrovetide, called *Maslenitsa*, Moscow, Petersburg and every Russian town had several days of processions and mass merry-making. Historically, any military victory worthy of fireworks had been celebrated almost on the scale of the great coronation festivals, when Moscow would be entirely decorated to designs by leading artists. Here again was a pattern which Bolshevik festivals like the parades for Congresses of the Communist International were again merely adapting to new content.[41] They derived a certain legitimacy in socialist theory from references to Paris in 1789, but fundamentally they were just the regular doses of mass colour and jostling humanity which had historically enlivened the life of all classes in Russia. With their policy of building new ideological messages onto those elements of cultural heritage which remained valid or adaptable, the Bolsheviks created a combination of simple fun with political education that evolved during the Twenties into a new genre of popular art.

This was their success, but to Lunacharsky as to some more radical avant-gardists it was also their dead baggage. As Lunacharsky himself wrote in early 1920, they were in danger of becoming no more than 'a lively noise and colourful party for festively dressed people'. 'Until social life teaches the masses an instinctive compliance with a higher order and rhythm', he wrote, one could not expect anything else.[42]

The most radical new conception was put forward to the Festivals section of Lunacharsky's commissariat Narkompros by the Moscow artist and designer Alexei Gan. In his earnestly political judgement the historical precedents 'from Biblical myths or Christian rites' were 'deposits of alien cults'. So too, in the end, were 'civic festivities of the French Revolution.' His new vision was of a 'mass action ... in which the whole city would be the stage and the entire proletarian masses of Moscow the performers'. These masses would invent the detailed scenarios for themselves 'in the process

Alexander Vesnin and Liubov Popova, their model of the 'capitalist fortress' to form one end of a vast installation on Khodinka Field, Moscow, for the 3rd Comintern Congress in June 1921.

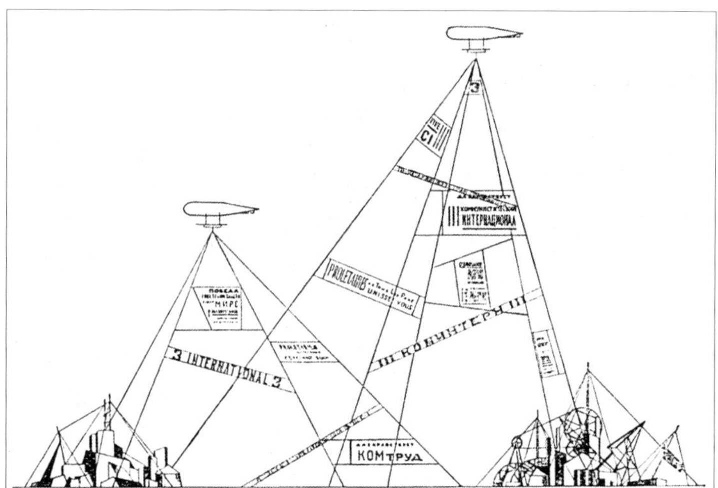

Vesnin and Popova's sketch for their whole installation on Khodinka: a cable structure suspended from two dirigibles, with 'the capitalist fortress', left, and 'the future Communist city', right.

of collective work'. Instead of 'decorating' the city, 'the whole city and its outskirts' would contain specially built stagings that were part of an imagined 'Communist city of the future'. At the summons of factory sirens, people in each district would rush out to enact their bit of the chosen theme (a history of the Three Communist Internationals was proposed for that year), moving to the next site for more. 'The main action' would be played out on the traditional festival ground of Khodinka in northeast Moscow, 'in a Field of the International set up with wireless station and aerodrome'.[43]

It seems clear to me that Alexander Vesnin's well known design with Liubov Popova for a vast installation on Khodinka, where the 'capitalist fortress' stands opposite a 'Communist city of the future', conceived as part of a 'mass action' to coincide with the Third Congress of the Third International a year later, was a belated development of this idea of their colleague Gan, though art history seems to have lost the connection. It was a natural collaboration: they were close colleagues in the new art research centre of the Moscow avant-garde, Inkhuk (see Chapters 4 and 5). When Gan published his book *Constructivism* in the next year, 1922, as their theoretical manifesto, its first sentence declared in dramatic typography that 'Constructivism arose in 1920 amongst the leftist painters and ideologists of "mass action".'[45]

These festivals were thus seminal in numerous ways. They were always parades of 'festively dressed people', but the danger of them losing political content was overcome as the Twenties progressed by selecting themes to reflect current government political or economic campaigns. If the former, foreign political leaders would be pilloried as evil capitalists in cheerful puppets or caricature. If the latter, factories would make displays of their products and the specialists in 'depictive statistics' kept up the pressure with ever more graphically rising curves of industrial output.

As festivals of the new religion, the continuing vigour of these events well vindicated the Party approach to cultural development, of building new content within familiar structures. For the avant-garde they provided a first chance to take over the entire public domain of their 'inherited capitalist cities' and to realise, as Gan put it in *Constructivism*, that the 'cramped spaces' of these 'material, technological "organs" of society' were 'obstructing the path of social reorganisation' and must be radically reshaped by a new architecture.

1 K. Paustovsky, *Story of a Life*, volume 3: *In that Dawn*, London, 1967, p.7 **2** L.Trotsky, *The History of the Russian Revolution*, London, 1967, vol.3, pp.228-30. For a wide variety of other eye-witness accounts see H. Pitcher, *Witnesses of the Russian Revolution*, London, 1994. **3** Trotsky, *History*, vol 1, p.243 **4** General aspects of this work are discussed, but unenthusiastically, in S. Fitzpatrick, *The Commissariat of Enlightenment: Soviet Organisation of Education and the Arts under Lunacharsky*, Cambridge, 1970. The most detailed factual accounts of Lunacharsky's life are Soviet ones, e.g. A. Yermakov, *A. Lunacharsky*, Moscow, 1975 **5** I have discussed this in more detail in Cooke, 'Socialist Realist Architecture', in M. Cullerne Bown & B. Taylor, eds., *Art of the Soviets*, Manchester, 1993, pp.86-105 **6** Z. A. Sochor, *Revolution and Culture: the Bogdanov-Lenin Controversy*, Cornell, 1988; also Yermakov, *Lunacharsky*, et al. **7** Cooke, 'Socialist Realist Architecture'; Sochor, *Revolution and Culture.* **8** Sochor, *Revolution and Culture*, pp.144-8 **9** ibid, pp.144-5 **10** V. P. Lapshin, *Khudozhestvennaia zhizn Moskvy i Petrograda v 1917 godu* (Artistic Life in Moscow and Petrograd in 1917), Moscow, 1983, p 416 **11** ibid, pp. 411-12 **12** Fitzpatrick, *The Commissariat*, p.122 **13** Lapshin, *Khudozhestvennaia zhizn*, pp.418-19 **14** One such reference is quoted in Fitzpatrick, *The Commissariat*, p.127 **15** For English sources on the Plan see B. Taylor, *Art and Literature under the Bolsheviks*, vol.1: *The Crisis of Renewal*, London, 1991, pp.56-63, and more schematically, V. Tolstoy, 'Art born of the Revolution', in V. Tolstoy, I. Bibikova & C. Cooke, eds., *Street Art of the Revolution: Festivals and Celebrations in Russia 1918-33*, London, 1990, pp.12-15 **16** See for example, A F Nekrylova, *Russkie narodnye prazdniki, uvezseleniia i zrelishcha, konets XVIII-nachalo XX veka*, (Russian Popular Festivals, Amusements and Spectacles, from the late 18th to early 20th centuries), Leningrad, 1988, and O. Nemiro, *Prazdnichnyi gorod: iskusstvo oformleniia prazdnikov. Istoriia i sovremennost'* (Festival City: the Art of Festival Decorations: Historically and Today), Leningrad, 1987. Some historical precedents are also discussed in the highly interpretative study of this topic, J. von Geldern, *Bolshevik Festivals 1917-20*, Berkeley-London, 1993, and other aspects in R. Stites, *Revolutionary Dreams. Utopian vision and experimental life in the Russian Revolution*, Oxford, 1989 **17** 'Dekret Sovnarkom na pamiatnikov respubliki' (Decree of Sovnarkom on monuments of the Republic), 12 April 1918, in Tolstoy etc, *Street Art*, p.39. For Russian texts of all documents in Tolstoy etc, *Street Art*, plus many more on these topics and more visual material, see the original two-volume Russian publication, V. P. Tolstoy, ed., *Sovetskoe dekorativnoe iskusstvo. Materialy i dokumenty 1917-32: Agitatsionno-massovie iskusstvo. Oformlenie prazdnestv*, Moscow, 1984 **18** Mossoviet archival documents, in Tolstoy etc, *Street Art*, doc. 2, pp.39-40 **19** ibid, note, p.40 **20** E. Ovsiannikova, 'Iz istorii komissii Mossoveta po okhrane pamiatnikov' (From the history of Mossoviet's Commission for the Protection of Monuments), *Sovetskoe iskusstvoznanie* (Soviet Art History), no.81, vol. 2, Moscow, 1982, pp.263-330 **21** A. V. Lunacharsky, Diary for 1 May 1918, *Vospominaniia i vpechatleniia* (Reminiscences and Impressions), Moscow, 1968, pp.208-9, quoted in Tolstoy, etc, *Street Art*, p.50. **22** Lunacharsky, ibid, p.51 **23** A. Blok, *Zapisnye knizhki 1901-1920* (Notebooks), Moscow, 1965, p 404, quoted in ibid, note to doc.8, p.53 **24** M. V. Dobuzhinsky, 'Bomba ili khlopushka' (Bomb or a firework), *Novaia zhizn* (New Life), 4 May 1918, quoted in ibid, pp.51-3 **25** Lunacharsky, Diary for 1 May 1918, quoted in ibid, p.50 **26** V. Mayakovsky, 'Prikaz po armii iskusstva' (Marching orders to the army of art), *Iskusstvo kommuny* (Art of the Commune), no.1, 7 Dec 1918, p.1 **27** P. M. Kerzhentsev, 'Iskusstvo na ulitse' (Art on the street), *Tvorchestvo* (Creative Work), 1918, No.3, pp.12-13, quoted in ibid, pp.53-4 **28** For a catalogue of them see ibid, pp.69-70, where many original drawings are illustrated in colour. Many originals were exhibited and catalogued, though not all illustrated, in S. Causey, ed., *Tradition and Revolution in Russian Art*, Manchester, 1990 **29** Photographs of the Bicentennial appear in Y. Barchatova et al, *A Portrait of Tsarist Russia. Unknown Photographs from Soviet Archives*, New York, 1989, front and back endpapers. Original drawings for the Tercentenary appear in Nemiro, *Prazdnichnyi gorod*, pp.39-42 **30** For designs by Shchuko and Lansere, see Nemiro, ibid. **31** N. Altman, 'Vospominaniia' (Reminiscences), archival materials, quoted in Tolstoy etc, *Street Art*, pp.70-1 **32** Altman's original colour drawings have been widely reproduced. See *inter alia* Tolstoy etc, *Street Art*, figs. 47, 48 and his own later reconstructions in figs. 49-53 **33** Altman, 'Vospominaniia', in ibid, p.71 **34** The original drawing is in ibid, fig. 48. The rest is illustrated from other archives here. **35** Nat. Al'tman, '"Futurizm" i proletarskoe iskusstvo' ('Futurism' and proletarian art), *Iskusstvo kommuny*, no.2, 15 Dec 1918, p.2. An English translation appears in J.E. Bowlt, ed., *Russian Art of the Avant-garde. Theory and Criticism, 1902-1934*, London-New York, 1976, pp.161-4, though wrongly paged to p.3. **36** L. Pumpiansky, 'Oktiabr'skie torzhestva i khudozhniki Petrograda' (October celebrations and the artists of Petrograd), *Plamia* (The Flame), no.35, 5 Jan 1919, pp.11-14, quoted in Tolstoy etc, *Street Art*, pp.81-2 **37** A. A. Sidorov, 'Dva goda russkogo iskusstva i khudozhestvennoi deiatelnosti' (Two years of Russian art and artistic activity), *Tvorchestvo*, 1919, no.10-11, p.43 quoted in Tolstoy etc, *Street Art*, p.68 **38** For a wide selection see D. King & C. Porter, *Blood & Laughter: Caricatures from the 1905 Revolution*, London, 1983 **39** Tolstoy etc, *Street Art*, Parts II & III **40** Examples may be found widely, eg.in A. Kopp, *Town and Revolution*, London, 1970, pp.46, 49; D. Elliott, *New Worlds. Russian Art and Society 1900-1937*, London-New York 1986, pp.72-3 **41** See sources in note 16 above. **42** A. Lunacharsky, 'O narodnykh prazdnestvakh' (On popular festivals), *Vestnik teatra* (Theatre Courier), no.62, 27 April - 2 May 1920, p.13, quoted in Tolstoy etc, *Street Art*, p.124 **43** 'Plan organizatsii pervomaiskikh torzhestv na ultisakh Moskvy ... Narkomprosa' (Plan for the organisation of May Day celebrations on the streets of Moscow ... from Narkompros), *Vestnik teatra* no.51, 5-8 Feb 1920, pp.5-6, quoted in ibid, pp.124-6 **44** See for example A. Rudenstein, ed., *Russian Avant-Garde Art. The George Costakis Collection*, London-New York, 1981, pp.388-9 **45** A. Gan, *Konstruktivizm*, Tver, 1922, p.1.

4: WHAT SHOULD A SOVIET ARCHITECTURE BE? PROFESSIONAL DIVERSITY AND ITS ORIGINS

In looking at the architectural avant-garde of Russia in the Twenties, it is important to distinguish between several distinctive theoretical approaches and to see the avant-garde within its larger professional context. Too often, all Modernist work of the period is labelled by the name of one group, the Constructivists, whereas superficially similar-looking work in fact derives from several quite different philosophies of architecture. It is also quite wrong to suppose that the Modernist avant-garde had the architectural field to itself, or that it emerged purely as a result of the 1917 Revolution out of a hitherto entirely conservative profession.

As Chapter 1 has shown, technical, formal and spatial innovations, as well as a concern with developing the new building types of a modern, more socially conscious society, had already developed considerable momentum in pre-Revolutionary architectural practice. As a result, the social priorities of the post-Revolutionary years were more or less accepted at a professional level, if not naturally embraced at a personal level, by the architectural community as a whole. On the other hand the question of the style in which such objects should present themselves, of the language with which they would most effectively convey the Revolutionary message, was a matter of heated debate. My aim here is to clarify the differences between those various strands of what were loosely 'modernist' approaches, to highlight the fundamental differences of theory behind buildings which often appear stylistically similar. Some of these approaches, in particular Constructivism, will be examined in greater detail later, or are further illuminated here by documents. Other approaches had a distinctive base of theory, but the architects concerned did not develop it so copiously in theoretical writings.

Diversity or pluralism?

The pluralism of architecture today may help us understand the arguments of various sides, but the diversity to be found in the Soviet Union of the Twenties is not properly described as Pluralism. Pluralism after all signifies a democratic acceptance of that diversity as the natural reflection of legitimately different political and philosophical viewpoints. Russian architectural circles of the Twenties were no more characterised by such mutual respect amongst the protagonists than Western architecture was in the heyday of the Modern Movement in Europe. My concern here is a positive one, of showing what each group believed should be the basis of a new Soviet architecture. I shall not confuse this by delving into the cross-currents of mutual recriminations and accusations more than is necessary for clarification of the essentials. But the general arguments made against all 'modern' building in the Soviet Union at that time are significant, for it was precisely to overcome or pre-empt such objections that some whom we must broadly describe as 'Modernists' were already formulating their approaches.

The arguments made against Modernist architecture in the Soviet Union of the Twenties were remarkably similar to those made against it fifty years later in the West. Modernist buildings were said to be joylessly 'industrial' in mood, to ignore the 'cultural heritage', and therefore not to communicate with the myths and aspirations by which the general population lived their lives. In this there was considerable truth, and Malevich's discussions of the relationships between abstraction and cultural development, discussed in Chapter 9 below, indicated some of the reasons why.

Even without seeking explanations, it is clear that some of these failures of communication were the result of deep differences of cultural origin between the population and the relatively very small architectural profession, and within that profession amongst the architects themselves, particularly as a new generation rose to greater influence during the Twenties. Other disputes were the result of the theoretical battle going on within Bolshevism itself over the proper balance between continuity and innovation in a proletarian culture. I have outlined these in discussing the revolutionary street festivals in Chapter 3.

The overlaying of these two factors – the actual cultural context and the theoretical debate on principles – produced the strange mix of alliances which brought the conservative, pre-Revolutionary generation of architects back to the top of professional hierarchies in the early Thirties, as executants of the historicist aesthetic chosen by the new dictatorship. As Chapter 1 has shown, the essence of the argument between innovation and the rhetoric of Historicism was already established in Russian architecture in the nineteenth century and years before World War I. In the West in the Eighties the argument re-emerged as Modernism versus Post-Modernism. In the Soviet Union in the Twenties it was Modernism versus an idea of synthesis with the cultural heritage that became called Socialist Realism.

The *dénouement* in that battle was the competition launched in 1931 for a vast Palace of the Soviets in central Moscow, but that is a saga in its own right on which I shall only touch peripherally in the essays here. Some consequences of its decisions for avant-garde design are touched upon in Chapter 12 below. Suffice it to note here that, even before such a philosophy was formulated with any clarity in the early Thirties, there was still a strong current in the profession itself which believed in the necessity to preserve a continuity with tradition. Whether it was the tradition of local vernacular building, or the tradition of high-art Classicism, both convictions were represented amongst those groups advancing what in general was a Modernist architecture.

In Russia as in Europe at that time, the new art was the most obvious and direct influence in shaping the theories and aesthetics of the architectural avant-garde. However, before looking at the artistic ideas which formed that aesthetic seedbed here in Russia, it is important to distinguish the various age- and interest-groups of that generally progressive front of the architectural profession which in some manner espoused Modernism, for the different reactions of the individuals were very naturally shaped by their differing personal backgrounds.

Four generations of the Revolutionary profession

Those architects whose offices had been the centres of innovation in the first years of the century were about sixty years old at the time of the Revolution, and plainly no longer leaders of change. Progressive free-thinkers like Leonti Benois in Petrograd or Fedor Shekhtel in Moscow became the elder statesmen of the profession during the first Soviet years. Thus Benois remained the central figure in balancing stability with innovation in architectural education in Petrograd-Leningrad right through to his death in 1928, when students and teachers alike accorded him a remarkable honorific funeral.[1] In Moscow, Shekhtel continued to be the doyen of the profession, remaining President of the Moscow Architectural Society, MAO, till 1922, and active in the organisation of architectural competitions and on their juries till his death in 1926. Some architects close in age to them perished in the upheavals, like Shekhtel's near-contemporary in Moscow, Lev Kekushev, or Benois' assistant in Petersburg-Petrograd, Marian Peretiatkovich. Very few of the Russian profession emigrated as a result of the Revolution: Fedor Lidval for example was unusual in emigrating to his former family home of Sweden. For the vast majority Russia was the terrain in which they were attuned to build, and the new regime promised every chance to continue a useful career.

Among those below Benois and Shekhtel in age who were young enough to lead the new profession forward, we are observing in the twenties the interaction of what were effectively four distinct professional cohorts.

The first and oldest of these had been born at the very end of the 1860s or in the early 1870s. By 1917 they were all well established, having had solid experience in good offices – sometimes indeed those of Shekhtel or Benois – before building significant projects independently. At the Revolution they ranged in age from forty to fifty but retained the flexibility to engage positively with the new situation. For them it was still possible to find a synthesis between the aesthetic positions they had established in the old society and the economic and ideological priorities of the new one.

The second cohort were under forty and also had solid professional experience, but they were young enough to seize the new theoretical challenge of the Bolshevik programme wholeheartedly. They became leaders of the main movements and approaches of the avant-garde.

The third, whom we may call the younger leaders, completed their training just as the 1917 Revolution broke. They had all the benefits of that solid pre-Revolutionary educational background, but had never built.

The fourth and youngest cohort were the first student generation of the Soviet period, taught in the 'Free' schools of the Twenties, particularly in Moscow, according to the new curricula which these older men created around their various theories.

In referring to these as the 'Russian' profession, not the 'Soviet', I do so advisedly. This progressive core which led the Soviet profession during most of the Twenties was precisely Russian. Indeed, anti-avant-garde protests of the 'proletarian' groupings of the late Twenties were directed more against the hegemony of this Russian-rooted elite than against the theoretical aspects of their architecture. Most of those architects who spearheaded the attack on the avant-garde within the profession were not bad modernists themselves, but they came from other, non-Russian republics [see p.87].

Looking in more detail at the membership of these four cohorts within the Russian profession of the Twenties, we see the rich variety of background and experience which the Soviet profession commanded at that date, and some explanation perhaps of its fertility.

The first and oldest of these four 'generations' had been practised exponents of Classicism or the *Moderne* before the Revolution, or were famous as innovators with the new technologies. They belonged to the artistic and educational elite trained in architecture faculties of the Academy or the Institute of Civil Engineers, IGI, in Petersburg, or the College of Painting, Sculpture and Architecture, MUZhVZ, in Moscow. Educational standards in all these schools rivalled the best in the West of that date. Most of these architects had also travelled or studied abroad.

Of those who were important in the Twenties, the oldest was Ivan Zholtovsky, aged fifty at the Revolution, who was a passionate advocate of Renaissance Classicism and in particular of Palladio. One year after him in graduating from the Academy School was Nikolai Markovnikov, whose career took him to work for the railways and become the leading Moscow advocate of small-scale low-rise housing development after the Revolution. Ivan Fomin was a talented designer equally fluent in Classicism and the *Moderne*. At the turn of the century his Academy training had been broken for several years following his expulsion for involvement in student protests, and he visited Paris and worked for Kekushev and Shekhtel before finally returning to graduate. Alexei Shchusev was another successful young Academy graduate who had split his career between the two 'alternate capitals' of Moscow and Petersburg, and could practise several styles with equal ease. Youngest of this senior cohort, aged forty-three at the Revolution, was Alexander Kuznetsov. A graduate of both the Institute of Civil Engineers and the Berlin Polytechnical Institute, he had published the first work in Russian on the theory of reinforced concrete design back in 1899, and eight years later, the first scientific paper in Russian on daylighting of buildings. At home and through conference papers abroad he was well known as one of the profession's most innovative designers of structures and services with many vast industrial buildings to his credit.

Rising fast beneath this oldest generation at the time of the Revolution was the second cohort of architects who were in their upper thirties, and in Russia as in any other country were thus poised to make their mark. Amongst the former pupils of Benois at the Academy in Petersburg was Vladimir Shchuko [pp.83-5], aged thirty-nine, with some inventively eclectic apartment buildings to his name, some *Moderne* interiors, much theatrical work, and some fine Empire for Russian exhibition pavilions in Italy. Boris Velikovsky had graduated from the Institute of Civil Engineers eight years after Kuznetsov, and already erected several buildings in Petersburg and Moscow [pp.68-71]. Amongst Velikovsky's collaborators in this latter work had been the three young Vesnin brothers, Leonid, Viktor and Alexander, who were rising stars of the Moscow profession [pp.38-45]. Though trained in Petersburg, they had increasingly figured in the prize lists of the Moscow Architectural Society's competitions during the last ten years. Between the Vesnin brothers in age was the Moscow educated Nikolai Ladovsky; whilst the Vesnins became leaders of architectural Constructivism in the twenties, he would lead the rival ideology he called 'Architectural Rationalism'. Other important future Modernists in this cohort were the Moscow-trained brothers Panteleimon and Ilia Golosov [pp.62-4; 69] and the Petersburg Civil Engineering Institute graduates Andrei Ol and Alexander Nikolsky [pp.52-5].

The third cohort comprised some highly talented architects born between 1890 and 1895 and thus still in their twenties at the Revolution. These differed from the second cohort in their lack of building experience, but subsequently contributed equally to theory and practice in the avant-garde. In this age-group backgrounds and education were more varied, but strong creative partnerships between these very talented young designers and members of the slightly older group were one of the distinctive features of the Soviet profession in the early twenties.

In this third cohort we find the key figure of Moisei Ginzburg, later, with the two younger Vesnins, a leader of Constructivism [pp.46-51]. Forced abroad by Russian educational restrictions on Jews, Ginzburg had taken a three-year course at the Milan Academy before returning to Russia to graduate from the more technical course at the Riga Polytechnic in 1917, which was evacuated to Moscow for the duration of the War.

The educational career of El Lissitzky, as another Jew, had been very similar: he graduated from the same Riga Polytechnic in Moscow one year later than Ginzburg, after a first degree in Darmstadt. Vladimir Krinsky [p.31], who like Lissitzky would later be closely identified with Ladovsky in Rationalism, had finished at the Academy in Petrograd in 1917. Nikolai Dokuchaev was another future Rationalist leader who completed his studies just as the 1917 Revolution brought education to a halt.

Among other key figures of the future avant-garde, Konstantin Melnikov [60-1] finished at the Moscow College in the same disrupted year but had managed to get building experience already; like his peers he would soon be back teaching in the reorganised schools, in this case with Ilia Golosov as his older partner. The distinctive figure of Iakov Chernikhov [p.114] also belonged to this age-group, but a fragmented educational career put him somewhat outside the general pattern. Indeed most of his study under Benois at the re-formed Academy in the middle Twenties overlapped with, and was financially supported by, his own teaching work in formal disciplines of design with boys in technical schools.

All these new recruits to the profession of 1917 knew the old 'styles' intimately, as their final diploma projects showed. In the Twenties this third cohort would argue fiercely amongst themselves over the principles that should generate a modern Soviet architecture, but they were united in regarding it as essentially a new phenomenon, not a reinterpretation of old canons. Within a year of the Revolution, as Chapter 10 describes, their old schools had been reorganised on freer lines by Government. Soon they were back in them and, especially in Moscow, passionately debating their new theories with colleagues from painting and literature in little 'research groups' even as they started teaching the next generation in the studios.

The fourth cohort were their students. The oldest of them were born in 1893 or soon afterwards, and their higher education was disrupted by the hostilities of Revolution and subsequent Civil War, which dragged on in some parts of the country till 1921. A few of them struggled through to be amongst the very first graduates of the new era – students like Georgi Simonov who graduated from the Institute of Civil Engineers in Petrograd in 1920, or Georgi Golts and Nikolai Kolli who left the reorganised Moscow school, Vkhutemas, in 1922. In general, however, this youngest of the four cohorts had not been born until about 1900. Professionally, they were the true children of the Revolution. Their whole training as well as their early professional experience was conducted under the new conditions, shaped by the new social programme, and limited by the new economic and technical constraints.

In Moscow the new multi-disciplinary school, Vkhutemas, had been formed by amalgamating the Moscow College of Painting, Sculpture and Architecture with the Stroganov College of Applied Arts. This Vkhutemas

Leonti Benois (1856-1928)

Alexei Shchusev (1873-1949)

Ivan Zholtovsky (1867-1959)

Alexander Kuznetsov (1874-1954)

Alexander Vesnin (1883-1959)

Alexander Nikolsky (1884-1953)

contained Moscow's most famous architecture school of the twenties, but not the only one. Under the pioneer of concrete structures, Alexander Kuznetsov, such emerging luminaries of Modernism as the Vesnins and Ginzburg also taught architecture at the city's other main school, in Moscow Higher Technical College, MVTU. Young stars like Ivan Leonidov, Mikhail Barshch and Andrei Burov emerged from these new curricula to join Constructivism, as Mikhail Turkus, Ivan Lamtsov and Georgi Krutikov emerged to join Rationalism. The former Academy school of architecture in Petrograd adapted less happily to its post-Revolutionary transformation into 'Free Studios' and had a period of chaos before Leonti Benois' leadership got it back to work in 1921-2. In the later twenties its graduates ranged from the formal speculator of Constructive design, Iakov Chernikhov, to the builders of some of Leningrad's best Modernism, Rationalist supporters Armen Barutchev and Iakov Rubanchik [pp.34-7].

I stress these age differences because they are fundamental to understanding the differences of emphasis and argument within Soviet Modernism in the Twenties. Informal teaching, free debate and open competitions enabled young talent to blossom rapidly, but very different levels and kinds of experience were being brought to bear on the problems by people of these widely divergent backgrounds, and this is reflected in the range of approaches.

In considering the kinds of prior experience which students brought to their studies, we also have to recognise the different spatial experience brought to urban architecture by students from rural, peasant backgrounds. Under the previous system of higher education such students would only have entered the elite colleges after initial study at provincial schools where this originality would have been tutored out in favour of establishment norms. Now, under the early Soviet regime there might be chaos in higher education, but it was open to all. Thus boys came fresh from Russian towns and villages that were still no more than a loose, low-density straggle of freestanding huts along a broad unsurfaced track. Here as in the wide-open countryside, a building constituted a powerfully three-dimensional event, rather than just being, as in dense cities, an object compressed and neutered to accommodate itself to the presence of others around it. Thus two of the greatest formal innovators of the architectural avant-garde, Ivan Leonidov and Iakov Chernikhov brought to architecture a primal, almost carnally brutal sense of form from childhoods spent in a formal environment totally different from the cubic matrix of the European city, which Moscow and Petersburg increasingly resembled, and which their Western-oriented teachers tended to see as essential to a modern urbanism. In Leonidov's work this open spatiality was immediately susceptible to the ordering system offered by Malevich's Suprematism, which Chernikhov also adopted, though less exclusively. Melnikov too, though picked up by a middle-class patron in his teens, was essentially a peasant boy who spent his formative years in that primitive environment, and the unneighbourly three-dimensionality of his building forms reflects the formal character of Russian rural building very directly.

As fellow professionals these people of very different social and spatial origins fitted in with their city-bred colleagues well enough in the *melée* of the Twenties. As personalities however, these three not only retained the fiery personal independence that makes difficult collaborators: their buildings also had in common this independence of form that makes them spatially unneighbourly within the general fabric of a city. The result of this influence from the Russian countryside was a marked formal difference between some of Russia's most original avant-garde Modernism and contemporaneous Modernist work in Europe.

If we consider the origins of avant-garde modernism's new language in Russia, as opposed to its spatial and social dimensions, then we are looking to quite another area of pre-Revolutionary activity: to art. Thus in 1914-15, as the War started to bite, it was the early constructed 'counter-reliefs' of former painter Vladimir Tatlin which first explored the way in which new materials might generate new artistic form and led, *inter alia*, to Constructivism. As Chapter 2 showed, these innovations of Tatlin's were precisely contemporaneous with those of Malevich, whose 'supreme abstraction' of form in a four-dimensional space is discussed further in Chapter 9. From that date through the Revolutionary years, these two would exhibit alongside each other in heated competition for the leading position in the avant-garde. Between the two of them, one focussing on material and the other on energetics of abstract form and colour, they provided that clean slate on which formal innovators of many different post-Revolutionary trends could build up new formal languages from first principles.

In this respect the position in Russia was similar to that in Europe of the Twenties, where the formal languages of the new architecture developed in close conjunction with, and indeed were often led by, explorations in the two- and three-dimensional areas of the fine arts. During the years when Russia was cut off from Western contacts and literature by the Civil War and the Western Entente's blockade, the Neo-Plasticism of Mondrian and Vantongerloo established the formal grammars for the architecture of van Doesburg and Rietveld in Holland. Likewise the Purism that Le Corbusier and Ozenfant juxtaposed to the complex spatial structures of Cubism became the test-bed for Corbusier's own essays on building in concrete. Social and intellectual linkages between painters and architects were of course a normal feature of traditional artistic culture in Russia as elsewhere, but Modernism's move away from representation towards abstraction naturally generated relationships that were more profoundly symbiotic, since architecture and the painterly or plastic arts now had far more of their aesthetic and formal territory in common.

Later in the Twenties, the work of these pioneer European Modernists would be well known and quite extensively published in Soviet Russia. The Constructivist group in particular came to consider themselves, in the title of a long article in the second issue of their journal, in 1926, an integral part of 'The international front of modern architecture'.[2] Through the most fertile years of artistic development however, up to about 1922, Russia was an isolated world, feeding off its own resources whilst the Bolsheviks gradually extended their conquest across the former Empire, and Western powers tried to cut their supply lines. Hence it was the internal conjuncture rather than external stimulae that gave unique coloration to Soviet artistic developments in this formative period.

From art to architecture

The Revolution of 1917 presented the architectural profession with new briefs, which were essentially concerned with helping to reorganise the life of the mass population according to the direction outlined in the Bolshevik party's Marxist programme. For pragmatic reasons as well as deep-held ideological ones, the party's main social priority was the introduction of cooperative and collective ways of living that would free women for useful work, provide some framework of daily life for the orphans and those uprooted by the hostilities and make better use of scarce resources, as well as fostering the new political consciousness. In the several years of Civil War before economic reconstruction could start across the unified territory, internal fighting almost wholly destroyed such building materials industries as brick-making, timber-cutting and cement production. Only when the building materials position revived somewhat in 1924 could any new building work actually be started. Before that, there was only the most basic of maintenance work done to buildings with scraps of black-market materials. There was no real work for architects except exhibition pavilions for state ventures like the All-Russian Agricultural and Handicraft Exhibition in Moscow, of 1923, or street kiosks for distribution of basic goods. Where peasants in the countryside could cut logs for themselves there were some new wooden huts, but architects could only dream on paper.

During these first post-Revolutionary years, as Chapter 3 has shown, there was extensive work for all artists willing to contribute to public celebrations and visual propaganda about the new regime. But the serious innovators amongst them soon started forming into discussion groups and 'institutes' to debate the theoretical underpinnings of a new art for a new society. Some of these groups and their debates were highly important, even seminal, for the development of new ideas in architecture.

The first important year for theory was 1919. In Petrograd, Tatlin designed his Monument to the Third Communist International to demonstrate a new conception of the 'revolutionary monument' as something other than the conventional portrait sculptures which Lenin's Programme of Monumental Propaganda was erecting to replace tsarist statuary. Tatlin had no 'group', at this time or later, beyond the students who worked with him, but the short statement they issued to accompany the showing of the Tower model, called 'The Work Ahead of Us' [Doc.2], was of seminal importance for the future relationship of the plastic arts in Russia and for the very concept of art itself amongst the avant-garde.

'What happened in a social sense [with the Revolution] in 1917 was already acheived in our work as artists in 1914, when we took "materials, volume and construction" as our basic principles.' Those functionless 'reliefs and counter-reliefs' had displayed 'combinations of materials' deriving from 'investigations into the use of materials themselves' and 'their mutual relationships'. These works done in the pre-Revolutionary period, they said, were the 'laboratory scale' research for a new formal language through which to respond, now, after 1917, to the new society's requirements for material objects. The pre-Revolutionary notion of a synthesis of 'painting, sculpture and architecture' had lost its way in 'individualism'. Shekhtel's venture in synthesis of 1902, with bas-reliefs and ceramics from Abramtsevo and Korovin's paintings, was their paradigm of what resulted, as it 'bequeathed us a series of "Iaroslavl Railway Stations" and other now-ludicrous forms'. In the revolutionary context, what were formerly three distinct arts would become part of a continuum of work with real materials whose end products served useful functions. From these studies of materials, they declared, a whole new set of 'disciplines' must be developed as the designer's tools, 'a modern classicism, equal in its rigour' to that derived from 'the marble of the past'. The Monument exemplified this union of 'purely artistic forms with utilitarian intentions'. From such work derived 'samples' or 'models', *obraztsy*, of 'something new which stimulate us to inventions in the work of creating a new world, and which call upon us to take control of the [physical] forms of the new way of life.'[3]

This potent challenge to a transformation of the notions of 'art' into elements of consciously created material culture was enormously influential, but Tatlin himself did not play a central part in the further collective development of these ideas. The action shifts to a group which came together in Moscow in 1919 for just that purpose, of finding a new kind of synthesis or common practice between the plastic arts. Its aspiration was embodied in its title, Zhivskulptarkh: literally, Paint-Sculpt-Arch, which soon became a slightly more formal research and discussion organisation called Inkhuk: the Institute of Artistic Culture.[4]

The programme for this Inkhuk, formed in May 1921 was written by the now fifty-five year old Kandinsky, and was a natural development of the ideas he had published a decade before in *On the Spiritual in Art*, whose essentials had of course been disseminated amongst Russian artists to great acclaim at the All-Russian Congress of Artists in December 1911, and were discussed in Chapter 2. His combination of Symbolism and psychology with abstract formal analysis was clearly echoed in the definition of that 'science of art' which Inkhuk would research. 'The first part of our programme' he wrote, 'consists of an analysis of the specific properties of each different artistic medium. The point of departure is to be the psychological response of the artist to that property – thus red, for example, is known to excite activity'.[5] This phrase 'psychological response' indicates the direction intended, and in circles increasingly fired by Tatlin's vision of a concrete and materialist art that would 'take control of the forms of production', it did not last long. When Kandinsky was forced to leave Inkhuk he took his ideas to the more establishment Moscow art forum called Rakhn: the Russian Academy of Artistic Sciences. Its different tone is indicated by fact that the principal architectural figure here was Zholtovsky. As a founder vice-president and chair of its Physico-Psychological Section Kandinsky delivered his line in several more papers here before leaving Russia with an invitation to return to Germany in December 1921.[6]

Kandinsky was replaced as head of Inkhuk by Osip Brik, a theorist of the movement 'into production' who was far more sympathetic to the majority of members. Meanwhile the artists and architects in the Institute organised themselves into Working Groups to investigate 'the specific properties' of painting, sculpture and architecture, with the latter group being led by the forty year old architect Nikolai Ladovsky. Ladovsky's 'work-plan' for the architecture group when they started in 1921 was:

'1: the assembly of theoretical studies and the existing theories of architecture of all theoreticians, 2: the extraction and assembly of relevant material from these theoretical treatises and from research in other arts that has a bearing upon architecture, and 3: the exposition of our own theoretical attitudes to architecture.' [7]

The other groups were working in parallel with them, as Ladovsky continued, and that included the Group of Objective Analysis, of which he was also a member, where 'top of their agenda right now is the investigation of [the principles of] construction and composition.' [Doc.3] It was from this Objective Analysis Group and this discussion that the ideas would emerge which defined the two main avant-garde architectural groupings for the rest of the Twenties.

The artists of the Objective Analysis Group, who included the most radically innovative abstractionists, were aware of the emergence of a new principle in their work, which differed significantly from the principles in which they had been trained, in most cases, before the Revolution. It was not their abstraction itself which was new, but a more self-consciously programmatic way of creating a form that involved 'building it up', literally 'constructing' it, rather than composing the work as a single perceived image.

The sheets on which each Objective Analysis Group member presented 'a composition' and 'a construction' to help clarify these emerging ideas amongst themselves are contained in that part of the George Costakis Collection of Russian avant-garde art which now resides in the West. Meanwhile Selim Khan-Magomedov has published the transcripts of their discussions of them, from Russian archives. These sources together illuminate this moment of the crystallisation of new perception and a new distinction of principle with remarkable vividness. [8]

For avant-garde architecture in particular, this debate marked a turning point. Those artists and architects who still believed in the primacy of the old-established notion of 'composition', and still sought to develop the psychological and perceptual direction outlined by Kandinsky's initial programme, were to become the 'Architectural Rationalists', led by Ladovsky and his colleague Krinsky. Two years after this Inkhuk discussion, in July 1923, they formed the first new architectural society of the post-Revolutionary period – first rival in the new capital to MAO – which they called Asnova, the Association of New Architects, to propagate this approach, particularly in teaching. [9] On the other hand those artists centred around Alexander Rodchenko and Alexei Gan who were convinced of the special importance of the new principle of 'construction' formed Inkhuk's First Working Group of Constructivists in March 1921. [10] In late 1925, as building work started reviving, some of these artist-designers linked up with architects Alexander Vesnin and Moisei Ginzburg and their students from MVTU to form a Constructivist architectural group under the name of OSA, the Union of Contemporary Architects.

These two groups, Asnova and OSA were to form the two main alignments of what we may call a scientific Modernism within the Russian avant-garde. Alongside them were a range of individuals pursuing variants of a more traditional approach. Some of this work is stylistically Modernist; some of it still Historicist, and others adopted various positions in between. I shall look first at the key identifying ideas of Rationalism and Constructivism, then at the most important of those others, some strongly principled, some more pragmatic, who were in any way Modernist.

Asnova and Rationalism

The work of this group was based on ideas about the psychology of perception, in particular the impact and reading of form. It developed, as I have indicated, from Kandinsky's inspiration as taken forward after 1921 by the 'composition' group within Inkhuk's Objective Analysis Group. Ladovsky and Krinsky, who were the the Rationalists' leaders, built virtually nothing. They were extremely influential however as teachers, especially in the Moscow Vkhutemas, and numerous Modernist architects amongst their pupils made their mark with powerful and inventive design work in competitions, and in some construction work such as housing in Moscow, and factory-kitchen complexes in Leningrad, later in the Twenties.

After the reorganisation of Moscow's two old art and architecture schools into 'Free Studios', in 1918, and into the more coherent 'Higher Artistic and Technical Studios', or Vkhutemas, in 1919, their integrated curriculum was based largely on the ideas of a continuum of the two- and three-dimensional arts developed in Zhivskulptarkh and Inkhuk. All students entered through a Basic, or Foundation, Course before moving on to their chosen disciplines, and this Basic Course was largely in the hands of Ladovsky and Krinsky. Whilst most architects of any note in the city were teaching in the school, even initially such old hands as Shekhtel, Ladovsky and Krinsky had a unique role in teaching all first-year students the fundamentals of formal composition and expression. Some examples of this curriculum were published in 1926 in the single issue of their group's journal, designed by Lissitzky, called *Asnova News (Izvestiia ASNOVA)* [Doc.18]. Much more of it was recorded in a book that in various versions remained central to Moscow architectural education to the very end of the Soviet period, *Elements of Spatial Composition in Architecture*, published by Krinsky with his pupils Lamtsov and Turkus in 1934 [pp.162-3]. [11] Ladovsky also taught a studio in the architecture department, based on their conception of 'architectural rationalism'.

In Ladovsky's definition of 1919, 'Architectural Rationalism stands for the economy of psychic energy in the perception of spatial and functional aspects of a building', and he specifically contrasted this to 'technical rationalism', whose priority is an economy of materials. [12] As he expanded this into his 'Foundations for a theory of architecture' [Doc.18] in the next year:

'Architectural Rationalism is founded upon the economic principle just as technical Rationalism is. The difference lies in the fact that technical rationalism is an economy of labour and material in the creation of a suitable and convenient building, but architectural rationalism is the economy of psychic energy in the perception of the spatial and functional properties of the building.

'Architecture operates by means of properties – like weight, density, mass, finiteness and non-finiteness, stability or dynamics etc – as specific quantities. The architect constructs a form, bringing together elements which are not technical or utilitarian ones in the normal sense of those words, but which can

Text continues on page 88 after the picture section.

ASNOVA: THE RATIONALISTS

a: Vladimir Krinsky, *skyscraper headquarters for the Supreme Soviet of the National Economy (Vesenkha USSR) on Lubianka Square, Moscow, 1923: photomontage from model.*

b: *notional plans, with partial elevation to the Square modelled in relief.*

c: *side elevational drawing,*

d: Ivan Volodko, *project for Vesenkha skyscraper: montage with (inverted) Ivan Belltower of the Kremlin, illustrating role of the Vesenkha tower as a second vertical in the central Moscow skyline.*

e: Krinsky, *competition project for the ARCOS building (Anglo-Russian Trading Company), Moscow, 1924: main street elevation.*

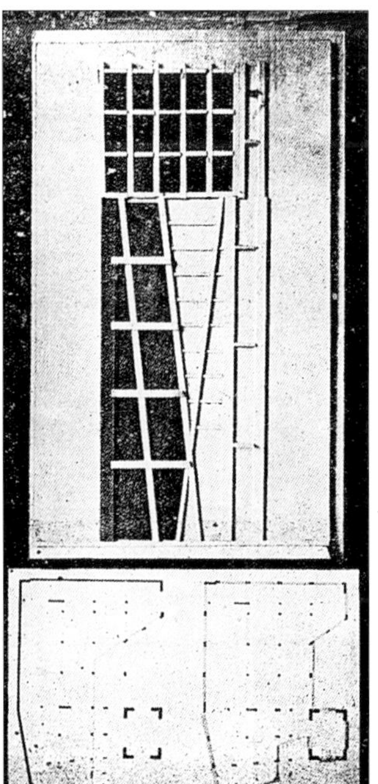

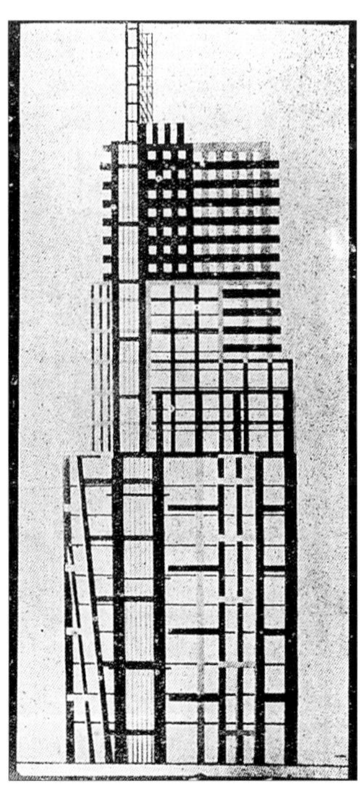

ЦИЯ — ЛЕ КОРБЮЗЬЕ ■ ГОЛАНДИЯ — МАРТ СТАМ ■ АМЕРИК
ЕЛЬ ТЕЙГЕ ■ ЮГО-СЛАВИЯ — ЛЮБОМИР МИЦИЧ ■ ЯПОНИЯ МУРА

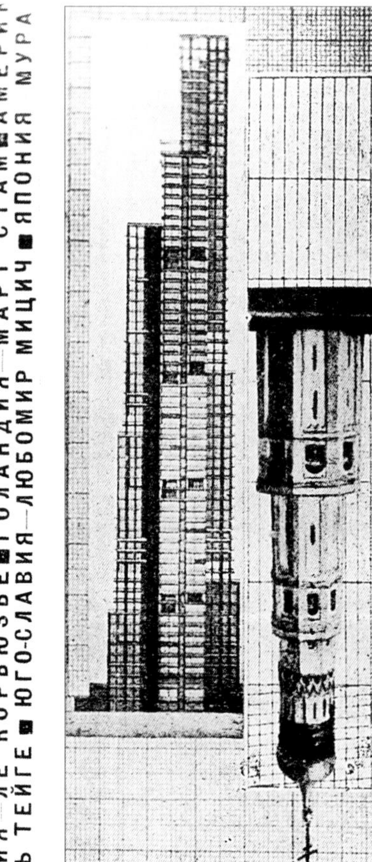

Buildings by Asnova members in Moscow

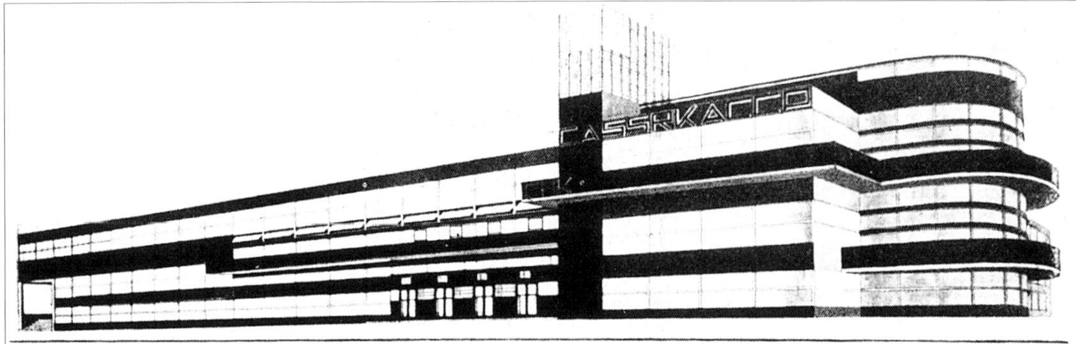

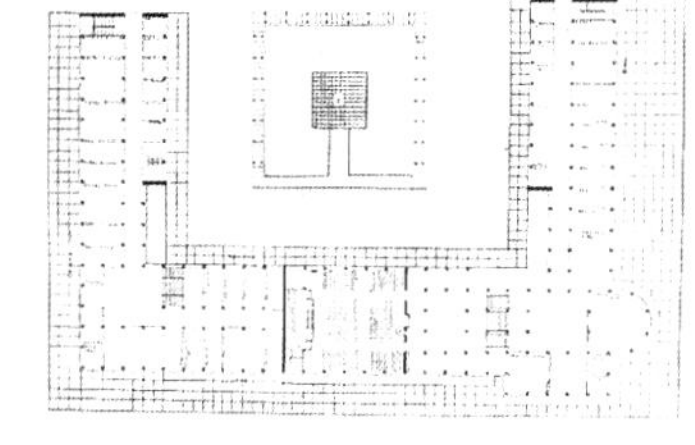

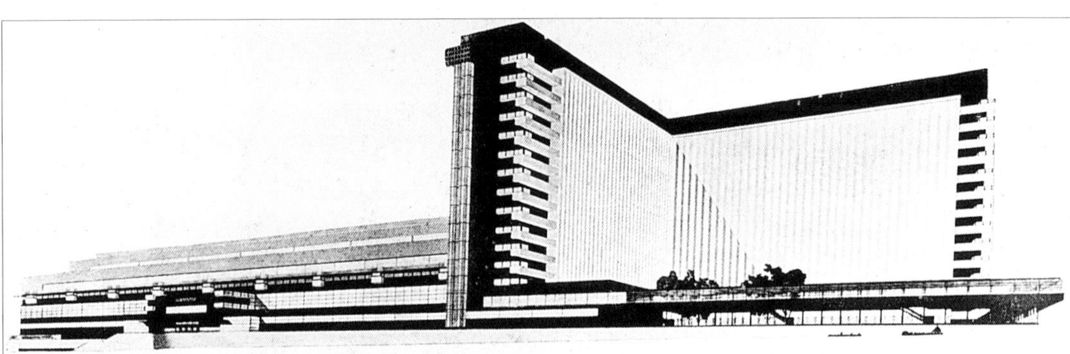

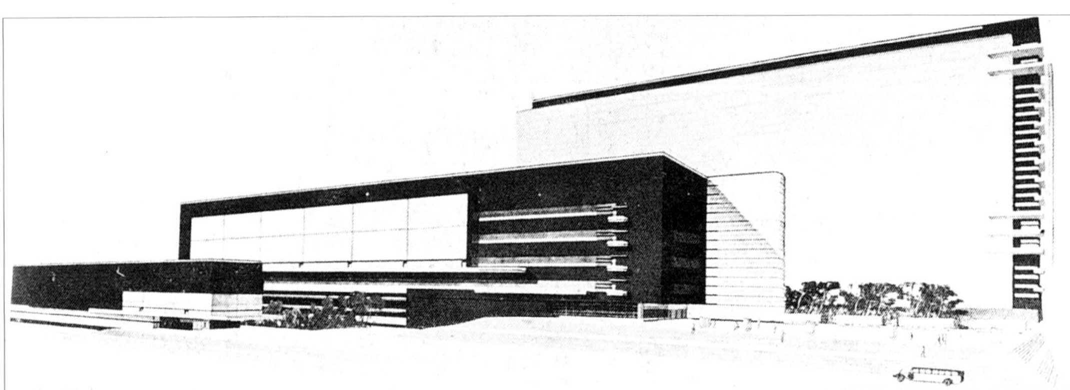

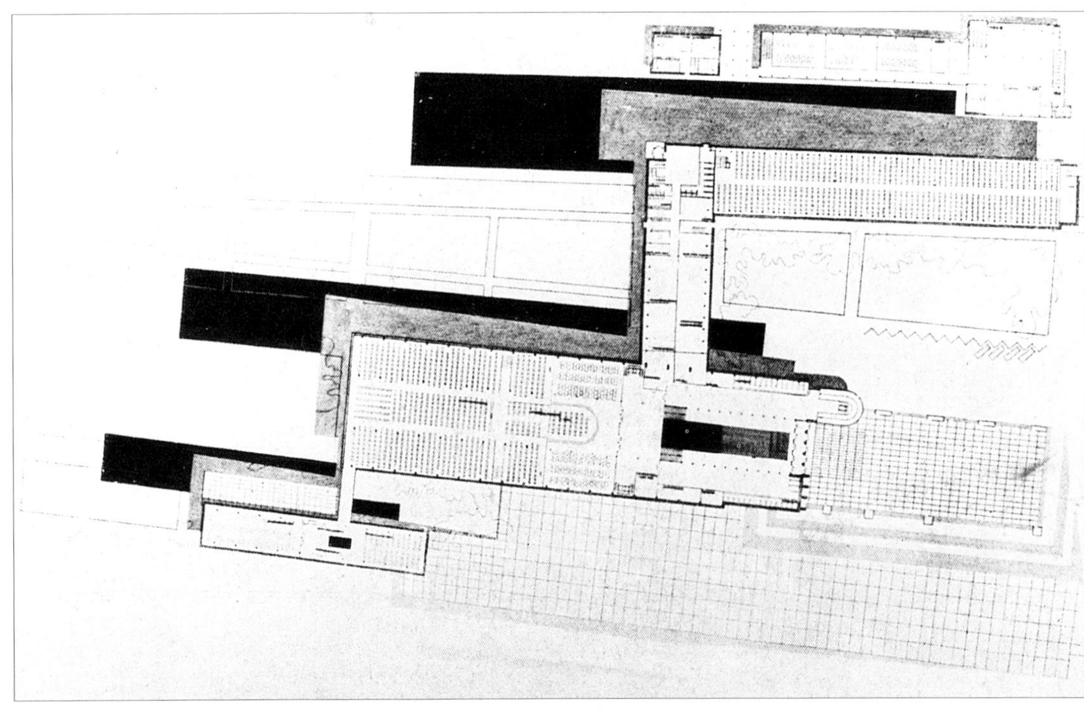

***a, b:* Daniil Fridman**, *5th prize-winning competition project for the House of Government in Alma-Ata, 1927: perspective, first-floor plan.*

***c:* Dmitri Markov, Daniil Fridman, Vladimir Fidman**, *competition project for the Lenin Library, Moscow, 1928, first stage: perspective.*

d: *second stage: perspective.*

***e:* Markov, Fridman, Fidman**, *Lenin Library competiton, second stage: ground-level plan.*

***f, g:* Andrei Bunin, Liubov Zalesskaia, Maria Kruglova, Mikhail Turkus et al**, *Competition project for the State Theatre of Massed Musical Activities, Kharkov, 1930: model, plan at upper level.*

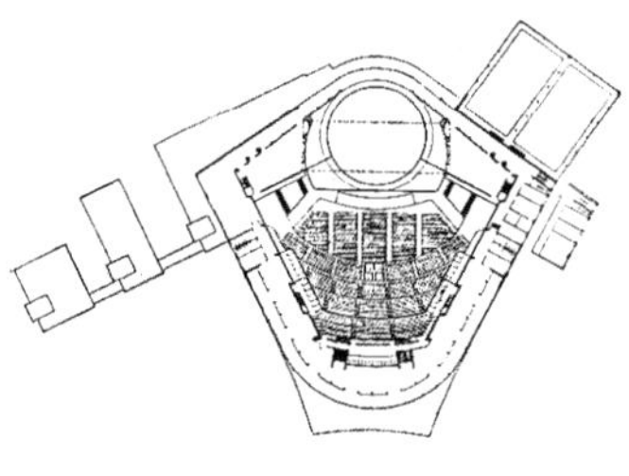

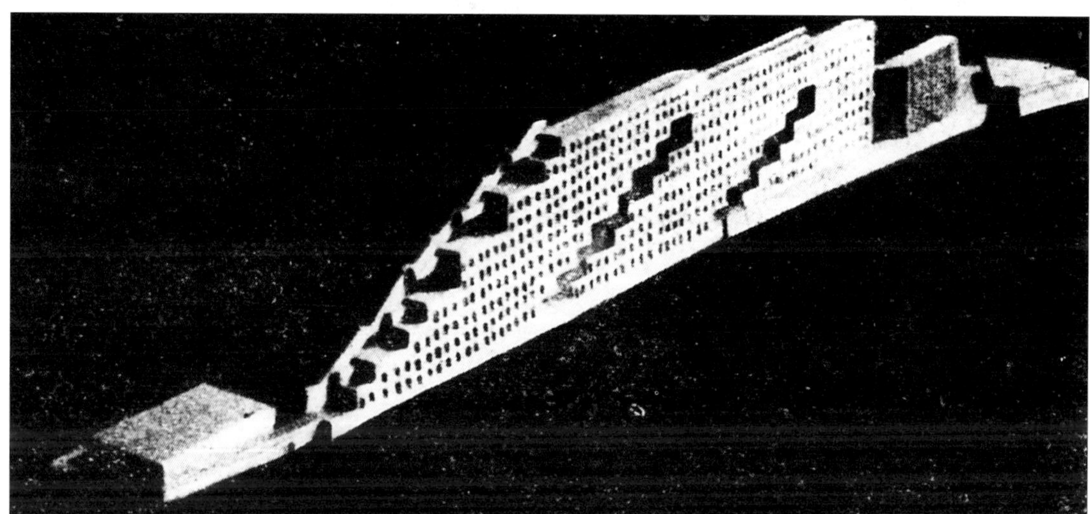

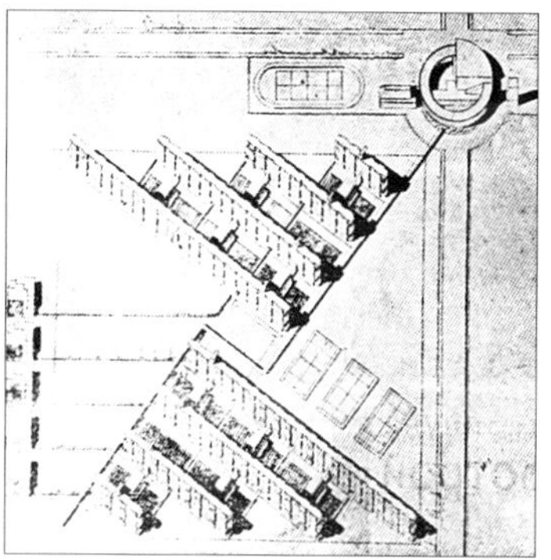

City-commune of the new car-production centre, Avtostroi:

a: Vikor Kalmykov, *skyscraper 'housing combines' for 700 people in general view of model.*

b, c: Kalmykov, Anatoly Kaplun, *terraced 'housing combines' for 1000 people: detail of model, perspective.*

d: Georgi Krutikov, Vitaly Lavrov, Valentin Popov, *competition project for the new city of Avtostroi, 1930: axonometric of part of the housing district, with sleeping blocks and circular social facilities building.*

e: *central strip with public buildings: model.*

f: *general view of model.*

g: *axonometric of rooms in communal housing blocks.*

h: *view of the city from the inter-urban highway.*

i: Unidentified Asnova team, *competition project for a Palace of Culture beside the Moscow River, 1930: model.*

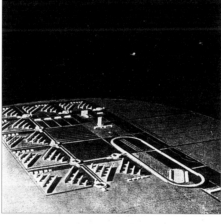

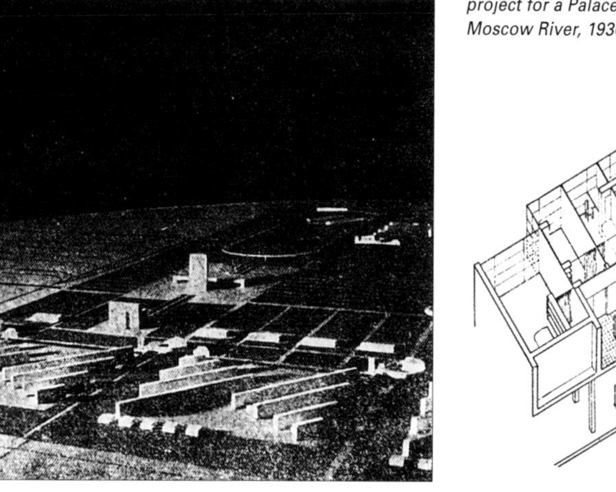

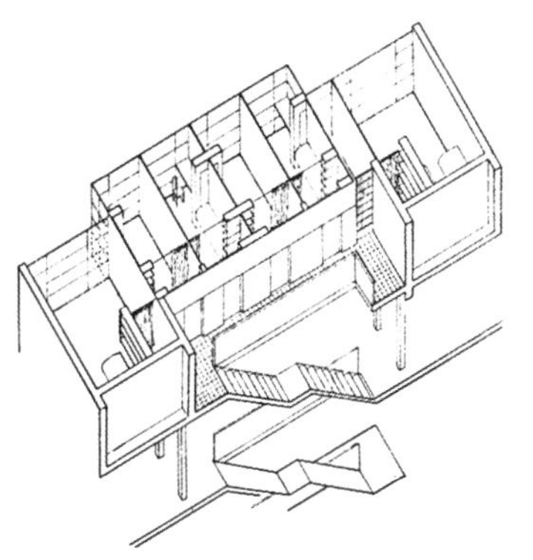

Buildings by Asnova members in Leningrad

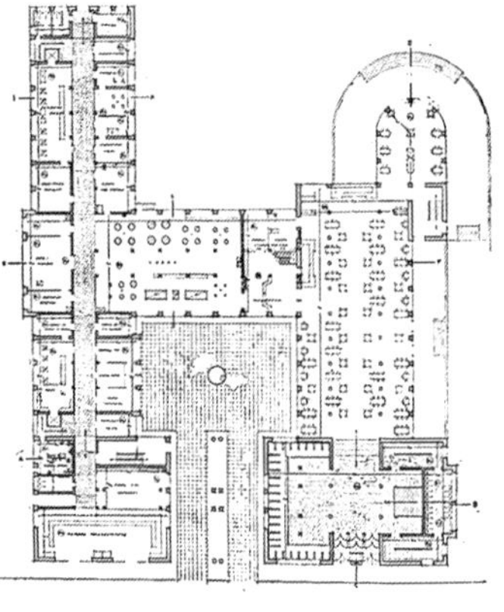

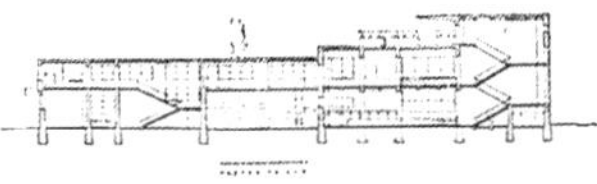

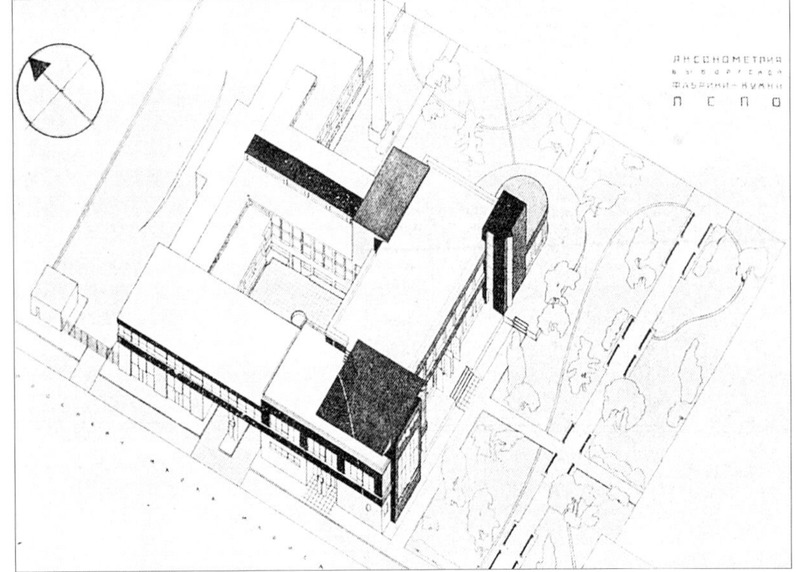

a: Armen Barutchev, Isidor Gilter, Iosif Meerzon, Iakov Rubanchik, *factory kitchen and public feeding complex for Viborg district of Leningrad, 1928-30: photograph, 1930.*

b, c: *ground floor plan, section.*

d: *photograph, 1989*

e: *axonometric drawing.*

f: *graphic statistics from* Our Achievements, *no.1, 1931: showing rise in 'Public feeding' outputs of USSR from 1929-1931, in millions of dishes served.*

g: *Viborg district complex: perspective.*

h: Barutchev, Gilter, Meerzon, Rubanchik, *factory kitchen and public feeding complex for Vasily Island, Leningrad, 1930-31: northwest corner, photograph 1989.*

i: *southeast corner, with semi-circular dining hall in trees, right, photograph 1989*

ДОМ
КООПЕРАЦИИ

НАРВСКИЙ УНИВЕРМАГ

НАРВСКИЙ УНИВЕРМАГ

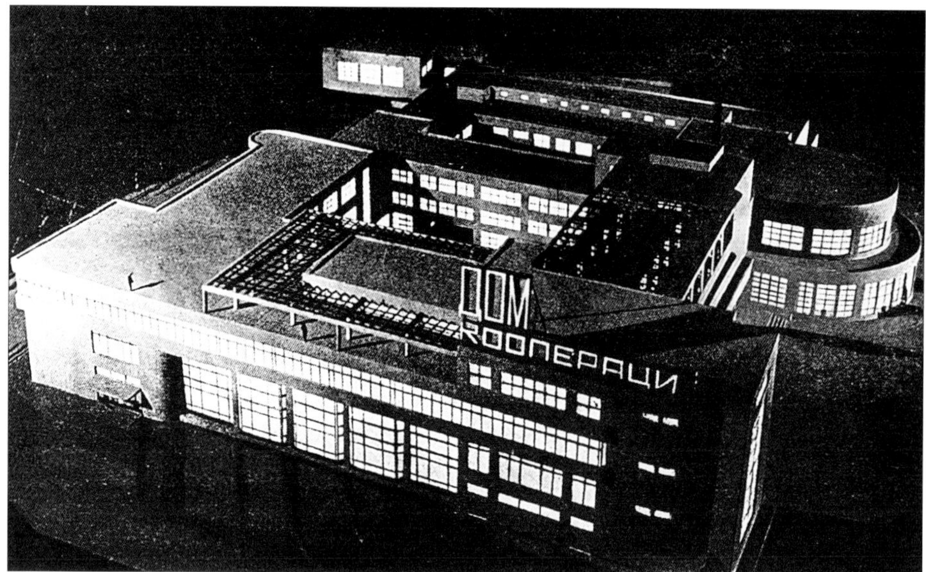

a: Armen Barutchev, Isidor Gilter, Iosif Meerzon, Iakov Rubanchik, *department store, factory kitchen and public feeding complex for the Kirov (Narva) district of Leningrad, 1928-31: perspective, showing the modernist building inserted in the classical city.*

b: *daytime photograph soon after completion.*

c: *night view soon after completion.*

d: *illuminated model of whole complex with department store along left part of main street front, and feeding accommodation behind entered front right.*

e: *view towards main entrance of feeding complex with department store beyond, photograph 1989.*

f: *semi-circular dining hall with central servery, perspective without furniture.*

g: *view along shop front from entrance to feeding section, soon after completion.*

h: *semi-circular dining room, evening view looking towards windows, soon after completion.*

OSA: THE CONSTRUCTIVISTS

Buildings by OSA members in Moscow: the Vesnin brothers

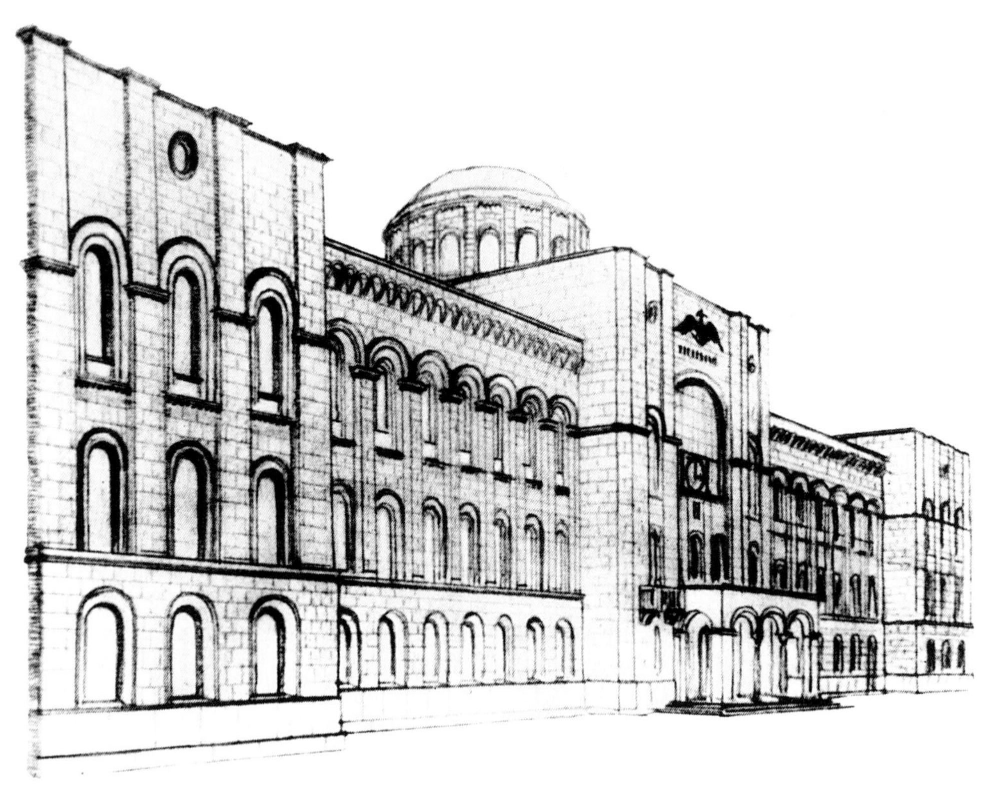

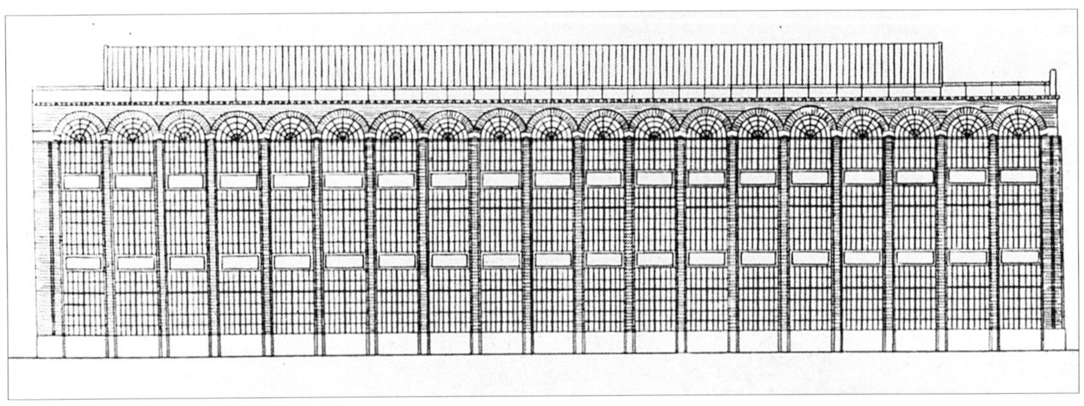

***a:* Vesnin brothers, for the office of O.R. Munts,** *Facade of the Moscow Central Post Office opposite MUZhVZ building, 1911: perspective.*

***b:* Leonid Vesnin,** *project for a dacha, 1908: perspective.*

***c:* Vesnin brothers,** *weaving shop for Tomna textile plant in Great Kineshemskaia, 1916-17: elevation.*

d: *competition project for Gostinyi Dvor (retail shopping centre), Nizhni-Novgorod, 1914: perspective.*

***e:* Leonid Vesnin with V.A. Simov,** *dacha for V. A. Nosenskov in Ivankovo near Moscow, 1909-11: photograph soon after completion.*

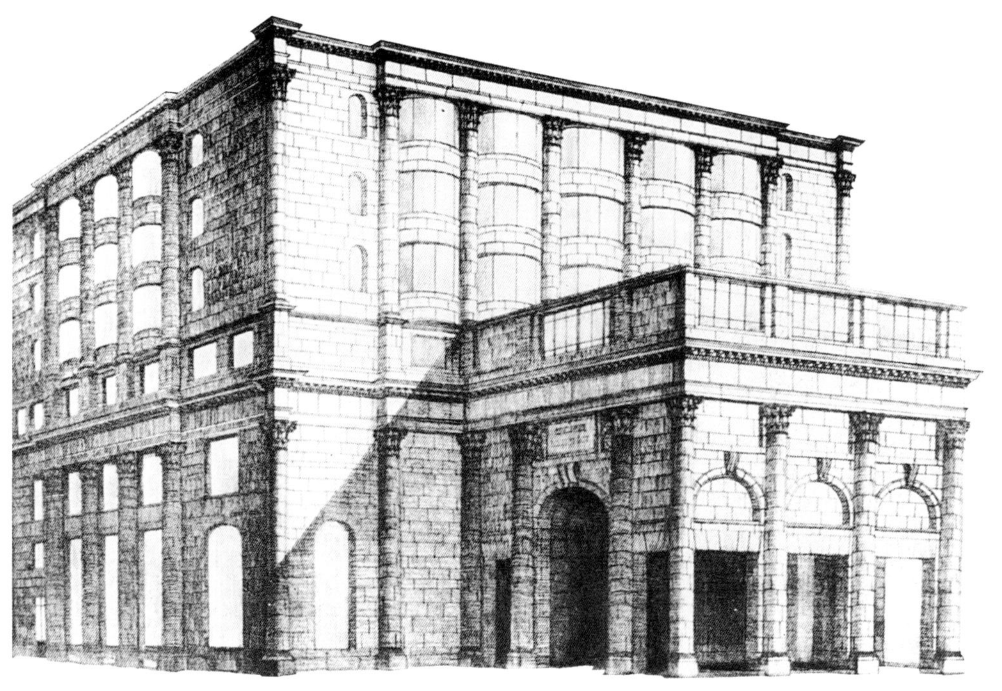

***a:* Vesnin brothers,** *development project for Mr. Roll, Moscow, 1913: perspective of the hotel.*

b: *Mansion for D. V. Sirotkin in Nizhni-Novgorod, 1915-16: perspective.*

c: *Project for the Dinamo Company's department store, Moscow, 1916-17: perspective.*

a: Viktor Vesnin, *Chernorechesky superphosphate plant in Nizhni-Novgorod, 1918-19: perspective.*

b: Alexander Vesnin, *stage set for G.K. Chesterton's play 'The Man who was Thursday', Kamerny Theatre, Moscow, 1923.*

c: Vesnin brothers, *Natural turpentine plant near Kostroma, 1922-24: sketch perspective.*

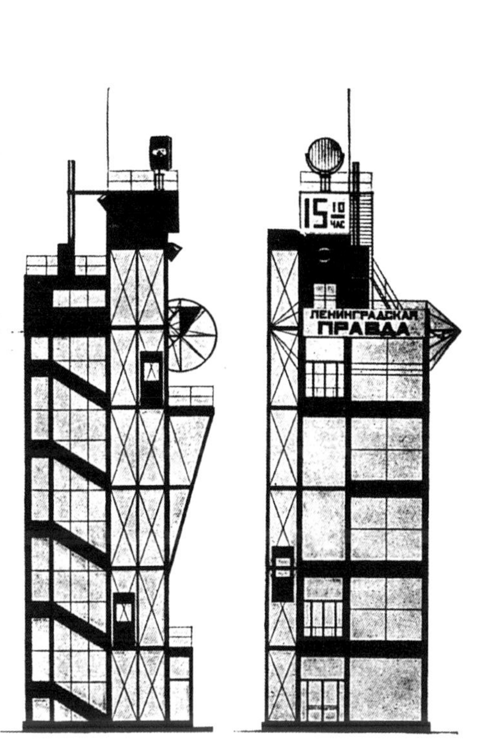

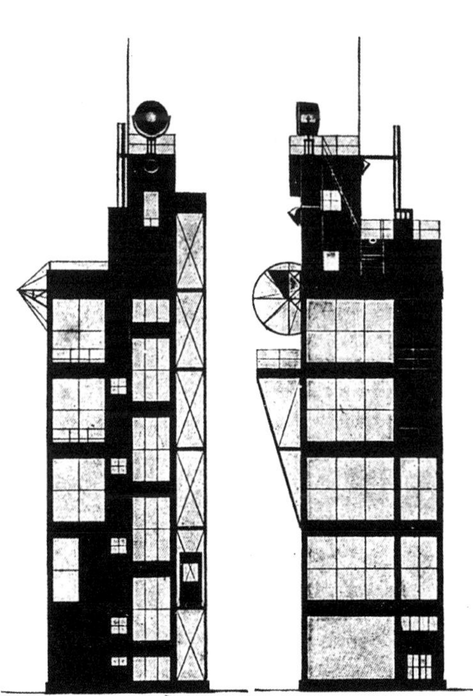

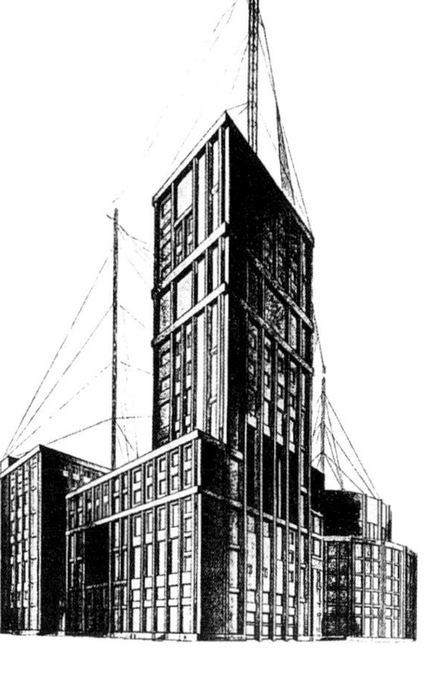

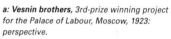

***a:* Vesnin brothers,** *3rd-prize winning project for the Palace of Labour, Moscow, 1923: perspective.*

b: *competition project for Moscow offices of the newspaper* Leningradskaia Pravda, *1924: four elevations.*

c: *perspective*

d: *first floor plan and ground floor with reception desk.*

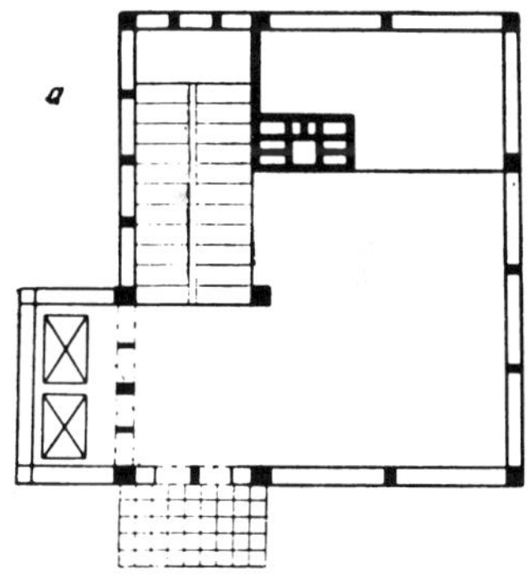

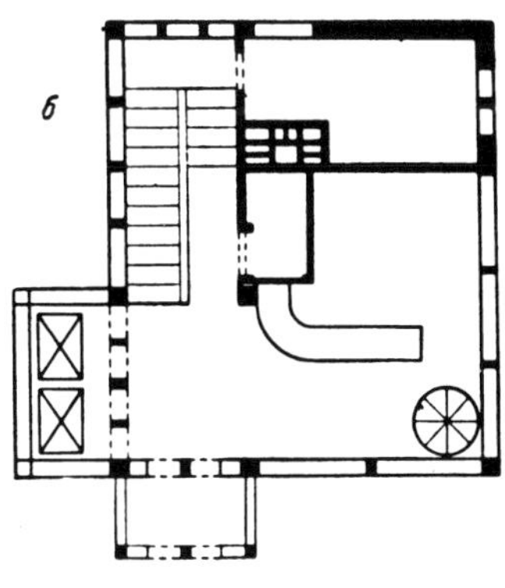

В. А. ВЕСНИН. ИВСЕЛЬБАНК
W. WESNIN. DIE BANK ZU IWANOWO-WOSNESSJENSK

a: ***Vesnin brothers,*** *Mostorg department store, Krasnaia Presnia, Moscow, 1927: photograph of entrance, 1928.*
b: photograph of front, 1928.
c: ***Viktor Vesnin,*** *Ivselbank Agricultural Bank, Ivanovo-Voznesensk, 1927: photograph during construction and perspective.*
d: ***Viktor Vesnin,*** *Institute of Mineral Raw Materials for the Scientific Section of Vesenkha, Moscow, 1925: general view during construction.*
e: view across the flat roofs.

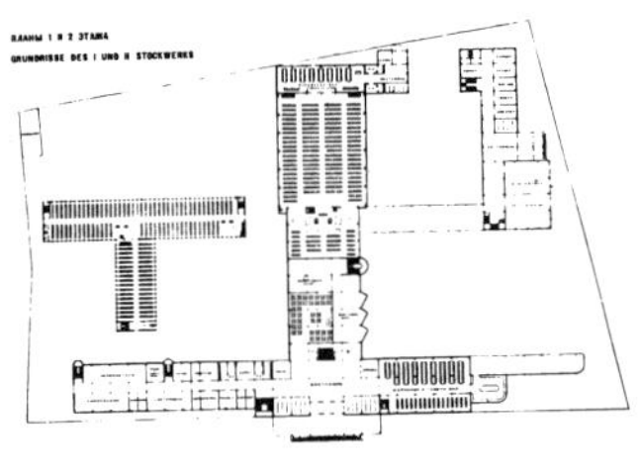

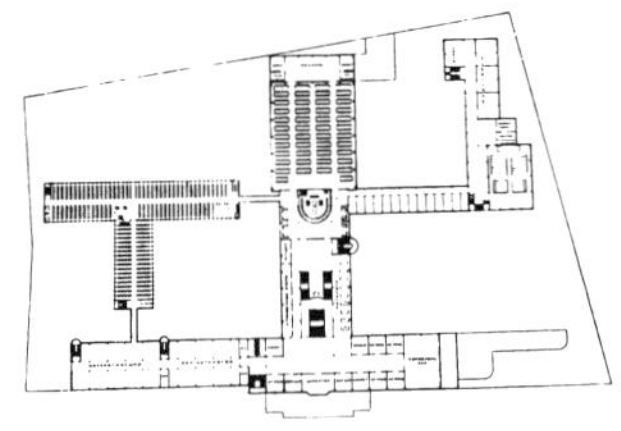

a: Vesnin brothers, *Second-stage competition project for the Lenin Library, Moscow, 1928: perspective of main entrance hall.*

b, c: *ground and first-floor plans.*

d: *Workers' club at Bailov in Baku, 1928: perspective.*

e: *Competition project for the Lenin Library: perspective.*

f: *Club for Society of Former Political Prisoners of Tsarism, Moscow, 1931-35: perspective (building only partially executed).*

g: *detail with entrance steps, photograph 1987.*

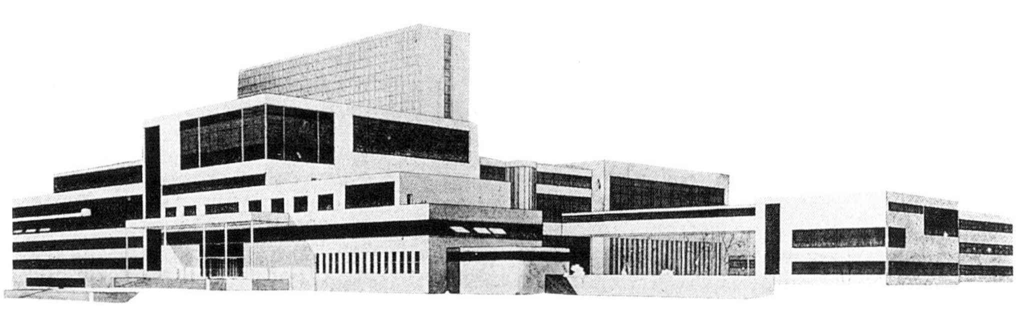

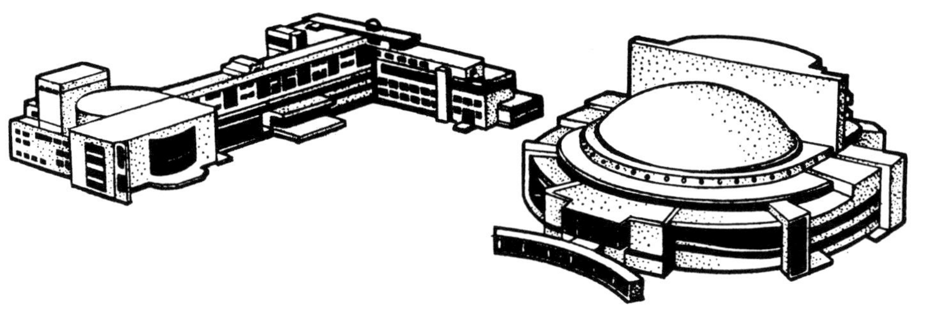

a: *graphic from* Our Achievements, *no.1, 1931, showing 'Palaces of Culture' (alternate name for workers' clubs) as centres of leisure and literacy for 'the working youth' of all Soviet nationalities.*

b: Vesnin brothers, *Palace of Culture of the Proletarsky district of Moscow, 1931-37: isometric drawing of the whole complex (theatre block, right, not built).*

c: *main entrance to foyers and smaller auditorium, photograph 1987.*

d: *first-floor foyer to the smaller auditorium, interior, photograph of 1930s.*

e: *entrance to Winter Garden with dome of astronomical observatory visible above.*

Buildings by OSA Members in Moscow: Moisei Ginzburg

АРХИТЕКТОР!

ТАК НУЖНО ПОНИМАТЬ МАТЕРИАЛИСТИЧЕСКИЕ ОСНОВЫ ЭСТЕТИКИ КОНСТРУКТИВИЗМА

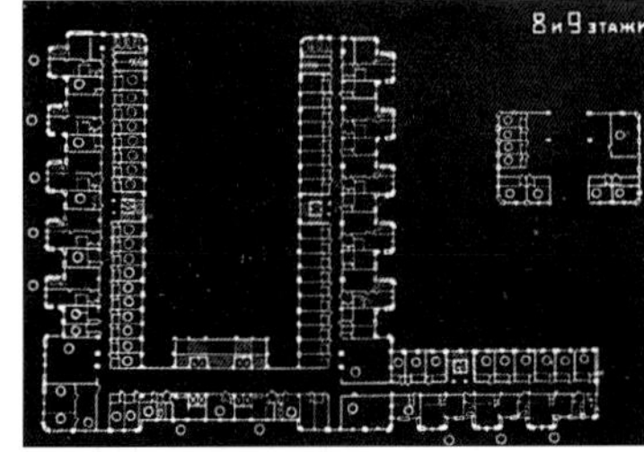

a: *typographical feature from* SA, *1926 no.3 (see pages 130-1).*

b: Moisei Ginzburg, *competition project for the Palace of Labour, Moscow, 1923: perspective of main entrance.*

c: *competition project for the House of Textiles, Moscow, 1925: section showing central courtyard and vehicle ramps to carparking below.*

d: *perspective.*

e-g: *plans of floors 7 & 8, floor 9, and of basement carpark.*

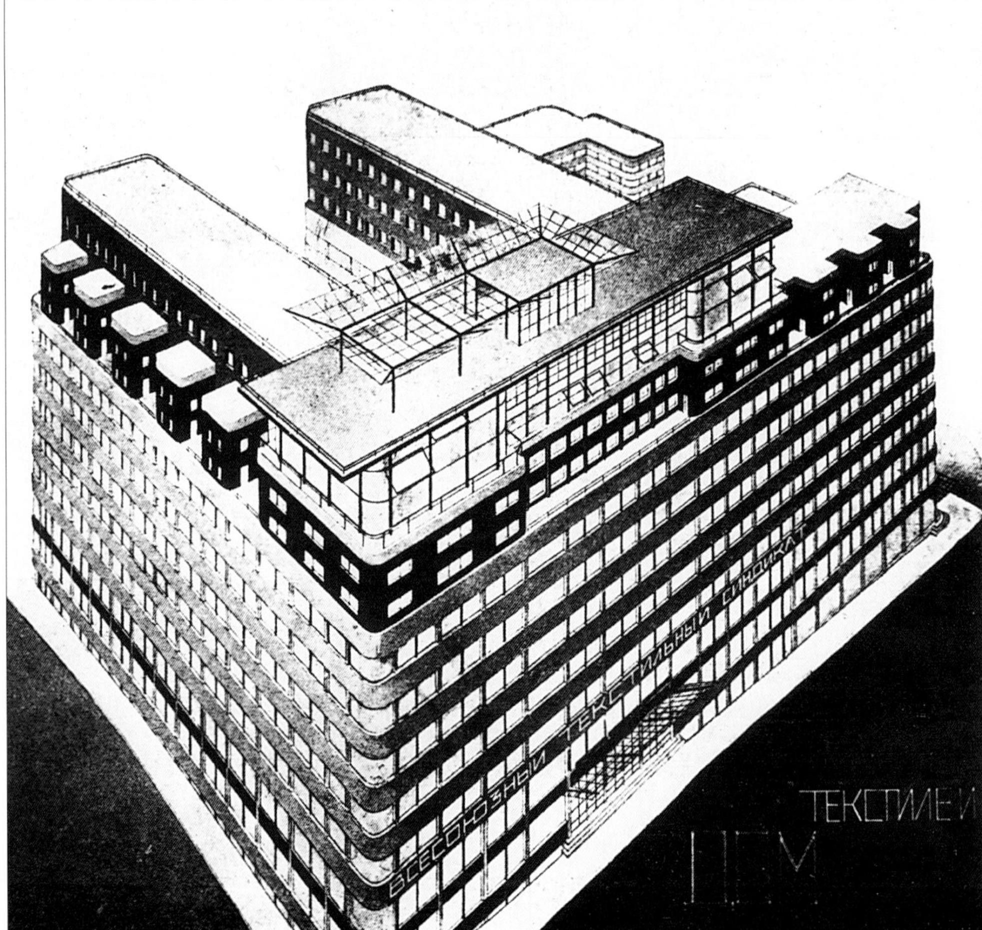

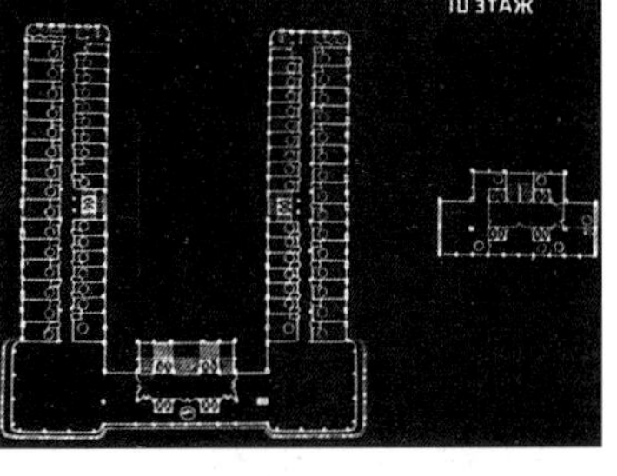

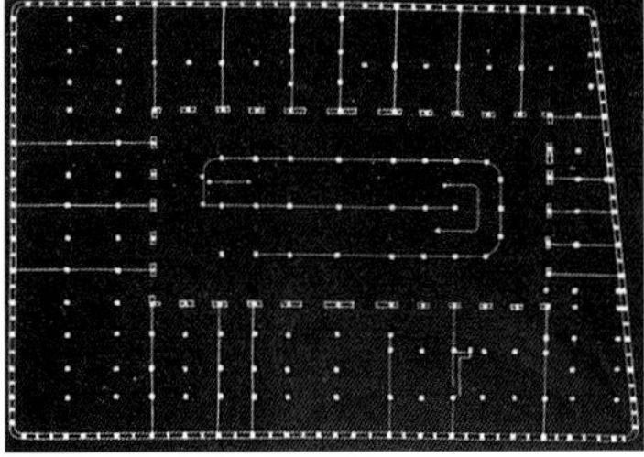

***a:* Moisei Ginzburg,** *Apartment and communal housing block for the State Insurance Bureau, Gostrakh, built 1926-27: photograph 1927.*

b: *view of roof terrace from adjacent building, photograph 1927.*

c: *axonometric.*

d: *Title to Ginzburg's article 'New methods of architectural thought' from the first page of SA's first issue, 1926 no.1 (see pages 129-30).*

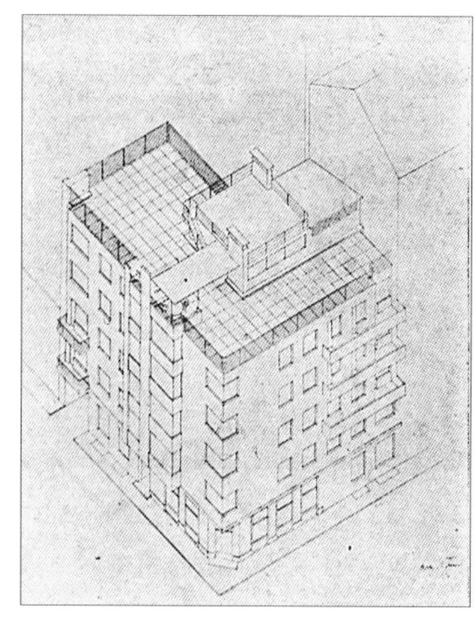

НОВЫЕ МЕТОДЫ
АРХИТЕКТУРНОГО МЫШЛЕНИЯ

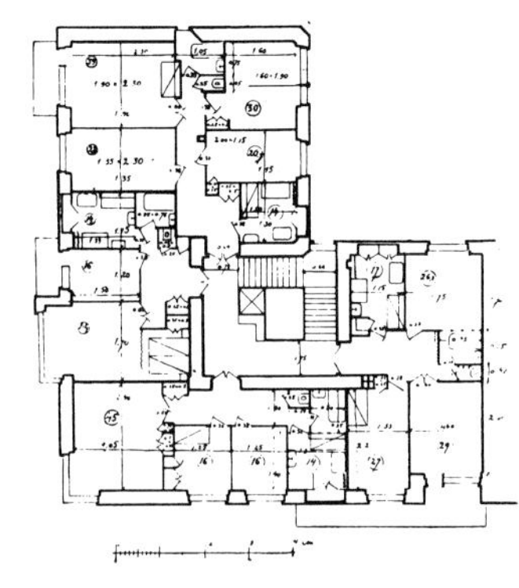

***a:* Moisei Ginzburg,** *apartment and communal housing block for the State Insurance Bureau, Gostrakh, Moscow, built 1926-27: upper corner from street, photograph 1927.*

b: *typical floor plan.*

c: *Ginzburg enjoying his Corbusian* toit jardin *in Moscow, 1927.*

d: *space-saving folding* couchette *('Cupboard-bed') used in this building.*

НОВЫЕ МЕТОДЫ АРХИТЕКТУРНОГО МЫШЛЕНИЯ

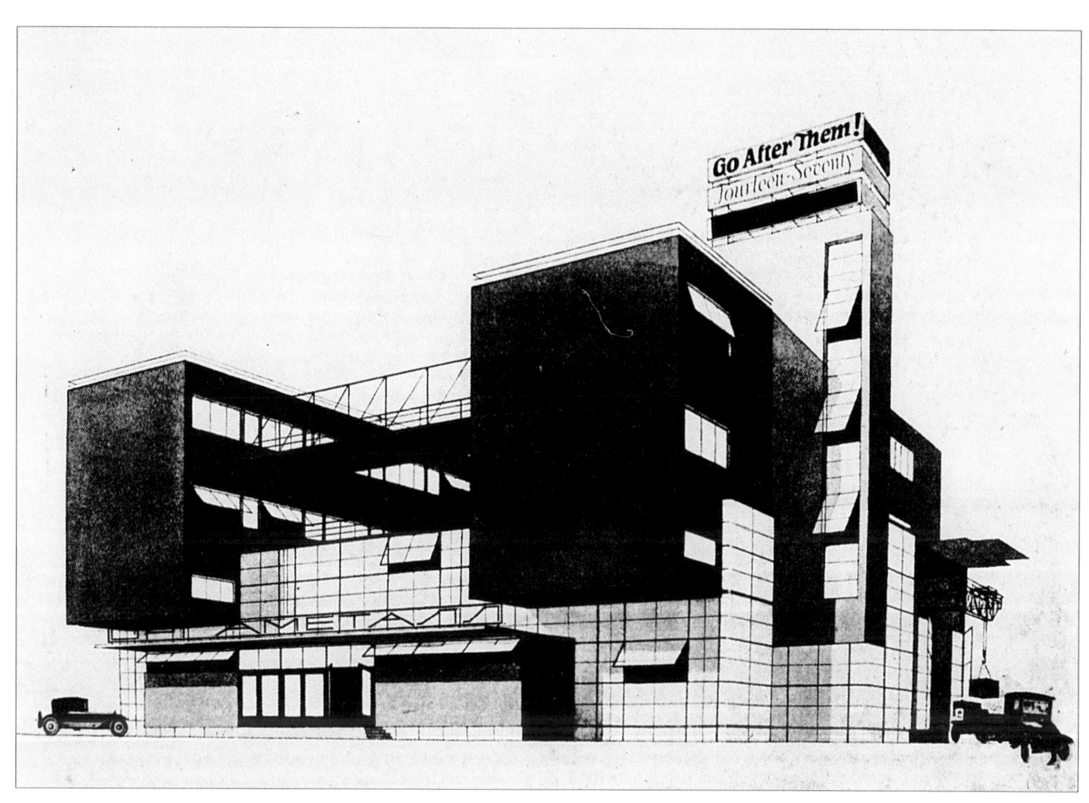

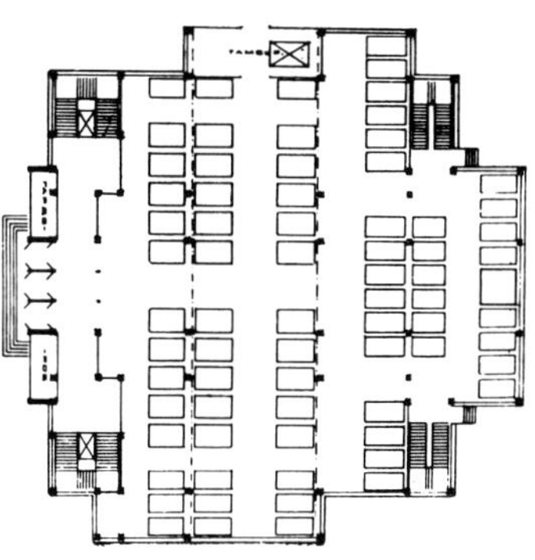

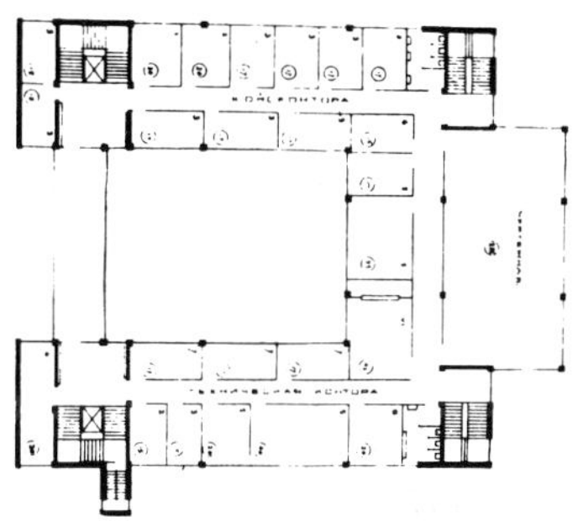

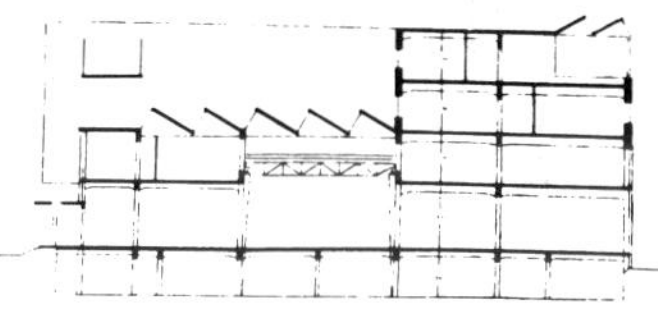

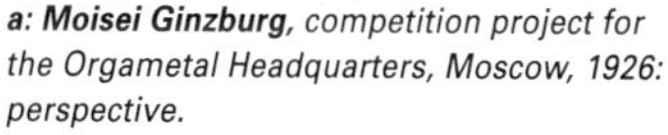

***a:* Moisei Ginzburg**, *competition project for the Orgametal Headquarters, Moscow, 1926: perspective.*

b-d: *ground floor plan with exhibition space for Orgametal's machines; plan of second and third floors, with offices and drawing office; section, showing top-lit central space at ground and first floors, and basement storage and parking.*

***e:* Moisei Ginzburg with Viacheslav Vladimirov, Alexander Pasternak,** *competition project for headquarters of the Russo-German Trading Company, Russgertorg, Moscow, 1926: perspective.*

f: *isometric.*

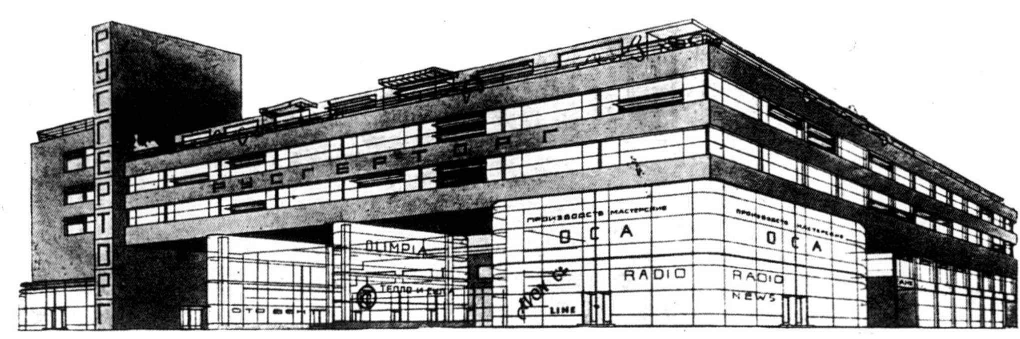

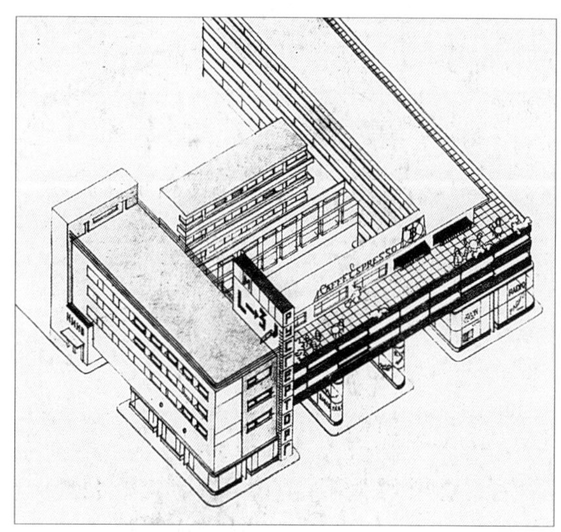

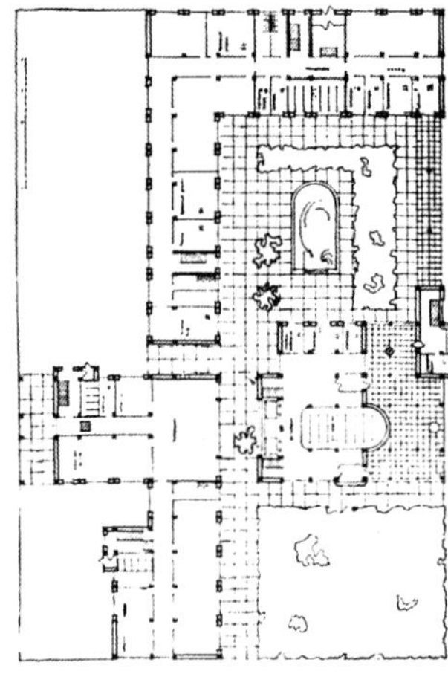

a, b: Moisei Ginzburg with Ignati Milinis, *competition project for the House of Government of the Kazakh Republic, Alma-Ata, 1928 (first prize: built 1929-31): axonometric and ground plan.*

c: *cutaway axonometric view of bridge 'court' and rear of auditorium.*

d, e: *first and second-floor plans.*

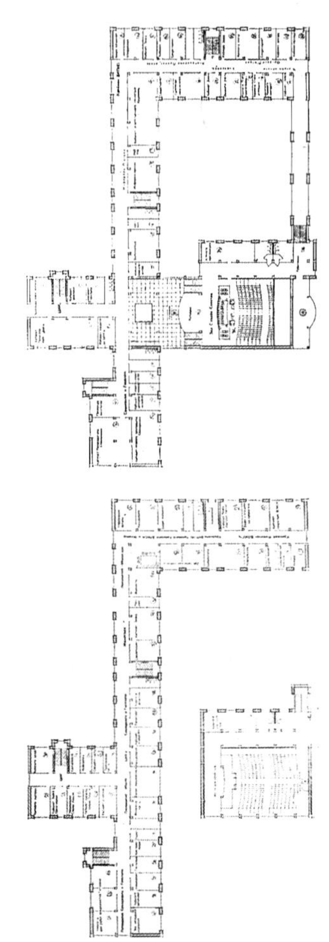

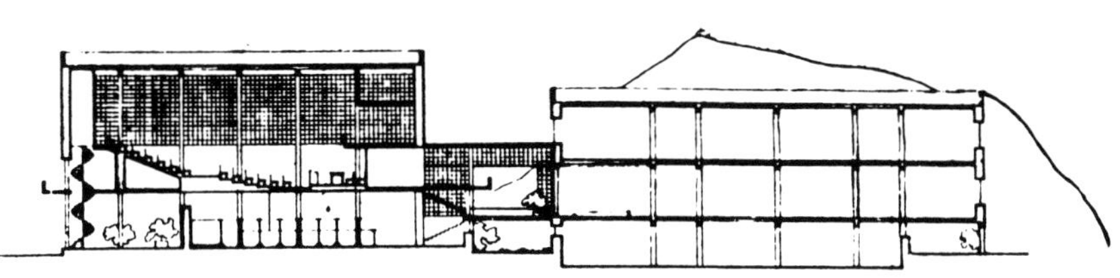

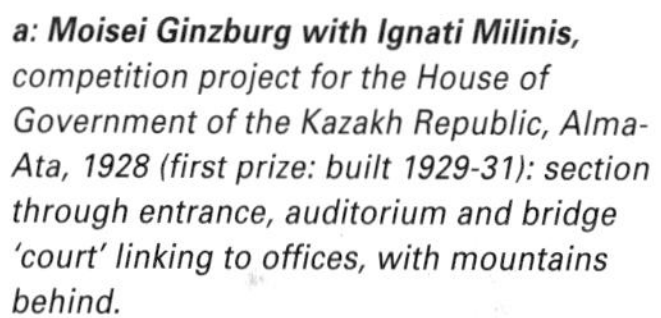

a: Moisei Ginzburg with Ignati Milinis, *competition project for the House of Government of the Kazakh Republic, Alma-Ata, 1928 (first prize: built 1929-31): section through entrance, auditorium and bridge 'court' linking to offices, with mountains behind.*

b: *perspective towards entrance.*

c-h: *six photographs of the model.*

i: *pictorial feature from* SA *1926 no.5-6.* Above, *'The Dead East' condemning 'the application of local style' as an approach to creating new architectures for the Soviet national republics (as Zholtovsky had done in a House of Government project for Dagestan), is contrasted with 'The Live East',* below, *where old courtyard housing in Bukhara illustrates the Constructivists' 'functional approach " of learning from how vernacular traditions handled climate (enclosure, shading, controlled fenestration), of enlarging accepted social spaces (family courtyard) to new social scale of the collective unit, etc.*

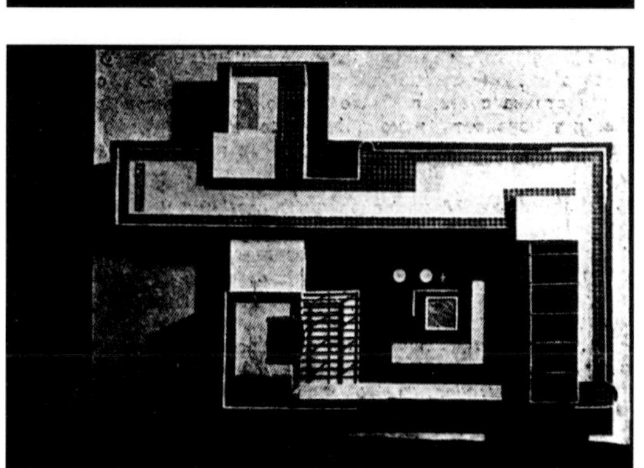

Buildings by OSA members in Leningrad: Alexander Nikolsky

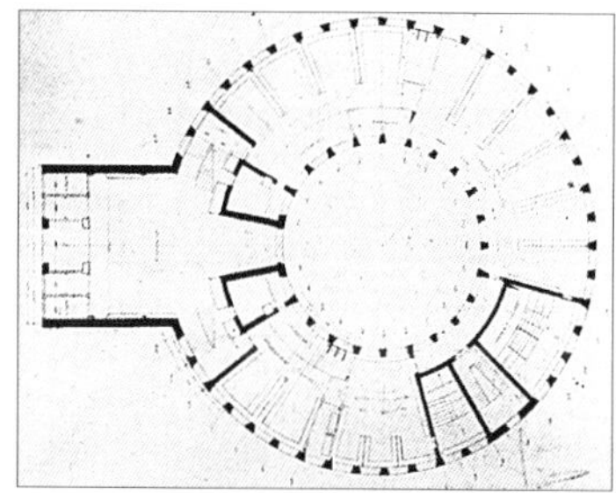

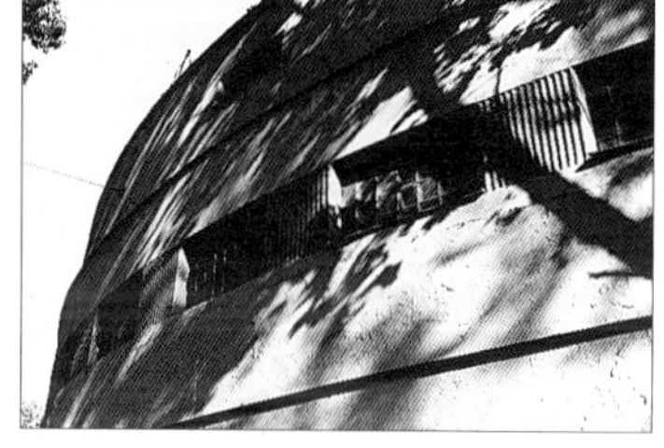

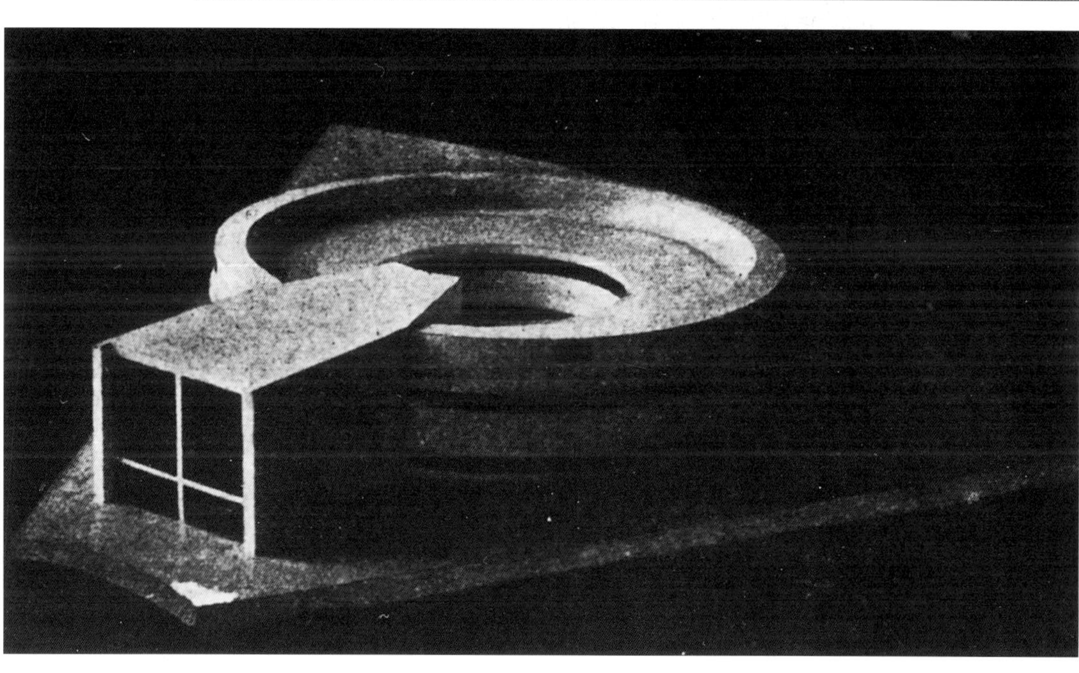

a: *typical interior of a former church converted to a 'club for atheists', with Communist portraits replacing icons, a stage for anti-religious plays, and political slogans replacing biblical texts.*

b: *a 'mockery procession' with 'red priest' in costume sings obscene songs about saints to church music, and Soviet emblems replace processional icons (cf. p.19: 'Krestnyi khod').*

c: Alexander Nikolsky, *conversion of former Russian Orthodox church at the Putilov factory, Leningrad, into a modernist 'CLUB OF THE RED PUTILOV WORKER', 1925-26: the new front.*

b: Nikolsky with Alexander Gegello, Georgi Simonov, *Tractor Street workers' housing development, Leningrad, 1925-7: detail, 1989.*

c: Nikolsky, *public bath-house with daily capacity of 2,100 baths, for the Lesny district, Leningrad, 1926-17: plan.*

d: *model.*

e: *external wall detail, photograph 1989.*

f: *Secondary School named for the Tenth Anniversary of the Revolution, Leningrad, 1927: detail of teaching block with astronomical observatory, photograph 1989.*

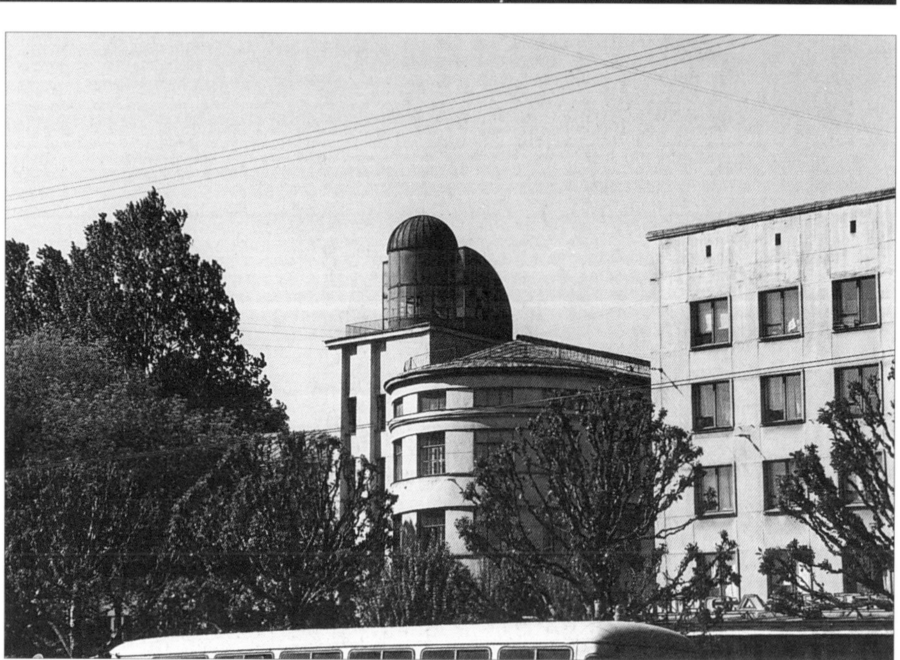

ЛЕНИНГРАД
LENINGRAD

ПЕРВАЯ ВЫСТАВКА СОВРЕМЕННОЙ АРХИТЕКТУРЫ МОСКВА ИЮНЬ ИЮЛЬ АВГУСТ 1927

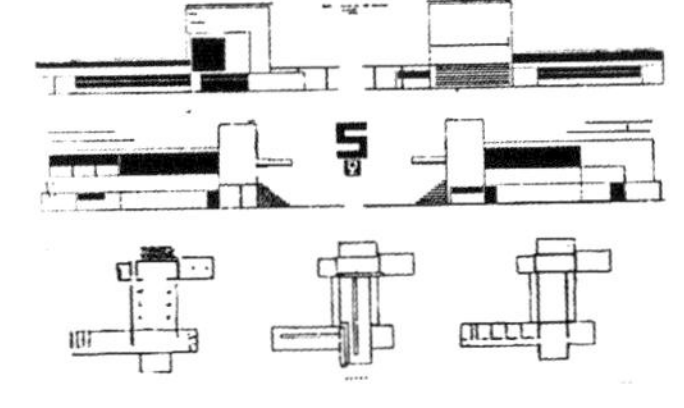

1 **АРХИТЕКТУРНАЯ МАСТЕРСКАЯ АЛЕКСАНДР НИКОЛЬСКИЙ И. БЕЛДОВСКИЙ В. ГАЛЬПЕРИН А. КРЕСТИН. КЛУБ С ЗАЛОМ НА 500 ЧЕЛ.**
ATELIER A. NIKOLSKY I. BELDOWSKY W. GALPERIN A. KRESTIN. KLUB FÜR 500

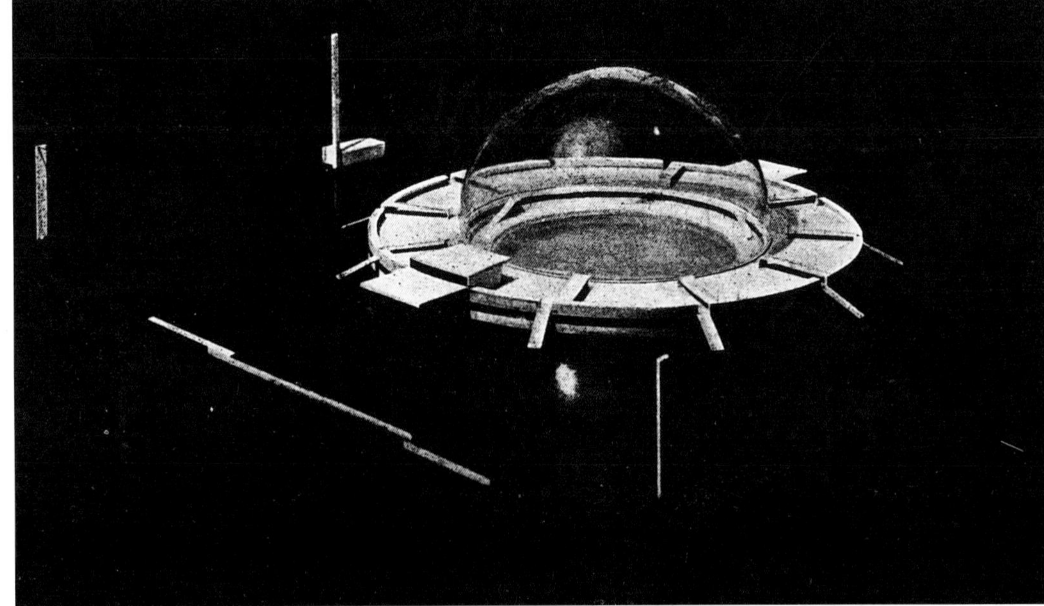

***a-c: Alexander Nikolsky with Ivan Beldovsky, Vladimir Galperin, Mikhail Krestin,** workers' club with auditorium for 500 people, 1927: view of model; plans and elevations; view of model.*

***d: Nikolsky,** public bath-house with daily capacity of 4,000 baths for the Moscow-Narva district, Leningrad, 1928: model of first project with glazed dome.*

***e, f:** axonometric and plan of second project, as built.*

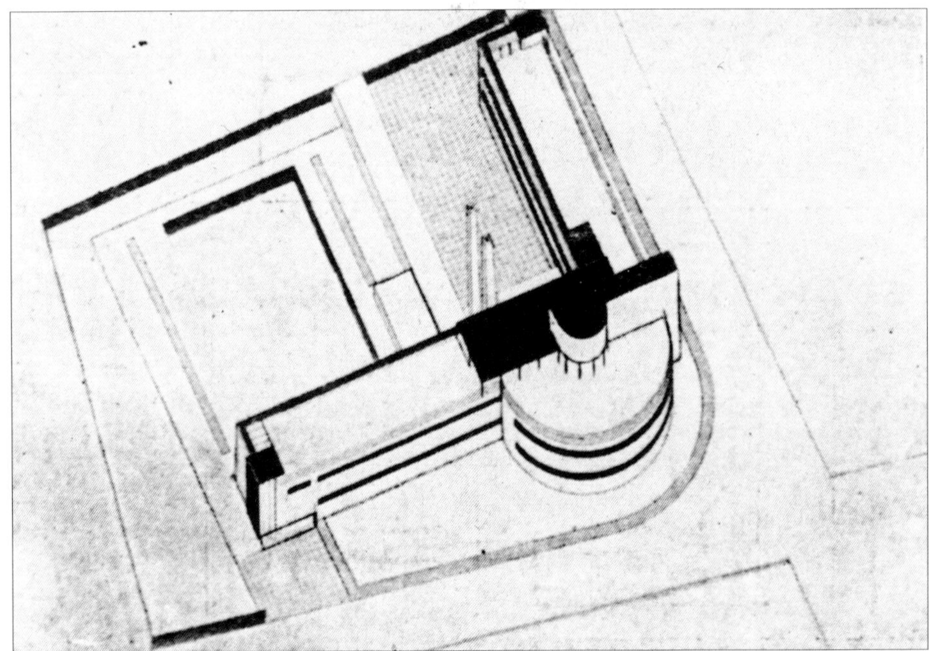

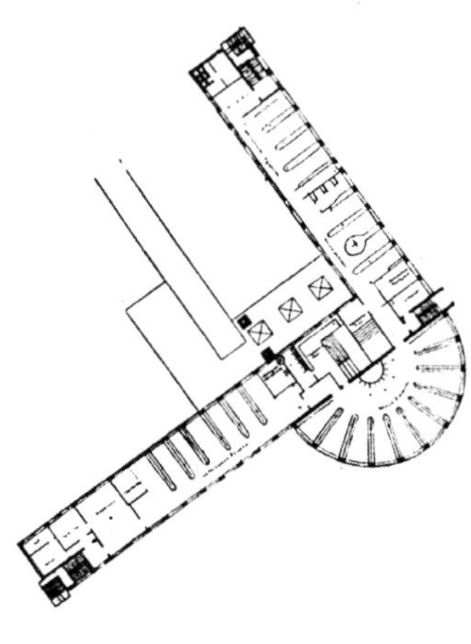

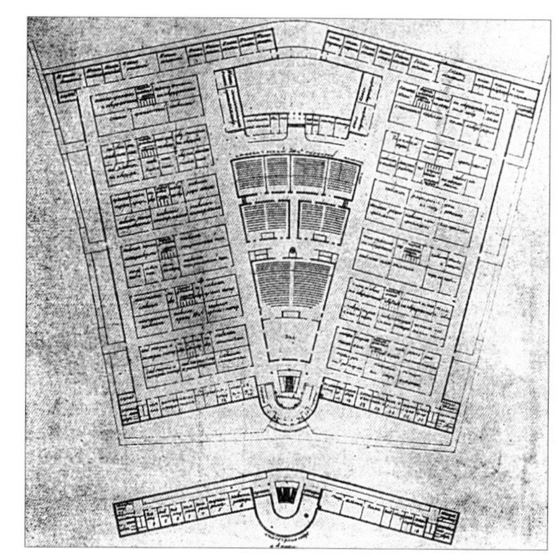

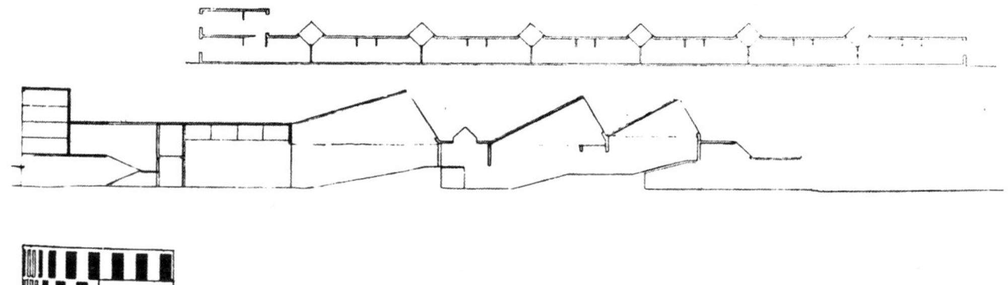

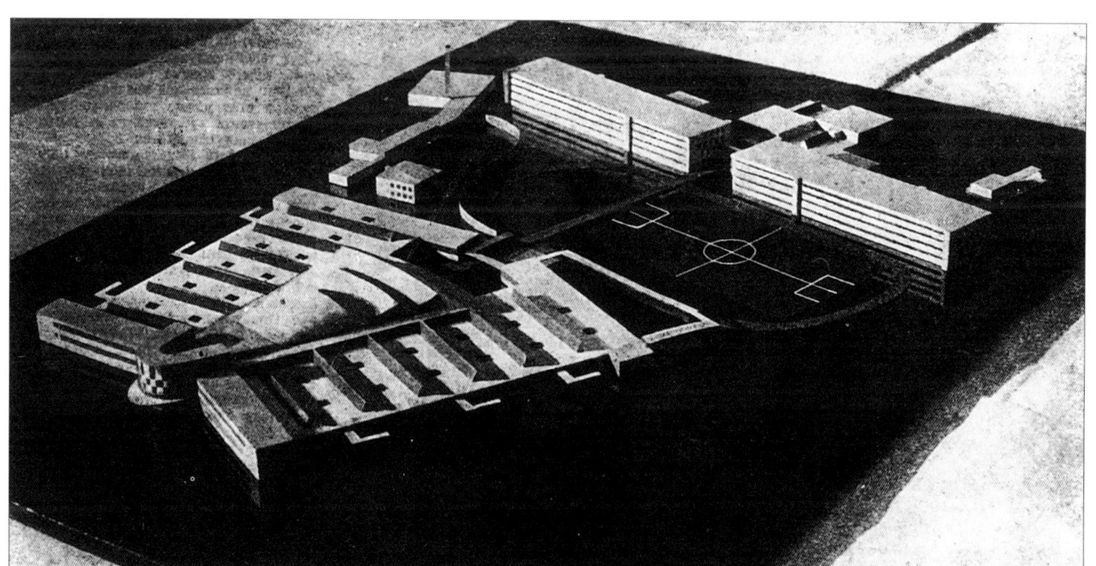

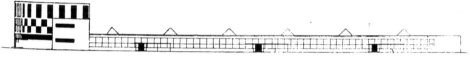

a: Alexander Nikolsky with Lazar Khidekel et al, *Higher Cooperative Institute, Moscow, 1930: ground and mezzanine floors of teaching block.*

b: *sections through classrooms,* top, *and auditoria,* centre; *side elevation.*

c: *model of whole development with teaching accomodation,* left, *and student hostel,* right.

d: *isometric of whole development.*

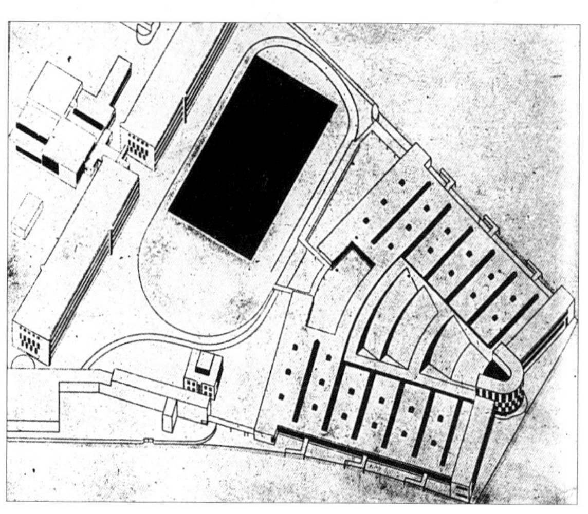

Younger Moscow Constructivists: Andrei Burov

***a*: Andrei Burov,** *model dairy breeding complex, built as film set for Eisenstein's 'The General Line' (released after Stalin's intervention as 'The Old and the New'): 1926, detail*

***b*:** *Burov,* right, *with Sergei Eisenstein,* centre, *and Le Corbusier,* left, *during Corbusier's visit to Moscow in October 1928.*

***c-h*:** *Film set for 'The General Line': six stills from the shooting in summer 1926, published in SA 1926 no.5-6.*

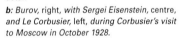

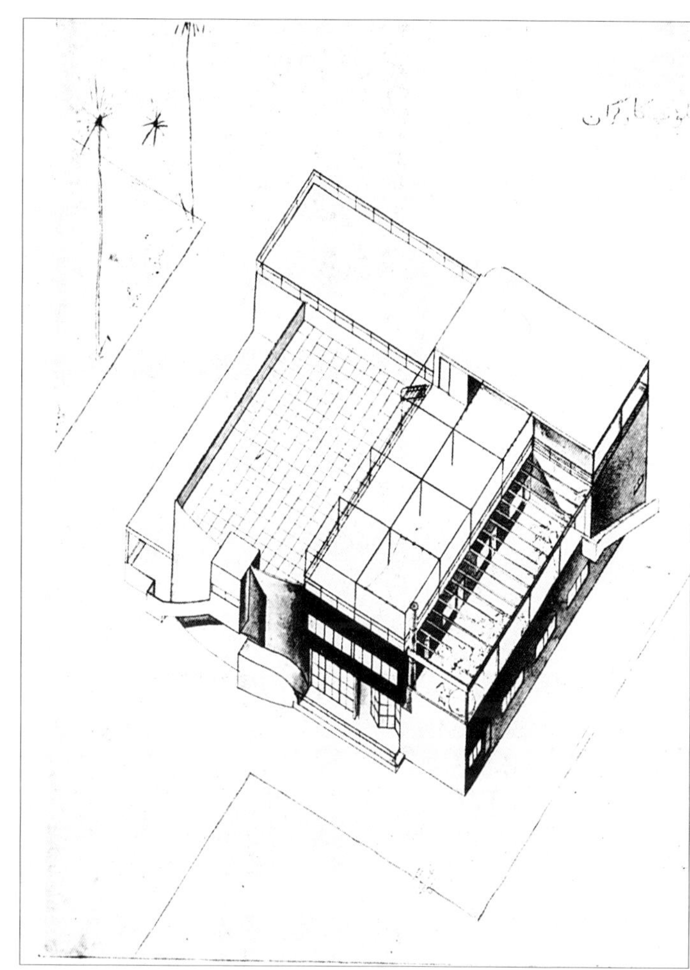

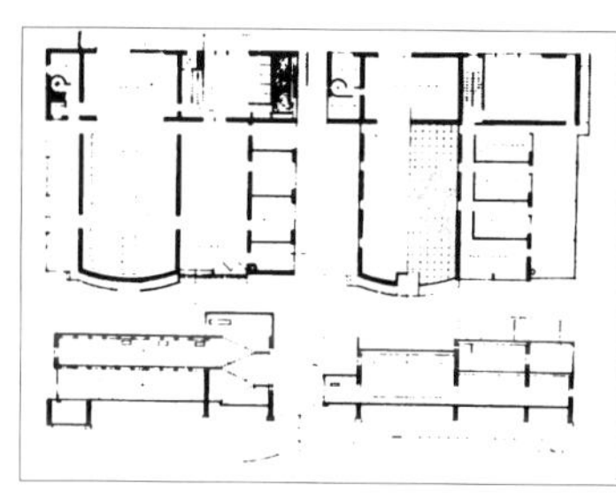

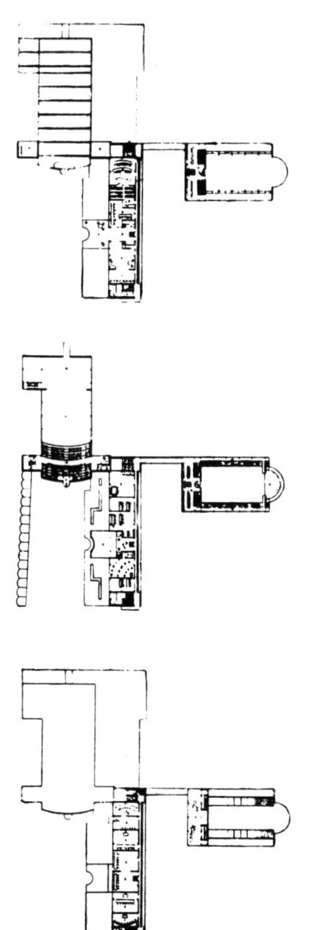

a, b: Andrei Burov, *standard 300-person workers' club of maximum compactness for Soviet Republics of the extreme south, 1927: axonometric; plans and sections.*

c-e: *Club complex for three factories of the Union of Food Industry Workers, Moscow, 1928: plans.*

f: *perspective of main courtyard looking past main entrance to the auditorium entrance.*

g: *axonometric, apparently from a nearby balcony.*

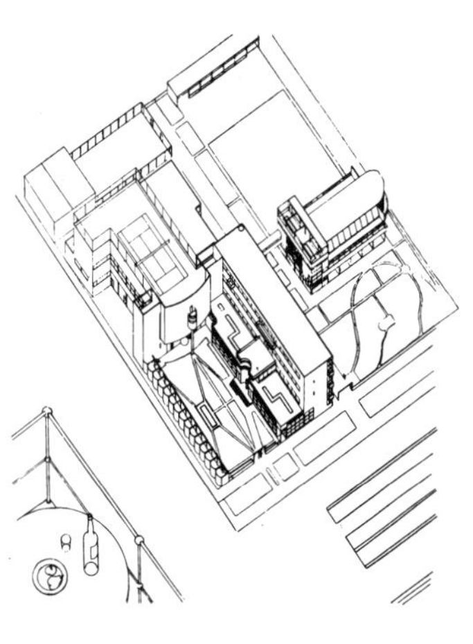

Younger Moscow Constructivists: Ivan Nikolaev

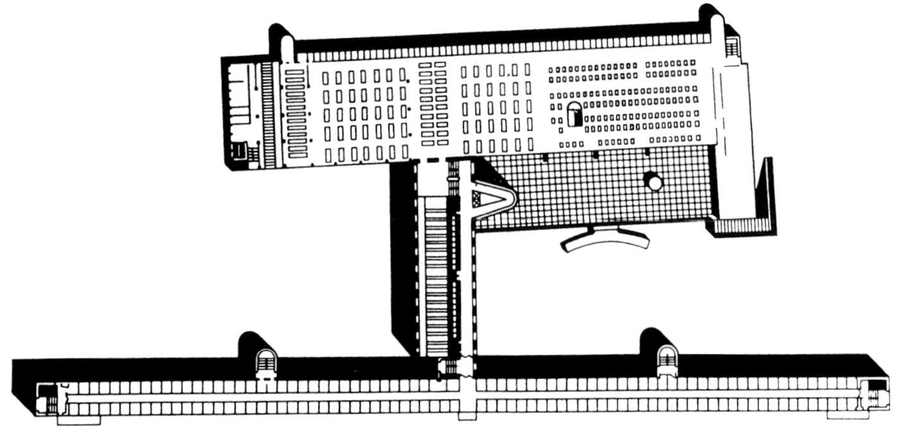

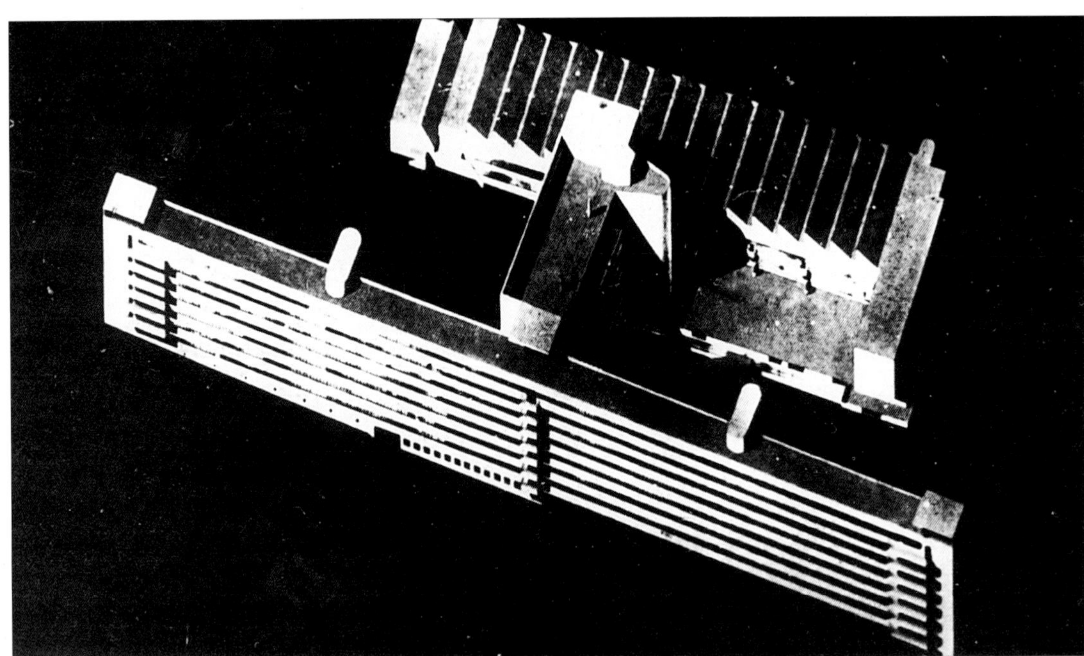

a: Ivan Nikolaev, *communal housing complex for trainees and apprentices of the Textile Institute, Moscow, 1929-30: ground-floor plan.*

b: *model, with T-shape block of minimal individual cabins running north-south, and lower block of communal feeding, study and recreational facilities to the East.*

c: *stair tower in north courtyard, photograph 1988.*

d: *sketches showing 1-4, exterior environments (Vladimir Shukhov's famous radio mast of 1922 visible right, in 4); 5, library; 6, entrance hall; 7, roof terrace outside library; 8, lounge area adjoining dining room; 9, sleeping cabins; 10, orientation, and study carrels on east face of library.*

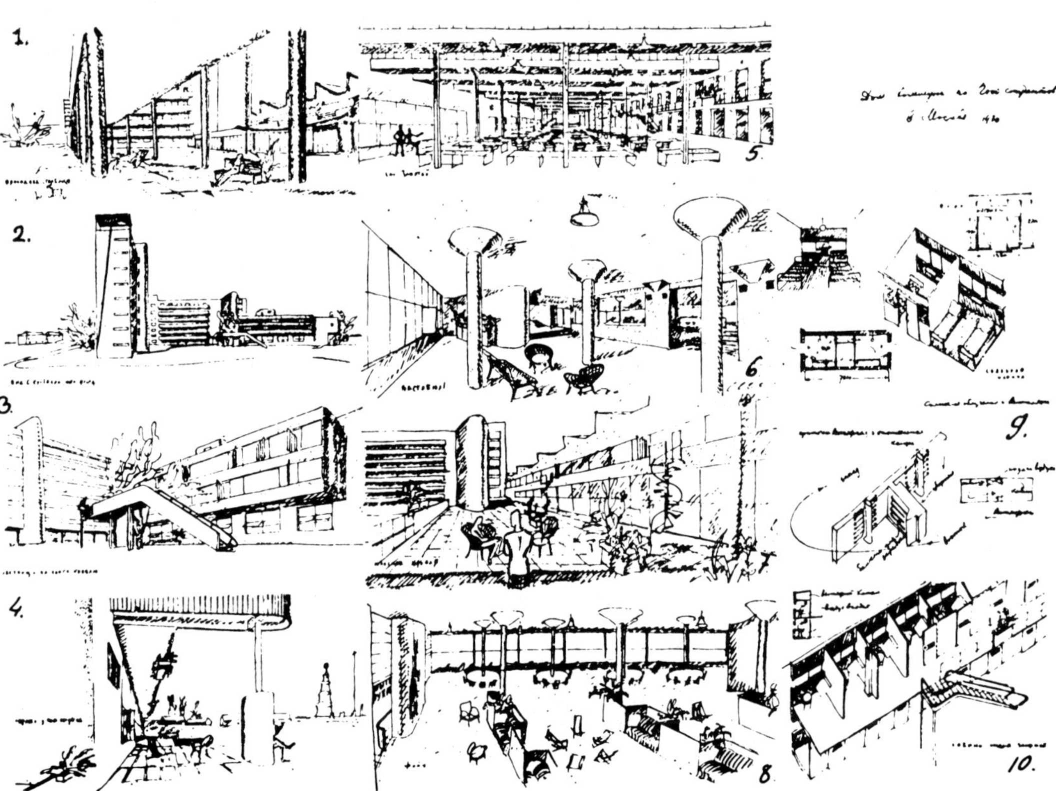

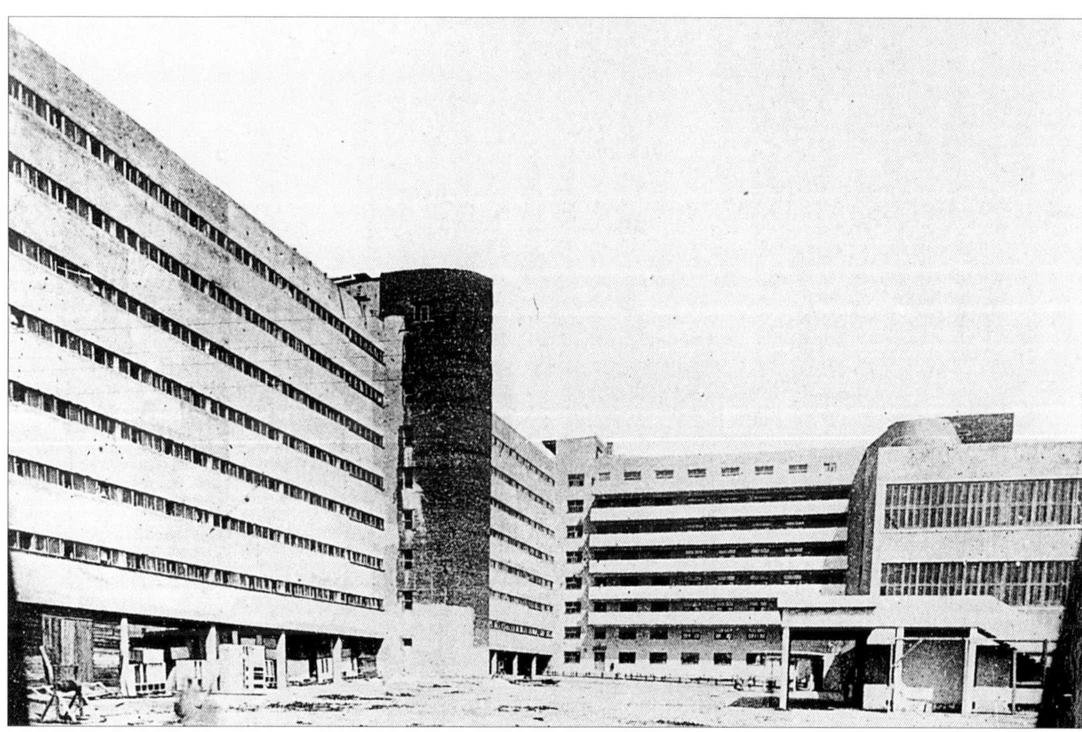

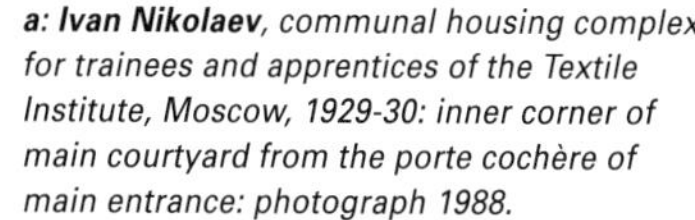

a: Ivan Nikolaev, *communal housing complex for trainees and apprentices of the Textile Institute, Moscow, 1929-30: inner corner of main courtyard from the porte cochère of main entrance: photograph 1988.*

b: photograph during last stages of construction, looking due north into main courtyard.

c: *east face of communal block with dining room at ground floor and two floors of library study carrels above.*

d-f: Nikolaev and Anatoli Fisenko under supervision of Alexander Kuznetsov, *All-Union Electrotechnical Institute complex, Moscow, central building, 1928: elevation; perspective; four floor plans.*

g: *laboratory building for Electro-Physics, 1928-29: the left-hand end of this building was the only image representing Soviet modernism in MOMA's 'International Style' exhibition, New York, 1932.*

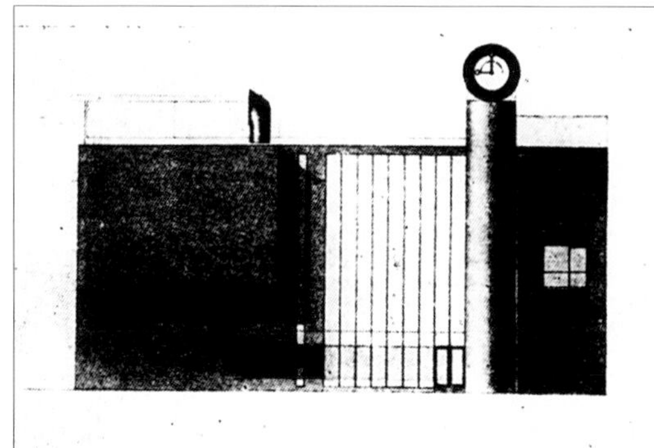

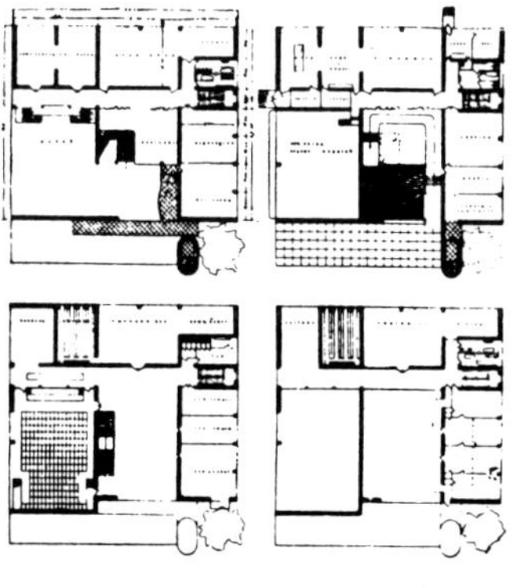

a: Konstantin Melnikov, *Own house and studio, Moscow, 1927-9, based on the principle of 'Equal value and evenness of loadings, light, air and heat': architect's model showing how the two cylinders interlock volumetrically.*

b: *Exterior detail, with the two stuccoed cylinders (garden-side, left, and street-side, right) separated by a strip of exposed structural brickwork. (For plans and construction of the house, see pages 136-9).*

c: *interior view of Melnikov family bedroom as designed, with parents' and son's beds separated only by a screen wall, to allow air circulation in the spacious room, and beds permanently built on solid sculpted pedestals.*

d: *competition project for model workers' housing, Moscow, 1922-23, first stage design: 'Every dwelling in a three-storeyed complex is like a free-standing villa': typical Melnikov presentation with all drawings on single sheet.*

e: *Competition project for the Palace of Labour, Moscow, 1923, where '8,000 people can all hear a speaker's natural voice': perspective with Theatre Square and the Bolshoi, bottom right.*

f: *New Sukharev Market, Moscow, 1924-26: timber floor frames laid out on site as first stage of construction.*

g: *'2,000 small traders all have corner sites': the market in operation, photograph of mid-1920s by Rodchenko.*

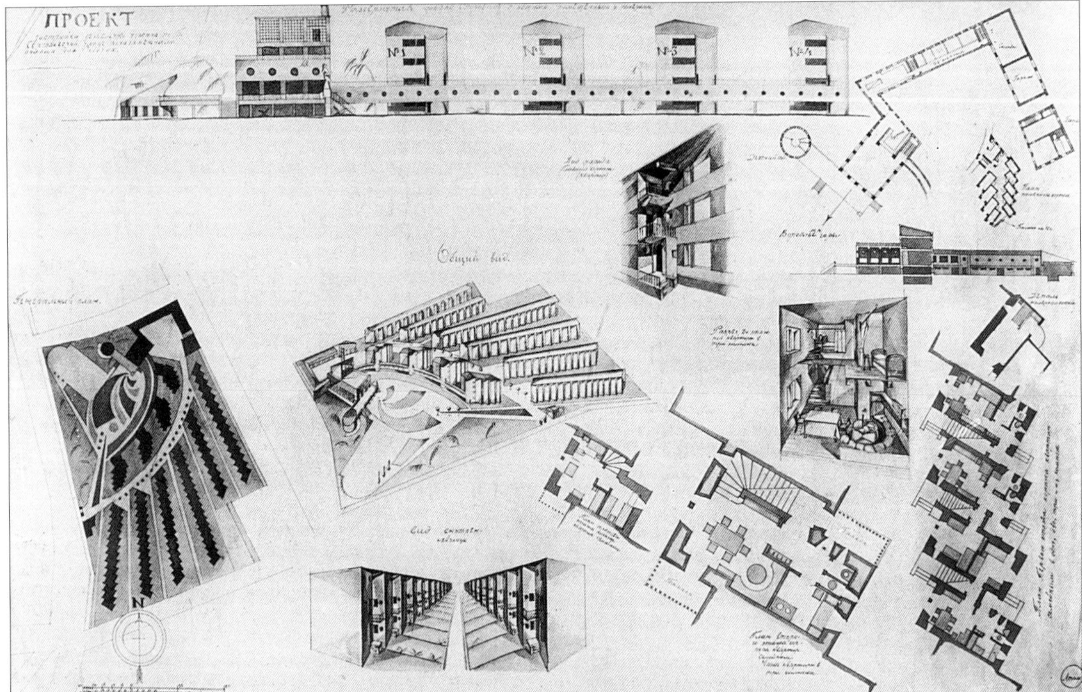

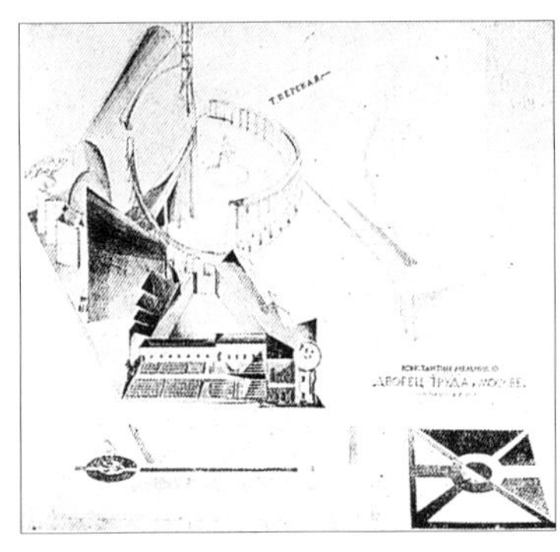

MODERNISTS OUTSIDE ASNOVA & OSA

Konstantin Melnikov

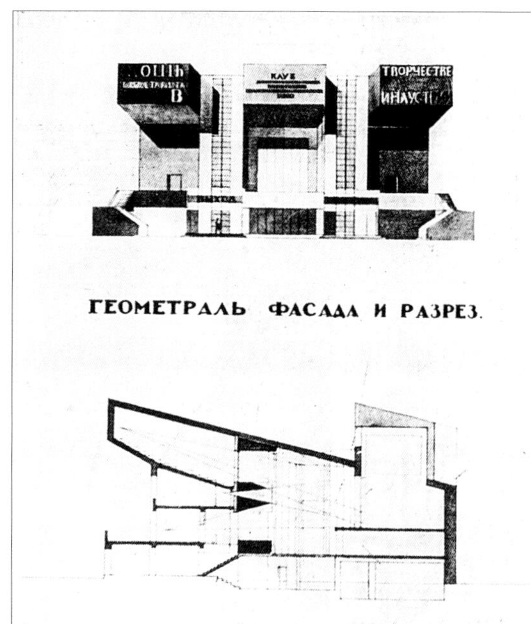

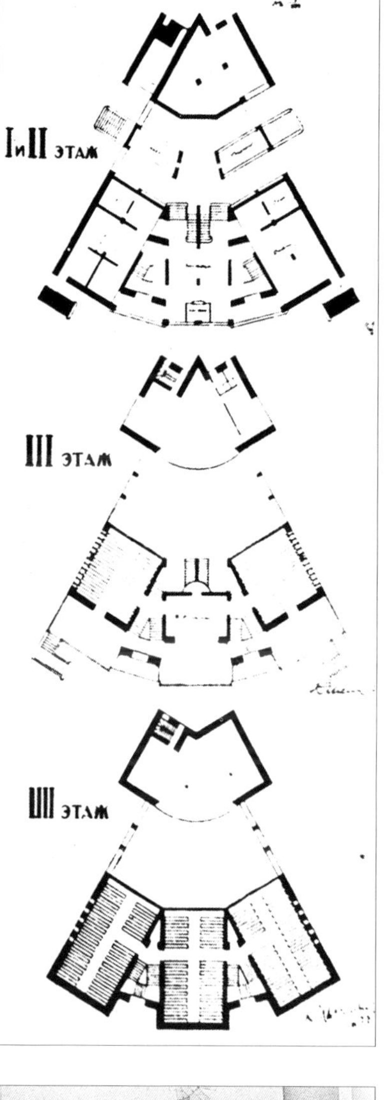

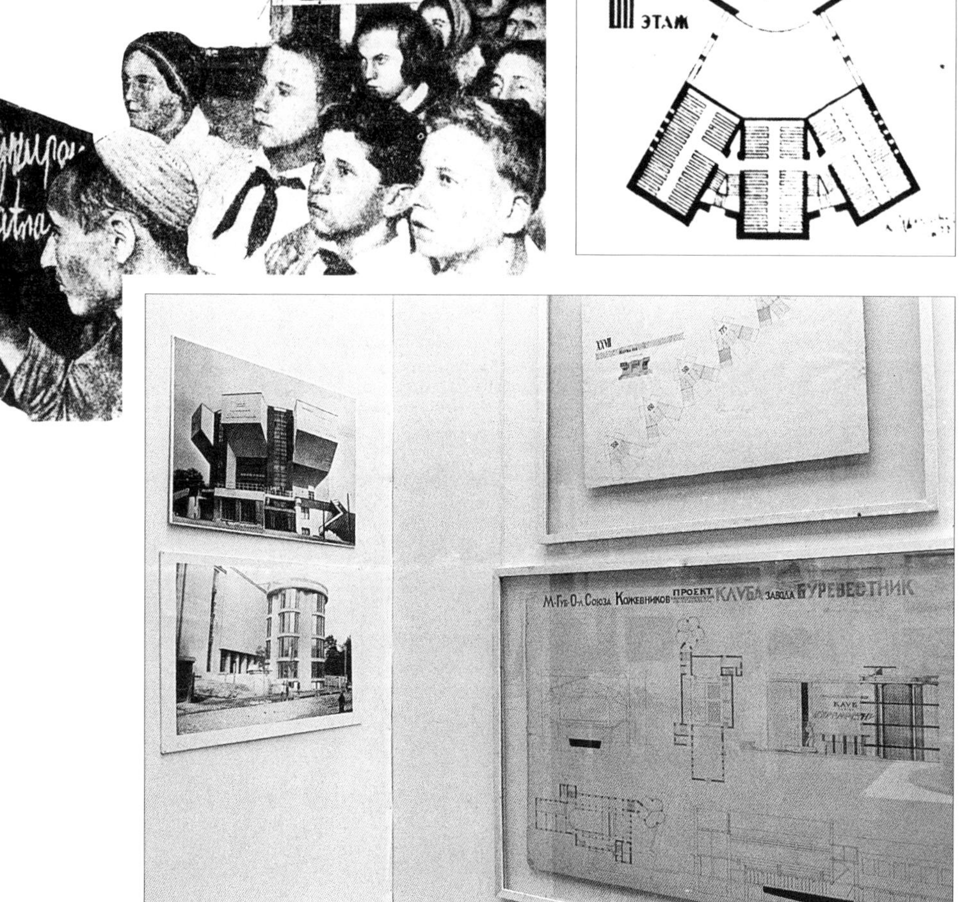

***a:* Konstantin Melnikov,** *Rusakov Workers' Club for employees of the Moscow Communal Economy, 1927-29: section, and Melnikov's elevational drawing showing the bas-relief slogans on rear of cantilevered auditoria: In this variant they read 'The force of the proletariat in the creativity of industry'. As built, they read 'The trade union is the school of Communism'.*

b: *plans of ground and first floors, second, and third, with the three cantilevered extensions to the main auditorium.*

c: *Rusakov club used as image in a montage celebrating Soviet achievements in 'raising the cultural standards of the population', and particularly literacy, across the whole USSR:* Our Achievements, *1931, no.1.*

d: *Drawings and period photographs of the Rusakov Club and Burevestnik Club, 1928-30, at the exhibition* Moskva-Parizh 1900-1930, *Moscow, 1981. Upper drawing is Melnikov's diagram of how 'Auditoria can be transformed for 350, 450, 550, 775, 1,000 or 1,200 people' in the Rusakov building. Lower drawing is a typical Melnikov composite, with plans, sections and elevation of his club for the Burevestnik Shoe Factory. Here main block and its segmented front tower were based on the principle of 'Living [ie. moveable] walls between every space'.*

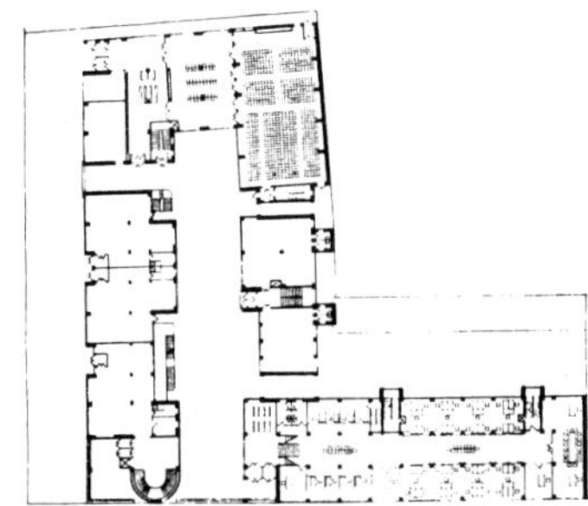

***a, b: Ilia Golosov,** competition project for the headquarters of the Russo-German Trading Company, Russgertorg, Moscow, 1926: perspective; ground-floor plan.*

***c:** competition project for the Lenin House of the People, Ivanovo-Voznesensk, 1924: perspective.*

***d:** graphic from* Our Achievements, *1931, indicating the propaganda pressure of First Five Year Plan period to compete with Western outputs and outstrip them, rather than develop the kind of trade for which organisations like Russgertorg, Amtorg, ARCOS had been founded in the early post-Revolutionary period. The graphic records projected 'Machine building abroad and in the USSR in 1931 as percentages of 1929 outputs: USSR, 257%. France, 86%. Germany, 60%. USA, 56%.'*

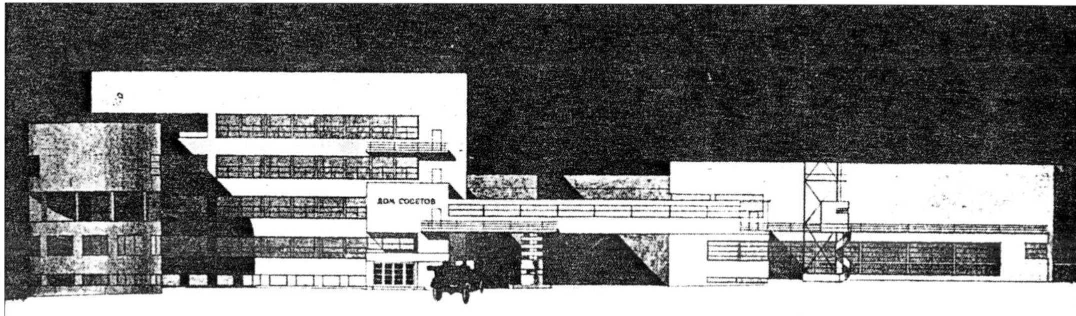

a:* *Ilia Golosov with Boris Ulinich, *competition project for the House of Textiles, Moscow, 1925: perspective.*

b:* *Ilia Golosov, *competition project for the House of Soviets, Khabarovsk, 1928 (built 1928-30): main elevation.*

c, d: *competition project for the Palace of Labour, Moscow, 1923: elevations.*

e: *Electrobank building competition project, Moscow, 1926: perspective.*

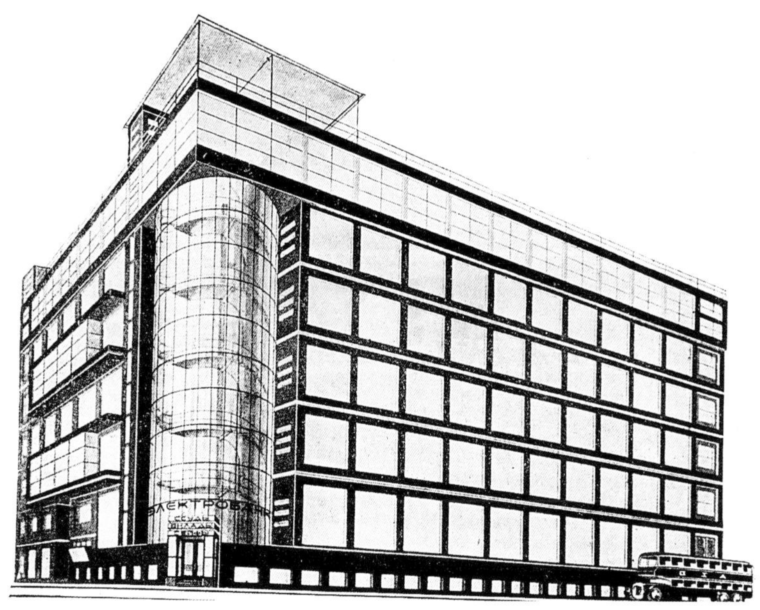

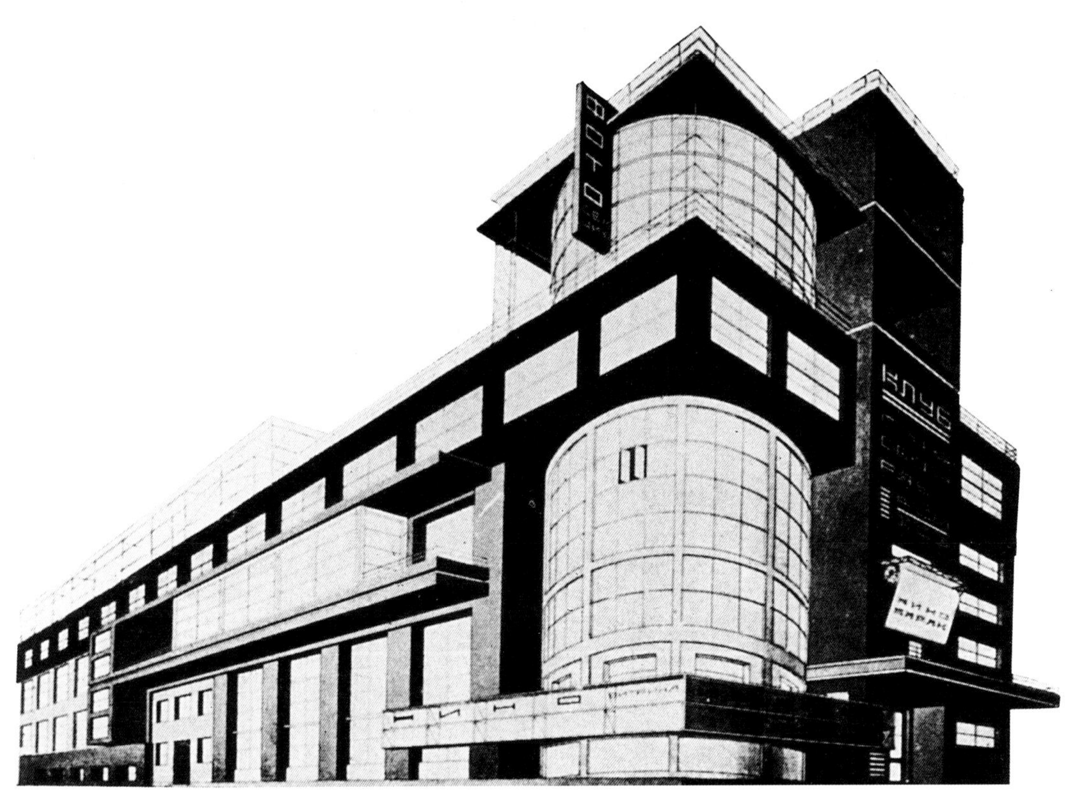

a: Ilia Golosov, *Zuev Workers' Club for employees of the Moscow Communal Economy, 1927-29: perspective.*

b: *interior view, corner stair rising from first to second floor , photograph 1989.*

c: *corner view, photograph 1989.*

d: *plans, from ground (top) to third floor (bottom).*

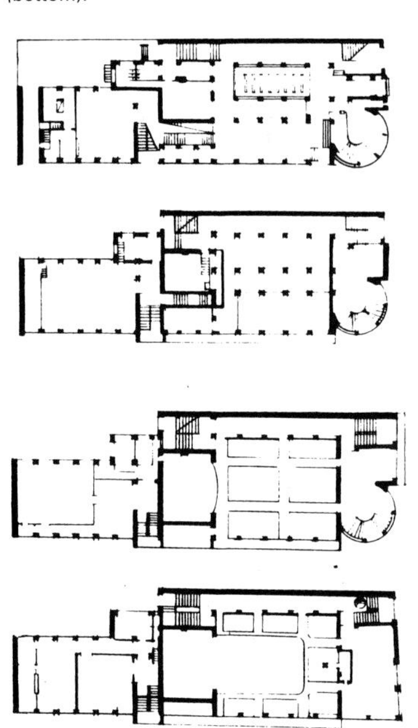

Grigori Barkhin

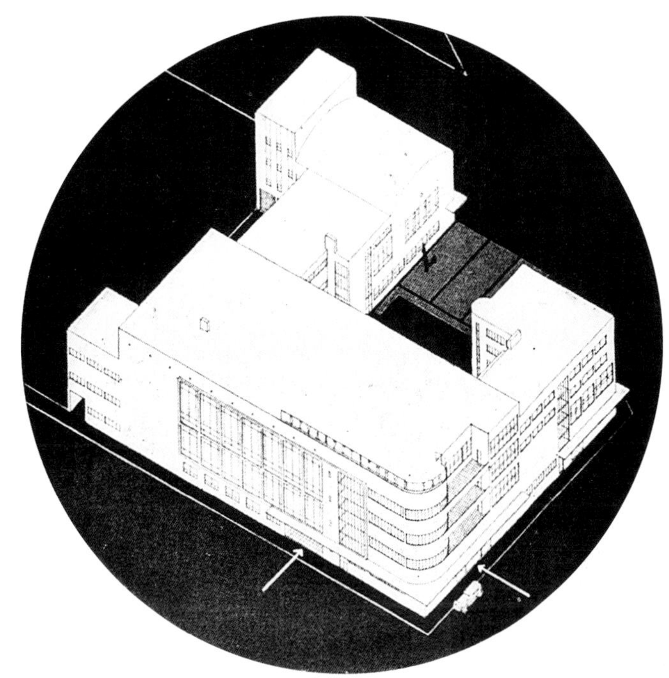

***a, b:* Grigori Barkhin,** *First-prize winning project for the State Bank in Novosibirsk, 1929: isometric of the whole complex; perspective.*

c: *ground and second floor plans.*

d, e: *illustrations from his book* Rabochii dom i rabochii poselok-sad *(The Worker's House and the Workers' Garden Settlement), Moscow 1922: the 'semi-detached' cottage, a concept unfamiliar in Russia, explained with a German examplef; a rationalised form of composite wall construction.*

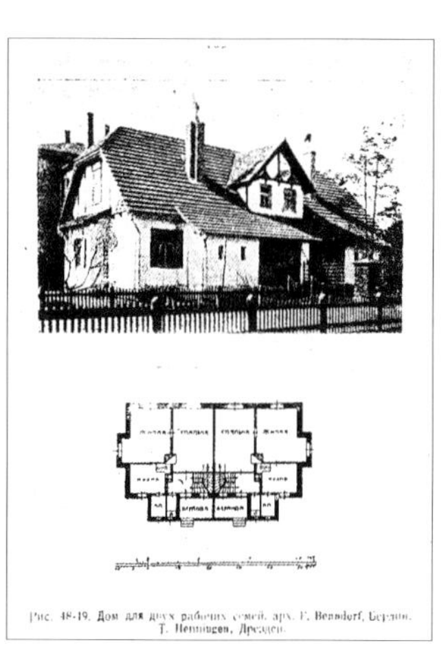

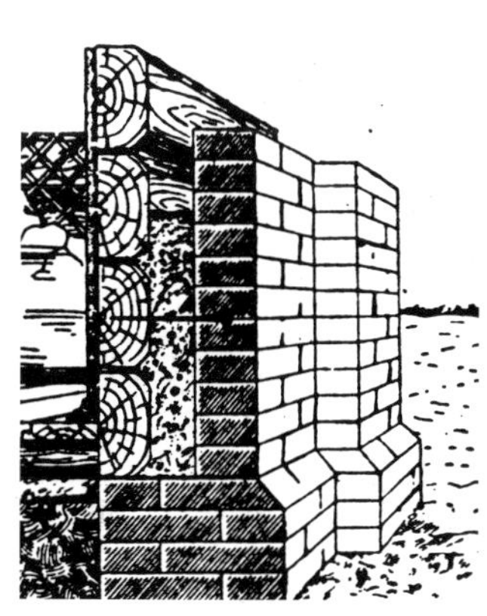

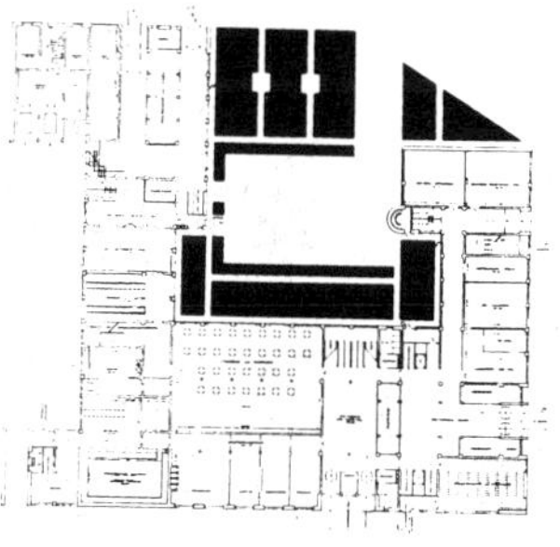

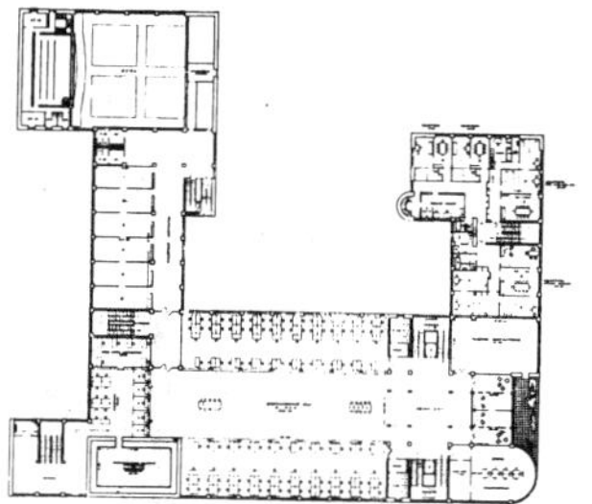

ДОМ
"ИЗВЕСТИЙ"
ИЗВЕСТИЯ
ЦИК СССР
и ВЦИК
НОВЫЙ МИР 2·68·26
КРАСНАЯ НИВА 2·52·53

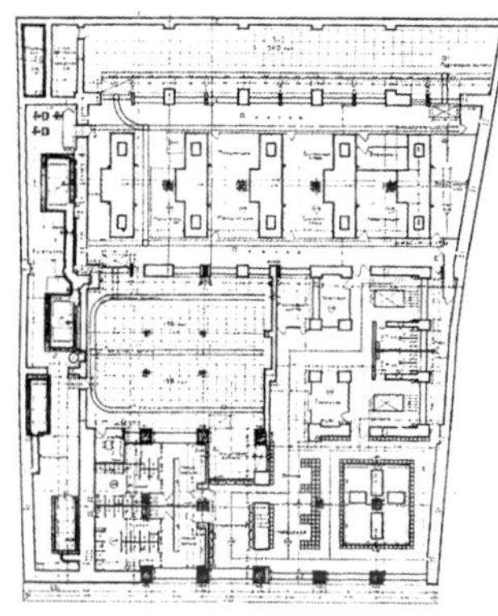

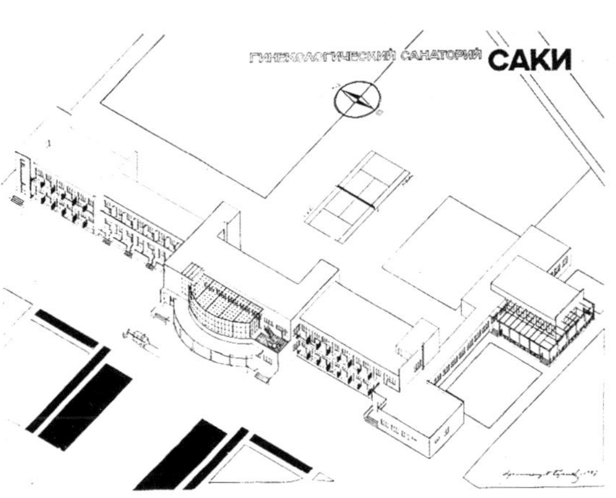

a: ***Grigori Barkhin**, editorial and production building for* Izvestiia*, newspaper of the Bolshevik Party Central Committee, and its associated periodicals, Moscow, 1925-27: perspective.*

***b:** exterior detail , photograph 1927.*

***c, d:** interior views of circulation space, 1927*

***e:** photograph soon after completion, showing modernist building rising above the historic city. In foreground, buildings of the Strastnoi Monastery, demolished early 1930s to leave an open square.*

***f:** basement plan with staff facilities and store of materials.*

***g:** Gynaecological sanatorium at Saki, Crimea, 1927 (built, 1928-30): perspective of main front.*

***h:** isometric of whole complex.*

Boris Velikovsky

a: Boris Velikovsky with Mikhail Barshch, Georgi Vegman, Maria Gaken, *Headquarters for the State Trading organisation, Gostorg, Moscow, 1925-27: perspective of the original scheme of 1925, with central tower prohibited by new height controls for central Moscow later that year.*

b: *main elevation soon after completion.*

c: *side elevation with what Alfred Barr, Director of MOMA, New York, described in 1927 as 'steamboat balconies', photograph, 1988.*

d: *concrete frame under construction.*

e: *view of central circulation space., 1927.*

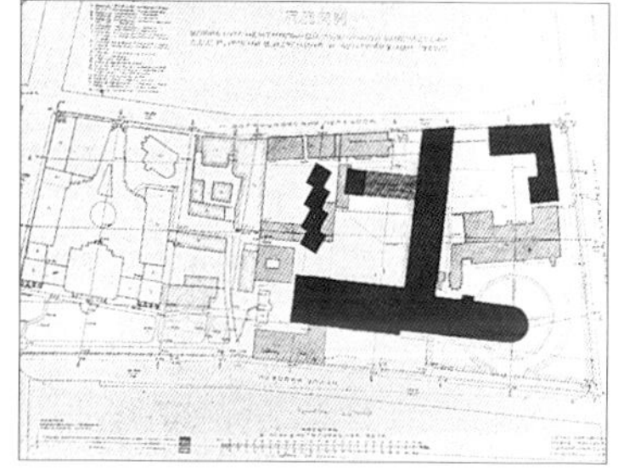

a: Boris Velikovsky with Alexander and Viktor Vesnin, *apartment and commercial building for I.E. Kuznetsov, Moscow, 1910: photograph, 1985.*

b: Boris Velikovsky, *workers' housing, Moscow, 1925: photograph soon after completion.*

c, d: Panteleimon Golosov, *competition project for the Lenin Library, Moscow, 1928: perspective; site plan.*

e: Panteleimon Golosov, *Headquarters and production building for the Bolshevik Party newspaper* Pravda *and its associated publications, Moscow, 1930-35: photograph of office block soon after completion, with production block,* right.

ВЭИ

170
СА № 5 1929

ВСЕСОЮЗНЫЙ ЭЛЕКТРОТЕХНИЧЕСКИЙ ИНСТИТУТ

Alexander Kuznetsov

***a, b:* Alexander Kuznetsov with Gennadi and Vladimir Movchan, Ivan Nikolaev, Anatoli Fisenko,** *All-Union Electrotechnical Institute, VEI, Moscow, 1928-1930: two photographs of the High Tension block during final stages of completion in summer 1929 from a feature on site progress in SA, 1929 no.5.*

***c:* Alexander Kuznetsov,** *Moscow Textile Institute, Wool Laboratory, 1926: perspective.*

d: *Headquarters of the Russian Polytechnical Society, Moscow, 1904-06: main elevation, photograph 1987.*

e: *Studio building for the Stroganov College of Applied Arts, Moscow (later part of Vkhutemas), 1913-14: entrance at angle to courtyard flanked by studios with old building, left. A pioneering work of reinforced concrete frame and staircase design in pre-Revolutionary Russia. Photograph, 1992.*

Leningrad: Noi Trotsky, Alexander Gegello, Georgi Simonov, David Buryshkin

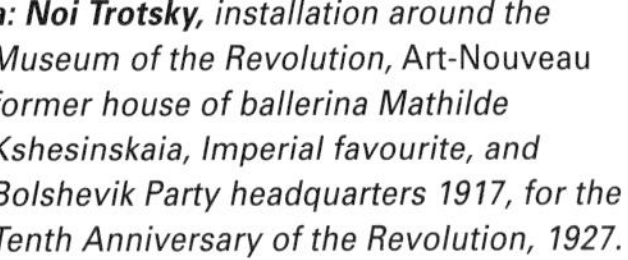

***a*: Noi Trotsky,** *installation around the Museum of the Revolution,* Art-Nouveau *former house of ballerina Mathilde Kshesinskaia, Imperial favourite, and Bolshevik Party headquarters 1917, for the Tenth Anniversary of the Revolution, 1927.*

***b*: Alexander Gegello, David Krichevsky, Alexander Dmitriev,** *Gorky Palace of Culture at the Narva Gates, Leningrad, 1925-27: detail of fenestration and stairtower, photograph 1989.*

***c*:** *main elevation, photograph 1989.*

***d*: Georgi Simonov,** *coeducational secondary school, Tkachei Street, Leningrad, 1927-29: gymnasium and changing-room block (girls-boys entrances), with classroom block* far right *and laboratory block* far left. *Photograph 1988.*

***e*:** *gymnasium and changing room block, detail, with sporthall at first floor, photograph 1988.*

***f*: David Buryshkin,** *installation around the Narva Gates for the Tenth Anniversary of the Revolution, 1927.*

Alexei Shchusev

a, b: Alexei Shchusev, *Convent of Martha and Mary, Moscow, 1908-12: interior perspective of the church looking towards sanctuary; the church.*

c: *Anatomical Institute for the First State University, Moscow, 1926: perspective.*

d: *The second temporary timber mausoleum for Lenin on Red Square, Moscow, 1924: perspective as built.*

e, f: *Final Lenin Mausoleum, in marble and granite, completed 1930: Stalin, Voroshilov and others taking the salute from the integral saluting base, as Red Army troops and tanks parade through Red Square, May Day, 1931.*

g: *October Revolution workers' club for railwaymen at the Kazan Station, Moscow, 1925-28: interior of auditorium.*

***a:* Alexei Shchusev,** *competition project for the Central Telegraph building, Moscow, 1926: perspective towards main entrance on Tverskaia Street (later Gorky Street).*

b: *Tverskaya (Gorky) Street as it was in the Twenties, before widening and straightening in 1930s: Telegraph site on left, opposite towers.*

***c:* Shchusev,** *Telegraph building: ground floor plan.*

d: *Competition project for the Ukrainian House of Industry, Kharkov, 1925: perspective of the whole complex.*

e: *perspective of the inner courtyard.*

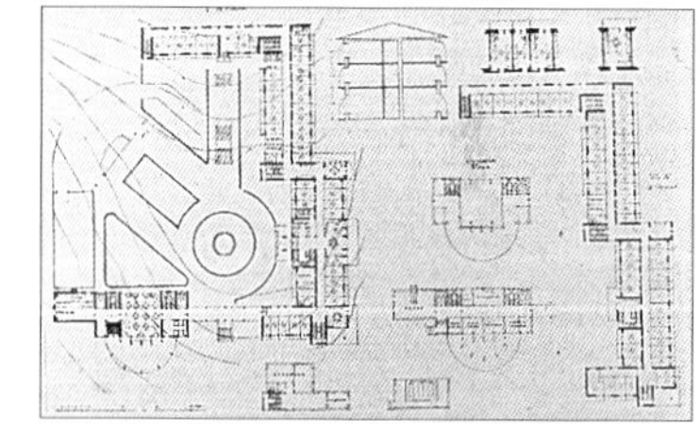

***a:* Alexei Shchusev**, *hotel-sanatorium in New Matsesta, Caucasus, 1927-28: rooftop terrace of guest-room block soon after completion.*

b: *perspective.*

c: *plans and section.*

d: *main block of guest rooms under construction.*

e, f: *details of exterior, soon after completion.*

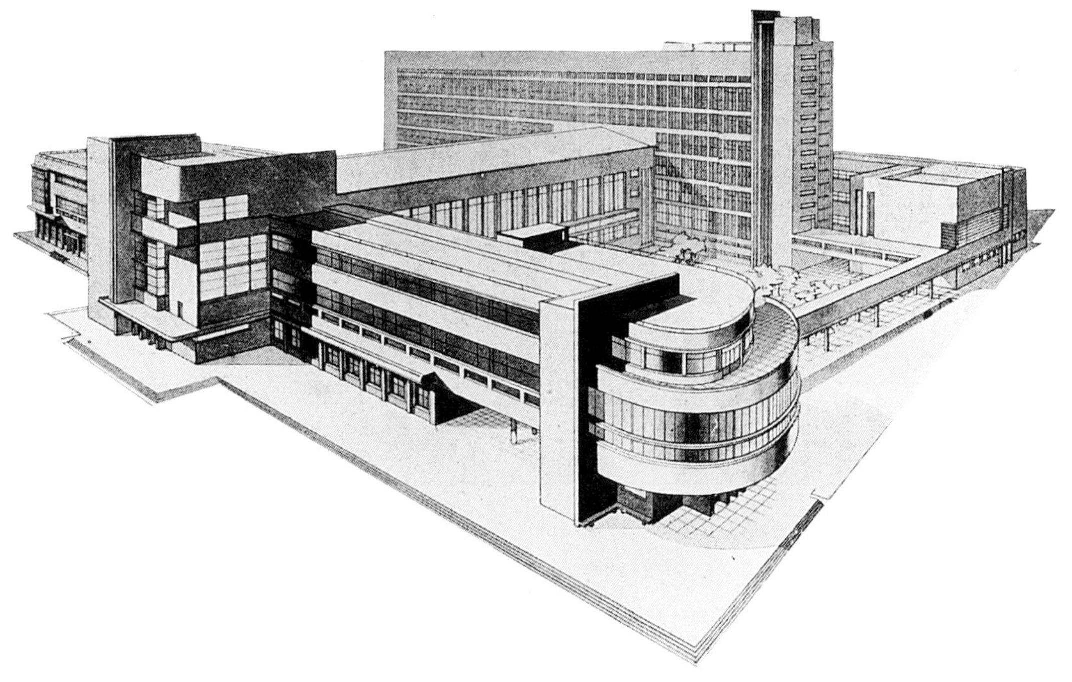

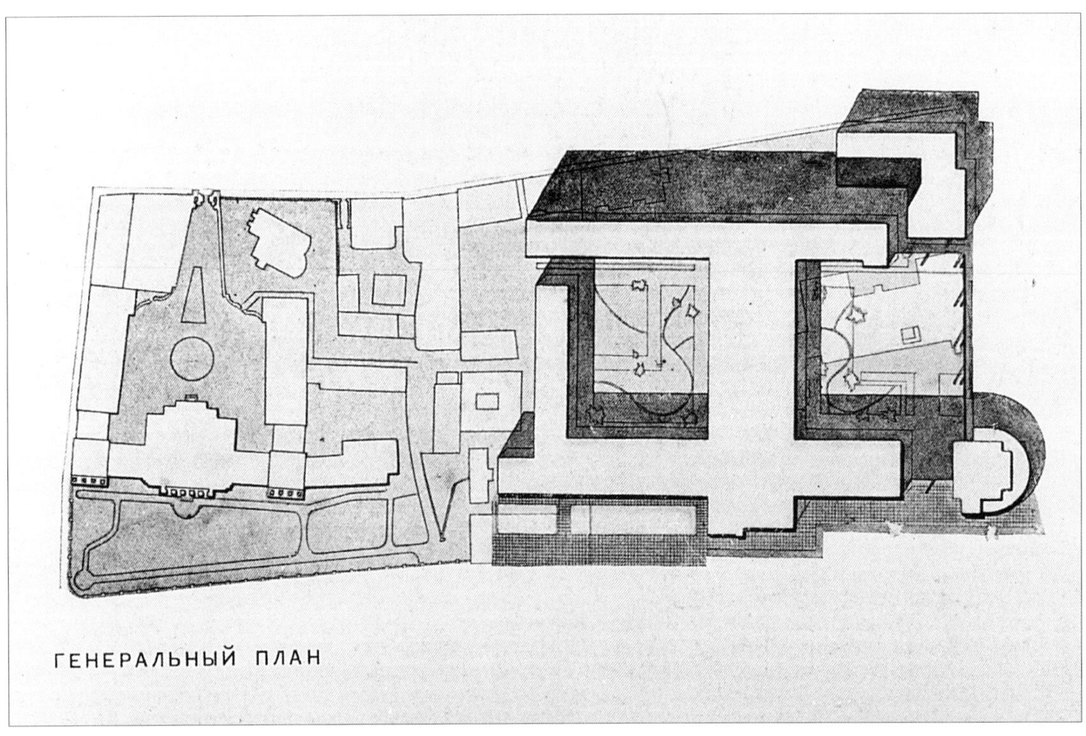

a: Alexei Shchusev, *Second-stage competition project for the Lenin Library, Moscow, 1928: perspective view of the whole complex.*

b: *site plan, with Pashkov Mansion, left.*

c: Vasily Bazhenov, *Pashkov Mansion, 1784-6, adjoining Lenin Library to the left.*

d: Shchusev, *Headquarters of Koopinsoiuz, later Commissariat of Agriculture, Moscow, 1928-33: general view, photograph 1985.*

e: *corner detail, photograph 1985.*

ON THE BOUNDARY WITH CLASSICISM

Ivan Zholtovsky and Pupils

a: ***Ivan Zholtovsky,*** *mansion and business offices for Gavril Tarasov, Moscow, 1909-12: detail of main street elevation, photograph 1985.*

b, d: *Pavilions of the Machine Building Industry, and Triumphal Arch of entrance, All-Russian Agricultural and Handicraft Industries Exhibition, Moscow, 1923, illustrations from Ginzburg's* Style and Epoch, *1924.*

c: ***Georgi Golts, Alexander Shvidkovsky,*** *project for Novosibirsk bank, 1926: entrance hall.*

АКАД.-АРХ.: И. В. ЖОЛТОВСКИЙ, — ПРИ УЧАСТИИ АРХ.-ХУД. С. Н. КОЖИНА — КОТЕЛЬНАЯ МОГЭС. МОСКВА 1927.

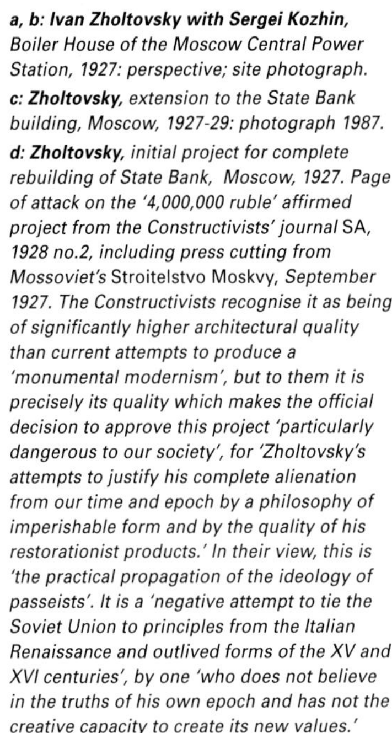

a, b: Ivan Zholtovsky with Sergei Kozhin, *Boiler House of the Moscow Central Power Station, 1927: perspective; site photograph.*

c: Zholtovsky, *extension to the State Bank building, Moscow, 1927-29: photograph 1987.*

d: Zholtovsky, *initial project for complete rebuilding of State Bank, Moscow, 1927. Page of attack on the '4,000,000 ruble' affirmed project from the Constructivists' journal* SA, *1928 no.2, including press cutting from Mossoviet's* Stroitelstvo Moskvy, *September 1927. The Constructivists recognise it as being of significantly higher architectural quality than current attempts to produce a 'monumental modernism', but to them it is precisely its quality which makes the official decision to approve this project 'particularly dangerous to our society', for 'Zholtovsky's attempts to justify his complete alienation from our time and epoch by a philosophy of imperishable form and by the quality of his restorationist products.' In their view, this is 'the practical propagation of the ideology of passeists'. It is a 'negative attempt to tie the Soviet Union to principles from the Italian Renaissance and outlived forms of the XV and XVI centuries', by one 'who does not believe in the truths of his own epoch and has not the creative capacity to create its new values.'*

2

Крупные постройки текущего сезона.

Дом Правления Госбанка.

Строительство первой очереди, начавшееся в июле с. г., должно быть закончено к концу будущего года.

Акад. И. В. Жолтовский. Проект дома Правления Госбанка.

АРХИТЕКТУРНАЯ КУНСТКАМЕРА

a, b: Georgi Golts, Sergei Kozhin, Mikhail Parusnikov, *Cotton-spinning factory at Ivanteevka for the Moscow Knitwear Trust, 1928-29: perspective; entrance hall.*

c, e: Golts, Parusnikov, *Boiler house at the Kiev Power Station, 1929: rear elevation; perspective of main front.*

d: *Boiler house: erection of structural frame.*

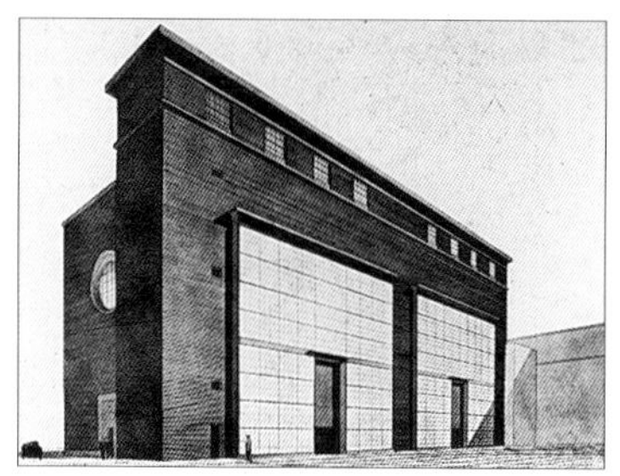

Ivan Fomin

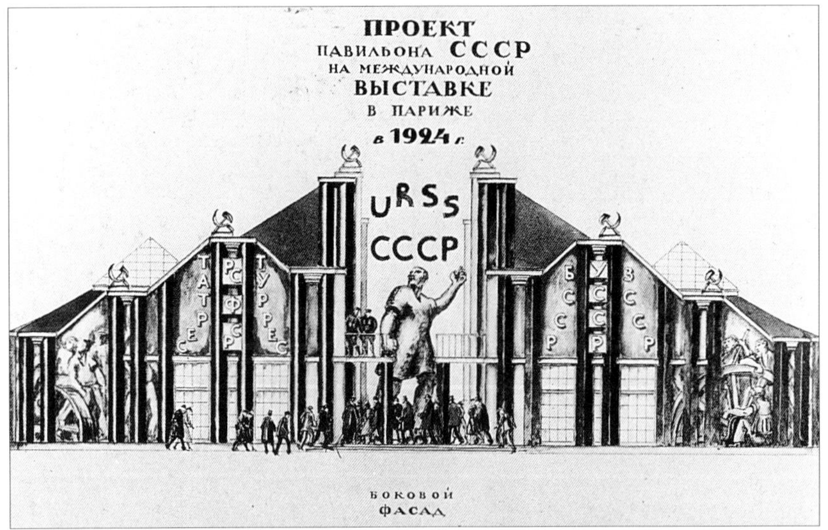

***a:* Ivan Fomin,** *dining table and chairs, in the 'New Style' exhibition, Moscow, 1902*

b: *New Petersburg housing development, 1912: elevational detail, photograph 1988.*

c: *Competition project for the Soviet Pavilion at the 1925* Exposition des Arts Decoratifs, *Paris, 1924: end elevation.*

d, f: *New campus for Ivanovo-Voznesensk Polytechnical Institute, 1926-28: perspective of central building; first-floor plan.*

e: *Preparatory Faculty for worker entrants (*Rabfak*): perspective.*

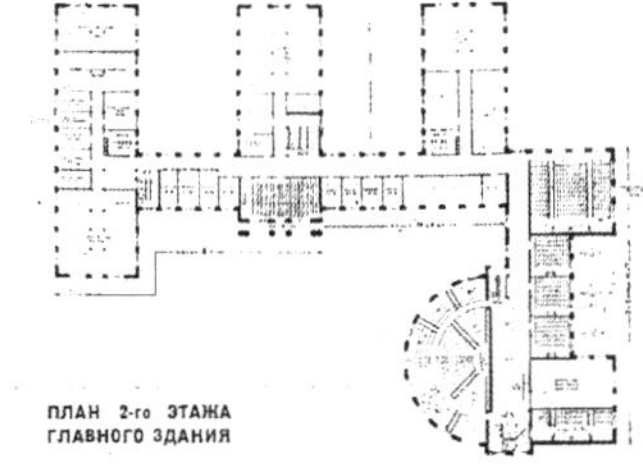

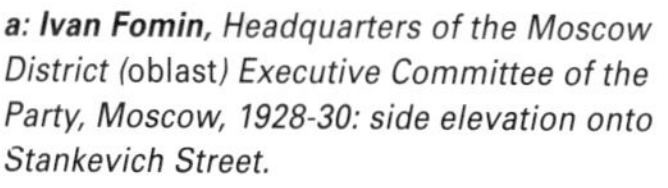

***a: Ivan Fomin,** Headquarters of the Moscow District (oblast) Executive Committee of the Party, Moscow, 1928-30: side elevation onto Stankevich Street.*

***b, c:** perspective into main courtyard; corner detail, photograph soon after completion.*

***d: Ivan Fomin with M.I. Roslavlev,** Sanatorium named for A. A. Smirnov, Zheleznovodsk, 1929: photograph soon after completion.*

***e: Fomin with Roslavlev,** Sanatorium 'For Industrialisation', Kislovodsk, 1929: photograph soon after completion.*

a: Ivan Fomin with Arkady Langman, *Dinamo Company complex central Moscow, 1929-31: Department store and office block, photograph soon after completion.*

b: *elevation to Dzerzhinskaia Street (left hand part only constructed).*

c, d: *covered walk under the housing soon after completion.*

Vladimir Shchuko

a:* *Vladimir Shchuko, *Markov's apartment building, St Petersburg, 1910: contemporary photograph.*

b: Vladimir Shchuko, Vladimir Gelfreikh, Nikolai Kolli, *Restaurant in the Foreign Section, All-Russian Agricultural and Handicraft Industries Exhibition, Moscow, 1923.*

c, d: Shchuko, *Competition project for Soviet pavilion at 1925 Paris* Exposition des Arts Decoratifs, *1924: perspective towards main entrance; side elevation.*

e: *Triumphal Arch to decorate Trinity Bridge, St Petersburg, Tercentenary celebrations of the Romanov Dynasty, 1913.*

a, b:* *Vladimir Shchuko, Vladimir Gelfreikh, *local transformer sub-station of the Volkovsky Power Station, on Belozerskaia Street, Leningrad, 1926: general view; entrance, photographed soon after completion.*

c: *transformer sub-station of the Volkovsky Power Station on Karl Marx Prospect, Leningrad, 1926-7: photograph 1988.*

d: *Lenin Palace of Culture, Leningrad, c.1927: entrance to cinema, photograph 1988.*

e: *rear with corner terrace, photograph 1988.*

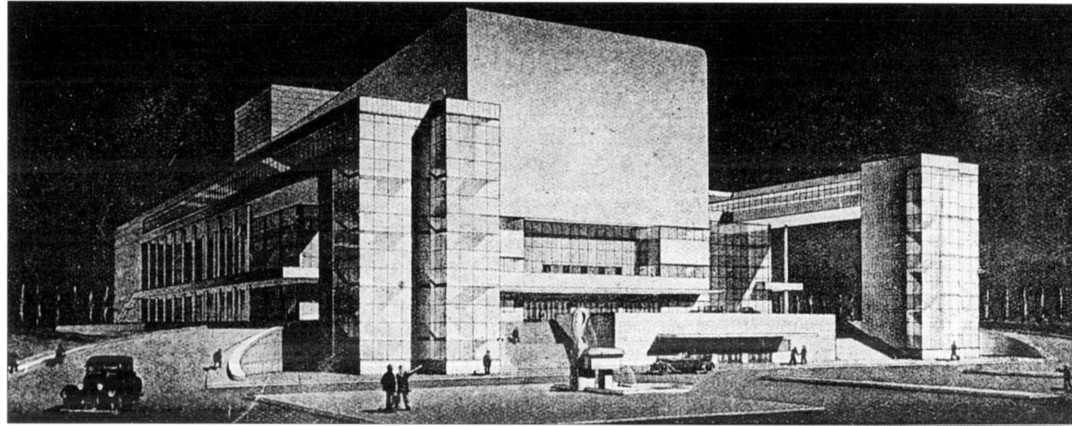

a: Vladimir Shchuko, Vladimir Gelfreikh, *project for Textile Workers' Club, Moscow, 1927: perspective.*

b: *City Theatre in Rostov-on-Don, 1930-31 (built 1932-35): perspective view by day.*

c, e: *perspective view by night; interior of main auditorium.*

d: *Lenin Library, Moscow: won in competition 1928-29 built 1930-40. Photograph soon after completion with entrance pavilion for Metro on street corner, later demolished.*

GARDEN-CITY MODERNISM

Nikolai Markovnikov

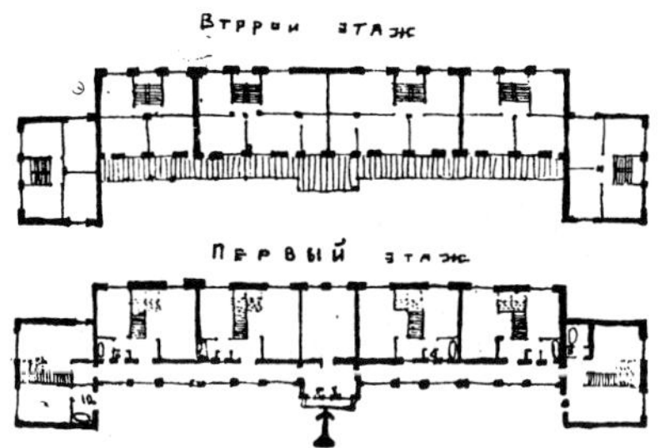

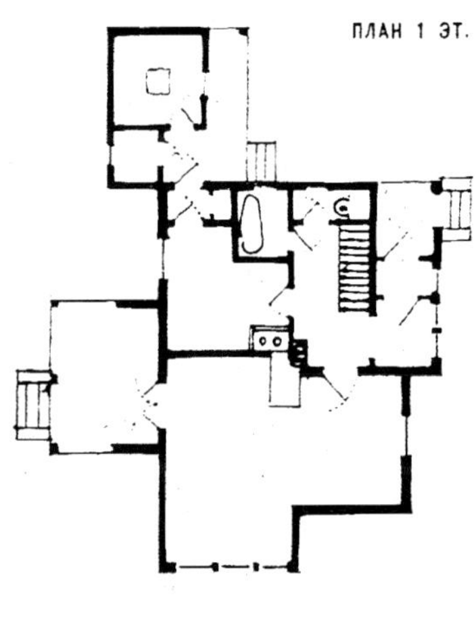

МОСКВА 1925—26 г.
MOSKAU.

*a: **Nikolai Markovnikov,** proposal for a two-storeyed terrace of semi-collectivised workers' housing with communal dining room, 1925: ground and first-floor plans.*

***b, c:** Housing type 60 in timber, for Sokol Garden Settlement, Moscow, 1925-6: photograph soon after completion; ground floor plan.* *(See also pages 136-7)*

***d:** Housing type 58 in the Gerard blockwork system, for Sokol Garden Settlement, Moscow, 1926: photograph soon after completion.*

e: Markovnikov's proposal for a two-storeyed 'Communal house of economic type', left, in courtyard form with central block of facilities, which he contrasts to the high-rise 'Communal house of the favourite contemporary type - a model which is without economic foundations and therefore represents an impractical architectural fantasy', 1928.

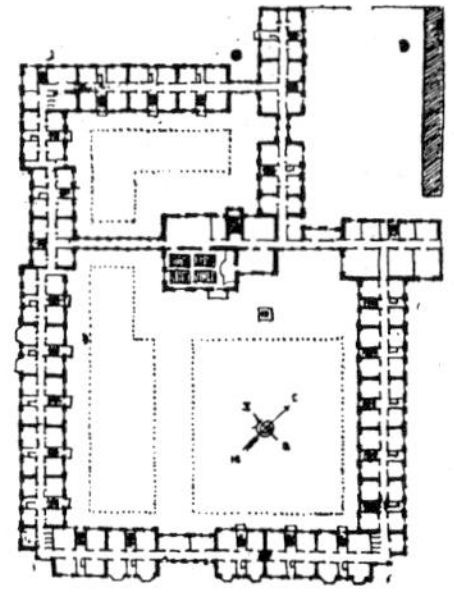

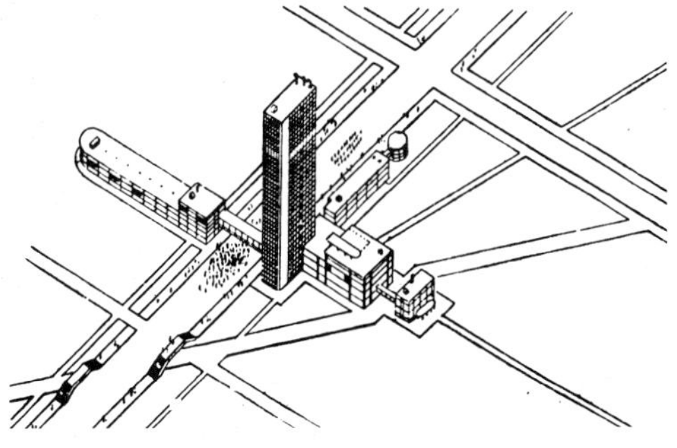

VOPRA

'Proletarian' modernists from the Republics

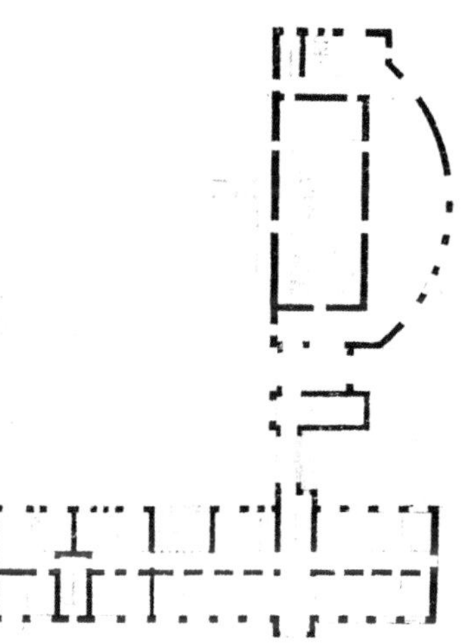

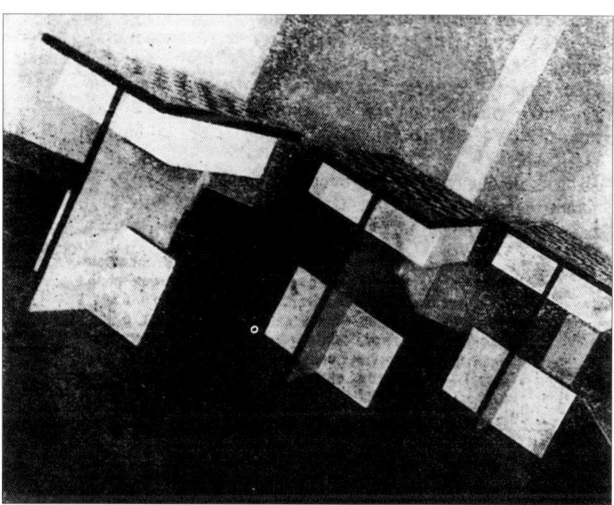

a-c: Karo Alabian, Mikhail Mazmanian, *Workers' club for Erevan, 1929: two photographs of the model; ground-floor plan.*
d, e: M. Arutchin, *furniture for the Club of Building Workers built by* **Alabian, Mazmanian, Gevorg Kochar,** *1929-31: equipment for art classes; chess tables.*
f: Alexander Vlasov and Vopra student team, *competition project for the State Theatre of Massed Musical Acitivies, Kharkov, 1930: perspective of entrance.*

be looked upon as "architectural motifs". In the architectural respect these "motifs" must be rational, and must serve the higher technical demand of the individual to orientate himself in space.

'The designer must take into account that approximation of the image which is obtained from perceiving real forms in perspective, the image given in the projection, ... with whatever accuracy and precision is required in the given situation.' [13]

On the process of designing he wrote in 1919, and always taught, that:

'In planning any given building, the architect must first of all assemble and compose only space, not concerning himself with material and construction. Construction enters into architecture only in so far as it determines the available concepts of space. The engineer's basic principle is to invest the minimum of material to obtain maximum results. This has nothing in common with art and can only serve the requirements of architecture accidentally.' [14]

In extending the concepts to the urban scale later in the Twenties the Rationalists' approach was equally distinctive. 'The architectural structure of the city', they said, 'directly influences the consumers of architecture by its appearance and by the way whole groups of structures are linked in a spatial system that evokes a particular attitude in the ordinary person.' Thus they declared:

'The Soviet state, which has put the principle of planning and control at the cornerstone of all its activity, should also utilise architecture as a powerful means for organising the pyschology of the masses. However, unfortunately, the objective level of development of the humanitarian sciences, the inadequate development of the science of art, and the trivial results that have emerged from modern psychology, do not give us the possibility to fully appreciate that psycho-organisational role which the spatial arts can have in life.' [15]

Research in this field however could 'give the Soviet architect the possibility to solve urbanistic problems by methods which are inaccessible to the Western architect and planner.' The uniqueness of this tool to Soviet architects resulted of course from a circumstance that needed no mentioning to their Soviet audience, the fact that all land and real estate had been nationalised.[16] The inherited cities were no longer packages of small development sites in differing ownership, but a continuous matrix that could indeed be shaped according to some overall schema of expressive or meaningful form.

By the time they wrote this declaration, in 1928, their attempts to get results from modern psychology had been quite thorough, and were particularly based on the experiments and theories of the German psychologist Hugo Munsterberg, then working at Harvard.[17] In their so-called Psycho-Technical Laboratory at the Vkhutemas they had tried to do such research, with strange equipment for testing people's perceptions of forms under different conditions of vision and movement [Docs.5 and 29].[18] Nothing very concrete emerged to be published, but Krinsky's teaching programme was highly influential and in the hands of good students their approach produced some striking architecture.

Fridman, Fidman, Bunin, Turkus, Krutikov were amongst their most productive pupils in Moscow, with such competitions as the Lenin Library (1928) or Kharkov Massed Musical Theatre (1930) demonstrating their capacity for lucid form, as well as some striking planning schemes by Ladovsky's senior students in Vkhutemas (Travin's Shabolovka housing in southern Moscow, 1927-28; group work on Avtostroi et al, 1930) [pp.32-3]. The most dramatic built work from adherents of Rationalism was done in Leningrad, in a series of factory-kitchen complexes (1929-31) by the young Asnova members Barutchev, Gilter, Meerson and Rubanchik [pp.34-7].

It is clear from these statements that the Asnova Rationalists of the Twenties distinguished themselves sharply from 'rationalism' as historically understood, i.e. from the nineteenth century Rationalism that they dismissed as 'Technical Rationalism' and which was amongst the lines of thought feeding into OSA's Constructivism. The distinction between these two groups is precisely that which Krasovsky had already seen when he distinguished the two types of rationalism he saw emerging within Russian architecture back in 1851. This passage from the preface to his magisterial *Civil Architecture* was quoted in Chapter 1 but for clarity it bears repeating here. Amidst a sea of Historicism, wrote Krasovsky, the growing body of anti-Historicists is determined that their art should reflect 'the contemporaneity that surrounds it'.

'Already those who do see and aspire to this [anti-Historicist] direction are tending to separate into two camps: the "aesthetic-rationalists" and the "technological rationalists". The slogan of the first is "form" and of the second, "construction".

'The "aesthetic rationalists" see architecture as an art of abstract form, to be composed according to rules that have been established a priori. *The "technological rationalists" approach the problem of form from the other side, and in designing they believe that everything in the parts and the whole must emerge purely in response to utility and construction.'* [19]

This latter formulation did not offer the sophistication of detail developed in the Constructivists' full 'method' of design, which followed more closely Krasovsky's own belief that 'the true path of architecture lies between these two', but it characterises quite accurately their starting point.

This contrast between the approaches of the Rationalists and the Constructivists was demonstrated clearly in 1923, with two projects for major buildings within a few hundred metres of each other in central Moscow. These were Krinsky's project for a 'skyscraper' to house the new Supreme Soviet of the National Economy, Vesenkha, on Dzerzhinksy Square [p.31] and the Vesnin brothers' third-prizewinning scheme for the equally new concept of a Palace of Labour on the site of today's Hotel Moskva [p.41], both regarded within their own groups as seminal schemes for defining their approach.

As Krinsky's own project description makes clear, his consciously anti-constructive tower was no more than sculpture: another vertical to balance that of the Ivan Belltower in the Kremlin, within the three-dimensional profile of the city centre. Lissitzky's well known Skyhook project, developed at about the same time, had a similar intention of providing points of 'orientation' and 'activisation' in the citizen's perception of the 'new' Soviet city.[20] This scheme is discussed further in Chapter 11 and his project description is Document 31.

The Rationalist approach was thus essentially sculptural, with these landmark buildings conceived from the outside, and internal organisation of their new functions playing no special role in generating their form. The Vesnin brothers' Palace of Labour scheme was characterised by being generated in precisely the opposite way. For this reason it was later described by their colleague Ginzburg as 'the first concrete architectural manifestation of Constructivism.'

'Here for the very first time we see the embodiment of the vital principles of our new approach to the solution of architectural tasks. This work is uniquely important and valuable for its NEW PLAN, which is not the old type of steroetyped symmetrical and ornamental image'.

On the contrary, it 'attempted the creation of a new social organism, whose inner life flowed not from stereotypes of the past but from the innovative features of the task itself.' 'A reinforced concrete frame' then provided 'a simple monolithic three-dimensional expression of the Palace ... that flows logically from its internal composition.'[21]

So this building's overall form had been generated by empirical investigation of this new social function, as the gathering place of mass representatives of labour, and the exterior form and treatment followed from this. In Krasovsky's formulation of seventy years earlier, 'the parts and the whole emerged purely in response to utility and construction', rather than as they did in Rationalist hands, as 'abstract form, composed according to rules established *a priori*.' The germs of these groups' two different design approaches were thus already clearly manifest in these two schemes of 1923.

OSA and Constructivism

The Constructivist group developed from several sources, of which the 'construction' faction in Inkhuk's Objective Analysis Group was perhaps the seminal one. However, the formal Constructivist architectural group, the so-called Union of Contemporary Architects or OSA, was not established till December 1925.

The central concern of the Constructivist architects was to develop a working method out of this simple rationalism of a spatial organisation and its technical expression which was demonstrated in the Palace of Labour. The method would enable the architect to produce this level of rigour and coherence every time, but with far more factors taken into account, including those of clear communication to building users. As Ginzburg put it later,

'Our work, the work of the architectural Constructivists, is different from both idealistic symbolism and this abstract formalism [of Asnova's]. It consists above all of the creation of a materialist working method which would make impossible in principle the dualism between social content and form, and which would guarantee us the creation of an integral, unified and holistic architectural system.'[22]

Chapter 5 describes in detail the various stages by which the ideas of Tatlin and Inkhuk's Working Group were developed during the middle Twenties into the Constructivist architects' 'method'. The most important texts were Alexei Gan's book *Constructivism* of 1922, and the writings of Moisei Ginzburg, starting with his book of 1924, *Style and Epoch*, and leading on into a series of theoretical articles in the Constructivists' journal *Contemporary Architecture* during 1926-27. This journal has always been known, at the time and since, by the initials of its Russian title, *SA*, and for concision I have used that throughout the book hereafter.

Gan's book *Constructivism* of 1922 was a highly political polemic which gave Marxist coloration to that shift in the artist's role which had been signalled by Tatlin. In Tatlin's language, the artist whom capitalism allowed only to 'embellish individual family nests' would now 'take control of the forms of the new way of life'. The fine-artist would become a designer. Gan was the first to identify these and other key ideas of emergent Constructivism not just with 'Revolution', but with Marxism, and to give a clearly materialist rationale for their engagement with architecture and city form. In drawing attention to how the old capitalist buildings were hindering social reorganisation, and how 'correct' buildings could conversely help it, he planted the notion of the building as social catalyst that Constructivist architects later formalised, on a chemical or electrical analogy (it is not clear which) as 'the social condenser'.

It was also Gan who demanded that the Constructivists' 'disciplines' must embrace everything from the most global factors of political principle to the smallest details of how materials can be manipulated and the relationships built up between them. Most importantly of all, he defined Constructivism more explicitly than the group in Inkhuk had, as an intellectual attitude to problem solving that was analogous to the logics derived from practical acts of 'construction', but not bounded by them. *Konstruktsiia* was an intellectual function, he said, a correct internal logic for the design process. In some way not yet defined that logic was to be a Marxist logic, and its practical embodiment would be a series of new 'disciplines'.

'In order to produce practitioners and theoreticians of Constructivism who are qualified, in a Marxist sense, it is necessary to channel our work into a definite system, to create disciplines, through which all the experimental work of Constructivists can be directed.'[23]

Ginzburg's book of 1924 then combined ideas about 'historical cycles' that come essentially from Wölfflin and Spengler with a focus on the machine as *Zeitgeist* that came in part from Corbusier, and he pointed to the machine as the proper source for this overall logic in their revolutionary society. At the more detailed level, he also saw the machine as a model for generating the spatial organisations of new building types from their social briefs. With a 'two stage analogy' between the machine and the factory, the factory and the 'civil building', he outlined how this might operate and in so doing took the first steps towards formulating the practical steps of a future method.[24]

Gan had insisted that design was no longer to be 'the communication of one's own fantasies'. The Constructivists believed that in a socialist society it must be an open, collective process to which specialists and laymen would contribute at appropriate points. None of this however was to eliminate either the architect, or the role of creativity. Thus Ginzburg wrote in 1927, in response to precisely such accusations of nihilism and 'removing the art' from design:

'There can be no question of any sort of an artist losing creativity just because he will know clearly what he is aiming for and in what consists the meaning of

his work. Thus subconscious impulsive creativity must be replaced by a clear and distinctly organised method which is economical of the architect's energy and transfers the freed surplus of it into inventiveness and the force of the creative impulse.' [25]

The procedures of their full method were described by Ginzburg in 1927 in a paper in *SA* entitled 'Constructivism as a method of laboratory and teaching work'.[26] This, like the development towards it, is described in detail in Chapter 5 and summarised in Documents 6 and 8. What matters here are its main features, first: that it was a linear process, based on the sort of linear determinism embodied in the machine and demonstrated in the engineer's method of designing it (see also Chapter 6); second: that it tried to embrace every kind of factor which influenced the building task and every relevant dimension of its wider context – political, technical, economic and aesthetic.

Whatever the building type concerned, as Ginzburg wrote in 1926, the architect should adopt the same approach, 'proceeding from the main questions to the secondary ones ... in a logical ordering of all the factors impinging on the task.' The result would be 'a spatial solution which, like any other kind of rationally generated organism, is divided into individual organs that have been developed in response to the functional roles which each one fulfils.' The 'new type of plan' which resulted would be 'generally asymmetrical, since it is extremely rare for functions to be identical.'

'These modern plans are predominantly open and free, not only to bathe the parts in sunlight and fresh air, but to make the functional elements more readable and to make it easier to perceive the dynamic life that is unfolding within the building's spaces.' [27]

The concern that forms be 'readable' was reflected in their more developed 'method' as a concern with perceptual clarity that embraced the whole content of Asnova's approach, as well as issues of proportion and formal articulation essential to acheiving an aesthetically coherent object. In that respect, their final method moved beyond the rather facile level of 'technical rationalism' as defined by Krasovsky and represented a more detailed elaboration than he ever ventured of design as a process of development from the technical to the aesthetic. Speaking rather imperiously in the third-person Krasovsky had insisted:

'In our opinion the path of architecture must not lie in the exclusive pursuit of either the beautiful or the utilitarian. The true path of architecture lies between these two. Our slogan is the transformation of one into the other: the transformation of what is functional into something beautiful.' [28]

When the Constructivists spoke of 'liberating surplus energy' for the 'creative' bits of design by bringing as much 'science' as possible to bear on generating the basic organism, their linear argument was essentially following Krasovsky's logic, just as the 'rational' strand of late nineteenth- and early twentieth-century architecture had done. In Krasovsky's formulation of this:

'The main source of architectural form is technology, or construction. Art participates in the creation of this architectural form only by communicating an aesthetic finality to the crude forms of technology.' [29]

In the Constructivists' 'functional method', each particular design problem was subject to 'the general characteristics of the epoch as a whole', which were the fact of a collective client and a new way of life; the fact that architecture was part of a larger state plan; the economic need to operate through norms and types; the ideological requirement to operate 'through one single monistic method'. [For these general factors see abstracted diagram on p.127.] 'Using the laboratory method', a design problem was first 'dismembered' for closer examination, then 'reassembled'.

'The first object' or 'stage' involved generating 'the basic spatial diagram of the building', which was that catalytic 'social condenser'. This was done through analysis of the 'flows' and 'needs' of social processes inside it, their environmental requirements, and 'revolutionary rethinking' of how the technical means available might be used. The second object demanded that 'the material forms crystallised as the social condenser be examined in terms of the problem of perception' to 'enhance the user's clear perception of it'. The third object involved more detailed examination of 'the elements of architecture which are the objects of perception', ie surfaces, incisions, detailed articulation of each part. The fourth object turned to production, and 'the particular processes of industrial production which leave their stamp ... on individual components and organisms within the building.' 'Reassembly' would then produce, they said, 'a logical building ... freed from handed-down models of the past'.[30]

One feature of this approach which they saw as inherently Marxist was its capacity to respond logically to change, in conditions and over time, by controlled and logical reconsideration of 'the values of the variables'. 'Form is a function, x', wrote Ginzburg, 'which has always to be evaluated anew by the architect in response to changes in the form-making situation.'[31] This mathematical language reflects another of the important lessons they took from engineering: that mathematical precision is necessary for a real understanding of the properties not just of materials, but also of the properly 'architectural' aspect of a building, which is its spatial organisation.

In diploma work by some of their students (see Chapter 10) this idea was projected forward to a situation where mathematics would make possible a genuinely multi-variate optimisation of building form. Given the very short period in which they were able to operate during the Twenties, and the amount of fundamental research required even in building science before such a rigorous and all-embracing logic as their 'method' could really be pursued – far less the students' vision, which only now after sixty years is becoming thinkable with computers – it is remarkable how much work on these lines the Constructivist group achieved. Their 'method' was a teaching and working discipline that produced some highly innovative designs. Their several years work on 'transitional' housing types was perhaps the most substantial and concerted body of design research done in the USSR in the Twenties. In competition schemes and their students' projects, they generated models for many other new socialist building types. [pp.40-59]

In the earlier and middle Twenties their work is generally characterised by a somewhat Gropius-like frame-and-skin. In the later Twenties it followed more or less rigorously the aesthetic of Le Corbusier and his Five Principles. Amongst students, as ever, there was a tendency to design 'in constructivist style', rather than pursue the method towards genuine spatial innovation, and the distinction was repeatedly being stressed by Ginzburg. One particularly talented and original student, Ivan Leonidov, designed for a far more advanced level of technology than existed (or was even conceivable) in the Soviet Union of the Twenties and attracted criticism to the group as a result. His Suprematist-inspired compositions of widely spaced prismatic volumes owed virtually nothing to the group's 'method' and too-readily became another student 'style', but as Ginzburg recognised, they were important as models of a new kind of urban space. OSA had local groups in several other cities besides Moscow. The largest of them was in Leningrad, led by the Vesnins' contemporary Alexander Nikolsky [pp.52-5], on whom Malevich and Suprematism were also a strong influences, though with less explosive spatial effect than on the young country boy Leonidov.

Melnikov and Golosov

Outside these two main groups, the most important of the other Soviet Modernists, and indeed the avant-garde architect who actually built most, was Konstantin Melnikov. With the exception of the Soviet pavilion for the Paris Exhibition of 1925, which brought him to international attention (see Chapter 8), his work was concentrated in Moscow [pp.60-1] where he grew up and trained. It comprised a series of highly individual workers' clubs, city bus garages, and his own private house which is discussed in Chapter 7.

At one stage Melnikov had informal connections with the Rationalists of Asnova, but he was not a man who liked either groups or theory. Even less did he like the Constructivists' emphasis on method and the mathematical approach of engineers. The approaches of Melnikov and Ilia Golosov, with whom he taught a studio in Vkhutemas in the very early Twenties [Docs.19-22], place them in a middle position between the two groups of more or less 'scientific' Modernists of their own age-group and the more pragmatic Modernists of the generation above them.

In the statement which launched their joint teaching programme in 1923 they asserted that:

'Architectural research should consist of the application of well mastered principles of study to the best monuments of historical architecture. Composition, as an exercise in the principles which have been mastered through experience and by experimental demonstration, is the achievement of a matching between creative intuition and the task posed.' [32]

It is easy to see how Melnikov came to occupy an isolated position. He wrote little but tended to oversimplify the positions of others in order to reject them. In a lecture of 1926 he said:

'Most widespread and mistaken ... is the view that architecture is style, since style in this context means only the sculptural establishment of parts.

'The Constructive trend treats architecture as if ... architectural practice is to be transformed into the necessity to master structural techniques. Since the engineer operates on the basis of mathematics, which is an incomplete science, he can never give complete answers. As a result, engineering will never produce architecture.' [33]

This parody of the Constructivists' view was typical of his refusal (or incapacity) to enter the deeper debates of architectural theory around him. For himself, he says, 'architecture is a volumetric and spatial art. It exists as the handicraft act of building, and only the development of this approach to building can produce such forms as we call architecture.' Perhaps the purest demonstration of this last statement was his own little house, based as it was on ideas about rationalising traditional handicraft techniques of Russian building. This is discussed in Chapter 7 and Documents 11 and 12..

The formal organisation of Melnikov's buildings was always derived from one single generating idea that originated in his personal response to the brief. This was the essence of his design approach, and the descriptions he later gave of the main spatial idea generating each of his most important designs [pp.60-1; 138-9] indicate the source of their power as images.

'Melnikov House: EQUAL VALUE AND EVENNESS of loadings, light, air and heat;
New Sukharev Market: 2000 small traders ALL HAVE CORNER SITES;
Rusakov Club: THE AUDITORIA CAN BE TRANSFORMED for 350, 450, 550, 775, 1000 or 1200 people;
Dulevo Club: sitting with ANTENNAE in a beautiful WOODLAND;
Model workers housing: now everyone can live in a three-storied complex AS IF IN A FREE-STANDING VILLA;
Palace of Labour project: every person in an audience of 8000 CAN HEAR A NATURAL VOICE.' [34]

These concepts represent bold and attractive thinking about the socially new architectural briefs, but the process by which Melnikov arrived at them was entirely traditional. It depended on exactly those chance factors of personal talent and inspiration which the Constructivists believed must be replaced if socialist architecture was to be socially responsive and responsible. Melnikov was unequivocal in rejecting their central tenets:

'There is no obligatory sequence whatsoever for the processes applied in the initial stages of work on any design. Very much depends on the intuition and what is still broadly known as "creative imagination". No work of any kind is possible on the conception of any building, of course, without some preliminary study of the technical and economic features of the task in hand. But it can happen that the spatial treatment and composition take shape in the architect's mind before the detailed work on the economic and technical considerations has started.' [35]

Grigori Barkhin (1880-1969)

Nikolai Ladovsky (1881-1941)

Ilia Golosov (1883-1945)

Georgi Golts (1893-1946)

Ivan Leonidov (1902-1959)

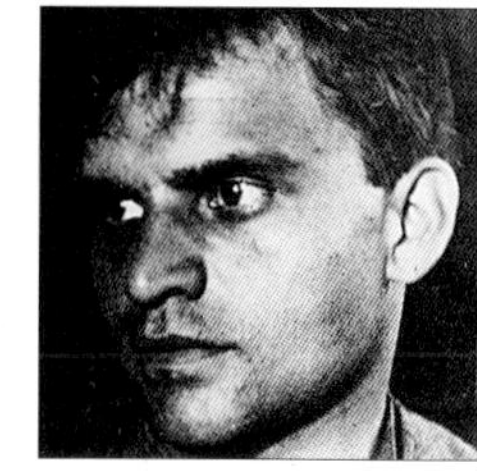
Georgi Krutikov (1899-1958)

This was precisely the kind of intuitive leap into formal solutions that Constructivists were trying by their method to prevent, especially amongst students, but Melnikov's teaching was as determinedly anti-theoretical as his own work. He typically announced to one set of students:

'In our classes we shall talk little and work a lot. We shall understand each other most quickly and fully through our practical tasks, and shall most easily master our subject through the processes of working together.' [36]

Behind this dogmatic refusal to engage in theory was in fact a sound if inarticulate grasp of the non-linear relationship of form to function whose complexity is perhaps more widely recognised now than then. To the same students he stressed the absence of any one-to-one relationship between function and form, insisting that 'one single [functional] theme leads very properly to 'a plurality of [architectural] form'. To him this was because the 'architectural' component of design is a symbolic one. As another lecture began: 'Architecture is a powerful language expressing the social structure of the age and its people.' [37]

Melnikov's buildings were often quirky, strangely proportioned and unneighbourly in comparison to the smooth elegance of much Constructivist or Rationalist work. However his focus on that still unexplained mental function which throws up 'concepts', draws our attention to the main problematic in the Constructivists' 'method': to that mysterious act, so summarily passed over, of 'reassembly' after the analysis. Within the Russian avant-garde as a whole Melnikov's work serves as the cautionary reminder of how easily those parts of the design process which are analytical or rational can override the synthetic element – what Melnikov insists on calling the 'intuition' – simply because they are more easily communicated, and in particular, taught, by formalised means.

Ilia Golosov also asserted that 'architectural form cannot be achieved through knowledge alone. Sensitivity and artistic intuition must also be present. Yet artistic intuition develops through knowledge' he conceded.[38] As we have seen, the Constructivists did not dispute that. It was merely their intention that rigorous organisation of the knowledge-based parts of design would liberate the architect's energies for the genuinely inventive part: for making the raw 'social condenser' into 'architecture'.

Golosov's theory, like the Constructivists' method, followed the underlying structure of the nineteenth-century Rationalists' concept of design, still current in the *Moderne*, where the first stage produced a crude functional form, and the second involved refining that form aesthetically.

Thus Golosov said:

'When composing a structure of whatever size, it is essential to distinguish MASS from FORM. Mass we define as any volume of the most rudimentary kind, devoid of any inner meaning, ie not resulting from any particular subjective architectural idea.

'Being without subjective content, an architectural mass is totally free in the shapes it adopts. The opposite is true of FORM. Form is the result of, and is responsible to, the MEANING which has brought it into existence. To perceive a FORM is to perceive an inner meaning. When a mass becomes invested with a meaning it becomes an architectural form. It is an expression of an architectural thought.' [39]

Melnikov's distinctive generative concepts exemplify what Golosov meant here by 'architectural thought'.

When Golosov discusses the principles which are to guide the architect in refining a design, the emphasis is clearly aesthetic:

'In analysis of architectural mass and form, one of the highest priorities in terms of perception must go to the principle of MOVEMENT. In every mass or form a correlation of forces expressing this principle of movement is always present in some way. Meaningful composition in architecture depends largely on a grasp of the properties in the configurations of masses and forms employed, in relation to their repose or dynamism.

'Each structure will have a dominant direction of movement. Achieving HARMONY amongst masses means achieving harmony amongst all the movements. Compositional innovation in architecture finds its starting point in the rhythm of the masses.' [40]

Here as with Asnova we see a preferential emphasis being given to what the Constructivists treated as just one factor amongst others. The notion of the new aesthetics as a balancing of dynamic movements was a strong theme in Ginzburg's *Style and Epoch* in 1924, where he saw it as one of the aesthetic lessons of the machine.[41] But he would never have contemplated making this the main focus of teaching, let alone the main determinant of an architectural system.

Ilia Golosov's most famous design, and the only one built in Moscow, was the Zuev workers' club, where it has to be said that the balance of the forms is more satisfactory from some viewpoints than others. He did an enormous number of competition projects, but his formal vocabulary is much less varied and inventive than Melnikov's [pp.62-4]. Very many of his designs depend for their formal coherence, as the Zuev club does, on a single cylindrical volume juxtaposed to a disparate assembly of rectangular ones.

Pragmatic modernists

Among those who must be considered the leading Soviet Modernists of the Twenties are four architects of the slightly older generation in what I have called the first and second cohorts. Contemporaries of the Vesnins and Ilia Golosov, they had experience before the Revolution but were still only in their early forties when building started up again in 1924. Whilst entirely sympathetic to the new regime, their less theoretical and polemic approach to the problems of design meant that they still operated under the banner of the old-established Moscow Architectural Society, MAO, rather than attaching themselves to the new groups. To these architects, Modernism in the twenties was not a sharply ideological battle, but a natural extension of forward-looking trends already developing before the Revolution.

The most broadly distinguished designer of these three was perhaps Grigori Barkhin, who was highly prolific in the innumerable architectural competitions of the twenties and became *pater familias* to a whole dynasty of teachers and practitioners that continues today. He is principally known, however, for his only Moscow building of the twenties, the editorial headquarters of the Party ºCentral Committee's newspaper *Izvestiia*, of 1925-7 [pp.66-7]. Compromised though this building was by the height limit introduced into central Moscow in late 1925, it was among the first built projects to raise the image of a modern future triumphantly above the old two-three storeyed city. With finish and fittings of a quality suited to its prestige down to the bronze doorhandles, it also offered a hope of continuity with pre-Revolutionary building standards that was soon to be dashed.

Immediately after the Revolution Barkhin had been involved with adapting peasant housing traditions and European Garden City ideas to the new Soviet situation. This practicality was fundamental to his teaching and practice. He wrote books on the wooden housing, but never engaged in theory for its own sake. He summed up his approach in his memoirs thus:

'However theoretical, or even at times abstract the problems with which I had to deal, I always believed that both one's analysis and one's conclusions must be closely intertwined with live practice, with the urgent concerns of the present moment. As I see it, this is entirely appropriate to architecture, which is simultaneously the most abstract and the most practical of all the arts.' [42]

This honest pragmatism and balance were combined with talent and experience to make Barkhin highly respected in teaching as in the profession.

Boris Velikovsky was a contemporary of Barkhin's whose approach was likewise rooted in solid experience of building, but who associated more closely with the Constructivists. He was a few years older than the Vesnin brothers, and Alexander and Viktor had worked in his office from 1908-10 whilst they were still technically students, doing elevational treatments for office and commercial buildings in the city centre [pp.68-9]. In the Twenties this collaboration continued with the next architectural generation. Thus Velikovsky's assistants on his major work of the Twenties, the headquarters of the state trading organisation Gostorg, of 1925-7, were three of the Vesnins' Constructivist students, Barshch, Vegman and Gaken.

Continuing where the pre-Revolutionary profession had left off with the boldest of their concrete frames – such as the Trading Centre (*Delovyi dvor*) by I. S. Kuznetsov, of 1912-13 – the Gostorg building was perhaps the most rigorous expression of a frame and glass Modernism actually built in the Twenties in the Soviet Union. Alfred Barr, founder of the Museum of Modern Art in New York and curator of the 1932 exhibition there which defined 'The International Style', saw this building in January 1928 and he described it as 'easily the finest Modern architecture in Moscow, very Gropius in style with all glass sections, steamboat balconies etc.'[43] Like Barkhin's *Izvestiia*, the Gostorg design lost its original central tower to the height regulations. More than any other Soviet building of the time however it managed to achieve interiors which genuinely possessed the flowing space, open celebration of vertical movement and multi-directional light which the modern frame could offer. His other work such as housing was constrained by exigent circumstances, but he was important as inspiration and practical tutor to the avant-garde students generation.

When it came to selecting Soviet work for inclusion in that definitive International Style exhibition, the single building selected was one part of the finest showpiece Modernist complex in the whole USSR, begun just after Barr's visit: the All-Union Electrotechnical Institute, VEI.[44] Lenin's National Plan for Electrification of Russia (Goelro) was the practical and symbolic foundation of all Soviet economic development. As this Institute was now the scientific centre for the whole Soviet electrification project, its new buildings in northeast Moscow were of the highest symbolic importance [p.70]. Here sleek Modernism of world class really was making an ideological statement.

Several architects worked on this, including the young Constructivist Ivan Nikolaev, the Movchan brothers and Fisenko, to whom it tends to be attributed. The senior figure behind it all, however, was the pre-Revolutionary pioneer of concrete frame construction Alexander Kuznetsov, who may be considered the third member of this 'pragmatic' category of modernists. He had built major projects for the Russian textile industry before the Revolution and his new buildings of 1926 for the Moscow Textile Institute were equally distinguished Modernism [p.71].

Immediately after the Revolution Kuznetsov had set up the architecture department in the new Moscow Higher Technical College, MVTU (see Chapter 10). From 1922 this was officially called its Faculty of Industrial Building but was effectively a whole school of architecture. Amongst those he invited to staff it were his near-contemporaries Viktor and Leonid Vesnin. When the younger Moisei Ginzburg returned to Moscow in 1921, it was here that he started teaching architectural history and theory. In the early years of the Constructivist movement in architecture, around 1924-5-6, this school rather than the Vkhutemas was thus its natural stronghold, and Kuznetsov was a father figure and teacher to the group rather than actually a member of it.

Kuznetsov was so active in building and teaching during the Twenties that no writings remain, but statements from just before and after this period show his absolute consistency across these two decades, and explain his influence on the Constructivists.

Speaking on 'Architecture and reinforced concrete' to the last Congress of Russian Architects, in Moscow in 1915, he said:

'In reinforced concrete we have not just a new material, but even more importantly, a whole new constructional system and a new method of designing buildings. Therefore in using this material we have to renounce old traditions and address ourselves to solving new tasks. Reinforced concrete cannot be left bare, as it emerges at present from the hands of engineers, but nor can the new material be finished with old forms deriving from masonry and timber. In order to create forms that organically derive from the very essence of reinforced concrete itself, it is necessary to master the technical and scientific aspects of the question.

'The architect, according to the definition advanced at the London Congress, "is an artist with scientific education". For working in reinforced concrete, more than in any other field, what is needed is the technically educated artist. The architect will not produce an expression of his epoch if he does not utilise the processes of technology of his own age in all their fullness. Architecture is the harmony of science and art.' [45]

In a paper published in the official Soviet architecture journal in 1934, well after the public demise of Modernism, his line was the same:

'In our socialist conditions the foundation of architecture is the contemporary science and technology of the constructional base. ...

'We study the heritage of the [distant] past but we forget about studying the more recent past of the late nineteenth century, in which humanity made greater progress than in all its previous history ...

> *'It is time to use the new constructional possibilities not only for narrowly technical purposes, but to link them to the architectonics of the building, to the articulation of its mass. For steel and concrete structural systems we have to find the appropriate laws of rhythm and proportions; to find other relations of the diameter of columns or protrusions of architraves, to the column height. We cannot dictate to the new through the laws of the old. It is time to give aesthetic expression to the individual details or parts and to the forms of the whole engineering structure. ... All parts of the building must be treated by the architect as obligatory objects for architectural treatment in this sense. ... But reinforced concrete is still awaiting this attention.'* [46]

A fourth man who has to be counted amongst the Modernists, though even older and more firmly rooted in eclectic and historicist practice before the Revolution than Barkhin, Velikovsky or Kuznetsov was Alexei Shchusev. He took over from Shekhtel as President of MAO in 1922 and stayed in that position till MAO was dissolved in 1930. Shchusev had quickly established himself in professional circles around the Academy of Arts in Petersburg after graduation, particularly through his scholarly restoration work on ruined provincial churches. In pre-War Moscow he had designed new religious and philanthropic buildings in a version of the *Moderne* style derived from simple medieval Russian stone architecture, and where appropriate (as for example in the Kazan Station development which spanned from 1913 to 1926), he used more elaborate historicist styles, both Russian and Classical.

Indeed it can be said of Shchusev that he was always contextual: he designed in whatever style was appropriate to the place, and even more, to the time [pp.73-6]. Entirely untouched by the notions of a new continuum between the three traditional arts such as unpinned the work of Asnova or OSA, he regarded Modernism as merely one such stylistic choice in architecture, a choice dictated to it not by the ideological 'demands of today' but by pragmatic demands. Thus he declared in a lecture of 1926:

> *'Amongst architects there is a battle for the new ideal, and we shall fight for it unrelentingly. Painting and sculpture have temporarily departed from architecture and now have to justify their presence again. In life today it is primarily economics that drive us forward, and economics is rooted in those same needs which make humanity turn towards building.*
>
> *'Style is not the product of the particular tastes of a few people. Style is a system of how things are decorated, which can be either luxuriant, or poorer. At the present time, we cannot aspire to the luxuriant. We must merely give form to that which derives directly from construction of the simplest of forms. Is this architecture? Does it represent its demise or its flowering? Simple treatments are closer to the latter than the former.*
>
> *'If we proceed from the demands of today, we must take account of the fact that right now, the most expensive materials [in our market] are brick and glass. All contemporary design, based on the simple forms of concrete, brick and glass, therefore shows itself not to be economic. On the contrary: all these aspirations to produce something economic crumble to dust even as a result of the high cost of plate glass. There is no way we can talk about architecture in today's context.'* [47]

In another speech later in the same week Shchusev took a more positive approach to the need to redefine the nature and role of architecture, himself preaching that 'high construction costs ... are why we need a new approach to designing and to the architecture of a building.' 'The architect's ability to solve spatial and volumetric tasks' he declared, could save 'the building technologist and the economist' from just that 'blind amateurishness which our epoch of social change is trying to eliminate.'[48]

Thus Shchusev may be seen as the most pragmatic of this category of Modernists. His buildings are generally too lacking in formal and stylistic clarity to be masterpieces. The exception is perhaps the most contextual of them: the Lenin Mausoleum on Red Square. Modernist in some respects while deeply atavistic in others, this sculptural object resulting from a several-year process of evolution is no measure of real design credentials. As a leading architect-planner in the post-Revolutionary years, Shchusev's contextualism was also manifest in his insistence on consideration of the formal and heritage aspects of city sites, and the Mausoleum is unquestionably masterly in that respect.

On the boundary with Classicism

Ivan Zholtovsky and Ivan Fomin were two architects who sought in different ways to produce a modern architecture that drew upon Classicism not just as a paradigm of rigour, as Tatlin had presented it, but for specific architectural qualities.

Zholtovsky was five years older than Shchusev, but their names are often linked as father figures to the young Moscow profession of the Twenties. Certainly they worked together as planners of Moscow when it first became the capital again in 1918, and both believed firmly in the traditional principle that any new building must respect its urban context, but otherwise their architectural philosophies were very different.

Where Shchusev could be negatively described as a weathercock, Zholtovsky consistently adhered to the Renaissance design principles in which he believed, and through which he had practised in Moscow before the Revolution [pp.77-9]. A brilliant and charismatic teacher throughout the Twenties, even to those not impressed by his personal architectural convictions, he considered Renaissance architecture to be the finest material for training the architect's eye in proportion and composition.

Zholtovsky's particular concern was the application of those aesthetic principles of proportion and composition to industrial architecture, as one of the most important areas of built environment to which working people, the new clients of architecture, were exposed. If this was an argument from expediency rather than conviction, it was still a valid one. Several electric power stations to designs by himself and his students in various parts of the country demonstrated the potential of his approach, notably his own Moscow City Power Station, Moges, built in 1927, and work by such talented pupils as Sergei Kozhin, Mikhail Parusnikov and Georgi Golts [pp.78-9]

Their elegantly formal designs, and Zholtovsky's whole attitude, made an illuminating contrast with Kuznetsov's approach to industrial building and the new structural materials. Where Kuznetsov insisted that new 'laws of rhythm, proportions, relations of diameter of column to column height, of protrusions to architraves ... must be found for steel and concrete structural systems', and that 'we cannot dictate to the new through the laws of the old', Zholtovsky's basic principle was the reverse. His concern was precisely to extract those 'laws of the old' in order to apply them to 'the new'.

His rather flat attempt at an a-stylar extension to the State Bank in central Moscow of 1927-9 may have been contextual, but it was mocked by the Constructivists for 'propagating the ideology of passeists and eclectics.'[49] Equally alien to the design philosophy of all true Modernists was his insistence on the continuing importance of the facade. However many of the young studied or worked under him to great advantage because of his emphasis on proportion, balance and the traditionally trained eye.

Ivan Fomin's approach was yet another response to the problem Kuznetsov had posed, of finding an architectural treatment for the concrete frame. Superficially, Fomin's work more explicitly retained classical 'motifs' than Zholtovsky's, but his approach actually represented the more radical and permissive reworking of Classical elements [pp.80-2].

An exact contemporary of Shchusev, though vastly more talented as a designer, Fomin had worked before the Revolution with the leading Classical architects in St. Petersburg. His period amongst the *Moderne* designers in Moscow included a very fruitful period in Shekhtel's office. His Red Doric and subsequent Proletarian Classicism of the Twenties were based on a belief that the proportions of Classicism must change as new materials generated different structural dimensions in building, but that the formal elements which expressed the underlying principles of trabeation, solid-and-void etc, remained valid. Zholtovsky was happy to abandon formal elements like columns in his industrial building but considered the important feature of Classicism to be its particular system of proportions. Fomin on the other hand stretched his simplified Classical elements into entirely new proportional relationships, but believed passionately that the key structuring elements of the formal language must be retained for their inherent 'internationalism' and 'democracy'. In his stripped-down version, Classicism would speak in a voice appropriate to the proletarian state. He presented his argument thus:

'The standards and discipline which are so essential to Classical architecture answer in full the needs of our own new way of life, and also of our new constructional practices and building materials, amongst which reinforced concrete occupies a large role.

'The repetitive rhythms of the column, on facades and inside the building, are entirely in accord with the repetitive frame of a reinforced concrete structure.

'There is no reason to suppose that the joyless look of naked construction represents the ideal of a reinforced concrete building. Classicism can teach us the appropriate language. This is why it isextremely timely to look backwards, to achievements of former epochs. However we do this not in order to repeat the old. Retrospectivism is not the right path for architecture in a revolutionary epoch. We do it in order to use a radical reconstruction of Classicism as the basis of our own, new, Soviet revolutionary style for this epoch.'[50]

Garden City modernism

At the opposite end of the appeal to tradition in the Twenties we find those who stressed the merits of dispersed, small-scale development of the type which traditionally characterised Russian towns. Amongst the explicitly avant-garde Modernists, both Barkhin and Melnikov argued from different points of view in favour of active development of the traditional one-family house, though both of them were principally concerned with the development of a new large-scale architecture of concrete. The leader of the movement which most explicitly continued the arguments and campaign of Russia's pre-Revolutionary Garden City movement was Nikolai Markovnikov, a Moscow architect born, like Zholtovsky, in the late 1860s [p.86]. Like Zholtovsky he was not only highly experienced, but was a teacher of architecture and urbanism who had influence far beyond the circles of those who followed his own particular design philosophy. His relationship with the Constructivists was a typical example of this. Reviewing the first issue of their journal, *SA*, in 1926 he wrote:

'If we progress only on paper, then it becomes all to easy to find that we have not moved forward in the direction real architecture must go, but are left aside, or even left behind.

'Our front-line practitioners have still not taken note of the already widely proclaimed slogan that construction must take account of economics. As a result they produce projects abounding in highly fragmented walls, with protrusions and overhangs, that are economically impossible because they lead to high costs in building housing accommodation.

'New forms in architecture can be achieved only out of new materials and through new modes of construction. Both of these will enter our practice with great difficulty and slowly, through the same sort of gradual development that produced such objects as the motor-car and the aeroplane. There is no way in which we can foresee the form which the final results of this development process will take.'[51]

For the primitive conditions of the Soviet Union in the early Twenties, Markovnikov believed that mass housing should be a rationalisation of the traditional low-rise cottage housing. In some cases, as in the Sokol Garden Suburb development built to a plan by Shchusev in 1923, certain of his houses used new materials like experimental types of hollow or foamed-concrete block. Other projects, not built, demonstrated that the ideologically approved *dom kommuna* type of social organisation (or 'communal house') need not be a monolithic block of expensive concrete or masonry, but could take the form of a low-rise courtyard using entirely traditional small-scale construction.

One thing that Markovnikov shared with the Constructivists was a concern to examine the real properties of a building form or urban layout through the hard realism of mathematics. Thus one of the most important episodes in Constructivism's history of public arguments over issues of principle was the battle between Barshch and Markovnikov over the relative economics of his scattered cottages or their compact integrated housing blocks 'under today's conditions'. Taking into account the prevailing economics of building and servicing, of the female workers' time budgets, transportation technologies and the collectivist lifestyle, both of them believed that mathematics proved their own form to be the most economic (see Chapter 11).[52] They differed, however, in the fact that the Constructivists believed that the methods of the engineer enabled the architect to produce a constant series of perhaps radically different 'correct new forms' as circumstances change, whereas Markovnikov saw the lessons of the car and the aeroplane as evolutionary rather than revolutionary.

The Soviet architectural profession of the Twenties was relatively very small. That was one of the problems facing the massive building programme that was launched under the Five Year Plans which began to get going in 1929-30. As a collaborator of Shchusev and a sparring partner of the Constructivists, Markovnikov serves as an important reminder of the extent to which key figures in the profession, focussed largely in the new capital of Moscow, were in close contact. The vigour and fertility of the avant-garde resulted not just from the high level of cross-fertilisation and competition amongst themselves, but from the urgency of the situation around them. It also resulted from the presence within their tight-knit professional environment of this range of quite different philosophies of what a Soviet architecture should be, equally passionately held and sharply argued, and all contributing some distinguished and inventive buildings to the early Modern legacy.

■

1 Described by his brother in Alexandre Benois, *Memoirs*, London, 1960, pp.162-3 **2** M. Ginzburg, 'Mezhdunarodnyi front sovremennoi arkhitektury' (The international front of modern architecture), *SA*, 1926, no.2, pp.41-6 **3** V. E. Tatlin, with T. Shapiro, I. Meerzon, P. Vinogradov, 'Nasha predstoishchaia rabota' (The work ahead of us), published in *VIII S"ezd sovetov. Ezhednevnyi biulleten s"ezda* (VIII Congress of Soviets. Daily Congress Bulletin), no.13, 1 Jan 1921, p.11. This statement was dated 31 Dec 1920 and accompanied showing of the tower model at this Party Congress in Moscow. **4** For further discussion and in particular extensive visual material from Zhivskulptarkh and Inkhuk see the following works of S. Khan-Magomedov: *Rodchenko*, London, 1986, Chaps 2, 3, 4 and *Pioneers of Soviet Architecture*, London, 1987, pp.67-70 & 78-89. Extremely full documentation will be found in Russian in his: *Zhivskul'ptarkh 1919-1920*, Moscow, 1993, and *Inkhuk i rannii konstruktivizm*, Moscow 1994. **5** 'Programma instituta khudozhestvennoi kul'tury, Izo-Narkompros', Moscow, 1920. For an English version of the first part see: Camilla Gray, *The Russian Experiment in Art 1863-1922*, London, 1971, pp. 234-5 **6** Kandinsky's contributions to Rakhn are documented in *Iskusstvo. Zhurnal Rakhn* (Art. The Journal of Rakhn), no.1, 1923, pp.412-17. His 'Programme for the Physico-Psychological Section', translated from there, appears in English in: J. Bowlt, ed., *Russian Art of the Avant-Garde: Theory and Criticism 1902-34*, New York, 1976, pp.196-8. Another of his papers to Rakhn appears in French in: D. Bozo, ed., *Kandinsky*, Centre Georges Pompidou, Paris, 1985, pp.158-9 **7** N Ladovsky, 'O programme rabochei gruppy arkhitektorov Inkhuka, 1921' (Programme of the working group of architects in Inkhuk), in M. G. Barkhin, ed., *Mastera sovetskoi arkhitektury ob arkhitekture* (Masters of Soviet Architecture on Architecture) , Moscow, 1975, vol.1, pp. 345-7 **8** A. Rudenstine, ed., *Russian Avant-Garde: The George Costakis Collection*, London-New York, 1981, pp.110-27; Khan-Magomedov, *Rodchenko*, pp. 83-9 **9** For some further detail in English see Khan-Magomedov, *Pioneers*, p.141 and documents on Asnova's constitution, pp.592-3. For full details on founding etc see: V. Khazanova, comp., *Iz istorii sovetskoi arkhitektury 1926-32: dokumenty i materialy* (From the History of Soviet Architecture 1926-32: documents and materials), Moscow, 1970, pp.39-40 **10** Khan-Magomedov, *Pioneers*, p.147 and docs. p.592 **11** V. Krinsky, I. Lamtsov, M. Turkus, *Elementy arkhitekturno-prostranstvennoi kompozitsii*, Moscow-Leningrad, 1934 **12** N Ladovsky, 'Iz protokolov zasedaniia komissii zhivskulptarkha 1919' (From minutes of meetings of the Zhivskulptarkh commission 1919), in Barkhin, ed., *Mastera*, vol.1, pp.343-4. For a general study of the Rationalists see: A Senkevitch, 'Aspects of spatial form and perceptual psychology in the doctrine of the Rationalist movement in Soviet architecture in the 1920s', *Via 6*, University of Pennsylvania, 1983, pp.78-115 **13** 'Osnovy postroeniia teorii arkhitektury - pod znakom ratsionalisticheskoi estetiki' (Foundations for building a theory of architecture - under the banner of rationalist aesthetics) 1920, in *Izvestiia ASNOVA* (Asnova News), no.1, 1926, p.3 **14** Ladovsky, 'Iz protokolov', in Barkhin, ed., *Mastera*, vol.1, pp.343-4 **15** 'Pervaia deklaratsiia ARU', 1928, *Ezhegodnik literatury i iskusstva na 1929 god* (Annual of literature and art for 1929), Moscow, 1929, pp.552-5, republ. in Khazanova, ed., *Iz istorii 1926-32*, p.125 **16** This nationalisation was effected by the Bolshevik government in its *Dekret o zemle* (Decree on the land), dated 26 Oct 1917 **17** N. Ladovsky, 'Psikho-tekhnicheskaia laboratoriia arkhitektury - v poriadke postanovki voprosa' (A psycho-technical laboratory of architecture - by way of posing the question), *Izvestiia ASNOVA*, p.7. For sources on Münsterberg's ideas and his contributions to applied psychology see: Senkevitch, 'Aspects', pp.113-4, n.49 **18** G. Krutikov, 'Arkhitekturnaia nauchno-issledovatel'skaia laboratoriia arkhitekturnogo fakul'teta Moskovskogo Vkhuteina' (The Architectural research laboratory of the architecture faculty at Moscow Vkhutein), *Stroitel'naia promyshlennost'*, 1928, no.5, pp.372-5. For other sources on the laboratory see Senkevitch, 'Aspects', p.113, n.48 **19** A. K. Krasovsky, *Grazhdanskaia arkhitektura* (Civil Architecture), St Petersburg, 1851, p. 27-9 **20** Both projects were published in the only issue of *Izvestiia ASNOVA*, produced by Ladovsky and Lissitzky in 1926 **21** M. Ginzburg, 'Itogi i perspektivy' (Achievements and prospects), *SA*, 1927, no.4/5, pp.112-118. For an English translation see: T. & C. Benton, D. Sharp, eds., *Form and Function. A sourcebook ... 1890-1939*, London, 1975, pp.156-160 **22** M. Ginzburg, 'Konstruktivizm v arkhitekture' (Constructivism in architecture), *SA*, 1928, no.5, pp.143-5 **23** A. Gan, *Konstruktivizm*, Tver, 1922, p.55. **24** M. Ginzburg, *Stil' i epokha* (Style and Epoch), Moscow, 1924, pp.18-29; 127-34 **25** M. Ginzburg, 'Tselevaia ustanovka v sovremennoi arkhitekture' (Aims in contemporary architecture), *SA*, 1927, no.1, pp.4-10 **26** M. Ginzburg, 'Konstruktivizm kak metod laboratornoi i pedagogicheskoi raboty' (Constructivism as a method of laboratory and teaching work), *SA*, 1927, no.6, pp.160-6 **27** M. Ginzburg, 'Novye metody arkhitekturnogo myshleniia' (New methods of architectural thinking), *SA*, 1926, no.1, pp.1-4. See full text in Document to Chapter 6. **28** Krasovsky, *Grazhdanskaia arkhitektura*, pp.27-9 **29** ibid, p.5 **30** Ginzburg, 'Konstruktivizm kak metod'; see Chapter 5 below. **31** ibid **32** 'Nakaz arkhitekturnogo izucheniia po programme masterskikh Novaia Akademiia' (Instructions for architectural study according to the syllabus of the New Academy studios), 1923, in I Kokkinaki & A Strigalev, eds., *Konstantin Stepanovich Mel'nikov*, Moscow, 1985, pp.93-4 **33** 'Arkhitektura: lektsii v tekhnikume kinematografii' (Architecture: a lecture to the Higher Technical College of Cinematography), 1926, in Kokkinaki & Strigalev, eds., *Mel'nikov*, pp.98-9 **34** 'Sut' riada svoikh proektov' (The essence of a series of my projects), 1965, in Kokkinaki & Strigalev, eds., *Mel'nikov*, pp.239-40 **35** K. Mel'nikov, 'Oformlenie proekta', *Arkhitektura SSSR*, 1933, no.5, p.35 **36** 'Konspekt lektsii na kafedre arkhitektury V-I. A, 14 aprelia 1932' (First lecture to the Department of Architecture, Academy of Military Engineers, 14 Apr 1932) in Kokkinaki & Strigalev, eds., *Mel'nikov*, pp.102-3 **37** 'Lektsionnyi obzor ... V-I A, noiabr 1933' (Lecture notes to architecture dept in Academy of Military Engineers, Nov 1933), in Kokkinaki & Strigalev, eds., *Mel'nikov*, pp.109-110 **38** 'Rukopis I. A. Golosova: II Arkhitekturnaia massa, Poniatie arkhitekturnoi massy' (Manuscript by I. A. Golosov: 2 Archiectural mass. The concept of architectural mass), in S. O. Khan-Magomedov, *Il'ia Golosov*, Moscow, 1988, pp.211-2. Extracts from this appear in English in his *Pioneers*, p.562 **39** ibid **40** ibid **41** Ginzburg, *Stil' i epokha*, pp.95-7 **42** A. G. Barkhina, *G. B. Barkhin*, Moscow, 1981, p.122 **43** I. Sandler & A. Newman, eds., *Defining Modern Art: selected writings of Alfred H. Barr, Jr.*, New York 1986, p.116 **44** H-R. Hitchcock and P. Johnson, *The International Style*, New York, 1966, reprint of the 1932 edition. The single detail image appears on p.234, as 'USSR Government architects (Nikolaiev & Fissenko): Electro-Physical Laboratory, Lefortovo, Moscow, 1927. Vertical and curved elements used with functional justification and aesthetic success.' **45** A. Kuznetsov, 'Arkhitektura i zhelezobeton' (Architecture and reinforced concrete), *Zodchii* (The Architect), 1915, nos. 19, 20; republ. in Barkhin, ed., *Mastera*, vol.1, pp.213-14 **46** A. Kuznetsov, 'Arkhitektura i stroitel'naia tekhnika v XIX i nachale XX veka' (Architecture and building technology in the 19th and early 20th centuries), *Akademiia arkhitektury* (Academy of Architecture), 1934, no.1-2, pp.51-2; republ. in Barkhin, ed., *Mastera*, vol.1, pp.214-16 **47** A. Shchusev, 'Lektsiia: stroitel'stvo naselennikh mest' (Lecture: the building of populated places), Paper to the First All-Union Congress on Civil and Engineering Construction, Moscow, 6-15 May 1926, in Barkhin, ed., *Mastera*, vol.1, pp.170-171 **48** A. Shchusev, 'Lektsiia: ekonomika, tekhnika i arkhitektura' (Lecture: economics, technology and architecture) to 1926 Congress as note 47, in Barkhin, ed., *Mastera*, vol.1, pp.169-170 **49** *SA*, 1927, no.2, p.49 **50** I. Fomin, 'Tvorcheskie puti sovetskoi arkhitektury i problema arkhitekturnogo nasledstva' (The creative direction of soviet architecture and the problem of the architectural heritage), *Arkhitektura SSSR*, 1933, no.3-4, pp.15-16, republ. in Barkhin, ed., *Mastera*, vol.1, pp.129-32 **51** N. Markovnikov, 'Novyi arkhitekturnyi zhurnal' (A new architectural journal), *Stroitel'naia promyshlennost'*, 1926, no.9, pp.654-55 **52** M. Barshch, 'Ekstensivnaia ili intensivnaia zastroika?' (Extensive or intensive development?), *SA*, 1927, no.3, pp.90-5. See also Chapter 11 below.

Doc. 2

VLADIMIR TATLIN, with TEVEL SHAPIRO, IOSIF MEERZON, PAVEL VINOGRADOV THE WORK AHEAD OF US

Moscow, 31 December 1920

The foundations on which fine art stood – the foundations of our craft – were all split apart, and all painting's connections with sculpture and architecture had got lost. The consequence of this was individualism, i.e. art had come to express only personal habits and tastes, and when artists addressed themselves specifically to material, they made a kind of eccentricity out of it in relation to one or other branch of fine art. Thus in the best cases artists embellished the walls of private mansions (individual family nests) and bequeathed us a series of 'Iaroslavl stations' and a diversity of now ludicrous forms.

What happened in '17 in social respects had already taken place in our art in 1914, when we adopted 'material, volume and construction (*konstruktsiia*)' as the foundation of our work.

Having declared our distrust of the eye, we place the eye under the control of the tactile, of touch.

In Moscow in 1915 there was an exhibition of material laboratory examples (*materialnykh laboratornykh obraztsov*), an exhibition of reliefs and counter-reliefs.

A further exhibition in 1917 showed a series of 'selections of materials' involving more complex investigations and manifestations both of material as such, and of what follows from its use (*ego sledstviia*), that is of movement, tension, and the relationships between them.

This investigation of material, volume and construction made it possible for us to move on, in 1918, to start creating selections of materials as an artistic form, using steel and glass, as the materials of a modern classicism, equal in their rigour (*strogost*) to the marble of the past.

In this way there now emerges the possibility of combining purely artistic forms with utilitarian intentions. An example of this is the project for a monument to the Third Communist International exhibited here at the Eighth Congress.

The fruits of this work are samples of something new (*obraztsy*) which stimulate us to inventions in the work of creating a new world, and which call upon us to take control of the [physical] forms of the new way of life (*formy novogo byta*).

Moscow, 31 December 1920.

This statement was published in the 1 January 1921 issue of the daily bulletin of the Eighth Congress of Soviets where the Tower model was exhibited, see n.2 opposite. The relatively unknown Pavel Vinogradov took no part in building the model, just helped re-erect it in the House of Unions (former House of the Nobility) for the Moscow show. The artists and students of Pegoskhum (Free Studios, see chapter 9) who helped the other three authors make the model were Terletsky, Dormidontov, Stakanov, Khapaev and two girls, Pchelnikova and Dymshits-Tolstaia.

Fedor Shekhtel, Iaroslavl Station, Moscow, 1902: the Moderne *approach to creating 'asynthesis of the arts' which Tatlin and colleagues dismiss here as 'ludicrous'.*

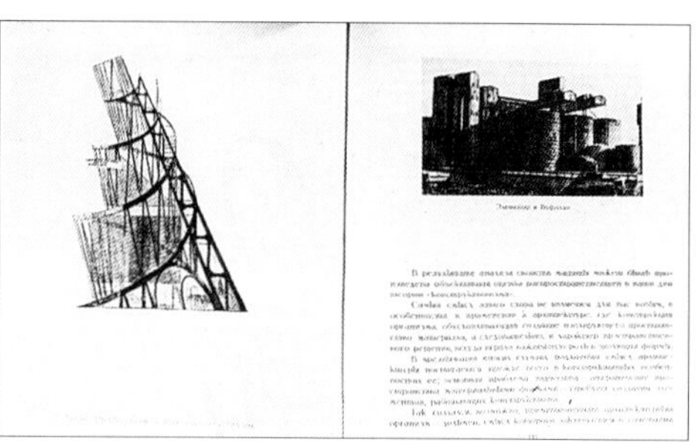

Opening spread to Chapter V 'Constructivism', in Moisei Ginzburg's Style and Epoch, *1924, juxtaposing Tatlin's Monument, and Buffalo grain silos derived from Corbusier's* L'Esprit Nouveau,as sources of 'the constructive style'.

Doc. 3

NIKOLAI LADOVSKY ON THE PROGRAMME OF THE WORKING GROUP OF ARCHITECTS IN INKHUK

From protocols of their meetings (26/27 March 1921 et al)

The task of our Working Group is to work in the direction of elucidating the theory of architecture. Our productivity will depend on the very rapid working out of our programme, on clarification of the investigative methods to be used and identification of the materials which we have at our disposal to supplement the work. The work plan can be roughly broken down into three basic points:

1: the assembly of appropriate theoretical studies and the existing theories of architecture of all theoreticians, **2**: the extraction and assembly of relevant material from these theoretical treatises and from research achieved within other branches of art, which have a bearing on architecture, and **3**: the exposition of our own theoretical attitudes to architecture.

The end-product of this work must be the compiling of an illustrated dictionary that defines precisely the terminology and definitions of architecture as an art, of its individual attributes, properties etc, and the relationships between architecture and the other arts. The three elements of the work plan relate, in the first case, to the past, to 'what has been done'; in the second, to the present, and 'what we are doing', and in the third, to 'what must be done' in the future, in the field of theoretical foundations for architecture. The commission which it will be necessary to set up for working out the detailed programme must develop the foundations for the programme we have proposed. ...

The task we are facing involves the study of the elements, attributes and properties of architecture. This is where we must begin the investigative work, on the one hand, with the absolutely central properties of architecture, and on the other, we must investigate those of its properties which, because they have a general family relationship to it, have been studied already by other Groups within the Institute [i.e. within Inkhuk, CC]. Top of their agendas right now is the investigation of construction and composition. For architecture, the most important elements are: space, construction, form, and its other elements follow those.

Here in condensed form is the schema for the programme. But certainly we have no need to confine ourselves dogmatically. For example, results emerging from investigations of questions that are not currently programmed might permit us to deviate from examining the questions in this order. The theory of architecture is an academic [*nauchnyi*, literally 'scientific'] field. And it would seem to require first of all a literary exposition in order to establish its concepts and terminologies with the greatest possible precision. But we must not eliminate graphic representation as one of the means of demonstration and proof. ...

It astonishes me that there can still arise amongst Group members questions such as 'Why is space to be studied as a first priority?'. In such a case would it not be better to turn to our relatives in art, where they will maybe explain to you 'why'?. Spatiality belongs exclusively to architecture, but architecture itself does not concern itself with investigating it, and uses it very badly. The dancer or the actor also work in space. It is from the theorists of these arts that we must work on questions of space and movement ...

Our colleague Petrov has touched upon two categories of question: firstly, the question of perception (of architectural action). But this is a field of psychology and philosophy. We cannot set up an sufficiently broad investigation of the question of perception, since we are not adequately competent in the question of psychology. We shall have to limit ourselves here to axiomatic givens, posited by the specialists on these questions.

Secondly, Petrov, in essence, is carrying out himself a bald classification of the properties of architecture, not according to its real characteristics, but according to purely accidental symptomatic features such as columns, bases, entablatures etc. But what is important in Petrov's words is the aspect of perception he has yet again underlined and his reference to the University as an architectural product. Would not an examination of this from the point of view of its organic and mechanical characteristics be an examination by analogy? But questions of analogy are questions of aesthetics. There what is being examined is a reincarnation of the individual: where for example a stone lying down calls forth, by analogy, a feeling of rest, and a standing stone, an aspiration upwards, and so on. Restlessness, peace, aspiration and so on are questions belonging to a special science, but not to architectural research. The latter already now gives, albeit temporarily, scientificly founded truths, and not analogous comparisons ...

We are not rejecting psychology, but we say that we are not specialists in it. The same is true with mathematics. But there is a field where we are Pythagorases, and that is architecture. And here we need defined premises to build on. These premises, even if only for today, must be immovable, otherwise proof is doomed to rapid ruin. Such premises, and directives of a general type, are what our programme provides.

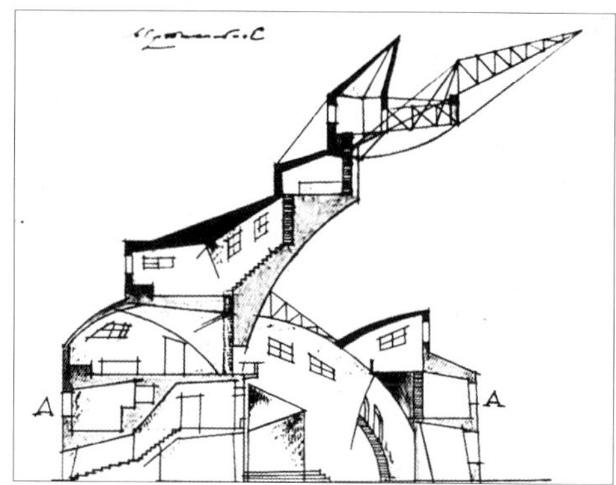

Ladovsky, project for a commual house, 1920: section

Doc. 4

ALEXANDER VESNIN
CREDO

Manuscript notes of a personal position statement to Inkhuk, in the context of the 'art into production' debates, April 1922

The tempo of modernity is fast, dynamic, and its rhythm is clear, precise, straight-lined, mathematical. Material and suitability to purpose (*tselesoobraznost'*) determine the structure (*stroi*) of an object created by the contemporary artist.

It is of no consequence whether the object serves a purpose and is utilitarian, like engineering structures and domestic artefacts, or only serves a purpose as laboratory work for the tasks of solving the problems of new contemporary forms. Each of these kinds of object created by the contemporary artist must enter into life as an active force, organising the consciousness of the individual, operating upon him psycho-physiologically, arousing an upsurge of energetic activity in him.

It is clear that objects created by the contemporary artist must be pure constructions (*konstruktsii*) without the superfluous ballast of representing anything (*izobrazitelnosti*), structured on the principle of the straight and the geometrically curved and on the principle of economy with maximum effective action.

Since the constructing (*konstruirovanie*) of any kind of object consists of a precise combination of basic plastic elements, such as material, colour, line, plane and surface treatment, the study of these elements must be given the first priority by the artist.

I regard all these elements as materialised energies, as possessing dynamic properties such as movement, tension, weight, velocity, which must be regulated to some purpose by the artist.

In just the same way as every part of a machine is a force materialised in appropriate form and material, which operates in and is necessary to the system of which it is part, and neither form nor material can be arbitrarily changed without damaging the operation of the entire system, so also in objects created by an artist, each element is a materialised force and cannot be arbitrarily thrown out or changed without destroying the effective operation (*tselesoobraznoe deistvie*) of the whole system, i.e., of the object.

The contemporary engineer has created objects of genius: the bridge, the steam-engine, the aeroplane, the crane.

The contemporary artist must create objects equal to these in the power, tension and potential energy of their psycho-physiological influence on the consciousness of the individual, and in the strength of their organising principle.

Popova, 'Construction with white half-moon', 1920, exhibited in the Erste Russische Kunstausstellung, Berlin, 1922

Vesnin (centre) and Popova (hat with pompom) with Vkhutemas students, 1922: left, Grushchenko; front left, Komarova, et al.

Doc. 5

NIKOLAI LADOVSKY
THE PSYCHOTECHNICAL LABORATORY OF ARCHITECTURE: POSING THE PROBLEM

29 March 1926, from Izvestiia ASNOVA, no.1, 1926

Even if only to an elementary level, the architect must be familiar with the laws of perception and the means by which it operates, in order to utilise in his practice everything that contemporary scientific knowledge can offer. Amongst the sciences which are facilitating the development of architecture, a very serious place must be given to the still young science of psychotechnics. This subsidiary science can undoubtedly look forward to a very large field of activity. It has already achieved recognition for itself in many fields of technology. Its influence becomes daily greater, as a result of the fact that it is throwing bridges between so called pure science and practical technology.

Amongst people of affairs the first to have recourse to it were representatives of the vast industrial and commercial companies of America, for the selection of employees, then business people used it in the advertising field, and then teachers used it in selecting and determining the capabilities of their students. At the present time there is no field of human activity to which psychotechnics is not making a claim.

In the field of aesthetics the well known psychologist Hugo Münsterberg works year by year in his Harvard laboratory. The following studies which have a relationship to architecture have been carried out there: Equilibrium of simple forms (Pierce); Unequal division (Anquier); Symmetry (Puffer); Repetition of spatial forms (Rowland); Vertical division (Davis) and so on.

The work which I, and subsequently also my colleagues, have carried out in the field of architecture in Vkhutemas since 1920, verified by the methods of psychotechnics, will help in creating a scientific statement of architectural principles on the basis of rationalist aesthetics.

The most correct approach to solving this question will be the organising of a psychotechnical laboratory for the study of questions of rational architecture through Asnova. To affirm the timeliness of a posing of this problem I can do no better than quote the words of Münsterberg:

'Psychotechnics cannot create artists ... but it can give them all a solid starting point from which they can achieve the aims to which they aspire by the most scientifically correct means, and by the same token avoid certain dangers. Through developing psychotechnics across the broadest front, it can in future pose its demands to the composers of art, whilst always affirming that genius will discover by unconscious means those things which science works out with great difficulty.'

Quite apart from the purely scientific importance which the work of such a laboratory can have, its activities must also have a practical importance in everyday architectural practice.

Such a laboratory could eliminate so many of those misunderstandings which arise in the evaluation of qualitative aspects of architectural work as a result of the absence of any agreed terminology even amongst specialists. It is only too well known that chance and accident predominate in the evaluation of competition projects. There can be no elimination of the passion that mutual incomprehension causes between teachers and pupils until the laboratory's work has been set up properly. In these and other cases the psychotechnical laboratory can play a large supplementary role.

On the resulting laboratory, see Document 29 pp.184-5.

Vladimir Krinsky, Project for a Temple of Intercourse between Nations, done in Zhivskulptarkh, 1919

5: CONSTRUCTIVISM: FROM TATLIN AND RODCHENKO TO A 'FUNCTIONAL METHOD' FOR BUILDING DESIGN

Constructivism in architecture has been subject to very various interpretations. By admirers and denigrators alike, it has been presented as a philosophy predominantly concerned with the function of architecture as a social catalyst, with what Soviet terminology calls literally 'social construction'. It has been presented as an obsession with the space-forming role of structural technologies, with 'building construction'. It has been presented as an obsession with 'constructing possible shapes', that is as an overwhelming concern for formal construction: at worst, as formalism. No wonder the literature and admirers of the resulting architecture are confused. How can a small corpus of work have acquired dogmatic labels of such diversity?

The answer is simple. Like any serious professional architects, the Constructivist group were obsessively concerned with all these dimensions of the architectural problem. They were practitioners *par excellence*, crippled though they were by poverty of resources. Leading members of the group were unquestionably amongst the finest practising architects of their period anywhere. Not for nothing did every one of them remain, through changing times, at the centre of Soviet architectural practice and education right through till death or old age. Unlike most others however, they were not prepared to leave questions of the interrelationships between these different dimensions of the architectural problem to chance, or to 'intuition'.

In the words of Lenin quoted in their journal, they believed that 'In order really to know an object, it is necessary to comprehend, to study, all aspects of it: all its internal and external connectivities.'[1] Their's was what today could loosely be called a 'systems' approach, or in the older and more general Russian term, a *kompleksnyi* approach. It addressed the design problem as an integrated complex; it was concerned with solving the problem as a whole. 'Form is a function, x,' said their leader Moisei Ginzburg, 'which has always to be evaluated afresh by the architect in response to the changing preconditions of the form-making situation.'[2] In modern jargon, which is not so far from their own at times, they aspired to model the entire decision space surrounding that form.

There is a direct generic relationship to much modern thinking here, but also a crucial difference from most of what has passed for systems thinking about built-environmental problems thereafter. The Constructivists were not nihilist in the face of architecture's traditional concerns with the delineation and organisation of real space, or with the necessity for expression in architecture through well-understood languages of form. Compared to the aesthetic concerns of the 1930s, or of recent years, their's was distinctly a poetry of the concrete rather than the rhetorical, but architects of Ginzburg's sophistication were too deeply rooted in what Russians call 'architectural culture' to deny that their objective must be poetry.

In this connection their essentially mechanistic method is very significantly a product of its time. Its aspiration was 'poetic' yet its method was 'mechanical'. In many periods and modes of thought those epithets are mutually exclusive. For much early modern art and literature, of course, the mechanical was indeed poetic: the Futurists and Le Corbusier are two relevant examples. But the difference here is that machines are not just the subject which has inspired the poetry. The poetry has been constructed according to a mechnically inspired method.

The notion of rules and principles for constructing effects, which is the basis of language, had been taken apart and made into a far more self-conscious and explicit tool than previously by such Russian Formalists as Viktor Shklovsky before the Revolution. In the post-Revolutionary years, Vladimir Mayakovsky in particular developed their ideas into a working method for producing poetry (or his advertising slogans, which he considered poetically at least as good), which assembled or 'constructed' the works according to a would-be mechanical method of 'manufacture'. This owes much to the whole armoury of Formalist concepts: of devices laid bare, the exposure of the process of making being the true aim of perception, and the interdependence of criticism and writing, i.e. of analysis and synthesis. These became the essence of Constructivism in all arts: in Sergei Eisenstein's film-making for another important example.

Mayakovsky: art as 'manufacture'

Mayakovsky laid out a description of how he 'manufactured' his poetry in a small book indicatively titled *Kak delat' stikhi?* usually translated as *How are verses made?* with the implication of 'how to do it'. This was written in 1926, just as the Constructivist architects were starting to work as an organised group on the parallel question which we might call *Kak delat' zdanii?* How are buildings made? Many of their number were involved with the circles around the group and journal *LEF*, 'Left Front of the Arts', whose leader, Osip Brik was a key theorist of the new 'production art' movement which on principle united these creative people from hitherto separate 'professions'.

As *LEF*'s founder-editor, Mayakovsky was a close colleague of all these artist-designers and architects, and the key ideas are identical. His text of 1926 however is a description *post hoc*. He had been working like this over several years and was a major influence on forming the approaches of those around him. I quote Mayakovsky's principles *in extenso* before proceeding further, so that they may echo through the development of others' ideas without explicit reference, as they would have done at the time.

1. Poetry is manufacture (proizvodstvo)*. A very difficult, very complex kind, but a manufacture.*

2. Instruction in poetical work doesn't consist in the study of already fixed and delimited types of poetical objects (veshchi)*, but a study of the means for executing all kinds of poetic work, a study of productive procedures that help us to make new things.*

3. Innovation in material and devices is the basis of every poetical product....

7. To understand the social imperative and task accurately, a poet must be in the centre of affairs and events. A knowledge of economic theory, a knowledge of the realities of everyday life, an immersion in the scientific study of history are the absolute fundamentals of a poet's work, more important than any scholastic textbooks by idealist professors who worship the past.

8. To fulfil the social task as well as possible you must be in the vanguard of your class, along with your class conducting the battle on all fronts. You must smash to smithereens the myth of an a-political art

9. Only by approaching art as manufacture can you eliminate chance, arbitrariness of taste and idividualism of judgement. ... Instead of mystically pondering a poetic theme you will have the power to tackle any pressing problem accurately with full poetic qualifications.

10. You must not make the manufacturing, the so-called technical process, an end in itself. But it is this process of manufacture that makes the poetic work fit for its intended use. ...

12. We poets of LEF never claim that we uniquely possess the secrets of poetical creativity. But we are the only ones who want to lay these secrets open, the only ones who don't want to surround the creative process with a cheap artistic religiosity as something to be worshipped.' [3]

Bogdanov: proletarian creativity

Another undoubted influence on Constructivism and on Mayakovsky himself were the theories of Alexander Malinovsky, known as Bogdanov, who had been the rival to Lenin in the Bolshevik party, before and after the Revolution, in the formulation of a Bolshevik theory of future socialist culture. They diverged in particular over how it would relate to the cultural legacy which the Revolutionary society had inherited from the 'bourgeois' past. He had been a close colleague of Lunacharsky and Gorky in their pre-war exile and back in Russia was a principal organiser of the agressively 'proletarian' culture movement, Proletkult. By 1920, Bogdanov was very publicly opposing Lenin's view that proletarian culture would 'emerge from steady development of reserves of experience which humanity has built up under the yoke of capitalism.' [4] In Bogdanov's view, the new culture would consist of 'forms of thought, feeling and daily life' that were 'socialist', entirely new and 'independent of all relations and other combinations of political forces', and 'created by the proletariat for itself'. [5] The community between Bogdanov and Mayakovsky is clear when he speaks of the 'methods' by which this would be created. Thus writing in the Proletkult journal in 1920 on 'The paths of proletarian creation' Bogdanov wrote:

'1. Creation, whether technological, socio-economic, political, domestic, scientific, or artistic, represents a kind of labour, and like labour, is composed of organisational (or disorganisational) human endeavours. It is exactly the same as labour, whose product is not the repetition of a ready-made stereotype but is something "new". There is not and cannot be a strict demarcation between creation and ordinary labour; not only are there all the points of interchange, but it is even impossible often to say which of the two designations is more applicable ...

'Creation being the highest, most complex form of labour, its methods naturally derive from the methods of labour. The old world did not understand ... this methodological connection, and dressed up "creation" in some kind of mystical fetishism. ...

'3. The methods of proletarian creation are founded on the methods of proletarian labour, i.e. on the type of labour that is characteristic of workers in heavy industry.

'The first characteristic of this is the unification of elements of "physical", i.e. muscular labour, which is now diminishing, and "spiritual" labour, i.e. calculation, concentration, control, initiative, which is now increasing in the worker's tasks. The result of this unification ... is monism, and ... it depends in turn on the scientific character of modern technology, in particular on the transference of the mechanical effort of the machine. The second characteristic of this new type of labour is the transparent unconcealed collectivism of its actual form. This

Vladimir Mayakovsky (1893-1930) as a young Futurist poet on the eve of the Revolution.

Masthead, Izo-Narkompros newspaper Art of the Commune *(Iskusstvo kommuny), with slogan: 'The way-of-life (byt) determines consciousness, not consciousness the* byt.*'*

Rodchenko cover, LEF*, 1923, no.3:* LEF *as aeroplane fires pen (ideas) at ape with only physical weapon*

depends on ... the close association between specialised types of labour within mechanical production. [As a result] the basis of work is becoming comradely, which entails mutual understanding, mutual sympathy, and an aspiration to work together extending beyond the confines of the factory, of specific trades and of production, to the working class on a national and universal scale. ...

'From the principle of methodological monism it follows that there can be no methods of practical work or science that cannot find a direct or indirect application in art and vice versa. ...

'The basic difference between the old and the new creative work is that now, for the first time, creative work understands itself and its role in life.'[6]

It was precisely the application of this to their 'art' of architecture that the Constructivist architects were pursuing, in the 'aspiration to work together' signalled by formation of their group OSA in late 1925. The political discrediting of Bogdanov's ideas in 1920 as 'complete nonsense'[7] and the disbandment of the Proletkults that followed, meant that any reference to him was politically inappropriate even till lately. So far as I have discovered, his name never appears in their writing. In the formative years of the avant-garde, however, just after the 1917 Revolution, his role was central and his ideas part of the common currency.

'Construction' as vocabulary and methodology

The characteristics of the building as a material, 'made' object and as a social object – the manner of its physical and psychological (Russians might say 'spiritual') interaction with people – these were the areas which the Constructivists saw it as their professional obligation to their Marxist-materialist society to develop organised bodies of testable knowledge – what Russian calls *nauki*: literally 'sciences' – out of which solutions could in the broadest sense be 'constructed'.

Some issues of vocabulary have to be elaborated here, in as far as English allows it. Whether we speak of 'designing', 'creating', 'building' or 'constructing', the Russian language has numerous words available, and each has a distinct meaning which only context can attach to their literal English translations.

If we return to the forms of 'construction' I mentioned earlier, we already encounter the distinction which is crucial to understanding the aims of Constructivism. In 'social construction' and 'building construction' the Russian noun is *stroitelstvo. Stroitelstvo* takes place in real space and time: the *stroitel* is the builder on a real site with muddy boots. 'Social construction' in this sense may be a strange concept to us, but this understanding of the phrase illuminates the way Soviet thinking envisaged possibilities in this area. In the phrase 'formal construction', by contrast, we are using the word *konstruktsiia*. Its meaning is indicated by the fact that a major Russian dictionary like Smirnitsky will indicate that this word often has linguistic connotations. A grammatical construction is a *konstruktsiia*. It should not be forgotten here, as I have already mentioned, that the Constructivist movement had some roots amongst those precursors of linguistic Structuralism, the Russian Formalists, and that one of its origins lay in the literary circles around the journal *LEF*. Thus in the final analysis *stroitelstvo* is a material process where *konstruktsiia* is an intellectual one.

When the early Constructivist artists like Alexei Gan and Alexander Rodchenko formulated the profile of that 'artist-constructor' whom they aspired to produce through their curricula in the Vkhutemas, he was not a *khudozhnik-stroitel* – an artist-builder, some legatee of the Arts-and-Crafts tradition which was well established in the old Russia. He was a *khudozhnik-konstruktor* – an artist-designer, even an artist-engineer. And here are further innuendos. The *konstruktor* is a specialist, highly qualified designer in industry: in engineering, for example, or today in electronics. *Dizainer* would be a term of insult implying the designer is a mere stylist, which is the current connotation of that international word in Russian. Already nineteenth-century Rationalists in Russia used the adjective *konstruktivnyi* as high praise for a manifestly 'built' piece of architecture. Smirnitsky represents the active verb *konstruirovat'* very precisely with the alternative translations 'to construct; to design; to form; to organise', and the Constructivists were the *Konstruktivisty*. They were concerned with how an architect organises or structures his thinking; how he organises the actual work of designing, and how he 'constructs' a set of appropriate forms.

They were also very interested in *stroitelstvo* in all its dimensions. As loyal Soviets, 'social construction', and particularly 'the building of socialism' were the unquestioned *raison d'être* of their work. Material construction is the physical means whereby architecture exists at all: the materialist, in particular, must have the constraints and possibilities of all its media at his finger tips. In problems of *konstruktsiia* however, the choices are rooted in philosophic or aesthetic principle rather than physics. Aesthetic principle defines choices amongst possible systems of formal construction. The overall approach to the task of designing; the ordering of data and prioritising of objectives; the methods of synthesis and the criteria of evaluation: these are the philosophic problems of *konstruktsiia*.

Moisei Ginzburg, leader of the Constructivist architects in their pursuit of theory, insisted

'There can be no question of any sort of artist losing creativity just because he knows clearly what he wants, what he is aiming for, and in what consists the meaning of his work. But subconscious, impulsive creativity must be replaced by a clear and distinctly organised method, which is economical of the architect's energy and transfers the freed surplus of it into inventiveness and the force of the creative impulse.'[8]

In the words of another, younger, founder-member of the group Nikolai Krasilnikov: 'Intuition is not eliminated thereby; it merely comes to occupy its proper place.'[9] The echoes of Bogdanov are clear. Constructivism was distinguished by its refusal to leave these methodological problems to the mercy of 'intuition'.

Again echoing Bogdanov, Constructivists believed that the Soviet architect's mode of working must exhibit the same holism as the material and cognitive worlds in which he was 'constructing'. Precisely in order to 'guarantee' that a monistic integration of the material and the cognitive aspects of the world was preserved in design work, they formalised their 'method of functional creativity' (*metod funktsionalnogo tvorchestva*), alternatively referred to as their 'method of functional thinking' (*metod funktsionalnogo myshleniia*), their 'functional method'.[10]

*'Our work, the work of the architect-constructivists, is different from the earlier stages of idealistic symbolism [he refers to Tatlin] and abstract formalism [Malevich's Suprematism and much student work in Vkhutemas]. It consists above all in the creation of a materialist working method, which would make it possible to create such a creative atmosphere as would in principle make impossible a dualistic posing of the problem, which would give us the guarantee of creating a holistic, monistic (*tselostnaia monisticheskaia*), architectural system.'*[11]

This 'monism' was precisely that which Bogdanov defined, that is a unifying of 'physical' factors and 'spiritual' or psychological ones in a manner they deemed impossible under capitalism. In capitalist systems, they maintained, 'dualism' is unavoidable, as the material or 'biological' nature of man's existence and 'the spiritual life' are condemned to remain 'opposed principles within every culture'.[12]

Thus in 'Constructivism as a method of laboratory and teaching work' Ginzburg wrote:

'Constructivism as a method aims ... for absolute monism, so that:

1) it does not permit any sort of non-working or "supplementary" elements in the formulation of its social condensers;

2) it solves the basic questions of the emotional perception by the actual way it organises the utilitarian-constructive set-up;

*3) it formulates each detail functionally, that is organising the material of the object (*veshch*) exclusively within the limits of its useful activity.*

*'Thus the integrity of the monistic aspiration of Constructivism (*tselostnost' monisticheskogo ustremleniia konstruktivizma*) is seen in the fact that it does not negate the emotional influence of material objects, as is usually assumed in order to incriminate Constructivism, but uses this emotional influence as one organising factor within the actual process of shaping the utilitarian-constructive solution of the object.'*[13]

Bogdanov's vocabulary also appears here in Ginzburg's statement that 'today the concept of "architecture" only has meaning' in relation to 'tasks of life-building (*zhiznestroeniia*), of organising the forms of the new life'.[14]

As was indicated in outline in Chapter 4, this method was a set of procedures whereby the totality of factors they saw impinging upon a design would be taken into account objectively, in an essentially linear process, 'moving from the first priority to the second', in generating a 'basic spatial organism' and proceeding 'logically' through its technical and formal refinement. Bodies of background knowledge were the subject of 'laboratory work'. As Ginzburg explained in 1927: 'Methodologically, in order to subject the whole productive process of the architect to evaluation, Constructivism has recourse to many other scientific disciplines and uses the laboratory method, of separating out one reaction, that is of taking one integral process' – in today's jargon, one subsystem – 'into temporary isolation from the others, in order to get the most favourable conditions for analysing it.'[15]

Extensive work was done by these Constructivist architects in generating new 'classes of spatial organism', or building types and in the exact analysis of their objective characteristics, as well as some of their more subjective, psychological properties. (As Chapter 4 has shown, this field generally belonged to Ladovsky's Rationalists and others). Given the very short period of barely four years during which they were working as an organised group, their oeuvre was an impressive demonstration of the standards they believed necessary. A range of the resulting designs and built work are illustrated on pages 41-59; 116, 120 and 134-5.

Quite apart from these extra-architectural influences in their own time, there is also of course a distinct continuity within architecture itself, between nineteenth- and early twentieth-century theorists and Constructivist architectural theory. These roots are undoubtedly real: as Chapter 4 has shown, there is a continuity of personal biographies across the divide of the Revolution amongst leading members of the profession, as there is of building technologies and much else, which conventional readings of this period wholly ignore. But given the political obligations to 'forget the old ways', these continuities were not part of the internally logical argument which the 'new men' were trying to construct. The continuities are therefore more appropriately separated from this discussion of the 'new' generation's thinking in its own terms. Some of them are discussed in Chapters 1 and 6.

Towards disciplines

The fullest exposition of the Constructivist architects' working method was published at the peak of their activity, in late 1927, as a paper by Ginzburg in their journal *Contemporary Architecture* (*SA*). The same issue contained much of the foreign work sent to the USSR's 'First Exhibition of Modern Architecture' which they had mounted in Moscow that summer.

This paper, already mentioned in Chapter 4, was entitled 'Constructivism as a method of laboratory and teaching work', and was 'a schematic plan of the course in the theory of architecture being given by the author in the architectural departments of Vkhutemas and MVTU [Moscow Higher Technical College]'.[16] This was how Constructivists taught design. It was how they themselves operated in designing. It was the framework whereby different 'laboratory investigations' by themselves and others – in building science, the social aspects of their briefs, visual psychology and the development of formal languages – were organised into the process of designing new buildings that would catalyse the process of 'building the new way of life'.

That five-part 'schematic plan' has been further edited into Document 8. Document 6 traces how Ginzburg's ideas developed through his successive earlier writings till they emerged in final form as the 'schematic plan'. These earlier writings stretch back over the two preceding years of *SA*'s publication, 1927 and 1926, beyond the formation of the Constructivist architectural group OSA in late 1925, back to Ginzburg's seminal 'manifesto' of a constructive architecture, the book *Style and Epoch* of 1924.

This consecutive enrichment and increasing detail of his thinking is a distinctive feature of Ginzburg's work in this period. A chronological reading of his papers makes it possible to recreate the evolution of the group's thinking as it happened, to follow their aspirations as they become clearer to themselves and in turn are further articulated to their readership. We shall follow this sequence in greater detail below.

Ginzburg was a man of broad, largely European education, of wide reading and already significant professional experience, hence the sources of his thinking are complex. In respect of the three main ideas concerning us here, namely: the catalytic role of architecture and the built environment in effecting social change; the need for an organised method of working whereby the designer can respond logically, and the proper range of factors to be embraced by that method, there are also direct sources within the thinking of Constructivist artists in the three years following the Revolution, when Ginzburg himself was far away from the Moscow-Petrograd avant-garde axis, working and writing down in the Crimea.

This exploratory and experimental work amongst artists is of course the familar territory of Constructivism's immediate roots. It embraces Tatlin's Tower of 1919-20, the geometrical 'structures' of Rodchenko and the First Working Group of Constructivists around 1921 and the ideas of Alexei Gan, revered as a founder theorist of Constructivism but noted professionally as a graphic- and exhibition-designer. As a portion of the history of art, this work has been documented in considerable detail in recent years through publication in the West as well as in Russia.[17] Here our concern is with the role of this work in laying foundations for architecture. If we examine what these artists said, in the texts with which they illuminated their intentions, we find a development of ideas that is directly continued into the thinking of Ginzburg and the other Constructivist architects through the middle and late Twenties. This too was outlined in Chapter 4: here I shall explore it in greater detail.

Much later, in 1928, Ginzburg was to dismiss Tatlin's Tower to his colleagues as 'idealistic symbolism'; as manifesting only 'the acute wish of a talented man to communicate emotionally.'[18] There was much truth in that. What else, after all, does most art manifest? When Ginzburg made that statement he was making a distinction that had become essential to reinforcing their public reputation as practical and engaged professionals, and, in a phrase redolent of Bogdanov and Mayakovsky, as 'builders' of the new reality rather than idealists in some way 'symbolising' it.[19] A few years before, in *Style and Epoch*, Ginzburg himself had included Tatlin's Tower in the canon of sources for a constructive architecture by using it as frontispiece to his fifth chapter, 'Construction and form in architecture. Constructivism'. The absence of textual commentary on the image suggests it was there more as gesture than as a step in his logic. Indeed at that time, front-line avant-garde art circles were not his home territory, as the typography of this book also indicates. For the Constructivist movement as a whole, however, Tatlin's grand and original scheme had been seminal to their own thinking.

Many putative 'sources' and 'meanings' have been attributed to this monument to the Third International.[20] Art historians have laboured points about Tatlin's youth on sailing ships and early familiarity with oil rigs down in Baku. To designers it is no surprise to find such formal imagery and technical knowledge reworked, consciously or subconsciously, in a highly creative new work. The most reliable source on any symbolising aspirations Tatlin may have had must be the commentary of 1920 by his close friend the Petrograd art critic Nikolai Punin, and Punin makes only passing allusions to the 'aspirational' quality of spirals amidst his technical description of the project.[21] Throughout this period it is more fruitful to examine the designer's own explanatory statements than to speculate on sources purely from visual similarities, for Russians of the Twenties did not use words pointlessly. Even paper, as Berthold Lubetkin has reminded us, was an extraordinarily precious commodity, making this in his nice phrase quoted from Ilia Ehrenberg, 'a wonderful time for poetry'.[22] Texts were concise and closely wrought; they deserve equally careful reading.

In 1919 Tatlin was running artistic and cultural affairs in Moscow for the Fine Art (Izo) section of Lunacharsky's Commissariat of Enlightenment, Narkompros. Having conceived his 'alternative' Monument as something non-figurative and non-sculptural, he went up to Petrograd for easier working conditions to build the model. When he and his student-assistants dismantled it and brought it to Moscow in December 1920 for display at the Eighth Congress of Soviets, they published a brief explanatory statement in the Congress newspaper which they entitled 'The work that faces us', usually translated, more passively, as 'The work ahead of us.' This is translated in full in Document 2.[23]

In this statement they explained the role which Tatlin's 'reliefs and counter-reliefs' had played, since 1914, as 'laboratory' scale preparation for the Tower project, and indicated how such explorations of 'materials, volume and construction (*konstruktsiia*)' could be the starting point for new disciplines. These disciplines would be 'equal in their rigour' to those of Classicism, but where the Classical language had been constrained by the structural limitations of marble, these new languages would be liberated by the potential of 'modern' materials 'like iron and glass'. 'In this way' they declared:

Vladimir Tatlin (1885-1953):
'Self-portrait as a sailor', tempera, 1911

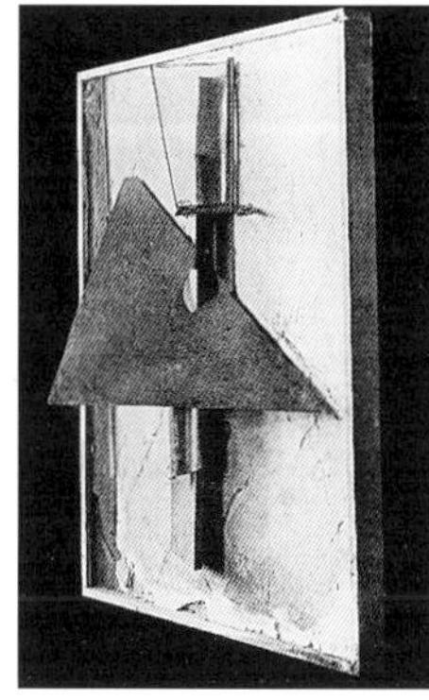

'Selection of materials: iron, stucco, glass, asphalt', 1914

'Suspended corner relief. Selection of materials: aluminium, primer, iron', 1916 (Three photos from Punin's Tatlin. Against Cubism, *1921).*

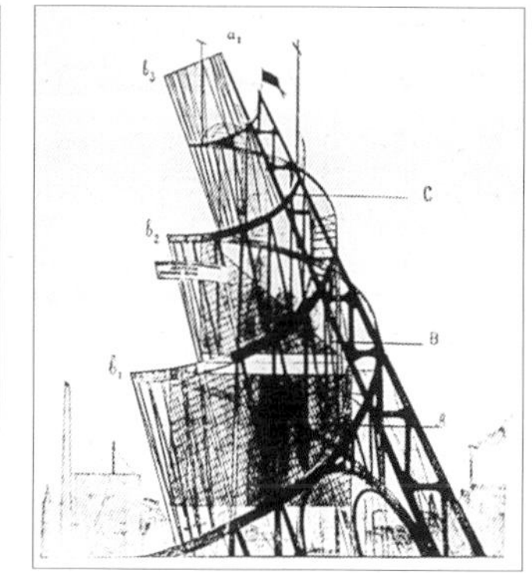

Monument to III International, 1919, side elevation (from Punin's pamphlet of 1920)

'there emerges the possibility of combining purely artistic forms with utilitarian intentions. ... The fruits of this are samples of something new (obraztsy) *which stimulate us to inventions in the work of creating a new world and which call upon us to take control of the [physical] forms of the new way of life.'*

Ridiculing Fedor Shekhtel's *Moderne*-style Iaroslavl Station in Moscow, with its representational paintings by Korovin and 'applied arts' from Abramtsevo, as an entirely bourgeois notion of 'integration of the arts', they postulated this new path to a 'synthesis of painting, sculpture and architecture'. Non-functional 'art', be it two- or three-dimensional, in modern technological materials, must now serve as investigative research for the formal aspects of functional tasks. They saw this as the proper parallel in 'art' to 'what happened in social respects in 1917'.[24]

During that same year of 1920 another group of artists, based permanently in Moscow and meeting in the little art-research 'institute' Inkhuk, had started talking in very similar terms. Chapter 4 has described the debates of early 1921 in which they juxtaposed the old artistic principle of *kompozitsiia* to their new concern with *konstruktsiia,* and recorded the emergence of a 'Working Group of Constructivists' within Inkhuk in the spring of 1921.[25]

Our interest here is this Working Group's declaration, written by Alexei Gan, where the vocabulary is already more explicitly politicised. 'The group's sole premise' they declared, 'is scientific communism, based on the theory of historical materialism.' These phrases were the common currency of the period: what matters is their interpretation of the underlying philosophical concepts. Of great importance for its continuity with Tatlin's statement was their affirmation of 'the necessity of synthesising the ideological and formal parts [of their task] so as to direct the laboratory work onto the tracks of practical activity'. 'Laboratory work' was to be the key concept in which this new relationship of 'art' work to 'design' was encapsulated.

Even more importantly, they started to frame some concepts which could help effect this synthesis operationally. Those 'elements of the group's work' which would make an 'organic link' here were three synthetic concepts which they termed *tektonika, konstruktsiia* and *faktura.* The definitions are brief but already they demand mastery of enormous and diverse fields.

Through principles of 'organisation' embraced by a 'science' of *konstruktsiia,* Constructivists will effect 'an organic link' between political values, industrial techniques and the specific possibilities of manipulated materials. *Tektonika* is a synthesis of the first two; *faktura* is the latter. '*Konstruktsiia* is formulating activity taken to the extreme.'[26] The First Working Group which was formed around these ideas comprised the seven artists Alexander Rodchenko and his wife Varvara Stepanova, who with Alexei Gan were the original 'initiative group', the brothers Georgi and Vladimir Stenberg, plus Konstantin Medunetsky and Karl Iogansen.

By the autumn of that year, 24 November 1921 to be exact, this group was at the core of the 'twenty-five leftist artists' in Inkhuk who finally declared an end to their concern with art that was in any sense 'fine' or 'pure' (in Russian *izobrazitelnoe, chistoe* or *stankovoe*). The influence came from their highly theoretical colleagues in the circle around Osip Brik, who had replaced the old conception of 'art' (*iskusstvo*) with 'artistic production' (*khudozhestvennoe proizvodstvo*). Brik had now taken over from Rodchenko as Chairman of Inkhuk's Presidium, and as Khan-Magomedov has newly shown, one major factor in this theoretical reorientation was in fact practical. Amidst many other reorganisations, as Brik told this meeting, Inkhuk was to be shifted from the cultural Commissariat, Narkompros, to come under the aegis of the national economic soviet, Vesenkha.[27] That plainly suited the 'production' theorists well enough, who were already thinking in terms more industrial than aesthetic.

With a new clarity they distinguished between the concepts which are distinguished in English as 'art' and 'artefact', insisting, in the words of one of their number, Alexei Filipov, that 'the production of duplicates of Nature' must be replaced in their work by 'the productive art of objects that are non-existent in Nature'.[28] Crucially, the aim of this new 'active art generated by exercising of the constructive imagination' was political:

'The aspirations of the new production art can be formulated by applying to artists K. Marx's ideas about scholars and scientists: artists have only in various ways depicted the world. Their task is now to change it.'[29]

In sessions of the Working Group of Constructivists Alexei Gan had been expounding some radical concepts as tools for effecting this 'change'.[30] In the next year, 1922, they were published and more fully developed in his book *Constructivism.* The book starts with blank pages bearing only their declarations in bold typography: 'We declare uncompromising war on art!' and then 'Welcome to the communistic expression of materials structures!' Punchy restatements followed of the Group's view that the traditional concept of 'art' must die naturally with the old culture, but here as throughout, Gan builds a yet more explicitly Marxist-materialist rationale around their thoughts.

Rodchenko: 1921, third series of c.25 'spatial constructions' in wood. Each explores possibilities of a given 'construction' principle with identical elements, or elements of standard section.

Gan, handcut lettering in red and black for his book cover: ALEKSEI GAN, KONSTRUKTIVIZM

Alexei Gan (1895-1940) at work on typography for Soviet journals, mid-1920s

'Constructivism is a phenomenon of our days. It arose in 1920 amongst the leftist painters and ideologists of "mass action"', he declared. 'The present publication is an agitational book with which the Constructivists begin the battle against supporters of traditional art.'[31] A comparison of Gan's typography with Ginzburg's, of two years later, indicates immediately the different worlds in which they were circulating at this time. Gan, as his own typographer, uses bold printer's rules and variations of typeface and size to reinforce the uncompromisingly political message. The enemy in this 'battle' are those unable to grasp the 'fact', which their own Marxist rationale makes logically inevitable, that there cannot be a peaceful evolutionary transition in Russia's concept of art if there has been a violent Revolution in her politics.

Portions of this book have been translated into English, but editing has distorted the emphasis.[32] Much of its explicit politicality has been drained by omitting long quotations from the Communist Manifesto. More significant here is omission of the climactic sections that direct Constructivist energies towards architecture and the whole urban environment, and of the full definitions of their three new 'disciplines'.

Artists who work 'on this side of October 1917' says Gan, 'should not be reflecting, depicting and interpreting reality. They should build practically and express the planned objectives of the new and actively working class ... which is building the foundation of the future society ... as an organised force in possession of a plan.' 'The master of colour and line, the combiner of spatio-volumetric solids ... must all become Constructivists.' But that too meant organisation. 'In order to produce practitioners and theoreticians of Constructivism who are qualified, in a Marxist sense' he warned, 'It is essential to channel [our] work into a definite system; to create disciplines through which all the Constructivists' experimental work would be directed.'[34] Having teaching jobs in the new Vkhutemas, 'the production of qualified Constructivists' or 'artist-constructors' became the aim of their curricula.

Here in Gan's 'definite system' is our first hint of a 'working method'. Its components would be those new synthetic 'disciplines' of *tektonika*, *faktura* and k*onstruktsiia*, but these now have fuller definitions.

> *'With* tektonika *as their first discipline, Constructivists are trying to chop away the ignorance and tyranny exercised by architects and builders under capitalism.* Tektonika, *or tectonic style organically emerges and is formed on the one hand out of the characteristics of Communism itself, and on the other from the appropriate utilisation of industrial material. The word tectonic is taken from geology, where it signifies violent restructurings coming out of the Earth's core.* Tektonika *is a synonym of organicness, of an eruption from the inner essence. As a discipline,* tektonika *must lead the Constructivist in practice towards a synthesis of the new content with new forms. He must be a person educated in a Marxist way, who has eliminated from his life all vestiges of "art" and has started advancing his knowledge of industrial material.* Tektonika *is his guiding star, the very cerebrum of his experimental and practical activity. 'Constructivism without* tektonika *is like painting without colour.'*[35]

Of the three concepts, this is perhaps the most obscure; indeed verbatim accounts of Inkhuk discussions recently published indicate that his colleagues, too, did not understand 'why comrade Gan keeps going on about geology'.[36] In fact the final sentence here, which seems to compound the obscurity, offers a key. Every professional act of the Constructivist must be 'coloured', or informed, by the understanding that a violent restructuring of underlying relationships has profoundly changed the way industry should shape and distribute material in space.

Faktura is simpler. This word emphatically 'must not be understood from the painter's point of view', 'as just the handling of a surface'. On the example of cast iron, it implies 'the character of the whole processing', the melting, casting and turning 'whereby it becomes an object'. As 'the appropriate use of material' *faktura* 'means the selection and processing from the raw material'. Also, 'more specifically, *faktura* is the organic condition of processed material or the new condition of its organism.' 'It is material consciously chosen and appropriately used in a manner that does not limit the *tektonika* or obstruct the *konstruktsiia*.'[37]

In the light of what I said earlier about vocabulary, the meaning of *konstruktsiia* should be clear. In Gan's words:

> 'Konstruktsiia *must be understood as the assembling and ordering function within Constructivism. 'While* tektonika *comprises an interconnection of the ideological and the formal and as a result gives a unity of conception, and* faktura *takes account of the state of the material,* konstruktsiia *reveals the actual process of putting together. Thus the third discipline involves giving form to the concept through the use of processed material.'*[38]

Konstruktsiia, in short, was design, but these expansive new synthetic disciplines still omitted the sciences of real space.

In challenging 'the combiner of spatio-volumetric solids' and 'the master of colour and line' to become Constructivists, Gan was not suggesting that they leave those skills behind them. On the contrary. 'A system must also

Мы об'являем непримиримую

войну искусству!

1-ая рабочая группа конструктивистов
1920 год
Москва.

Gan, 1922: typographical feature that opens his book Konstruktivizm, *reading: 'We declare uncompromising war on art! – First Working Group of Constructivists, 1920, Moscow'.*

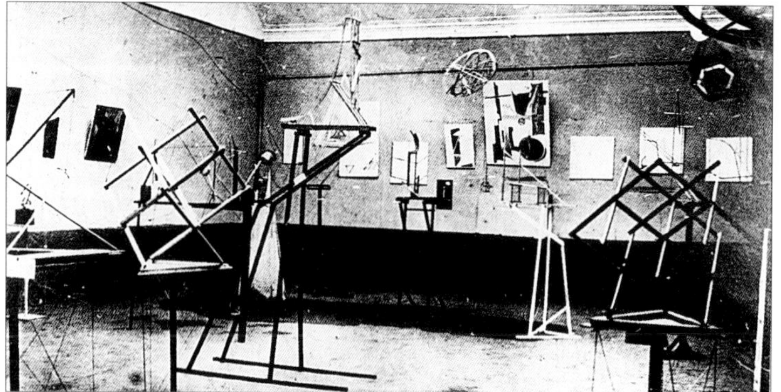

'Spatial constructions' by Rodchenko (his second series, 1920-1,'Similar figures', hanging) and by Stenberg brothers (on stands), 2nd Spring Exhibition of Obmokhu (Young Artists), May 1921

be worked out in the field of producing forms', and he explained how that system would be developed by quoting his colleague 'the Constructivist Rodchenko', 'elucidating one of his experiments in spatial Constructivism.' The works concerned would-be items from his 'spatial inventory' or studies of similar geometrical forms from the period around 1920-21, which as art-works are well known. Rodchenko had written:

*'I have devised these latest spatial constructions as experiments, specifically to make the designer (*konstruktor*) bound by the law of appropriateness of applied forms, to constrain him to assemble the forms according to laws, and also to show their universalism, how from identical forms he may assemble (*konstruirovat'*) all possible constructions, of diverse systems, kinds and applications.'* [39]

Here was 'art' already consciously executed as laboratory work for design. Contemporaneous photographs indicate that such exercises were already central to Rodchenko and Stepanova's teaching. [40]

Towards architecture

Rodchenko and his immediate colleagues did not pursue these ideas into architecture. Others were to carry the baton forward in that direction and Gan thrust it at them unequivocally.

'The planned working out of the whole area of the urban territory, of its individual districts and also its proper solution in the vertical dimension, in the tektonika *of its masses and volumes, in the* faktura *of its materials and the* konstruktsiia *of its structures – these are the basic tasks of our Constructivism, which arose in the fresh cornfields of the proletarian revolution and is actively and consciously fighting for communism.'* [41]

In developing their 'definite system', their 'primary objective' must be 'to establish a scientific foundation for the approach to constructing buildings and services that would fulfil the demands of Communist culture in its transient state, through all stages of its future development out of this period of ruin'. [42]

This bold extension to the scale of architecture is striking. In the natural continuity of the artistic community in Russia, as I have commented in Chapter 4, one flank of the profession was always close to the fine-artists. Indeed 'architect-artist' (*arkhitektor-khudozhnik*) was the standard appellation and official qualification of architects graduating from the Academy school before the Revolution.[43] In emerging Constructivist circles, Alexander Vesnin formed the first integral link with architecture, though his 'Credo' of this date, April 1922, Document 4, is still merely seeking inspiration for art in the qualities of engineering, rather than calling for a leap across the historic divide of the professions. Indeed, as Khan-Magomedov has pointed out, it is curiously defensive of the historic notion of 'art' at a time when his artist colleagues have abandoned that.[44]

It may be that for someone as political as Gan, the imperative to embrace architecture was a reaction prompted by the very dismissive and conceptually limited view of architecture's 'propaganda' potential which Lunacharsky was currently disseminating. 'For the moment we are not in a position to make use of architecture on a wide scale for propaganda purposes', he had said, but 'perhaps in the near future' architecture could again contribute, like the 'temples' of old which were such 'an extremely powerful way of influencing the social soul'.[45] To artists following the line of thought opened up by Tatlin or Brik's 'production art' theorists, however, and seeking to shape 'the world', architecture and the city were their natural horizon. Already here in Gan, if vaguely, is the idea later central to architectural Constructivism, that form must accommodate or respond to social evolution. Yet more importantly, however, he introduces the notion that architecture, by its spatial organisation, itself actively influences that evolution. He raises the question negatively:

'As the material, technological "organs" of society, the capitalist towns that we inherited are staunch allies of counter-revolution. Soviet communism has already discovered that the capitalist town not only cannot accommodate even the most timid measures of Revolutionary reorganisation, but more than that! It stubbornly obstructs the path of that reorganisation. Its small and awkward buildings have been totally unable to accommodate the operational requirements of the various new Soviet organisations. They are too cramped, just as the streets and squares which we inherited have not afforded the spatial conditions that we need for mass parades and vast assemblies.' [46]

'We must get human consciousness organised' he declares. 'We must force the active revolutionary groups and the working masses to see this disformity, this misfit, to see it just as clearly as they see a misfit when some reorganisation brings disorder into their own home.'[47]

The logical implication is present here, though Gan does not develop it: if a 'misfitting' environment can obstruct social change, a 'fitting' one can foster it. If spatial organisation can be a negative catalyst, it can also be a positive one. Over the next few years, that view of architecture was to become the central motivation of the Constructivist architects, as they also pursued in greater detail the implications of Gan's other injunction, 'to develop a system of forming objects in general'.[48]

Gan's book *Constructivism* came off the presses in 1922, to spread these ideas beyond the confines of Inkhuk. During the previous year there had returned to Moscow a young architect who previously spent three wartime years there, from 1914-17, studying engineering at the Riga Polytechnical Institute which was evacuated to the Russian capital for the duration of the war with Germany. Son of an architect in Minsk, this twenty-nine year old Moisei Ginzburg had had a head-start to early professional maturity. He had been amongst the last young Russians to complete a university education abroad before the First World War. At one of Europe's most interesting moments, immediately prior to the outbreak of the War, he travelled through France to Italy to spend three years at the highly traditional architecture school of the *Accademia di Belli Arti* in Milan. Graduating in mid-1914, he was there in May of that year for the revelations of Sant'Elia's *Citta Nuova* exhibition, and no doubt read the remarkable *Messagio* that accompanied it, where for all the iconoclasm, so much of what would later emerge as the positive aspects of architectural Modernism were already expounded and amongst it, much of Le Corbusier's later programme.

Three years at the Milan Academy had left him experienced in both the beneficial disciplines and the inhibiting limitations of the classical architectural education.[49] But behind the verity and appeal of Marinetti's vision he plainly also perceived the lack of any practical signposts for the professional. Returning to Russia in 1914, he balanced his education with the engineering-oriented courses at this highly regarded European-style Polytechnical Institute. It was a stimulating atmosphere: one Englishman teaching there at this time remarked of Moscow as a whole and this school in particular, how 'even during the war ... the thirst for knowledge and study continued without appreciable abatement'.[50] Ginzburg followed this by four years down in the Crimea during the Revolution and Civil War, building some houses and studying the region's vernacular architecture. After this he was an exceptionally travelled young architect amongst the generation to which he returned in the decimated and isolated Moscow of 1921.

Ginzburg's student years in Moscow, during the War, had been the period of Tatlin's first experiments into three-dimensional 'constructions' and the 'culture of materials'. His four years absence had seen those beginnings evolve into politically committed programmes and educational curricula. By 1922-3, architect friends of Tatlin like the Vesnin brothers, all a decade older than Ginzburg, were already engrossed in exploring the consequences of this commitment for architecture through the first architectural competitions organised by a revived post-Revolutionary Moscow Architectural Society (MAO), where Shchusev had just replaced Shekhtel as Chairman. At a time when words attracted more attention than designs for which there were no materials, these older people were more at home at the drawing board than the typewriter. Ginzburg, though, was a scholarly young man already experienced in journalism and seeking to make his mark.

Like Alexander Vesnin, he was becoming attracted by ideas being expressed by Mayakovsky, Brik and others in the journal *LEF*, and during 1922 Vesnin and Ginzburg became the nucleus of a small architectural group amongst these literary Constructivists. Already having several articles to his name in the journal *Amongst the Collectors*,[51] Ginzburg also moved quickly to the centre of reviving professional circles in MAO, and a year later, plainly to mutual advantage, he became chief editor of its new journal *Architecture*.[52] During the next few years talking, writing and teaching were an active architect's most rewarding media, and Ginzburg used them all.

As indicated in Chapter 1, MAO was the main forum for progressives of the pre-Revolutionary generation. Ginzburg's two colleagues on *Architecture*'s editorial board were Leonid Vesnin, eldest brother of the successful pre-War trio and Edgar Norvert, an established expert on building rationalisation. Amongst their larger editorial committee were two leading pioneers of new building techniques Ivan Rerberg and Alexander Kuznetsov, and two leading architects-turned-planners, MAO Chairman Shchusev and Vladimir Semionov (see Chapter 11). The new position in which the whole profession found itself was expressed by the latter in the first issue of *Architecture*, under the title 'Priority tasks', in terms which show the young avant-garde was far from alone in its concerns. 'It will soon be ten years since any of us built anything' began Semionov.

'Our very approach to work has to change. Where previously we converted reliably proven technical knowledge into concrete facts, we now have to blaze entirely new trails not just in architecture, in the narrow sense of that word, but also in the broadest sense of architecture, as creative construction (stroitelstvo)*, where logic, the way of life, community attitudes and every side of civil life all make their demands equally. Before the Revolution we knew neither this complexity, nor this responsibility.'*

Professionally, he wrote, it will be 'the task of the future public architecture to understand these new conditions, these new requirements of the present time, and to find forms answering the real situation'. But 'The battle requires organisation, and the changed circumstances call for new methods.'[53]

As editorial writer for this issue, Ginzburg took the opportunity to offer some pointers from other circles. 'Contemporary researches in the field of artistic form' he wrote, 'are speaking of a new phase of creative activity' which must take account of 'that new element of our lives, our psychology and aesthetics: the machine.' 'Architecture today must find sources of inspiration in the achievements of engineers and of industrial architecture' he declared, and in a four-page article, all six illustrations were 'Grain elevators in Buffalo, New York.' With 'the descent of artists from Olympia' to become 'master-craftsmen in the real world' said Ginzburg, they have brought a 'healthy coarsening of our concept of the creative process'.[54]

The other Moscow forum where the serious young Ginzburg was active was one fully sensitive to the traditional refinements he invoked in that remark. Rakhn, the Russian Academy of Artistic Sciences, was formed in 1921, largely under the influence of Kandinsky, as a talking shop on a modernised model of eighteenth-century European academies. It was dedicated 'to discovering the inner, positive laws on whose basis aesthetic works are produced in each branch of art, and to deriving from that the principles of synthetic artistic expression'.[55] Ginzburg read numerous papers in the architectural section led by Ivan Zholtovsky. In February 1924 he presented the argument of a book he had already completed entitled *Style and Epoch*. The book was typical of the approach observed by one recent Soviet writer to be characteristic of Rakhn, in that 'theory and history were bound together as a single topic of investigation.'[56] On the other hand the old-style typeface and traditional design characteristic of Rakhn's own publications did not immediately identify it as a radical or avant-garde work.

Style and Epoch

In fact *Style and Epoch* was seminal to the whole development of Constructivist thinking about architecture. It also provides an important point of comparison with Western thinking, in particular that of Corbusier, who to Soviets always occupied the foreground of it.

With its further illustrations of Buffalo grain silos, and now also of aeroplanes, the book looks sufficiently like *Vers une Architecture* for Corbusier to have felt no doubt immensely flattered when his inscribed copy arrived in the mail.[57] One can only speculate as to how it might have influenced his approach if he had been able to read the text. Precisely how and when the message of *L'Esprit Nouveau* arrived in the Soviet Union remains uncertain, but as far as has been recently ascertained, the first copies to arrive were those which 'Le Corbusier sent to the Commissar of Enlightenment A.V. Lunacharsky ... in 1922, long before the establishment of diplomatic relations between the Soviet State and France.'[58] In early

1923 MAO's *Architecture* referred in its 'Survey of journals' to there being 'a few copies in Moscow in private hands' with more expected by the 'university and neo-philological libraries soon'.[59] The strength and authority of Ginzburg's ideas already derived, however, from the very wide range of stimuli on which he drew. The architectural philosophy expounded here can be seen as a natural, indeed logical synthesis of the various influences in his training, his early professional life, and the Moscow circles around him.

While *L'Esprit Nouveau* was not the only influence behind Ginzburg's book, the end product was plainly modelled closely upon it. *Style and Epoch* shows us that this material which the West has always found to be an indigestible lump had already been critically digested in the Soviet Union. Yet more significantly, it had already been used as the first stepping stone to an operational method that would bring to architecture the qualities so lauded in engineering, rather than just the forms. Indeed the Russians themselves were aware of this. Thus Leonid Vesnin wrote to his brothers in a holiday letter of summer 1924, on his re-reading of Corbusier's *L'Esprit Nouveau* material lately published as *Vers une Architecture*:

> *'I am reading Corbusier-Saugnier but fairly slowly and therefore more carefully than I did last winter. I see that there are certain questions on which one could already disagree with him. We have gone further and we look more deeply.'*[60]

Out of those initial observations about the honesty of form in grain silos, cars and aeroplanes, Ginzburg had built a consistent little Marxist-theoretical work (though he did not call it that), which makes *Vers une Architecture* look more than ever like a loose piece of journalism. Although then and later, Corbusier made many comments upon historical architecture, he never attempted to pull them together into any theory of the general development of architectures. Gan had insisted that 'The theory of historical materialism through which the Constructivists are assimilating history in general and the basic laws of society must serve them equally as a method of studying the history of art' to develop 'a science of the history of its formal development.'[61] Here Ginzburg produced a first such analysis of architecture.

For all Corbusier's eulogies on the logical and precise methods whereby engineers create forms, nowhere did he really attempt to build a bridge into the practice of architecture. (Further aspects of this are discussed in Chapter 6.) All too clearly Corbusier had no aptitude for the sort of calculations involved. Ginzburg by contrast, with the engineering emphasis of his polytechnic degree, was a prototype of his own vision of the architect. It was a vision close to that which his mentor in teaching at MVTU, Alexander Kuznetsov, had described to the last pre-War Congress of Russian Architects a decade before as 'an artist with a scientific education.'[62] Ginzburg insisted that architectural creation is a monistic process and a distinct activity (though elements from many others are synthesised into it), but he saw that only those whose central concern was architecture could build a bridge from engineering that was useful to it. While circumstances made Corbusier's fundamentally romantic book a major inspiration to architectural thinking world-wide, there is no doubt that Ginzburg's is the more useful and thoughtful work, which would have served the practice of architecture better in that role. To those exploring Constructivism's implications for architecture, it provided both historical legitimacy, and an operational starting point for their approach to building design.

To Corbusier, 'style' was never much more than an attribute of artefacts. To Ginzburg it was 'some kind of regularity, a similarity through conformity to the same laws (*zakonomernoe edinstvo*)'[63] which relentlessly characterises every branch and product of the life of a historical period. It can only be identified through as intimate an understanding of the period's 'social, economic, climatic and national particularities' as of its 'artistic environment'.[64] Wölfflin's *Renaissance and Baroque* had influenced him here, and he quotes it widely.

Briefly summarised, it was Ginzburg's observation from extensive historical study that what one might call the 'health' of architecture follows that of cultures and their respective *Weltanschauungs*, as they pass through phases of fresh, creative 'flowering', 'organic' maturity and decline into 'decorative' rhetoric.[65] It was to illustrate this theory of a cyclical process that he used the historical examples which Corbusier would have found familiar. With his concern for historical objectivity and dynamic processes, Ginzburg also paid considerable attention to the Gothic, which had never fitted Corbusier's formal predilections.

Ginzburg called the first phase of a typical architectural cycle *konstruktivnyi*: 'constructive'. Neatly he spans the gap here between the limited nineteenth-century architect's understanding of that term and the broader meaning already established amongst Soviet artists. In a constructive phase, says Ginzburg, unprejudiced responses are being made to the mass of what are, axiomatically, new social and technical problems. In these periods, the chief task in every field of design is that of 'devising the characteristic plastic types for the epoch', and the present coincidence of social and technical revolutions made their own period unquestionably such a 'constructive' phase.[66] In these periods, 'the new style will always be aesthetically strong and organically logical'.[67] In Viollet-le-Duc's terms, the *'principes'* will be pure, for 'the architect is facing the very basic problem of the delimiting of space with material forms and this requires the creation of elements working constructively'.[68]

In the present, early-Soviet period however, Ginzburg perceived factors making their's a 'doubly constructive' phase. Exceptional economic stringency required the maximum possible economy of material in that 'delimiting' and therefore a maximising of the constructive work done by the building elements. But it also happened that the principles on which every branch of their contemporary life was organised, or more accurately aspired to be organised, were precisely those embodied *par excellence* in the machine: the principles of honesty, structural simplicity, objectivity, precise organisation and thus economy of means. Returning to themes we have already observed in his writings he declared: 'The essence of this machine, which is beginning to play such an exceptional psychological role in our lives, consists in the naked constructiveness of its component organisms.'[69] 'The machine is creativity at its most organised, the greatest clarity and power in the formulation of the creative idea.'[70] 'In the machine there can be nothing superfluous, accidental, "decorative"', and never forgetting architectural history: 'In essence we find in the machine, before all, the clearest expression of that ideal of harmonious creativity long ago formulated by the first Italian theoretician, Alberti.'[71] It was in this sense that the machine was the symbol of their present epoch, and these characteristics of the style of every 'constructive' period thus happened, in this one, to be also the characteristics of its own particular *Weltanschauung*. How then could the correct architectural style of the young Soviet Union be anything but 'constructive'?

This argument was unquestionably the primary source of the Constructivist architects' strong self-confidence. It gave them a conviction that their stance was historically 'correct' – a conviction quite as strong as the parallel one which motivated their political leaders. Moving to a higher level of detail, the particular characteristics and prototypes of modern 'organisedness' then gave them the starting point for their method of design.

'As forms', said Ginzburg in *Style and Epoch*, 'neither the engineering structure nor the machine gives us an expressive spatial solution, which is what constitutes the distinguishing mark of architecture'.[72] 'How,' he asked, 'are we to build a bridge between these contemporary ensembles and the architectural monuments, once we realise that this is possible only through the principles of creativity and not through the actual forms? We will try to continue our analysis.'[73] His 'continued analysis' showed the machine to be potentially an appropriate model for the organisation of any functionally interconnected agglomeration of specialised and diverse activities, dynamic and static. Here was already a quite sophisticated methodological concept that left Corbusier's mere image of the house as a '*machine à habiter*' in the realm of aphorisms.

From this general idea of the machine as an organisational prototype, Ginzburg developed a two-stage analogy. The first stage was an analogy between the machine and the factory, which is:

> *'a collective of machines; ... all linked together by desirable necessity just as the parts of an individual machine are, ... and at the same time is also a "dwelling", primarily for machines not people, but [in a way that makes it] an architectural object none the less, with all the spatial connotations of that.'*[74]

'Industrial architecture' therefore 'serves as the connecting link, ... but factories and silos cannot be the sole contents of modern architecture.'[75] So, secondly,

> *'Precisely as we established the analogy between the machine and the industrial building, an analogy may be established between the industrial building and the architecture of the dwelling or the community building. Just precisely as the industrial building is not the conscious imitation of a machine, but comprises forms that have been generated organically and quite independently, while reflecting the same contemporaneity through whatever are their own unique characteristics, so here in precisely the same way is it a question of building an analogy.'*[76]

Style and Epoch did not pass unappreciated by the Soviet architectural profession. 'In the excellent book of M. Ginzburg,' said the old-established Leningrad architect and planner Professor Karpovich, reviewing it for the city's main environment journal *Questions of the Communal Economy*, 'the reader will find not only theoretical discussions on style in architecture, but also

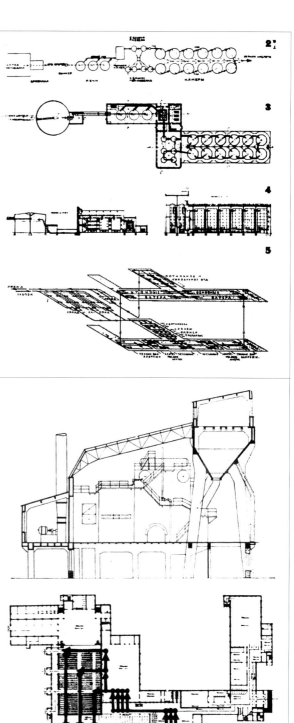

ЦЕЛЕВАЯ УСТАНОВКА
В СОВРЕМЕННОЙ АРХИТЕКТУРЕ

Производственные, или трудовые, процессы ассоциируются обычно в нашем представлении с фабрикой, заводом; **общественно-бытовые** — с жильем, общественным зданием. Разницы по существу здесь не имеется.

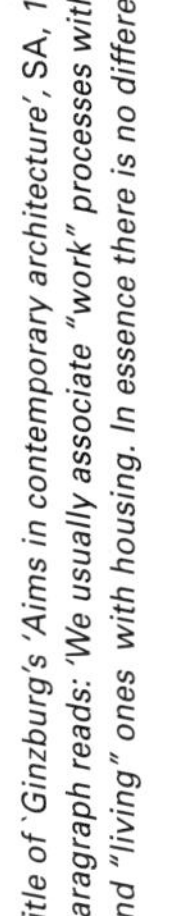

Title of 'Ginzburg's 'Aims in contemporary architecture', SA, 1927, no.1. Paragraph reads: 'We usually associate "work" processes with factories and "living" ones with housing. In essence there is no difference here.'

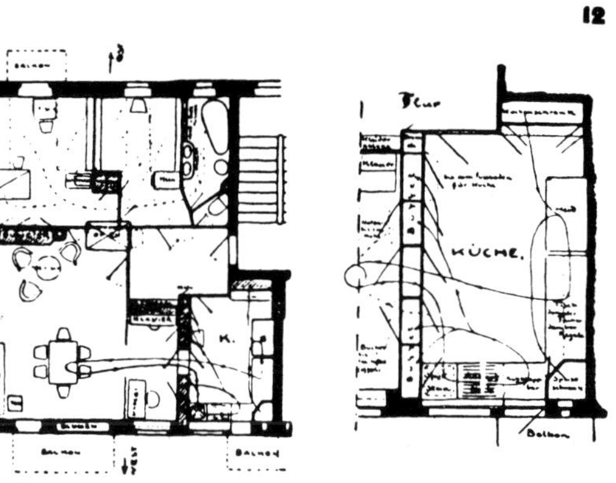

Ginzburg illustrates his 'two-stage analogy' between machine and factory, then factory and workers' club or kitchen, from 'Aims in contemporary architecture'.

absolutely practical approaches to the creative problems of contemporary architecture.' 'The book demonstrates', said Karpovich, that 'the study of the machine can give a new stimulus to the creation of new architectural forms', though 'it shows us how far today's Constructivists are from the creation of such new forms'.[77] Karpovich was a relevant and objective commentator on the book's originality. Removed from the fray of avant-gardism, he was all the same a free-thinking, even radical figure from pre-Revolutionary days. He well knew that nothing else emerging in Moscow was comparable. Architectural research circles in Rakhn, which Ginzburg had used as a testing ground, were dominated by the Classicist Zholtovsky. Architecture in Inkhuk was by now predominantly the terrain of Rationalists Ladovsky, Krinsky and Dokuchaev. *Style and Epoch*'s main competitor in sophistication at this date, in the pursuit of an approach to the whole architectural problem, was the work of his younger Leningrad colleague Alexander Rozenburg, a hospital design specialist before the Revolution, whose book of the previous year, *A Philosophy of Architecture*, was more synoptic, but infinitely less topical and less pregnant.[78] Ginzburg's natural allies were the people in LEF, amongst whom this book must have provided him with impeccable credentials.

OSA's 'method of functional creativity'

From the 'two-stage analogy' and other principles established in *Style and Epoch*, Ginzburg and his colleagues developed the central concepts and procedures of their design 'method'. First however they formed themselves into a group, and started a journal.

As the city's established professional organisation, MAO had proved itself inadequate as a platform for advancing genuinely new aesthetic ideas. A society headed by the compromising Shchusev could hardly be their scene. Anathema to the young and *engagés* was the passive 'professionalism' of Edgar Norvert's view that 'the posing of general social questions and questions about the new way of life is outside the domain of the architect'. Too dominant was his opinion, expressed in *Architecture* in 1923, that architecture could not serve society until distinct social forms had crystallised out of the present transitional period.[79] This was the opposite of the emerging Constructivist view, encapsulated by Gan, that buildings themselves influenced the social change. The psycho-formal work of Nikolai Ladovsky and his colleagues in Asnova, said the Constructivists, 'could only acquire a genuinely scientific materialistic basis if it was always made clear what real problems the theoretical work was directed at', and 'if the methods being applied in solution of these tasks were fundamentally those of the architect, so that they could be put to real and practical use in the present-day architect's work as an organiser of building.'[80] By the end of 1925, serious construction work was starting again across the Soviet Union. They clearly needed to be organised if any part of that cake was to come their way. Of all Moscow architects, the Vesnins had most consistently been successful, both officially and in the eyes of their colleagues, in the new wave of architectural competitions. On housing they took First Prize as a trio for oil workers' housing for Grozneft in 1922; Leonid took First in MAO's Moscow competition of 1923. As a trio they took Third in the government's prestige Palace of Labour competition of 1923 with a building whose social, spatial and technical novelty made it 'canonical' for Constructivism [p.41].[81] In 1924, they took First for the ARCOS company headquarters in central Moscow. In the inconclusive closed contest for tiny Moscow headquarters of *Leningradskaia Pravda* in the same year, they produced one of the most dramatic and seminal schemes of the whole decade [p.41]. By 1925, Ginzburg and some of their students were starting to enter this league in competitions, and real commissions were in hand such as Mostorg department stores, the Raw Materials Institute or Gostrakha's housing [pp.42-3, 47-8]. They were legitimately confident. Thus in late 1925, Ginzburg and the Vesnins formed their own Constructivist architectural group to fill the gap, and called it OSA: the Union of Contemporary Architects.[82]

Between them Ginzburg and the three Vesnins, Leonid, Viktor and Alexander, represented a bridge between progressives of the older generation and the younger avant-garde. From the architectural group which had coalesced in LEF came Vesnin himself and Mikhail Barshch, Andrei Burov, Ivan Sobolev, Nikolai Krasilnikov who were his students in Vkhutemas. Ginzburg's students in MVTU were represented by Georgi Vegman, Georgi Orlov, Viacheslav Vladimirov and the older Kasilnikov brother, Vasili. Other students amongst founder members were Fufaev, Kornfeld and Kapustina. Alexei Gan was a central participant from the beginning, as theorist and publicist, designing their journal *SA* which started during the next year, and later in staging their exhibition. He and Alexander Vesnin brought a direct link to the aesthetic debates of the Inkhuk's original Working Group of Constructivists and the attitude to materials of Tatlin, whom Vesnin knew well since the period when they shared a studio before the Revolution. Ginzburg and Leonid Vesnin brought the experience of pre-Revolutionary Russian pioneers of a technologically and aesthetically 'modern' architecture, particularly through their connections with Norvert, Artur Loleit and Kuznetsov. Much of the group's authority derived from the fact it was a synthesis of this broad thinking and very substantial experience. Their method sought to formalise 'correct' relationships between these very diverse components.

After the demise of MAO's short-lived *Architecture*, and an attempt to revive the pre-Revolutionary journal *The Architect* (*Zodchii*) in 1924, OSA's journal *Contemporary Architecture* (*SA*) was the USSR's only purely architectural magazine of the later Twenties. It published six bi-monthly issues a year, with bold Modernist typography, good photographs and serious writing, from 1926 to 1930. The title of the very first article, 'New methods of architectural thinking', encapsulated its programme.[83] This paper by Ginzburg is translated as Document 9 in Chapter 6. Here as in his next two major articles on this theme,[84] and already in *Style and Epoch*, he addressed both theoretical and operational questions. (The continuity and development of ideas is schematically summarised in Document 6.) In 'New methods of architectural thinking' these two classes of questions became two distinct categories of 'variables': the 'general unknowns' and the 'particular' ones.

'General unknowns' were those identifying 'characteristics of the epoch as a whole' whose influence must permeate the entire design and construction process of the new society. In *Style and Epoch* he had discussed these 'social, economic and national peculiarities' of a culture as inevitably influencing building form.[85] From further analysis of their own emerging culture Ginzburg now identified four such 'peculiarities' of the Soviet situation. The first was that individual clients had been replaced by a collective one, a whole society, which was trying to build 'a new way of life'; the second was the concomitant shift in architecture's position, to become one part of a larger social and economic plan. The third was the conjunction of these factors to produce a new, ideological and technical status for norms and standard types. The fourth and final one was an overriding methodological obligation under the new ideology, to 'solve the architectural task, like any other, only through precise evaluation of its "unknowns" and the pursuit of a correct method of solution'.[86] The deductions were not all novel, but the codified statement was new.

By now, Tatlin's Tower, so complex and unrealisable in the decimated state of Russia, had been reduced to a piece of technological symbolism in the public mind. By now this iconic object had therefore become an example of how not to proceed. Ginzburg condemned it here as 'merely naive ... an attempt to replace the complexities of the art of architecture by forms, which however sparkling' were derived as 'symbolism ... from other aspects of technology'. Architecture was not symbolism, but 'invention like another other', a task of 'organising and giving form to (*skonstruirovat'*) a concrete practical problem not only for the dictates of today, but to fit the needs of tomorrow'. 'From the inventor the contemporary architect must take only his creative method.'[87] A future issue of *SA* drove home the difference from Corbusier here, with a feature on calculations underlying the design of those seductive biplanes that is also discussed in Chapter 6 and is translated as Document 10.[88]

Developing the qualitative features of this 'method' further, Ginzburg declared that the conditions that had produced the architect's 'new social consumer' had also 'freed him' from being a 'peacemaker in irreconcilable conflicts of interest', operating (if only in self-defence) behind closed doors. By the 'method of functional creativity' they as Constructivists aspired to make design 'a unified organic process'. Having a 'single clear aim', the task could be 'hammered out logically ... from first priorities to second ... from skeleton to envelope, from inside to out, as a conscious process from beginning to end'.[89] Such a process would be open to scrutiny of its data and decisionmaking, and thus publicly accountable. It would be a collective act of 'construction' as the public and specialists contributed their components, and much of *SA*'s campaigning was thereafter directed at stimulating that participation. The architect's specialism however, was the synthesis: the *konstruktsiia*.

The main rules for that process of *konstruktsiia* had already been worked out. They are only outlined at this stage, but the Constructivists' view of what should be primary in design and what secondary, is clearly indicated by the ordering of stages within their 'logical process'. 'Spatial parameters, their dimensions and interconnections are the first function of the brief'; 'the spatial organisation is the starting point of the design and the place to which the main thrust must be directed'. Then secondly, the architect must establish the appropriate building materials and method of construction 'as functions of the basic spatial solution'. Thirdly, he must order the 'external interrelationships of spatial elements'. 'The grouping of the architectural masses, their rhythms and proportions will derive naturally from the first half of his activity: they are a function of the material envelopes and inner volumes he has "constructed".' Finally, he will give form to individual components and elements: to apertures, overhangs etc 'all on the basis of calculations or other types of consideration within the brief'.

In this linear process, 'one task leads logically from another'. The architect 'is freed from the handed-down models of the past' and is 'forced to seek artistic expressiveness in that which is most important and necessary'. If the resulting architecture is currently 'ascetic', that is not the result of the process, merely of 'youth' in both the builders, and the new life they are building. New systems of compositional principles will develop from the typical spatial patterns of the new problems themselves.[90]

Ginzburg's categories of 'general' and 'particular unknowns' correspond to today's 'state' and 'decision variables'. Gan and the Working Group in Inkhuk had established a role for the former category of unknown within the design process, but the mapping of Ginzburg's classification onto their concepts of *tektonika*, *faktura* and *konstruktsiia* is not exact. The notion of *konstruktsiia* had been absorbed as the premise of their whole approach; that is clear. The concept of *faktura* lay beneath all references to materials and 'appropriate' building methods in Ginzburg's 'second stage', and in his fourth, but more as an assumed rigour of analysis than as an explicit operation. Notions of an 'expressive' relationship between materials and their spatial possibilities stretched back to Tatlin. The complex 'geological' concept of *tektonika* as a synthesis of deep political and technological 'restructurings', is largely subsumed within Ginzburg's category of 'general unknowns', but technological elements of the concept, in particular, also permeate the rest. Gan's 'three new disciplines' had constituted a first redefinition of the 'whole' design problem in their expanded, Marxist-materialist context, but it was crude. However in moving from Gan's 'general system' towards the first outlines of a 'method', the architects had articulated the intuitive categories into something approaching real tools.

In his next two papers Ginzburg elaborated certain ideas and introduced others, as Document 6 indicates. In 'The functional method and form', published later in 1926, he established a role within his four-stage process for those issues of visual psychology and of 'economy of perceptual energy' being explored by Asnova under Ladovsky.[91] From within earlier Constructivist thinking he took up the question of how form should relate to an evolving content. Gan had spoken in general terms; Ginzburg was now explicit. The Constructivist must 'calculate correctly' the complex overlapping relations between old and new within 'the dialectical development of life' at any given time. Then 'the functional method of thinking must always take as the precondition of its material forms not the areas of backwardness, but the landmarks of the new way of life and advanced technology'.[92] How he should take the new way-of-life as his starting point, and why, were the most important topics of his next paper, 'Aims in contemporary architecture', published early the following year.

Here two of the most powerful ideas in earlier Constructivist writing come together. Developing his own 'two-stage analogy' with the machine, and harnessing it to Gan's vision of spatial organisation as a catalytic force in social change, Ginzburg formulated the concept which henceforth became central to all his colleagues' propagandising and design work, the concept of 'the social condenser'.

Out of the basic analogy he identified in *Style and Epoch*, Ginzburg develops the two concepts of the 'scheme of equipment' and the 'flow diagram', which will be the tools for establishing the 'first spatial diagram of the building' in the first stage of the method. The 'scheme of equipment' is a description of the hardware involved in each of the myriad specialised and identifiable events within a building. In a machine, these correspond to the components of its specialised sub-assemblies. The 'flow diagram' describes the multiple human movements between them, which correspond to the conveyor belts of the factory or the drives of a complex machine. Henry Ford in his autobiography had described achieving great spatial economies in his production lines through rationalisations of this kind: plainly, as Ginzburg reasons, such economies must be equally accessible to the architects of a building. 'For Palladio in the Villa Rotunda' or the pre-Revolutionary palace 'accommodating only the mazurka or the polonaise', functions were not distinguishable, said Ginzburg, always enjoying the historical example. 'With building in a socialist country' however, 'the difference is basic, and one of principle'.[94]

The influence of Russia's Taylorist movement for the 'Scientific Organisation of Work' (N.O.T) was certainly also strong here. Led by a Futurist poet, member of Proletkult and occasional contributor to *LEF*, Alexei Gastev, this was one facet of a larger preoccupation with the rationalisation of time-use and of all forms of motion that permeated Soviet daily life as well as industry in the early Twenties. Though sometimes a little comic in its experiments and obsessive in its campaigns, this was a serious attack on the problems of making an effective industrial workforce from a predominantly illiterate, non-numerate and peasant population. Gastev's poetry on industrial themes was less subtle than Mayakovsky's, but had its 'commercial' strand in slogans for time-and-efficiency campaigns where Mayakovsky's was in product advertising. Gastev's campaigning extended to the rationalisation of language and modernising of proletarian emotions through exposure to rhythms of the industrial world. In his Central Institute of Work in Moscow, Gastev's laboratory recorded human bodily movements in performing industrial tasks in order to eliminate all superfluous elements of the movement and the wastage of energy involved in them.[94] In one direction, this led to the theatre director Meyerkhold's system of gesture and stage movement called Biomechanics. In another, it was manifestly influential on the development of Constructivist ideas of efficient 'flow' in buildings. One early explicit reference appears in *SA* where the Vesnins' competition scheme for the Central Telegraph Building in Moscow is designed around 'a rationalisation of work-processes based on N.O.T.'[95]

Use of time-and-motion as a basis for space planning was of course part of the armoury of serious Modernists in the West. It is not clear when the Constructivists first learnt of the Germans' use of such ideas in building design; probably not by 1925-6 when they started formalising their method, but in 1927 they used material from Bruno Taut and others as illustrations to their articles.[96] They also noted that Frank Lloyd Wright's houses were models of economic movement.[97] Eclectic or not in its origins, the status and role which OSA accorded to the resulting 'basic spatial diagram' was uniquely defined by Ginzburg's conception of their period as 'doubly constructive'. It constituted an empirical solution of a socially and technically new brief, in the fresh, creative 'flowering' stage of a new era. Within Ginzburg's historical schema it was thus one of the means to generate 'the characteristic plastic types for the epoch'. With the materialist's view of the power of organised matter, the Constructivists saw these incarnations of the advanced 'landmarks' in Russia's social evolution as the architect's most important contribution to Soviet revolutionary objectives. Through the circuitry of these 'social condensers', low-voltage activity and a weak consciousness would be focused into high-voltage catalysts of change in the habits and attitudes of the mass population. This contribution to the act of 'social construction' was OSA's social mission as architects; it was their methodological objective that identified them as Constructivists.

The method of laboratory and teaching work

The last column of Document 6 shows how these arguments in Ginzburg's writings from 1924 to early 1927 developed finally into the full procedures of the 'method of laboratory and teaching work', detailed in Document 8, which he published at the end of that year.

Though numbering has been slightly altered the logic of the process is unchanged. Thus Stage 1 or 'the 1st object' involved generating 'the basic

Alexei Gastev (1882-1941), poet and founder of Soviet Taylorism, c.1924

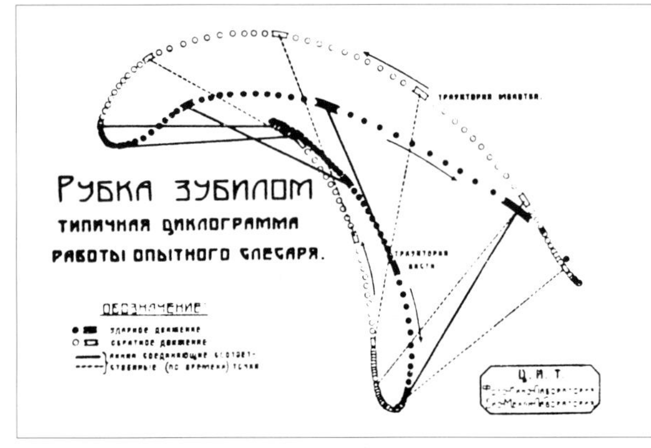

Gastev's Institute of Work Processes, TsIT, Moscow, c.1925: left: *record of 'expert metal-worker's chisel movement';* above: *filming hammer-swing.*

spatial diagram of the building', the 'social condenser', through analysis of the 'flows' and 'needs' of the revolutionary social processes inside it, through examination of their environmental requirements and through 'revolutionary rethinking' about how the technical means available might be utilised, stressing always 'rationality' and 'practical realisation'. Stage 2 demanded that 'the material forms crystallised as this social condenser be examined in terms of the problem of perception, so that the useful activity of the condenser is enhanced by the user's clear perception of it.' This stage embraced topics investigated by the Rationalists and basic issues of formal clarity. For Constructivists they are only one among many generative factors in determining building form and certainly not the most important.

Stage 3 involved a more detailed examination of 'the elements of architecture which are the objects of this perception: surface, volume and the volumetric co-existence of bodies in space.' It stressed the importance of those 'types of transformation', like cutting holes in surfaces, changes in the relationships of parts or in the material, that offer the architect means of making formal responses to changes in the brief. This was the area to which much of the Constructivist teaching about abstract form in Vkhutemas was directed, in particular the serial and combinatorial ideas first developed in the artistic work of Rodchenko.

Stage 4 reasserted the importance of *faktura* in its concern with industrial production processes. It involved detailed examination of 'the particular processes of industrial production which leave their stamp ... on individual components and organisms within the building'. A 5th stage of 'reassembly' would then 'restore organic wholeness' to produce 'a logical building ... freed from handed-down models of the past'. As I commented in Chapter 4, that final synthetic act remained mysterious. This was the aspect of designing which their abhorrence of 'intuition' left the Constructivists least equipped to discuss, let alone to investigate.

Very importantly, though, this full description of their method has re-embraced that category of 'laboratory work' pioneered and developed in teaching by Rodchenko to create, in Gan's words, 'a system for producing forms'. Rodchenko had insisted that the designer must be 'constrained to assemble forms according to laws'; he must be able to make 'all possible combinations, of diverse systems, kinds and applications' through understanding the fundamentals of formal 'construction'.[98] In Ginzburg's new '3rd object' Rodchenko's 'rules' have been aggregated into 'types of transformations', whose logic will ensure that the clarity, consistency and flexibility of response to be achieved through the rest of the method are matched in the logic of an architect's formal vocabulary.

These grammars and disciplines of formal construction were the essential prerequisite if the architect was to respond with perfect fluency to the new social briefs, to handle the logical evolution of his own design solutions and to refine those solutions to the point of perfect formal and stylistic coherence. 'Constructivism never admits the fixing of forms' writes Ginzburg,

> *'Form is an unknown, x, which has always to be evaluated anew by the architect. ... We have therefore to study not just the elements of architecture, but the methods of transformation of those elements, to understand how changes in the brief must affect the form.'*

'Three points are vital here', he stresses, namely

> *'that this method of formal transformations be understood as an essential component of the architect's working tools; that this transformation process is never just an aesthetic one but involves reorganisation of the working, constructive elements of the building; and that what we are changing is the material object itself, but that this is done in the context of its essential purpose and of its perception by the building user.'*[99]

This is the point at which the particular concerns of the Leningrad 'constructive' architect Iakov Chernikhov engage with the larger programme of the Moscow-based Constructivist group OSA. OSA had its own local branch in Leningrad, as it did in several other Soviet cities. The Leningrad group was centred on the old-established architecture school of the Institute of Civil Engineers, IGI, now LIGI [see Chapter 10], and was led by Alexander Nikolsky.[100] It contributed actively to the journal *SA* and to its 'Modern Architecture' exhibition in 1927, as well as executing some good buildings [pp.52-5], but was not particularly significant for its theoretical contributions.

Chernikhov had nothing to do with this or any other group. Professionally, he was a relative loner, earning a livelihood through industrial building and a vast amount of teaching, according to his particular programme, in industrial and labour schools, whilst still himself studying under Leonti Benois at the Academy school to get full architectural qualifications. While not a member of the inner circles of the avant-garde, he attended some of their discussions and lectures. But he was always surrounded by numerous passionately devoted students who were also his assistants in preparation and execution of his abstract and architectural 'constructions' on paper.

Chernikhov's theory of the role of the machine as the proper inspiration and logical paradigm of contemporary architecture was independently derived. Influenced though it may have been by contemporaneous work around him, it is a self-sufficient argument. Whilst his numerous books generally presuppose some larger 'model' of the design process outside his own special topic, he does not refer to any wider context very often or very explicitly. On the other hand, his whole training programme was premised upon the value of what the Moscovites called 'laboratory work', and he pursued this problem of 'the method of formal transformations' and the possible 'organisations of the building's working, constructive elements', at the level of detail, energy and rigour far greater than was achieved, amidst their other concerns, by the members of OSA.[101]

Synthesising formal and theoretical principles derived variously from Suprematism and mechanical engineering, Chernikhov produced an analysis and programme aimed even more exclusively than the Moscovites' professionally-oriented work, at architectural training, but only at a part of that training. In his chosen field, of 'constructive' formal languages, which is what Chernikhov calls 'Constructivism', the two programmes match very closely. Ginzburg's list of the 'types of transformation' to be mastered [Doc.8] is almost identical to Chernikhov's list of 'the fundamentals of Constructivism' in the second part of *The Construction of Architectural and Machine Forms*, where he says:

> *'The fundamental elements of Constructivism consist of all the various possible unions of elements which go to make up a structure. The following formal*

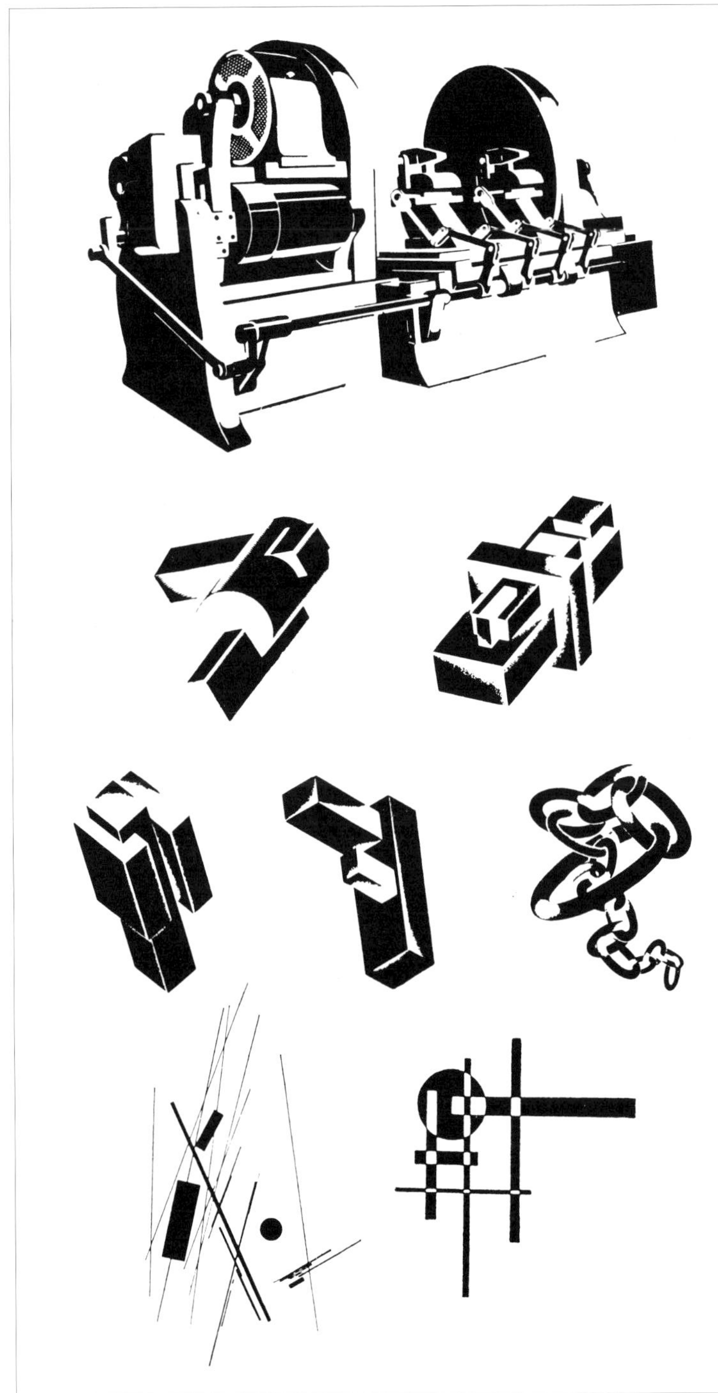

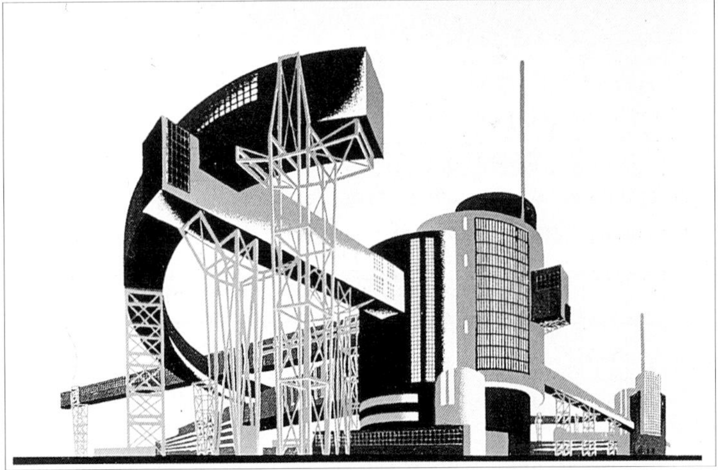

Chernikhov: Machine as 'constructive assembly'. 'Constructive principles': Penetration; Embracing; Mounting; Linkage. 'Compositions of linear and circular elements'. 'An architectural fiction'.

relationships of elements must therefore be recognised as the basic principles of Constructivism: a) Insertion, b) Clamping, c) Twisting, d) Embracing, e) Mounting, f) Bending, g) Coupling, h) Piercing, and so on. All these fundamental relationships are in essence simple but they can create complex combinations which amaze us by the refinement and richness of the shapes they produce. As a supplement to these essentially static relationships there is the possibility of a dynamic element. Knowledge of these fundamentals of formal construction greatly helps in the elucidation of the essence of Constructivism, but it is not enough to be familiar with the forms themselves. Complete familiarity with the principles underlying them is essential. One must study the insertion of one element into another with all the possible individual variations and combinations. Training, practice and innate flair play no small part in this, and exactly the same approach must be applied to study of all the other fundamental elements.' [102]

The theory and programme which Chernikhov expounded in that book, and in the preceding *Fundamentals of Contemporary Architecture*, present this 'approach' in exhaustive detail, from its starting point in the simplest exercises of linear construction through to the fully developed fictional building complexes which form his well known 'fantasies'. 'This approach requires that there be specific, clearly defined tasks set as examples,' he says, 'which clarify in detail the essence of the specific formal constructive problem we are studying thereby.'[103] The illustrations to all his books are just that: solutions to clearly defined tasks of formal construction or composition. Some of them, where the objectives set were expressive rather than purely mechanical, were similar to the products of equally precisely-defined tasks which the Rationalists set in the Basic Course of Moscow's Vkhutemas. As a result Chernikhov was accused at one stage of copying their pedagogy, but he defended himself by insisting that he could not know it as they had published nothing.

Chernikhov was as dedicated as the Constructivist group proper to the pursuit of a 'new' architecture inspired by the machine. As he wrote in *Fundamentals*, 'We must ask the general question as to which factors in contemporary technology and our modern way of life have the power to determine the character of the new architecture?' The answer lay in 'the multiple principles and properties of engineering.'[104] Though he does not deploy the Moscovites' mathematical vocabulary, his approach to achieving this aim is the same. 'The replacement of outdated forms in architecture can only be achieved' says Chernikhov, 'through a radical reconstruction of the basic architectural means and devices. The elements of that new architecture will emerge as a result of the limitless varying of the abstract (non-objective) forms which are at architecture's disposal.'[105] Though he does not use the phrase 'laboratory work', the function of abstraction or 'non-objectivity' in this process is quite explicity this. The concept is identical to that which emerges in the Moscow Constructivists' teaching via Rodchenko, in particular his notion of the formal data-bank or 'spatial inventory'. In Chernikhov's words:

'With the help of so-called non-objective elements we have the possibility for creating a series of the most fantastic formal constructions which are not initially constrained by any direct practical application, but in return possess properties which make them available for real and direct application in the future. Having been trained through the development of multiple series of

constructive structures and through designing multiple diverse combinations, we shall be fully equipped for the moment when a completely new and original formal solution is required of us in the future.'[106]

As he wrote here in *The Construction of Architectural and Machine Forms*, by this rigorous training in the generation of architectural 'fictions' or *fantazii*, 'our inventive capacities will be developed to their full potential'. As he put it in his *Architectural Fictions*, the aspiration is to develop 'the ability of the individual in question to imagine different forms in all their possible inter-relations and combinations.'[107]

Herein of course lies the value of Chernikhov's analyses and grammars in an age that can now generate 'all possible inter-relations and combinations' of its selected formal vocabularies automatically, with electronic technology, and can exploit the ruthlessly clear logic of relations which he codified to make different, but equally lucid, relational statements.

For the sake of history, however, it should be recorded that this complementarity of Chernikhov's work to their own was not admitted (even if it was perceived) by the Constructivists in Moscow. The work's reception manifestly suffered from the delay which separated the development of his ideas in the mid-Twenties from the publication of them. By 1930, when his first major architectural treatise came out (there were small ones earlier), the Modernist groups in Soviet architecture were already embattled against the growing opposition. Moreover that first big book, *Fundamentals of Contemporary Architecture*, being as much concerned with architectural expression as with pure formal construction, was not the best exemplar of the complementary relationship (not that these were years for vaunting the 'machine' inspiration of architecture either). Thus *SA*'s review of Chernikhov's *Fundamentals* was dismissive. 'Our architecture has long ago outlived the "symbolic" formalism of Iakov Chernikhov,' wrote the young critic Roman Khiger. 'If this book had appeared in 1921-22, when symbolism was flowering here, and we were concerned with the "dynamic" in all its forms and diversity, ... it might perhaps have played a certain role.'[108] In the longer historical perspective, however, Chernikhov's work on the formal principles of a Constructive architecture represents an important elaboration of the general theory in areas where the Constructivists themselves have not left us records of anything so exhaustive.

The application of mathematical methods

In the paper preceding his full exposition of 'Constructivism as a method', Ginzburg had recognised that 'the whole Soviet community must be drawn into solving the task' which that 'functional method' outlined. The task which it defined was 'not within the powers of the single architect or even a collective of architects'.[109] The exhaustive precision to which they aspired also demanded bodies of data and research that were decades beyond the Soviet Union's horizon at that time. All the same, some remarkable work was done in broaching these topics.

Working with leading structural engineers, for example, they themselves explored the relative economics of various new structural systems. (Some of this is discussed in Chapter 7.) Using the latest foreign data and research they advanced building science aspects. On lighting issues, they made pioneering studies of the relationships between colour and working efficiency, between fenestration and illumination patterns. This work is published in their journal and elsewhere. Most advanced for its time however was their work on optimising the parameters of their 'spatial prototypes' by quantitative methods.

As can be seen from its centrality in their method, all their design work sought compactness through minimising the lengths of 'flow diagrams'. Housing was the area of design research into which they put most intensive effort, in a three-month research study for the Construction Committee (Stroikom) of the Russian Republic's Economic Soviet (Ekoso RSFSR), during 1928. Here their method was first an analytical, then a synthetic tool, as they investigated the superfluities and inefficiencies of the established apartment types for 'the new way of life', and for the new densities at which people were living. 'Is it possible' they then asked themselves, 'to make a one-roomed apartment [for one couple or family] which is as economic in terms of the standard ratios adopted by Mossoviet as a three-roomed one [now shared by several of them]?' The usual answer was No. 'We have shown it is Yes.' 'On the basis of the new processes of domestic work and way of life, we then devised new sizes and forms of accommodation, analysing the forms we had built up on the basis of movement diagrams and of the schemes of equipment that will serve the accommodation.' The result was a series of six entirely new compact apartment types labelled A-F, mainly one-storeyed but best known for the split-section type, 'F' which Corbusier saw and developed further in his *Unités d'Habitation*. They were ingenious, but their main interest historically lies in the quantified methods by which Ginzburg and his team evaluated their relative merits and established a 'best' design.

The reactions produced when this research was presented to representatives of thirty-five state economic and housing bodies were indicative of the novelty of their approach and the up-hill struggle they faced in advancing any systematic approach to design.[110] Zhukov from the Russian Supreme Economic Soviet, Vesenkha RSFSR, saw that the work was 'unique for embracing the social dimensions of the housing question at the same time as the purely economic ones', and Kurella from the art administration Glav-iskusstvo grasped the originality of 'creating stimulae to the transition from a purely individualistic life to a more collective one', rather than simply imposing the change. Rukhliadev of the Cooperative Housing Union, Tsentrozhilsoiuz, saw this was 'the first time anyone has begun to tackle the question of getting some order into the kitchen'. One Kopeliansky showed a glimmering of deeper understanding when he spoke of the inherent difficulty of resolving such multivariate problems:

'All mathematicians know full well that in order to construct a triangle it is necessary to take not more than three corners, but solution of the task of low-cost housing is a triangle with too many sides, therefore its solution is very difficult.'

Lissitzky, representing Asnova, opined that 'this particular triangle has some 20 sides.'[111] But most comments focussed on insignificant detail in the drawings. Thus when Ginzburg as team-leader concluded the discussion his

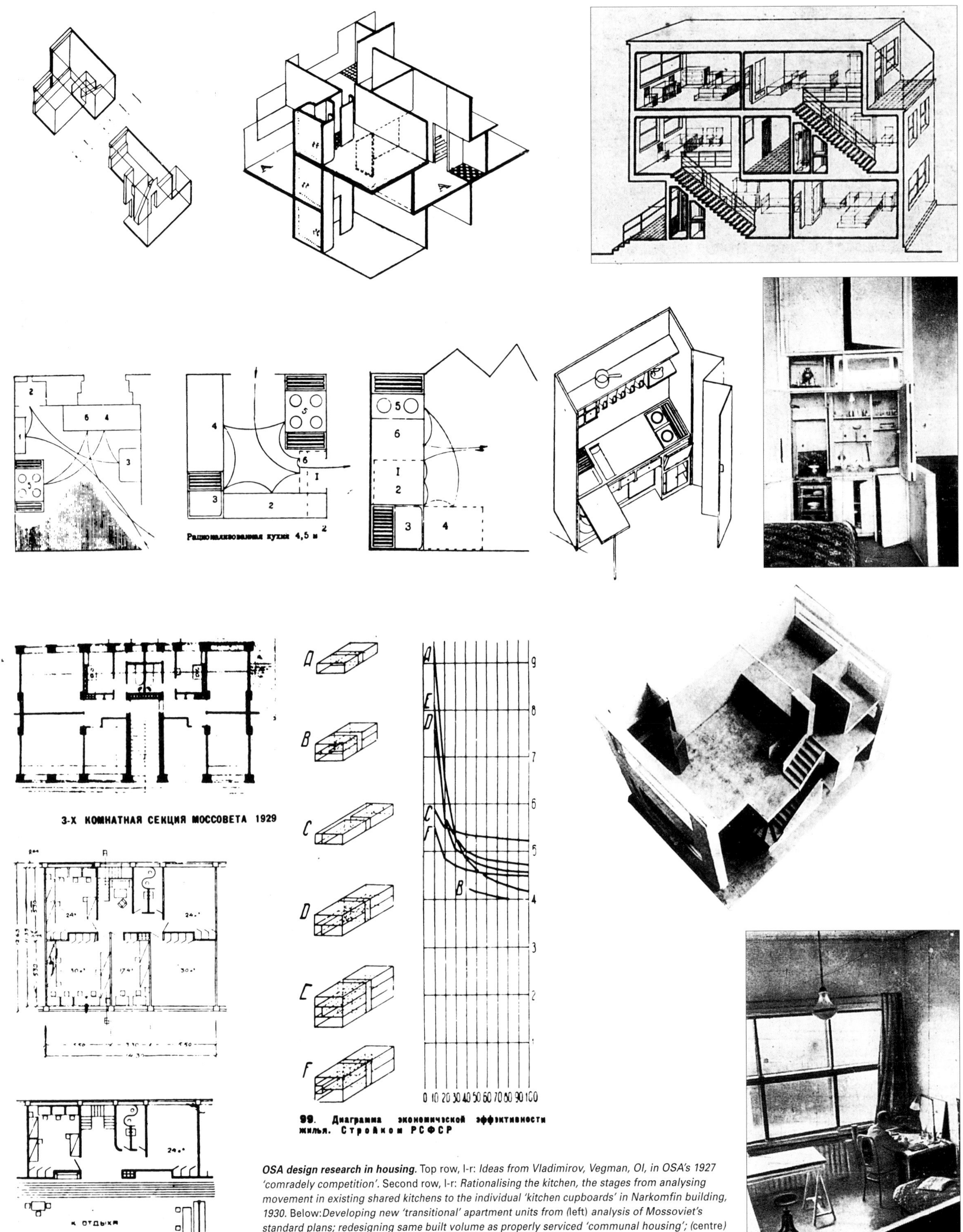

OSA design research in housing. Top row, l-r: *Ideas from Vladimirov, Vegman, Ol, in OSA's 1927 'comradely competition'.* Second row, l-r: *Rationalising the kitchen, the stages from analysing movement in existing shared kitchens to the individual 'kitchen cupboards' in Narkomfin building, 1930.* Below:*Developing new 'transitional' apartment units from* (left) *analysis of Mossoviet's standard plans; redesigning same built volume as properly serviced 'communal housing';* (centre) *graphs of living-to-circulation ratios in six new types, A-F;* (right) *model and photo of Type 'F'.*

exasperation is palpable from the published account, and precisely reflects their own central focus on the conditionality of all solutions, and on working method.

> *'The inadequacy of almost all criticisms we have heard lies in the fact they suppose we have been seeking some kind of universal answer to all our ills. Our work is not outside time and space, but is a response to certain criteria and types defined by Mossoviet, and builds upon certain specific data. ...*
>
> *'I am very surprised also by the fact that no-one amongst our comrades here has said anything about what interests us most of all. We were seeking to validate our method of working, but no-one seems interested to give this any consideration.'* [112]

They had in fact produced very interesting work not just on new housing units, but on the static (i.e. volumetric and areal) parameters of spatial organisations resulting when apartment units were linked by circulation into whole buildings. The work's relevance and originality was recognised by commissions for several demonstration buildings (of which the Narkomfin complex, discussed in Chapter 7 was one), and it was developed in a further contract from Stroikom to produce the new set of 'obligatory designs for use throughout the Russian republic in new housing construction of 1930'.[113] But the time when such socially and technically inventive housing could be 'afforded' was in fact passed, trampled underfoot by the industrial imperatives of the first Five Year Plan. The fate of all their work was represented in microcosm by the fate of this housing research.

More complex interactions of 'flow' factors were the focus of their mathematical arguments with Garden City adherents, on the relative economic and human merits of 'extensive or intensive' residential development. (This is discussed in Chapter 11.) However, as one young founder-member of OSA pointed out in his Vkhutemas final diploma thesis in 1928, whilst these limited and essentially technical studies gave 'undeniably useful results', they were still 'considering requirements too much in isolation'.[114] They did not tackle the problem of synthesis. Ginzburg's conspicuous silence on the nature of the 'reassembly' process in the '5th object' of the functional method made it all too clear that this young Nikolai Krasilnikov was right.

Here in the very heart of the architect's province, any question of 'a scientific ... replacement for the habitual intuitive-graphic method of designing [had] hardly been broached' he insisted.[115] In his own diploma work and in a joint paper with fellow-student Lidiia Komarova in the next year, Krasilnikov 'tried to open up this question ... and to creep towards ... a mathematical-graphic method' of solving it.[116]

Krasilnikov was convinced that:

> *'A scientific theory of the design of form is possible through the dialectical method of thinking by the application of mathematical methods of analysis; that is, by analysis which uses the infinitesimal concepts underlying analytical geometry and the differential and integral calculus, and the theories of probability and mathematical statistics.'* [117]

His thesis was devoted to demonstrating how these techniques could be used to optimise 'the actual form of the building' in terms of 'the material resources for constructing and running it'; 'amortisation and repairs'; 'the time spent by people in all kinds of movement'; 'amortisation of the health of the individual', which was a function of 'sanitary-technical and psychological factors'; the extent to which 'conditions in particular parts of it favour the maximum "productivity" of mental or physical work and of leisure'. His particular objective was 'the building form which diverges least from the maxima or minima of each of these factors' whilst also achieving 'the maximum cubic volume of building on a given site area'. At the planning scale, he then optimised 'conditions of daylighting, exposure to wind, and ventilation of the whole administrative complex, and links between this building and other parts of the town'.[118] An edited version of his mathematical paper appears as Document 30 in Chapter 10 with its key illustrations.

As architecture, Krasilnikov's circular town of skyscraper office-blocks was somewhat traditionally conceived, but his concern was as ever with method. His attempt to combine objective factors of building science with parameters of human space use in the same evaluation process was important. His procedure for optimising, however, remained linear. He established the 'best' spatial configurations 'in relation to each of these factors individually'. He still started from the optimal flow diagram – albeit one now defined in greater detail, and probabilistically – and compared that to other optima by inspection, in a pre-established order of priorities. Thus far he had not moved beyond the linear *konstruktsiia* of the functional method under which he had been taught.

Krasilnikov recognised this, as he did the primitiveness of his techniques by the standards of 'higher mathematics', even then. In the subsequent paper with Komarova he recognised that this was still essentially the age-old process whereby the architect examines a series of discrete, alternative forms 'and divines empirically ... the most successful combinations of those variants he has put to the test'. Under the title 'A method of investigating the generation of building form' they declared, 'Our aim must be to advance this process in order to make possible an objective scientific assessment of all the possible variants available to the designer.'[119]

It was the conceptual step embodied in that 'all' which was historically important. Since Rodchenko first spoke of 'showing the designer how he may assemble *all possible* constructions' (my italics), this concept of exhaustiveness had remained a chimera to them even in Rodchenko's easier field of form generation, far less in relation to evaluation.

From the premise that 'the form of any body is a function of many variables', Krasilnikov and Komarova argued that a dialectical process takes place in which even purely quantitative changes in the brief lead to a qualitatively different form, and the 'correct' form emerges from a resolution of competing or conflicting demands. Moving beyond the series of discrete alternatives they saw that 'a continuous sequence of variants therefore exists' for which 'we can build up into a surface, or system of curves in space' on which to locate their optimum solutions.[120] The paper is discussed further in Chapter 10.

This clear mathematical formulation of the concept of a multi-dimensional solution 'surface' seems to be unique in the architectural context for its time. It was to be about four decades before automated data-processing techniques emerged and any architects started handling the enormous computational operations involved in an integrated, multi-variate optimisation of this kind. This work was the high point of the Constructivist architects' research in the methodological field, which was their central interest and as they saw it, their central ideological responsibility.

With his realistic understanding of engineering, Ginzburg's 'functional method' was an almost literal response to the observation in Bukharin and Preobrazhensky's *ABC of Communism*, of 1919, that 'Marx's chief instruction to his followers was that they should study life as it actually is, ... precisely after the manner in which we might study a machine.'[121] In its *konstruktsiia*, his whole, essentially linear process was also rooted in a mechanical analogy. With their grasp of mathematics, Krasilnikov and Komarova sought to indicate the ultimate implications for architecture of a remark from Engels' *Dialectics and Natural Science*, and the almost identical one from Lenin which headed their papers, that 'In order to really know an object, it is necessary to comprehend, to study, all aspects of it: all its internal and external connectivities.' With this concept they brought the functional method several stages closer to later concepts of systems theory, and to later techniques for solving such multi-variate problems. The same two, canonical, ideas had lain behind the early Constructivists' redefinition of design as a function of '*tektonika, faktura* and *konstruktsiia*', but whilst the content and interrelationships of these three 'disciplines' remained ill-defined, their's was a very general model.

As a group, the Constructivist architects refuted charges of trying 'to eliminate the aesthetic emotion'. They were merely seeking to recognise that 'the character of it has changed under the influence of changed conditions of life, new economic priorities and new technology'.[122] Nor, Ginzburg insisted, did 'the functional method of thinking in any way eliminate the extremely complex tasks of architectural form-making'; 'it merely establishes a framework of procedures for that process'.[123]

In what sense was their approach Marxist?

These architects, like most of their contemporaries, had little background in the Marxist philosophy on which they premised their design approach. Like the vast majority of Soviet people at that date, they had only the most cursory grasp of its history or its theory. Their understanding of its implications reduced itself to five essential principles.

First, it meant concerning oneself with reality and how it really operates. As Gan wrote in his *Constructivism* in 1922, quoting Marx in *The Poverty of Philosophy*:

> *'The theoreticians of the proletariat must set themselves the cognitive task of giving themselves an account of what is really going on in front of their eyes, and of becoming the interpreters and explainers of that reality.'*[124]

Second, it meant looking at problems and events in their total context, not compartmentalising them off from factors that were in reality having an influence on them. This was the sense in which their's was essentially a 'systems' view. It meant not artificially dividing the world into 'designed' material and stuff not worthy of 'design'; not separating design from social and economic determinants. This is what Gan spelt out in his definitions of *tektonika, faktura* and *konstruktsiia*. In Rodchenko's design teaching and in the Constructivist architects' design method these were articulated in far greater detail.

Third, being Marxist meant looking at things in terms of how they are changing. As Communist Party Secretary Kaganovich said, talking of housing and planning in 1931, 'It would be entirely un-Marxist to try to foresee what exactly the form of the communist way of life will be in the distant future: we know only that it will change.'[125] Ginzburg embodied precisely this in his principle, enunciated in 'Constructivism as a method', that 'form is a function, x, which must always be evaluated anew by the architect ... in accordance with changes in the form-making situation'.

Fourth, it meant recognising their own place within a collective process. Specifically, this meant that design was no longer to be (in Gan's words), 'the product of extreme individualism'.[126] As Ginzburg put it later, 'Abstracted and individualistic inspiration' must be replaced by 'a precise elucidation of the unknowns of the problem and pursuit of the correct method of solution.'[127] That 'precise elucidation' demanded maximum possible objectivity, and the collective responsibility meant operating through an 'open' process that could be participatory and accountable.

Fifth and finally, it meant seeing the products of their work as proactive, as agents of specific social change. In Filippov's words of 1921 it meant 'applying to artists K. Marx's idea about scholars and scientists', that instead of merely depicting or describing the world, 'their task is to change it'.[128] Instead of merely providing passive commentaries on the social structure and values around them, or just 'following in the tail of events' – the heinous political offence of *khvostizm* – their buildings must be, as Gan envisaged them, actively 'revolutionary'. In Ginzburg's phrase, they must 'work', in a materialist sense, as active 'social condensers'.

Whilst far from denying the elegance of the architectural forms they produced, these were ultimately the criteria by which the Constructivist architects judged the success or unsuccess of their own labour.

■

1 *Sovremennaia arkhitektura* (Contemporary Architecture, or *SA*), 1928, no.6 p.170 **2** M Ginzburg, 'Konstruktivizm kak metod laboratornoi i pedagogicheskoi raboty' (Constructivism as a method of laboratory and teaching work), *SA*, 1927, no.6, pp.160-6 **3** V. Mayakovsky, *Kak delat' stikhi?* (How to make poems), Moscow, 1926. My translation is from an edition of 1931. For an English translation of the whole book, with excellent commentary and introduction, see V. Mayakovsky, *How are verses made?*, translated etc by George Hyde, Bristol, 1990. **4** V. I. Lenin, 'Speech to the Third All-Russian Congress of the Komsomol', 2 October 1920, in Lenin, *Collected Works*, vol.31, Moscow, 1965, pp.283-99 **5** 'Ot redaktsii' (From the Editors), *Proletarskaia kul'tura* (Proletarian Culture), no.3, (Aug 1918), p.36, quoted in Z. A. Sochor, *Revolution and Culture: The Bogdanov-Lenin Controversy*, Cornell, 1988, p.148. The extent to which Bogdanov became a non-person can be seen from a Soviet study such as V. V. Gorbunov, *V. I. Lenin i proletku'lt*, Polit-izdat, Moscow, 1974. **6** A. Bogdanov, 'Puti proletarskogo tvorchestva (Paths of proletarian creative work), *Proletarskaia kul'tura*, no.15/16, 1920, pp.50-52, translated in J. Bowlt, ed., *Russian Art of the Avant-Garde: Theory and Criticism 1902-1934*, London-New York, 1976, pp.178-82 **7** Lenin, 'Speech to the Third All-Russian Congress of the Komsomol'. **8** M. Ginzburg, 'Tselevaia ustanovka v sovremennoi arkhitekture' (Aims in contemporary architecture), *SA*, 1927, no.1 pp.4-10 **9** N Krasil'nikov, 'Problemy sovremennoi arkhitektury' (Problems of contemporary architecture), *SA*, 1928, no.6, pp.170-6 **10** In *SA*, 1926, no.1 he speaks of a 'metod funktsional'nogo tvorchestva'; in no.4 he speaks of 'metod funktsional'nogo myshleniia' though the article is entitled 'Funktsional'nyi metod', and through 1927 onwards that phrase appears generally. **11** M. Ginzburg, 'Konstruktivizm v arkhitekture' (Constructivism in architecture), *SA*, 1928, no.5, pp.143-5 **12** Ginzburg, 'Konstruktivizm v arkhitekture', p.144, quoting Firkant's *Dualism in the Contemporary World View*, via Adolf Bene's *Der Moderne Zweckbau* **13** Ginzburg, 'Konstruktivizm kak metod' **14** ibid **15** ibid **16** ibid **17** L. Zhadova, ed., *Tatlin*, Budapest, 1984 & London, 1988; A. Strigalev & J. Harten, comp., *Vladimir Tatlin: Retrospektive*, Cologne, 1993; S. O. Khan-Magomedov, *Rodchenko*, London, 1986; S. O. Khan-Magomedov, *Inkhuk i rannii konstruktivizm* (Inkhuk and early Constructivism), Moscow, 1994 **18** M. Ginzburg, 'Konstruktivizm v arkhitekture'.**19** ibid, and M. Ginzburg, 'Funktsional'nyi metod i forma' (The functional method and form), *SA*, 1926, no.4, p.89 **20** See for example K. P. Zygas, 'Tatlin's Tower reconsidered', *Architectural Association Quarterly*, vol.8, no.2, 1976, pp.15-27; J. Milner, *Vladimir Tatlin and the Russian Avant-Garde*, Yale, 1983, pp.151-80 **21** N. Punin, *Pamiatnik III Internatsionala* (The monument to the Third International), Izo-Narkompros, Petersburg (sic), 1920 **22** Lecture, 1 May 1969, Cambridge; a version published in: P Coe & M Reading, *Lubetkin and Tecton*, London & Bristol, 1981, pp.191-9 **23** V. E. Tatlin, T. Shapiro, I. Meerzon, P. Vinogradov, 'Nasha predstoishchaia rabota' (The work ahead of us), *VIII s"ezd sovetov: ezhednevnyi biulleten' s"ezda* (8th Congress of Soviets: Daily Congress Bulletin), Moscow, no.13, 1 Jan 1921, p.11 **24** ibid **25** Khan-Magomedov, *Rodchenko*, pp.83-99; Khan-Magomedov, *Inkhuk i rannii konstruktivizm*, pp.36-72; 89-112 *26* The authoritative text appears in Khan-Magomedov, *Inkhuk i rannii konstructivizm*, pp.95-6, its origins explained on p.91. An approximate version, first published in the West in *Egyseg*, Vienna, 1922, appears as 'The programme of the Productivist Group' in S. Bann, ed., *The Tradition of Constructivism*, London, 1974, pp.18-20, also in N. Gabo, *Gabo*, London 1957 **27** Khan-Magomedov, *Inkhuk i rannii konstruktivizm*, pp.232-3 **28** A. Filippov, 'Proizvodstvennoe iskusstvo' (Production art), *Iskusstvo v proizvodstve* (Art in production), no.1, 1921, pp.9-12. An English translation appears in Bann, *The Tradition*, pp.22-25 **29** Filippov, 'Proizvodstvennoe iskusstvo', p.10 **30** Paper of Alexei Gan to Inkhuk, 28 March 1921, 'O programme i plane rabot Gruppy konstruktivistov' (On the programme and work plan of the Group of Constructivists), full text in Khan-Magomedov, *Inkhuk i rannii konstruktivizm*, pp.98-100 **31** A. Gan, *Konstruktivizm* (Constructivism), Tver, 1922 **32** Bann, *The Tradition*, pp.32-42; Bowlt, *Russian Art*, pp.221-5 **33** Gan, *Konstruktivizm*, pp.20; 53 **34** ibid, p.55 **35** ibid, p.61 **36** See verbatim texts of their discussions in Khan-Magomedov, *Rodchenko*, pp.93-4; Khan-Magomedov, *Inkhuk i rannii konstructivizm*, pp.102-7 **37** Gan, *Konstruktivizm*, p.61-2 **38** ibid, p.62 **39** ibid, p.65 **40** cf D Elliott, ed., *Alexander Rodchenko*, Oxford 1979, p.46 **41** Gan, *Konstruktivizm*, p.64 **42** ibid, p.53 **43** The professional association of Academy-trained architects, for example, was the Obshchestvo arkhitektorov-khudozhnikov (OAKh, Society of Architect-Artists), as opposed to the more catholic Petersburgskoe obshchestvo arkhitektorov, (POA, Petersburg Society of Architects) **44** A. Vesnin, 'Credo', in M. G. Barkhin, ed., *Mastera sovetskoi arkhitektury ob arkhitekture* (Masters of Soviet Architecture on Architecture), Moscow, 1975, vol.2, p.14. Ms. reproduced in facsimile in Khan-Magomedov, *Inkhuk i rannii konstruktivizm*, pp.226-7 **45** A. Lunacharsky, 'Revoliutsiia i iskusstvo' (Revolution and art), *Kommunisticheskoe prosveshchenie* (Communist enlightenment), 1920, no.1, translated in Bowlt, *Russian Art*, pp.190-3 **46** Gan, *Konstruktivizm*, p.63 **47** ibid. p.63 **48** ibid, p.64 **49** He discusses these limitations in M. Ginzburg, *Stil' i epokha* (Style and Epoch), Moscow, 1924, pp.9-10 **50** R.O.G. Urch, *We Generally Shoot Englishmen*, London, 1936, pp.27-8 **51** *Sredi kollektsionerov*, articles in 1921, nos.11-12; 1922, nos.1, 3, 7-8 **52** *Arkhitektura*, monthly of MAO; only 2 issues published: 1923, nos.1-2; 3-4 **53** V. Semionov, 'Ocherednye zadachi' (Priority tasks), *Arkhitektura*, 1923, no 1-2, pp.28-30 **54** Editorial, 'Estetika sovremennosti' (Aesthetics of contemporaneity), *Arkhitektura*, 1923, no.1-2, pp.3-6 **55** N T Savel'eva, 'Organizatsiia nauki ob arkhitekture v gosudarstvennoi akademii khudozhestvennykh nauk' (The organisation of architectural research in Rakhn-Gakhn), in A A Strigalev, ed, *Problemy istorii sovetskoi arkhitektury* (Problems of the History of Soviet Architecture), Moscow 1983, pp.48-56; *Iskusstvo: zhurnal Rakhn* (Art: Journal of Rakhn), no.1, Moscow, 1923, pp.5-12, 407-13, et al; also Bowlt, *Russian Art*, pp.196-8 **56** Savel'eva, 'Organizatsiia', p.53 **57** Ginzburg, *Stil' i epokha*. For an English translation with Introduction and extensive notes see M. Ginzburg, *Style and Epoch*, introduced and translated by A. Senkevitch, Jr, Cambridge Mass., 1982 **58** I. V. Kokkinaki, 'K voprosu o vzaimosviazakh sovetskikh i zarubezhynkh arkhitektorov v 1920-1930-e gody' (On the connections between Soviet and foreign architects in the 1920s and 1930s), in *Voprosy sovetskogo izobrazitel'nogo iskusstva i arkhitektury* (Questions of Soviet Fine Art and Architecture), Moscow, 1976, pp. 350-82. She also mentions that Lunacharsky published a translation of 'Les yeux qui ne voient pas' in the journal he edited, *Khudozhestvennyi trud* (Artistic Labour), 1923, no.2 pp.25-8 **59** Edgar Norvert, 'Obzor zhurnalov', *Arkhitektura*, 1923 no.1-2 pp.42-4 **60** Letter from L. Vesnin, archival material quoted in A G. Chiniakov, *Brat'ia Vesniny* (The Vesnin Brothers), Moscow, 1970, p.99 **61** Gan, *Konstruktivizm*, p.54 **62** A.V. Kuznetsov, 'Arkhitektura i zhelezobeton' (Architecture and reinforced concrete), *Zodchii* (The Architect), 1915, no.19-20; version of a speech to the 5th Congress of Russian Architects, Moscow, 1913 **63** Ginzburg, *Stil' i epokha*, p.13 **64** ibid, pp.13-20 **65** ibid, pp.119-20; on the cultural dimension he refers to Russian editions of N. Danilevsky's *Russia and Europe*,1888, and O. Spengler's *Der Untergang des Abendlandes*, 1923 **66** Ginzburg, *Stil' i epokha*, pp.78, 73-89, 121 **67** ibid, p.121 **68** ibid, p.111 **69** ibid, p.121 **70** ibid, p.94 **71** ibid, p.93 **72** ibid, p.131 **73** ibid, pp.128-9 **74** ibid, p.132 **75** ibid, p.133 **76** ibid, p.134 **77** Prof. V.K. Karpovich, review of Ginzburg's *Stil' i epokha*, in *Kommunal'noe khoziaistvo* (The Communal Economy), 1925, no.2, pp.167-8 **78** A. V. Rozenberg, *Filosofiia arkhitektury* (A Philosophy of Architecture), Petrograd, 1923 **79** E.Norvert, 'Priemy planirovki', in V N Semionov, ed, *Udeshevlenie stroitel'stva*, Moscow, 1925, pp.15-26 **80** '*SA* privetstvuet vykhod ASNOVA' (*SA* greets the publication of [*Izvestiia*] *ASNOVA*), *SA*, 1926, n.2, p.59 **81** M. Ginzburg, 'Itogi i perspektivy' (Achievements and prospects), *SA*, 1927, no.4-5, pp.112-8. For an English translation see T. & C. Benton, D, Sharp, eds., *Form and Function. A Source Book*, London, 1975, pp.156-60 **82** On the founding of OSA see: V. E. Khazanova, comp., *Iz istorii sovetskoi arkhitektury 1926-32; dokumenty i materialy*, Moscow, 1970, pp.65-8 **83** M Ginzburg, 'Novye metody arkhitekturnogo myshleniia', *SA*, 1926, no.1, pp.1-4 **84** Ginzburg, 'Funktsional'nyi metod' & 'Tselevaia ustanovka' **85** Ginzburg, *Stil' i epokha*, later parts of Chapter 1 **86** Ginzburg, 'Novye metody', p.1 **87** ibid, p.2 **88** K. Akashev, 'Forma samoleta i metody ego proektirovaniia', *SA*, 1926, no.3, pp.65-6. See translation in Chapter 6 below. **89** Ginzburg, 'Novye metody', pp.1, 3 **90** ibid, pp.3-4 **91** Ginzburg, 'Funktsional'nyi metod', p.89 **92** ibid, p.89 **93** Ginzburg, 'Tselevaia ustanovka', p.6 **94** A. Gastev, *Poeziia rabochego udara* (Poetry of the working class attack), Moscow, 1918. On his Central Institute of Work (TsIT) the richest source is R. Fülöp-Miller, *The Mind and Face of Bolshevism*, London-New York, 1927, pp.205-16. On other aspects of its influence see N. Misler, 'Designing gestures in the laboratory of dance', in N. van Norman Baer, ed., *Theatre in Revolution: Russian avant-garde stage design 1913-35*, London-San Francisco, 1992, pp.157-70 **95** L. & A. Vesnin, 'Konkursnyi proekt' (Competition scheme), *SA*, 1926, no.2, p.53 **96** Ginzburg, 'Tselevaia ustanovka', p.6 **97** ibid, p.7 **98** Gan, *Konstruktivizm*, p.65 **99** Ginzburg, 'Konstruktivizm kak metod', p.165 **100** On Leningrad OSA see Khazanova, comp., *Iz istorii 1926-1932*, p.85 **101** On Chernikhov's theories and teaching see C. Cooke. *Chernikhov: Fantasy and Construction. Iakov Chernikhov's Approach to Architectural Design*, Architectural Design Profile, no.55, London, 1984 **102** Ia. G. Chernikhov, *Konstruktsiia arkhitekturnykh i mashinykh form* (The Construction of Architectural and Machine Forms), Leningrad, 1931, pp.93-96. NOTE: All Chernikhov's theoretical and teaching work dates from middle-late Twenties though his main books were not published till the end of the decade. I have therefore not quoted publication dates in the text as they somewhat misrepresent the real chronology of ideas. **103** Ia.G. Chernikhov, *Osnovy sovremennoi arkhitektury* (Fundamentals of Contemporary Architecture), Leningrad, second edition, 1931, p.49. This book was first published in a slightly different format in 1930. **104** Chernikhov, *Osnovy* (1931) , pp.58-9. See also Cooke, *Fantasy and Construction*. **105** Chernikhov, *Osnovy* (1931), p.51 **106** Chernikhov, *Konstruktsiia*, p.139 **107** Ia. G. Chernikhov, *Arkhitekturnye fantazii: 101 kompozitsii v kraskakh* (Architectural Fictions: 101 Compositions in Colour), Leningrad, 1933, p.43 **108** R. Khiger, review, in *SA*, 1930, no.3, inside back cover. **109** Ginzburg, 'Tselevaia ustanovka', p.10 **110** 'Slushali: Problemy tipizatsii zhil'ia RSFSR. Doklad M. Ia. Ginzburga' (They listened: the problem of housing standardisation in the Russian Republic. Lecture by M.Ia. Ginzburg). His lecture on Constructivist housing proposals and subsequent discussion amongst specialists in Stroikom RSFSR, *SA*, 1929, no.1, pp.4-36 **111** 'Slushali', pp.6, 12, 22, 26, 28. **112** 'Slushali', p.30 **113** V.I. Vel'man, ed., *Tipovye proekty i konstruktsii zhilishchnogo stroitel'stva rekomenduemye na 1930g* (Standard designs for housing construction recommended for use in the 1930 season), Moscow, 1929. Besides the Narkomfin complex at ul. Chaikovskogo, 25B, others in Moscow were at Gogol bd, 8, and at Galushkina ul., Rostokino. For provincial projects see M. Ginzburg, *Zhilishche* (Housing), Moscow, 1934. On the broader social context of this work see V.A. Buchli, 'Narkomfin *dom-kommuna* Moscow', PhD thesis, Cambridge 1995 **114** Krasil'nikov, 'Problemy' **115** ibid, p 170 **116** ibid, and N. Krasil'nikov and L. Komarova, 'Metod issledovaniia formobrazovaniia sooruzheniia' (A method of investigating the generation of building form), *SA*, 1929, no.5 pp.183-4 **117** Krasil'nikov, 'Problemy', p.170 **118** ibid, pp.174-5 **119** Krasil'nikov and Komarova, 'Metod', p 183 **120** ibid, pp 183-4 **121** N. Bukharin and E. Preobrazhensky, *Azbuka kommunisma* (The ABC of Communism), 1919; London, 1969, pp 66-7 **122** Ginzburg, *Stil' i epokha*, p.122 **123** Ginzburg, 'Funktsional'nyi metod', p 89 **124** Gan, *Konstruktivizm*, p.12 **125** L.M. Kaganovich, 'O Moskovskom gorodskom khoziaistve i o razvitiem gorodskogo khoziaistva SSSR' (On the Moscow urban economy and on the development of the urban economy of the USSR), speech of L. Kaganovich to the June Plenum of the Communist Party Centre Committee, *Pravda*, 4 July 1931, pp.3-4 **126** Gan, *Konstruktivizm*, p.18 **127** Ginzburg, 'Novye metody', p.1 **128** Filippov, 'Proizvodstvennoe iskusstvo', p.10.

Doc. 6

MOISEI GINZBURG: Development of ideas in the 'functional method' through his writings of 1923-4 to 1927: resumé

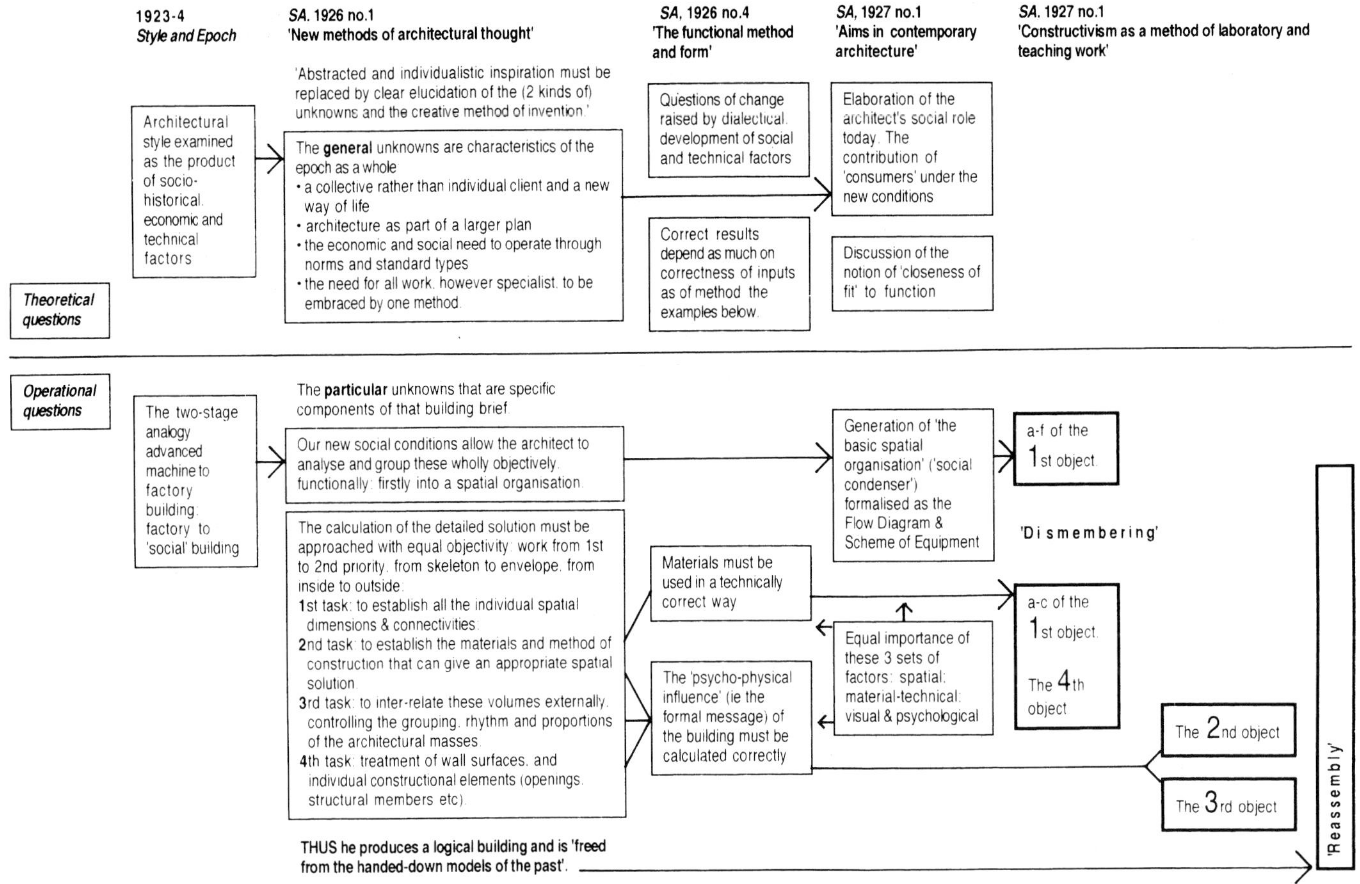

1923-4
Style and Epoch
SA, 1926 no.1
'New methods of architectural thought'
SA, 1926 no.4
'The functional method and form'
SA, 1927 no.1
'Aims in contemporary architecture'
SA, 1927 no.1
'Constructivism as a method of laboratory and teaching work'
Theoretical questions
Architectural style examined as the product of socio-historical, economic and technical factors
'Abstracted and individualistic inspiration must be replaced by clear elucidation of the (2 kinds of) unknowns and the creative method of invention.'
The **general** unknowns are characteristics of the epoch as a whole
• a collective rather than individual client and a new way of life
• architecture as part of a larger plan
• the economic and social need to operate through norms and standard types
• the need for all work, however specialist, to be embraced by one method
Questions of change raised by dialectical development of social and technical factors
Correct results depend as much on correctness of inputs as of method: the examples below.
Elaboration of the architect's social role today. The contribution of 'consumers' under the new conditions
Discussion of the notion of 'closeness of fit' to function
Operational questions
The two-stage analogy advanced: machine to factory building, factory to 'social' building
The **particular** unknowns that are specific components of that building brief
Our new social conditions allow the architect to analyse and group these wholly objectively, functionally: firstly into a spatial organisation.
The calculation of the detailed solution must be approached with equal objectivity: work from 1st to 2nd priority, from skeleton to envelope, from inside to outside.
1st task: to establish all the individual spatial dimensions & connectivities.
2nd task: to establish the materials and method of construction that can give an appropriate spatial solution
3rd task: to inter-relate these volumes externally, controlling the grouping, rhythm and proportions of the architectural masses.
4th task: treatment of wall surfaces, and individual constructional elements (openings, structural members etc).
Materials must be used in a technically correct way
The 'psycho-physical influence' (ie the formal message) of the building must be calculated correctly
Generation of 'the basic spatial organisation' ('social condenser') formalised as the Flow Diagram & Scheme of Equipment
Equal importance of these 3 sets of factors: spatial; material-technical; visual & psychological
a-f of the 1st object
'Dismembering'
a-c of the 1st object
The 4th object
The 2nd object
The 3rd object
'Reassembly'
THUS he produces a logical building and is 'freed from the handed-down models of the past'.

Doc. 7

MOISEI GINZBURG
HOUSING COMPLEX FOR EMPLOYEES OF NARKOMFIN, MOSCOW
SA, 1929, no.5, pp.161-2

This complex is required to accommodate fifty families who would largely retain their old individual character. It is therefore of a 'transitional' rather than fully communal type.

1: The dwelling block. This mainly comprises types F and K worked out with my colleagues in Stroikom RSFSR. Access to the two floors of type F, above, is by a glazed corridor on the fourth floor. Access to type K units below is from an open balcony-corridor at first floor. These are the horizontal arteries of the building, connecting to the staircases at each end and by the first-floor bridge to the communal centre.

The whole living block is raised on circular columns so that no-one lives at ground level (which is always considered lower value), and the park flows underneath. There is another garden on the roof.

2: The communal centre. This comprises two double height storeys, each with mezzanine. The lower one is a sports hall. The communal dining room, reading and other recreational rooms are above, with summer dining on the roof. Two separate buildings will contain the children's centre, and laundry, garaging etc.

My colleague in design and execution is I.F. Milinis. Structural engineer is S.L. Prokhorov of Tekhbeton.

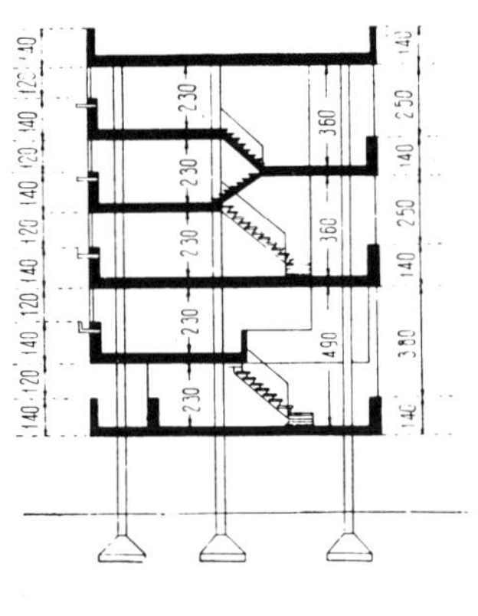

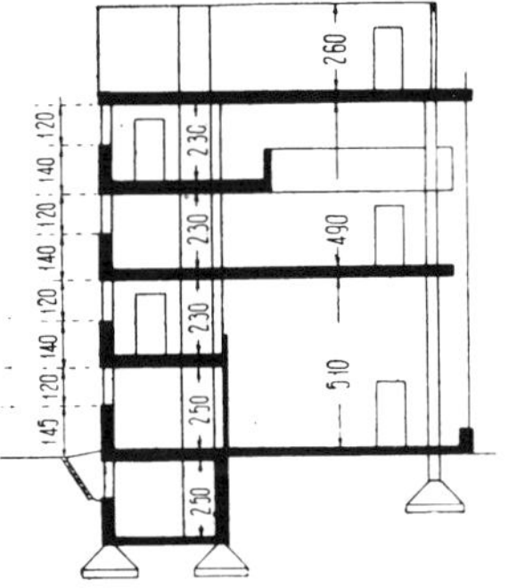

Right: *Inhabitants on the terrace outside the communal centre, photographed soon after completion in 1930.*
Far right: *Sections: top, the dwelling block with types F above (see p.116) and K below; bottom, the communal centre with dining and recreational rooms above and sports hall below.*

Doc. 8

The Constructivist architects' 'functional method': diagrammatic resumé of MOISEI GINZBURG, 'Constructivism as a method of laboratory and teaching work', SA, 1927, no.6, pp.160-6

Dismembering: **The 1st object is to establish the FORM of the SOCIAL CONDENSER as the product of:**

Consideration of all the PRECONDITIONS: both REQUIREMENTS and POSSIBILITIES.

1: The social and productive preconditions of the BRIEF:

- a **Study of how these preconditions may CHANGE through social and technological changes**, stressing not the dimensions but the dynamic of how use of spaces is changing over time.
- b **Build up the FLOW DIAGRAMS** - from local ones to the overall one, which is THE FIRST SPATIAL DIAGRAM OF THE BUILDING.
- c **Study the SCHEMES OF EQUIPMENT** that these require.
- d **Establish the DIMENSIONS of that equipment**, and the correct SPATIAL PLACING of it.
- e **Study the ENVIRONMENTAL REQUIREMENTS** of the activities and processes taking place: temperature, light, accoustics.
- f **Build up from this the scheme of the SOCIAL CONDENSER**, establishing an integrated organism as a SPATIAL PROTOTYPE.

2: The technical and constructional preconditions of the REALISATION:

- a **Study of BUILDING MATERIALS at the architect's disposal**, stressing the maximally revolutionary reassessment of them, as far as possible using the most ADVANCED, ie the MINIMUM MASS.
- b **Study of the STRUCTURAL METHODS AND SOLUTIONS that are appropriate** in relation to preconditions of the brief; study their character and technical possibilities, stressing the most RATIONAL construction methods in relation to their SPATIAL POSSIBILITIES.
- c **Study of the conditions and methods of PRACTICAL REALISATION involved** in relation to each detail and the architectural whole, the actual METHODS OF BUILDING, seeking the maximum INDUSTRIALISATION, 'assembly' rather than 'building', with all its architectural consequences.

Consideration of PERCEPTION and VISUAL CLARITY.

The 2nd object is to thus look at the MATERIAL FORMS crystalised as the social condenser, in terms of the PROBLEM OF PERCEPTION, so the useful activity of the condenser is enhanced by users' clear perception of it.

Constructivism sees FORM as ACTIVE, not passive. It considers the ORGANISATION OF PERCEPTION of equal importance to the organisation of material factors.

There are 2 stages to this:

A: The following must be studied IN ORDER, from PARTICULAR properties of the particular object, to GENERAL questions:

1. **The FUNCTIONAL CHARACTER of the object, its purpose**
2. **Its STATE - static or moving?**

→ A: Perception in respect of the object's fundamental characteristics

3. **Material - its properties and faktura, colour etc**
4. **The RELATIVE SCALES of parts and whole**
5. **The TEKTONIC STRUCTURE of the object: how it is structured; the links of parts and whole; the principles by which its parts are related.** → C: Perception of UNITY and WHOLENESS
6. **FORM AS A BOUNDARY, a 3-D volume, a defined space**

→ (3–6) D: How to ORGANISE PERCEPTION to make CLEAR the relationships of the elements comprising the object, their absolute & relative SIZES, clarity of the OVERALL SPATIAL FORM.

7. **The main distinguishing marks of the object as a SPATIAL ORGANISATION** → B: Perception in respect of SPATIAL INTER-RELATIONSHIPS and of SPACE in general.

B: In relation to the perception of these characteristics, **the second stage** of the studies **ARE THEN GROUPED AS ABOVE, A to D**

Consideration of the RATIONAL USE of the FORMAL ELEMENTS of the architecture.

The 3rd object is to study THOSE ELEMENTS OF ARCHITECTURE ITSELF which are the OBJECTS OF PERCEPTION, namely, in order of COMPLEXITY:

A: SURFACE **B: VOLUME, as a system of surfaces**
C: The volumetric coexistence OF MANY BODIES (intersecting, or contiguous, or related but separate)
D: SPACE: TIME and MOVEMENTS as METHODS OF ORGANISING SPACE; space as the inter-relation of individual volumes TO EACH OTHER and the whole; LOCATION of an object in space; space as an ISOLATING factor; space as the ORGANISATION of UNRELATED or PARTIALLY RELATED dimensions (space-street-town)

TWO IMPORTANT PRINCIPLES are to be observed THROUGHOUT THIS PROCESS:

1: None of this laboratory dismemberment must concern itself with ARTISTIC EXPRESSIVENESS IN GENERAL, for Constructivism only understands expressiveness CONCRETELY, in relation to DEFINITE AIMS AND INTENTIONS, as something specific to its context.

2: All such studies carry the basic danger of CANONISATION of certain forms, of their becoming fixed elements of the architect's vocabulary. Constructivism is LEADING THE BATTLE against this phenomenon, and it studies these basic elements of architecture as something CONTINUOUSLY CHANGING in connection with the changing preconditions of the form-making situation. It NEVER ADMITS therefore the FIXING OF FORMS. **Form is an unknown, 'x', which is always evaluated anew by the architect.**

Therefore we have ALSO TO STUDY not just the ELEMENTS OF ARCHITECTURE, but the METHODS OF THEIR TRANSFORMATION; we have to study HOW THAT UNKNOWN, 'X', CHANGES, **how changes in the brief affect the FORM.**

Amongst such TYPES OF TRANSFORMATION we may include:

1. Change in the building's external relationships;
2. Vertical or horizontal dismemberment of it;
3. Cutting of the surface or volume from inside (doors, windows etc)
4. Cutting of the surface or volume from outside (change of silhouette);
5. Difference in the material, colour or faktura;
6. Change in the spatial relationships of parts;
7. Introduction of mobility into the parts or the whole;
8. Introduction of new (working) elements, and so on.

In all this, 3 things are vital:

1: This method of transformations is PART OF THE ARCHITECT'S REAL, PRACTICAL TOOLS;
2: That TRANSFORMATION involves not just AESTHETICS, but reorganisation of the WORKING, CONSTRUCTIVE ELEMENTS;
3: That what we are changing is the MATERIAL OBJECT, but this is done IN THE CONTEXT OF ITS ESSENTIAL PURPOSE, and of its PERCEPTION BY THE USER.

Consideration of the POSSIBILITIES of INDUSTRIALISED BUILDING.

The 4th object is the study of INDUSTRIAL PROCESSES, not as FETISHISM, not to IMITATE industrial FORMS, but to identify THOSE CHARACTERISTICS that will be the HALLMARKS OF INDUSTRIALISATION in ARCHITECTURE. Thus we study:

1: How industrial technology CREATES a functional form. **2:** The particular industrial processes which LEAVE A STAMP on the character of its products.

This must be done both in relation to INDIVIDUAL COMPONENTS of the building and in relation to WHOLE ORGANISMS within it (kitchens etc).

Reassembly: **The 5th object is the RESTORATION OF ORGANIC WHOLENESS.**
This applies whether the functional method is being used for ANALYSIS of an EXISTING DESIGN, or for CREATION OF A NEW ONE.
Either of these involves all four objects above.

6: GINZBURG AND LE CORBUSIER: ENGINEERING AND THE MODERN STATE OF MIND

One glance at a building like Ginzburg's Narkomfin housing complex is enough to indicate that Corbusier was a major influence on the Constructivist architects. But the influence, as I have already indicated in Chapter 5, went far deeper than 'style' or even the subtler questions embodied in Corbusier's 'Five Points'.[1] The Constructivists revered him from the beginning of their activity as someone who 'opened our eyes' and had taught them how to analyse. Boris Korshunov, a contemporary of the Vesnins, wrote in the first issue of *SA* in mid-1926, of how they had grown in their own understanding through his successive publications.

> *'In* Vers une Architecture *... he opened our eyes to truths already existing but unrecognised. In* L'Art Decoratif *he showed us how machines ... have been gradually teaching us a new way of life entirely different from that of previous decades ... In* Urbanisme *[we see how] our cities have got left behind by life; how mechanisation ... has so changed the tempo of urban life that we can no longer fit ourselves into our streets.'*[2]

Even then, when the Constructivist architects' group was just starting out they recognised that Corbusier's writing 'has a very special importance for us.' In early 1930, only three-and-a-half years but a vast collective oeuvre later, Ginzburg gave this a personal dimension in a letter to Corbusier:

> *'Like all my friends I value you tremendously not only as a subtle master architect but also as a man with the ability to solve radically and fundamentally the problems of organisation.*
>
> *'For me you are today the greatest and most brilliant representative of the profession that gives my life content, goal and meaning. That is why your ideas ... have a quite exceptional interest and importance for us.'*[3]

One must allow for hyperbole here, or at least *politesse*, as Ginzburg was writing after Corbusier's Moscow visit with the confidence of a nearer-equal to say 'But my dear Le Corbusier, you are wrong' (over the future of the Soviet city). Even so, he ends his letter with the continuing hope 'that in the future as in the past we shall learn much from you to help solve our problems.'

From the first reading of Corbusier's texts, however, and before any of the politicisation which underlay Ginzburg's confident 'you are wrong' in 1930, the Russians had not read uncritically. In Chapter 5 I quoted what Leonid Vesnin wrote in a letter to his brothers in 1924. His holiday reading was *Vers une Architecture* which they had previously only seen as articles in *L'Esprit Nouveau.*

> *'I am reading Corbusier-Saugnier but fairly slowly, and therefore more carefully than I did last winter. I see that there are certain questions on which one could already disagree with him. We have gone further and we look more deeply.'*[4]

In what particular respects could they legitimately claim that they had 'gone further and deeper' in mid-1924, and did it continue to be true later?

Rhythms beneath the surface

In comparing *Vers une Architecture* with Ginzburg's *Style and Epoch* in Chapter 5, I have already indicated my judgement on its truth at that date, which coincides exactly with Leonid Vesnin's letter. The Russians had already started to build organisational analogies with machines that could indicate how the architect might work in order for buildings to emulate their success in achieving 'the greatest clarity and power in the formulation of the creative idea', even to the level 'formulated by Alberti'.[5] That embryo of a design method was certainly already a step beyond Corbusier operationally, and led to the work described in Chapters 5, 7, 11. Here I want to look at how they pursued what must have struck them as one of the most important and pregnant phrases in the book, his assertion that 'All these objects of modern life create, in the long run, a modern state of mind.'[6]

As ever with Corbusier, the remark was unexplained and undeveloped. To Russians in the early Soviet years it would particularly have attracted attention because of its inherently materialist premise that the material environment which a society constructs under influence of its technology in turn shapes its social superstructure and its worldview. At this date, in the very early Twenties, thinking artists and architects who sought any form of engagement with the new régime around them were struggling to get some intellectual foothold in a world of ideas with which they previously had no connections. In Chapters 4 and 5 we have seen it happening amongst the frontline avant-garde. Almost more revealingly, because rather more explicitly and naively, we can also see this process taking place in the early discussions of the Russian Academy of Artistic Sciences, Rakhn. I have already mentioned this new style 'academy' several times because it was largely created by Kandinsky, and provided his intellectual refuge when the young turks of Inkhuk rejected his old-style concept of art; it was also the forum in which Ginzburg read the papers which became *Style and Epoch.*

In this academic research and discussion society of relatively traditional profile, the papers presented during the formative years 1921-3 range from such traditional topics as 'Right and reversed perspective in art and in perception of real space', 'The elements of music' and Kandinsky's thesis on 'Basic elements of painting', to Zholtovsky attempting to be modish on 'The state and prospects of industrial applied arts (*khudozhestvennaia promyshlennost*) in Russia'.[7] More politically oriented were Lunacharsky on 'The tasks of the state in the art field', and from further Left there were some radical views from Lunacharsky's party enemy Bogdanov in his paper on 'The organisational role of art', plus several others attempting to establish a foothold in the new world of ideas around them. Thus the physicist Professor N.E. Uspensky on 'The role of positivist sciences in art' was complemented by 'The role of art in the positivist sciences', and all of it was paralleled by a research study on behalf of the whole Academy by one Iu.P. Denike into what Marx had actually said about art, conducted through 'kind permission of the Institute of Marx and Engels of the Communist Academy for use of their magnificent library'.[8]

From Denike's report published in the first volume of Rakhn's proceedings, one senses on one hand their slightly bewildered, even desperate desire for guidance. But equally clear was the complementary fact, that despite its apparent centrality to work on a broad cultural front, this issue was obscure and hardly documented. At the moment when the Soviet art community was dedicating itself to obey the canon, it was clear there really wasn't one. As Denike reported after his research, there were only 'fragments of thought, sometimes not even set out in a fully resolved way, even only half thought out'. But they had

'great value and must without fail be included in the field of view of everyone who themselves seeks to work out or study historical materialism, as a theory of society's development and as a conception of social determinism which must be verified and justified in all spheres of live phenomena, including also the phenomenon of art.'[9]

One problem that Denike had uncovered immediately, was that Marx's knowledge and sympathies in the field of 'art' were with literature and poetry. Even the 'fragments of thought' therefore touched directly on only a small section of the Academy's members' interests.

Their ultimate mission was outlined by Lunacharsky in a programme paper on 'The role of the Academy in the study of art in a social direction'. Being so straightforwardly scholarly, however, they were more aware than most enthusiasts that they set off into this 'role' with no real information as to its parameters. Almost the only solid guidance which Denike could offer his colleagues was qualititative rather than substantive: that these questions required deep, non-superficial study.

'And in order to understand what was Marx's theoretical approach to the questions of art, we already have something to go on [literally, a certain point of support] in those few unarguable bits of information which tell us first of all, that Marx was not a superficial reader of literary works, but in this one branch of art at least had a profound and rich aesthetic experience. And that is very important.'[10]

If nothing more specific, therefore, following Marx meant probing beneath surfaces.

One theme that figures constantly in the general current of looking 'beneath surfaces' at this time is that of rhythm, rhythms of movement, periodicity. One of these first papers in Rakhn was by the crystallographer Professor G.B. Vulf on 'Rhythm in the creations of nature'. This of course was to be Moisei Ginzburg's entry point into the serious architectural debate around him, through his first book *Rhythm in Architecture*. This opened with the observation that whether we encounter it 'in the movements of the planetary system, in a person working, in the swerving movements of a wild beast, in the spurting flow of a river', rhythm is everywhere.[11] For some people this particular theme derived from Marx's historical economics and sociology. For others, as in Ginzburg's cyclical theory of relationship of cultural 'health' to architectural style in *Style and Epoch*, it came from Spengler, or in a more narrowly art-historical way, from Wölfflin.

In *Rhythm in Architecture*, however, as no doubt for more people than were publicly daring to quote him, Ginzburg's text was a passage from Nietzsche's *Joyous Science* which he places at the head of his first page.

'Rhythm is compulsion. It exerts an irresistible impulse to continue chasing, to follow it, to coordinate oneself with it; and not only in the pace of the feet: the spirit also follows the beat of the bars, and thus certainly commits itself to the spirit of the gods. And they have tried with the help of rhythm to compel them, and to acquire power over them.'[12]

In the second paragraph of his text Ginzburg brings this a little closer to materialist modernity where he insists that 'All scientific hypotheses, laws and philosophical views of the world are nothing other than attempts to find the formula and definition which can express the rhythmic pulsation of the cosmos.' On the next page he continues: 'The essence of any kind of rhythmic phenomenon consists above all in movement (the word "rhythm" in Greek means "flow").' After all the history from the Gothic cathedrals, Chaldean ziggurats and the Pazzi Chapel, he concludes the book with the assertion that 'The task of contemporary architecture is to find those elements of form and those laws for combining them, in which the rhythmic pulsation of our days manifests itself.'[13]

Number as a state of mind

This is the line of thought which leads directly into investigations of architecture's formal language. Ginzburg himself took it up in the next year in his next book, *Style and Epoch*, in discussion of the new aesthetics of asymmetry, dynamism and ultimate economy of material and movement that the machine established as a new paradigm of 'organisedness'. The concern with rhythm and dynamics in this formal area was more fully developed by others like the Leningrader Iakov Chernikhov and by the Rationalists, though Ginzburg, as his lectures on composition show [Doc.26], continued to teach the contents of this book to his students. But both Chernikhov and these aesthetic Rationalists in the end belong in the same category as Corbusier, in addressing only the products of design as a generators of 'sensations', not the inner organisation of human movement within the spaces, or the 'flow' of ideas which constitute the design process itself. In Ginzburg, by controther hand, it is always implicit the 'movements' which are to be objectively studied are of two types: movement within the object (for which the dynamic organisation of the machine offers a direct model), and the movement of the architect 'through the problem', i.e. the process of design.

What, in that context, did it mean to pursue 'a modern state of mind' in relation to the way a designer worked or viewed his work?

Firstly, and probably under inspiration of Bogdanov, it meant self-awareness. Bogdanov had encapsulated this idea in the crucial statement in his 'Paths of proletarian creative work' of 1920, that 'the basic difference between the old and the new creative work is that now, for the first time, creative work understands itself.'[14] And secondly, also from Bogdanov and with different nuances from others in the Marxist tradition, it meant that design was one operation within a larger 'monistic' system made possible by modern science's elimination of religious mystification. Here practical and philosophical spheres of human existence were of one whole, no longer separate planes of existence in constant conflict.

The physical organisation and dynamic rhythms of the machine were the key to this new monistic unity of form and content. Machines were that 'supremely organised' construction of science within the material world. But the key to acheiving that reintegration, the unifying language at one level deeper, was number. To an extent it is impossible and inappropriate to pursue in detail here, mathematics and number were an almost magical touchstone to Russian speculative thought in this time, as it had been since well before the 1917 Revolution.

The passion for number in the Twenties was reinforced by the injunctions to quantified precision which rang through all the Soviet government's campaigns for rationalisation and efficiency, in social as well as industrial and economic fields. In the illiterate, still religious, still largely medieval Russia, where most workers could not count far less tell the time, only the dissemination of a primitive sense of number could tighten up any organisational or productive activity. In the arts and in this case in Constructivism, however, the more sophisticated concern with number is a result of its long-established links with avant-garde literary circles.

A seminal paper here was that of the Formalist critic and theorist of language Victor Shklovsky entitled 'Art as a device', of 1917, which discussed the ways in which conventional language-use already operates through simplification and abstraction of a quasi-mathematical kind. He discusses there how 'habituation' in the use of language leads to 'the process of "algebrisation", the over-automisation of a symbol [which] permits the greatest economy of perceptive effort' and how 'this characteristic of thought not only suggests the method of algebra but even prompts the choice of symbols, i.e. letters.' To Shklovsky, rhythm, or rather the 'disordering' of rhythms to break through these 'over-automised' readings of words and images, was one of art's most important 'devices'.[15]

At the high point of Constructivist literary debate in *LEF* during 1922-3 Shklovsky was temporarily abroad, but these Formalist ideas were being developed in Russia by his colleagues Brik and Mayakovsky. They laid out their programme of 'Our linguistic work' in *LEF*'s very first issue. It was their declared aim to reintegrate different social usages of language into 'a single linguistic material, and to process it according to today's methods, ... not as an aesthetic end in itself but as a workshop for the best expression of the facts of the contemporary era.'[16] The self-styled 'transrational' (*zaumnyi*) poet Velimir Khlebnikov, close colleague at one stage of Tatlin, equally delighted to express semantic and linguistic relations in quasi-mathematical formulae. In 1922 he expounded the 'facts of the contemporary era' that interested him, which were the key events of Russia's revolutionary history, terms of a complex periodicity he claimed to have found, in rhythms based on powers of 2 and 3.[17]

An example closer to art was the formula 'devised by Lev Bruni in 1916 and developed in our joint investigation of Tatlin's work' with which another of Tatlin's friends, the critic Nikolai Punin, explained the relationship of Tatlin's work to preceding art movements in 1921 in his booklet *Tatlin: Against Cubism*. Where Malevich had explained the painterly development from nineteenth century Realism, through Impressionism, Cubism and Futurist to his own Suprematism in terms of the formal devices he called 'additional elements' (see Chapter 9), Punin described the same development towards the seminal breakthrough of Malevich's rival Tatlin in the 'painterly reliefs' according to Bruni's 'formula of successive loadings' (*formula nagruzheniia*). As his final set of formulae put it:

'Therefore our sequence can be finally established as:

$$\frac{d}{d^1} > \frac{c}{c^1} > \frac{b}{b^1} > \frac{a}{a^1}$$

where a/a¹ is Impressionism, b/b¹ is Expressionism, c/c¹ is Cubism and d/d¹ is the type of painterly relief devised by Tatlin. Each relationship in this series increases successively as each absorbs all preceding relationships. Such is the volume of formal achievements in Tatlin's work, going back genetically to Impressionism, that it covers everything which has been achieved by humanity in the field of plastic art, as it aspired to realise its fundamental law - the law of successive loadings.'[18]

In dedicating his little study 'To participants in the State Free Artistic Studios', i.e. to the new art school in the old Academy (see Chapter 10) it is clear Punin does not intend this language of art criticism only as a game for a few research colleagues. I quote it to show how far the picturesque but profoundly rooted determination to mathematicise went at this time, which is hard to imagine if one is not accustomed to Russian thought. These were the normal terms of critical and creative discourse surrounding the Constructivists, out of which arose their desire to mathematicise design.

The engineer's state of mind

This therefore was the equipment and the set of imperatives with which Ginzburg approached the question posed in their different ways by the manifestos of both Marinetti and Corbusier: the profound if simple question: 'What, if anything, has the architect to learn from the engineer?' In different ways it underlay all modern architectural programmes, and Ginzburg's writings of the Twenties perhaps made a uniquely clear-headed contribution to it.

This clarity emerges if we examine the related question of 'What can the architect learn about architecture from the machine?' In Corbusier, as in most modernist writing, the two questions are fatally confused. Ginzburg, with his focus on the designer's working method, made an important contribution to theory of modernism by reminding us they are different.

Returning to the theme of the dynamic, implicit in all concerns with both machinery and 'rhythm', we see the limitations of Corbusier's thinking at this point. When he insisted that 'the purpose of architecture is to move us', the terrain is of course not physical, but emotional and spiritual. The greatest emotive power, in his judgement, lay with 'primary geometrical forms', and the reason for emulating 'the engineer's aesthetic' was that these were precisely his vocabulary.[19] As usual, he had waved a gallic hand towards something deeper but did not probe far. 'The engineer shows the way because he proceeds on the basis of knowledge', he wrote, 'and architecture in its own domain should also begin at the beginning'.[20] Ginzburg took the message, but injoined like all around him to follow Marx in 'probing deeper', he found himself up against the next question. As he put it in *Style and Epoch* 'How are we to build this bridge between engineering and architecture once we understand that it is possible only through principles of creativity and not through actual forms?'[21] Corbusier offered hints for those who agreed that architecture is 'a matter of plastic emotion'. But he gave little guidance on how the architect might proceed in the task of 'organising life' which Ginzburg and his colleagues took as the premise for a socialist Soviet architecture.[22]

In *Style and Epoch* there was a clear endorsement of Bogdanov's crucial insistence that 'the new kind of creativity' would be distinguished from the old by the fact that (with my italics) 'it understands *itself*'. Ginzburg follows by insisting that the incarnation of this self-understanding would be some objectively formalised 'method' for performing that creativity.

> *'There can be no question of any sort of artist losing creativity just because he knows clearly what he wants, what he is aiming for, and in what consists the meaning of his work. But subconscious, impulsive creativity must be replaced by clear and distinctly organised method, which is economical of the architect's energies and transfers the freed surplus of it into inventiveness and the force of the creative impulse.'*[23]

That was in 1924. As indicated in Chapter 5 and Document 6, the next stage in developing this self-conscious method of working was Ginzburg's lead paper in the very first issue of the Constructivist architects' journal *SA* in 1926, entitled 'New methods of architectural thinking'.[24] With slight editing, this is translated as Document 9.

In a very real sense, this paper set the agenda for the group's next five years' work, till they effectively ceased operating in 1931. Here Ginzburg insists that the true radicalism of form which the engineer achieves requires absolute clarity of 'knowledge' about both aims and architectural means. The first agenda of the 'clearly organised working method' is to ensure objectivity and rigour in bringing together the various bodies of knowledge that bear upon a design. Underneath that is the second agenda of self-understanding, whose converse is social accountability to the new proletarian client of which the architect himself is an integral part.

Already here the main stages of the eventual 'functional method' are presented in outline form in the latter part of the article. The method was to form 'a unified organic creative process in which one task leads from another with all the logic of a natural development' and where 'no part is

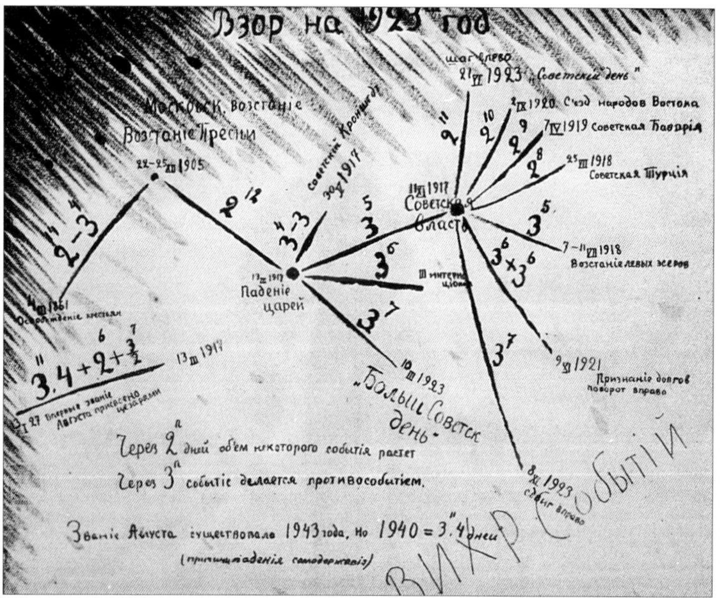

Moisei Ginzburg (1892-1946), photograph of late 1920s. Khlebnikov, periodicity of Revolutionary events, from his Vestnik, 1922. Le Corbusier: photograph from SA. Leonidov, slogan 'Architect! Do not imitate the forms of technology but learn the method of the engineer', SA, 1926, no.3.

arbitrary'. Lest the message of this was not clear, it was reinforced and given a real 'shape' in *SA*'s third issue. This gave the most prominent place to an article on 'The form of the aeroplane and methods of designing it', not signed by Ginzburg, but manifestly written by an obliging aeronautical engineer to a brief from him.[25] A typographic feature by Ivan Leonidov on the editorial page of this issue summed up the message readers should take from this un-architectural piece: 'Architect! Do not imitate the forms of technology, but learn the method of the engineering designer.'

Here too Corbusier had given the clue and the cue when he insisted that 'The lesson of the aeroplane is not primarily in the forms it has created; ... the lesson of [it] lies in the logic which governed the enunciation of the problem and which led to its successful realisation.'[26] But the nature of that logic had never been explained. Here in *SA*, they were explicit about what they understood its nature to be. The obliging engineer Akashev ran through the main stages of the basic aerodynamic and loading calculations by which he could create a plane that flies. He said all the right things on the way: the designer of aeroplanes knows what he wants, and he knows his science and technology. 'The last thing he is thinking about initially is beauty' of course, but he ends up, after following the 'strict and rigid' logic of the mathematics and the chemistry, with an object which 'evokes an aesthetic sensation in every viewer'.[27]

That was exactly Corbusier's dream, but here was concrete proof that it is not 'romanticism or heroism of the inventor' which has at last enabled man to fly, but what Corbusier himself called 'cold calculation'. *SA* left nothing to chance in the communication, however. The calculation was not simply presented as information: the typographical layout created a clear visual model of that essentially linear logic which Ginzburg had described in his paper two issues previously as 'the inventor's creative method'. Here was precisely the 'unified organic creative process where one task leads from another with all the logic of a natural development', a literal 'calculation' of form, in which 'no single part of the thinking is arbitrary'.[28] Lest any reader should still miss the point, a typographical feature within the article itself stressed again the centrality of this material to the development of their creed: 'Architects! This is how you must understand the materialistic foundations of the aesthetic of Constructivism.'

The model for the epoch

In this pair of papers, one by Ginzburg and one plainly commissioned for its purpose by *SA*'s editors – i.e. by himself and Alexander Vesnin – we see the moment of crystallising the key step beyond Corbusier. Here was fulfilment of the claim made by Leonid Vesnin two years earlier when he wrote 'We have already gone further'. Ginzburg devotes a passage in this paper to endorsing Corbusier's observation that the end products of engineering become at their best the pure paradigmatic 'perfectly evolved' artefacts he called '*objets-types*'. Much of the Constructivists' later work sought to develop equivalent new socialist architectural '*types*', notably for housing. These two papers together document the critical moment in their response to a different but complementary assertion, that the engineer also offers the architect a '*processus-type*' – a standardised and self-conscious creative process which will generate the new architectural *objets-types* for the new mass Soviet client.

If we step aside from the Corbusian comparison and look back to Bogdanov's challenge to create 'a creativity that understands itself', it is perhaps useful to place this work in a larger context not just of 'states of mind', but more specifically of mental models.

The development amongst designers themselves of self-conscious descriptions of their own activity is an under-developed aspect of design history, because unfortunately there is little raw material for it. Highly complex as that activity is, its analysis is also complex, both intrinsically and in its relation to larger cultural processes. Potentially, however, it offers an intellectual challenge whose attractiveness lies precisely in the unusual character of design, as a synthesis of seemingly quite separate and non-commensurable dimensions of human affairs.

That complexity alone may explain why there has been relatively little of this reflective activity, but the Russian Constructivist movement, as I see it, occupies a unique place in twentieth-century thinking about this topic. Amongst the models with which theorists or analysts of the design process have sought to describe it (or in the Constructivists' case, to dictate it) the most interesting common feature is the use of analogies with the front-line science or technology of their time. We can see the Constructivists' model for designing man's largest artefacts – buildings, towns and settlement systems – as the centrepiece of a triad of such models in this century, each reflecting the modes of thought emerging with a new stage of scientific and industrial development as it generated the modern and then the post-modern world. By going back to a natural-science model at the turn-of-the-century we see some of the origins of this thinking within Russia. Moving forward to the sort of probablistic, information theoretic models we would use today, we can see the Constructivists' mechanistic paradigm more clearly in its historical perspective. I have clarified them further in three diagrams.

The most potent natural science model of design in pre-Revolutionary Russia was that developed by the Moscow engineer and philosopher Peter Engelmeier discussed in Chapter 1 [p.13].[29] Like most of his class in Russia he has disappeared from the intellectual history books, but in the immediate post-Revolutionary years he was still occasionally referred to, as for example significantly in Rakhn, where Professor Uspensky's lecture mentioned earlier, on 'The role of positivist sciences in art', took Engelmeier's ideas as their starting point.[29] He himself was still personally active. As late as 1929 we find him still trying to advance the case for a 'Philosophy of Technology'. In January that year, in the journal *Engineering Labour*, he referred back to his initatives in 1927 within the All-Union Association of Engineers, VAI, to 'construct a philosophy of technology' that would examine it as 'a biological phenomenon, and anthropological phenomenon' and from points of view of 'the history of culture, economics, art, ethics and other social factors'.[31]

Even in 1927 VAI was politically suspect as a group of 'old specialists' propagating 'non-class' values, attacked in the same campaigns that hit Vkhutemas [Chapter 10]. By 1929 it was plain Engelmeier's ideas must be dismissed for giving no place to Marxism.[32] Thus by the Twenties he was obscure, but his pre-Revolutionary contribution had ensured that the factors which should bear upon the shaping of any artefact of industrial man were already identified before the process of a socially-conscious, Soviet industrialisation began and had been brought together within a very powerful general model.

His model had gone no further than to identify the broad categories of factors: the ethical, the aesthetic, the pure-scientific and the technological; to model their interconnectedness as some kind of 'valency', and to offer a formula for representing their degrees of presence or absence in all 'acts of technological will', what Bogdanov would have called technological creativity. Diagram 1 here shows this in graphic terms. In mathematical terms his was essentially a set-theoretic model, and is powerful, of course, because the precise elements of each set, and the manipulations that will be performed between sets, are not specified. Questions of how a political factor might determine the use of certain utilitarian potentialities in a given technology, for example, remain to be established for each era and culture by its own techniques of speculation and testing. But he had issued the next generation with the challenge of establishing the proper balance and relationship between those factors. His earlier work may have been one contributor to Bogdanov's conviction that a self-aware theory of creativity was possible.

A decade later, when Gan and his colleagues picked up that challenge, Gan's new set of 'disciplines' for the task of design synthesised a range of human and technical factors as broad as Engelmeier's [Chapters 4 and 5]. By looking back to Engelmeier's chemical model we see more clearly that the novelty of the Constructivists' mechanical one lay not in its scope, but in its structure. And further, that it proposed a procedure for the act of designing, rather than just a descriptive model of factors that had shaped its end products.

The simplest of Gan's triad of disciplines was the second, *faktura*, which covers the territory of Engelmeier's *istina* and *polza*: of scientific knowledge or of 'Truth', and of 'Utility' or use. The one which Gan's colleagues found most difficult to grasp was his first, *tektonika*: the science which described how 'the appropriate use of industrial material' was determined by the system of socio-economic and political intentions – in their case specifically by 'the characteristics of Communism itself.'

Engelmeier's model helps to show why they found it so difficult: the interface under scrutiny here is precisely that between two of Engelmeier's hybrid factors, 'applied technologies' and 'applied ethics'. Gan did not get far in charting the contents of such a science or 'discipline', but when he talks about *tektonika* as a concept analogous to that of 'tectonics' in geology, 'where it signifies violent restructurings coming out of the earth's core',[33] today's systems-trained mind has less difficulty understanding it.

With Gan's third discipline, *konstruktsiia*, we come to the heart of our present topic, for this was 'the assembling and ordering function within Constructivism which 'reveals the actual process of putting together.'[34] As I have described in Chapter 5, this word *konstruktsiia* implies that the 'assembly function' is an intellectual one. It refers not to physical components, but to the kind of logic governing the whole process. In these

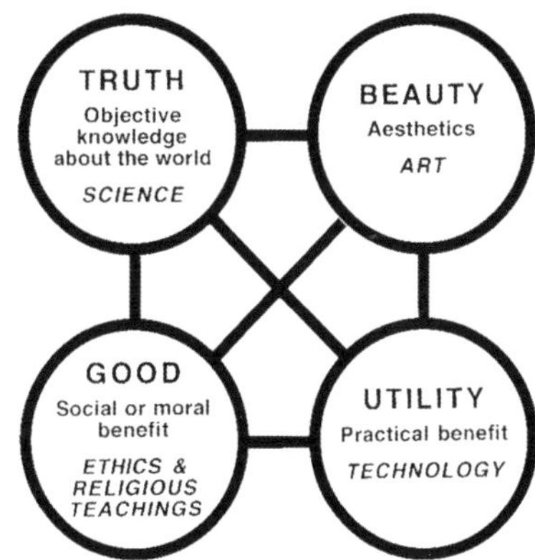

Diagram 1: *Schematic structure of Engelmeier's analogy between 'acts of technological will' and an organic molecule; the four 'elements' with a valency-like potential to interact [compare p.13].*

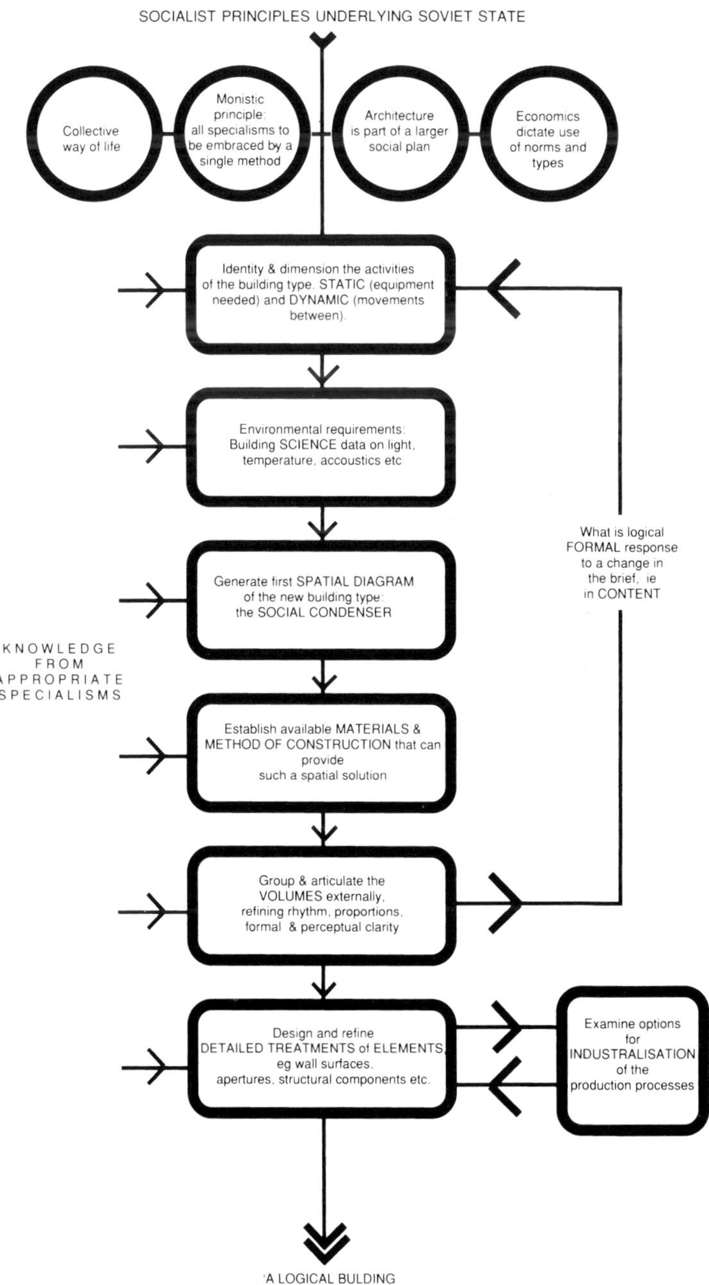

Diagram 2: *Further abstraction of the Constructivist architects' 'functional method' [compare Document 8, p.121], underlining its dependence on 'general unknowns', linearity, determinism.*

two papers we see how literally the logic is mechanical: one process leading quasi-automatically to the next. The parallel with the Constructivists' Functional method is clear from Diagram 2, which is further simplified from the summary of Ginzburg's exposition in Document 8 [p.121]. Back in 1918, Mayakovsky had made this identity between mental structures and mechanical ones a theme of his poem 'The Poet-Worker'. 'Hearts are just like motors; the mind is like an intricate engine' he declared, and its thought processes could be changed by rasping away at it with a file. He precisely encapsulates the reassuring certainty which pervaded his whole generation, that causes and effects, material and psychological, were indeed directly related, even literally 'mechanically', that is with 100% probability.[35]

The linearity of the Constructivist process also had precedents in the nineteenth century Rationalist architects' approach discussed in Chapter 1 whereby a 'crude form' generated by technology was then subjected to aesthetic refinement. However they had expanded this to embrace the full range of considerations embraced by Engelmeier's model. By inspection we can identify his elements arranged in different ways within it. Their most important additions were the stages and criteria embracing Engelmeier's ethical category of Good. The 'general [or 'state'] variables' which reflected and enacted the new ethical values of Soviet socialism led directly to such operational principles of their own daily work as standardisation, typisation, accountability, openness to public participation. In the field of 'particular ['decision'] variables' relating to each specific problem, as we see in Ginzburg's paper here, their method now demanded a clear statement of whose 'welfare' was to be enhanced, and by precisely what new 'benefits' or changes of life-style, as a result of each 'act of design'.

To my knowledge this 'design method' of the Constructivists was the most explicit and detailed formulation from any country, as well as the most all-embracing, of a design approach 'proper' to the First Machine Age. In scope and rigour it goes far beyond anything produced, for example, by Hannes Meyer at the Bauhaus. The reasons for their own comparatively greater territory and rigour were well understood, moreover, at the time. At OSA's First Conference in 1928 Ginzburg expounded on precisely this, and on the relatively limited decision-making territory accessible to their Western colleagues thanks to 'the system they work under.'[36]

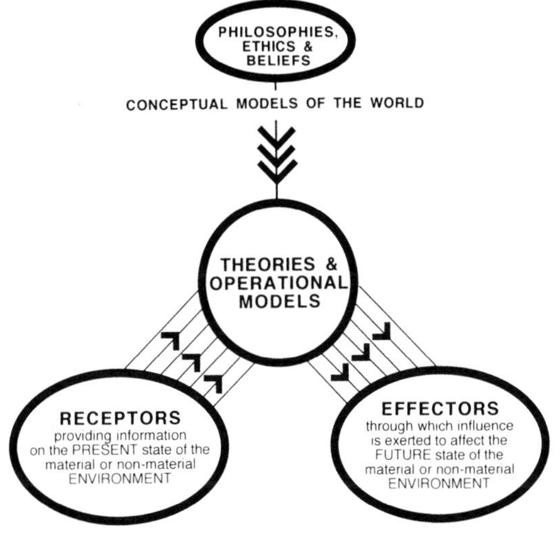

***Diagram 3:** Information-theoretic model of design as pluralist, probablistic.*

Thus Soviet Constructivism is important for providing the most explicit and rigorously formalised paradigm of a design process 'correct' for what Reyner Banham thirty years ago taught us to call the First Machine Age. Banham was already aware then, that what distinguished the newly-crystallising Second Machine Age from the First was 'a revolution' in the nature of power and the mechanisms of control, as well as a new importance for 'mass communications'. Still, as he admitted, 'we yet lack a body of theory proper to our own [Second] Machine Age. We are still free-wheeling along with ideas and aesthetics left over from the First.'[37] But that was a full generation ago. By the mid-nineties the Second Machine Age is a daily reality in the West and its 'technology' is information itself. On the basis of an information-theoretic perception of human affairs, the linearity and deterministic certitude which characterised the mechanical model of design activity in the First Machine Age have perforce dissolved again into highly generalised, that is to say powerful, models but ones that are firmly probabilistic rather than mechanistic.

In the Second Machine Age the principles of information theory have taught us to recognise the relativistic nature of our knowledge about the world and to see the effects of our designs only in terms of the possible or at best the probable. An information-theoretic model of the design process builds on those perceptions. The model I illustrate here in Diagram 3 is derived with certain modifications from the work of March and Stiny.[38] Where they regarded 'languages' as the main data-bank feeding 'theory', however, I would prefer to see it as one – albeit key – parameter within the processes of conceptual and operational model building. In my view it is ever more important to make this explicit statement of the all-determining role of value-systems and world-views in shaping the entire intellectual apparatus of theories and models whereby design activity proceeds.

Through a description of this kind, design theory can embrace the pluralism of both world-models and intentions that are created today by widely differing values for the ethical variable, found even within one society. Such a model refuses to identify any one 'correct starting point' for the design process, or any uniquely appropriate 'ordering of priorities' within it. It therefore ceases to prescribe a 'method' and returns to the sort of system diagram conceived by Engelmeier. Where the Constructivist model saw every stage of decisionmaking as a 'transmission of force', the contemporaneity of this model lies in its classification of every 'action' as a 'transmission of information', whether the reality is a process of data collection, of deduction, of proposition or of actually pushing the material environment into a new shape.

Thirty years ago Banham observed we were in a transitional period, aware that a whole new perception of our affairs was emerging but still operating with models 'left over' from the old structure. Now that theory has caught up, we can see how completely the mechanical, linear notion of a unitary 'design method', which is certainly not entirely dead within some fields of design theory even today, was modelled upon the larger cultural and philosophical prototypes of its day. Taking these successive models from the eras of chemistry, mechanical engineering and information technology as a starting point, we can move towards general observations on the manner and path by which thinking about the design process relates to other fields of intellectual endeavour.

By formulating the Modern paradigm so exhaustively the Constructivists perform a service even today. In rejecting such confident and mechanistic determinism, we then perhaps better understand the paradigm shift in the Post-Modern debate as it insists that design should draw at least equally upon the aspirations of the humanities.

■

1 Corbusier's '5 points of the new architecture' (raising buildings up on pilotis; using the flat roof as a roof-garden; free plan form in a framed structure; horizontal sliding continuous windows; free functionally-generated composition of elevations) were presented to Russians in *SA*, 1928, no.1, pp.23, 25 **2** B. Korshunov, 'Urbanisme', SA, 1926, no.1, pp.37-8 **3** Correspondence between Le Corbusier and Ginzburg, SA, 1930, no.1-2, p.61 In English in A. Kopp, *Town and Revolution*, London-New York, 1970, pp.252-4 **4** Letter from L. Vesnin, archival material quoted in A.G. Chiniakov, *Brat'ia Vesniny* (The Vesnin Brothers), Moscow, 1970, p.99 **5** M. Ginzburg, *Stil' i epokha* (Style and Epoch), Moscow, 1924, p.93 **6** See the English edition of *Vers une Architecture*, which is collected articles from *L'Esprit Nouveau*, viz: Le Corbusier, *Towards a New Architecture*, London, 1946, p.256 **7** *Iskusstvo: zhurnal' RAKhN* (Art: the journal of Rakhn), no.1, Moscow, 1923, pp.412-3 **8** Iu.P. Denike, 'Marks ob iskusstve' (Marx on art), *Iskusstvo*, no.1, pp.32-42 **9** ibid, p.32 **10** ibid, pp.35-6 **11** M. Ginzburg, *Ritm v arkhitekture* (Rhythm in Architecture), Moscow, 1923, p.9 **12** ibid, p.9. On the fate and influence of Nietzsche's ideas in the USSR see, B. Glatzer Rozenthal, ed., *Nietzsche and Soviet Culture: Ally and Adversary*, Cambridge, 1994. In the architectural article here, M. Bliznakov, 'Nietzschean implications and superhuman aspirations in the architectural avant-garde', pp.174-210, it is erroneously stated (p.175) that 'Nietzsche is never mentioned by name' in any texts of the Russian avant-garde architects. This prominent quotation by Ginzburg seems to have been missed. For the pre-Revolutionary situation over Nietzsche see E.W. Clowes, *The Revolution of Moral Consciousness: Nietzsche in Russian Literature 1890-1914*, DeKalb, Ill., 1988 **13** Ginzburg, *Ritm*, pp.9, 10, 116 **14** A. Bogdanov, 'Put'i proletarskogo tvorchestva' (Paths of proletarian creative work), *Proletarskaia kul'tura*, no.15/16, 1920, pp.50-52, translated in J.E. Bowlt, ed., *Russian Art of the Avant-garde: Theory and Criticism 1902-1934*, London-New York, 1976, pp.178-82 **15** V. Shklovsky, 'Iskusstvo, kak priem' (Art as a device), 1917, in English translation as 'Art as technique' in L.T. Lemon and M.J. Reis, eds., *Russian Formalist Criticsm: Four Essays*, Nebraska-London, 1965, pp.3-24 **16** V. V.Mayakovsky, O. M. Brik, 'Nasha slovesnaia rabota' (Our linguistic work), *LEF*, no.1, 1923, pp.40-41. For an English translation see A. Lawton, ed., *Russian Futurism through its Manifestoes 1912-1928*, Cornell, 1988, pp.202-3 **17** These theories and the diagrams appeared in his two lithographed broadsheets, *Vestnik Velimira Khlebnikova* (Velimir Khlebnikov's Herald), Moscow, 1922 & 1923 **18** N. Punin, *Tatlin. Protiv Kubizma* (Tatlin. Against Cubism), Petersburg (sic), 1921, pp.17-19 **19** Le Corbusier, 'The engineer's aesthetic and architecture', *Towards a New Architecture*, p.23 **20** ibid, p.20 **21** Ginzburg, *Stil' i epokha*, p.28 **22** ibid, p.140 **23** ibid, p.142 **24** M. Ginzburg, 'Novye metody arkhitekturnogo myshleniia' (New Methods of Architectural Thinking), *SA*, 1926, no.I, pp.1-4 **25** Engr. K. Akashev, 'Forma samoleta i metody ego proektirovaniia' (The form of the aeroplane and the methods of designing it), *SA*, 1926, no.3, pp.65-66 **26** Le Corbusier, 'Airplanes', in *Towards a New Architecture*, p.102 **27** Akashev, 'Forma samoleta', p.66 **28** Ginzburg, 'Novye metody'. **29** P.K. Engelmeier, *Filosofiia tekhniki* (A Philosophy of Technology), Vols.I-3, Moscow, 1912. **30** On this discussion of Engelmeier's work in the Rakhn in I922, see: Iu.P. Volchok, 'Vliianie nauchno-tekhnicheskikh znanii na teoreticheskie problemy vzaimosviazi konstruktsii i arkhitekturnoi formy', in Volchok et al, *Konstruktsii i forma v sovetskoi arkhitektury*, (Moscow, I980), pp.38-39. **31** P. Engelmeier, 'Is a philosophy of technology necessary?' (presumably: 'Nuzhna li filosofia tekhniki?') *Inzhenernyi trud* (Engineering Labour), 1929, no.2, pp.36-40, quoted in K.E. Bailes, *Technology and Society under Lenin and Stalin*, Princeton, 1978, pp.105-7 **32** ibid **33** A. Gan, *Konstruktivizm*, Tver, 1922, p.55; on the difficulties of understanding, see S O Khan-Magomedov, *Rodchenko*, London, I986, pp.92-93 **34** Gan, *Konstruktivizm*, p.62 **35** V. Mayakovsky, 'Poet-rabochii' (The Poet Worker), *Iskusstvo kommuny* (Art of the Commune), no.3 (22 Dec 1918), p.1 **36** M. Ginzburg, 'Konstruktivizm v arkhitekture' (Constructivism in architecture), *SA*, 1928, no,5, pp.143-5 **37** Reyner Banham, *Theory and Design in the First Machine Age*, London, 1960, pp.10, 12. **38** Lionel March, 'The Aesthetic State', *Design*, Sept 1981.

НОВЫЕ МЕТОДЫ
АРХИТЕКТУРНОГО МЫШЛЕНИЯ

Doc. 9

MOISEI GINZBURG
NEW METHODS OF ARCHITECTURAL THOUGHT

SA, 1926, no.1, pp.1-4

One decade separates us from the architectural 'affluence' of the pre-Revolutionary era, when in Petersburg, Moscow and other great centres the best Russian architects lightheartedly cultivated every possible 'style'.

Is a decade so much?

It is a small fissure in time. But the Revolution, in sweeping away the stagnant prejudices and outlived canons, has turned the fissure into an abyss. On the far side of that abyss remain the last witherings of the already decrepit system of European thinking, of that unprincipled eclecticism which always has a thousand aesthetic recipes at the ready, all of them approved by our grandfathers and great-grandfathers. Such thinking was ready to ladle out truth from wherever suited – provided only it was from a source in the past.

On this side of the abyss is opening up a new path which still has to be paved, and great new expanses of space which still have to be developed and populated. The outlook and worldview of the contemporary architect is being forged in the circumstances of today and new methods of architectural thinking are being created.

Instead of the old system in architectural designing, where the plan, construction and external treatment of the building were in a state of constant antagonism, and where the architect had to use his powers to the full as peacemaker in irreconcilable conflicts of interest, the new architectural work is characterised above all by its single indivisible aim and aspiration. It is a process in which the task is hammered out logically and which represents a consciously creative [*sozidatel'nyi*] process from beginning to end.

In place of the abstracted and extremely individualistic inspiration of the old-style architect, the contemporary architect is firmly convinced that the architectural task, like any other, can only be solved through a precise elucidation of the factors involved [literally: the unknowns] and by pursuing the correct method of solution.

The architect sees around him the fearless creativity of inventors in various fields of contemporary technology, as with gigantic steps it conquers the earth, the ocean depths and the air, winning new bridgeheads by the hour. It is not difficult to see that these astonishing successes of human genius are explained, in general, by the fact that the right method was pursued in tackling the task. The inventor knows full well that however energetic the upsurge of his creative enthusiasm may be, it will be useless without a sober consideration of all minutiae in the circumstances surrounding his activity. He is fully armed with contemporary knowledge. He takes account of all the conditions of today. He looks forward. He conquers the future.

Certainly it would be naive to replace the complex art of architecture by an imitation of even the most sparkling forms of contemporary technology. This period of naive 'machine symbolism' is already outdated. In this field it is only the inventor's creative method that the contemporary architect must master. Any mould or model from the past must be categorically repudiated, however beautiful it may be, for the pursuits of the architect are in their essence precisely such invention, just like all other invention. His is a work of invention which has set itself the aim of organising and constructing a concrete practical task not just in response to the dictates of today but as something that will serve the needs of tomorrow.

Thus first and foremost we face the question of clearly exposing all the unknowns of the problem. First among these are the unknowns of a general character, dictated by our epoch as a whole. Here we are identifying those particular features of the problem which derive from the emergence of a new social consumer of architecture - the class of workers, who are organising not only their own contemporary way of life but also the complex forms of new economic life of the State. It is not a question, of course, of adapting to the individual tastes of this new consumer. Unfortunately, in posing the problem it is often reduced to precisely this, as people hastily try to attribute to the worker tastes and preferences which are essentially echoes of old pre-Revolutionary attitudes.

Least of all is it a matter of tastes here at all. What we are concerned with is elucidating the characteristics of the new consumer, as a powerful collective which is building a socialist state.

It is a question, above all, of the principle of plannedness. This must not just be a feature of the way leading state organs operate, but must become part of the work of every architect. It is a question of how the solving of individual problems becomes part of the larger productive network of the country as a whole.

The character of a contemporary architect's work is radically altered by the fact that he recognises his activity to be the establishing of architectural standards for the organisation of new dwellings and towns, rather than the fulfillment of individual commissions. He sees it as his task to be continually advancing and improving those standards, in connection with the larger characteristics of production and with the advancing technological levels both here and internationally. In the conditions through which we are living as we develop socialism, each new solution by the architect, be it a dwelling block, a workers club, or a factory, is conceived by us as the invention of a more advanced model or type, which answers the demands of its brief and is suitable for multiple production in whatever quantities the needs of the state require. From the very start, this situation diverts the architect's energy away from the pursuit of a solution answering individual tastes, and redirects it towards further improvement of the standard type which he has devised and a fuller, more sophisticated standardisation of its details. But in order that these type-solutions may undergo a genuinely radical renewal, in order for them to become genuinely new architectural products, they have to be thought out, of course, not for some specific individual site, not in accordance with arbitrary whim. On the contrary, they must derive from the general whole, from the new principles of rational urbanism which will satisfy tomorrow's needs as well as today's. ...

The social conditions of our contemporary world are such that questions of individual aesthetic developments in architecture arise only secondarily. Today's conditions focus our attention first and foremost onto the problem of rational new types in architecture, and by including the architect within the overall production chain of the country, they abolish the isolation which previously existed between various forms of architectural and engineering activity. Certainly the complex development of our life is such that more than at any other time, it compels the architect to specialise in a specific field, but at the same time the firm conviction has arisen amongst all contemporary architects that their different specialisms – housing, community buildings, factories – are merely subsections of a homogenous territory *[ubezhdenie v odno-znachnosti ikh tvorcheskoi deiatel'nosti]*. ... Not only has the boundary between engineering structures and public architecture been wiped out of our thinking, but those very engineering structures themselves have come to be seen as front-line pioneers in the shaping of a genuinely contemporary architecture.

Sober consideration [lit: calculation] of all these circumstances, which have been created and intensified by our present social conditions, is not just the first condition for a correct solution of our architectural tasks. It is also the source of all those purely architectural possibilities which lie concealed within the changes which have taken place in our mode of life.

But alongside these, there is a series of other 'unknowns' facing the architect, which derive quite separately from the particularities of each factor of the given piece of work, from the particular features of the task in hand, from its functional requirements and from the productive and locational conditions obtaining in that situation.

The solving of these 'unknowns' leads to an entirely new method of architectural thinking: to the method of functional design [lit: functional creativity].

Free from the handed-down models of the past, from prejudices and biases, the new architect analyses all sides of his task, all its special features. He dismembers it into its component elements, groups them according to functions and organises his solution on the basis of these factors. The result is a spatial solution which can be likened to any other kind of rationally conceived *[razumnyi]* organism, which is divided into individual organs that have been developed in response to the functional roles which each fulfils.

As a result of this we are seeing in the works of contemporary architects the emergence of entirely new types of plan. These are generally asymmetrical, since it is extremely rare for functional parts of a building to be absolutely identical. They are predominantly open and free in their configurations, because this not only better bathes each part of the building in fresh air and sunlight, but makes its functional elements more clearly readable and makes it easier to perceive the dynamic life that is unfolding within the building's spaces.

That same method of functional creativity leads not only to clear calculation of the 'unknowns' of the task, but to an equally clear calculation of the elements of its solution.

The architect has then to establish his route from the first priorities to the second, from skeleton to envelope. It is only this functional architectural thinking which strictly establishes the spatial organisation as the starting point of the design and the place to which the main thrust must be directed. It demonstrates that the first function of the concrete requirements of the brief must be a clearly established set of individual spatial parameters, their actual dimensions and the links between them. For the contemporary architect this is the principal starting point. It forces him to develop his conception from the inside outwards and not the other way round, as was done in the period of eclecticism. It sets up the direction he will follow from then on.

The second factor to be considered is the constructing of these spaces which have been developed from inside outwards, by means of specific materials and specific structural techniques. It is clear that these are unavoidably a function of the basic spatial solution.

A further step in the work of the new architect is the inter-relating of volumes from the outside. The grouping of architectural masses, their rhythm and proportions will derive naturally from the first half of his activity. This part of designing now becomes a function of the material envelopes and inner volumes he has 'constructed' in the design.

And finally he comes to the treatment of this or that wall surface, the detailed treatment of individual elements: the apertures, piers and so on. All of these are functions of one element of what has been enumerated, or of other considerations within the brief.

Thus the very method of functional creativity leads us to a unified organic creative process where one task leads from another with all the logic of a natural development, instead of the old-style chopping up into separate independent tasks which are usually in conflict with each other. There is no one element, no one part of the architect's thinking which would be arbitrary. Everything would find its explanation and functional justification in its suitability for purpose. The whole unifies everything, establishes equilibrium between everything, creates images of the highest expressiveness, legibility and clarity, where nothing can be arbitrarily changed.

In place of ready-made models of the past which have been chewed over endlessly, the new method radically re-equips the architect. It gives a healthy direction to his thinking, inevitably leading him from the main factors to the secondary ones. It forces him to throw out what is unnecessary and to seek artistic expressiveness in that which is most important and necessary.

There is absolutely no danger in the asceticism of the new architecture which emerges from this method. It is the asceticism of youth and health. It is the robust asceticism of the builders and organisers of a new life.

ФОРМА САМОЛЕТА И МЕТОДЫ ЕГО ПРОЕКТИРОВАНИЯ

DIE FORM DER LÜFTFAHRZEUGS UND DIE METHODE SEINER BERECHNUNG, VON ING. K. AKASCHEFF

Всем известна форма самолета, его смелые и оригинальные линии, его законченные контуры. Вся его конфигурация на фоне неба неустанно приковывает внимание каждого, будь то простой обыватель или художник; в каждом из них форма самолета вызывает эстетическое ощущение.

Спрашивается, чем и как достигается эта оригинальность и смелость линий, каким путем идет и какими методами пользуется конструктор, чтобы получить эту эстетическую форму самолета?

Исходным пунктом при расчете самолета является требуемая грузоподъемность, т.-е. конструктор должен знать цель своей постройки: надлежит ли ему построить тяжелый бомбовоз, пассажирский самолет или легкий одноместный истребитель?

Имея это основное задание — грузоподъемность,—определяющее тип самолета, перед конструктором встает вторая задача для некоторых типов самолета, не менее первостепенная, чем первая,—вопрос о скорости самолета, хотя в конечном итоге она является функцией первого условия.

Для разрешения своей задачи конструктор определяет размеры самолета и мощность двигателя, т.-е. размах и ширину крыльев и величину хвостового оперения с общим центром давления или поддерживающей силы и центром тяжести самолета.

Решение этих вопросов построено на основной формуле аэродинамики

$$R = KSV^2 \bullet$$

Из этой формулы следует, что при данной поверхности

$$S$$

движущегося тела сопротивление воздуха

$$R$$

увеличивается пропорционально квадрату скорости движения. Разложив сопротивление

$$R$$

по координатам x и y, имеем

$$R = R_x + R_y.$$

$$R_y$$

называется полезное сопротивление, т.-е. это есть та сила, которая поддерживает самолет в воздухе, а

$$R_x$$

—лобовое или вредное сопротивление, которое необходимо преодолеть при движении самолета по горизонтальной линии. Возьмем элементарный пример. Если взять

$$S$$

равную 1 $м^2$, то при скорости

$$V$$

равной 150 км в час, сопротивление

$$R_x$$

будет равняться 44 кг, при

$$V = 200 \text{ км в час},$$

$$R_x = 79 \text{ кг, а при}$$

$$V = 250 \text{ км в час},$$

$$R_x = 123 \text{ кг}.$$

Законы вещей — законы мышления

Для преодоления этого сопротивления, на поверхность 1 $м^2$, при скоростях в 150, 200 и 250 км в час, соответственно для каждого случая потребуется мотор мощностью в 25, 60 и 15 лс. Цифры взяты на основании современных аэродинамических опытов, проверенных практикой самолетостроения при K = 0,025 и α = 90°.

Отсюда следует, что конструктору самолета весь свой опыт и знание приходится сосредоточить на устранении вредных сопротивлений R_x. Здесь не приходится думать о красоте формы самолета. Вся мысль конструктора сосредоточена на уменьшении вредного сопротивления R_x, так как уменьшение R_x означает уменьшение мощности мотора или, если мощность мотора останется той же, уменьшая R_x, мы увеличиваем R_y, т.-е. полезное сопротивление или грузоподъемность самолета.

Этот закон аэродинамики слишком суров и строг, чтобы позволять конструктору увлекаться изящными формами самолета, т.-е. ставить перед собой эстетическую задачу—создать элегантный, красивый самолет.

АРХИТЕКТОР!

ТАК НУЖНО ПОНИМАТЬ МАТЕРИАЛИСТИЧЕСКИЕ ОСНОВЫ ЭСТЕТИКИ КОНСТРУКТИВИЗМА

• $R = KSV^2$ — основная формула аэродинамики, где K есть коэффициент, зависящий от характеристики окружающей среды (воздуха) и формы движущегося тела; S — поверхность движущегося тела в $м^2$ V — скорость движения в м в секунду и R — общее сопротивление воздуха в кг.

65

First page of Akashev's article, 'The form of the aeroplane and the methods of designing it', from SA 1926, no.3, translated opposite

Doc. 10

ENGINEER K. AKASHEV
THE FORM OF THE AEROPLANE AND THE METHODS OF DESIGNING IT

SA, 1926, no.3, pp.65-66

Everyone is familiar with the form of the aeroplane, with its bold and original lines, its complete and self-contained contours. Its whole configuration against the background of the sky endlessly attracts the attention of the simple man in the street and the artist alike. The form of the aeroplane evokes an aesthetic sensation in each of them.

The question that is asked is how is this orginality and boldness of line achieved, what approach and what methods does the designer use in order to obtain this aesthetic form of the aeroplane?

The starting point in calculating the aeroplane is its required load-carrying capacity. That is to say, the designer has to know the aim of his structure: is he required to build a heavy bomber, a passenger aircraft or a light single-seater fighter plane?

Having this one central piece of data, i.e. the load-carrying capacity, which determines the type of plane required, the designer is faced in most cases with a second question, no less fundamental than the first. This is the question of the aeroplane's speed. In the ultimate analysis, of course, this is a function of the first criterion.

In order to solve his task the designer determines the size of the plane and the power of its engines. Thus he has to decide the span and width of the wings, and the size of the tail unit, with the overall centre of pressure or lifting forces and the plane's centre of gravity.

Solution of these factors is built upon the fundamental formula of aerodynamics:

$$R = KSV^2$$

where K is a coefficient depending on the characteristics of the surrounding environment (in this case air) and of the form of the moving body; S is the surface area of the moving body in square metres; V is the speed of movement in metres per second and R is the average air resistance in kilogrammes.

From this formula it follows that for a moving body of given surface area,

S

the air-resistance,

R

increases in proportion to the square of the speed of movement. Expanding

R

into its coordinates, x and y, we obtain:

$$R = R_x + R_y.$$

R_y

is called the useful resistance, ie it is that force which supports the plane in the air.

R_x

is the frontal or obstructive resistance, which has to be overcome in the aeroplane's horizontal movement forward. Let us take an elementary example. If we take

S

to be lm^2, then at a speed of V = 150 km/hour, the resistance

R_x

will equal 44 kilograms. Or if:

V = 200 km/hour,

R_x **= 79 kg,**

and if:

V = 250 km/hour,

R_x **= 123 kg.**

To overcome this resistance, for a surface of lm^2, at speeds of 150, 200 and 250 km/hour, motor powers of respectively 25, 60 and 150 horsepowers are required. These figures are based on today's aerodynamic experiments, confirmed in practical aeroplane building, which takes K = 0.025 and ê = 90°.

From this it follows that the designer of the aeroplane has to concentrate all his experience and knowledge on eliminating the obstructive resistance, R_x. The last thing to be thought about at this stage is the beauty of the plane's form. The designer's thinking is concentrated entirely upon reducing the obstructive resistance, R_x, since reduction of this variable means reduction of the motor power, or for a constant motor power, a reduced R_x means an enlarged Ry, that is an increase in the useful resistance and hence the carrying capacity of the plane.

This law of aerodynamics is too strict and rigid to permit the designer to get carried away with beautiful forms, i.e. to set himself the aesthetic task of creating an elegant and beautiful aeroplane.

ARCHITECT!
THIS IS HOW YOU MUST UNDERSTAND THE MATERIALISTIC FOUNDATIONS OF THE AESTHETIC OF CONSTRUCTIVISM

Besides this inexorable law of aerodynamics – of air resistance being proportional to the square of the speed and the cube of engine power – the aeroplane designer faces a second problem. This is to give the aeroplane stability, i.e. to make it capable of resisting wind forces and of getting out of any position relative to the earth, if for any reason its flight regime should have a problem. Any aeroplane structure which does not satisfy these conditions must sooner or later hit catastrophe: if the plane should lose stability, it will crash.

And finally there is a third condition which requires the designer to minimise the aeroplane's weight. This is the question of calculating the aeroplane's static properties. From each detail and component he must remove all material which does not contribute to its strength. Every few grammes of material that adds to the static loading is literally cut out.

Thus is created a machine which has maximal strength for minimum weight without carrying any load which is dead, i.e. non-functional.

When an aeroplane has some 3,500 components, this application of the 'regime of economy' [current jargon of Soviet economic policy, CC] to the weight of each one, results overall in such an reduction in the aeroplane's weight that its fuel-carrying capacity can be reduced, or alternatively that its flying range can be increased by, say, an hour or hour-and-a-half, or another 150-200 kilometres.

ARCHITECT!
ARE YOU CUTTING OUT EVERY GRAMME OF MATERIAL THAT DOES NOT ACTUALLY CARRY A STATIC LOADING?

In brief, there are three conditions to be met in calculating the design of an aeroplane:

1. The aerodynamic form of the external components and their general mode of assembly, must be based on the principle of maximum elimination of obstructive resistances, R_x, which impedes the forward movement of the aeroplane.

2. The distribution of the centres of gravity and resistance (for both R_x and R_y must be the very best possible for providing maximum stability of the plane in the air), and

3. Cutting out of the components all material that does not carry a static loading, will create in the end result an aeroplane invested with those beautiful forms so well known to all.

ARCHITECT!
PAY ATTENTION: THIS IS THE METHOD OF FUNCTIONAL THINKING

If we survey the evolution of aeroplane form from the first designs at the very dawn of aviation, around 1909-10, up to our own times, then the present day aeroplane will be seen to have considerable aesthetic superiority.

The earliest type of plane, with its layer upon layer of components, with its several hundreds of metres of wires and cables, linking all the various components together, has now given way to aeroplanes with a minimum number of components in its shape and with actual forms that are as smooth and simple as possible.

This evolution in the areoplane's form is the result of an evolution in the methods of designing it, or, more accurately, in the scientific foundations on which calculations are based. The absence of exact knowledge, about the conditions of dynamic and static work being done by each component of the aeroplane, meant that the designer was forced, in his aim of achieving stability and improving the plane's aerodynamic (flying) qualities, to complicate the design with superfluous components and details and to shape the forms of these things quite arbitrarily.

The aeroplane became heavy, unrefined in its details and its overall form gave the impression of a series of different configurations assembled haphazardly.

АРХИТЕКТОР!
И ТЫ УДАЛЯЙ КАЖДЫЙ ГРАММ
МАТЕРИАЛА ЕСЛИ ОН НЕ НЕСЕТ
СТАТИЧЕСКОЙ НАГРУЗКИ

It is only contemporary achievements in aerodynamics and aviation technology that permit the designer of our own day to make components which answer the real demands of their purpose and do it without overloads of superfluous material. The end result is the contemporary form of the aeroplane, as the embodiment of the designer's ideas achieved through scientific structural calculations, and as a final result, a refined and beautiful form that evokes aesthetic sensations.

The evolution of methods of calculation for aeroplane design during the last eighteen-twenty years, when the designer can at last realise the age-old dream of humanity to fly in the air, is the result of explorations of human thought over many centuries. It is not the romanticism or heroism of the inventor which we observe in the attempts of medieval flying-machine designers, that has given contemporary technology the possibility to build the aeroplane. It is purely the contemporary state of chemistry, metallurgy, thermodynamics and aerodynamics, in a word, the whole totality of the latest achievements of scientific thinking.

In building a new life, in creating its new forms, we are making scientific thinking the foundation of all that we do. We are strong enough, and our aims are too well defined, for contemporary construction to decorate itself pretentiously or with the artificiality of 'beautiful' forms.

АРХИТЕКТОР, ВНИМАНИЕ
ВОТ —
МЕТОД ФУНКЦИОНАЛЬНОГО МЫШЛЕНИЯ

7: APPROACHES TO RATIONALISING SOVIET BUILDING PRACTICE: CONSTRUCTIVISTS AND MELNIKOV

High-Tech or Low-Tech? Modern building or traditional? A conventional technology or an 'appropriate' one? Since Peter the Great these alternatives had had connotations of 'Western' versus 'Russian'. That polarity itself had philosophical and political dimensions which ramified throughout Russian society in the eighteenth and nineteenth centuries, and ran through every issue it debated. In the Soviet building industry after the Revolution the issue of Western versus Russian was as current as ever.

Before the First World War, in the last years of the Tsarist regime, building in Russia's main cities was in boom. Technically, the peaks of sophistication in these metropolitan centres were on a level with comparable work abroad. Advertisements from architecture journals, for example [cf. p.12], indicate not only the current levels of indigenous craftsmanship in building finishes and purpose-made fittings, but the extent of foreign capital involved in engineering aspects of construction, both in structural engineering and in such equipment as lifts. Whatever their national sources, latest advances were displayed proudly across the whole range of architecture from industrial buildings to the domestic; from ever vaster Orthodox churches reasserting autocracy to the entirely new building types like schools, hospitals, 'people's palaces' arising from the pressures to democratise. Men like Artur Loleit, Alexander Kuznetsov, or in lightweight structures Vladimir Shukhov, had pioneered the introduction of techniques that were on the front line of current processes world-wide. Reinforced concrete became a major factor in the architecture of the *Moderne* period just as cast iron techniques had been a rallying point for the Rationalist movement of the nineteenth century. But these pockets of modernity had existed within a sea of entirely traditional building technology that was still largely medieval.

That traditional technology was dominated by timber. Whole tree-trunks may appear the most primitive of construction materials, yet as practised in Russia, even in the Middle Ages, the technique was sophisticated. Whole houses could be bought in knocked-down form as standardised pre-packages in the markets. The fires that periodically swept through Russia's timber-built towns would leave only the masonry churches and defensive structures standing when the overall matrix of building was razed. That matrix would then be reconstructed with these standardised, prefabricated units. European visitors since the intrepid Adam Olearius, in 1639, repeatedly described these 'markets for the sale of ready-made houses'. Thus Archdeacon Coxe in his account of travels in 1784:

> *'Amongst the curiosities of Moscow, I must not omit the market for the sale of houses. ... The purchaser who wants a dwelling repairs to this spot, mentions the number of rooms he requires, examines the different timbers, which are regularly numbered, and bargains for what suits his purpose. The house is sometimes paid for on the spot, and removed by the purchaser; or the vendor contracts to transport and erect it upon the place where it is designed to stand.'* [1]

At the same time much apparently masonry building in Russia was in fact logs or brickwork faced in stuccoed lath-and-plaster. The classical and neo-classical architecture of Russia was likewise rarely built in stone. Peter the Great's edict that all stone must go to Petersburg was one reason for this, but the tradition was already strong. Thus a major domestic complex like the Razumovsky Palace in Moscow of 1801-3 was grandly Westernised in its salons and composition, but the structure beneath its European costume was the age-old logs, brickwork and lath-and-plaster; hence the almost insuperable problems of conserving this urbane city fabric today as it reaches the end of its natural life.

The Soviet problem

By the early 1920s five years of civil war had wreaked havoc in factories and industrial plants across the whole Soviet Union. In 1922-3, when specialists in the new State Planning Bureau, Gosplan, faced the problem of Russia's reconstruction, they encountered at the very foundations of their task a set of building materials industries that were the worst decimated of all industries in the country.

Building work had effectively ceased with Russia's entry into the First World War, and that was already nearly ten years previously. At that date the major industrial cities like Moscow or the textile centre of Ivanovo were boom towns on the peak of a building explosion. From that period derived most of the middle-class apartment blocks in central Moscow, for example, into which the homeless working classes had now been resettled out of their grossly crowded and fetid basement 'corners' by some of Lenin's first legislation. In the intervening decade, however, almost every brickworks in the country had become ruined; the situation with cement works was only marginally better. Glass was nearly unobtainable. Steel production was on its knees. Even skilled labour for felling and dressing timber was dispersed and depressed. Those planners in Gosplan's Building Sector fully understood that their industry must be the keystone on which Russia's whole industrial capital was reconstructed, and with it her economy. As ever, though, it was hard to persuade politicians of the urgency and logic of that priority. Those debates can be traced through Gosplan's journal *The Planned Economy* (*Plannovoe khoziaistvo*), where careful statistics alternate with near-despair throughout the Twenties.

Amongst the practice-oriented members of the architectural avant-garde this crisis in the building industry, like all other dimensions of their 'reality', was a central concern. Professor Bernatsky, leading construction economist in Gosplan, was constantly drawing attention to the issues it raised and in particular, during the middle Twenties, the threat it represented to government aspirations to eliminate the urban housing crisis. Thus in June 1925 Bernatsky wrote in the Gosplan journal:

'It is clear that a vast building programme lies before us and that even a small reduction in construction costs per cube of building will make a real impact on total house-building costs nationally. This forces us to give the most serious attention to determining the most favourable type of structure. Two alternative paths immediately present themselves: that of capital construction in brick, reinforced concrete etc, applied to large multi-storeyed buildings with only a small percentage of timber; or of predominantly light-weight timber construction ... which has the advantage of speed and cheapness but has the disadvantages of high cost in use, short lifespan, large areas of dispersed development requiring high investment in utilities, roads etc. ...

'We can only progress at full speed by establishing rational types of structure at the same time as we work to reduce detailed construction costs. This question of the choice of type - or more precisely of types - of structure has cardinal importance as in this are resolved the fundamental factors of cost reduction, as well as the sanitary and aesthetic priorities of the inhabitants. The types will vary according to climatic region, as will appropriate materials. For example reinforced concrete with steel frame is far less suitable in Moscow's climate than further south. ... However only a rational choice of types, along with [all these technical issues] will create the healthy base on which our national construction programme can be realised.'[2]

Among the key questions raised by such attempts at cost reduction were those of the labour force. Its seasonality as well as its low skill were perennial Russian problems. Thus Bernatsky's colleague Smurgis insisted in 1928 that 'It is absolutely necessary to find ways of economising on skilled workforce. We must find ways of executing building work that enable us to make wider use of labour that is unskilled.' On the negative side, that approach would further consolidate the building industry's deep-rooted conservatism, which was already inhibiting both the more economic use of traditional materials and the introduction of new techniques. Smurgis showed that Gosplan fully recognised this:

'In reality our so-called shortage of building materials is a consequence of the conservatism of the construction industry, which has no desire to apply solutions different from those to which they are accustomed. The shortage of building materials should be focussing our attention not on reducing the amount of building we do, but on reducing the amounts of material used per unit of a job, and on seeking to replace scarce building materials by others which are not scarce.'[3]

Russian building had always been famous for its extravagance with materials. Most construction was done to very generous rules-of-thumb. Safety factors, if calculated at all, were several times higher than any in Western practice. How should they build now, when 'economy' and 'rationalisation' were central planks of the regime's survival campaign and the subject of repeated decrees and slogans? Even in early 1930, when the First Five Year Plan and its massive construction programmes were well under way, the nature of 'rationalisation' in building was still at issue. Thus Bernatsky was writing in January 1930:

'The concept of "industrialisation" in its simple aspect, i.e. as continuous mass production by machines in closed accommodation, is far from being applicable to all branches of the national economy. One area to which it does not apply is construction, where full "industrialisation" is prevented by many factors which include dispersedness of the structures being built, the necessity to make buildings up from separate and often very small components, the extreme diversity of their functions as objects and hence their shape and size. ... If full industrial rationalisation is impossible, however, it is entirely possible to achieve an approximation to it which we can call "the industrialisation of building", ... and its starting point has to be the correct choice of construction methods and structural types.'[4]

These technical questions were ringing in the ears of all architects throughout the Twenties. Some of the more practice-oriented members of the Modernist avant-garde addressed them seriously and behind the stylistic similarities of their work some very different approaches to the rationalisation problem were being advanced, and demonstrated in some of their best known buildings.

OSA argues by demonstration

Even by the time the architectural avant-garde first became professionally active, in the middle Twenties, Gosplan's Building Sector had grappled with these problems long enough to know that their whole edifice of plans for reducing building costs was fatally weakened by lack of data on the real possibilities of particular building techniques. They had no detailed figures about either the built area of each building type bought by a given sum of money, or about the quantities of each building material consumed in constructing it. Any 'normative consumption' data they could construct, through dividing areas output by gross materials input, was highly aggregated, and based on the archaic techniques habitual to the building industry from that half-affluent, half-medieval past when it last built anything.

In the end data bases, like their whole 'new world', could only be reconstructed from the bottom up, from attacking the grass roots. Arguments on the relative merits of 'high technology' versus the labour intensive approach permeated all of the Bolshevik government's national economic planning. As we have seen, the same argument ran through the state planning agency's Building Sector, but in the hands of local authorities and lumbering industrial agencies very little real progress or even experimentation took place. As in many other fundamental issues, the sharpest thinking

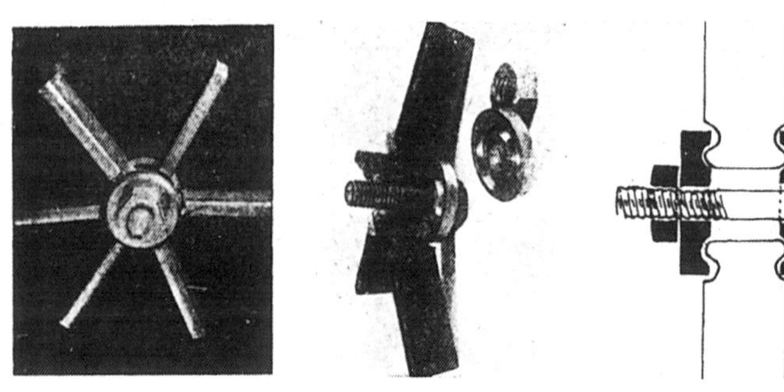

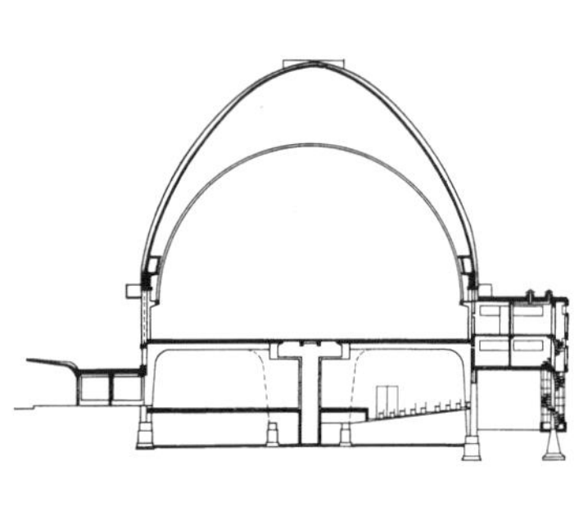

***Barshch and Siniavsky, Moscow Planetarium, 1927-8:** from top: General view from Zoo side; Inner Netzwerk dome before covering; Netzwerk details; Section, entrance left; Entrance hall.*

and most practical demonstrations took place in less official circles. In this case, both sides of the argument found their most energetic and inventive propagandists amongst the avant-garde architects.

As might be expected from their intellectual preoccupation with the machine and their extensive European contacts, the Constructivists' approach to these technical aspects of Soviet architecture was a Westernising, 'high-tech' one. In a typographical feature in the middle of Ginzburg's article on 'The international front of modern architecture', in the second issue of their journal *SA* in 1926, 'the technical task [of] building rationally on the basis of the latest achievements of technology' was presented as an integral part of the 'social task of architecture, of creating the new architectural types on the basis of new relationships in production and the new way of life'.[5] This belief and their campaign for application for 'building rationally on the basis of new technology' continued throughout OSA's existence, and like the rest of their work it was quantified wherever possible.

Later that year, *SA* published detailed exposures of structural wastefulness in the building forms which Moscow City Soviet's building department were passing off as 'economic'.[6] By amassing and publicising all available data from specialists on the economics of frame-and-infill construction, and of the flat roof – both of which remained little more than stylistic issues to most of their fellow professionals – OSA contributed significantly to a turn-around in government attitudes to these innovations.[7] When Mossoviet issued a decree on replacement of load-bearing masonry building in the city by greater application of framed structures, OSA's ally, the leading engineer Prokhorov observed with satisfaction in *SA* that this was a major step towards disseminating the attitudes they had pioneered, since masonry could be done by rules-of-thumb, but a frame had to be calculated.[8] OSA challenged Vesenkha's Scientific and Technical Administration to produce some studies as serious and scientific as their's on these and other new structural forms.[9] They published numerous studies of foreign building techniques and components.

One of their main campaigns was for the mechanisation of construction. With the government currently trying to engage the whole Soviet production operation in a 'regime of economy', *SA*'s third issue in mid-1926 launched their attack on this front with the slogan 'Give us machines for building! The regime of economy in construction means mechanisation of building work.'[10] They ridiculed the wastages taking place through outdated techniques on even 'model' public building sites like the new Institute of Marxism-Leninism in central Moscow. Here donkeys were carrying bricks to the upper floors of wooden scaffolding, and at best the hoists were wooden gantries. The construction site for the equally prestigious new Moscow Telegraph Headquarters was 'Wood, Wood, Wood' and the only technology was 'Machines of the age of Leonardo da Vinci'. Demanding that the government give the highest priority to importing such equipment, their engineer correspondent Erlikh declared 'No-one can doubt the necessity for machines', and presented fully costed examples of the labour- and time-savings available through use of just the simplest mechanical lifts, crushers, diggers or mixers, as well as more sophisticated tower cranes.[11]

A year later in mid-1927, when a Central Committee decree heralded a replacement of the 'regime of economy' by campaigns for 'the rationalisation of production', *SA* printed the editorial eulogies from *Pravda* and *Izvestiia* in full, without comment, as if to say 'At last!'[12] They then renewed the battle by arranging through the state trading agency Gostorg for a Moscow exhibition of certain German machinery, which Erlikh had urged they could now import on very favourable terms, just as a start. This coincided with their staging of the Soviet Union's 'First Exhibition of Modern Architecture' in the Vkhutemas building in June-July 1927. European architects had contributed from France, Belgium, Holland, Germany, Poland, Czechoslovakia, and the identification of 'mechanisation' with Westernising was clear.[13]

Two real building projects in particular served as demonstrations of OSA's belief that 'rationalisation' of Soviet building meant introducing mechanisation and advanced technology on Western models. These were the Moscow Planetarium built by the young Barshch and Siniavsky in 1927-8, and the complex of 'transitional housing' for the People's Commissariat of Finance, Narkomfin, built by Ginzburg and Milinis in 1928-30. Each in its way represented the development of a politically important new building type that would be a catalyst or 'condenser' of the new socialist values.

With the Moscow Planetarium, the opportunity to demonstrate advanced technology came with the job. As an element of the government's virulently anti-religious education policy, this first planetarium had an ideological importance now hard to conceive. When foreign currency was extraordinarily scarce, the Moscow City Soviet was 'motivated by the possibility of promoting a wholesome scientific worldview in the population' that still clung to the creation myths of Genesis.[14] As one of OSA's most ideological members, Alexei Gan extolled it on the pages of *SA* as 'Our [Soviet] kind of theatre' where the individual 'extends his senses and perception ... through a technological apparatus, allowing him to "see" twenty-six thousand years backwards and forwards.'[15] Given its prestige, any visitor will be struck by the awkwardly narrow site. This too resulted from deep, and indeed imaginative, educational principle. As its architects explained in 1928: 'In the USSR, a planetarium must naturally be a place for popular dissemination of the theory of evolution.' Mossoviet and the scientific clients Glavnauk had therefore wanted it near the Moscow Zoo, 'in order to present as one whole the exhibition of non-organic evolution comprising the planetarium's astronomical museum, and the evolutionary sequences already planned in the Zoo Park directly alongside this site.'[16]

The 119-lamp optical unit from Carl Zeiss came as a package with Zeiss' hemispherical 'screen' and their patented anti-echo system of steel ribbons behind it. Plainly a little exhilarated by their contact with real Western technology, the architects commented on the extreme ease of erecting this Netzwerk hemisphere. The outer cupola was also a Netzwerk structure, with a thin concrete covering and insulation outside that, though its precise form was delineated 'for the Moscow skyline' by the founder-Constructivist artists, the Stenberg brothers. The architects were equally proud of their fine concrete frame below, and their neat flow diagrams of visitors' movement. However, an intelligent and sympathetic critique in Mossoviet's *Construction of Moscow* (*Stroitel'stvo Moskvy*) criticised these for not maintaining the standards of 'logic and rationality' displayed by Zeiss. Real 'economy' they

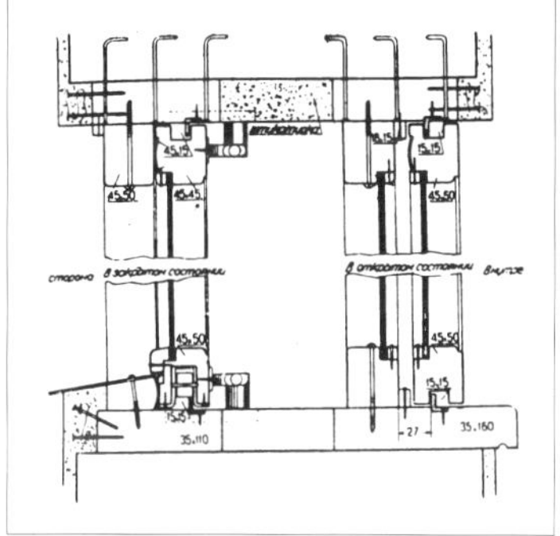

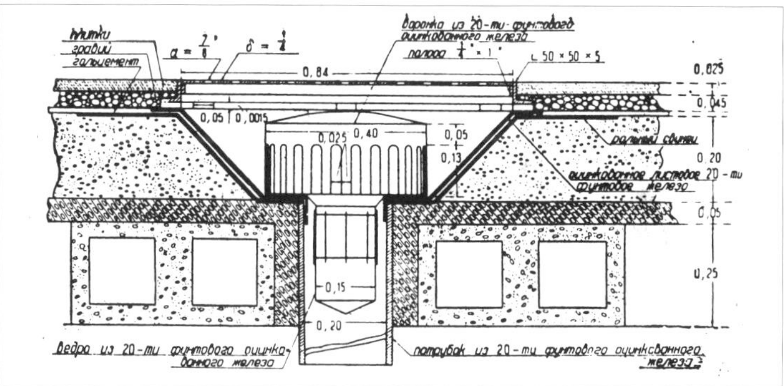

Ginzburg and Milinis, 'Transitional' housing complex for employees of Narfomfin, 1928-30: *from top: Perspective, communal block left and housing units right; Inside foyer of communal block; Laying up hollow-pot floor; Sliding windows; Pipework in hollow block walls; Flat roof at drain.*

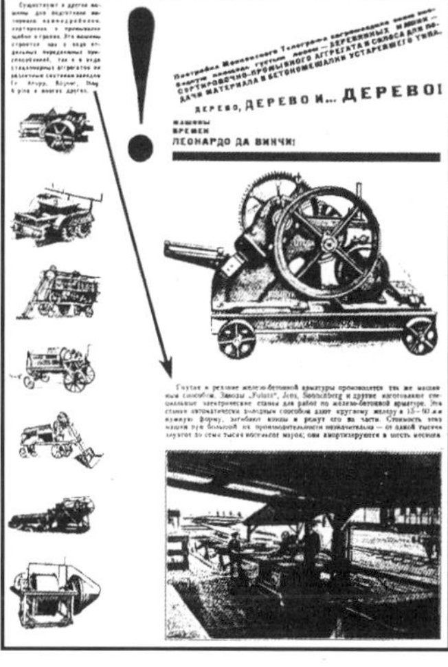

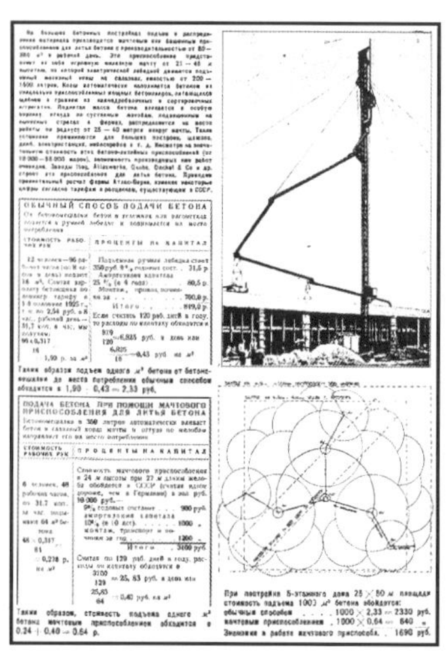

SA campaigning, 1926, no.3: *left: Deploring Soviet building industry's dependence on 'Machines from the age of Leonardo da Vinci'; right: Expounding the economics of tower cranes.*

declared would have avoided taking heavy audiences up to the first floor at all, and saved much concrete thereby. For all that they were clearly comfortable with this identification of new architecture with the atheist message, and they described the architectural treatment as a model to its 'bourgeois predecessors abroad.'[17]

A planetarium would always be a one-off project, but Moisei Ginzburg's housing complex for fifty families of the Finance Commissariat Narkomfin was treated as a test-bed for the application of 'modern' techniques throughout state housing construction. Its social aspirations, as the 'condenser' of a 'transitional' life-style, were an exemplary political statement [see Chapter 5]. Stylistically, it followed Corbusier's 'Five points of the new architecture'. Technically, however, its importance in Soviet building was as 'an experiment in the possibilities of using concrete and reinforced concrete within an industrialised, mass-production system of housing construction'; in 'using new materials', and in 'examining the possibilities and cost-effectiveness of pre-casting components, by factory methods.'[18]

Totally new in Russia were the 'cold' (i.e. non-insulating) hollow blocks which the engineer, S. L. Prokhorov of Tekhbeton, applied for internal walls and the floor slabs. Blocks of identical form from 'slag concrete' used for outside walls were already known as the 'Peasant' system. (Unfortunately these are now the main cause of the building's decay.) Also new were the horizontal sliding windows, whose many space saving and draughtproofing advantages they advanced. They admitted learning much about the brittleness, heaviness and handling problems of precast elements; of exposure problems in stuccoed walls without protecting cornices. Here long built-in window boxes had proved an unexpected if partial palliative.[19] In these discussions of their technical experiments, the avant-garde's excitement as their principles become materialised is palpably real.

Melnikov's low-tech alternative

Konstantin Melnikov's awareness of the injunctions to seek economies and 'rationalise' was no less, but his technical approach was diametrically opposite to the that pursued by the Constructivists.

Melnikov was never a man for rigid uniformity of principle. He used building techniques according to context. The great steel girder structures the pioneer Shukhov designed for his two bus garage roofs in 1926 were exploitations of a modern technique stretched near its maximum spans, and were suitably poeticised in photography by Rodchenko. The bold cantilevers central to the formal idea of his Rusakov Club of 1927 relied on the properties of reinforced concrete. Neither of these expanded the repertoire of proven construction techniques which the Soviet regime had inherited. His own little house, however, was conceived as a demonstration of 'rationalisation' through the original and in some senses more practical approach, of updating traditional artisan building techniques.

As Melnikov saw it, 'structural stability, heat insulation and daylight penetration' were the three basic problems to be 'unified through technology and architectural analysis'. He would explore here 'the materials most common in our country', namely bricks and timber boarding.[20]

Most advocates of a rationalised small-scale building in the Twenties were not members of the architectural avant-garde but adherents of the old Garden City movement and its new Soviet legatee, the Housing Cooperative movement. Chief among these people in the mid-twenties was Nikolai Markovnikov. He wrote regularly in *The Building Industry* (*Stroitel'naia promyshlennost'*) and *Construction of Moscow* to publicise their particular views, engaging on occasion with the Constructivists, specifically Barshch, to quantify relative advantages (see Chapter 10). The building branch of the Housing Cooperative movement consistently pioneered any form of small-scale mechanisation or mass production that could offer them benefits, as well as rationalisation of site practices and paper-work. Markovnikov's approach to constructional issues was cautious however. He demonstrated new kinds of foamed concrete block in small-scale housing, but at the same time he fully recognised the potential disadvantages of facing the conservative, largely peasant workforce with new materials or unaccustomed techniques.[21] His campaigning was thus mainly for compacted space and reduced scantlings out of brick and timber which were still used in the traditional ways [p.86].

Melnikov by contrast devised a quite new approach to the use of these materials in his own house:

> *'The fundamental principle of existing building is a concentrating of stresses into specific parts of the structure. My principle is the opposite, characterised by equal distribution; the essence of my system lies in the dispersal of stresses over all parts of the structure.'*[22]

He saw this as the key to using low-grade, cheap materials that were familiar to workers and readily available even in the currently stretched and erraticly supplied Soviet market place. His 'opening up' of the traditional stuccoed-brick wall produced a load-spreading cage into which windows and

Typical Soviet building labourers on a Moscow site, mid-1920s, with primitive hand tools and wooden scaffolding. Most were seasonal workers who returned to their villages for harvest.

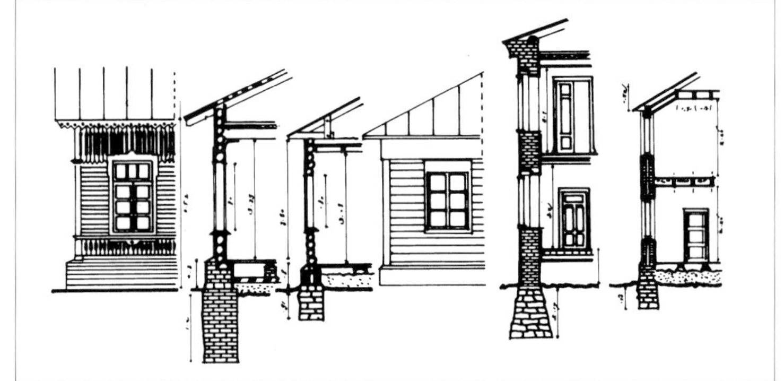

Markovnikov: Rationalising traditional timber and brick construction by reducing storey heights and scantlings. Use of roof pitch for habitable space was called the 'English cottage' section.

insulation could be inserted as desired, further saving brick by maximum fill with 'building rubbish' of higher density and thermal storage capacity. His floors required no beams but were entirely constructed of small scantlings: a two-way grille of notched planks stiffened by a 'structural' ceiling and floor of diagonal tongued-and-grooved boarding, to produce a modern, lightweight stiffness in place of traditional massive 'strength'. The brick structures were circular, to get maximum floor area for the structural circumference, and these cellular 'plates' filled with further insulation were notionally 'inserted like the base or the top of a large barrel.'[23] The advantages which he believed would follow from this were numerous. These are recounted in Documents 11 and 12, which are his own description prior to building, and critic Nikolai Lukhmanov's sympathetic commentary from *Construction of Moscow* in spring 1929, when it was near completion.

What the latter article particularly highlights, however, are the difficulties encountered by even such supposedly modest innovation in Soviet building practice at that date. In attempting to respond to government injunctions to demonstrate 'economies' and 'rationalisation', and to Gosplan's calls for development of 'new types of structure', Melnikov hit the problems Gosplan also identified, of unskilled labour and its inherent conservatism. Long before their specialist Smurgis wrote in 1929 of a construction industry 'which has no desire to apply solutions different from those to which they are accustomed', Markovnikov too had made that fact of life the premise of his whole approach. When Soviet building was just waking up 'from its ten years asleep' in early 1924, he wrote in the first issue of the Housing Cooperative movements journal:

> *'From the very start, in setting ourselves the aim of reducing construction costs, we must not diverge far from the practical conditions of our reality. We must be very careful in applying any new methods that are not familiar to our workers and must avoid using any materials that are not generally known to them. For it is well known that all deviation and even the most desirable improvements or inventions, whilst they are new and unaccustomed for the workers, will increase the cost and complicate the work.*
>
> *'Improvements must therefore be introduced gradually, as part of a naturally progressive move forward, but we must start by working with the methods that are usually applied.'*[24]

Five years later Lukhmanov's article described how Melnikov's experiment in 'rationalising traditions' fell foul of precisely these problems.

While Melnikov was trying to rationalise 'what he knew', so too in their different way were the Constructivists. As colleagues and pupils of Alexander Kuznetsov, Ginzburg and his young assistant Ignati Milinis were steeped in the science and potential of reinforced concrete. It is not clear why Gosplan's Bernatsky had considered 'reinforced concrete with a steel frame' to be somehow unsuited to Moscow's climate, unless he imagined it always fully glazed. Neither frame nor over-glazing were problems with the Narkomfin housing. Indeed structural surveys of the late 1980s have shown that the frame itself remains in excellent condition, and amounts of glazing were always very controlled. The long-term structural problem, as mentioned earlier, has been caused by the element that was far more experimental: the slag-concrete infill.

What commentators at the time saw as most problematic however was the extreme constructional complexity of the intricate spatial structure demanded by OSA's theoretically 'economic' housing units and their low 'coefficients' in relation to conventional formulae.[25] The Narkomfin building site was a model of advanced technique in the new, more economical use of materials, and offered many lessons for the training of Russia's mass unskilled labour force. The ultimate lesson it fed back to the architects, however, was the fundamental one identified at the beginning of the technical debate within Gosplan: that technology and 'building type' – what Lukhmanov discussed in his paper on Melnikov as building 'shape' – are not separable factors in the equation of building cost. Whilst building economists debated, however, these avant-gardists had made the running in practical design research on these issues.

■

1 W. Coxe, *Travels in Poland, Russia, Sweden and Denmark*, London, 1784, vol.1, p.348. Further descriptions may be found in George Heard Hamilton *The Art and Architecture of Russia*, London, 1975, pp.114-5 and James Cracraft, *The Petrine Revolution in Russian Architecture*, Chicago, 1988, p.34. **2** L.N.Bernatskii, 'Zhilishchnyi krizis i zhilishchnoe stroitel'stvo' (The housing crisis and housing construction), *Plannovoe khoziaistvo* (The Planned Economy), 1925, June, pp.36-55 **3** Iu. Smurgis, 'Voprosy stroitel'nogo dela' (Questions of the building business), *Plannovoe khoziaistvo*, 1928, November, pp.102-114 **4** L.N.Bernatskii, 'Puti industrializatsii stroitel'stva' (Paths of the industrialisation of construction), *Plannovoe khoziastvo*, 1930, January, pp. 149-165 **5** Slogans in *SA*, 1926 no.2 p.44. **6** G.Vegman, 'Rabochee stroitel'stvo v Moskve' (Workers' housing construction in Moscow), *SA*, 1926, no.1, pp.9, 1 **7** Flat roof survey: *SA*, 1926 no.4, pp.98-103; Prefabricated steel housing: *SA*, 1927 no.6, pp.170-8; Hollow-block techniques: *SA*, 1928 no.2, pp.49-60; New concrete techniques: *SA*, 1928 no.6, pp. 188-93. **8** Engr A.L. Prokhorov, 'Poslednye dostizheniia v stroitel'stve iz betonnikh kamnei' (The latest achievements in building with concrete blocks), *SA*, 1928, no.2, pp.49-60 **9** Editorial, *SA*, 1927, no.2, p.50 **10** *SA*, 1926, no.3, p.86 **11** A.N. Erlikh, 'Mekhanizatsiia stroitel'stva' (The mechanisation of construction), *SA*, 1926, no.3, pp.80-86 **12** *SA*, 1927, no.3, pp.82, 84 **13** *SA*, 1926, no.4, p.108 and *SA*, 1927, nos. 4-5 and 6 on the exhibition. For a detailed discussion of its planning, contents and critical reception see: I. Kokkinaki, 'The First Exhibition of Modern Architecture in Moscow', *Architectural Design*, 1983, no.5/6, pp.50-59 **14** M. Barshch and M.Siniavskii (assumed), 'Planetarii', *SA*, 1927 no 3, p 80. **15** A.Gan, 'Novomu teatru, novoe zdanie' (A new building for a new kind of theatre), SA, 1927, no.3 p.81 **16** M. Barshch and M. Siniavskii, 'Planetarii v Moskve' (The planetarium in Moscow), *Stroitel'stvo Moskvy*, 1928 no 8, pp 1-3. **17** A. Zil'bert, 'Pervyi planetarii v SSSR' (The first planetarium in the USSR), *Stroitel'stvo Moskvy*, 1930, no.1, pp.30-32 **18** M.Ia. Ginzburg, *Zhilishche* (Housing), Moscow 1934 (written 1930-1), pp.98-102 (Chapter 5): 'Konstruktsiia, material, metody stroitel'nogo proizvodstva: opytny dom NKF' (Construction, material, methods of building production: the experimental building for Narkomfin). **19** ibid. **20** Melnikov, quoted in N. Lukhmanov, 'Tsilindricheskii dom', *Stroitel'stvo Moskvy*, 1929, no.4, pp.16-22. Melnikov's elegant coloured site plans are reproduced in: A. Calnek, ed., *The Great Utopia*, Guggenheim Museum, New York, 1992, figs.706-8, also with archival photos of the house, the terraced variants and other buildings, in S. Khan-Magomedov, *Konstantin Mel'nikov*, Moscow, 1990. **21** N. Markovnikov, 'Zhilishchno-kooperativnoe stroitel'stvo' (Housing cooperative construction), *Zhilishchnaia kooperatsiia* (Housing Cooperation), 1924, no.1, pp.12-14 **22** Mel'nikov, quoted in Lukhmanov, 'Tsilindricheskii dom', p.18 **23** Lukhmanov, 'Tsilindricheskii dom', p.18 **24** Markovnikov, 'Zhilishchno-kooperativnoe stroitel'stvo', p.14 **25** 'Slushali: Problemy tipizatsii zhil'ia RSFSR. Doklad M.Ia. Ginzburga' (They listened: the problem of housing standardisation in the Russian Republic. Lecture by M.Ia. Ginzburg). His lecture on Constructivist housing proposals and subsequent discussion amongst specialists in Stroikom RSFSR, *SA*, 1929, no.1, pp.4-36.

Doc. 11

KONSTANTIN MELNIKOV CONSTRUCTION OF HIS HOUSE

Manuscript notes, 7 August 1927

A: Construction of the walls

Architecturally the house consists of two cylinders, 8 and 11 metres high, which intersect each other to one-third of their 10-metre diameter.

External walls are made of ordinary red brick. These are laid up according to a special system to form columns that describe broken vertical lines forming a chequerboard pattern in the walls, around apertures of rhomboid form whose dimensions are multiples of brick dimensions.

This system of brick coursing, especially when done in a circle, provides a perfect answer to the problem of distributing stressses evenly throughout a whole wall.

As ties, certain bricks are cut to 3/4 dimension and the courses are displaced in two dimensions: along the length of the wall in a given course, and through the wall on every second course. This produces vertical and horizontal set-backs of 1/4 brick depth that are filled with stucco of a simple lime mix, which supplements the thermal insulation of the wall where it is 2-bricks thick.

Of the total 124 apertures in the whole external wall, half are used for windows and half are used as a thermal storage (closed and filled).

The foundations are a ribbon of rubble ashlar.

B: Floors and roof

The horizontal structure to all floors is identical, of 9 metres diameter and made of timber. In accordance with the overall structural idea, these floors do not have any concentrated points of support.

Their construction consists of a two-way grid, 0.5 x 0.5 metre, executed from planks of 2.5 x 22 cm section, used on edge and tied together above and below by planking with clean grooved boarding of 2.9 x 9 cm. This planking is laid at 45 degrees to the framing, with top and bottom layers running perpendicular to each other. The cubic spaces formed inside the framing serve as convenient places for packing with thermal and acoustic insulation material.

Since creating the frame to the precise dimensions on site is highly labour intensive, these gridded frameworks for floors and ceilings were prepared on the site alongside the building, and assembled in place on temporary supports with wedges.

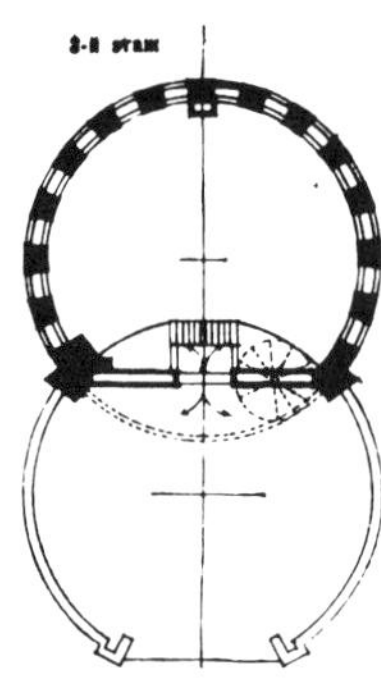

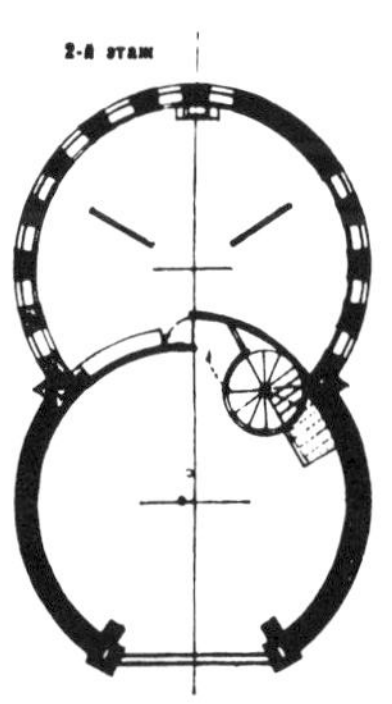

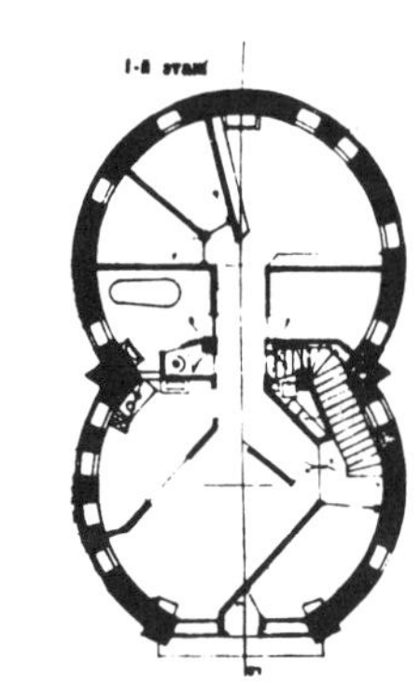

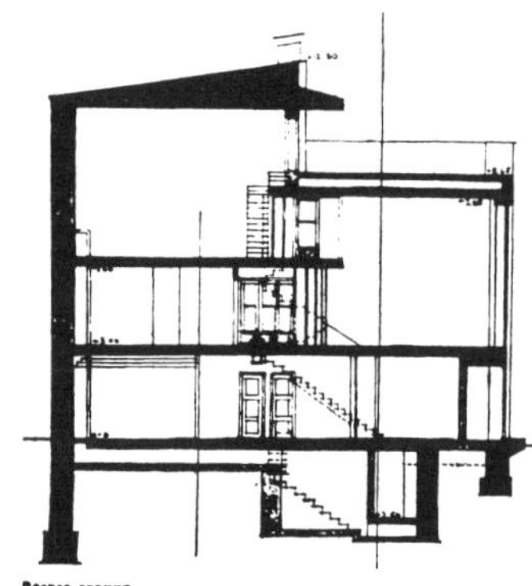

Right, from the top:
Plans of the house: ***Second floor****, with Melnikov's double-height studio on garden side;* ***First floor****, with common family bedroom (see photo p.60), rear, and double-height living room, glazed full-height onto street (cf. photo far right);* ***Ground floor****, with entrance from street, dining room set diagonally on front, kitchen, all sanitary accommodation and utility rooms behind, and stairs to first floor.*
Section *through long axis of the two interlocking cylinders (see model p.60), street side right, garden left.*

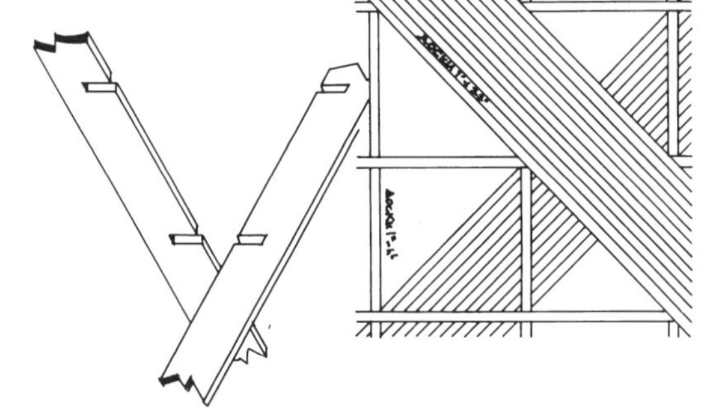

Far right, from the top:
Site at foundation stage, with Melnikov and his schoolboy son Viktor (present inhabitant);
The two-way spanning floor plates, upper one boarded, lower one before boarding, and below it, Melnikov's drawing of this two-way system;
Finished house, from an apartment across the street, showing roof terrace, full-height French windows open to living room, and entrance;
Melnikov in spats and his wife Anna in high heels, posing beside the bare brick 'cage' of their new property before infill and stuccoing.

Doc. 12

NIKOLAI LUKHMANOV
THE CYLINDRICAL HOUSE

Stroitel'stvo Moskvy, 1929, no.4, pp.16-22

New constructional forms are very much lacking in our building practice. The old rectangular ways of making a building are still applied on a mass scale with us, regardless of their advantages in use, of the possibilities for rationalising work operations within them, or of their appropriateness to the new way of life. Whether the building is of a commercial or industrial type, housing or for administration, everything is built here in the form of a cube, despite the fact that many of these buildings would profit greatly from being in other shapes: triangular, rhombic, circular. This lack of new structural shapes in our building practice has an important impact on the rationalisation of construction and on our capacity to improve the functioning of our industrial and urban way of life through use of new architectual structures.

It is the practical and political role of the architect to manage these functions through new architectural erections and constructions that accord with the requirements of the cultural revolution and the industrialisation of the country, .

Bold and courageous experiment is required in our construction work if we are to get new architectural forms introduced into practice, and it cannot happen without architecture taking the lead over construction.

One of the latest works of the architect-artist K.S. Melnikov is the experimental structure of a one-family house on Krivo-Arbatsky Lane, and has great interest in this respect. Melnikov, the project's author, is convinced of the necessity for a reconstruction of our building practice. He says:

'The underlying principle of all present construction work is the concentration of stresses into specific elements of the structure. My principle is the precise opposite: the dispersal of stresses, their even distribution over all parts of the structure.'

Architect Melnikov already designed this house in 1927. Now, when the structure is already more than 80 per cent completed, we can usefully disseminate some information about this experiment.

The house is constructed of two vertical cylinders, intersecting each other to one-third of their diameter. The cylindrical form of the building is called forth by: 1) the cylinder's economic advantages of shorter enclosing walls for a given area compared to walls around a square; 2) by the living conditions which circular rooms create, of which I shall speak separately. The figure of eight plan form resulting from this cylindrical construction is the basis for the exterior walls. The construction of these walls is then a standard grid, laid up in brick, beginning from the foundations and ending with the roof. It is the same throughout, with individual details of the brick construction repeating themselves again and again, thus eliminating the concepts of 'vertical and horizontal', 'column and beam' which characterise existing structural systems, and dispersing stresses throughout the whole wall. All dimensions in the wall of solid load bearing elements and of apertures, are determined by the dimensions of the brick. Despite the complexity of this manner of laying up and the vast number of apertures (the two cylinders contain in total about 200 of the hexagonal 'windows'), and despite the strict observance of cross-links in the coursing, the walls were laid without cutting any brick. This was achieved by shifting the courses in each row by 1/8th of a brick in one direction or another. The hexagonal apertures in the standard brick coursing were distributed in diagonal lines and can be used in a diversity of ways: some of them for windows, some to increase the wall's insulation value (the aperture is filled with building rubbish, earth and so on, producing a wall which amounts to a thermal accumulator.)

The structure of the floors and roof is of great interest. There are no beams, secondary floors or trusses. All these have been replaced by boarding. The structural network - the future basis of floors, ceiling and roof, - is itself made up of boarding. The floors and roof elements are inserted into the cylinders like the base or the top of a large barrel. This framework is then tied together above and below with grooved boarding. This boarding forms the floor and ceiling, which thus become working parts of the structure, unlike in the old building system where they were only an unavoidable ballast.

Thus in the new construction those parts which were formerly secondary elements become the working parts. A building constructed like this distributes stresses uniformly, spreading them evenly over all its parts. This very principle of evenness of stressing reduces the quantity of building materials required, and gives the possibility to utilise materials of less strength, which in turn guarantee a lower thermal conductivity. The experimental work of architect K.S. Melnikov is executed from those materials which are most widespread and common in our country. Precisely for this reason, brick and timber were the most difficult to experiment with in new ways, but successful conduct of such an experiment has shown the great flexibility which in fact exists within such a system of building. Stability, thermal insulation and light penetration are the main factors to be combined with the technology of construction plus the self-analysis of architectural creativity to produce a design, and they have led the author of this building to invent a new constructional system.

The final cost of the building came out at 32,000 rubles for an overall cubic volume of 1,350 cubic metres, giving a cost per cubic metre of 24 rubles.

In scrutiny of these figures it is necessary to allow for the conditions applying to all experimental work, as well as the purely local and private circumstances of this particular project. The combination of these has significantly increased costs. Thus ground conditions on the site that was allocated required the foundations to be dug to great depth – down to 4 metres in some places; thanks to the tightness of funds overall, the construction period extended over almost two years, which raised 'imposed' costs such as lodgings, periods of time casually wasted, temporary heating in winter, and so on. Other extra costs resulted from organisational shortfalls in the procurement of building materials and from the typical sins of the experimenter in correcting details for purely compositional reasons during the process of construction (e.g. changing the construction of the window frames, the method of laying up the walls and the brick-laying of the walls in closed 'triangles'). By eliminating these extras which so characteristically accompany any sort of experiment, the cost for such a building could come down to about 18-19 rubles per cubic metre. Even that sum might be reduced further in future, notably through a more qualified workforce. In particular, the circular form of the building, the system of coursing the bricks, and the method of making the horizontal elements of floor and roof, were seen here by the bricklayer and the carpenter as 'making their work more complicated'. They had to learn a new standard way of bricklaying and a new standard way of laying boards for the floors.

We still have not given full recognition to the specific conditions of our everyday life that favour such cylindrical constructions.

These conditions are characteristic for our epoch, which is conquering the old culture of everyday life through the help of industry and technology, and with the help of a prophylactic policy for health care, physical culture and hygiene in the dwelling. The circular room, which is the aim and concomitant of cylindrical construction, does not have corners, those concentrators of dust and dirt. However much we insist that flat walls are obligatory so that objects can be stood right against them, in fact they cannot if there is to be any of the necessary circulation of air. The perimeter of the circular walls is also shorter than in our usual buildings. All this guarantees greater cleanliness of the accommodation with less expenditure of effort. Finally, the cylinder represents the opportunity for fuller and more even air changes for the given volume and apart from that, as with any kind of circular enclosure, it creates a feeling of spaciousness.

K.S. Melnikov's house contains five circular rooms. Two are on the ground floor, which is essentially given over to the 'laboratory-dwelling'. Also on this floor are the entrance vestibule, dining room and kitchen. On the first floor is the wardrobe accommodation, toilet, two rooms for family workshops and studios, bathroom and lavatories (thin straight lines on the plan indicate partitions, separating the various elements of accommodation). Of the two large rooms on the first floor the first is a guest room or common, family room, and the second, with two partitions and 14 windows, is a bedroom. The fifth large room with forty windows is intended as a studio for the architect himself. All rooms are intended to be equipped with permanent, fitted furniture – cupboards, wardrobes, tables and beds, will be specially constructed, hermetically sealed to the walls and the floors. Besides this, with the exclusive aim of furthering hygiene in the house, floors, ceiling and walls of the bedroom will be coated in alabaster, polished till it shines. The various rooms and level in the house are linked by a spiral staircase, which starts in the ground floor vestibule and in effect ends on the gallery which leads onto the balcony. The floor of the balcony has an extremely original system of pipes for drainage.

The architect has also devised 'a scheme for applying the principle of the cylindrical house in a terraced system'. Its importance for our construction effort is mainly in the housing cooperative sector. It successfully solves the question of the building of small housing units of 1-2 rooms with all conveniences, and offers of chance to reduce the construction coefficient (relation of cubic volume to housing area): it would be 5.97 for a one-roomed apartment on this pattern and 5.50 for a two-roomed one, in contrast to the current coefficient in Moscow of 7.35 (the costs of building are reduced by 10-15 per cent in the terraced form). Apart from this, Melnikov's design offers the possibility for an even wider choice of building materials (the lack of concentration of stresses into individual parts of the building also makes it possible to cast the walls).

Thus the experiment in that old architectural form, the one-family house, offers possibilities for a new form of mass housing construction.

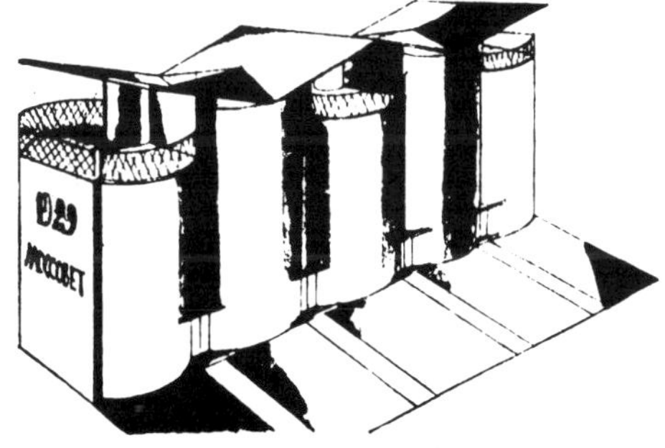

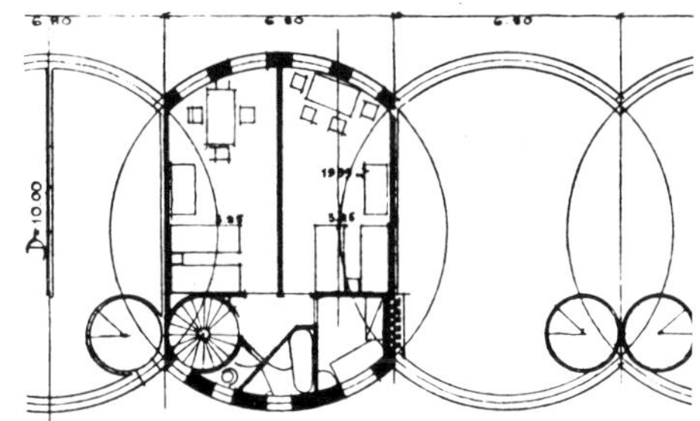

Melnikov's proposal for a 'terraced' version of his house to provide public housing: perspective and first floor plan.

Konstantin Melnikov, Soviet pavilion at the Exposition des Arts Decoratifs et Industriels, Paris, 1925: entrance.

8: MELNIKOV AND THE CHANGING FOCUS OF WESTERN LITERATURE ON THE RUSSIAN AVANT-GARDE

'The undiminished interest of the international architectural community in the achievements of Soviet revolutionary architecture manifests to the vitality of the creative ideas generated by the October Revoluton of 1917. One can hardly find a great architect in any part of the world today who has not in some way or other addressed himself to this period of Soviet architecture ... and the jubilee of Konstantin Melnikov has generated a new flow of interest. On a Soviet initiative, UNESCO has included the name of Melnikov amongst the officially listed "major figures of world culture" to be commemorated by events in 1990.' [1]

Thus the Union of Architects of the USSR wrote in its 'Programme' for a Festival to coincide with Melnikov's centenary in 1990.

Naturally we must make allowances for some patriotic hyperbole. However something has plainly changed from the situation when Melnikov's Western biographer Frederick Starr wrote in 1969, that:

'Among the consequences of Melnikov's suppression [ie exclusion from the Union of Soviet Architects and profession in the mid-Thirties, CC] is the fact that his work has not been well enough known to exert any discernable influence on either Soviet or world architecture'. [2]

Plainly the truth of his influence lies somewhere between these two extremes. However, neither reputation nor influence can be formed without information, and the closed nature of Soviet society and its territory until recently have been the major factor in hiding Soviet work of the Twenties, as of other periods, from objective judgement of Western historians and critics. In the absence of personal contact with a work, literature forms a surrogate contact.

In Melnikov's case, the literature appears at first sight to have been fickle. Interestingly, however, the changing levels of attention devoted to Melnikov have not been related solely to any general political 'opening up'; nor even, I think, to the 'professional demise' to which Starr attributes it, for Melnikov starts disappearing from the literature before that occurred. The change was a relatively independent phenomenon, and seems to me attributable to three factors: firstly, to the vast quantity of other work, as good and often better, which started to appear after Melnikov's Paris debut in 1925 as the only Soviet modernist the international world knew; secondly, to the West's interest in coherent, verbally expressed theory, which Melnikov eschewed, and thirdly, consolidating these two, the dominance of others in the few internationally accessible publications produced by Russians themselves, such as the Constructivists' journal *Contemporary Architecture* (*SA*), published from 1926-1930, and El Lissitzky's book *Russland: Die Rekonstruktion der Arkhitektur in der Sowjetunion*, published in 1930.

Before focussing on an examination of the ideas elicited and developed in the writings of the 1970s by Frederick Starr, whose 'meticulous labour of love', as Charles Jencks rightly called it, restored Melnikov to prominence, even dominance, in Western perceptions of Soviet avant-garde architecture, it is interesting to trace how it was that Melnikov moved so dramatically from spotlight to obscurity in the previous decades. Apart from the specific interest of the Melnikov case, it is a cautionary tale in the power and potentially distorting effect of the architectural literature, and one example amongst many of why the revisionist histories now beginning to emerge are so important to our proper understanding of Modernism and its legacy.

What was Melnikov's unique contribution?

Today, with directors of Melnikov's workers' clubs offering guided tours to foreign architectural tourists, and cafés installed to make dollars from each party; with both Western and Soviet guide books to Moscow identifying these clubs and his house as 'monuments' on the tourist itinerary, it is hard now to grasp the truth of Starr's observation in his pioneering article of 1969. Outside the Soviet Union, he wrote, Melnikov's name 'is known in connection with no more than two or three buildings and he is absent from all the major encyclopedias of modern architecture.'[3]

Starr is not an architect, and there are certain items of the literature which even his best advisors would reasonably not have brought to his attention. But the essential observation here was true at that date. Indeed, perhaps, in the canon of world architecture in his time, that representation of Melnikov is a fair one.

On the basis of technical sophistication or even competence of execution, one could argue that almost no Soviet building merits inclusion amongst the great products of the last eighty years or so. But if architectural achievement is to be limited by technical sophistication of the realised work, there is much else that would be excluded too. If the criterion is to be theoretical interest, much Russian work must qualify, though probably not Melnikov. If the criterion is to be formal inventiveness, then even Melnikov's small production of fully resolved and successful buildings must qualify him, quite apart from the extraordinary unrealised oeuvre of his years of disfavour in the early Thirties.

Melnikov's formal inventiveness owes much, in my view, to a characteristically Russian formal sensibility, rooted in the broad, open tedium of the Russian landscape where three-dimensional form makes a powerful statement of 'presence', both as volume and as silhouette. This is perhaps where Melnikov in particular adds something to the vocabulary of international Modernism, for having liberated itself from the confines of the party wall to free-up site planning and the volumetric composition of the city, most Western Modernism in fact refilled these empty spaces with very soberly cubic volumetric compositions. Of Melnikov's works, by contrast, there is hardly one which is not conceived as a sculptural object rather than as a sub-unit of a three-dimensional city grid.

When Starr's ground-breaking monograph on Melnikov appeared in 1978, Charles Jencks was known for his *Modern Movements in Architecture* and was asked by the London *Architects' Journal* to review it.[4] To its shame, the journal illustrated Ilia Golosov's Zuev Club as a Melnikov building alongside his Paris Pavilion and Rusakov Club. Certainly Melnikov and Golosov were close colleagues in the very early Twenties, five years before the competition for this Zuev Club, and had taught a joint studio as 'The New Academy' for a while in the Vkhutemas. By 1927, however, as Chapter 4 has shown, their design strategies had diverged. The erroneous labelling of these juxtaposed photos jars enough, therefore, to draw our attention to this unique three-dimensionality of Melnikov's work.

Despite its dramaticly glazed circular stairtower on the corner, Golosov's famous building is so much a piece of the cubic space-matrix of the street and the city that it could never, to the well familiarised eye, be by Melnikov. Melnikov's own scheme for that site (from which he claimed Golosov stole the circular motif), comprised four cylinders, freestanding from the party walls along this linear site. Where Golosov plugged in awkwardly to the cubic matrix of the city fabric, Melnikov would have stood free of it. Consciously or not, his spatial model is fundamentally that of the innumerable Russian churches, some medieval and others, even more similar, with classical rotundas, which in the Twenties still stood on almost every Moscow street corner. In 1979, Jencks had lately published *The Language of Post-Modern Architecture*, and he used the Melnikov book review to make a comparison, then topical, between aspects of Melnikov's career and Bruce Goff's. His final comment on the value of rediscovering the Melnikov oeuvre links the two architects' contributions to design:

> *'If only Melnikov, Goff, the Expressionists, had carried the day over the international style, we would have had a richer language of architecture. As it is, they remain a missing link back to the fuller language of romantic classicism.'*[5]

This theme of Jencks' is close to an idea expressed by Starr in his small monograph on Melnikov's Soviet pavilion for the 1925 Exposition in Paris. 'Admired but not emulated,' he writes, 'Melnikov's building proved to be the international swansong of those currents [of Modernism] that were not compatible with the rapidly evolving International style'.[6]

This is a gross exaggeration of its uniqueness, certainly, but read in the context of Russian Modernism, rather than international Modernism, it hints at the explanation for what happened, as I see it, to push Melnikov out of the spotlight, in the Western perception of the Russian scene.

Paris 1925: the world's first view of Soviet architecture

Before 1925, almost nothing of what Soviet architects had been doing since the Revolution had been seen in the West. Indeed only a few projects had risen above the level of romantic sketches or lumpish attempts to resolve over-blown briefs. Architecture was only just beginning to be a serious area of concern within the literary or artistic movements of the avant-garde.

The most solid early architectural text, by Melnikov's contemporary Moisei Ginzburg, had just been published in 1924 as *Style and Epoch*. Amongst forty-one pictures which Ginzburg selected as a fair coverage of innovative Russian work he considered to be in the spirit of Modernism, there were two photographs of Melnikov's Makhorka tobacco pavilion at the Moscow Agricultural Exhibition of the previous year, and a sheet detailing his prize-winning competition project of 1922-3 for workers' housing.[7] In the context, that was very fair coverage. Both designs derived their relative strength and plausibility from being projects of modest and manageable scale, but except for the copy which Ginzburg sent to Le Corbusier, few people abroad would have seen this small and rather serious book.[8]

Street-corner churches, round towers: Moscow, drawn 1610.

Golosov's Zuev club, below, erroneously shown as Melnikov's, Architects' Journal.

Melnikov's own scheme for Zuev club, 1927, from street corner (plan right)..

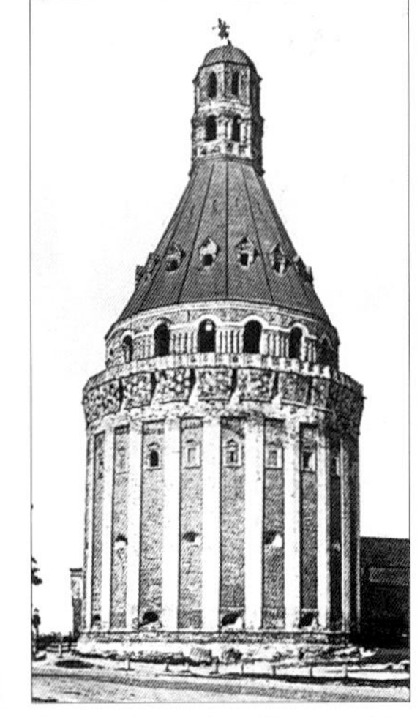

Simonov Monastery, Moscow, 16-17C, famous circular brick tower.

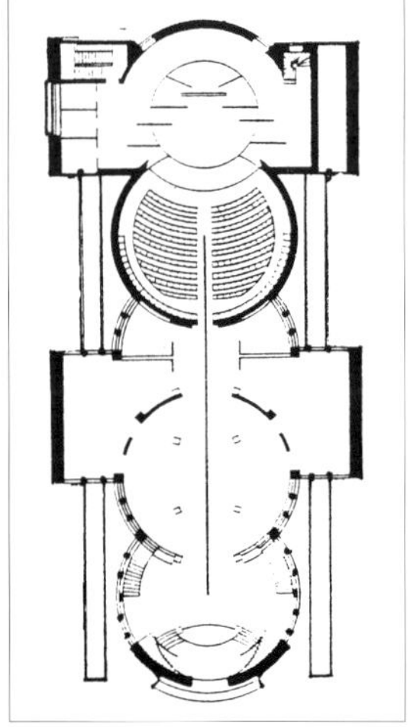

Melnikov, 1927, plan of Zuev club design with four cylinders enfilade.

At this date, Russia's avant-garde artists were in advance of the architects in their exploration of Modernist vocabularies. To Western eyes, the aesthetic level of the abstract and broadly constructive work they saw in Berlin in 1922, in the Erste Russische Kunstaustellung at the Van Diemen Gallery, was far more sophisticated than anything they had yet seen by Soviet architects. Not till Melnikov's pavilion went up in Paris in 1925 did that judgement have reason to change.

The Paris Exposition des Arts Decoratifs in 1925 offered an enormously larger audience, and Melnikov profited from the groundwork laid since the turn of the century by Diaghilev. Here was a city that expected a thrill of 'exoticism' from things Russian. Thus as Reyner Banham put it,

> *'At such a time, [Russia's pavilion] could hardly have gone unnoticed however it had been designed, but Melnikov's deceptively simple structure in wood must have looked as if it had been deliberately conceived to excite and annoy, ... [with] a form of symmetry, but not one listed in the Academic recipes.'*[9]

It did shock, negatively as well as positively. *The Architectural Review*, as Britain's principal architectural journal, merely mentioned 'the Russian pavilion composed cubistically of plate glass and steel' (sic) as one extreme of the 'heterogenous' range of architectures to be expected in such shows. 'Picture them all side by side, discovered by the eyes' wrote their editor, 'then be grateful for the trees'.[10] The American *Architectural Record*, writing specifically of the Melnikov, went a lot further.

> *'The most eccentric of these buildings is dividing the opinion of the many who have stood aghast before it, some declaring it a practical joke on the Exposition, and the others warmly asserting this monstrosity to be rich in symbolism and an advance in the direction of a new art millenium. This building is the contribution of the Soviet Russians to the new modern school and it follows closely the formula which banishes completely all curves and ornament. A facetious writer in the Paris press hazards the guess that this edifice must have been completely constructed in Russia and then taken down, piece by piece, for shipment to Paris. It is quite clear, says this humorist, that some of the packing boxes were mistakenly labelled and that in reconstructing the Soviet monument the workmen have mixed up the various units.'*[11]

Equally derogatory views were to be read elsewhere, notably in the Italian *Architettura e Arti Decorative* and the French *Le Revue de L'Art*, and *L'Intransigent*. They offer a welcome antidote to the ecstatic writing that is to be found in most of the French press, which derived its confidence from the fact that the Exhibition Committee had awarded Melnikov's building the Grand Prix.[12] Indeed, to be cynical, one can see the prize as a good way to hype up the public interest in the show itself, as full of unexpected novelties. The relative stylistic uniformity of the largely-French show made it difficult to premiate one above the other. Foreign exotica is always better value for a prize: it prevents local jealousies and keeps everyone happy.

The success of Melnikov's building with the design fraternity certainly owed much to this factor. Its integrity as an exhibition object derived greatly, as Jean-Louis Cohen has pointed out, from the fact it was conceived purely for that function, not, like Corbusier's pavilion for *L'Esprit Nouveau*, as a demonstration of something else – in that case, of 'the realism of the *immeuble-villa* cell' within his Plan Voisin. Much of the 'scandal', derived from precisely the 'nakedness' of Melnikov's undecorated structure and open glazed walls. Even that *vulgarité* alone would always have produced a pleasant *frisson* in France, with a cultural disposition to enjoy nakedness as much in engineering as in human flesh.

In relation to the stress placed by contemporary commentators on the pavilion's 'symbolism', which has been nurtured by most writers ever since, it is worth noting here that Melnikov's line in interviews in Paris was to divert attention from suggestions of symbolism onto precisely this quality of directness. The best example of this was the interview with him published in *Le Bulletin de la Vie Artistique*. After some obligatory ramblings about how the October Revolution has changed the world, the interviewer tried to divert Melnikov into 'telling us in more detail about your Paris pavilion. What is the basic idea behind it?' Melnikov replied unequivocally.

> *'This glazed box is not the fruit of an abstract idea. My starting point was real life, I had to deal with real circumstances. Above all, I worked with the site that was allocated to me, a site surrounded by trees: it was necessary that my little building should sharply distinguish itself amidst their shapeless masses by colour, height and a skilful combination of forms. The means available to me were very meagre: this limited the choice of materials. I wanted the pavilion to be as full of light and air as possible: that is my personal predilection and I think it reasonably represents the aspiration of our whole nation. Not everyone who walks past the pavilion will go inside it. But each of them will see something of what is exhibited inside my building, all the same, thanks to the glazed walls and the staircase which goes out to meet the crowd, passes through the pavilion and enables them to survey the whole of its contents from above. As far as the intersecting diagonal planes raised over that route are concerned, may they be a disappointment to the lovers of completely closed roofs! [In the recently published Russian version Melnikov's phrase is the typically colourful 'corked-up' roofs, but the milder French 'couvercles' may be closer to his original. CC] This roof is no worse than any other: it is so made as to let in the air and yet protect the passage from the rain, from whatever direction it beats on it.'*

'But don't you think that all this glass and this strange roof make your pavilion much too light-weight?' asked the interviewer, focussing on the aspect that must have been most conspicuous amongst the heavy marble Art Deco around it. Again Melnikov was almost brusquely direct:

> *'You are really saying that you would prefer something more heavy-weight. But why should a building whose function is temporary be given false attributes of the everlasting? My pavilion doesn't have to keep standing for the whole life of the Soviet Union. It is quite enough for it to keep standing till the exhibition closes. To put it briefly, the clarity of colour, the simplicity of line, the abundance of light and air which characterise this pavilion, whose unusualness you may like or dislike according to taste, have a similarity to the country from which I come. But do not think, for goodness sake, that I set out to build a symbol.'*[13]

Even later in life, when very prone to ascribe romantic symbolic intentions to his works, Melnikov again described the generating idea here, as in his Makhorka pavilion two years earlier, as the simple desire to get maximum walking route through a minimal building. His trick was to give it an impression of size from the outside by extending one horizontal dimension to maximum length, and by raising one corner to maximum height[14] [Docs. 13, 14]. These are the simple devices of an intelligent architect and there is no doubt that those co-professionals who praised his building recognised that.

The spotlight moves

After the Exhibition closed the Soviet pavilion was donated to Paris trade unionists for re-erection elsewhere, and lost to international attention. Quite numerous pictures had appeared, but in obscure Parisian journals. For the world architectural public, all that remained of this building after autumn 1925, as Starr has pointed out, were 'a couple of pictures from which it is very difficult to form any useful impression of the whole building.'[15] Meetings in Paris led to Melnikov getting 'a whole section' amongst other Soviet artists and architects at the Machine Age exhibition in New York in 1927, but Russian material arrived too late to be properly published, and in a small, shortlived show in obscure premises, their participation made little impression.[16] Back at home no one showed much interest in engaging with events abroad. Melnikov himself described the general lack of interest in his success on his return from Paris. The reasons were as much practical as ideological: to public and profession struggling with the lively challenges of Soviet reality, international exhibitions were a total irrelevance.

During the rest of the Twenties there was not much information in any Western architectural literature about developments in the Soviet Union. It was difficult to get there, though once arrived, as Alfred Barr noted on his trip during the winter 1927/8, no one worried much what one did, as Intourist had not yet got organised to control people.[17] The rich cultural study by Rene Fülöp-Miller in his *Mind and Face of Bolshevism* was based on travels in 1925, which therefore pre-date any significant architectural activity.[18] Barr's visit, as a front-line Modernist art critic, produced some interesting comments in his diary, now lately published, on 'the four "modern" buildings in Moscow' and his very domestic meetings with Lissitzky, Burov, Rodchenko and 'a brilliant young architect, Moisei Ginzburg by name'. He visited Ginzburg's Gostrakha apartment building [pp.47-8], saw issues of *SA* (plainly for the first time) and was given some 'back numbers'. He saw such other modern buildings as had by then gone up, notably Barkhin's *Izvestiia*, and Velikovsky's Gostorg.[19] But Melnikov had nothing built yet at that date.

Not surprisingly it was the French critics who kept up a trickle of coverage, with a few pieces in such journals as *Cahiers d'Art*. But the main lines of East-West contact through the later Twenties were those developed by the Constructivists, who documented their own work as well as that of 'foreign colleagues' like Corbusier, Gropius or Hannes Meyer in their elegant bi-monthly *SA*. This was received in Europe and East-coast America by various organisations trading with the USSR, various national and specialist libraries, and various individuals within the European avant-garde network.

Given the difficulties of communication at that time, *SA* was the main source of information on Russia for others in 'the international front of modern architecture'. Just as one can recognise some of Corbusier's illustrations offset into Ginzburg's early writings, so European architects' occasional writings on Russia returned the compliment by offsetting from *SA*. As they could not understand the text, what they said was often a personal meditation prompted by the images, rather than factual reportage. Van Doesburg's three articles in *Het Bouwbedrijf* during 1928-9 are typical: where the rest of his writing is sharp and factual, the Soviet pieces are rambling, and whilst reproducing images, he feels a capitalist compulsion to issue warnings against being deceived by Soviet images as much as by Soviet words. Thus whilst declaring *SA* to be 'very well edited', he feels compelled to warn against being too impressed by the pictures.

> *'In evaluating designs, models and realised projects as shown in modern [Soviet] periodicals such as* SA *etc, one should keep in mind that the photographs may be tricked, and one should be aware of technical and architectural flaws which can easily be disguised by this technique. In France this kind of modern photography is called photogénique. It has already caused a great deal of confusion in modern architectural production.'*[20]

SA was the only properly architectural magazine of the Twenties in the Soviet Union, but as Starr has already rightly observed, Melnikov did not appear in it once during the whole five years of its publication. And understandably, for as Chapter 4 has shown, he had nothing in common with these theoretically-minded people and consistently adopted a proudly anti-intellectual attitude to them. Looking back on Asnova and OSA in his later autobiographical notes, for example, he wrote:

> *'These architectural groups dominated innovation. The difference between them amounted only to the fact that one lot described themselves as the "new" architects and the other as the "contemporary" ones. Out of all of us at that time, I least of all understood the torrent of words they produced'.*[21]

But it was a two-way hostility. Melnikov had building commissions for the workers' clubs in hand, to which most of the Constructivists, and rightly in my view, would have closed their eyes in horror at the messy compositions and uncomfortable proportions.

One very indicative question arises here. Melnikov later told Starr how Corbusier had spent 'several days' showing him around modern buildings in Paris.[22] So what happened when Corbusier himself made the return visit a mere three years later? Melnikov must have been the only 'Modernist Russian architect' he knew personally. He had been the much-fêted star of Paris whose Exhibition building was the only one 'apart from my own' which Corbusier reputedly admitted to be 'interesting'. But did Corbusier renew this acquantaince with Melnikov when he finally visited Moscow himself, only three years later? The answer seems to be a clear 'No'. From Melnikov's side no mention was made to Starr by the architect himself, determined though he was on a position amongst 'the great names'. Likewise Kokkinaki in Moscow, intimately familiar with the Melnikov family and archive, confirms no mention of such contact in papers or family memories, bent on hagiography as they have always been.[23] From Corbusier's side there is no mention either, as Cohen confirms, who has made the most detailed study of Corbusier's Russian travels.[24] It is plain that when Corbusier first went to Moscow in autumn 1928 about the Tsentrosoiuz project he was now 'taken over' by the Constructivists. I suspect Melnikov had written himself out of any such contact by his determined indifference to 'theory'. His own statement, quoted earlier, and Starr's admissions, recognise that this was rooted in a deep anti-intellectualism, and his innate lack of aptitude for disciplined and analytical thinking.[25]

In 1929, Lissitzky wrote his *Russland. Die Rekonstruktion der Arkhitektur in der Sowjetunion*, which was published the next year in Vienna. Lissitzky's text was not deeply theoretical (and has been fattened up for the later, English-language editions). But it focussed more on ideas and approaches than individual buildings. Thus for all Melnikov's peripheral relationships to Asnova, with whom Lissitzky had earlier associated himself in Moscow and propagandised abroad, Melnikov is never mentioned in the text. The section on 'The club as a social force' is illustrated only by a particularly abstract Leonidov plan. In the main plates, a side elevation of Melnikov's Paris pavilion was accompanied by a close-up of the roof over the staircase. Rodchenko's dramatic angled shot of a bus garage roof paid greater homage to the engineer Shukhov than to Melnikov as architect. One plate showed his Paris garage drawing, and two close-up shots of the Rusakov club did little to explain the form. But six Melnikov images amongst sixty-two plates was reasonable, given the glittering array of talent and invention amongst his colleagues.[26]

The early Thirties saw several solid articles published in the West on Soviet Modernism. One on clubs in *L'Architecture d'aujourd'hui* in 1931 gave Melnikov due attention.[27] Two important articles by the emigré Russian Modernist Berthold Lubetkin in the *Architectural Review* concentrated on ideas, and associated Melnikov firmly with Ladovsky's Asnova group, which alliance he was now tending to claim in the Soviet press presumably to reduce the vulnerability of being a loner. A photograph of the Rusakov club was captioned 'This building is a typical expression of the "formalistic" aesthetic of the Asnova group, combined with a certain ingenuity of planning.' With two other photographs, this was fair representation in a wide-ranging cultural and documentary study.[28]

War and after

In the political situation of the Soviet Union in the Thirties, after the widely proclaimed 'demise' of Modernism resulting from the Palace of Soviets competition judgement in early 1932, only a few vignettes on Soviet architecture naturally emerged in the Western professional press. Corbusier's humiliation in the competition and the saga of the unfinished Tsentrosoiuz meant the changed atmosphere in Moscow was well known throughout European Modernism. Across the Atlantic, Hector Hamilton's success in the Palace of Soviets had made the new atmosphere unusually well publicised in the more distant and less *engagé* profession in America.[29] Whilst all this proceeded, Hitchcock and Johnson were planning their 'definitive' International Style show of 1932 for Alfred Barr's Museum of Modern Art, where the stylistic range was narrowly restricted to frame-and-skin games and ribbon windows.[30] There was far more they could have included from Russia beyond the single token image of the Electro-Technical Institute by Nikolaev and Fisenko [p.70]: the Narkomfin building [pp.120, 135] must have qualified if they had been attempting authority rather than journalism. But certainly nothing of Melnikov's.

Amidst the West's own problems of the Thirties, professional interest cooled even further. A very mixed selection of Westerners was invited to the visciously anti-Modernist First Congress of Soviet Architects in 1937. To Clough Williams-Ellis, the dramas passed by as an 'atmosphere' which 'not surprisingly seemed to me somehow tense and oppressive' despite 'the gargantuan feasting'.[31] Frank Lloyd Wright enjoyed the ego-trip.[32] Others, more alert, shuddered when they saw how Vopra's Alabian, as Simon Breines reported in the *Architectural Record*,

> *'attacked the "formalists" like Melnikov who are "indifferent to living reality" and whose experimental pursuit of architecture as a sort of sculptural problem resulted in the cubistic and extremely freakish buildings which were so well known after the Revolution.'*[33]

In the following two years, when Seigfried Giedion gave the Harvard lectures that became *Space, Time and Architecture*, Russia barely existed in his 'new tradition'. One sentence claims that Tatlin's tower expresses 'the same kind of feeling' as Borromini; another labels Malevich as a 'constructivist'. There is no mention of Soviet architecture, but not through Giedion's ignorance. As Secretary of CIAM he had written a protest on the Palace of Soviets result to Stalin in spring 1932 and gone to Moscow that autumn to discuss CIAM's ill-fated Fourth Congress. Fingers bitten therefore, he merely noted that 'the avant-garde had no place is Stalin's Russia'.[34]

A different view was maintained on the European side of the Atlantic. In the middle of the Second World War, a remarkably direct and objective little popular *Introduction to Modern Architecture* was published by J. M. Richards, then Deputy Editor of *The Architectural Review*. Its broad geographical balance is conspicuously different from the highly partisan accounts of Hitchcock and Johnson or Giedion. Amongst the forty-five architects whom Richards listed as having 'contributed most to the development of Modern architecture in the last twenty years' are Poles,

Moscow sources and precedents for Melnikov's Rusakov Club, 1927-8. Left to right: *Erich Mendelsohn, 'Sketch for an industrial complex', 1914, shown in his Moscow lecture. Sukharev Tower, 1692-1701, one of Moscow's most important landmarks, with typical old-Russian broad external stair to first floor. Melnikov, Rusakov Club, entrance side. Poteshny Palace, Kremlin, 1652-79, cantilevers.*

Czechs, Hungarians, and 'Tatlin, Lissitzky and Ginzburg in Russia'. Even more unusually Richards grasped the nettle of 'the unfortunate association of architecture with politics' which elsewhere was so studiously avoided.

> *'It is in a way natural that modern architecture should be ... looked upon with disfavour by anti-progressive political dictatorships; not as the dictatorships themselves have suggested, because it is a "Bolshie" architecture devised by Reds or by Jews, but simply because it is rational and matter-of-fact, by-passing as architecturally irrelevant the pomp that would make architecture a useful medium for glorification of the state.'* [35]

Noting that Russia had produced much positive work, Richards had the wisdom and modesty to write that 'This strange reaction' which had taken place in Russia 'since about 1928', 'is difficult to explain, so complex, obscure and hard for us to understand are the various factors at work moulding Russian life today. Partly', he conceded, 'the explanation' was

> *'a reaction against the technical failure of the early modern architecture, put up in a hurry, without skilled labour, often in unsuitable materials and certainly without backing of the highly organised and highly mechanised building industry such as modern architecture in Europe had grown up with.'*

Partly, 'it was also a matter of propaganda and prestige'.[36] Such soundly practical judgement augured well for the post-War relationship between professionals in the two allied countries.

In the immediate post-war years there was considerable contact between the professions of Europe and Russia over common problems in post-war reconstruction. In Britain Lubetkin was an active agent of that contact, and the RIBA gave its Royal Gold Medal to the veteran Viktor Vesnin as a distinguished senior member of the post-war Soviet profession. But in general the Twenties receded from the spotlight.[37] In part this certainly reflected an awareness of the personal risks which survivors of that 'bourgeois internationalism' still faced, under the ever more virulently nationalist cultural policies of Stalin. In part, it reflected the universal unawareness of modern architectural history in the post-war period.

Almost the only serious mention of Russian Modernism in the new literature of that time seems to have been that in Alberto Sartoris', in his *Encyclopedie de l'Architecture Nouvelle*, published in Milan in 1948. Somewhat randomly he grouped Soviet Modernists into 'the avant-garde' and 'the younger generation'. Melnikov is amongst the former.[38] In the United States at Stanford, Arthur Voyce enlarged a short pre-war article on 'contemporary Soviet Architecture' into a text on 'The Revolutionary period' for his book *Russian Architecture: Trends in Nationalism and Modernism.* It is slender and generalised, but not unintelligent.[39] There is a photograph of the Rusakov club, but the complete lack of any textual mention of Melnikov probably reflects the extent to which he had been 'written out of existence' already by the profession even in the middle Thirties.

In 1958, Hitchcock's would-be encyclopedic account of *Nineteenth and Twentieth Century Architecture* referred to Russia only in a footnote, to explain why Corbusier suddenly went there.[40] In those days of very scanty architectural publishing – hard now to imagine – the next important study of Modern architecture, Banham's *Theory and Design*, had the same gap in it. Thus Anthony Vidler wrote in *Oppositions* in 1976,

> *'The evident lack of serious assessments of Constructivism in the English speaking world has been compounded by the notable omission of any treatment of the Russian Constructivists [ie. Modernists. CC] in that by now standard text, Banham's* Theory and Design in the First Machine Age, *which formed the historical understanding of so many generations of architectural students.'* [41]

'So many generations' was a misleading phrase to cover fifteen years: Banham's book was in fact published in 1960. He had occasionally dropped the names of Lissitzky, Malevich or Ladovsky, but more to give effect than to give information. Melnikov appeared briefly as the architect of the Paris pavilion, in the passage I have already quoted, which was accompanied by the entrance closeup from Lissitzky's *Russland.*

Filling the historical gap

The first serious attempt to fill this gap caused by absence of Soviet work from the standard view of Modernist history was Vittorio de Feo's *URSS: Architettura 1917-36* three years later. Here again, attention was focussed on those who wrote quotable theory, though the theory was never very adequately recounted. Melnikov figured visually with images of the Seine Garage and Rusakov club; a spread on his Paris pavilion included a Malevich 'Planeta' drawing of 1924 alongside the plans as if to imply influence. For the first time in many years, however, there was some attempt at characterisation: Melnikov's *metafisica* is defined as a 'recognition of the vacuity of mechanistic symbolism'. Three sentences praise the Paris pavilion as displaying Melnikov's capacities and representing 'a crystallisation of the ideas of Asnova', to which he is again linked, and the group's emerging 'maturity'. Another florid sentence praised the felicitous matching of 'programme' and 'composition' in his clubs, and from Breines de Feo summarised the accusations of the 1937 Congress.[42] Here though was a first serious monograph on Russian Modernism which started from 'The World of Art and Art Nouveau', wove together some relevant poetic and artistic texts (albeit from secondary sources) to present an outline history of the period. This was again mainly from Western-language materials, but the bibliography of those sources, particularly the journal sources, remains valuable today. This, like the copious visual material filling half the book, was groundbreaking in its time.

In the same year, a decade after Stalin's death, serious publication on the architecture of the Twenties was also beginning in the Soviet Union itself. Thus 1963 saw the first of several very substantial volumes of documentary materials from the Twenties compiled by Vigdaria Khazanova at the Institute for Art History in Moscow, under general supervision of former Constructivist Kirill Afanasev (see pp.174-5], and the son of another Twenties Modernist, Oleg Shvidkovsky [cf. p.77].[43] For all that Khrushchev is said to have decried Melnikov's clubs as 'ugly', it was his reorientation of Soviet architecture, admitting that not everything done in the Twenties was bad, and his general political thaw, that made possible a rediscovery of this period in certain circles of the Soviet profession itself. There were numerous people who had documents or 'remembered', and as the only leading name still alive, Melnikov profited greatly.

Khazanova went on to produce an important scholarly book in 1970 on the period 1917-25, with due attention to Melnikov's early work.[44] Meanwhile the Soviet architectural press was beginning to respond with articles on leading avant-garde figures by several dedicated researchers, including the then young Selim Khan-Magomedov. In 1965, as Iuri Gerchuk reported in the official Soviet monthly *Arkhitektura SSSR*, 'the seventy fifth birthday of Konstantin Stepanovich Melnikov, one of the founders of Soviet architecture, was celebrated by Moscow architects with an evening in his honour and a large exhibition of his work'. According to Starr's later account, this exhibition had been prepared by Melnikov himself.[45]

Gerchuk's essay had particular importance in the Western literature as the first serious Soviet commentary on Melnikov to be translated into English. It went all over the world in the internationally-read journal *Architectural Design*, in a special issue of early 1970 coinciding with the London exhibition *Art in Revolution*, organised by the pioneering historian of Russian avant-garde painting, Camilla Gray. The same material then entered the standard literature in British and American editions as a book.[46]

Gerchuk's account of Melnikov went boldly beyond being factual. He sought 'to describe the particular character of his architectural thought', stressing the fact that for all his fantasy, Melnikov had been an active builder. On his general judgement of Melnikov's talent, however, I would not myself concur. Gerchuk wrote of 'Melnikov's inclination towards experiment, towards maximum refinement of architectural form, his acute sense of formal balance, the complex and dynamic way in which he interlocked exterior and interior space in a building', as if they were features of all his work, not just of the exhibition pavilions, 'to which his talent was sympathetic'. The rest however was less questionable. No one could disagree that his clubs were 'disturbing, paradoxical and extraordinary, neither familiar nor even alike'. They had in common only an auditorium 'planned with consideration of its possible use in parts by movable screens', but 'technical problems prevented the realisation of most of this' so that criticism at the time had 'made no allowance for their real incompleteness'. That was an accurately aimed question about the 'realism' of which Melnikov was so proud.

Gerchuk rated highly Melnikov's 'principle of fluid space, which is not related solely to a proposed function but undergoes transformations and develops quite freely', seeing him here adopting 'a functional attitude ahead of that of the Constructivists, whose "functional method" led rapidly towards a fragmentation of the building by clear emphasis on the individual function of each element'. Certainly a comparison of their workers' club designs with those of Melnikov shows the validity of Gerchuk's distinction here. 'Paradox' was the particular characteristic of Melnikov's work on which Gerchuk focussed, a paradox resulting from 'the extraordinary use of a strict logic entirely of his own'. Given that Melnikov was still alive, Gerchuk was commendably frank, in my judgement, about his Narkomtiazhprom (NKTP) scheme of 1934 [see p.201]. Unfamilar criteria, he said, had 'transformed his strong qualities of acute imagination and a willingness to reach extreme conclusions, into weaknesses'.

The *Art in Revolution* show which coincided with Western publication of Gerchuk's article included good photographs and some new models of Melnikov designs, but the catalogue essay by Khan-Magomedov was brief and anodyne. That was explained by the censorious climate under which any such presentation of Soviet material abroad was still conducted. A certain free speech had been achieved in circumscribed circles of 'those who understood' at the heart of the Soviet profession. On the other hand, all ventures abroad amongst the ideological enemy still ran the gauntlet of Party supervisors, and this one had its share of *skandaly*, or rows, so that a portion was shown elsewhere (Lissitzky's 'Proun' room) and the host side added a second 'unofficial' catalogue for materials the Party men disapproved.

New critical engagement

While *Art and Revolution* was in preparation for London, two more monographs on Soviet architecture of the Twenties appeared in Europe.

Anatole Kopp's *Ville et Revolution* of 1968 was a text born of personal architectural convictions. 'Readers should be warned: the author is a Marxist, and much of this book is blatant propaganda' wrote the editor of London's *Architectural Review*, a little oversensitive to its enthusiasm.[47] Kopp's study in honour of the fiftieth anniversary of the Revolution was concerned primarily with showing 'architecture as a tool for "transforming mankind".' It therefore concentrated on those who most directly addressed the issue of architecture as a catalyst in this process, which was the Constructivists. Melnikov's pavilion, his house and his clubs were visually better documented than ever before, but in this context there was again little to say about him, in a book that placed great emphasis on 'illustrating the battle of ideas ... through documents'. In the following year, 1969, Vieri Quilici's *L'architettura del construttivismo* came out in Rome, again with a very catholic definition of 'constructivism', and with a text that focussed on the early Twenties, but

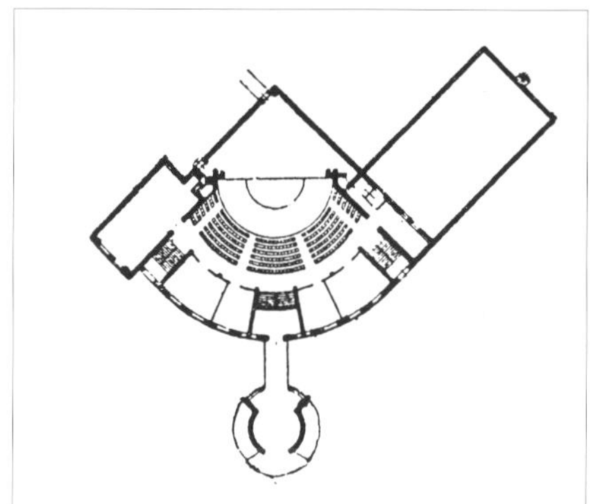

Melnikov, club of the Kauchuk factory, Moscow, 1927: ground floor: feeding left, and sports-hall right.

Photo of 1929, showing outdoor stairs rising to upper (auditorium) entrance, with general entrance in circular pavilion at ground.

Embedded corner rotunda: common device of Moscow Classicism: University Library, K. Bykovsky, 1901.cf. MUZhVZ, p.9.

it joined the valuable trend in Italy (in series like *Rassegna Sovietica*) of publishing extensive translations of documents. In that context Melnikov only got passing mention, though as ever he figured in the illustrations.

Amongst the general discussions of modern architecture published at this time, Manfredo Tafuri's *Teorie e storia dell'architettura* dropped Russian names at several points with an eye to the fashionable allusion. Thus Melnikov appeared bracketed with Sant'Elia, Duchamp, Ladovsky and some others who 'look at the new nature of industrial "things" for new emotional occasions, ... in Benjamin's words, who are not yet free from the equipment, of those who look at it excitedly, rather than go behind it and use it.'[48] To which one can only respond: Maybe.

Tafuri's collaboration with Francesco dal Co on *Modern Architecture*, published in 1976, was more illuminating. How they construed Melnikov as 'undoubtedly the best qualified personality in Soviet Constructivism' is not clear. But on the development of his Paris scheme they were perceptive, and the serious study of *avant-projets* as well as final designs was a new step in the analysis of Soviet work.

'There is no point in reading those intersections [of deformed geometrical masses] as metaphors of the socialist dynamic; the preparatory drawings for the pavilion show circular buildings broken up, inclined and intersected in an informal manner, indicating beyond a doubt that what interested the architect was only experimentation with a language made up of alienated objects, of volumes designed to deform their own geometry and in fact clashing with one another.'

That observation seems to me apt. More generally, they saw Melnikov's work as:

'derived from the Cubo-Futurist ... provocative use of form and from the Formalist method of semantic distortion. The materials of the architectural language, the geometrical forms and also the kitsch elements like the gesticulating statues on his garage for Paris and the NKTP project, were treated as neutral elements rendered active and expressive by means of a skilfully programmed play of oppositions, the entire language itself being a kind of game. From that standpoint, Melnikov was the most coherent analyst of the architectural syntax of the twenties and thirties in Russia, in line with the theories of V. Shklovsky or Eichenbaum, that form should be independent of all other aspects ... having nothing to do with any revolutionary or propagandist aims.'[50]

Here it seems to me we are close to the truth. We can easily read this to imply intellectual underpinnings to Melnikov's work which I would doubt, but the phrasing carefully indicates a parallelism not a direct influence. This seems to have been the first general history of Modernism to locate the Russian avant-garde naturally and adequately amongst the rest. The next such study, and the first in English, was Kenneth Frampton's *Critical History of Modern Architecture*. Though published in 1980 after Starr's work on Melnikov, it is worth noting it before focussing in detail on that work.

Frampton's chapter on 'Soviet Union 1918-32' is more documentary than 'critical' or even interpretative. Some of the allusive phrases in his earlier Oppositions article on Russian Modernism also seem to me rather insubstantial. I would entirely concur, however, with his firm judgement that 'nothing Melnikov was to achieve in his later career – his workers' clubs of the late twenties was to equal his early structures in wood.'[51] I shall return later to the reasons for that.

Melnikov finds his champion

It must have been sometime between late 1972 and his death in 1974 that Melnikov wrote the following passage in the 'Autobiographical Notes' he had begun in the Sixties.

'From 1922 onwards, my success with my own style raised me rapidly to the zenith of the architectural art in its highest forms. The scarlet sunrise blazed through the decades from the heights that had been conquered. All the triumphal arches of unique events, both here and abroad, belonged to me, to Melnikov: the first All-Union architectural competition; the first Agricultural Exhibition; the first sarcophagus; the first pavilion of the USSR; the first worldwide architectural competition; the first Festival of World Names.

'But the attention of the press is a gift from heaven, and taking even the facts by surprise, the press forgot its celestial function. With monographs serving as a form of "advance", the patents for architectural innovation were distributed to Ginzburg, Lissitzky, the Vesnins and Leonidov. It is but sophism, however, to search for architecture in the empty desert of drawings.'[52]

Thus spoke a man who built, seeing two of the first Soviet monographs on architects of the Twenties devoted to people who built nothing, and two, to people whom he regarded with contempt as word-mongers. Perhaps the same resentments expressed in conversations with Frederick Starr were the prompt to the latter's 'labour of love'. Starr must answer for himself on that. Certainly those conversations gave his extensive writings on Melnikov a unique authenticity, but in places I have to admit to thinking they perhaps also led to an imaginative speculation that is not supported by evidence, as I shall explain.

Starr dates his interviews with Melnikov to 1966 and 1967. In 1969, he published an extensively illustrated article in *Architectural Design*. Its text was mainly factual, but much of the information, like much of the visual material, was previously entirely unknown in the West. The most interesting interpretative passages concerned Melnikov's own house. Starr ascribed the extraordinary levels of light and free-flow of air in the open plan, unconventionally including even the sleeping area, to a desire not just for 'nature unpolluted', but also for 'purity ... in the metaphysical sense evoked by the German Expressionist Bruno Taut in 1922'. He quoted the passage from Taut's *Frülicht* where he proclaims 'Hail transparency, clarity ... the flashing, the airy – Hail to eternal architecture'. In relation to Melnikov's late-Twenties project for the Green City recreational village, he ascribed his use of sleep as the medium for reviving the tired city-dwellers' spirit, to Melnikov's 'particularly Russian obsession with elemental forces'.[53]

Between completion of the manuscript for his major monograph on Melnikov in 1974, and its eventual publication in 1978, Starr published an article in *Lotus International* in 1977 which questioned whether Melnikov could be called 'a Soviet Expressionist'. Though published before the book, it was plainly written after the shorter discussions of this theme which appear there, and develops them in greater detail. Since Melnikov had died in 1974, and Starr had not seen him again since 1967, it is not clear what the source was for the new information on such topics as Melnikov's 1926 meeting and conversation with Mendelsohn (who did indeed visit Russia while building a textile plant in Leningrad [54]). Like further information on the Expressionist tracts contained in Melnikov's library, it may have derived from meetings with his widow and son in 1976.

In this article however, Starr no longer speculates on the influence of a Mendelsohnian form as source for the Rusakov Club, on the Sheerbartian influence on his Expressionist interest in crystals, or the influence from Taut's *Stadtkrone*: on the basis of biographical facts and the contents of Melnikov's library, he asserts them to be facts. He justifiably notes that 'What distinguishes Melnikov from the Futurists and links him with the Expressionists is his indifference to technology as such, and his coolness towards industrial civilisation.'[55] Starr's evidence seems to me very convincing on the formal influence of Mendelsohn's 'sketch for an industrial complex' of 1914 on the Rusakov club. On the matter of the pyramid as a theme of death, I am more sceptical. As a diagram of the structure of Russia, it was no invention of Melnikov's but a common image, much played with, for example, by cartoonists during the 1905 Revolution.

In an extensive discussion of the Paris pavilion that formed a small book, Starr claimed there was an analogy in Melnikov's mind between the route he had planned around a crystalline sarcophagus of Lenin, in 1924, and his plunging of the Paris crowd 'through' the split crystal structure of the pavilion in 1925, as a penetration of the very 'body' of the revolutionary society.[56] In this case the fuller development lies in his book of 1978, appropriately titled *Melnikov: Solo Architect in a Mass Society.*[57]

This book was a pioneering model of a genre till recently too rarely explored, which presents architecture through an integrated view of the architect's life and times. As such, it profits greatly from the breadth of knowledge of an author who is not an architectural specialist. On the other hand, some passages on ideas and influences do not ring true from the point of view of a designer, and of how the processes of generating and developing ideas operate. Deep analogies are discussed between different schemes, as between the sarcophagus and Paris, where I would say we are only seeing the natural tendency of a designer, as of a writer or any other creative artist, to circulate a constant set of formal themes throughout a certain period of work, even when the external circumstances or objective demands of the tasks appear on the surface unrelated. The bulk of the book is a biography of Melnikov as individual and as artist, seen amidst his colleagues and his denigrators. The visual material is extremely rich. Later work by Khan-Magomedov in particular has shown that there is little extant material which Starr did not already show, especially amongst preliminary sketches.[58] If his study had stopped at Chapter IX, however, it would be stronger.

To my mind the tenth and last chapter, entitled 'Architecture against Death: the System of Melnikov's Art', conceived as a climax, in fact shakes much of the edifice. Why? Because there is no evidence for any of the sweeping claims that are made. More than that, it draws our attention to the number of occasions earlier in the book when there is also, in fact, no evidence for interpretations which at the time convinced us. Careful examination of the footnotes will show repeatedly that there are detailed sources for everything except the crucial ideas attributed to Melnikov. At best, they are paraphrases attributed to 'Conversation with author'. Here we see in hypertrophied form the danger that has beset much of this writing on Soviet Modernism which I have reviewed, and much later work too: the danger of over-interpretation from 'outside' the real development process of the designs concerned.

What really is the design theory?

The contention of Starr's concluding chapter is that Melnikov's entire mature architecture should be seen as 'a record of his profound and enduring preoccupation with the problem of death'.[59] But here I think we see the weakness of this genre; we see an interpreter who knows more about history and cultural context than about the substantive topic, in this case the production of architecture or other creative work.

The chapter is a very rich evocation of the atmosphere of wild, mystical convictions that is intensively experienced by many Russians and is most characteristically different from any cultural space inhabited by post-Enlightenment Europeans. In the end it is the bedrock of fatalistic determination not to engage with reality and objectivity which Russians will claim is the basis of their 'spirituality', but in practical aspects of life is a

Typical depiction of Russian society as pyramid of mutually-exploiting layers, cartoon of 1905.

Melnikov, personal counter-project for the Palace of Soviets, 1932, with pyramid of Soviet society symbolically split: a vigorous form of conical pyramids, jagged silhouette, in Russian tradition, cf. right.

Typical 17th C Moscow street church: Trinity in Nikitnikakh, 1635-53.

constant downfall. Starr writes here that:

'Melnikov's refusal to become identified with any ideology of the day was due not so much to his opposition to their substance as to his belief that they were all irrelevant to architecture.'[60]

I doubt that. In my judgement, there is a more literal truth than Starr admits in Melnikov's own words, distancing himself from his colleagues of the Twenties, when he said in that passage I have already quoted: 'Out of all of us at that time, I least of all understood the torrent of words they produced.'[61] Actually Starr came close to the nub of the issue when he wrote that:

'By the late Twenties, Melnikov was living a life for which neither his upbringing nor his education had prepared him. The acclaim that had been lavished on him brought wearisome social obligations, while the more he dressed himself up in felt hat and spats, the further he moved from the simple life he had hitherto always lived. None of this sat well with Melnikov's innate austerity, and he was later to recall having come gradually to fear for his own corruption.'[62]

That, in my view, is one of the most accurate judgements in the book. The pseudo-philosophical ramblings of Melnikov's writings on 'theory' come from an empty mind, not an over-filled one. The supposedly 'great revelations' are mere common-places, but such was the theatrical 'tragedy of Melnikov' that Starr was only one of the many, Russians as well as Westerners, who fell for them.

All creative work, as is surely agreed, represents some little stab, however trivial, against the vacuum of annihilation and oblivion in death. If you are in the game yourself, you know it does. But Starr, like most of those who write 'art history' is a commentator not a creator. Melnikov is earnestly quoted as obsessed with the architect's universal obligation 'to communicate the agitation of his spirit to others',[63] which again, if read less melodramatically, is no more than a reaffirmation of the role of any artistic activity. The key evidence of the death preoccupation in his work is Melnikov's report of some moments in his life when 'there existed for me no world at all ... and a "nothingness" that shook my whole spirit'.[64] But this is common enough experience, surely, and not the secret revelation of an inner architectural programme. When it comes to attributing analogies of death to the parked cars in his Paris garage,[65] I have to admit that I think Starr is lost. Too many vodkas or a joke over the drawing board – maybe. But not here: this is serious. 'Up to now,' he writes in the middle of this last chapter,

'we have been grouping together diverse projects in order to show the extent of Melnikov's apparent preoccupation with the problem of man's mortality and his need for rebirth. But a sharp distinction must be drawn between the projects of the late NEP period (1925-8) and those before and after. ... Only at Dulevo [club], built [on a supposedly anthropomorphic plan. CC] at the height of the cultural revolution in 1929, do we see the problem once more stated in public terms. This time the change in focus was to be permanent. From that date on Melnikov concentrated exclusively on the analogy that he perceived between social revolution and the physical resurrection of the dead.'[66]

There follows more detail on the theories of Russian philosophers and eccentrics, but absolutely nothing that I can see, except speculation and implication, to link this with Melnikov's architecture. All Starr actually says here is that this thinking is an important part of the cultural climate in which Melnikov lived. Noone who has sat through nights of Russian ramblings over vodka glasses and samovars would question that. But then at last it dawned on Melnikov, as Starr presents it in his final paragraphs, that the good aspects of life and human values exist only through a relativism which is defined by the bad aspects.[67] It all seems extraordinarily facile.

This discussion is worthy of careful analysis, but for its technique, not for its content. The latter is not worthy of great probing, for the explanations seem to me simpler. As Lubetkin observed back in 1932, Melnikov's work demonstrated 'a certain ingenuity of planning',[68] though the results are not objects which sustain Melnikov's (or Starr's or Gerchuk's) high claims for their aesthetic sophistication. And Melnikov was no great intellect. Isolated for so long, in highly frustrating and difficult circumstances, he did not have the inner intellectual resources to fill the vacuum with anything really positive, as some of his contemporaries might have done. Sitting in solitary state in his conspicuously unique house, in itself a daily reminder of his earliest successes, he rambled mentally around certain constantly recurring themes. He had built a positive credo around the unalterable fact that, in Starr's opening words to this final chapter, 'Melnikov was the very antithesis of a systematic thinker.'[69] As I see it, detestation of any form of systematic attack on the design problem, his insistence that it all comes out of 'intuition', and that a single generative idea is all that each building requires, are precisely the causes of the weakness in his design. Put in another way, what 'the solo architect' actually needed most was the additional filtering and criticism that comes from working with others.

The longer view

The Paris pavilion was a good example of the positive results of both collaborative work with his peers, and the discipline of technical criteria which he so despised. The idea of the diagonal pathway is splendid for the purpose. Let no one take that away from him. As Jean-Louis Cohen has written, 'the sequence leading the public under the laternation of the covering panels to the first floor, is one of the most dramatic architectural itineraries ever conceived by a twentieth-century architect.'[70] But in all the initial sketches up to the stage when decisions of 'making' had to be faced, the project is messy and over-complex for its size. The rigour to which Western eyes were responding in 1925, as they still do, derived from the modularity of parts and simplicity of elements which fabrication from standard pieces dictated. Let us not forget that, as Cohen's research has shown, the detailing was largely done by French carpenters, with less of it brought from Moscow than Starr and some press reviews have suggested.[71] The effect of this was a practical reality on site, which history has merely forgotten. Thus on 25 March 1925 Rodchenko wrote from Paris to his wife, the artist and designer Varvara Stepanova,

'The pavilion is nearly finished. Tomorrow I begin setting up my club stuff and today I got my own drawings to go on there, which arrived in the Diplomatic Bag. Our pavilion will be the very best in terms of novelty. The principles of construction here are entirely different from how we do things – altogether lighter and simpler. It's a good thing I hadn't done working drawings in advance,

as everything would have had to be redone here anyway.'[72]

The colour treatment of Melnikov's original scheme is likewise a mess of small-scale graphics.[73] The clarity of the final version has never seemed to me consonant with other Melnikov work, and here too we must be grateful for Cohen's research and recent publications of documents. These have shown that the visual impact of the building owes a vast amount to Rodchenko's bold and highly selective eye for articulating the elements of a constructive composition by colour.[74] Rodchenko's letters home reveal his resentment than no one was giving him credit, here or elsewhere in the Soviet displays, for this most decisive contribution to their public impact. On 17 April he wrote:

'They have painted the pavilion, just like I coloured the project: red, grey and white. It came out terrific, but no one says a word about the fact I did it. They just ask advice the whole time – so everything all around is mine. In the Grand Palais section we've got six rooms, where the whole colour scheme is also mine. And yet again they never mention my name. ... But I don't mind: let them get on with it.'[75]

So, less of this is Melnikov than received accounts have claimed. And the business which Starr elaborates of everyone being 'temporarily coloured pink' by passing under the red roofs? Well, a good student could surely rise to that.

Every one of Melnikov's schemes was better in the execution than the drawings, and precisely because of the discipline of those elements which he refused to accept as determinants of his forms. Take the Lenin sarcophagus, which is a simple enough thing, and be thankful they did not have the glass-cutting and resin glues to make that first Cubist form he designed. Starr suggests Melnikov's 'exhaustion' was some kind of creative burn-out resulting from supreme designerly effort here.[76] On the contrary, as would be the case in Moscow even today, he was worn out by the sheer nightmare of getting plate glass cut from shop windows in order to have any glass at all for this highest-prestige state job.

Jencks' review of Starr's book, quoted earlier, picks up this point in relation to Melnikov's work of the early Thirties. His Palace of Soviets project, as Jencks notes,

'uses representation, ... metaphor, ... anthropomorphism, ... abstraction, ... colour, lettering, conventional signs, classicism – the works. The result not surprisingly is awful ... and yet judging from his built work, the bombast and inhumanity might have disappeared in the realisation. Often an initial poetic inspiration, an overstatement, is transformed for the better as cost, actual fabrication and his sensitivity enter the picture.'[77]

In short, it would profit from some objective disciplines. The same point underlies Frampton's distinction between his timber buildings and the clubs.

'Nothing that Melnikov was to achieve later in his career – his workers' clubs of the late Twenties – was to equal his early structures in wood – his dismountable Sukharev market erected in Moscow in 1924, and his pavilion and Gostorg kiosks built in Paris in 1925.'[78]

The need for objective disciplines was a truth that Melnikov tried to avoid throughout his work, at cost of its genuine aesthetic quality. It was precisely the detail in Starr's several writings on Melnikov that enabled us to start penetrating through the skin in which this enigmatic figure clad himself. But some of Starr's judgements, as I see it, should be taken as provocations rather than answers.

As a designer, not a social historian, I do not see here a story of 'solo versus mass', but an object-lesson in the fact that only a genius can afford to deny himself the disciplines of collaborative interaction with colleagues, and as the geniuses best of all know, there is no real creativity without humility in response to the objective discplines of form-making and material. If he had not been so determinedly 'solo', both socially and intellectually, I think Melnikov would have been a better designer.

Whatever the judgement on that, his position in the interface between Russian avant-garde work and the Western perception of it has been a unique one. Through the Paris pavilion he was the first Soviet architect to come to Western attention. The records of that, and his enigmatic clubs and house, kept him in the spotlight. They so obviously pursued a different line from Western Modernism, and, *pace* Van Doesburg, generated strikingly memorable photographic images. He also lived longer than anyone of comparable importance in the avant-garde, long enough to be a barometer of changing regimes and to acquire a heroic status amongst the more romantic observers in both Russia and the West. The squalid family battles over the fate of his little house now threaten to degrade some of that. But

Konstantin Melnikov (1890-1974), photographed in his house, 1972, aged 82, by Cartier-Bresson.

Melnikov, 1924-5, final design for Soviet pavilion at the Paris exhibition of 1925: main elevation – compare modularity and clear articulation of building erected, p.153, bottom.

Soviet pavilion under construction, 1925, by French carpenters with Melnikov in group standing right.

still today he remains the only Soviet architect, of the avant-garde or any other period, to have been the subject of a full-scale Western biography. If only because of that, his life and career are an important reference point for Soviet architectural history and its Western historiography as a whole.

■

1 Soiuz arkhitektorov SSSR (Union of Architects of the USSR), 'Programma festivalia sovetskogo arkhitekturno-khudozhestvennogo avantgarda 20-x -30-x gg, priurochennogo k 100-letiiu so dnia rozhdeniia K S Mel'nikova' (Programme for a festival of the Soviet architectural and artistic avant-garde of the 20s and 30s to mark the centenary of K S Mel'nikov), Moscow, 1989 **2** S. F. Starr, 'Konstantin Melnikov', *Architectural Design*, 1969, no.7, pp.367-373 **3** ibid, p.373 **4** Charles Jencks, 'The lone star', *The Architects' Journal*, 16 May 1979, pp.1009-1010 **5** ibid, p.1010 **6** S. F. Starr, *K. Mel'nikov: Le Pavillon Soviétique*, Paris 1925, Paris, 1981, p.40 **7** M. Ia. Ginzburg, *Stil' i epokha* (Style and Epoch), Moscow, 1924, plates XXI-XXIII **8** The inscribed copy which Ginzburg sent Corbusier is still in the Fondation Corbusier. **9** Reyner Banham, *Theory and Design in the First Machine Age*, London, 1960, p.216 **10** H. de C., 'A general view', *Architectural Review*, 1925, July, pp.3-14 **11** W. Francklyn Paris, 'The International Exposition of Modern Industrial and Decorative Art in Paris', *Architectural Record*, 1925, Oct, pp.365-85 **12** For a very full listing and extensive extracts assembled by J-L. Cohen, see, Starr, *Le Pavillon*, 'Documents', pp.129-178 **13** 'Le pavillon des Soviets', *Le Bulletin de la Vie Artistique*, 1925, no.11 (1 June), pp.231-3. The full feature, pp.231-7, includes other material on pavilion and Mel'nikov. Text of the interview in French in Starr, *Le Pavillon*, pp.142-3, and as retranslated into Russian, in I. V. Kokkinaki & A. Strigalev, eds., *Konstantin Stepanovich Mel'nikov*, Moscow, 1985, pp.96-8 **14** Mel'nikov's manuscript notes on the form of the Makhorka pavilion are published in Kokkinaki & Strigalev, eds., *Mel'nikov*, pp.155-6. This is translated here as Doc.13 **15** Starr, *Le Pavillon* **16** *Little Review* et al, *Machine Age Exposition*, May 16 to May 28, New York, 1927. Russian materials, pp.32-5 **17** I. Sandler & A. Newton, eds., *Defining Modern Art. Selected Writings of Alfred J. Barr, Jr.*, New York, 1986, p.103 **18** René Fülöp-Miller, *Geist und Gesicht des Bolschewismus*, Zurich-Vienna, 1926; English edition as *The Mind and Face of Bolshevism*, London-New York, 1927 **19** Barr was in Moscow 26 Dec 1927 to 16 Jan 1928. See Sandler & Newton, eds., *Defining Modern Art*, pp.105-34. In Leningrad he met only artists – and indeed little modernist work had yet gone up there. **20** T. Van Doesburg, 'Kunst- en archi-tectuurvernieuwing in Sovjet-Rusland', *Het Bouwbedrijf*, 1929, 1 Feb, pp.49-53. The other articles appeared under the same title in 28 Sept 1928, pp.395-400 & 26 Oct 1928, pp.436-441. All three appear in English in: C. & A. Loeb, trs., Theo van Doesburg, *On European Architecture*, Basel, 1990, pp.183-209 **21** K. Mel'nikov, 'Arkhitektura moei zhizni' (The architecture of my life), 1967 onwards, in Kokkinaki & Strigalev, eds., *Mel'nikov*, pp.57-91 (p.72) **22** Starr, *Melnikov*, p.108 23; Starr, *Melnikov* & *Pavillon*. **23** Kokkinaki, personal communication. **24** J-L. Cohen, *Le Corbusier and the Mystique of the USSR*, Princeton, 1992. Also S.F. Starr, 'Le Corbusier and the USSR: New Documentation', *Oppositions*, no.23, Winter 1981, pp.122-137. **25** Melnikov, 'Arkhitektura moei zhizni' (as note 21); also Starr, *Melnikov*, p.116 **26** Text forms the first section of El Lissitzky, *Russia: an Architecture for World Revolution*, Cambridge, Mass., & London, 1970. Plates 13, 14 refer. **27** M. Ilyine, 'L'Architecture du club ouvrier en URSS', *L'Architecture d'Aujourd'hui*, 1931, Nov, pp.17-19 **28** Berthold Lubetkin,'The Russian Scene: Part II, The Builders', *Architectural Review*, 1932, May, pp.201-14 **29** On the Palace of Soviets competition and its outcome see: C. Cooke, *Architectural Drawings of the Russian Avant-Garde*, New York & London, 1990, pp.37-42; C. Cooke & I. Kazus, *Soviet Architectural Competitions 1920s-1930s*, London, 1992; C. Cooke, 'Mediating creativity and politics: 60 years of architectural competitions in Russia', in A. Calnek, ed., *The Great Utopia*, Guggenheim Museum, New York, 1992, pp.680-715 (pp.707-9) **30** H-R. Hitchcock & P. Johnson, *The International Style*, New York, 1966, reprint of 1932 edition. **31** C. Williams-Ellis, *Architect Errant*, London, 1971, p.188 **32** Frank Lloyd Wright, 'Architecture and life in the USSR', *Architectural Record*,1937, Oct, pp.58-63. See also Williams-Ellis, *Architect Errant*, pp.187-8 **33** Simon Breines, 'First Congress of Soviet Architects', *Architectural Record*, 1937, October, p.63. For an account of the Congress as it impacted on Melnikov see S. F. Starr, *Melnikov: Solo Architect in a Mass Society*, Princeton, 1978, pp.215-277. On the wider preparations and proceedings see Hugh D. Hudson, *Blueprints and Blood. The Stalinization of Soviet Architecture 1917-1937*, Princeton, 1994, pp167-202. **34** S. *Giedion, Space, Time and Architecture. The Growth of a New Tradition*, Cambridge, Mass., 1941. Page references to fifth edition (1982) pp.117, 439-41, 698 **35** J. M. Richards, *An Introduction to Modern Architecture*, London, 1940 pp.73-4 **36** ibid, pp.76-7 **37** Lubetkin's activity on this front is one topic not covered in John Allan's *Lubetkin*, London, 1992. He edited a *Soviet Architectural Reconstruction Bulletin* published by the Society for Cultural Relations with the USSR, London, visited the USSR etc; Viktor Vesnin's receipt of the Gold Medal in 1945 is fully documented in the British architectural press, eg *RIBA Journal*, 1944, Dec, pp.31-2; *The Builder*, 1945, 5 Jan, p.13. **38** A. Sartoris, *Encyclopédie de l'Architecture*, Milan, 1948 **39** A. Voyce, *Russian Architecture: Trends in Nationalism and Modernism*, New York, 1948 **40** H-R. Hitchcock, *Nineteenth and Twentieth Century Architecture*, London, 1958, Chapter 22, note 35. **41** A. V. (A. Vidler), Introduction to Frampton, 'Constructivism', *Oppositions*, no.6, Fall 1976, p.25 **42** Vittorio de Feo, *URSS: Architettura 1917-1936*, Rome, 1963, pp.31, 37, 43, 75. **43** V. Khazanova, comp., *Iz istorii sovetskoi arkhitektury 1917-1925. Dokumenty i materialy*, Moscow, 1963 **44** V. Khazanova, *Sovetskaia arkhitektura pervykh let oktiabria* (Soviet architecture of the first years after the Revolution), Moscow, 1970 **45** Iu. Gerchuk, 'Arkhitektor Konstantin Mel'nikov', *Arkhitektura SSSR*, 1966, no.8, pp.51-55. Starr, Melnikov, pp.236-7 **46** *Architectural Design*, special issue on Russian avant-garde architecture, February 1970, republished as O. A. Shvidkovsky, ed., *Building in the USSR 1917-32*, London & New York, 1971. Gerchuk's article on Melnikov is pp.57-66 **47** A. Kopp, *Ville et Révolution. Architecture et Urbanisme des Années Vingt*, Paris, 1967. English edition, *Town and Revolution*, London-New York, 1970. S. Cantacuzino, 'Up the Revolution', *Architectural Review*, March 1971, pp.195-6 **48** M. Tafuri, *Teorie e storia dell'architettura*, Rome, 1968. English edition, *Theories and History of Architecture*, London, 1980, p.32 **49** M. Tafuri & F. dal Co, *Modern Architecture*, Milan, 1976, p.180 **50** ibid **51** K. Frampton, *Modern Architecture: A Critical History*, London, 1980, pp.167-77, and 'Constructivism: the Pursuit of an Elusive Sensibility', *Oppositions*, No.6, Fall 1976, pp.25-44 **52** Mel'nikov, 'Arkhitektura moei zhizni', section XXVI, in Kokkinaki & Strigalev, eds., *Mel'nikov*. The successes to which he is referring here were: prize in Moscow model housing competition of 1922; the Makhorka pavilion at the 1923 All-Russian Agricultural Exhibition, Moscow, 1923; Lenin's sarcophagus, 1924; the Paris pavilion, 1925; the competition for a monument to Christopher Columbus at Santo Domingo, 1929, and the exhibition of his work at the Fifth Milan Triennale of 1933. The monographs to which he refers are: Sophie Lissitzky-Küppers, *El Lissitzky. Maler, Architekt, Typograf*, Dresden, 1967 (though published in East Germany, this originated from his widow who still lived in the USSR); A.G. Chiniakov, *Brat'ia Vesniny* (The Vesnin Brothers), Moscow, 1970; P. A. Aleksandrov & S.O. Khan-Magomedov, *Ivan Leonidov*, Moscow, 1971, and S. O. Khan-Magomedov, *M.Ia. Ginzburg*, Moscow, 1972. **53** S. F. Starr, 'Konstantin Melnikov', *Architectural Design*, 1969, no.7, pp.367-73 **54** During 1925-7 Erich Mendelsohn designed and partially built the Red Banner textile works in Leningrad. The protests it aroused etc are discussed in Cooke, 'Mediating creativity', p.697. His visits etc are recorded in 'Pis'mo Erika Mendel'sona', *SA*, 1927, no.3, p.108. Melnikov attended a lecture he gave in Moscow in 1926. **55** S. F. Starr, 'Konstantin Melnikov: a Soviet expressionist?', *Lotus International*, Milan, No.16, October 1977, pp.13-16 **56** Starr, *Le Pavillon*, p.105; and Starr, *Melnikov*, pp.94 & 247-250 **57** Starr, *Melnikov*. Full details in note 33 above. **58** S. O. Khan-Magomedov, *Konstantin Mel'nikov*, Moscow, 1990. This elegant volume contains paintings, drawings, new documentary photographs, some in colour, but the range of project sketches etc in Starr's Melnikov remains unsurpassed. **59** Starr, Melnikov, p.245 **60** ibid, pp.240-1 **61** As note 21 above **62** Starr, Melnikov, p.252 **63** ibid, p.244 **64** ibid, p.244 **65** ibid, p.251 **66** ibid, p.253 **67** ibid, p.256 **68** Lubetkin, 'The Russian Scene', pp.201-7 **69** Starr, *Melnikov*, p.240 **70** Jean-Louis Cohen, 'Il padiglione di Mel'nikov a Parigi: una seconda ricostruzione', *Casabella*, Milan, 1986, Nov, pp.40-51 **71** Cohen, 'Il padiglione', pp.44 & 50. Starr, *Melnikov*, p.99; Starr, *Le Pavillon*, ch.4, pp.60-98 **72** V. A. Rodchenko, comp., *A. M. Rodchenko: Stat'i. Vospminaniia. Avtobiograficheskie zapiski. Pis'ma* (A. M. Rodchenko. Articles. Reminiscences, Autobiographical notes. Letters), Moscow, 1982, p.89. An edited version of this letter was published in *Novyi Lef*, 1927, no.2, pp.11, 12, 15, but omitting some of the more revealling comments. **73** This drawing appears in black-and-white in Starr, *Melnikov*, p.95, fig. 79. It appears in colour in Kokkinaki & Strigalev, eds., *Mel'nikov*, plate 37; *Architettura nei paese dei Soviet* (Exhibition catalogue), Milan, 1982, p.129, plate 116; Khan-Magomedov, *Konstantin Mel'nikov*, p.87 **74** Cohen, 'Il padiglione', pp.42 & 50 **75** Rodchenko, *A. M. Rodchenko. Stat'i*, pp.93-4 **76** Starr, *Melnikov*, pp.83-4 **77** Jencks, 'A lone star', p.1010 **78** Frampton, 'Constructivism: an elusive sensibility', p.39.

Doc. 13

KONSTANTIN MELNIKOV
MAKHORA TOBACCO TRUST PAVILION, ALL-RUSSIAN AGRICULTURAL EXHIBITION, MOSCOW 1923: THE DESIGN PRINCIPLES

Typed notes, 11 December 1933, private archive, Moscow

THE REQUIREMENTS OF THE BRIEF:
On 60 square sazhen [272 m^2], with a volume of between 150 and 200 cubic sazhen [1,455 - 1940 m^3], to build a factory with accommodation for displays. The material for the building was to be a strict system of timber construction.

1 GENERAL PRINCIPLES
Givens: The passage of the fabricate through its successive stages of sifting.

Lightness of weight of the equipment (dispersion).

Lightness of weight of the fabricate.

Form of the solution: The sequence by which the fabricate passes through the individual stages of its processing is distributed in.the vertical.

2 EXTERNAL CONDITIONS ON SITE :
Givens: Direction of movement of the visitor is from the exhibition's main entrance along the river bank.

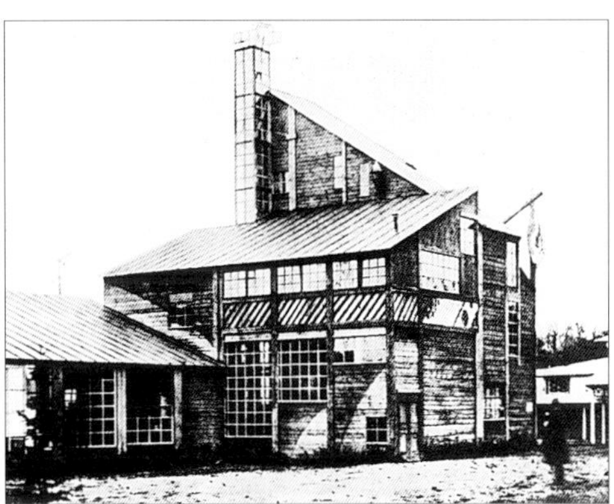

Form of the solution: The sharp fall of the intersecting planes and the gradual thickening of the space at the entrance to the pavilion.

The spiral form of the open staircase (rhythmic, coming closer and moving away, it deforms the vertical plumb line).

3 THE INTERNAL CONDITIONS:
The movement of the visitor is only in one direction.

The broken line on the horizontal and the diversity of volumes in the vertical creates complexity.

Different parts of the pavilion have different volumetric form (to create contrast).

4 RESULT – THE EXPRESSION:
Despite the building's minimal dimensions (it is essentially no more than a kiosk), a powerful impression of size is achieved by the compositional devices:

I. The total path length traversed by the visitor as he moves through the changing pictorial perspectives of this pavilion of only 60 square sazhen [272 m^2] and 4 sazhen [8.52 m] height, is 1/5 of a verst [213 m].

II. The exterior surface area of this little building, which is what operates upon the viewer's perception, totals 200 square sazhen [908 m^2].

III. The height of the volume that creates its perceived scale is 9 sazhen [19.17 m].

IV. The vertical scheme I devised for the demonstration of Makhorka's production process replaces the conveyor belt by a system of gravity feeds.

Doc. 14

THE PLASTIC EXPRESSION OF FORM: THE PARIS PAVILION

Lecture to the Architecture Faculty, Academy of Military Engineers, November 1933

I draw your attention to one principle which is purely architectural, and is self-evident and clear in its definitions, namely this: any building, in producing an impression of some kind on us, will have a greater effect of surprise on our feelings if we perceive that its actual dimensions are far smaller than our impression led us to believe. This is what one might call an artistic illusion of the parts of the building, and is achieved not through rhythmic combination of those parts, but mainly by an aesthetic concept underlying the design. The questions are interesting, but ... difficult to define. ... There are a great number of these aesthetic rules, and each epoch has its own; indeed in any given epoch the rules differ between diffferent peoples and nations, and are often in contradiction with each other. ... I shall talk about those things that are not matters of argument in aesthetics, which can be demonstrated and can be physically felt.

Looking at this column from the Parthenon, I draw your attention to one detail in particular: the flutes. Each flute has an outward circular continuation whose measure is unquestionably greater than that of the column's diameter, that is than the line defining the body of the column. Thanks to this the column seems fatter than its real size. By their vertical upward movement these flutes also strengthen the column's verticality. Thus on the one hand it seems that the column is fatter than it really is, on the other hand, it seems taller. As a whole this aesthetic device imparts to the column a fascinating harmoniousness.

We come on to the enlargement of volume by planes. This device is to be seen in at every step in the great historical monuments of architecture. In this respect, creative imagination is not confined to any single geometrical structure.

Here in the famous caryatids of the Temple of the Erechtheion we see columns replaced by the figures of women. For centuries the sculptural pediments of the Parthenon have served as sources of imitation for this same device: the introduction of sculpture into a piece of architecture, so that the rich volume of the sculptural form has an effect on the impression we receive, giving greater overall strength to the form of the building. The pleasant impression we get from the vaults of Rome, Byzantium and the medieval period is explained by this same law: that the curved surface is larger than the straight one, and therefore the space which is covered by it seems to be larger.

This aesthetic rule, with its possibility for physical calculations of the image reinforcement achieved, was familiar and well studied amongst the designers of Ancient Egypt.

The Great Pyramid of Cheops produces its stunning impression by its grandiose dimensions a) its volume (the quantity of materials); b) its perimeter; c) its area, its surface; d) its height relative to its cubic volume.

Amongst contemporary works in which this same principle applies, I draw your attention to the building I myself constructed in 1925 in Paris, at the International Exhibition of Decorative Arts. Here [below] we have the plan of the USSR Pavilion. The site we were allocated was extremely small. Its overall dimensions were a mere 11 m x 29.5 m.

In order to enlarge it, I took the diagonal as the main axis of the architectural composition, this being the longest dimension in a rectangle.

I would further draw your attention to the design of the staircase. It is not broad, but because it is on the skew it seems very large and ceremonial. I would also point out that as a result of this device, it turned out that the shifted volumes of the interior space also worked on the elevation, by in fact enlarging the number of square metres of wall on the facade. The roof too was fragmented into elements. Thus overall this structure of small physical dimensions had the appearance of a large celebratory building. The effect was enhanced by the special mast with its red flag, which announced its presence to the whole exhibition.

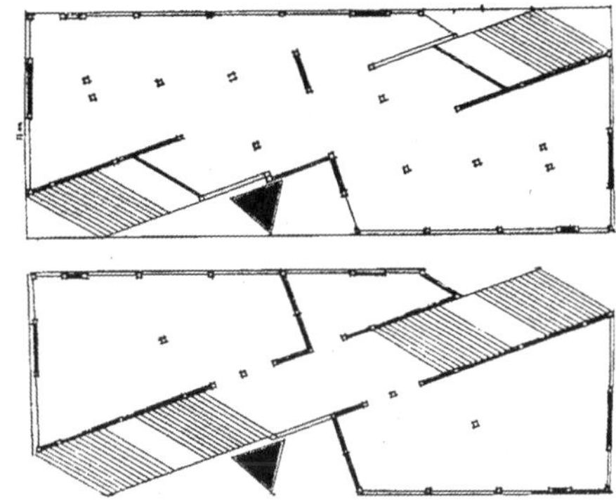

***Melnikov: USSR Pavilion, Paris, 1925:** plans as built.* Above: *Ground floor;* Below: *Upper floor. Black triangle is the mast.*

Main elevation (cf plans left). Whole diagonal wall alongside stair was red. Entrance was at left end – see photograph p.140.

9: MALEVICH: SUPREMATISM AS THE SPACE OF ENERGY

Soon after the 1917 Revolution, as Chapter 3 described, Malevich and other radical young artists became directly involved in the new government's cultural programmes and in 1920 Lunacharsky welcomed how 'talented publicists and theorists of artistic revolution such as Brik and Punin, outstanding representatives of the left such as Tatlin, Malevich and Altman' had been 'the stronghold' of his Commissariat's art section, Izo.[1] But as Chapter 3 already hinted, that official appreciation of them did not last.

Tatlin produced very little written theory during the Twenties but Malevich wrote a great deal. By this and by advancing a theory which directly related the 'appropriate' artistic language to the state of a population's cultural and technical development, Malevich and Suprematism became Lunacharsky's easiest target amongst the artistic avant-garde. In the longer term it is precisely Malevich's account of modern art as a development through 'systems' which are correlates of states of awareness of modernity, and of Suprematism as a climax of that development, that is of continuing interest.

New Systems in Vitebsk

It was typical of those fluid times time that artists moved around as sympathies or hostilities dictated. Through the accident of Marc Chagall becoming 'artistic Commissar' in his native Vitebsk, this obscure little town in Western Russia became the centre of Suprematism. Chagall invited graphic artist and fellow Jew El Lissitzky to join him. Izo then appointed Malevich there in 1919 to reduce the 'conservative' impact of Chagall in the good local art school.

Life was tough and uncertain in Russia that autumn: the first campaign of the Entente powers against the new Soviet government had been defeated in July, only to be replaced by a second that would not be defeated till the next March. Individual precariousness was well described that July by the philosopher P.D. Ouspensky, whose *Fourth Dimension* of 1909, *Tertium Organum* of 1912 and *New Model of the Universe* of 1914 had much influenced Malevich. Wandering the provinces he wrote to London of the 'occult' situation in which 'I personally am still alive only because my boots and trousers are still holding together. When they end their existence, I shall evidently end mine.'[2] On 10 October, the Entente powers launched an all-out economic blockade of Russia as the Red Army continued fighting successful battles Westwards. This Blockade isolated Russia from all foreign literature and contacts. For arts already self-sufficient of Europe and pregnant with extraordinary new visions, the results of several years isolation at this point were entirely positive, forcing them into undistracted pursuit of their own profoundly original ideas. Thus civil war and the emergency rationing of War Communism was still at its height when Malevich arrived in the embattled area of Vitebsk on 5 September 1919. As one local student Lev Iudin recorded, his impact was immediate in 'spreading a different atmosphere and a different frame of mind.'[3]

Hand-lithographed publications which Malevich produced in the school here contain the clearest surviving expositions of Suprematism's relationship to preceding 'systems' in art and of its own formal vocabulary and intentions. His first little book, plainly needed as manifesto and textbook to establish his line in the school, was called *On New Systems in Art* and written in late 1919. This elaborated the ideas he had sketched in *From Cubism and Futurism* in 1915. The second, an essay accompanying '34 drawings' in 1920, spelt out the meanings of colour and form within the Suprematist language.[4]

His vague inspirations of 1915 had now become a clear vision of 'intuition and creativity' and everything else as 'energetic forces'. Already he had a distinctive geographical model of how this energy was hierarchically distributed which is unusual amongst the generally city-focussed avant-garde.

> *'Man is an organism of energy, a grain striving to form a single centre. ... Villages are small organisational centres of energy which in turn form new centres with a more complex and powerful form of energy; for the villages, the towns are the major centres, and they in their turn single out power for the central cities of the country as a whole ... A supreme town will be formed as a product of the forces of the towns of whole peoples: by this time the latter will have formed a single moving force.'*[5]

His account of the 'new systems' in painting stresses the slow incremental process through which new artistic languages emerge to solve new painterly problems in response to changing 'environments'. In his own period, the key features of that environment were a new questioning of 'what is an object', and a new focus on the phenomenon of 'movement'. No explicit references to cognitive psychology or theoretical physics were needed to justify his assertion that these were the main intellectual perceptions of his era, but such connections were implicit. Malevich insists however (as any serious artist would) that it is not art's role to re-process the discoveries of science into the languages of art as a 'popularisation'. Art's role is to investigate the same territory through its own particular modes of analysis and expression. Society, of course, does not understand art's potential here. With what sounds like a dig at Lunacharsky he laments that:

'even the most cultured socialists ... always demand that art be comprehensible, but they never demand of themselves that they adapt their mind to its comprehension. Many people, especially socialists, think that art exists for the purpose of painting comprehensible bread-rolls.' [6]

From Cézanne he says, painters inherited 'the realisation that ... an object has six, five, ten aspects, and to convey it more fully as it is in actuality, it is essential to portray all these sides ... from outside and inside.' Thus early Cubists 'began to build objects' rather as 'in a complex engineering drawing'. This was naturally as incomprehensible to the average person as engineers' drawings of motorcars, 'because they could not comprehend how all the shapes came together as one whole.' Later stages of Cubism followed the 'purely painterly' logic of this process, to explore a kind of painting 'that rejected all objects as such', seeking not 'the object's totality but its dissolution into the component elements needed to create painterly statements'. The object became just 'the starting point for building a new painterly construction' and 'this marked the beginning of pure painting.' [7]

Futurism made two leaps beyond Cubism's residual concern with 'the world as a collection of objects'. Firstly, 'the dynamics of the energic power of things was discovered'. Where previously 'the painter could only show that a railway engine was moving by showing the smoke going backwards', Futurism found a way to convey 'the sensation (*oshchushchenie*) of movement itself'. Secondly, 'it clarified the position of the painter' who 'is now the *centre* around which the movement is going on'. Here the communication problem got worse. For 'the man in the street used to seeing just a few carriages, it was naturally difficult to make out what was what in this image of the total movement of the city'.[8] For artists however this change of position was seminal, as 'fixing in our minds a new real concept of the contemporary state of our understanding of the world'. Suprematism took forward Futurism's unfinished agenda by engaging with the 'reality' of that 'contemporary state' as a 'reflection in our consciousness' of 'the purely energetic power of movement.' [9] His reference to Suprematism as 'the new painterly realism' is confusing. This 'realism' is the appropriate painterly response to the new intellectual reality which sees the world as energy; it is thus pure Suprematist abstraction.

In language prescient of the information culture two generations later Malevich sees both material objects and non-material factors like 'initative' as energy, or 'energic forces'. Suprematism's concern is to chart this energetic dimension of existence. In the final paragraph of *New Systems* he challenged his future students to recognise the nature of their own times:

'Today the world's intuition is altering the system of our vegetable world of flesh and bone; a new economic order is being brought about to smooth the ruts in our creative minds, in order to carry forward its plan for moving forward into the infinite: this is where the philosophy of contemporaneity lies, and the philosophy of our creative days must follow.' [10]

As he evocatively but accurately described his world of Russia in the Twenties: 'We are living in a special time: perhaps there has never been such a time, a time of analyses and results for all the systems that ever existed.'[11]

Unovis

When Inkhuk was formed in Moscow in March 1920 around Kandinsky's programme for 'research into the fundamentals of art', it affiliated with its colleagues in Vitebsk. A meeting of Malevich's adherents on 14 April agreed that 'our designation is to be Unovis (*Utverzhditeli Novogo Iskusstva*) affirmers of the new art'. Soon virtually all studios in the Vitebsk School had 'united under the Unovis banner' and thus been taken over intellectually by Malevich. It was the signal for Chagall to leave and Malevich replaced him as Director.[12] Lissitzky was now a Unovis man and having spent the winter developing his concept of the Proun, he stayed too.

The 'Proun', meaning 'project affirming the new', is the main theoretical concept linked with Lissitzky's name and like much associated with him, has got inflated in the West through his self-publicity. It is a limited parallel to the 'laboratory work' concept launched by Tatlin and developed by the Moscovites in Inkhuk around Rodchenko [see p.106]. A Proun was an abstract formal composition of Suprematist type in isometric or perspective projection conceived as 'a half-way station between painting and architecture'. As a formal model of non-specific scale, such a painting or drawing provided a step towards use of the Suprematist language in 'applied' fields, but Lissitzky never took the idea much further than relief decorations on the walls of 'Proun rooms'.[13] It is impossible to distinguish its influence on architecture from the greater influence of Malevich himself, manifested particularly through Khidekel in Leningrad [p.167] or Leonidov in Moscow [pp.175-6; Ch.12]. Lissitzky was a journalist and graphic designer not a fundamental thinker, and Malevich's later remarks indicate he found Lissitzky's popular 'politicising' of Suprematist language unhelpful to his serious theoretical purpose.[14] Later in 1920 Lissitzky was attracted back to Moscow by the growing activities of Inkhuk. In 1921 he started teaching at the Vkhutemas, mainly in furniture [p.184] and he spent much of the Twenties in Europe.

Malevich's notion of modern painting as a succession of definable and rule-based perceptions of the world became the basis of his teaching method. In the work of individual Vitebsk pupils we can see them being taken through each successive 'system' till they reach their own 'level'.[15] From the questionnaire which every applicant had to fill in we see the rigour and awareness Malevich demanded of the annual one-thousand-odd teenage aspirants.[16] Their extreme youth was remarkable. Thus Lazar Khidekel was only fifteen when he joined Malevich in 1919 after studying with several teachers already. Lev Iudin was sixteen. Ilia Chashnik was seventeen that year and Nikolai Suetin was by far the oldest of his core group at twenty-two.

The book which explained Malevich's own 'system' to his students came off the school press in December 1920 as *Suprematism: 34 Drawings*. Its illustrations trace the development of an increasingly complex spatial vocabulary out of the Black Square. The short text described the stages of planar Suprematism, and his conception of the Suprematist canvas as 'a window through which we discover life' as 'a state of dynamism'.

'Suprematism is divided into three stages according to the increasing numbers of black, red and white squares: the black, coloured and white periods. In the latter, the forms are painted white on white ... conveying the power of statics or apparent dynamic rest by the planar surface alone'. [17]

'The form clearly indicates a state of dynamism ... It conquers space' not like Futurism, by depicting 'clumsy machines ... with wings, wheels and petrol' but 'by means of specific magnetic interrelations on one form.' Suprematism's 'technical organisms' are autonomous. They are solutions to problems on another 'planet or entire system', or in today's phrase, 'in another universe of discourse', and in relation to their purpose 'have achieved utilitarian perfection'.

> *'The three squares of Suprematism represent specific types of* Weltanschauung *and world-building. The white square is a purely efficient movement of the form embodying the whole new, white, world-building. It also evokes the establishment of world-building as "pure action", as self-knowledge in a purely utilitarian perfection of "all man" ... The black square constitutes economy, which I introduced as the fifth dimension in art.'* [18]

His energy-based rationale for the selection of colours is explained thus:

> *'The Suprematist canvas reproduces space as white, not blue. The reason is obvious: blue does not give a true impression of the infinite. Suprematist infinite white allows the optical beam to travel unimpeded. ... The construction of Suprematist colour forms is in no way connected with aesthetic requirements ... The colour or tone in a work ... depends on the composition of elements which create the lump or form of energy. ... [As] movement changes the form in accordance with economic considerations, the colouring also changes.'* [19]

Even here Malevich does not miss the chance to spit at Tatlin's 'real materials in real space'. 'Suprematism's attitude to materials is directly opposed to the agitation which is now going in favour of the culture of material'. 'This obsession with material surfaces is a psychosis of contemporary aesthetics'; it is a concern with 'the organism's feathers instead of the utilitarian perfection of economic necessity'. Malevich had left the world of the material. As he wrote at the end of this text, 'I myself have entered a remote and for me new realm of thought. As best I can I shall give account of what I see in the infinite space of the human skull.' [20]

This text was dated '15 December 1920'. In the pamphlet of January known as *Unovis' Second Almanac* we see the agenda of politicking and creative work through which his group projected this vision into their own lives. Its three most illuminating articles form Document 15.

During that month, January 1921, Malevich went hear to Inkhuk debate whether his paintings were 'constructions' or 'compositions' [cf.p.30]. They reckoned them 'essentially compositional' though Ladovsky more categorically declared 'There is no construction in Suprematist works'. [21] By December he was trying to get Unovis out of Vitebsk but Inkhuk declined to help him relocate in Moscow. Petrograd was more tolerant of differing approaches and he had old friends there like Matiushin. Thus in 1922 he returned there with Suetin, Khidekel, Iudin, and Chasnik. Pegoskhum had just become the Academy again [p.162] and it made him a professor. Avant-garde activity was focussed on the new Museum of Painterly Culture which in 1923-4 Malevich transformed into an institute called Ginkhuk, akin to Moscow's now-defunct Inkhuk. Matiushin headed the department confusingly named 'Organic Culture' whose concern was his 'theory of expanded seeing' and the operation of perception, psychologically and phsyiologically, through the senses of the whole 'organic human being'. In 'Material Culture' Malevich was stuck with Tatlin, seeking new uses of materials in industrial goods. (His famous energy-saving coat and stove were developed here and initial ideas for his Flying Machine.)[22] 'General Ideology of Art' was headed by the critic and Tatlin supporter Nikolai Punin. Malevich led formal theory in the 'Artistic Culture' department and the whole institute aimed 'to study phenomena of the spatial arts by methods of natural science'. [22] At the practical level his colleagues seized the big city's opportunities to start 'devising utilitarian forms for new objects', notably in ceramics factories.

The 'additional element'

With his concept of the *pribavochnyi element*, conventionally translated as 'the additional element', Malevich identifies that new painterly device which is the kernel of each painterly 'system' and embodies its particular perception. By analogy with a 'new pattern of behaviour' in the human body, that a doctor diagnoses as the symptom of some 'extras' (*pribavki*) invading a patient's organism, he seeks the new pattern of painterly behaviour which identifies a new 'system in art'. His main argument is built around a sequence of four issues: (1) What is happening when a painter makes an image? (2) How does the 'system' which determines the shape of that image relate to his cultural condition? (3) In any particular case, is there a fit or a misfit between the formal system underlying the image and the system of the painter's own consciousness or cultural condition? (4) How should teaching, as a process of diagnosis and therapeutics, ensure these two are in proper synchrony in a given individual who is trying to be a painter?

The whole process is rooted in the fact that 'what what we call nature is our own mental construct (*sobstvennaia vydumka*) which has nothing in common with original reality (*podlinnost'*).' 'The diversity of painterly blobs and lines [which the painter produces] derives from the form of irritation (*razdrazhenie*) which 'the original reality' causes in him.' [24] Whether consciously or not, this is close to the orthodox Marxist view of art and cognition as forms of 'reflection' (*otrazhenie*) endorsed by Lenin in his

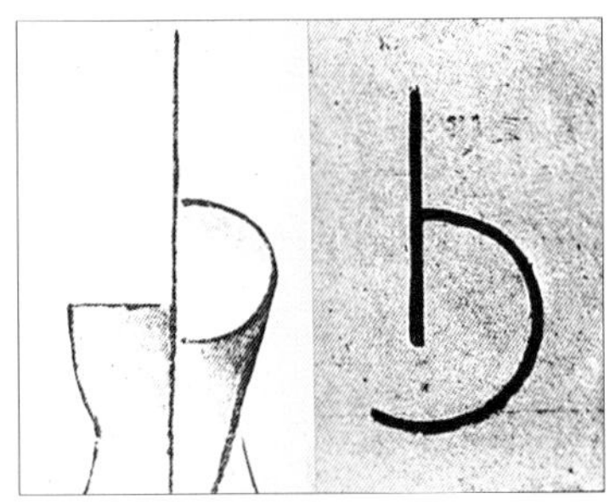

Right, 'sickle'-shaped 'additional element' of Cubism. Left, *derivation from plan + elevation*

Supremamatist equipment for daily life: tea cup by Malevich, from Russkoe iskusstvo, *1923*

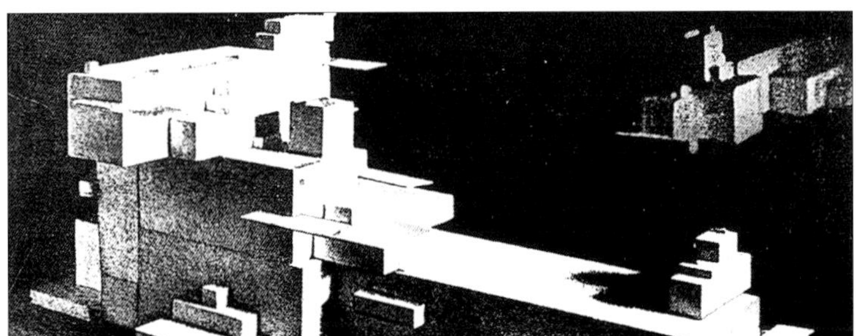

Arkhitektons by Malevich, Chashnik and Suetin in the dramatically lit Ginkhuk show, June 1926, which caused AKhRR to write in Leningradskaia Pravda *of 'An ivory tower at state expense'.*

Materialism and Empiriocriticism of 1908. This theory involves the two key concepts 'irritability' (*razdrazhimost'*) or the ability to receive environmental stimulae, and 'sensation' (*oshchushchenie*), which is the consciousness of having received that stimulous, ie its registering in the brain.[25]

In Malevich's exposition of the additional element 'the term stands for a whole culture of activity which can be defined by a typical or characteristic condition of straight and curves lines in the painter's behaviour'. The Cézannist additional element was a 'curved fibrous' form. A 'Cubist condition' of the canvas 'is a plane of six dimensions' allowing a multi-directional depiction. The device for handling this six-dimensional representation, hence its 'additional element', is the 'sickle', or straight line intersecting a curve.[26]

'The additional element of Suprematism is the Suprematist straight line. The environment corresponding to this new culture has been produced by the latest achievements in technology and especially of aviation. It can be manifest either as dynamic Suprematism of the plane, where the additional element is the "Suprematist straight line", or as static Suprematism in space – abstract architecture – with the additional element being the "Suprematist square".'[27]

Here Malevich's observations about cultural differences become linked up with his art-historical analysis. He unequivocally identified the transition from Cézannism through Cubism to Futurism and Suprematism with stages in society's material and hence cultural modernisation, from rural existence as a part of the natural world ('corresponding to Millet'), through the urban existence of the small town, to metropolitan existence in the modern city and hence to the world 'of communications in the air'.[28]

He unflinchingly spells out this sequence of correspondences between given cultural condition and its correct painterly 'system'. Indeed his prescription to students who were painting 'in Suprematist style' but not genuinely perceiving the world 'mechanically', let alone 'as energy' was to send them to the villages to 'start again' from Millet. Given the 'cultural condition' of Russia at this date, this theoretical position was as near as anyone in the avant-garde came to shooting themselves publicly. Lunacharsky had railed against his 'incomprehensible' theory many times.[29] Already in 1920 however he had spelt out with brutal clarity a view of the irrelevance of 'abstraction' to the Russian populace for which Malevich's own theory now gave 'proof'.

'Within the line of development of European art, Impressionism, all forms of Neo-Impressionism, Cubism, Futurism and Suprematism are natural phenomena. ... All this work, conscientious as it is, has the character of laboratory research. ... But the proletariat and the more cultivated sections of the peasantry did not live through any of the stages of European or Russian art. They find themselves at an entirely different stage of development.'[30]

Nothing could have been clearer. In view of this it was strange that officialdom took so long to destroy Malevich's professional base.

Bauhaus and architecture

In October 1925, after more feuding with Malevich, Tatlin quit Leningrad for Kiev and thence for the Vkhutemas in Moscow. Malevich used his workshop as a studio for developing his own ideas about a 'Suprematist architectural order' in the wooden and plaster block models he called arkhitektons. Soon Ginkhuk was inspected by its official parent body Glavnauk, and this 'so-called architecture' left them disgusted at its 'abstracted character'. In February 1926 Malevich was fired as Director.[31] In summer an exhibition of these arkhitektons got fierce criticism from the pro-Party and doggedly Realist AKhRR, Association of Artists of Revolutionary Russia, and Malevich's paper on 'The theory of the Additional Element in Painting' was forbidden publication by the notorious Glavlit censors. In December Ginkhuk was closed.[32]

Malevich had an invitation to Germany pending for the next spring, and prepared twenty-two panels explaining his theories of modern art's development and his teaching method to accompany his lectures. In March he left for Warsaw, Berlin and the Bauhaus in Dessau. This trip had several concrete results. First, the panels remained in the West and became divided between the Stedelijk Museum and MOMA in New York. Those describing how the 'systems' concept was used as diagnosis and prescription for his painting students are translated as Document 16. Second, Moholy-Nagy published his censored text as a *Bauhausbücher* entitled *Die Gegenstandslose Welt: The Non-Objective World*. The text was cut, as Kandinsky's English edition had been, and only lately has it been possible to compare with his original.[33]

Thirdly, through Hugo Häring's association of progressive architects in Berlin a room was organised for him in the Grosse Berliner Kunstausstellung that summer. Lunacharsky reviewed this show irrately, insisting that 'Malevich's "theoretical texts" embarrass even the Germans'.[34]

Soon after Malevich returned home the Constructivist architects' journal *SA* suddenly carried three pages about him – perhaps as a gesture of moral support, perhaps under influence of Leonidov who increasingly used his language. Between Malevich and Gan, who wrote the appreciation, there were also personal links going back to 1918. Malevich later told *SA* firmly that 'your magazine has nothing to do with architecture' and 'I wish to be only occasional in it', but 'in friendship I shake your hands'.[35] Gan's piece however indicates an attempt to see complementarity in their two movements as both suffered increasing official hostility. Extracts appear here as Document 17.

■

1 'Ob otdele Izo', 1920, in A.V. Lunacharsky, *Ob iskusstve*, vol.2, Moscow, 1982, pp.79-83 **2** P.D. Ouspensky, *Letters from Russia 1919*, London, 1978, p.6 **3** Quoted in S. Compton, *Chagall*, London, 1985, p.40 **4** Both discussed in more detail in Cooke, 'Malevich: from theory to teaching', *Art & Design*, 1989, no.5-6, pp.6-47; K. Malevich, *O novykh sistemakh v iskusstve*, Vitebsk, 1919; refs here to English in T. Andersen, *K.S. Malevich: Essays*, vol.1, Copenhagen, 1968, pp.83-117; *Suprematizm. 34 risunka*, Vitebsk, 1920, English, ibid, pp.123-64 **5** ibid, p.116 **6** ibid, p95 **7** ibid, pp.95-6, 99 **8** ibid, pp.115-6 **9** ibid, p.116 **10, 11** ibid, p.117 **12** On this period see Compton, *Chagall*; L. Zhadova, *Malevich*, London, 1982; W. Beeren & J. Joosten, eds., *Malevich*, Amsterdam-Leningrad, 1988 **13** S. Lissitzky-Küppers, *El Lissitzky*, 1968; J. Debbaut, ed., *El Lissitzky*, Eindhoven, 1991 **14** Andersen, vol.1, p.127 **15** Khidekel's family have typical work. **16** A. Rudenstine, ed., *Russian Avant-Garde Art: George Costakis Collection*, London, 1981, p.261 & A. Nakov, *The Suprematist Straight Line*, London, 1977, p.45 **17** *34 risunka*, in Andersen, vol.1, p123 **18** ibid, pp.123-7 **19** ibid, p.126 **20** ibid, pp.126-8 **21** S. Khan-Magomedov, *Rodchenko*, London, 1986, p.85 **22** L. Zhadova, ed., *Tatlin*, London, 1988 **23** Beeren etc, *Malevich*, p.80 & L. Zhadova, 'Ginkhuk v Leningrade', *Prob.ist.sov.ark.* 4, Moscow, 1978, pp.25-8 **24** Andersen, *Malevich: Essays*, vol.3, Copenhagen, 1976, pp.147-94 (151-3) **25** Fuller discussion in Cooke, Malevich' **26** Andersen, vol.3, pp.155-6; 177 **27** K. Malevich, *The Non-Objective World*, New York, 1959, p.61 **28** Andersen, vol.3, pp.187-8 **29** Eg. Lunacharsky, *Ob iskusstve*, vol.1, p.293; vol.2, pp.435-6 **30** Lunacharsky, 'Ob otdele', p.82 **31** H. Klotz, ed., *Matjuschin und die Leningrader Avantgarde*, Stuttgart, 1991, p.43 **32** Beeren etc, *Malevich*, pp.81-2 **33** 1980 edition of Bauhausbucher-11 has Malevich's ms. in facsimile. **34** Lunacharsky, *Ob iskusstve*, vol.2, pp.214-8 **35** A. Gan, 'Spravka o Kazimire Maleviche', *SA*, 1927, no.3, pp.104-6; Malevich's letter to *SA* and its reply, *SA*, 1928, no.5, p.156. Full texts in Cooke, 'Malevich'.

Doc. 15

UNOVIS GROUP, VITEBSK ALMANAC NO.2

Hand lithographed pamphlet, January 1921

'The overthrow of the old world of the arts will indeed be delineated on the palms of your own hands.'

UNOVIS

1. *Partiinost* in art. M. Kunin.
2. Unovis in the studios. L. Khidekel.
3. Architecture faculty. I. Chashnik
4. On still life. L. Iudin.

2nd publication of the Vitebsk Creative Commitee of UNOVIS
Vitebsk, 1921, January
Bukharinskaia Street, No.10

PARTIINOST [THE NATURE OF PARTY] IN ART

A party arises when there is a specific class of people following the same aim and the same set of interests. Those aims comprise the party's programme, clearly spelling out what each member must do to achieve the stated aims. All people who seek to better defend their own opinions and to see their aspirations realised must organise themselves into a party.

At present, all the young have recognised the essence of the new art, but adherents of the old art (even when they wear the dress of youth) are erecting all possible obstacles to the realisation of its aims – aims which answer the requirements of today and are necessary to everyone who has creative blood flowing in their veins.

Партийность в искусстве.

Партия возникает тогда, когда есть определенный класс лиц, преследующих одни и те же цели, одни и те же интересы. Те цели к которым стремится партия составляют программу партии, ясно указывающую на все те пути по которым должен следовать каждый член партии для достижения намеченных целей, и всякий желающий как-бы лучше защитить свои взгляды и проводить их в жизнь должен организоваться в партию.

И теперь, когда вся молодежь осознала сущность нового искусства, приверженцами старого [будь они облачены в одежду юности] чинятся все возможные препятствия к осуществлению тех целей, которые отвечают запро-

So, it is time to get organised into a party.

There are two entirely different ideas here that are in danger of getting mixed up: the idea of party, and the idea of loyalty to a particular artistic direction. So I will spell out clearly the difference between them.

The crucial difference is that all members of a party work in one direction conforming to the agreed programme, but in art there is no one single direction. The members of any artistic 'party' do not follow identical programmes, though their work produces no results if it lacks a larger system. It is in the nature of a party, by contrast, to propagate its opinions and structures COLLECTIVELY, in an organised way, to dictate its convictions and principles to everyone.

In art there are primitive parties, when small circles of artists form 'groups'. These are the best proof that it is necessary to unite to achieve one's aims, but the short-coming of these groups is their exclusiveness.

Thus knowing what factors a party pursues, I pose the question: do we need a party in art, which must be free, creative and making things? Should it be tied up by party discipline and lose its essential freedom?

Yes! In the present chaotic moment in art, they would like to permit artists only one kind of canvas, namely: monuments; there is a class of artists wanting to resurrect the rotted trash which is no use to anyone; they want to squeeze our new ideas, and our new thinking on the structures of the new world into the framework of the departed world.

In this advanced revolutionary moment, when we are craving the real emancipation of art, the affirmation of new forms and the realisation of those forms, it is necessary to organise ourselves into a party.

How are we to deal with the individualists, if they are not to be organised into a party? Clearly each will pursue his own tasks. ... In allowing the individualist freedom of action we are announcing that there will be no place for him in the proletarian communist structure and that the future, which only the collective can construct, belongs to us.

All this can only be realised with an organised, cohesive UNOVIS party as the leader.

M. Kunin

UNOVIS IN THE STUDIOS

In their second year our studios have shown a real mastery of the practical and theoretical foundations that we have developed. Since we organised UNOVIS the fogginess has gone. Each studio now has solid foundations for its investigation of a particular aspect of our work, and has set itself do-able tasks for achieving its aims.

Amidst the chaos which has continuously reigned here, we have laid down an orderly and correct path for the under-masters' work (*podmastery*: this was UNOVIS's term for students), though much depends on their own energy and attitudes.

Those that have followed the programme correctly are now fully cogniscent of the line of development of painting. They pass through all the basic painting modes of the contemporary schools: Cézannism, Cubism, Futurism and Suprematism, and through this acquire knowledge of all types of creative composition, and of the constructing of painterly elements, which serve as the basis of our further progress from here.

More than this, the UNOVIS method leads to a purely creative path of creating new forms, affirming Suprematism as the fundamental systematising new form of the world.

In the equipping of the techno-electrical society there is no place for the artist with his aesthetic rubbish. Every kind of creator will in future be required to participate in this strong and powerful culture, which is imminently coming into being in our communist state.

In this work we must participate on an equal level with the engineer the agronomist and the workers of all specialisms.

From all this it is clear that artistic aestheticisation seems insignificant in this approaching situation. Only by pursuing a pure creative route of construction and invention shall we serve as a force for giving expression to the future of culture.

Laz. Khidekel

ARCHITECTURAL AND TECHNICAL FACULTY

The architectural and technical studio is the culmination of all our knowledge in the painterly field to which the under-master who has passed through painting and material faculties moves on. This is the laboratory for the pure creative work of inventing new constructions, which is leading Suprematism out of its draughtsmanly plan-making to devising the organisms of utilitarian forms for new objects.

The systematic study of all the stages and principles of Suprematism, is the first starting point of the movement towards invention of new utilitarian Suprematist organisms. The processes of geometricisation in Cubism and Futurism are only the preparation for studying Suprematism's systems and principles, for elucidation of its planned movement in space.

The constructions underlying Suprematist structures are the working drawings on which to build and develop the forms of utilitarian organisms.

As the architectural and technical faculty develops it is becoming a vast studio-laboratory, equipped not with the pitiful little mechanical tools and paint-pots of the painting faculties, but with machines that are electric, with foundries and with all the means and wealth of the technology of material forces. In unison

„Ниспровержение старого мира искусств да будет вычерчено на ваших ладонях"

„Уновис"

Содержание:
1. Партийность в искусстве. М. Кунин.
2. Уновис в мастерских. Л. Хидекель.
3. Архитектурный факультет. И. Чашник.
4. О натюр-морте. Л. Юдин.

II^ое издан. Вит. творкома „Уновис"

Витебск 1921 г. январь.
Бухаринская № 10.

with astronomers, engineers and mechanics it shares the unified aspiration of constructing organisms of Suprematism, as the new forms of economy of the utilitarian system of the present day.

The faculty has two sections, the architectural and the technical. The first involves the study of systems of drawn Suprematism and the construction of them in plans and drawings, ruling out earthly space to give each energy cell its particular place in the overall plan. It involves the constructing of all the component elements and the allocation of space on the earth's surface to each of them, delineating those places and lines from which the forms of Suprematism will rise and extend in space. All work in this section leads to drawings and plans, to a diagram of earthly energy cells, to the placing of cells of Suprematist forms of space.

The second section is constructional-technical. It involves the systematic constructing of individual energy-elements in the time of space (*vo vremeni prostranstva*), and the building up of force-forms of an organism into a Suprematist construction of a utilitarian kind (*postroika silovykh form organizma v utilitarnost' suprematisticheskoi konstruktsii*).

Here are the engineer-technologist, the astronomer, the chemist and mathematician. Here the organism's parts are assembled, cast and constructed. From here they go out to display their refinement to the world. The architectural and technical studio is crucible of all the other faculties of the UNOVIS school to which every kind of creative personality must strive in a unified collective of builders of the new forms of the world.

Long live the party of UNOVIS, which is affirming the new forms of utilitarian Suprematism.

I. Chashnik

COMRADES!

Get ready for the All-Russian Spring Exhibition of UNOVIS in Moscow.

Lithog. printing works of Vitebsk Art Studios.

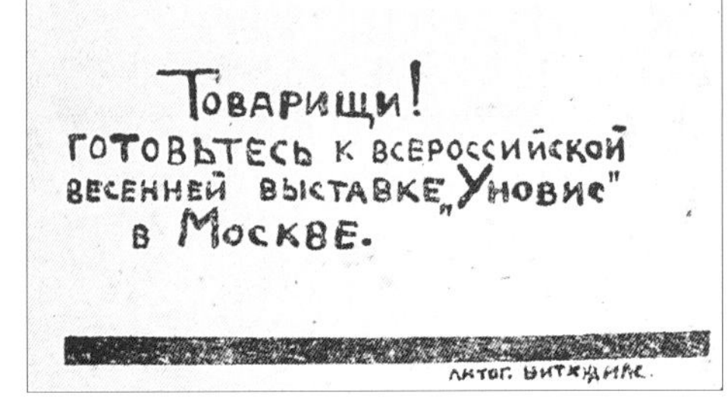
Товарищи!
Готовьтесь к всероссийской весенней выставке „Уновис" в Москве.

Литог. Витхудмас.

Doc. 16

KAZIMIR MALEVICH
DIAGNOSIS AND PRESCRIPTION OF THE STUDENT PAINTER'S 'HEALTH'

Pedagogical panels prepared in Ginkhuk, taken to Poland and the Bauhaus, 1927

INVESTIGATION OF PAINTERLY CULTURE AS A MODE OF BEHAVIOUR OF THE ARTIST
For us a painting has become a body (*stala telom*) in which are laid out for inspection the causes of what a painter does, and his condition (*prichini i sostoianiia*), as well as the way his whole understanding of nature is structured and the relations between these things.

PANELS 1-8: ANALYSIS OF WORKS OF ART
The artist's behaviour is manifested in the structure of forms and colours that he uses. Through an analysis of the colour and form in a work, we can cognise the mood of what his soul is living through (*nastroenie dushevnykh perezhivanii*).

PANELS 9-16: ANALYSIS OF SENSATION
Breaking down the painterly behaviour into its component elements of sensation.

PANELS 17-21: THE PEDAGOGICAL METHOD
There follows an example of the application of the new pedagogical method to two individual students

PANEL 17: Diagnosis of the image (*uiasnenie obraza*)
The purpose of these exercises is

1: To investigate the individual's painterly manifestations in order to determine what is his characteristic way of structuring things (***stroi***);

2 To break down the individual's painterly manifestations into component elements of sensation, to establish which of them are extraneous factors drawn into the work and which are genuine characteristics of the individual's own system that should be fostered.

The exercises are divided into two parts:
a) Collecting data on the individual and processing it;
b) Making a diagnosis from the processed data.

The data is divided into:
a) Direct data from:1 The questionnaire; 2 Examining the student's work and asking him questions about it; 3 Incubation (*inkubatsiia*).
b) Data obtained by experimental means which results from: 1 Psychological tests; 2 Colour tests; 3 Tests of colour-association.

Prescription for development of the image:
The purpose of this is to eliminate the disease of eclecticism from the body, if it is present, and develop the individual's sensations to 100% functioning.

This is achieved by a prescription appropriate to the the individual's observed painterly behaviour.

If necessary, the prescription may use these supplementary methods: 1 Isolation; 2 Prescribed (*retsepturnye*) exercises in still life; 3 Incubation; 4 Analysis of a work of art; 5 Discussion.

Observations on the work can be made by means of: 1 Notes; 2 Bulletins; 3 Conversations and questions.

PANEL 18: Applications of the new method
This shows practical work executed with two individuals who have differing sensation structures.

Direct data: After the works themselves have been examined, the questionnaire asks about the school where the student studied, the various artistic influences he has encountered and various examples of painting that are around him now. All this produces:

1 Data indicating how consistent are the artistic behaviour and sensations of the individual concerned, resulting in a typical behaviour graph.

2 Information on the individual's circle of sensations. This data derives from classification of the individual's works according to groups of sensation or according to stages in the development of a particular sensation or sensibility.

Incubation: From this data is obtained on the individual's sensations at present. The individual's own free manifestation of his sensations is observed without interventions from the investigator.

Conclusions about these two students

1 The first student's influences are primarily mystical. Methodologically, he is constantly developing one and the same sensation. The circle of sensations on which he draws is a lyrical one, inclined to mysticism.

2 The second student showed evidence of influence from the systems of Painterly Realism. His underlying painterly temperament is unstable. The circle of sensations is that of Cubism and Suprematism. Eclectic forms arise because he combines these two systems.

PANEL 19: Data gathered by experiment
Two types of experiment are used: Colour tests and Form tests, both of which are done in the Organic Culture Group's laboratory [in Ginkhuk].

Three examples of colour tests
1: Aim: To elucidate the colour wave (*tsvetovaia vol'na*) in which the student is located, and to determine its position in relation to the overall system of waves.
What it involves: the student making a free selection of available tones from their own spectrum.

Conclusions from the two students concerned
The first is located in the tonal area; he has an individual colour spectrum which is post-Impressionist in its general culture. The second has an eclectic spectrum, combining colour waves of Cubism and Suprematism.
2: Aim: To explain the logic of connections (*poriadka sviazok*) between the colour units he has employed.
What it involves: Selection of colours which are supplementary to the colour unit (*tsvetovoi edinits*) in question. Grey is used as the example in both cases.
3: Aim: To test colour associations and mood induced in the student while creating the painterly image
What it involves: Associations with the colour unit being used, or the colour series. Red used as example.
Conclusions: First individual's associations were: Hot day, a castle in the sun with festivities in front of it; dancers relaxing. Thus his associations are of a literary, romantic type. All connection with the actual colour as such has been lost. Second individual's associations were: A tram-car, a brilliant red surface, a painting by Léger. His associations are shown to retain a direct connection with the colour itself.

PANEL 20: Summary of the diagnoses
First student's *stroi* is lyrical with mystical inclinations; His sensations are basicly Painterly Realist, but a little eclectic in their expression. Second student's *stroi* reveals pure sensation. His sensations are eclectic in expression, combining elements of Cubism and Suprematism. Earlier his work manifested the influence of Cézanne, but now Cubist elements are dominant.

PANEL 21: Typical prescriptions for restoring students' contact with their own real sensations
First prescription (for eliminating the Suprematist additional element) ***Student should undertake:*** Liberating conversations and 100% still-life painting. ***Results that will be observed:*** Suprematist elements disappear rapidly. Raw painterly elements appear in the surface treatment and the 'sickle' structure. Student gets pleasure and satisfaction from work on painting. ***Conclusions:*** It is essential to use the data of this new work to check again and establish how far the new painterly sensations are now genuinely inherent to the make-up of the student concerned.

Second prescription (to test how far the student can resist a weakening of the painterly structure) ***Student should undertake:*** A prescriptive still-life with a strong dose of purely painterly sensations, aimed at the condition of painting in First-stage Cubism. ***Results that will be observed:*** There will be further loosening of painterly structure as the student moves onto a First-stage Cubist painting. His contact with his painting is stronger. ***Conclusions:*** Student to go on working within the painterly sensations of First-stage Cubism.

Third prescription (to weaken the Cubist structure, and get the student working at the level of painting that is appropriate to him). ***Student should undertake:*** Painterly still-lives of a first-stage Cubist type and be entirely isolated from the influence of Second- or Third-stage Cubism. ***Results that will be observed:*** The individual will be in total contact with his own work. ***Conclusions:*** Student to continue working in this way.

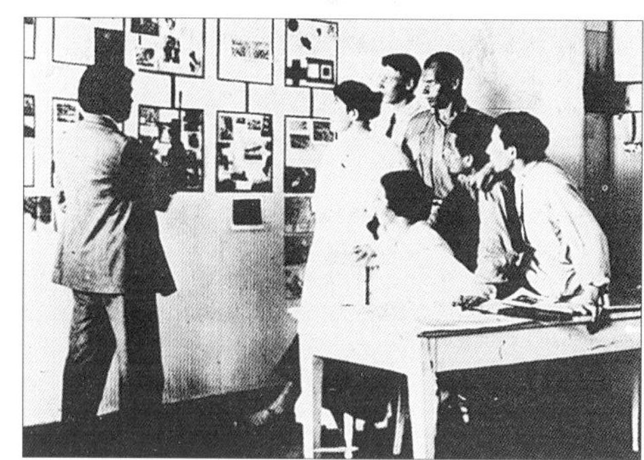

Malevich, left, *discusses work with his assistants in Ginkhuk. Ermolaeva stands nearest him, Iudin sits on table,* right.

Doc. 17

ALEXEI GAN
NOTES ON KAZIMIR MALEVICH

Extracts from SA, 1927, no.3, pp.104-6

During recent years comrade Malevich has worked exclusively in the field of volumetric Suprematist compositions, on problems of the volumetric and spatial forms of material masses. This is somewhat related to the tasks facing creators of contemporary architecture.

Malevich works intuitively. ... His experience is not organised by consciousness. ... So while volumetric Suprematism does not yield objects of that concrete social utility without which contemporary architecture is not architecture at all, they have vast importance as abstract research of new form, as such. ...

Kazimir Malevich does not accept either [Rationalism or Constructivism]. He pursues his own 'purely suprematist' path, on the principle of its 'primacy' or 'superiority' (*pervenstvo*). What then is a Suprematist architecture? It is 'the primacy of volumetric masses and their spatial solution in consideration of weight, speed and direction of movement.'

True, this metaphysical formulation does not yield much, to put it mildly, to an intellect thinking materialistically. But Malevich does not only speak, he does, and what Malevich does, we repeat, has great psychological importance. In his new Suprematist volumes and volumetric combinations there is not the smallest particle of atavism.

This is where Suprematist studies can be very important. They could be very beneficially introduced into the Basic Course of the Vkhutemas, in parallel to those exercises currently conducted under the influence of the psychologist Münsterberg's Harvard Laboratory.

The novelty, purity and originality of abstract Suprematism fosters a new psychology of perception. This is where Malevich's great contribution will lie.

10: STUDENTS AND TEACHERS: AVANT-GARDE ARCHITECTURE IN THE SCHOOLS

Moscow's bohemian 'artistic and technical studios', the Vkhutemas, have come to occupy a dominating position in the history of Soviet architectural education in this period, both in Russia and abroad, not least for parallels between elements of their pedagogy and work at the Bauhaus. Indeed links were fostered by both sides at the time. In the fine arts, Kandinsky found the Bauhaus a welcoming employer when the new politically-conscious avant-garde in Moscow rejected him in 1921 (see chapters 4 and 5). As typographer, publicist and furniture designer the peripatetic Lissitzky formed a two-way link in the middle Twenties.[1] In the later Twenties the Constructivist group OSA assiduously kept in touch with the Bauhaus architects through correspondence, publication and exhibition of their work, and hosting their German *confrères* who came to Moscow when they themselves had no chance to travel there.[2]

These links have been extensively documented. My concern here is to rectify the impression which this traffic has created, that Russia had only one school of architecture of any interest in the Twenties. At the same time the documents make it possible to bring to life something of the reality of work and teaching in those schools which is recorded, as they struggled to make 'the new architecture' in a generally hostile environment across the larger USSR.

Launching a 'free' system

Historically, Russia's students had always been a relatively radical political force, especially in St. Petersburg. As Chapter 1 showed, the tsarist government's fear of their influence was one of the reasons for its conservative and at times highly restrictive higher educational policies. As was also mentioned in Chapter 1, the social origins of art and architecture students tended to be broader in the late tsarist period than those of the student body as a whole, because sheer talent, rather than prior tutoring, was such an important criterion for obtaining entry. The network of regional schools like Odessa and Kiev brought local talent forward to the Academy or to MUZhVZ, and served to spread the ultimate recruitment net very wide. This was not however a cause of particular radicalism in the student body of art or architecture schools. Rather the opposite. The pressures on government came from students of law, philosophy or literature in the Universities. When there was trouble in art and architecture schools it was usually over internal details of curriculum, equipment or domestic facilities, and sometimes, if they felt trapped by inflexible teaching, over the composition of the staff.

There was trouble of this kind in the architecture department of MUZhVZ even during the War. In 1915, some of the older architecture students including Nikolai Ladovsky sought to celebrate the school's fiftieth anniversary in 1916 with an exhibition that would raise the question of 'The flowering of contemporary Russian architecture and the relation to this of MUZhVZ'.[3] As Russian architecture readjusted after the Moderne and sought to reinterpret its own classical traditions, they wanted new staff brought in. Specifically they wanted people whom they called 'the living classics': Alexei Shchusev, Vladimir Shchuko, Ivan Zholtovsky, Marian Lialevich, whose recent work in Moscow and Petrograd (formerly St. Petersburg) seemed to represent a new force in the Russian profession.

In mid War nothing changed, but immediately after the February 1917 uprising they started battling again, in particular for a structural change that would halt their constant rotation from class to class, between different studio teachers, and create long-term studio groups where each student stayed with the same master. In autumn 1917 just after revolutionary takeover, Zholtovsky was brought onto the staff at MUZhVZ, and though only officially teaching upper years, everyone went to his classes to study Italian Renaissance in a new way,

By April 1918 the Soviet Government's Council of People's Commissars, Sovnarkom, had decided the whole academic system of art education must go. The Art School of the Academy was still the country's leading one, although Moscow had just become the capital. The Academy was closed by Sovnarkom's decree of 12 April and reformed as Petrograd State Free Art-Study Studios (PGSKhUM) or Pegoskhum, under the aegis of Narkompros's art department, Izo. Lunacharsky set the tone in his opening speech to these first new Free Studios:

> *'Socialist society can give the life of the artist an endlessly richer content than the society in which he has lived till now. ... Maximum freedom ... resulting from this moment of transition in world history, and briefs set not by the merchant classes but by the people, with it creative freedom, and a free structure for all art establishments. These are the principles which can uniquely answer to the great perspectives now opening up to art.'*[4]

On 5 September 1918, as Commissariat responsible for education, Narkompros opened the whole country's art schools in a similar way as

'State Free Artistic Studios' (GSKhM) or Svomas. They were open to all comers regardless of prior training, and once enrolled they had total freedom of pursuits. Teachers must be invited by students: in Petrograd, for example, twenty votes were needed for a teacher to run a studio.[5] A total of 700 students signed up for the former Academy which previously taught half that number.[6] The system was explicitly conceived as a return to the Renaissance apprenticeships which had preceded the routinised European Academies, and the discontented students of the pre-Revolutionary period found themselves in a more radically changed situation than they could have dared propose. At the same time, experienced traditionalists were proving the most popular teachers amongst this new student body. Thus in the first voting in Petrograd, the elderly Leonti Benois got 99 votes from aspirant architects, his former pupil Ivan Fomin, 53, and amongst artists the established realist Kardovsky got 83 pupils, the slightly more modern Petrov-Vodkin got 40 pupils, and only two signed up for the front-line avant-gardist Vladimir Tatlin.[7]

When this process was applied in Moscow, the Stroganov College of Applied Arts on Rozhdestvenka Street became the First Svomas and the Moscow College of Painting, Sculpture and Architecture, MUZhVZ, on Miasnitskaia Street, became the Second Svomas. Regional art and architecture schools went through similar changes.

Architecture in the former Stroganov College was never a strong subject and was now taught in a tepid and conservative way by the oldest of the Vesnin brothers, Leonid, himself Academy trained and not yet converted by his PIGI-trained younger brothers to a thoroughly forward-looking view; by Fedor Shekhtel, whose inaugural lecture to his students is preserved as a rather sad text, and the worthy Sergei Chernyshev.[8] This soon ceased to be a separate department, as Shekhtel retired old and sick, and the other two moved over to the Second Svomas at the former MUZhVZ.

Here things were much livelier. The students' own initial invitations to teach them went to Shchusev, Zholtovsky and the established teacher Ivan Rylsky, all seen as experienced but 'new'.

Across the country there followed two academic years, 1918-19 and 1919-20, when not only the constraints had gone, but the good teaching of artistic skills too. Chaos reigned in differing degrees in different art schools. Petrograd suffered particularly from an extreme and largely incompatible mix of students. The highly skilled and serious ones who were the cream of the old system were now swamped by entirely unskilled enthusiasts with no conception of discipline.[9] As Alexander Benois later wrote of his brother Leonti's efforts at this time, 'His lectures underwent no change during the revolution and were untouched by the disturbing reforms which introduced such chaos into academic teaching.'[10] Even amidst the government's other problems this increasing shambles caused concern, as cultural policy, and the arts within that, were central planks of the Bolshevik programme. At the same time, with a hope of reviving industries like furniture and household-goods production for the rehoused and increasingly devastated population, the economic policy-makers were recognising the importance of producing designers where before the Revolution there had been training in crafts.

During 1919 new thinking was bubbling everywhere. Radical but official arts publications like *Art of the Commune* (*Iskusstvo kommuny*), in Petrograd, and parallel, often shortlived ones elsewhere, were reporting and leading an active redefinition of the role and nature of art. Experimental work abounded. In Petrograd, Tatlin's widely publicised tower model was built in the old mosaic workshop at the back of the Academy. Architecture students in the Moscow Svomases, like the whole art community, were exposed to its extraordinary fresh imagery and were more susceptible to such stimulous than the still heavily romantic studios of Petrograd itself. Here in what was now the capital, discontent with eternal study of the orders and outdated building types spread: those teachers like Zholtovsky who had seemed 'new' seemed to many increasingly dated.[11] The radical Ladovsky who had been a pre-Revolutionary agitator was now leading the experimental art-synthesis group Zhivskulptarkh (see Chapter 4), whose exhibition in summer 1920 was a revelation and inspiration to the restive young discontents in the architecture school. A group of three students in Zholtovsky's studio at the Second Svomas, Sergei Mochalov and Victor Balikhin from the top of the school and Nikolai Krasilnikov lower down, lead a protest.[12] This was the start of a process that ended with Ladovsky heading not just half of the architecture faculty, but a whole 'foundation course' shared by all students entering the school.

Vkhutemas and the revived Academy

In June 1920 there had been another conference of those involved in policy and administration in this field, and by autumn the result was another national reorganisation. Five months later, by a decree of Sovnarkom on 29 November 1920, the Moscow situation was reorganised to amalgamate the two Svomases into one school, to which existing students could transfer immediately. After four years study they would get proper qualifications regulated by Narkompros, Vesenkha and the State Committee for Labour Conscription, which would have the right and responsibility to distribute the trained people to wherever they might be needed on graduation.

Thus was formed the 'Moscow Higher State Artistic and Technical Studios' or Vkhutemas. In the words of the decree it was to be:

> *'a specialised higher education establishment for artistic and higher technical and industrial training whose aim is to produce master-artists of high qualification to work in industry, and to be instructors and leaders of technical education elsewhere.'*[13]

The seriousness of government intentions was indicated by clauses in the decree which awarded the students military status: the downside of this was penalties for desertion, but the advantage was a firmer-than-otherwise supply of rations. The intake should as far as possible be of 'workers'.

Lenin signed the decree on 18 December 1920, and a couple of months later on 25 February 1921 he and his wife Krupskaya visited the school's hostel for a 'meeting with students'. According to the founding decree, Vkhutemas students, like all others, were to have 'obligatory education in political literacy and the fundamentals of the communist world view on all courses'.[14] Maybe encouragement to those studies was the visit's intention but it left the students concerned professionally unimpressed by their leader. In the way of such meetings he met a selected group of five, including architecture student Nikolai Krasilnikov, and talked to them 'about their studies, literature and art'. As one reported on their meeting,

> *'Lenin liked our youthful enthusiasm, directness and unconditional disdain for oldstyle routine and passionate desire to serve the revolution. But from everything he said with such animation, it was clear that neither Lenin nor anyone around him had a correct understanding of the future development of art. We could all agree on one thing, that art must go in step with the revolution, but ... we each had our views what this means. And Vladimir Ilich strongly defended realistic art.'* [15]

Some kind of writing was plainly already on the wall.

Up in Petrograd at the Pegoskhum the student-elected architecture teachers were Leonti Benois, Ivan Fomin, Oskar Munts, Georgi Kosiakov, all leading professional figures and respected teachers in the old academy school, and the much younger Ernest Shtalberg, who had graduated there himself in 1914 under Benois, with some 180 students between them. It was largely through Benois' leadership that any structure remained to the architecture curriculum, as he organised it into a shared initial course backed up by specialist lectures, before an upper course in a single professor's studio – all rather on the Academy model as before. At the same time he ensured that design tasks set were relevant, with 'public dining rooms' and 'buildings for district soviets' treated with the same seriousness as the Imperial and capitalist briefs had been formerly.[16] Their first four post-Revolutionary graduates emerged in autumn 1921,[17] Noi Trotsky being later the best known, with a massively monumental diploma scheme for an industrial complex, whose idiom was continued in the first-prize winning Palace of Labour competition project that thrust him to prominence in 1923.

During this year, 1921, the whole of Pegoskhum 'Free Studios' underwent a reorganisation parallel to that which had created Vkhutemas in Moscow, in this case reinstating the name of Academy. The underlying aim within the school was now a changeover 'from the exclusively individual method of teaching to a method of objective, common courses'.[18] There was a first-year foundation course for students of all specialisms, largely conceived by the new Dean, Andrei Belogrud. This comprised three 'streams' of work, 'general', 'programmatic' (*programmnoi*) and constructive (*konstruktivnoi*) intending as he put it that 'all three kinds of composition serve one and the same aim, which is to develop the student's capacity for free creative work, and pedagogically these three complement each other'.[19]

The 'general' stream involved mastery of 'rhetorical and abstract factors'. Here 'tasks involve architectural concepts which do not require the students to have close involvement with specialised details of a brief and can give them open space for their artistic inventiveness'. 'Programmatic' composition aimed 'to develop the capacity to solve a task of a utilitarian kind'. 'Constructive' composition required designing building structures in which 'the constructional factors lie at the very basis of the form-making'.[20] Each carefully worked-out exercise was basicly set and taught by one particular professor, but students could consult with any member of the faculty.

This foundation course was plainly an attempt to find some middle way between the highly 'formal' teaching of the first year developed in Moscow, and the traditional approaches to composition historically taught in the old Academy. so certain drawing classes remained obligatory throughout a student's whole career. Above that basic course, five faculties were created: architecture, painting, sculpture, polygraphy and the now-obligatory and highly necessary Preparatory Faculty for worker-entrants, the *'rab-fak'*.[21] Now Rector of the whole Academy, Andrei Belogrud was an architect of the kind Moscow might have called 'the living classic'. Indeed his own pre-Revolutionary style had been freer than any of those four, Shchusev, Shchuko, Zholtovsky and Lialevich, whom the MUZhVZ students had sought as their teachers back in 1915. But those who were regularly called 'leftists' also had every encouragement and increasing influence in the school.

Under the new statutes it was again Benois who set the serious professional tone for the whole architecture faculty. As he said at this time:

> *'With the introduction of a whole new structure to our lives, changing everything public and private, there has to be a profound influence on our art in general and on our building in particular. Rich private villas and commercial buildings have gone and as artist-architects we must be ready, just as the painters and sculptors must be, to bring our talents and knowledge to bear on producing the very best solutions possible under the new economic and political conditions. ... It will require of us more work than ever, in acquiring the new scientific and technical knowledge without which we cannot be architects.'* [22]

Given his central concerns on the eve of the War, discussed in Chapter 11, his emphasis on planning is not surprising. As he continued in the same

Vladimir Lenin (1870-1924), with his sister in a Moscow street, July 1918.

A group of Vkhutemas students on the balcony of their hostel, mid-1920s.

Vkhutemas: *Samples of student work in the 'Space' (three-dimensional) section, Basic Course.* Left: *Assembly of 2 and 3 rectangular solids.* Right: *Articulation of surfaces in relief.*

paper: 'First place in our attentions must go to the building of our towns: to their planning and reorganisation and as far as possible improving the whole level to which they are equipped'.

At the Vkhutemas in Moscow, Ladovsky and his colleagues Vladimir Krinsky and Nikolai Dokuchaev had a scheme for dividing their studios of the architecture faculty by the specialisms of monumental buildings, planning, spatial problems.[23] They ran in roughly this way for a year, till autumn 1922, when they got their subsection of the faculty established as a parallel studio in its own right. Zholtovsky, Shchusev and the other 'living classics' were now the 'Academic studio' and this trio formed the core of the other, with equal status, called 'the New Researches studio' and subsequently the 'Unified studio' or Obmas. With increasing confidence Ladovsky, Krinsky and Dokuchaev officially formed themselves into the first new architectural society of the Soviet period in the following July, 1923, under the name of Asnova: the Association of New Architects.[24] (See Chapter 4.) Their power increased further that autumn when reorganisation of the Vkhutemas curriculum led to the 'basic course' in such concepts as spatial composition, colour, rhythm, which they had created for their students became the obligatory entry path for all students in the school, whatever their later professional specialism would be.[25]

Their increasing success irritated others of their generation, however. In that autumn term of 1923, not persuaded by either of the increasingly polarised approaches being taught in what was historically also 'their' school, Ilia Golosov and Konstantin Melnikov launched a third studio. Its name, 'The New Academy' was intended to signal its position between the other two, and Documents 21 and 22 indicate their stance.

In Ladovsky's teaching method for architecture, which he called 'psychotechnical', an 'abstract' (*otvlechennyi*) and a 'real' or 'productive' (*proizvodstvnnyi*) task always hand in-hand, first the abstract exercise, then a task with a 'brief' using that formal theme. The 'abstract' themes were exercises and combinations of rhythm, metre, proportions, and in his terminology, 'contrast and nuance; geometrical properties of form; physico-mechanical properties (mass and stability; mass and equilibrium etc).' Thus a student might tackle an abstract formal exercise in, say, 'the manifestation of dynamism and vertical correlation of parts' [eg. Silchenko, p.163], and then design 'a silicates pavilion for the USSR' with those same formal properties. An abstract exercise in 'volume' at the top and 'space' below might typically be reworked in a 'productive' exercise as a 'water tower'. In another example illustrated here [p.164, top, by Grushchenko], a task where 'volume and space' were to be integrated rather than related vertically, the 'productive' task was a 'caustic soda processing tower'. Sometimes this stage would demand the use of specific materials, but this dimension, which was a key part of the foundation method which Belogrud devised at the Academy in Petrograd, was generally underplayed here.

Document 18 gives the full text of one of the 'abstract' exercises Ladovsky set, dating originally from 1920. The task here was 'manifestation of the inherent geometrical properties of a form'. The text was published by Ladovsky himself as an example of his method in the first and only issue of Asnova's *News* (*Izvestiia*), produced in 1926, with illustrations from the work of one student Petrov. Solutions done at the same time by Turkus and others have been published more recently.[26]

In the theory of Ladovsky and his Rationalist colleagues, discussed in Chapter 4, this mastery of formal and spatial organisation as an expressive means was the real content of architecture. This is the skill which only the architect brings to a problem of building. As is clear from his statements which I have quoted in Chapter 4, all the rest is considered necessary but is only the 'means' and 'conditions'. In teaching practice his fundamental principle was the use of models, from the very first lessons through the whole of an architect's training and practice. In such an intensively worked-out system, it was more than usually natural that his teaching assistants were always older students newly graduated through his studio. Also illustrated here are applications of these formal concepts as the generating principles for planning schemes (see also Chapter 11), which were amongst Ladovsky's main personal interests in the later twenties.

Through student exhibitions as well as the professional grapevine, the essentials of this approach, albeit in simplified form, became known throughout the architectural community, and applied in primitive versions in some provincial schools. Archival material has lately shown that Krinsky at one stage regularly travelled back and forth to Leningrad (as Petrograd had been named since Lenin's death in 1924), to do some form of teaching at the

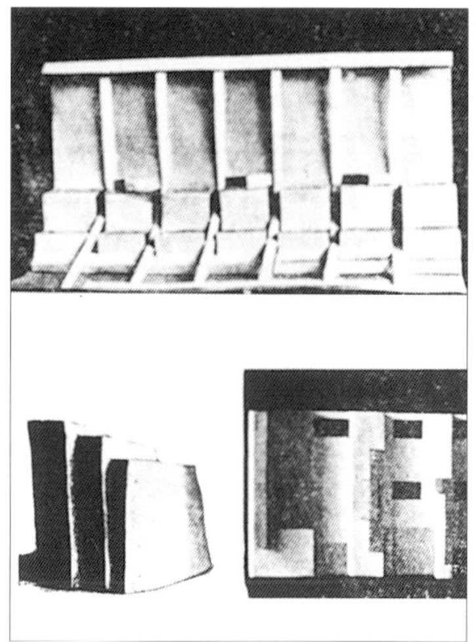

Exercises in constructing regular and irregular rhythmic sequences in the horizontal.

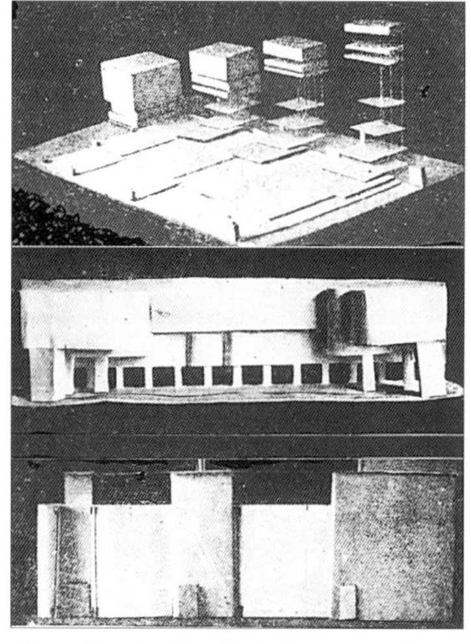

Above: Constructing rhythmic sequence in the vertical. Below: Frontal compositions.

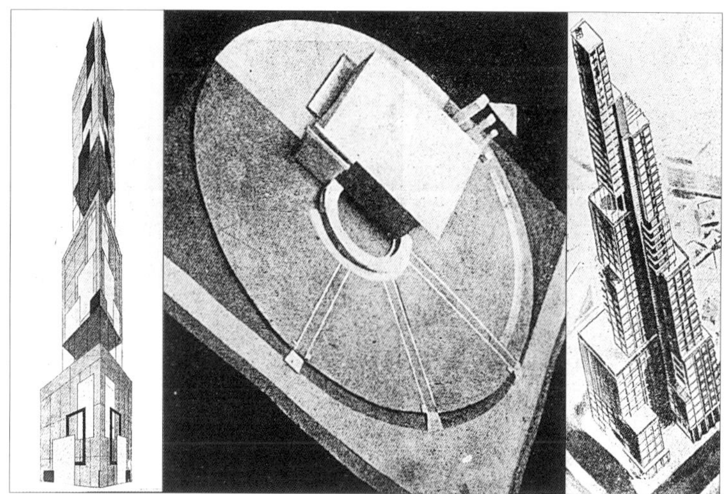

Centre: *Exercise in volumetric composition.* Left and right, *2nd year work under Ladovsky, 1924: Silchenko, 'Manifestation of dynamism'; Lopatin, 'Dynamic & rhythm in vertical: Vesenkha HQ'*

Vkhutemas: *Grushchenko, 2nd year 1922 under Ladovsky: 'productive' exercise 'volume and space in a soda-processing plant'. Gelfeld 4th year 1927 under Vesnin, 'building for Vkhutemas'.*

Academy of Arts.[27] For all that, when Leningrader Iakov Chernikhov was accused in 1930 of 'copying Ladovsky's method', it was reasonable for him to protest that he could not have done, because what Ladovsky taught was closely guarded and had not been published in any detail.[28] Historically our main source of information on this Asnova teaching work is Krinsky's book of 1934.[29]

Above this foundation level, in the architecture studios not run by Rationalists, quite different philosophies of architecture were being taught in Vkhutemas throughout the Twenties. These ranged from relics of historicism, through Shchusev's solid pragmatism, discussed in Chapter 4 and reflected in his paper to the Vkhutemas curriculum conference of 1926 reported in Document 27, to the Constructivist line of Alexander Vesnin's studio, underpinned by theory from Moisei Ginzburg. Documents to which we shall return below give a picture of the student experience this was creating by the mid-Twenties.

Architecture at MVTU

If the emerging group of Constructivist architects in 1923-4 did not feel so threatened as Golosov and Melnikov by the Rationalists' ever-expanding dominance of Vkhutemas, it was probably because their own main powerbase was elsewhere, in the Architecture Faculty of the Moscow Higher Technical College, MVTU. Less famous because less flashy, being technically rather than artistically based, this second Moscow school of architecture had serious claims to be the capital's leading professional school.

By the nature of its origins industrial buildings were its specialism, which made it a natural post-war resort for the Vesnin brothers, as Leonid and Viktor particularly had acquired extensive building experience in this field during the War years and after [p.40]. Indeed, when it came to getting official Mossoviet registration for their Constructivist architecture group OSA, in 1925-6, it was as 'specialists oriented towards industrial buildings' that their sponsors vouched for the group's legitimacy and desirability to the registration authorities.[30] This was the specialist field of the scholarly Alexander Kuznetsov (see Chapters 4 & 5), who had enormous experience all over late tsarist Russia in building major industrial complexes.[31] In 1913 he had sought to create a specialised architectural school for this field in Moscow, but war intervened. In 1918 he achieved this as founder-head of the Department of Factory and Industrial Building in MVTU, a historic and distinguished technical college tracing its origins back to the College for Artisans (*Remeslennoe uchilishche*) founded in 1830.[32]

More immediately, MVTU inherited an architecture faculty from the Polytechnic (*politekhnikum*) that was formed in Moscow as parallel school to IGI in Petrograd in early 1917, when it seemed the end of the War might be near. The Polytechnic had two faculties, Architecture and Constructional-Engineering, and soon after the Revolution itself became called an Institute of Civil Engineers. Through habit the name MIGI continued well after its amalgamation into MVTU in the early years after the Revolution. (Sources are vague.)[33]

The Polytechnic's Architecture Faculty had started in 1917 with four professors, of whom the housing specialist Nikolai Markovnikov and the ubiquitous Shchusev were historically the best known. By 1918, the staff included Boris Korshunov and Edgar Norvert, whom we encounter later on the pages of the Constructivists' journal *SA*, as well as Leonid Vesnin. In the amalgamation with MVTU this team was complementary to Kuznetsov's. His department was the former Constructional-Engineering one, and in 1922 acquired virtually independent status as an Institute in its own right.[34] By that time Vladimir Semionov, architect turned leading planner (see Chapter 11) was on the MVTU architecture staff, joined shortly by Ivan Rylsky, and Panteleimon Golosov, the elder brother of Ilia. Re-establishing himself in Moscow a year after his return from the Crimea, Moisei Ginzburg had applied for a job at Vkhutemas in 1922 and been turned down, in the retrenchment of staff due to curriculum reorganisation.[35] This served only to strengthen the team at MVTU. Khan-Magomedov has published a photograph of him with Leonid Vesnin and their MIGI-MVTU students soon after this.[36]

The architecture curriculum at MVTU was more conventional than that at Vkhutemas, but in its preservation of nineteenth-century polytechnical traditions, such as Kuznetsov, for one, had acquired as a student in Berlin in the 1890s, or as LIGI continued in Leningrad, it was a far more liberating education for the practical architect than Vkhutemas. Many MVTU staff were themselves trained in the Institute of Civil Engineers in Petersburg (then PIGI), rather than in the art-school traditions of the Academy or MUZhVZ. In the Twenties in Moscow there were always some serious students (Vegman and Vladimirov amongst them in Constructivist circles) who studied at both Vkhutemas and MVTU simultaneously.[37]

Alongside its industrial specialism, architecture at MVTU had two thematic disciplines, architecture proper, for civil buildings and housing, and town planning. Its first year course devoted heavy attention to a grounding in representation, both technical drawing and freehand sketching, which continued as formal subjects through to the third year. In the second year students began their main discipline. In architecture this meant 'design of buildings through all stages of their development, from the simplest tasks to complex projects in the higher years and the diploma.'[38] Thus in the second year they did housing and smaller, mainly rural buildings. In their third they did larger scale housing as well as 'public buildings for urban use, such as schools, medical facilities, railway stations, local government buildings.' By the fourth year they were dealing with 'whole complexes of multi-storeyed buildings posing complicated problems within a larger planning solution', and these might be whole institutions of higher education, club and leisure complexes, cooperative developments of a new residential district and its facilities. The final diploma was then 'a brief taken from that year's all-union [i.e. national] competitions or other concrete projects under way, which have included the Palace of Labour, the Moscow House of Textiles, the Central Telegraph, the *gubernia*-scale [i.e. regional] hospital competition, and so on.'[39] The fourth year planners would be doing urban servicing systems, local government economics, city structure, and design work for sections of cities or whole villages. 'In the 1926 diploma year, they did schemes for Riazan, Evpatoria, Matsesta, Penza and for workers' settlements in the Tula area.'

The faculty saw itself as producing a 'thoroughly modern type of architect' who has combined 'properly developed compositional works with a profound theoretical training'. Before the Revolution Kuznetsov had preached the view that an architect is 'an artist with a technical education' (see Chapters 4 and 5). This balanced synthesis was precisely the philosophy followed by MVTU now. As the School officially stated it in 1927:

> *'In contrast to the curricula of architectural education in the former schools or to others today, the Architecture Department of MVTU does not give over-riding preference to either artistic, or mathematical and technical orientations. ... Eclectic education in an "aestheticising" conception of architecture has been replaced here by a profound training in composition of architectural masses that continues over several years, in the sound solution of planning aspects of the building, and in rational and serious study of real-life themes.'*[40]

As the staff of the Architecture section themselves declared, 'the quality of our graduates is best of all testified by their performance in all-union architectural competitions.' In the three years 1924-7, 'fifteen national competitions were won by architects from our department. Members of staff took thirty prizes overall, and our students achieved some eighty prize places'. This reflects the vast numbers of architectural competitions conducted in the USSR during these years, of which only a few have become famous in the general literature through particularly seminal schemes by avant-garde leaders.[41] But more locally it reflected 'the priority which this school gives to practical experience on the major building sites of Moscow, and to its links with the real organisations of the country such as administrative agencies, the Commissariat of Internal Affairs (NKVD) and government bodies'.[42]

As far as the international Modern Movement is concerned, it was of course a work of MVTU staff and graduates that represented Soviet Architecture in the canon-defining Museum of Modern Art show of The International Style in 1932, where one photograph of the VEI Electrotechnical Institute complex was the only Soviet work included. The elegance of this extensive area of Modern Movement buildings, now sadly destroyed except for one small block, would have been enough on its own to indicate the success of the MVTU vision of 'the artist with a technical education', as produced by a combination of pre-Revolutionary disciplines and Constructivist theory [p.70]. Another canonical work of Soviet Modernism, the Communal House of Textile Apprentices [pp.58-9] is equal testament to the aesthetic power MVTU was capable of fostering. Alexander Vesnin's studio in Vkhutemas produced some of the dazzling stars of the younger-generation avant-garde, but the theoretical approach recorded in Ginzburg's articles on their 'functional method' was the basis of Constructivists' teaching in both schools. If never as formal as it appears on paper, comments from their students and published curricula indicate that.[43] Ginzburg taught his courses in 'theory of architecture' in both schools: the published paper on 'Constructivism as a method of laboratory and teaching work' states precisely that (see Chapter 5),[44] and there is no reason to imagine it was not true of his earlier courses like that of 1923,[45] or its updated form of 1926, outlined in Document 26, which owes much to his first book of 1923 on *Rhythm in Architecture*.

The Architecture Faculty in LIGI

The nearest Leningrad equivalent of MVTU was the institution on which it was partly modelled, and whence many of its staff had graduated: the architecture faculty of the Institute of Civil Engineers (IGI).

The academic tradition here went back through such technical pioneers as Ieronim Kitner, doyen of the Petersburg profession around 1910 who worked with Baltard in Paris on early iron structures, to Apollinari Krasovsky, first theorist of technical Rationalism in Russian architecture whose work of 1851 is discussed in Chapter 1. In the immediate post-Revolutionary years it was not untypical of such technical institutes in losing a sense of direction, and losing students. Thus the student body of PIGI (as it was till Petrograd became Leningrad in 1924) fell from 900 in 1914 to only 140 in January 1920.[46] With more positive prospects for engineering and construction work, students then started returning until by the start of academic year 1921-2 they were over 500, and now many of them of worker origins and having war service behind them.

Amongst architects the elderly Kitner emigrated to Germany in 1918, but in the next generation of teachers most continued. These were highly capable professionals like German Grimm, Adam Ditrikh, Alexander Dmitriev [p.72] and Vladimir Pokrovsky who had many buildings scattered round the city, but they were not charismatic or innovative figures. Leonti Benois did some teaching here again, as he had in the 1890s, and the teaching of aesthetic and technical disciplines continued much as before.[47] The innovator who brought Modernism into IGI studios was one of its own former students, Alexander Nikolsky, who had graduated in 1912 and had extensive building experience as well as the rare benefit, for Russians, of travel abroad. In 1920 Nikolsky came onto the IGI architecture school staff full-time as lecturer in 'architectural composition and measured drawings'.

One of the prompts towards reform was an exhibition mounted (perhaps by him) in LIGI in autumn 1923, showing MIGI-MVTU projects alongside their own student work.[48] Beside the Moscow schemes, their's were manifestly 'plans and facades reworked from the best of the pre-Revolutionary classics' whereas 'the Migi-ites were ignoring the old gods. Their projects were somewhat sketchy, but they were searching for new forms, new compositional concepts, new spatial solutions to their briefs'. They were 'not decorating form, but in everything were obviously going somewhere, on a live path'. The result was 'a storm of protest in LIGI', and soon after it, 'there appeared the first "style-less" scheme in the school – a cinema – a simple box without articulation', that represented the first signal for 'a renewal ... for ever greater use of reinforced concrete, and exploration of the constructive possibilities of new materials.'[49]

In leading the reform of the curriculum towards 'encouraging students' own invention' Nikolsky was far from rejecting 'what can be learned about articulation, about relations of parts and modules, from Vignola and others'.[50] 'Architecture operates by elements that are common to all periods, styles and epochs' he wrote in 1925, 'surface, volume, construction, space, concepts of rhythm and so on. These elements in their diversity of combinations have given, now give and will give us in future works of architecture.'[51] With another well known younger member of the pre-Revolutionary profession, Andrei Ol, he devised the programme for a new foundation discipline in the Institute, called 'Introduction to Architecture'.[52] As a sequence of exercises in abstract composition removed from materials, function, construction, what Nikolsky called the '*arkh-skhema*', it was not unlike Ladovsky's approach but without the metaphysical overtones. Here too they developed those abstract themes into real design exercises with specific briefs and structural systems, but with the aim of 'training the eye, the organ without which you cannot become an architect, to its most disciplined and sophisticated'. As their published work showed, among it that later sent to OSA's Exhibition of Modern Architecture in Moscow in 1927 [pp.57-8], Nikolsky's teaching method stressed the development of projects through models, 'which have every advantage over the drawing both for expressing your thoughts and for emergence of new ideas as you work on the task'.[53]

For those students seriously interested in pursuing modernist languages of architecture, the northern city of Petrograd-Leningrad offered a somewhat different environment of artistic experiment from that surrounding Vkhutemas down in Moscow. It was more pluralist, more tolerant of diversity than the new capital, where the internal politics of Inkhuk or *LEF* created orthodoxies and jealousies immediately. Petrograd had its own Inkhuk, known initially as the Museum of Artistic Culture and then as the 'State' Institute, Ginkhuk,

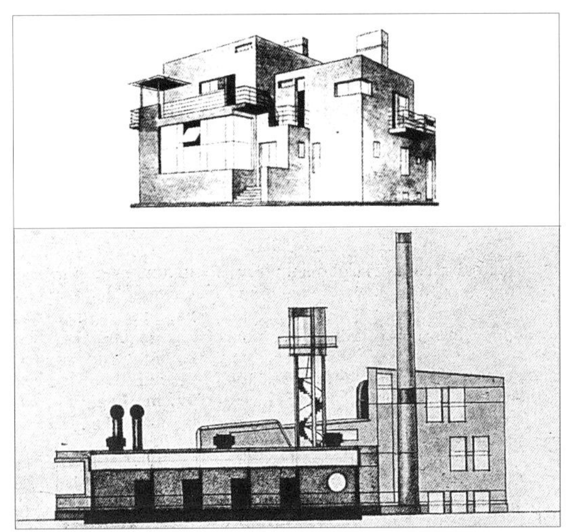

MVTU: Chernov, 'House for an architect', 1927. G. Movchan, diploma project 1926: Mechanised bread factory for northeast Moscow.

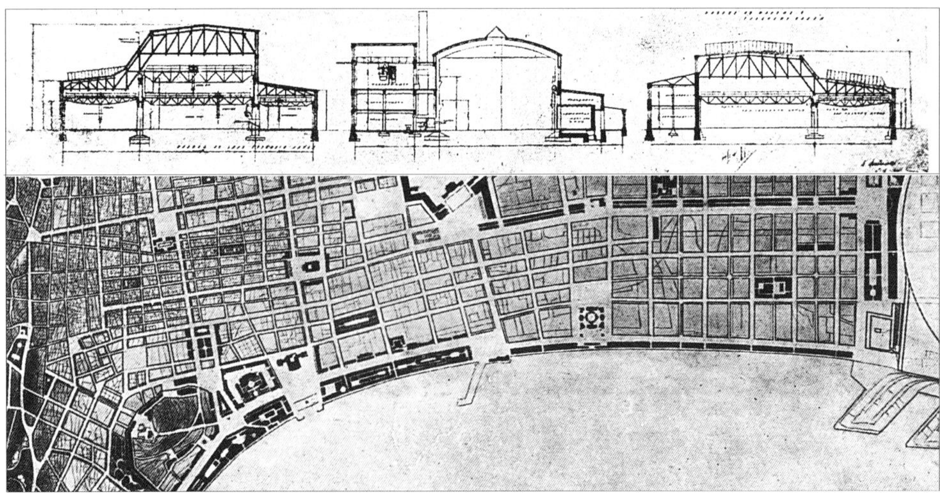

Anatoli Fisenko, diploma project 1925: an iron foundry, cross-sections.
Tatiana Chizhikova, diploma project 1927, replanning of seafront area of Baku.

where artists likewise lectured on their work and debated their theoretical ideas. For the progressives in IGI the most significant difference from Moscow was the presence in these circles of Malevich, who moved there from Vitebsk with several of his pupils in 1922 (see Chapter 9).

Their interest in pursuing Suprematism into architecture had started in Vitebsk, and is recorded for example in their *UNOVIS Almanac No.2*, translated in Document 15. Once the group got to Petrograd, Ilia Chashnik who wrote there on architecture shifted his interest to ceramics, and it was Lazar Khidekel who enrolled under Nikolsky at IGI in order to get a proper architectural training. Where Moscow Modernism's two main formal strands grew out of the construction-composition split in Inkhuk, which in personal terms one might characterise as the split between Ladovsky and Rodchenko, Petrograd-Leningrad Modernism thus acquired quite another formal strand from the volumetric experiments and *arkhitektony* of Suprematism, a strand virtually excluded amongst other polemics in Moscow. Khidekel's own work shows this directly, and as a student in the school his influence was extensive, not least in broadening the experience of fellow students by attracting them into the extra-curricular debates at Ginkhuk.

In 1923, continuing a habit of the pre-Revolutionary profession, Nikolsky expanded his students' experience and the life of the school still further, by forming a small 'office' of his pupils and other young architects. Khidekel was subsequently a member of it. The first ones were Ivan Beldovsky, Vladimir Galperin, and the brothers Alexander and Mikhail Krestin. For these students, who graduated respectively in 1924, 1925, 1925 and 1929, the regular gatherings on Thursdays at Nikolsky's flat offered the same sort of intensive professional maturing process that Moscow Constructivists got, as described below by one of them, from gatherings at the Vesnins' flat. They worked together on projects, often for competitions. Nikolsky described his intention:

> *'on the basis of participation by everyone present in contributing to the thought and work of each of the others, to dispel the anonymity and isolation of them as workers, which is so different from the old system of mutual reinforcement and consolidation that we took for granted amongst architects in the former times.'* [54]

Later this group work extended into an office for architecture and building technology formed within the school itself on Nikolsky's initiative. One of the main research topics here was daylighting, particularly of school buildings [p.55] which were amongst the main new 'types' being built around Leningrad in new workers housing districts at that time.[55]

The teaching developed in LIGI owed a great deal to the ideas and procedures of Moscow Constructivism. From 1926-28 Nikolsky was an active member of the group, head of OSA-Leningrad, but always saw and taught their 'method' as one of several approaches to design. Like the best Modernists to emerge later from the Academy School, he saw merit also in Asnova's approach. The young Academy quartet, Armen Barutchev, Isidor Gilter, Iosif Meerzon and Iakov Rubanchik [pp.34-7], were actually members of Asnova and later of Ladovsky's 'urbanism' group ARU. Nikolsky did not go that far, but Alexander Vesnin accused him in a letter of getting too close:

> *'For us [i.e. OSA] what is important is the rational solution of the functions and the constructive side. To us, new form must be what emerges when the functions have been solved in a new way and new construction systems have been applied. Your work is done much more formally than functionally, and is closer to Asnova than to OSA.'* [56]

In building up a design Nikolsky taught students to start by 'eschewing all detail', concentrating on critical scrutiny of any relevant existing building type as well as the brief itself, to identify its 'points of weakness' (*slabye mesta*). From this would come the 'main idea' out of which a spatial composition could be built that could be 'carried through to architectural finality'.[57] He admitted to Vesnin that in his teaching, the 'functional method' was valuable just as 'a means to give a more organically constructive logic' to a building.[58]

In a report sent to *SA* in late 1926, LIGI member V. Malinovsky, who sounds like a young lecturer, described the limitations of what most students could actually absorb from this training:

> *'Speaking of the architectural trends amongst the students of LIGI, it has to be recognised that the vast majority cannot even enter the orbit of serious design work as a result of their lack of preparation for such training, and the academic overload. We really need to spend far more time giving them that basic training which is necessary for a student to be independent. We need to stimulate greater activity by the student society (*kruzhok*) and get the really keen ones gathered around us. Putting the best of today's projects alongside old ones you*

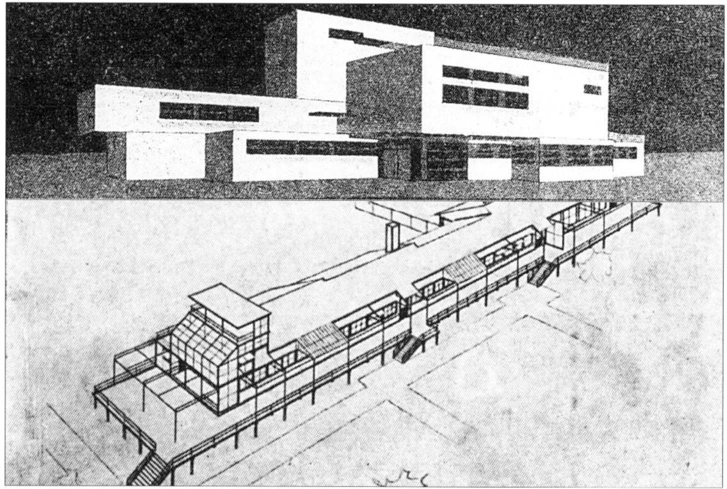

***LIGI:** Lazar Khidekel, second year studio, 1926: a workers' club. Konstantin Ivanov, second year studio, 1926, a sanatorium.*

LIGI project work in the Architecture Schools room of OSA's First Exhibition of Modern Architecture in the Vkhutemas building, Moscow, June 1927.

can see what a great leap forward the Institute has made. But we need a really active body of students, really serious teaching on the engineering side, strict preparation of students for design work, plus a genuine cultivation of the new movement in architecture, and there would undoubtedly be no small benefit to the process of creating the new style, whose logical movement forward is irrepressible.'[59]

Whether or not this diagnosis is right, the student societies in the two Moscow schools were certainly very active in broadening and supporting academic work. Reports on their activities during early 1926 are reproduced from *SA* in Documents 24 and 25, as voices from the students themselves.

Pressure to be 'relevant'

At just this time, in November 1926, academic conferences in all faculties of the Moscow Vkhutemas indicate rather different battles under way. Internally the struggles were less with student unpreparedness or lack of energy than between the staff's ideologies and against lack of material resources. Externally, there was increasing pressure to be 'relevant'. The government was currently campaigning for a 'regime of economy' in all aspects of life: greater efficiency but also elimination of activities that did not directly contribute to social and economic reconstruction. In June, just as the new Rector, Novitsky, took over at Vkhutmas, the Party Central Committee issued the first of several demands for more participation by genuinely 'working class' elements in all branches of education and training. The staff and student body had sent '150 letters of invitation' to industrial and economic organisations, trade unions, official establishments in Moscow, to get their judgement on the school's products and usefulness to the outside world.[60]

The first real threat to the exploratory, art-based nature of the Vkhutemas architecture faculty had come back in Spring 1924. The Narkompros department for Professional and Technical Training, Glavprofobr, under whose aegis the school operated, had proposed that Vkhutemas architecture should be amalgamated with the faculty at MVTU. There was a general problem in higher education of too many one-specialism schools, and widespread amalgamations were under way nationwide.

Seventeen of the Vkhutemas professors wrote a letter of protest to Lunacharsky, as head of Narkompros to insist that architecture was absolutely essential to the school. 'As the most socially oriented of all the arts, its departure would leave the departments of painting etc without direction.' At the same time, MVTU 'has architects and structural engineers from Vkhutemas on its staff, precisely because MVTU cannot take the aesthetic side of architecture to the levels that Vkhutemas can'.[61] The proposal lapsed, and in April 1925 Lunacharsky personally endorsed precisely this view of architecture as 'organically necessary' to the school', although 'externally', that is in material conditions, it was 'in a bad state and needed to be restored'.[62]

The architecture faculty was reprieved, but in 1926 the whole school reduced the 'artistic' content of the Basic Course. Its second year became part of the specialist teaching, and with the start of the new academic year that autumn, upper levels of architecture ceased to be structured as studios under individual professors. The same people taught, but in three specialised studios of Housing (chaired by Ladovsky), Community Buildings and Industrial Architecture (chaired by Shchusev), and Spatial Architecture and Planning (chaired by Ilia Golosov). The other professors, Rylsky, Dokuchaev, Kokorin, Alexander and Leonid Vesnin moved between them.[63]

More changes followed in 1927, but this basically refashioned the school in a less individualistic, more task-oriented mode.

At the conference in November 1926, invited representatives of the government and client bodies spent two days hearing papers and seeing around the architecture faculty. The report published in *SA* covered both the faculties where Constructivists had strong representation, Architecture, and the Wood-and-Metal Working Faculty to which Rodchenko had brought such official approval by the international success of its furniture in Paris the previous year. These two reports are translated as Document 27.

Kornfeld's report on the architecture conference loses no chance to point out that OSA's teaching is relevant and useful whereas Asnova's produces in students 'a new metaphysical understanding of space quite removed from real life'.[64] The battle lines seem as jealous here as when the school started half a decade earlier. Amongst the detailed itemisation of all Resolutions which appeared in the *Building Industry* journal, however, a more intelligent agreement about their complementarity is indicated over the key question of who should give a new course on 'Theory of architectural composition'.

On a motion proposed by Dokuchaev it was agreed that:

'The novelty of such a course, which is not given anywhere else up till now, forces us to recognise the correctness of running two parallel lecture series on this theme during the current year, according to the two outlines proposed by professors Ginzburg and Dokuchaev, having in view that both programmes, different as they are, have very significant interest.'[65]

Dokuchaev's course followed a predictable Asnova line about 'combining forms' and their 'clear perception of buildings by their users'.[66] Ginzburg's course outline is translated here as Document 26 because it shows the firm historical basis of Constructivist teaching continuing as they develop their preoccupations with 'functional method'. In fact it shows Ginzburg using his first book, *Rhythm in Architecture*, to continuing effect: large sections of this course plainly assume this as the students' textbook. As a whole it also shows both the extent of a continuity between Asnova and OSA teaching in this field, and the contrast between them, one abstracted, and Ginzburg's solidly rooted in historical examples.

Returning to Kornfeld's account of the faculty conferences, we see Shchusev's line ridiculed by simply reporting it, and both faculties imputing incompetence and inappropriate interference to Glavprofobr. In *SA* it is only the design people, however, who really assert themselves over the inadequacy of their accommodation, basic equipment and materials for the socially important tasks they are tackling. In the full list of Resolutions in *The Building Industry*, by contrast, this is a constant theme. The architecture faculty is recognised as needing 'financial reinforcement', probably from those economic organisations 'having an interest in construction'. It needs 'material resources and equipment'. From construction organisations it needs 'all sorts of technical drawings, models, statistical data, literature on standards, albums of projects, architectural and technical literature and information on new constructional systems', and there should be a special reference room where this library of technical material can be consulted.[67]

From this we have a picture of the school's reality that corresponds to repeated comments of individuals in this school and most others in Russia in the Twenties. So acute was the lack of any publishing on architecture, even, that when building activity started reviving back in 1924 it had been suggested the numerous entries for increasing numbers of architectural competitions should be distributed around the schools as a means of disseminating knowledge simply of good architecture, quite apart from 'new' architecture. The same *Building Industry* journal had declared:

> *'When architectural circles in the capitals [i.e. Moscow and Leningrad] are discussing contemporary trends in architectural composition with ever greater breadth and subtlety, students across the country who are also future builders have little available to them but albums of railway structures or total trash in their libraries. Meanwhile MAO's recent competitions have produced dozens of talented and well-worked-out schemes for various new types of building ... which we are too poor to publish. Mounted on pin-up walls in the schools, as the basis for group discussions and seminars, ... they would cease to be "wasted work" in their designers' portfolios.'*[68]

There is no record of action, but the proposal is indicative of the isolation from ideas that poverty imposed on most of the country, and which their own accounts constantly confirm.

Modernism in the regional schools

For all this disorder, Moscow and particularly Vkhutemas were inevitably looked to as the fount and inspiration of their own battles by those variously called 'the young' and 'the left' who fought even larger inertia in the regional schools of Russia and the non-Russian republics. They not only lacked communication with the centre, but local lack of communications and resources made it difficult to have any impact on local opinion, local clients or the conservative professional establishments around them.

We have two vignettes of the situation in regional schools, mainly in other Soviet republics, through two events organised by OSA.

In summer 1927 their 'First Exhibition of Modern Architecture' opened in the Vkhutemas building on Rozhdestvenka Street which they inherited from the Stroganov School, where the Architecture Faculty was now centred. This included invited projects from several groups of Modernists and individuals in Europe – from Bauhaus, Poland, Switzerland, Holland, France, Belgium, Czechoslovakia, as well as materials from Constructivist sympathisers across the Soviet Union. Asnova were invited to contribute but characteriscally declined and were represented only through student work in the Vkhutemas section.[69] Several schools had submitted for a special 'schools room'. It was dominated by LIGI, MVTU and Asnova's work from Vkhutemas, but other modest schemes came from such distant schools as Kiev and Tomsk. Students of the Constructivist members showed in the OSA room alongside their teachers: thus Leonidov's diploma project for the Lenin Bibliographical Institute, for example, was a focal point of their room with his model dramatically lit by the window.

If the provincial student work in the show itself was modest, the impact of the show on schools was significant. Amongst the reported 5,000 visitors from thirty towns across the country were 'about forty special excursions organised from institutes of higher education in Tomsk, Kiev, Odessa, Baku and Saratov' as well as Moscow and Leningrad.[70] With so little possibility of publication at that time, such study tours were a normal means of communication.

The Asnova students represented were names that have later become well known: Lamtsov and Turkus who became Krinsky's teaching assistants; Krutikov, known for his 'Flying City' diploma scheme but now Ladovsky's assistant in his Psycho-technical Lab; Travin who was soon doing some interesting Moscow housing; Volodko whose early abstract work was published and became well known.

Other walls of the same room showed student work from two other centres of Constructivist activity, MVTU and LIGI. The MVTU students were also soon to make a professional mark with real building in such developments as the Electrotechnical Institute, where Nikolaev, Fisenko and Movchan were already working under their professor Kuznetsov. Others showed almost exclusively industrial projects, done under Viktor Vesnin.

As might be expected from the state and approach of the school, work

Academy of Arts, Leningrad: *Igor Fomin, son of Ivan [pp.80-82], 3rd year project, 1926, for a House of Scientific and Technical Congresses: the Academy in its traditional mode.*

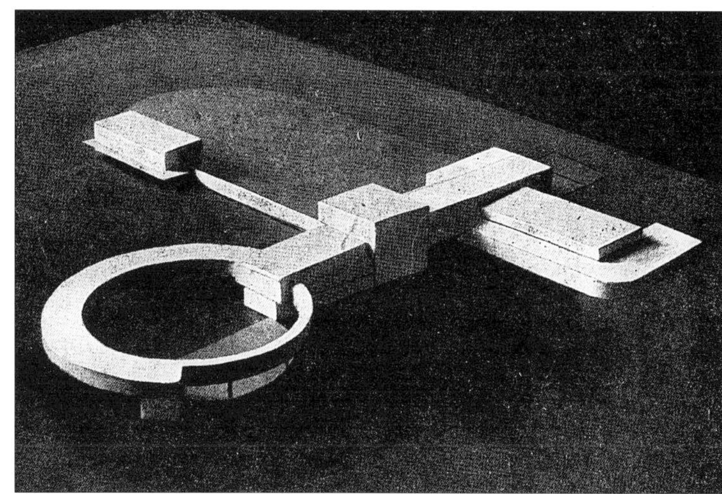

Olga Ivanova, 3rd year project, 1929-30, for a workers' club complex with 500-seat auditorium block model, exemplifying the partial penetration of Modernism into the Academy studios.

by LIGI students under Nikolsky was of more mixed genre. Mainstream Modernism came from the Krestin brothers, who became regular members of Nikolsky's office. But the range extended from the Suprematism of Khidekel's workers' club to the more classical formalism of a covered market area by a student called Lavrinovich.

From Kiev Art Institute were a few works by students of A. F. Aleshin who were the core of Ukrainian OSA – cinema, a scheme for the Moscow House of Textiles competition, a Museum of the Revolution from the highly talented Ignati Milinis, who was soon to become Ginzburg's assistant, notably on the Narkomfin housing complex (see Chapters 5 and 7). Odessa Polytechnic of Fine Arts sent some schemes, as did the Siberian Technical Institue in Tomsk, both of which soon had embryonic OSA groups.

Several of these schools also sent reports on their courses and circumstances, which were published in *SA* and reinforce the picture of under-resourcing, lack of information on the new architecture, and hostile 'stylistic' environments.

The Odessa Building Polytechnic (*Stroitel'nyi tekhnikum*) described in detail a rich curriculum of technical subjects in its three-year courses 'with a tenth trimester for the diploma project'.[71] But very little actual design took place till 'three obligatory projects in third year'. And worse than that: 'shortage of resources' meant that 'there was only one senior teacher of architectural design. Which means that apart from the impossibility of one person doing so much, there is an even more important result: so much influence from one teacher, passing on his habits and tastes to the majority of students.' Their response had been self help, through active use of their student society to organising discussions of their own.

The architecture students in Kiev Art Institute reported that their student society had run out of steam through lack of ideological direction. But the school as a whole was 'decisively fighting against all attempts at a rebirth of the dead styles' and trying to develop a new architecture through 'rigorous analysis and study'.[72]

The enthusiasts in the Siberian Technological Institute of Tomsk reported 'a strong desire to work on the level of the latest architectural trends, though only isolated works bear any relation to Moscow Constructivism as represented by OSA.' This was 'explained by the fact that teaching staff follow a different train of thought from the students, and by the absence of relevant literature.' They set up discussion groups, but the turning point had been 'during the winter holidays.'

'Through support of the Institute's administration, the architecture section organised a study visit to Moscow and Leningrad, for detailed familiarisation with the architectural life of these two centres. After the visit, there was a markedly greater similarity of work to that going on in Moscow, although there remained many convinced opponents of the flat roof, the large areas of glass and so on, for our Siberian conditions. This is a question we should like to see discussed in the national press too. Meanwhile we are trying to strengthen our contacts with Vkhutemas, as that is very important for us.'[73]

Tomsk seemed to be winning the battles, but the situation reported from Kharkov's three architecture schools, particularly the Artistic Polytechnic, reflected all the familiar problems simultanously:

'Our problem is that Narkompros decided to "Ukrainianise" the polytechnic and therefore designing has to be done in Ukrainian style, which comes in two versions: Ukrainian Baroque and Ukrainian Art Nouveau.

'Some students have submitted to this pressure but others, despite the hostility of one group of professors, came over to Constructivism. The position of this part of the student body is very difficult: they have no materials whatever for learning about this kind of design, since the school's library only has old materials, other libraries have nothing, and it is useless to seek help from the school Council since they are old-style people of another persuasion.'

On top of that, staff had been reduced now 'to two architects running the whole faculty', and 'had not the students run things for themselves the situation would have been deplorable. But things cannot continue like this for long. Narkompros must give some attention to this, raise the level of teaching to a reasonable level and give the school a decent teaching staff.'[74] Compared with all this, Moscow and Leningrad were certainly in luxury.

Fighting classicism and baroque

At OSA's First Conference nine months later, in late April 1928, further informal reports from these and other centres give a unique picture of the battle that modernism was fighting out in the provinces, in particular inside the schools.[75]

Leningrad was the senior provincial group, with Nikolsky as their leader, but their report gives a refreshingly direct picture of what Modernism meant for them in reality, as well as their outsiders' view of the situation in the Academy.

'The Leningrad OSA was formed in our IGI, three years ago, and then comprised 3-5 people. It followed our visit to Moscow when we saw work on Gostorg building and realised this was the right way. In general our students now follow the OSA line, but not necessarily 100 per cent.

'Now as to our teachers. We had a professor with a European name: Benois. Certainly such a professor was valuable, but he was old. [Leonti Benois had died two months previously in February 1928. CC] The person we follow is Nikolsky. There are also 2-3 research people. With us in LIGI students and staff have close connections, and as a result staff have a strong influence on the students' methods of designing. But we feel our courses are not as good as those for the engineers, and we are currently looking at all teaching of design right from first year through the whole school to the final year. We had a debate about approaches and methods of design and the students got so involved it had to continue into a second session.

'In relation to other schools, we have to say we don't have much contact. But we are thinking of linking with the Academy of Arts and with the [engineering people at the] Polytechnical Institute. Before coming to the conference I sent the Academy some materials. Students seemed attracted by it and we reckon we may establish a group amongst the young who come from working backgrounds there. We are also working on the people [mainly in Construction courses, CC] in the Technological Institute. Under Nikolsky we are trying to develop some scientific underpinning for contemporary architecture. We have created a scientific research group in which active and talented students are working.

'It should be possible to do a lot in the Academy of Arts school as there are several young teachers there, but it is a "sad situation". They had a discussion after ours, on similar themes, and to try to do something we have formed a "Union of proletarian students on architectural questions" to tie the schools together. Now concerning the professors there. When we had our conference, they thought they could stand aside and regard it as amusing. For one there is Fomin with his so called "proletarian classicism or any other kind of classicism". In architect Trotsky, on the other hand, we found a person who, if not entirely independent minded, then at least has some leftward leanings. There is also Serafimov, who oscillates for and against our side. But the young there more or less follow Rudnev. We have to keep up the ideological work in their direction.' [76]

At least Moscow and Leningrad had robust Modernist elements in the art scene, if they were not as strong as they would like in architecture. In the provinces, the only city with a comparable artistic background seems from these reports to have been the ancient Russian and Tartar city of Kazan.

Here, as they reported to OSA's conference, things had started well due to the presence of a strong branch of LEF in Kazan in 1923-4. The head of Architecture at the Kazan Artistic and Technical Institute, Professor Gavrilov, had been one of its leaders, so early Constructivism in architecture had 'great support' in that school. But he had died in 1926. They were now helped by 'the very high level of the technical people at the Kazan Polytechnic (*tekhnikum*), who see the point of what we are doing'. They had formed 'OSA-Kazan' in September 1927 under the name of OMA, the Society of Young Architects, but like all the other provincial groups, this was a very small gang, comprising just 'four architects, three newly graduated engineers, and three students, one from the Tekhnikum and two architecture students from their own school'. For all this their representative gave a long detailed account of research and design projects they had completed, which left other delegates apologising that 'they had not brought formal papers like that from Kazan'.[77]

The Ukrainian groups from Kharkov, Kiev and Odessa used the Moscow conference as the occasion to form themselves into a 'Ukrainian Society of Modern Architects' to pursue 'methods of constructivism in research and practice'. Their reports indicate they still needed all the solidarity they could muster. Odessa's representative reported that 'we have people in the Odessa Society of Architects who are still building in the baroque style, or with German tiled roofs'. He reported his own first success with constructing a 'thoroughly designed and insulated' flat roof, only to get a letter from an old engineer who warned him as a 'young boy' of his technical errors. The OSA group in Odessa was the only Modernist group there, and 'is concentrated in the studios of our school of architecture'.

In Kiev too, the new architecture was a phenomenon of the younger generation, but had now built up enough power 'within the very conservative situation' to have 'frozen out' the elderly opposition somewhat. 'It is a generational thing' their man said. 'Even amongst the young there is a split between those to whom the new architecture is a formal thing, and those who are really tackling new tasks.' Interestingly he said quite explicitly something that is implicit elsewhere but not always stated: 'We follow OSA because we need to follow a firm line, not something unclear.' And they were giving 'maximum attention to propagating its ideas in the school and informally through the student society (*kruzhok*).' Kharkov said nothing about their school, but still – and surprisingly, for a city soon internationally famous for major Modernist projects of the next few years – it was 'a generally very conservative situation'.[78]

The extremes of north and south were also represented, from Baku as well as Tomsk, and both stressed the importance of *SA* as a focal point for their group, an information source, and a tool for propagating modern architecture more widely. In the rich old oil capital of Baku on the Black Sea, there were ripples amongst the young: 'With us all the older generation gets all the architectural work. But the students are not in agreement with this and have started to protest. What is published in *SA* helps to inform them, and they have grouped around the journal.' In Tomsk, up in the Siberian north, debate was clearly more lively.

'In Tomsk architectural life centres around the School. We still only have a few OSA members, and their influence is not very strong as we are so far from Moscow. But we are trying to modify the curriculum throughout the school to get it closer [to what we see in Moscow], and 80 per cent of it has now been reformed. On the school walls, we make a strong impact and teachers are starting to follow our line because "they don't want to get left behind". We use

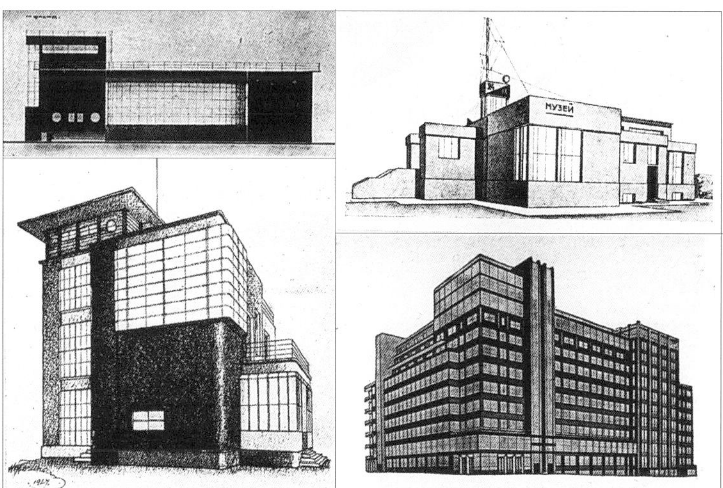

Regional schools: *Agaev (Tomsk), 1927, cinema; Savatov (Odessa), 1926, local museum.* Below: *Kiev Art Institute, 3rd year: Grechina, 1927, Art centre; Malozemov, 1926, House of Textiles.*

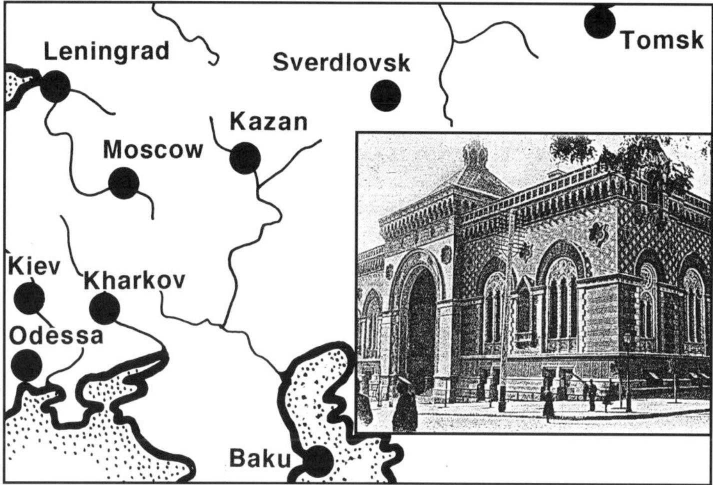

Locations of the architecture schools. Inset: *'Ukrainian Baroque' which the die-hards continued: Stock Exchange 1900 by doyen of pre-Revolutionary Odessa school, Prof. A.A. Bernardatsi.*

material from SA *as the basis for open lectures to students and staff which are highly influential.'* [79]

Again the Tomsk representative spoke of the attractiveness of Constructivism because it was explicit. As he concluded, 'We have looked at Asnova's ideas, but they do not have a dialectical method to follow, so after detailed discussion we decided to follow OSA.'

Sverdlovsk made no mention of their school, but like all other provincial centres mentioned their dependence on Moscow and Leningrad, particularly as the source of 'many specialists who come to build and bring their ideas'. But their OSA group had held twenty meetings with well attended lectures.

Moscow pluses and minuses

The Moscow to which these provinces looked for leadership had its own increasing troubles. As the front line of advance it was naturally the vulnerable first point of attack when the official attitudes became less tolerant to experimentation and long-term thought. At the same time, the experience it offered to students through its traditions of close contact with their world-class teachers was incomparably rich, and produced student work of historic originality and importance.

In mid-1928 the journal *Building* (*Postroika*) attacked the Vkhutein architecture faculty for producing 'pure artists' and 'fantasists' not 'good young specialists for building' and cited as 'proof' the fact that amongst sixty-two diploma projects lately defended in this VUZ [higher education establishment] there was one for a 'flying city'. This was Georgi Krutikov's now-famous scheme.[80] As Rector of the school, Novitsky replied with a sharply defensive 'letter to the editor' that was later republished in *SA*.

He diplomatically (and probably factually) admitted that:

'there is a lot I do not agree with in the teaching of the faculty, but the author does not understand that an artistic VUZ as opposed to a technical VUZ is precisely based on a certain "cutting off from real life" and life today demands the training of an architect of a new type, who is artist and engineer-builder simultaneously'.[81]

This was the basis of the 'specific ideological position' the school has always maintained.

As I have already hinted, there was a larger context to this, beyond mere issues of architectural 'ideology'. Soviet government bodies had initially not paid great attention to any form of technical education, either to its quantitative outputs or to its qualitative makeup in 'class' terms. Now, by the later Twenties, the expanding industrial and construction programmes were manifestly lagging behind government aspirations, and in official minds, objective shortages of trained people were being reinforced by 'lack of ideological commitment' in the cadres of professionals educated before the revolution. Inevitably, in architecture as elsewhere, these people were the ones with practical experience, but when scapegoats were sought, it was easy to blame late projects, technical failures, unfulfilled norms and the like on their political 'unreliability'. In June 1926 and again in April 1927 and February 1928 the Central Committee of the Party had urgent discussions and issued edicts on improving the political composition of student bodies by admitting more 'of worker and peasant origins'.[82] In his

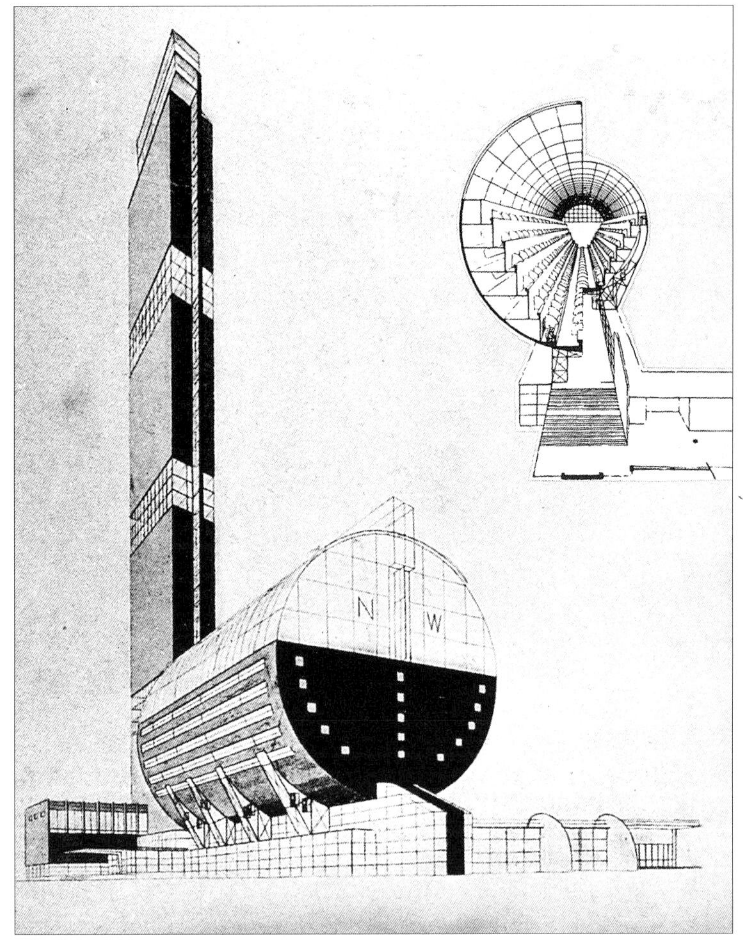

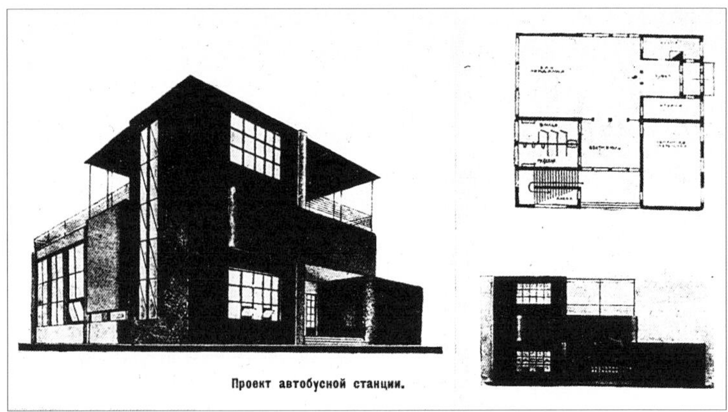

Vkhutemas studios. Top: *A. Vesnin's studio: Viktor Pashkov, diploma project for a Lenin Institute of Librarianship, 1927, perspective and inset, section of reading room inside the tank-like volume: a classmate of Ivan Leonidov's [pp.175, 202] tackling same brief.* Below: *Shchusev's studio for industrial and public buildings: D.D. Bulgakov, 4th year project, 1926, for a garage; by the same student, 3rd year project, 1925, passenger building and offices for a bus station.*

letter of mid-1928 Novitsky had offered some defence of Vkhutein in this respect, but the facts were not reassuring. His figures revealed that of 300 students in Architecture Faculty of Vkhutein only thirty were members of the Communist Party itself and 39 members of Communist Youth League, Komsomol. As to class origins, 56 had come in through the Rabfak, 69 were workers and children of workers, 63 were peasants and children of peasants, making 43 percent in total from the preferred 'worker and peasant classes'. Against this 125 were white-collar workers or their children, and of the 'labour intelligentsia' there were 45, and of the non-working element, seven people of whom three are Party members. This was better than the accusations claimed, however: 'The criticisms are saying there are no workers in the Vkhutein architecture faculty and all are NEP-men [the new-rich bourgeois of post-Revolutionary years, CC]. As Novitsky concluded, 'The social make-up is not as good as it should be, but it will not be corrected by lies.'[83]

In relation to the eternal complaints at Vkhutemas-Vkhutein and all other architecture schools, it is significant that the whole through-put of technical personnel in Soviet higher education, not just of architects, was more constrained by lack of facilities in the institutes than by any lack of candidates to enter the courses.[84] But increasingly there was pressure from technical departments of government and from industry itself, to remove this whole area of education from the hands of Narkompros. Being 'culturally' oriented, they were seen as worsening the situation by keeping the long, rich, theoretical courses which had characterised pre-Revolutionary professional education. As E. H. Carr has described it, the national conference on industrial and technical education held in September 1927 'seems to have been the first concerted attack from the side of industry on this easy-going tradition'.[85] Lunacharsky, still head of Narkompros, tried to blame the problem on industry's indecision as to what specialist manpower it needed.[86] In fact the relevant arm of Narkompros, Glavprofobr, had tried to follow such a demand-led model back in the early Twenties.[87] But like all other attempts at keeping ahead of requirements at this time, the lack of resources accompanied by the speed of change had overtaken it.

Much acrimony led to a decree in August 1928 that restructured higher technical education to produce more so-called 'red specialists' or 'specialists of the new type'. It shifted many institutes from the aegis of Narkompros to control by such economic bodies as Vesenkha.[88] In this process, during 1927 and 1928, Vkhutemas became an 'Institute', Vkhutein, rather than just *masterskye* or 'studios', and further tightened its curriculum. When Novitsky took over from the painter Favorsky as Rector in 1926, he had already seen this had to be the future, and in 1927 started discussions with Glavprofobr to that effect. But 1928 was the year of the change-of-name, of serious reduction in the role of the Basic Course, and likewise of increasing exposure to accusations of political unreliability when 'fantasy' projects occasionally caught the hawk-eyed attention of hard-liners.

At the opposite end of this situation was the personal experience of individuals and the quality of work being done.

Two memoirs published in the mid-1980s by veterans of this period, both Constructivist students in Vkhutemas-Vkhutein, reflect the same quality of

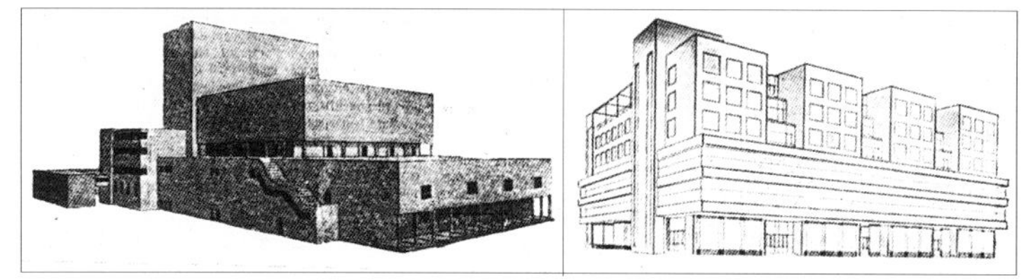

From top: *A. Vesnin's studio: M. Barshch & M. Sinavsky, joint diploma project, 1926, for covered market and offices development, Bolotnaia Sq., Moscow.* Andrei Burov *[pp.56-7] diploma project, 1925, Central railway terminus, Moscow.* V. Ershov*, course-work, 1927: sugar refinery.* Mikhail Mazmanian*, 4th year studio, 1927, theatre in Erevan and 3rd year studio, 1926, Commercial building.* Bottom: *Nikolai Dokuchaev's studio:* Trifon Varentsov*, diploma project, 1928, administrative district of a new city.*

staff-student relationship and the climate of debate thus created, which we saw being preserved in Leningrad by Nikolsky.

The first reminiscences come from Kirill Afanasev, who was born in 1909.[89] He graduated from Vkhutein in 1930 and must therefore have entered Vkhutemas about 1925.

'Study was not divided in the first two years, as we all took the Basic Course. After that we students chose our own professor, we chose the creative direction we wished to follow. These professional architecture courses were concentrated on Miasnitskaia, in the Bazhenov building [former MUZhVZ] opposite the Post Office [pp.9; 38]. It was literally necessary to run there, in order to successfully enrol in the design studio of one's favourite professor.

'Division of students amongst the professors was very symptomatic. Shchusev was primarily respected as a practising architect, so the majority of students aspired to study under him. He was popular because he stood aside from this heated discussion between Constructivists and Rationalists. His was the third force, and at this time it had great importance amongst architects of the older generation too, who already had experience and popular reputations.

'Next in popularity came Alexander Vesnin, Ilia Golosov and Sergei Chernishev. In the main, the architecture studios of Ladovsky and Dokuchaev in the upper years had a shortage of students.'[90]

How they came to their choice was often an accidental matter. As Afanasev continues:

'I recall one episode that changed my life. In the second year of the Basic Course I did some rather ordinary project. Alexander Vesnin came to the show, and was talking with Krinsky. I hid round the screen and heard Alexander Alexandrovich ask about my scheme: "Vladimir Fedorovich, what is the idea on which this project is based?" Krinsky answered, "The student has tried to manifest the rectangularity of the forms of the building." "But what takes place inside this building?" "Oh, this is a bus stop, and here are the public phone boxes." "How very interesting! You don't think that it would be good to show those telephones, as from the project you would never know that?"

'This accidentally overheard conversation had a great impression on me and on my biography. I literally ran to Miasnitskaia to enrol in Vesnin's studio. From that moment I became a fully and passionately convinced Constructivist.'[91]

We see some of the nuances which emerged once the 'functional method' hit the studio:

'Amongst the OSA people there were two slightly different trends, those who emphasised more the "functions" side in form making and those more stressing the "construction" side. Alexander Vesnin was on the functional side. I went for the side where construction dominated, along with Burov and Leonidov.

'Burov used to express it very clearly and graphically: "Gloves which you wear on your hand – this is Functionalism, but the telephone, where the constructive box determines the form of the apparatus by its construction – this is Constructivism." In their approach, the execution of building works had a greater form-making importance, and function less.'

The role of theoretical approaches and the traditionalists scepticism of them come comes over clearly:

'I must stress that this Formalism and Constructivism were just means of finding form, but not themselves architecture. For that one is talking of genuine mastery – of art. The professional mastery of the younger teachers, and hence of the many students, was often not at a high level.

'All this attracted sarcasm from Shchusev. He used to say: "You cherchery*" – meaning seekers, from* chercher*, in French, or "You Robinsons [presumably from Robinson Crusoe, CC], you begin from taming the nanny-goat. But where is tradition, where is mastery, where is culture?" It was true that in those times we did not hear anything much about our Russian traditions or of the classics, nor did we students discuss them.'*

Most remarkable however, as I have commented, was the direct contact between the best students and the teachers.

'Very often a student would go and work alongside a professor at home, helping to execute his commissions or competition work. This domashinstvo *as it was called [*domashnyi *means 'domestic' from* dom*, 'home', CC] was almost obligatory and extremely advantageous.*

'On Alexander Vesnin's recommendation, I spent three years as such a domestic student with Ginzburg and took part in the building of the house on Novinsky Boulevard [ie Narkomfin, p.135], in design of the Green Town [Disurbanist project, see Chapter 11] and many other things.

'In this way the students saw the teachers' successes, and believed in them.

'In the end the main quality, the main contribution, of the architecture school of Vkhutemas was this highly creative environment which was fostered in the upper courses by both the teachers and the students.'[92]

The second reminiscences come from Lidiia Komarova, a little older than Afanasev.

'I studied under Alexander Vesnin first, from 1922, in his studio with [the painter and designer] Professor Liubov Popova on the Basic Course, and then

Lidiia Komarova as a student in Alexander Vesnin's studio, 1922 [see also p.98].

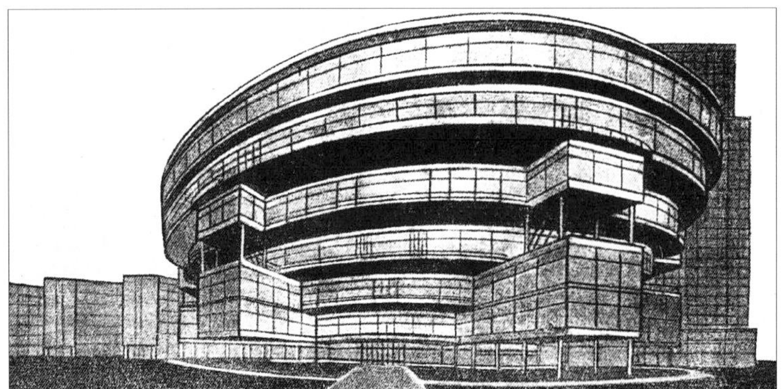

Lidiia Komarova, diploma project under Alexander Vesnin,1929: Headquarters building for the Communist International (Comintern), Moscow.

Ivan Leonidov, diploma project under A. Vesnin 1927, for Lenin Institute, detail of model.

from 1923 in his architectural studio. The Vesnin studios – of Alexander and Leonid Vesnin in Vkhutemas, and Victor Vesnin in MVTU – were the heart of Soviet Constructivism.

'Many of Alexander Alexandrovich's students were active in OSA, and some, including me, became editorial board members on SA.

'We gathered for very interesting discussions, usually in the apartment of Alexander Vesnin on Denezhny Lane, now Vesnin Street, which was SA's editorial offices.

'Moisei Ginzburg was the editor. Often here would be Brik, Gan, Leonidov, Khiger, Burov, Okhitovich, Sokolov, Vladimirov, Barshch, Siniavsky, Zhirov, Nikolai Krasilnikov, Yalovkin, Vegman, Milinis.

'In a very natural and unconstrained atmosphere, till late at night, we discussed the problems, the trends, the tasks of contemporary Soviet architecture. The main thing was in working out the group's theoretical position – the credo of Constructivism as a method of creative work. There were interesting arguments, and people gave papers to stimulate our discussions on aspects of functional design, the method of form-making etc. The sort of themes we took, for example, were "functional appropriateness and architectural form", "the development of technology and industrialisation". Everyone was speaking out against the new "stylisers", the epigones of the "constructive style" and so on.

'In the schools, diploma projects took big building tasks ... and inventiveness was unlimited ... The diploma project and discussion of it was always a significant event in the students' and teachers' lives. In the SA *editorial meetings we had heated discussions over projects and student work of the studios, and deciding which we should publish in* SA.*'*[93]

From a photograph taken when Le Corbusier attended one of these meetings, we can sense something of the ambience in which this took place.

Diplomas: formal and methodological

As these comments from all over the Soviet Union have shown, these Moscow circles, and particularly the Vesnin studios in Vkhutemas, were the fount and epicentre of ideas that inspired efforts in many distant, far less privileged, schools. Historically, they also produced work at the cutting-edge of architectural development in their time, nationally and internationally. In terms of impact and prescience, two in particular stand out, which represented climaxes of different strands within this avant-garde work.

Ivan Leonidov's Diploma project of 1927 for a 'Lenin Institute of Librarianship' has become one of the most enduring images bequeathed by this period. Looked at as design, the almost equally radical, and far more workable scheme of his class-mate Victor Pashkov perhaps has almost equal claim to this status. It is a work that might come from the drawing board (or computer screen) of some leading high-tech office today, equally pursuing the aim which Leonidov stated for his project: 'To answer the needs of contemporary life through maximal use of the possibilities of technology.'[94] Such is fate, when aided by a good model dramatically photographed, that Leonidov's more abstract and more purely Suprematist piece of supposed Constructivism transmits that vision better.

It was precisely this hybrid nature, in design approach and formal language, which made Leonidov's scheme radical. Even more than Krutikov's Flying City which we saw causing upset a year later, this scheme provided the Achilles heel to which anti-Modernist officialdom, as well as the building industry, could direct its attacks on Constructivism and 'the new education'. *Leonidovshchina* (Leonidovism) was the word coined by the press, meaning technically unrealisable fantasy that is generally wasting collective time, insulting the proletariat and sabotaging the national economic and ideological effort.[95]

In having somehow to defend the scheme in *SA*, but also indicate its real failures in relation to Constructivism's proper intents, Ginzburg identified precisely that feature which has made it influential again recently: its new conception of urban space. The work 'is economically and technically impossible to execute today'. In that sense it was 'utopian', not properly Constructivist. 'Whilst in principle a work of our philosophy' it in fact resulted 'from a purely space-oriented architectural treatment' in which 'Leonidov is not really able to prove that his constructive conundrum was actually necessary, that this solution and only this will solve the problem concerned.' For all that, there was a sense in which 'this work constitutes a landmark and reference point for our future work', as Ginzburg put it, because:

> *'it represents a categorical break with that whole system of techniques, schemas and elements which have inevitably become common and habitual with us, and which at best result from a unity of method, and at worst, threaten us with a stereotyped stylistic template.'*[96]

It was important precisely because of this 'space-oriented architectural treatment', what we would see historically as the Suprematist compositional system, 'which leads away from the traditional conception of building, and

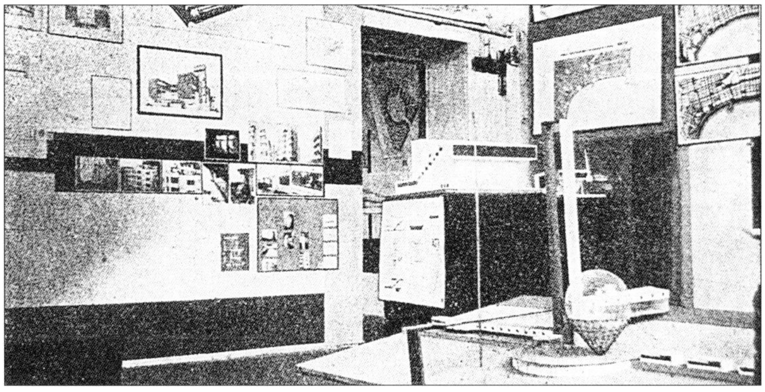

OSA's own room in their First Exhibition of Modern Architecture, Vkhutemas building, June 1927, with student work from LIGI, MVTU [cf. pp.166-7], and Leonidov's diploma model, right.

Gathering of SA *editorial board in the Vesnin flat, Denezhny Lane, with Le Corbusier, Oct. 1928: Leonid, Viktor, Le C., Alexander, Burov, the Vesnins' sister Anna, two other women unidentified.*

towards a reorganisation of the very concept of the public space and the city in which such a building might stand.' It is no surprise that such a work should have been an inspiration to Koolhaas and OMA.

Out of the same studio a year later, but pursuing quite another approach, was the diploma project of Nikolai Krasilnikov already discussed in Chapter 5, which is translated as Document 30.

This scheme developed a vision of where Constructivist design method might go, as opposed to their formal or urban language, and though not through any direct line of influence, but merely through its right understanding of where computational techniques would go, it was equally prescient of work current six decades later.

Just as the sight of these students' faces in a typical student snapshot brings refreshingly to life the reality from which this work comes, so too does the discovery, when recomputing Krasilnikov's solutions with modern equipment, of a mistake in his maths. It indicates the extent to which the group as a whole were using their mathematics to the limit, when *SA* published one graph whose strange changes of gradient immediately attract the mathematical eye. It results in fact from an arithmetical mistake when Krasilnikov evaluated his own complex and mathematically non-trivial formulae, to which one would have expected this visual evidence to have alerted someone – if only Professor Lakhtin, director of the Vkhutemas mechanics laboratory, whose textbook on *Distribution Curves* he has used.[97]

A further year later, as also mentioned in Chapter 5, Krasilnikov published a joint paper with Lidiia Komarova, which moves the speculation, or rather prediction, a crucial stage further. In the light of Komarova's reminiscences quoted above, it gives a further vignette onto the sort of discussions that went on 'till late at night' in Alexander Vesnin's flat.

Krasilnikov's diploma work had sought to optimise his building form by a process that was still essentially dependent on a linear, sequential set of priorities in which each decision about 'best form' followed, as Ginzburg had said of his functional method, 'logically from one to the next'. This was still effectively old-style design by inspection rather than a true optimisation. As quoted earlier, the work with Komarova had as its aim 'to advance this process in order to make possible an objective scientific assessment of all the possible variants available to the designer'.[98]

From the premise that 'the form of any body is a function of many variables', Krasilnikov and Komarova argued (in the approved vocabulary) that a 'dialectical process' takes place in which even purely quantitiative changes in the brief lead to a qualitatively different form, and the 'correct' (ditto) form emerges from a resolution of conflicting or competing demands. Hence, 'a continuous sequence of variants exists'. This was a concept itself qualitatively different from the series of discrete alternative forms which had hitherto been the extent of the Constructivists' vision.

With two examples, the students then outlined a mathematical procedure 'for finding the most advantageous possible dimensions' of a given spatial organisation in terms of 'cost, for any given form of construction'. This involved 'drawing up equations' describing 'costs of a specific form of any one part of the building in relation to all different forms of each other part.' These equations would produce 'a series of cost curves. These we can build up into a surface, or system of curves in space, which will give us the position of the minimum cost'.[99]

In their list of 'all the requirements' for which they would establish curves were included all the organisational, material, environmental and social factors contained in Krasilnikov's earlier list of a building's five measures of 'cost-effectiveness, in the very broadest sense'. These in turn embraced the whole 'first object' of the functional method, from structural questions through to 'the flow diagrams and schemes of equipment, always remembering sanitary and hygiene factors such as daylighting'.

This clear mathematical formulation of the concept of a multi-dimensional solution 'surface' seems to be unique in the architectural context anywhere for that date. Leonidov's ambition 'to answer the needs of contemporary life through maximal use of the possibilities of technology' addressed a future construction technology. In looking to 'the further development of higher mathematics', beyond 'analytical geometry and the differential and integral calculus, and the theories of probability and mathematical statistics',[100] his fellow students Krasilnikov and Komarova were addressing the possibilities of an information technology, before knowing it would be called that. All of their work was in that respect 'utopian'. In Ginzburg's words about Leonidov's project, they had 'forgotten about those real conditions in which our practical activities have to take place'.[101] Lenin, whom Krasilnikov had met in his first days in the school, and who 'only liked realism', would not have approved this as work for students. On the other hand time has shown, as the party spokesman admitted of the Constructivists' 'disurbanist' planning proposals soon after Krasilnikov and Komarova's paper was published (see Chapter 11), 'they may be right about the future.'

Ultimately the greatest credit must go to their teachers. Neither Leonidov's nor Krasilnikov's diploma schemes had stayed within the bounds of what their teachers had already conceived: they took key streams of their thinking so far forward as to mark out the next horizon.

Difficult as the political conjuncture may have made it at the time, that must be the vindication of any pedagogy.

1 El' Lisitsky, 'Baukhauz v Dessau', *Stroitel'naia promyshlennost'* (The Building Industry), 1927, no.1, pp.53-4. The fullest account of Lissitzky's travels and connections remains: S. Lissitzky-Küppers, *El Lissitzky*, Dresden 1967 & London-New York, 1968 **2** This starts with 'Sud'ba Veimarskogo Baukhauza' (The fate of the Weimar Bauhaus), *Sovremennaia arkhitektura* (*SA*), 1926, no.1, pp.24, 30, and the Taut-Mendelsohn visit, *SA*, 1926, no.2 p.60; other items in 1926, no.4; 1927, no.1, pp.42-4; 1927, no.6, pp.163-8; 1928, no.2, pp.69-71; 1928, no.5, pp.146-53. This Bauhaus parallel was assiduously preserved, eg. V. Tikhonov, 'Tri arkhitekturnye shkoly XX v', and Kh. Shedlikh, 'Vkhutemas-Baukhauz', in A. V. Stepanov, ed., *Vkhutemas-Markhi, 1920-80*, Moscow, 1986, pp.36-9 **3** S.O. Khan-Magomedov, *Obmas Vkhutemasa*, Moscow, 1994, p.21 **4** V.G. Lisovsky, *Akademiia khudozhestv* (The Academy of Arts), Leningrad, 1982, pp.153-4 **5** V.G. Lisovsky, *Arkhitekturnaia shkola akademii khudozhestv* (The Architecture School of the Academy of Arts), Leningrad, 1981, p.29 **6** Lisovsky, *Akademiia*, p.155 **7** ibid p.156 **8** Khan-Magomedov, *Obmas*, p.34; For

Shekhtel's lecture to Architecture Department of First Svomas, 'Skazka o trekh sestrakh: zhivopis', arkhitekture, skul'pture' (A tale of three sisters: painting, architecture, sculpture), 15 April 1919, see M. G. Barkhin, ed., *Mastera sovetskoi arkhitektury ob arkhitekture* (Masters of Soviet Architecture on Architecture), Moscow, 1975, vol.1, pp.14-22 **9** Lisovsky, *Arkhitekturnaia shkola*, p.30 **10** A. Benois, *Memoirs*, London, 1960, p.163 **11** Khan-Magomedov, *Obmas*, p.31 **12** ibid, p.31 **13** Text of the decree, 'Dekret sovnarkoma ob organizatsii Moskovskikh vysshikh gosudarstvennykh khudozhestvenno-tekhnicheskikh mastershikh (Decree of Sovnarkom on the organisation of the Moscow Higher Artistic and Technical Studios), 29 Nov 1920, in: V.P. Tolstoi, ed., *Sovetskoe dekorativnoe iskusstvo. Materialy i dokumenty 1917-32: Farfor, Faians, Steklo* (Soviet Decorative Arts. Materials and documents 1917-32: China, Porcelain, Glass), Moscow, 1980, doc.37, pp.102-3 **14** ibid, clause **15** *V.I. Lenin i izobrazitel'nom iskusstve. Dokumenty, pis'ma, vospominaniia* (Lenin and Fine Art. Documents, letters and reminiscences), Moscow, 1977, pp.83-4 **16** Lisovsky, *Arkhitekturnaia shkola*, p.30 **17** ibid, p.30 **18** Archives, quoted in ibid, p.31 **19** ibid, p.31 **20** ibid, p.32 **21** Lisovsky, *Akademiia*, p.158 **22** Documents in Academy of Arts Library (NBAAKh), fond 16, cat.1, doc.316, pp.35-7, quoted in Lisovsky, *Akademiia*, p.16 **23** Khan-Magomedov, *Obmas*, pp.36-7 **24** V. Khazanova, comp., *Iz istorii sovetskoi arkhitektury 1926-32. Dokumenty i materialy*, (From the History of Soviet Architecture 1926-32: Documents and materials), Moscow, 1970, p.39 **25** Khan-Magomedov, *Obmas*, p.61 **26** Much of Khan-Magomedov, *Obmas*, is the text of successive exercises set to students in Obmas, and the projects founded on each. **27** Khan-Magomedov, *Obmas*. **28** Ia.G. Chernikhov, *Osnovy sovremennoi arkhitektury* (Fundamentals of Contemporary Architecture), Second edition, Leningrad, 1931, p.11 **29** V. Krinsky, I. Lamtsov, M. Turkus, *Elementy arkhitekturno-prostranstvennoi kompozitsii* (Elements of Spatial Composition in Architecture), Moscow, 1934. Abstract exercises in 'Space' from Basic Course, illustrated here, are reproduced from this source. **30** 'Zaiavlenie ... v Administrativnyi otdel Mossoveta' (Statement to the Administrative Dept of Mossoviet), in Khazanova, *Iz istorii 1926-32*, p.68 **31** V.N. Perlin, 'Aleksandr Vasil'evich Kuznetsov', *Arkhitektura SSSR* (Architecture of the USSR), 1967, no.7, p.44 **32** A. Fisenko, 'Razvitie sovetskoi promyshlennoi arkhitektury' (The development of soviet industrial architecture), *Arkhitektura SSSR*, 1967, no.7, p.14; and 'VTU im. Baumana' (The Higher Technical College named for Bauman), *Moskva. Entsiklopediia* (Moscow. Encyclopedia), Moscow, 1980, p.193 **33** Fisenko, 'Razvitie', p.14 **34** ibid, and M.P. Makotinsky, 'A. Kuznetsov 1874-1954', in M.I. Astafeva-Dlugach et al, comps., *Zodchie Moskvy* (The Architects of Moscow), vol.2, Moscow, 1988, pp.104-8 **35** H. Hudson, *Blueprints and Blood. The Stalinization of Soviet Architecture 1917-37*, Princeton, 1994, p.232, n.16 **36** S.O. Khan-Magomedov, *Pioneers of Soviet Architecture*, London, 1987, p.571, fig.21 **37** Khan-Magomedov, *Obmas*, p.97 **38** Prezidium Otdeleniia, 'Arkhitekturnoe otdelenie MVTU: k 10-letiiu sushchestvovanniia' (The Architecture Department of MVTU: for ten years of its existence), *Stroitel'stvo Moskvy* (Construction of Moscow), 1927, no.6, pp.14-16 **39** ibid. **40** ibid. **41** C. Cooke, 'Mediating creativity and politics: sixty years of architectural competitions in Russia', in A. Calnek, ed., The Great Utopia, Guggenheim Museum, New York, 1992, pp.680-715 **42** Prezidium, 'Arkhitekturnoe otdelenie', p.16 **43** eg. L. Komarova, 'Arkhitekturnyi fakul'tet Vkhutemasa: masterskaia A. A. Vesnina', in Stepanov, *Vkhutemas-Markhi*, pp.33-35; and A. Vesnin (attrib), 'Opyt primeneniia metoda materialisticheskoi dialektiki k postroeniiu uchebnoi programmy po arkhitekturnomu proektirovaniiu' (Experiment in applying the method of materialist dialectics to constructing a curriculum for architectural design), *SA*, 1930, no.5, front and back covers. **44** *SA*, 1927, no.6, p.160 **45** Hudson, *Blueprints*, p.230, n.55, to TsGALI, f.681, cat.2, doc.106, pp.28-9 **46** G.A. Ol', *Aleksandr Nikolsky*, Leningrad, 1980, p.41 **47** ibid, p.42 **48** V. Malinovsky, 'LIGI v novykh iskaniiakh' (LIGI work in new directions), *SA*, 1926, no.5-6, pp.138-40 **49** ibid, p.139 **50** A. Nikolsky, 'Ob arkhitekturnom obrazovanii' (On architectural education), ms. in GMIL (State Museum of History of Leningrad), published in Barkhin, *Mastera*, vol.1, p.494 **51** ibid. **52** Ol', *Nikolsky*, p.46; Nikolsky, 'Vvedenie v arkhitekturu: 1-e sobesedovanie 16.XI.27' (Introduction to architecture: first conversation, 16 Nov 27), in Barkhin, *Mastera*, vol.1, pp.495-6 **53** '2-e sobesedovanie' (Second conversation), ibid, p. 496 **54** Nikolsky, unidentified article, in Ol', *Nikolsky*, p.47 **55** *SA*, 1928, no.4, pp.113-7 **56** A.S. Nikolsky, *Leningradskii albom*, Leningrad, 1984, p.28 **57** Ol', *Nikolsky*, p.52 **58** Nikolsky, *Albom*, p.28 **59** Malinovsky, 'LIGI', pp.139-40 **60** Decree of 8 June 1926, see E.H. Carr & R.W. Davies, *Foundations of a Planned Economy 1926-9*, vol.I, part II, London, 1969, pp.590-1; Ia. Kornfel'd, 'Konferentsiia vo Vkhutemase' (Conference in Vkhutemas), *SA*, 1926, no.5-6, pp.135-6; N. Lakhtin, 'Akademicheskaia Konferentsiia Arkhitekturnogo Fakul'teta Vkhutemasa i rezul'taty ee raboty' (The academic conference of the Vkhutemas Architecture Faculty and the results of its work), *Stroitel'naia promyshlennost'*, 1927, no.1, pp.70-2 **61** L. Zhadova, 'Istoriia arkh-faka Vkhutemasa' (History of the Vkhutemas Architecture Faculty), in Stepanov, *Vkhutemas-Markhi*, pp.25-30 **62** A.V. Lunacharsky, 'Osnovy khudozhestvennogo obrazovanniia' (Fundamentals of artistic education), *Sobranie sochinenii v 8-mi tt, t.7* (Collected Works in 8 volumes, vol. 7), Moscow, 1967, p.455 **63** Zhadova, 'Istoriia', p.29 **64** Kornfel'd, 'Konferentsiia'. **65** Lakhtin, 'Akademicheskaia Konferentsiia', p.71 **66** N. Dokuchaev, 'Zapiski po kursu "Osnovy arkhitektury"' (Notes for the course 'Fundamentals of Architecture'), in Khazanova, *Iz istorii 1926-32*, p.45 **67** Lakhtin, 'Akademicheskaia Konferentsiia', p.71 **68** N. Sheviakov, 'K voprosu ob ispol'zovanii rezul'tatov arkhitekturnykh konkursov' (On using the products of architectural competitions), *Stroitel'naia promyshlennost'*, 1924, no.5, p.360 **69** I. Kokkinaki, 'The First Exhibition of Modern Architecture in Moscow', *Architectural Design*, 1983, no.5-6 (*Russian Avant-Garde*), pp.50-9 which has full bibliography. **70** ibid p.50 and reports in *SA*, 1927, no.4-5 **71** *SA*, 1926, no.5-6, pp.140-1 **72** SA, 1927, no.3, p.110 **73** ibid **74** 'Zhizn Vuzov' (The life of the Schools), *SA*, 1926, no.1, pp.23-4 & 'Pervaia konferentsiia OSA v Moskve' (First conference of OSA in Moscow) *SA*, 1928, no.4, pp.116-23 **75** ibid **76** ibid, p.120 **77** ibid, pp.119-20 **78** ibid, p.118 **79** ibid, p.116 & 'Pis'mo iz Tomska' (Letter from Tomsk), *SA*, 1928, no.3, pp.103-4 **80** P. Novitsky, 'Restavratory i arkh-fak Vkhuteina' (Restorationists in the Vkhutein Architecture Faculty), *SA*, 1928, no.4, pp.109-110. For Krutikov's scheme see Khan-Magomedov, *Pioneers*, figs 791-801 and more fully in C. Cooke, *Architectural Drawings of the Russian Avant-Garde*, New York-London, 1990, pp.98-101 **81** Novitsky, 'Restavratory', p.110 **82** Carr, *Foundations*, I part II, pp.590-2 **83** Novitsky, 'Restavratory', p.110 **84** Carr, Foundations, I part II, p.592. **85** ibid, p.593 **86** ibid, p.593 **87** S. Fitzpatrick, *The Commissariat of Enlightenment*, Cambridge, 1970, pp.64-7 et al. **88** Carr, *Foundations*, I part II, p.595 **89** K. Afanas'ev, 'Borba techenii vo Vkhutemase' (The battle of different trends in Vkhutemas), in Stepanov, *Vkhutemas-Markhi*, pp.31-2 **90** ibid, where records in TsGALI for Nov 1924 give figures: A. Vesnin had 45 students; L. Vesnin 43; Shchusev 34; Rylsky 32; Ladovsky 28; Kokorin 18; Dokuchaev 12. **91** Afanas'ev, 'Borba', p.31 **92** ibid **93** Komarova, 'Arkhitekturnyi fakul'tet', pp.33, 35 **94** Leonidov's project and notes, in *SA*, 1927, 4-5, pp.119-24; in English: A. Gozak & A. Leonidov, *Ivan Leonidov*, London-New York 1988, pp.42-9 **95** For documents on Leonidovism see Gozak & Leonidov, *Leonidov*, pp.94-8 **96** ibid, p.42 for English. Full text is M. Ginzburg, 'Itogi i perspektivy' (Achievements and prospects), *SA*, 1927, no.4-5, pp.112-4-6-8 **97** The irregular dip in his plot of total building volume in his city against number of rings of development is visible on the right-hand page reproduced in Document 30, p.187, below, and arises from an arithmetic error in his calculations. Full explanation appears in my earlier publication of this paper, ref. p.187, top right. **98** N. Krasil'nikov & L. Komarova, 'Metod issledovaniia formobrazovaniia sooruzheniia' (A method of investigating the generation of building form), *SA*, 1929, no.5, pp.183-4 **99** ibid **100** N. Krasil'nikov, 'Problemy sovremennoi arkhitektury' (Problems of contemporary architecture), *SA*, 1928, no.6, pp.170-6 **101** Ginzburg, 'Itogi', p.116.

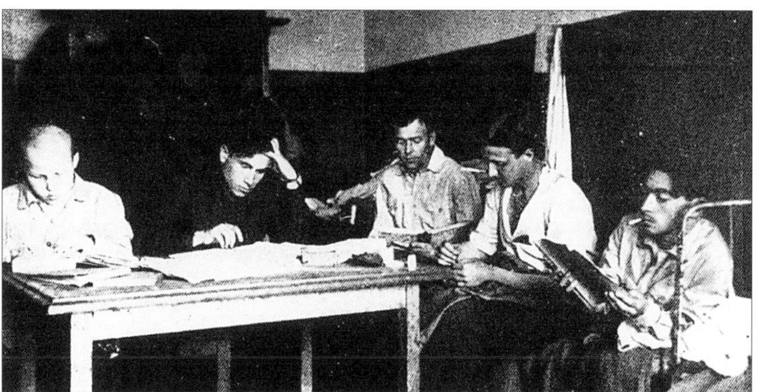

Typical living conditions of Moscow students in the Twenties: like most families after the government 'evictions and compressions' of 1918-19, sharing one room in a former middle-class apartment.

Senior students in Alexander Vesnin's studio, Vkhutemas, 1927: Lidiia Komarova, centre back; Ivan Leonidov sitting, lowest, in front of her, and Nikolai Krasilnikov, to the left shaded between them.

Doc. 18

NIKOLAI LADOVSKY
FOUNDATIONS FOR BUILDING A THEORY OF ARCHITECTURE (UNDER THE BANNER OF RATIONALIST AESTHETICS)

20 & 30 October 1920, published in Izvestiia ASNOVA, no.1, 1926, pp.3-6

Architectural rationality is founded on the principle of economy just as technical rationality is. The difference lies in the fact that technical rationality is an economy of labour and material in the creation of a suitable and convenient building, but architectural rationality is the economy of psychic energy in the perception of the spatial and functional properties of the building. It is a synthesis of these two forms of rationality into one building that creates ratioarchitecture (*ratsioarkhitektura*).

Part 1: ON FORM

1 In the perception of material forms as such we can simultaneously see in them the expressiveness of properties that are:

1) Geometrical – the relationships of sides, edges, angles, characteristics of surface etc;
2) physical – weight, density, mass;
3) physico-mechanical – stability, mobility etc;
4) logical – expressiveness of surface character as such and of delimiting volumes.

According to the expressiveness, sizes and quantity we may speak of:

a: strength and weakness;
b: greatness and smallness;
c: finiteness and non-finiteness (*konechnost i beskonechnost*).

2 Architecture operates by means of these 'properties' as specific quantities. The architect constructs a form, bringing together elements which are not technical or utilitarian ones in the normal sense of those words, and which can be looked upon as 'architectural motifs'. In the architectural respect these 'motifs' must be rational, and must serve the higher technical requirement of the individual to orientate himself in space

As an illustration of one type of work on the geometrical expressiveness of form let us examine the following.

Example 1

3 Two projections of a rectangular solid give a geometrically precise **representational image** of it (Fig.No.1)

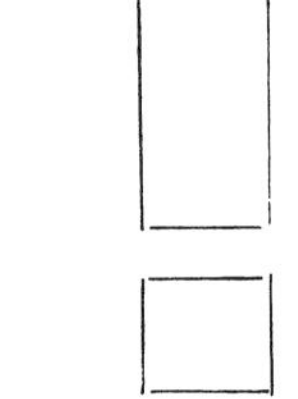

Fig. No. 1

The real perspective of it, represented in the series of static moments 1, 2,... (Fig.No.2) gives an approximated image, which tends towards the geometrical one expressed in the two projections, as its limit.

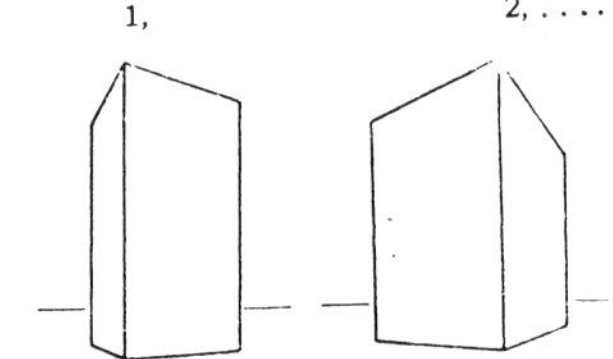

Fig. No. 2

4 The work of the architect on the geometrical expressiveness of form, which we always perceive in perspective, consists in approximation of the image obtained from the perceiving of real perspective, to the image given in the projections.

The degree of approximation depends on the quantity and quality of the element-signs entering into the system of definitions constructed by the architect. It is usually visible technical construction that provides this system of element-signs. Where it can be utilised fully, a synthesis of architecture and technology results, and where it cannot be done, the architectural construction of the element-signs is created by relief components of the surface of the form, as the technically simplest and most economical means of performing this. As a concrete example of the posing and solution of a problem of this type, I quote an exercise which I first set in the Architecture Faculty of the Vkhutemas in 1920.

Exercise No. 1
(Architectural-geometrical form)

5 Given: **1.** A right rectangular solid in horizontal projection, comprising a 20x20 m square with height of 30 m.

2. The height of the viewer's eye at 1.60 m, the distance of the viewpoint being not more than 30 m, the viewpoint moving at a speed of not more than 15 m per second.

3. Solar illumination.

Note. In solving the exercise it is necessary to take into account the movement of the sun and the possibility of a position in which there might be simultaneously an equal volume of illumination on the two sides of the rectangular volume.

It is required to communicate to the viewer:

1. the direction of the surfaces forming the sides of the volume, in relation to coordinate surfaces i.e. its spatial orientation. (Note. The spatial coordinates are those which are adopted in the theory of perspective.)

2. a clear reading of the edges;

3. equality of the sides;

4. the relationship of side of the base, and to height;

5. the right-angular relationship of the surfaces forming the sides;

6. the right-angularity of the corners.

The permitted means of expression and representation are: vertical and horizontal delineations, tone and treatment of the surfaces.

It is required that the following be presented:

1. a model or perspective view;

2. drawings of two elevations which meet at a corner;

3. a horizontal and a vertical section, all at a scale of 1:100.

20.X–1920. N.L.

6 As is evident from this statement of the task, the main work involved is that of manifesting to the viewer the geometrical properties of the rectangular solid. But what does it mean to manifest the geometrical image? Perhaps we see in the mathematically correctly constructed rectangular solid some quite other form – a sphere, a cone a cylinder etc? No, we do not see in it a sphere or a cone, nor do we see a rectangular solid with those geometrical properties given in the problem.

It is enough to examine the perspective series 1, 2, ... (Fig.No.2) to realise that it does not contain enough information for us to determine, say, that the sides of the base are equal, or that the relationship of the side to the height is 1.5:1.

Can we allow that the architect, in constructing the form, did not know how it would be perceived by the viewer? To allow that would be to accept complete lack of principle and the impossibility of any real control in the field of geometrical expressiveness. It is necessary to establish the principle that the architectural-geometrical task consists in such a treatmentof a material form as permits the viewer to really perceive its geometrical characteristics with whatever accuracy and precision is required in the particular situation.

What needs to be done for this purpose in the case in question?

7 It is necessary to establish some mark or identity between each pair of simultaneously visible sides of the rectangular solid, and therefore to do this between all sides of it.

This means that subdivisions made on the surfaces of all sides of the solid must be identical .... **(1)**

If for example we draw a circle onto each surface of the solid in such a way (Fig.No.3) that the viewer may determine in perceiving it that the diameters of each simultaneously visible pair are equal, then the image will have been rendered into a close approximation of its real geometrical character, and the equal distances of each edge from the other will be clear. .... **(2)**

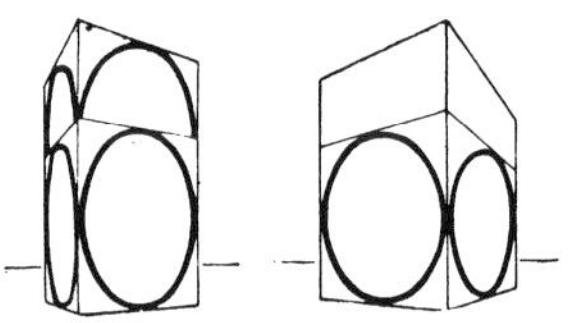

Fig. No. 4 Fig. No. 3

If we also draw the semi-circles (Fig.No.4), we demonstrate that the relationship between the base and the height is 1.5:1; we demonstrate the equality of the sides and all the properties that follow from that, all to a given degree of approximation. .... **(3)**

Continuing with this kind of analysis, we find those other elements needed to solve the task that is posed.

Having compared the architectural images obtained as a result of this procedure, with the perspective series 1, 2, (of Fig.No.2), under these particular conditions of viewing, we can be convinced to a large extent of the approximation of the architectural image (in Fig.No.4) to the image given by the projections. (i.e. in Fig.No.1).

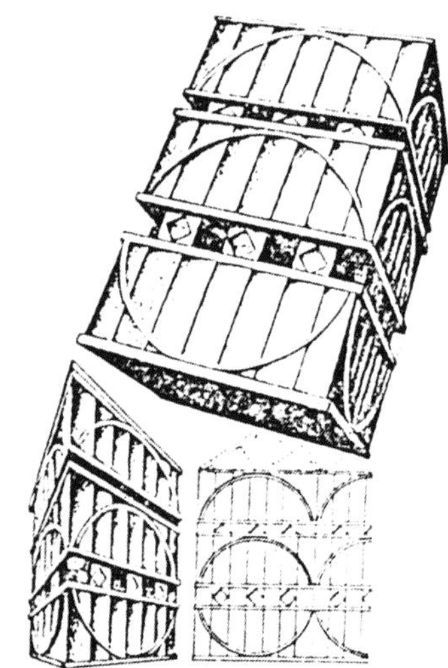

Fig. No. 5.
Work by student Petrov under N. Ladovsky, Vkhutemas, 1920

Основы построения теории Архитектуры
(Под знаком рационалистической эстетики)

The action of light on the modelling of an object is well known and understood. Requirement 3 is posed here. A possible solution to this problem would be:

a) either different textural treatment of each pair of simultaneously visible surfaces ....**(4)**, or

b) a breaking-down of one of each of the two simultaneously visible surfaces into parts making an angle with the surface of which they are a part, ...**(5)**, or

c) a division of both visible surfaces as in (5) but with the angles of the parts of the surface of one side being unequal to those of the other surface ....**(6)**.

8 In the solution shown here, by student Petrov, (under N.L., Vkhutemas 1920) requirements 1, 2, 5 and 6 of the task were manifested in the following manner:

1 & 2, by the double-square repetition of the horizontal projections of the rectangular solid,

5, by vertical and horizontal straight lines, mutually perpendicular to the surfaces,

6, by showing small squares visible from below in the corners of the horizontal projections, which are read as such directly thanks to their small size, and hence small perimeters.

Exercise No. 2
(Architectural-geometrical form)

9 Given:

1. The drawing of the geometrical form supplied
2. the normal horizon of view, mobile point of view with a speed of movement of not more than 15 m, maximum distance of the viewpoint 30 m.
3. illumination by sunlight.

It is required to manifest to the viewer:

1. All surfaces as such,
2. surfaces A & B as forming an angle,
3. the inclination of surface B,
4. the cylindrical or conical character of surface K,
5. the clear delineation of all angles.

It is required that the following should be presented: Model and drawings at a scale of 1:100.

Vkhutemas
30.X–1920 ***N.L.***

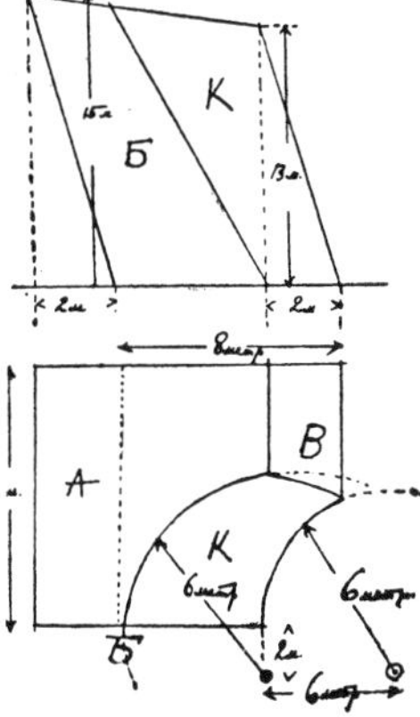

Fig. No.6

Doc. 19

ILIA GOLOSOV
LECTURE NOTES FOR A PROGRAMME OF ARCHITECTURAL EDUCATION
8 April 1921, from the State Archives of Literature and Art, TsGALI, Moscow

Study of the styles which have existed in past architecture is essential. Style is not the essence of architecture, however, and what really matters is to learn to distinguish true artistic spirit from mere style and material values.

A free arrangement with contrasts and movements is the essence of the artistic process, and content, which must be examined independently from style and which in essence can adopt any specific form, is entirely independent of style. Thus the study of style does not offer a path to understanding the essence of architecture. That is why it should not be seen as part of the course of study of architectural structures.

The study of traditional architecture must undoubtedly enter into the programme of teaching on architecture but under no circumstances should it be taught on the level of its external appearances as style. It should aim to convey an understanding of its essence: of the principles for building up masses; of the placing of masses and of the ways of perceiving them; of the relationship of plans to elevations; of functional suitability of form and so on.

This is the only viewpoint from which historical architecture should be examined in a foundation course of architectural design. They should have been given the necessary factual information on the classics of architecture and such topics as the Orders in advance, through conventional lecture courses of the kind used in all architectural schools as the main means for teaching Classical proportions in particular.

The study and knowledge of proportions as such is necessary in the early part of architectural education, but must not be based exclusively on the examples of the classics. In these artistic works which constantly repeat the same overall structure, as do Greek temples for example, students can work out for themselves the more or less constant relationships of different parts of the building. But in the study of proportions in general, we must not be lead only by those principles, since the sets of proportions necessary for certain given kinds of design work must be created afresh. They cannot always conform to a definition of the relationship of elements that has been established once and for all time. ...

I consider that the programme which has currently been accepted for the basic course of architectural study does not satisfy the above mentioned principles, therefore I propose to replace architectural drafting exercises by the study of how architectural form is structured, in accordance with the following schema:

Programme for conducting architectural training in the First Course:

I. General concepts of architecture, its tasks, and its significance in the life of humanity.

2. The architectural mass:
The concept of architectural mass.
The placing of masses.
The relationship of masses.
The scalar qualities of masses.

3. Architectural form:
The concept of architectural form.
How form depends on content.
The relationship of forms.
The scalar qualities of form.
Composition of simple architectural structures in terms of their plan, elevations and sections.

4. The architectural treatment of masses and forms:
The significance of a different architectural treatment of one and the same mass.
The manifestation of scale in a mass through the treatment of its parts as architectural details.

5. Means of expression:
Manifestation of the powerfulness of a building.
Manifestation of the grace of the building.
Manifestation of the idea of the building.
Compositions of a simple piece of monumental architecture showing plan, elevations and sections.

6. The significance of spatial relationships.

7. Rhythm in architecture.

Doc. 20

ILIA GOLOSOV
THE CONCEPTS OF MASS AND FORM IN ARCHITECTURAL COMPOSITION
Early 1920s, from the State Archives of Literature and Art, TsGALI, Moscow

In aspiring to get as close as possible to a solution of the tasks I have defined, I have conceived the present text as an attempt to establish a firm conception of architectural masses and forms, and some understanding of the usefulness of these concepts in the process of architectural composition.

The underlying concept here is essential to the disciplines which should be studied in artistic education. The decisive lack of creative thinking in contemporary architectural design, which is manifesting itself so clearly at the present time, undoubtedly results from the complete lack of an education that touches upon such issues.

An architectural structure only possesses value when an aesthetic idea is present in it; when it is the result of a clear idea about architectural mass and form.

We have to recognise that the first essential condition of value in an architectural composition is the presence in the creator's mind of a correct starting point for architectural thinking about the manifestation of the *primitiv* of that building or combination of buildings. By the term *primitiv* I mean here the primary and fundamental concept that embraces the entire subject-matter of the building.

Without manifestation of this *primitiv* there cannot be a clear concept about any kind of building as a product of architectural composition. ...

The first thing that has to be studied is how to embrace conceptually the general idea of a building from the point of view of its *spatial* characteristics, since each building is first of all perceived from precisely this standpoint.

The initial perception of a structure is the feeling of its relationship in space, of the suggestive power of its mass. Consequently the concept of mass as something that explains its own make-up, or in other words, the formulation of the *primitiv* of the building as the indicator of its general spatial idea, is a factor of extreme importance in the process of architectural composition.

In what follows ... I am trying as far as possible to lay out principles that can be accepted as giving a conventionally agreed definition of the concept of mass and form in architecture, as the firm and necessary basis for deductive architectural thinking.

The concept of the architectural mass

The existing concept of the physical mass, as the quantity of matter and material which an object contains, cannot serve as a starting point for the study of mass in architecture as a product of *aesthetic* activity.

The mass that interests us has to be understood as neutral in respect of all its usual inherent properties, which have interest here only to the extent that they influence its spatial character and its relation to other masses. We therefore use the word as a new conventional or technical term with a new meaning to signify these other characteristics.

We shall call the kind of mass that interests us ***architectural mass.***

By this term we understand a mass that does not have a specific content of function or meaning, that is completely free in the forms it adopts and bears no responsibilty for them.

The architectural mass, or the *primitiv* of the building, which is the same thing, is the phenomemon existing in architecture that is perceived with the help of our deductive thinking independently of all other phenomena in this field. Our consciousness of it is directly dependent upon our methodological study of this phenomeon as one of the specialised disciplines of our aesthetic science.

This study must be conducted only on the level of abstract concepts. ... This conventionally defined concept of mass requires an abstract presentation in order to better explain its significance in architecture.

The architectural mass always has a volumetric value. It is characterised by the complete absence of any internal content over and above its significance as volume and the spatial characteristics it possesses of itself and in the context of masses related to it.

Architectural mass being mainly a phenomenon of volume is not conceivable as a concept outside its dependence upon a form, therefore there is always some form or other inherent to any architectural mass.

Such a form is as a whole dependent on the mass and its volume, and in essence has the features of the mass. Therefore I shall designate it by a special term: ***geometrical volumetric form***, ie it is a spatial form as distinct from an architectural form – of which I shall speak later.

Thus: **architectural mass is the most rudimentary volumetric form carrying no inner content and having meaning only in relation to space and other masses.**

The subjective architectural mass

The subjective architectural mass is that mass on which the idea of the overall architectural composition is concentrated. It bears the whole weight of responsibility for the unity of all the masses coexisting as a composition. The objective masses are those subordinate to this subjective mass. ... We shall introduce the concept of 'organism' as meaning a group of structures standing apart in a spatial respect and connected into one unbroken whole.

The subjective mass, as the nucleus of the live organism is the thing that gives life to the objective masses which organically depend upon it. This subjective mass is absolutely independent from those subordinate to it and is a function of the overall architectural and spatial idea. As such it expresses its essence in its own geometric and volumetric form. Figures 1 and 2 give examples. The subjective masses here represent slightly different responses to the same essential idea, which is defined by the following conditions:

1 the static character of the subjective mass relative to the others [i.e. not active in the horizontal – see later, CC], and its aspiration upwards;
2 the closed character of its development in one direction and the possibility of free development in the other, this being determined by the placing of the subordinate masses;
3 manifestation of the significance of each of its four sides;
4 subordination to itself of the masses manifested by it.

Here we see the vast importance which the subjective mass has in the overall distribution of masses. Correct solution of the whole depends directly upon the specific individual characteristics of the subjective mass. If this mass is right, it is no great labour to achieve harmony in the general composition of masses around it, as the subjective mass will clearly establish and indicate the possibilities for doing this. ...

Lines of gravitation

In studying the process of dividing architectural masses into the subjective and the objective, we encounter another esssential principle which also demands definition. This is the principle of gravitation.

This is the main factor in the relationship between individual organisms: the gravitation of one organism towards another.

In each group of coexisting organisms there exists without fail a system built upon the principle of a unification of individual parts into one whole. This system is nothing other than an abstract representation of the links which develop between the masses through the presence in each one of a main line. This main line gives direction to the individual organism and is the basic connecting factor between different organisms.

Each organism contains within itself a force, which is its live impulse or energy. This force has the property of forming tensions which operate in various ways between the elements of the organism, and it will be expressed graphically as a line of some kind.

The direction of that line, as the sum of all the forces existing within the organism, expresses the gravitation of it in any specific direction.

We call that directional line of the organism its ***line of gravitation.***

In a simple organism, this line will be simple; in a more complex organism, the line will be complex. ... This line of gravitation is an indication of the spatial potency of the organism, being the sum of the architectural and spatial ideas of its constituent parts.

Such lines are of very diverse type ... and here we consider only the two main ones:

1 the ***active or vertical line of gravitation;***
2 the ***passive or horizontal line of gravitation.***

The vertical line always runs towards the centre of the earth, ... and expresses itself as an upward aspiration of the form. ...

Let us take the cylinder in figure 3, whose height is equal to its diameter.

This relationship of horizontal to vertical does not generate any notable gravitation in any direction, and may be called a state of latent gravitation.

As soon as the relationship of vertical and horizontal changes, ... a line of gravitation develops upwards. ... The circular cylinder, the circular cone and the symmetrical pyramid are all forms which latently or explicitly embody the principle of a line of gravity through their central axis. ...

There exist organisms of masses which have a clearly manifested dominant gravitation towards one side or another. This is the generally horizontal category, and usually it is this gravitation which creates links between one organism or form and another. ... These horizontal lines of gravitation may be of two general types: ***centrifugal or centripetal.*** ...

Figure 4 shows the simplest case of horizontal gravitation. It may also be distributed as a curve in the horizontal plane. Figure 5 shows this, with a horizontal line of gravitation consisting of a series of weaker ones. Their slight vertical gravitation is overwhelmed by the strength of the horizontal. ... In figure 6 we see the process of confluence of the two directions of gravitation, horizontal and vertical ... and in figure 7 we see the absorption of two horizontal forces into a single vertical one.

The objective architectural mass

Objective masses are dependent on the subjective mass; they are passive and have no individual life. ... There can be no element in an organism which is outside the sphere of influence of the subjective mass. Any element of the composition has objective value, as a node of the organism, but it lives only through the existence of the nucleus. Such an objective element has all the attributes of an architectural mass, and may be called an architectural mass of objective value, or ***an objective architectural mass.*** Such masses play a lesser role, but they also contribute their constituent lines of gravitation to the overall organism.

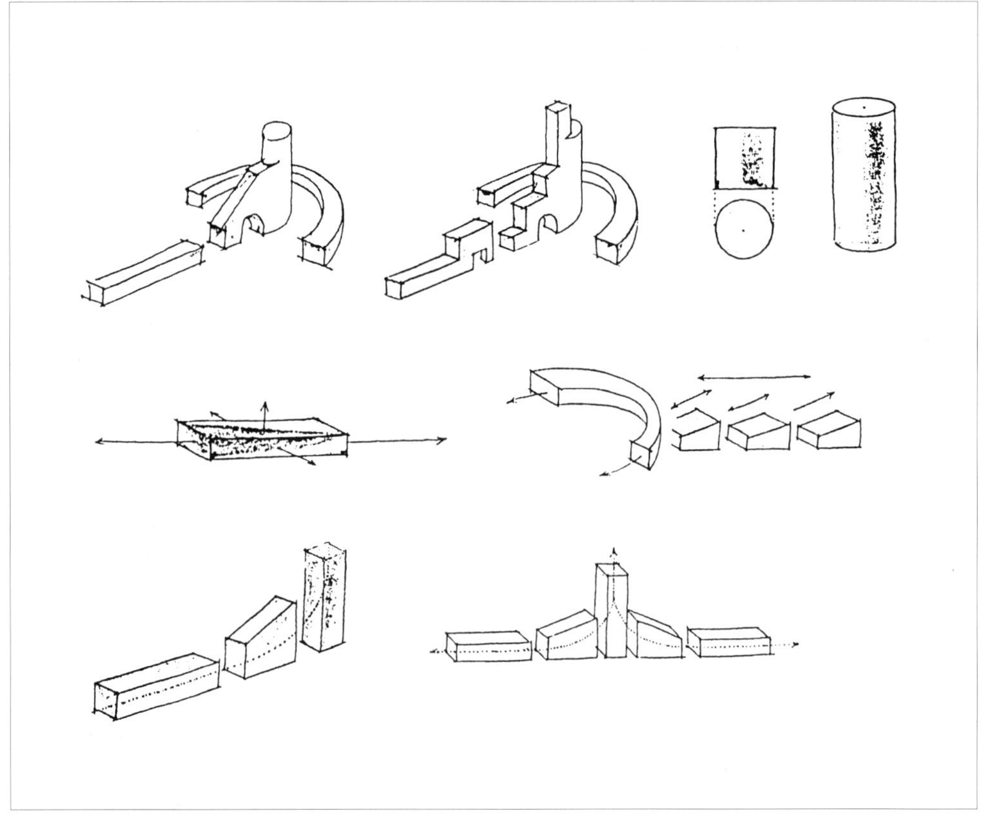

Golosov's diagrams.
Top row, left to right: Figures 1, 2 and 3. Middle row: Figures 4 and 5. Bottom: Figures 6 and 7.

Doc. 21

KONSTANTIN MELNIKOV & ILIA GOLOSOV SLOGANS OF THEIR VKHUTEMAS STUDIO 'THE NEW ACADEMY'

10-15 November 1923, from TsGALI, State Archives

The true mark of architecture that is NEW is that it does not simply reuse *forms*, but it is based through-and-through on reusing the established *perceptual gradations* of the architecture that is OLD.

Let the architecture of the past show you that your own ventures have a blood-connection with it.

To the academicist [i.e. those in Zholtovsky's Vkhutemas studio, CC], *convention* is the law.

To the Obmas designer [Rationalists of Ladovsky's studio, CC], the *model* is the law.

To us, the law is the application of one to the content of the other

We take not a specific form of the OLD architecture, but all its degrees and gradations, which have brought its inspiration to the building task.

The law by which artistic form affects us is eternal. As it was in the past, so it will also be in the future. The absence of this law in new work leads to *decadence*.

The application of old forms is *imitation*.

Without the principle of the old, the new form is decadence.

The method is intuition: of FORM

For the academicist, form is the END PRODUCT (a synthesis)

For the Obmas designer, form is the STARTING POINT (a principle)

For us, form is the TOTALITY (principle and synthesis).

The NEW is only new when the OLD is known: knowing the old, you will legitimate the new.

Without the old, everything new is decadence.

Doc. 22

INSTRUCTIONS FOR ARCHITECTURAL STUDY IN 'THE NEW ACADEMY'

November 1923

The process of building up an architectural object proceeds by the scrutiny of one and the same volume in space from the most diverse points of assimilation of it.

Architectural research should consist in the application of well-mastered principles of study to the best monuments of historical architecture. Composition, as an exercise in the principles which have been mastered through experience and by experimental demonstration, is the achievement of a matching between creative intuition and the task posed.

Doc. 23

KONSTANTIN MELNIKOV 'ARCHITECTURE': FROM A LECTURE TO THE TECHNICAL COLLEGE OF CINEMATOGRAPHY, MOSCOW

16 November 1926

Here are some common definitions:

a) architecture is style;
b) architecture is construction;
c) architecture is a spatial art.

Architecture = a + b + c.

The first of these definitions is the most widespread and the most mistaken, since style in this context means only the sculptural embellishment of the building's parts.

The Constructive movement regards architecture as a function of the art of building, so that architecture is transformed into a mastery of structural devices; thus the brothers Perret in France, for example, build like engineers, and manage the whole construction of a building themselves.

Architecture is a volumetric and spatial art.

In the broad sense of the meaning of architecture, these definitions only serve as starting points.

I affirm that architecture exists as the handicraft act of building, and only the development of this approach to building can produce such forms as we call 'architecture'.

In as far as engineering operates on the basis of mathematics, which is an incomplete science and still developing, to that extent engineering cannot give precise answers on construction.

As a result, engineering will never produce architecture.

Doc. 24

'LIFE IN THE SCHOOLS': STUDENT SOCIETIES IN THE MOSCOW SCHOOLS

SA, 1926, no.1, pp.23-4

THE ARCHITECTURE STUDENTS' SOCIETY (*KRUZHOK*) IN VKHUTEMAS

After almost a year's break in its activity the architectural *kruzhok* [literally 'circle, i.e. students' society, CC] in Vkhutemas began to operate again in November 1925.

A temporary committee was elected. A plan of work was drawn up that included the organisation of a lecture series on questions of architecture and construction. In order to work these topics out in greater depth discussion groups were created for the history of architecture, building technology, N.O.T., and photo-kinematography.

One aim of the plan of activities is to provide all-round assistance to the student body in their academic work by means of organising special lectures on the topics of their current projects.

A library-cum-reading room is being organised, and subscriptions to journals taken out. Great attention is also being given to preparations to publish a journal of the architectural *kruzhok* itself. Articles and illustrative material are being assembled for this.

The journal will illuminate questions of life in the school, links with production, questions of architecture and art.

The *kruzhok* held a lecture by students who have returned from a trip to Paris, about the architecture of the Paris exhibition.

THE ARCHITECTURAL STUDENTS' SOCIETY IN MVTU

During the current academic half-year the Architectural *Kruzhok* of MVTU has been doing preparatory work on the business of finding funds and securing some accommodation for it to operate in, as well as organising a library and subscriptions to foreign literature.

Given the acute shortage of printed material on architecture, the *kruzhok* has made an album, with its own resources, of the best student work on the themes of housing, schools, clubs, hospitals, and so on. This album material will be a great help to students in forthcoming design work.

Amongst the *kruzhok*'s activities, it conducted lectures and a visit. Amongst the lectures, architect LISSITZKY spoke 'On contemporary architecture', student KHIGER spoke on 'Creative work, art and architecture', and Professor SERK spoke on 'Construction legislation, the public-servicing of towns and housing construction in Germany'. Two trips to peformances in Moscow theatres were also organised.

Our next events will be lectures by professors and students on themes of current interest to the student body, dealing with the basic problems of contemporary construction.

The following lecture themes are partially in process of planning, partially already fixed:

'Workers settlement construction in the USSR'
'Garden cities or skyscrapers?'
'Standardisation and mechanisation in construction'
'N.O.T. in construction'
'Architecture and engineering'
'Marxist method in the study of architecture'.

The most interesting element in our activity is the work on design of the building for Perovsky Theatre-Club.

The administration of the club of railway workshops in Perovo approached the architectural *kruzhok* with the proposal to set up a competition amongst students for design of the theatre-club, to include accommodation for a theatre of 1000 people, a sportshall for 300 people, library-reading room, lecture hall, accommodation for evening classes and theatre *kruzhok* activities etc.

The competition brief was linked to the 4th course of the architecture department and is being carried out as school work with students being supervised by professors. Twenty-five people are working on projects for it, and six money-prizes have been announced.

After the jury scrutiny of the projects we propose to have an exhibition of them in Perovo.

The Perovo workers will have their own representatives on the jury in order to express their judgement on which are the best projects.

This work has a series of positive aspects: the fact of a concrete task, concrete local conditions, and the fact it is definitely intended to built a building to the winning design for spring of this year, obligates people to adopt a more responsible and careful attitude to the working out of the design from the students' side, and to more attentive scrutiny of the schemes by the professors.

ЖИЗНЬ ВУЗОВ

The exhibition is also of interest as it creates a direct link between designers and client – the working mass. It will provide a check on how far the project answers the concerns of the working people in architectural respects, and how far they in their turn are able to raise their own understanding of architecture.

In concluding this survey of the work of the architectural *krukhok* in MVTU, it has to be said that although its work is still weak and small, it is genuinely the collaborative work of students. As such it has set itself the task of deepening its members' knowledge of architecture, and thereby advancing the school's aim of producing qualified specialists. It helps the development of people who in future may contribute to the school as research colleagues and makes some attempts to link the whole school closer to industry, and to make more direct links between the proletarian student body and the working population as a whole in creative work on architecture.

A. M.

Doc. 25

STUDENT SOCIETY, INDUSTRIAL BUILDING DEPARTMENT, FACULTY OF CONSTRUCTIONAL ENGINEERING, MVTU
SA, 1926, no.5-6, p.141

The *kruzhok* is a voluntary research society of students which aims to reinforce and extend work in the school through deeper study of: industrial processes; the latest construction methods and their applications in factory design; advanced methods of contemporary architecture as they assist in design of rational industrial buildings.

One aim is to make available literature, and despite problems in reliable supply of the latest Russian and foreign literature it has assembled an exceptionally valuable library of some one-thousand volumes ranging from structural theory to the fine arts. Journals received include *SA, The Building Industry* (*Stroitel'naia promyshlennost*), *Industriebau, Betona-Eisen, Stavba.*

At present the *kruzhok* is working with recent graduates on compiling a fundamental work on factory building design, under editorship of Prof.Kuznetsov, which will cover structural principles and building design as well as essential information on industrial processes themselves. The former part will derive from the lecture course Prof. Kuznetsov gave here in 1925-6. He has entrusted its editing to Ivan Nikolaev. Chapters on industrial processes come from relevant literature, prepared by A.S. Fisenko and V.Ia. Movchan (metallurgical); I.S. Nikolaev (textiles); V.G. Kalish (silicates); B.N. Varbazin (paper); S.A. Maslikh (cement).

Recent lectures have included Prof. Kuznetsov on 'Building in America' after his recent visit; Prof. A.F. Loleit on his trip to Germany; I.S. Nikolaev on Spinning mill design, A.S. Fisenko on Iron foundries and student S.A. Varga 'On calculating statically indeterminate structural systems by the focuses method'.

Amongst excursions, we have visited numerous industrial complexes in Moscow and Leningrad: AMO, Hammer and Sickle, Red Putilov, Baltic Shipbuilders, the former Tsindel factory, Moscow timber processing plant no.1, the Triangle Brewery Works, and numerous chemical plants. Alongside these were numerous visits to museums and art collections in both cities.

The *kruzhok* envisages its future will be closely connected with OSA and the journal *SA.*

Doc. 26

MOISEI GINZBURG
COURSE PROGRAMME: 'THEORY OF ARCHITECTURAL COMPOSITION'
Vkhutemas, 1926, from the State Archives of Literature and Art, TsGALI, Moscow

I: The psychology of the creative process in architecture

1 The creative process as a result of the interaction between the external world of forms and the interior world of the artist. The three factors of the creative process. The nature of the influence from the external world of forms on the architect's creative process.
2 The material world and its interpretation by the architect. The limits of creativity. The character of need. Material possibilities in creative work.
3 The external world as submitted to the legitimate interests of the artist. Objective and subjective factors.
4 The creative personality. The psycho-physical element. The abstract and cognitive element. The emphasis on abstract beauty. The interior world of the artist as a spiritual world. The philosophical dimension of cognition. The abstract and formal field.
5 The evolution of architectural form. Its boundaries, aesthetic concerns and decorative character. Creative conception and material realisation.

II: Rhythm as the essence of architecture

1 The cosmic and universal character of rhythm. Active and dynamic rhythm, static rhythm.
2 The rhythm of a closed architectural form. Repetition and alternation. Harmony. The rhythm of symmetry. Arhythmia.
3 The rhythm of an architectural grouping of spatial forms. The quantitative influence of symmetry. Integration of the rhythm. Rhythms. Rhythms of progression and unifying rhythms. Architectural details as rhythmic sequences. Partial rhythms.
4 Mastery of rhythm. The mathematical essence of rhythm. Rhythmic modules and harmonic modules. Harmony.
5 Attempt at systematising rhythm. The transcription of rhythms.

III: Architectural processes

1 **Mass and the decorative element.** The origin of mass. Its relationship to organic structure. Its relation to the specific aesthetic solution of the problem. Subdivision of the mass. The decorative element.
2 **The fundamental laws of rhythmic composition of masses.** Vertical and horizontal forces. Collision of these forces and the various principles this generates: monumental, harmonious, rhythmic, picturesque. The vertical enlarged towards the base. Forms which tie space together: the parallelogram. Rounded forms: cylinder and cone. Complex forms.
3 **Organic, aesthetic and decorative styles.**
4 **The problem of monumentality.** Sense of scale. Absolute measure. Theory of contrast. Massiveness. Textural treatment of walls. The use of illusory masses. The law of symmetry. Unity of the design, the coherence and limits of subdivision. Unity in the vertical development. Unity in the horizontal development. Sensation of calm.
5 **Harmony.** The concept of harmony. The value of modulation of forms. Law of relationship of building elements: geometrical and numerical rules. The rule of three, rule of simple numbers, 'pure' relationships, law of the Golden Section. Law of similar forms. Interconnection of forms and their independent values. Perfection of details.
6 **Rhythm.** The element of movement. The character of movement. The unity of rhythm across the space of an opening and in the mass of a solid wall. The rhythmic value of the column, pillar and pilaster. Accessories of rhythm. Horizontal and vertical rhythm. The development of problems in rhythm and their complexity.
7 **Picturesque expression.** The concept of pictureque expression. Force and power in the action. Indeterminacy. The absence of boundaries and limits. Fortuitous elements. Optical symmetry and asymmetry. Richness of subdivisions. The value of light and shadow. Lighting. Choice and character of mouldings. The profile of the cornice. Emphasis.
8 **The simultaneous solution of several problems**. Monumental rhythm. Picturesque monumentality. Picturesque rhythm. Harmony.
9 **Sculpture, painting, decorative and applied art.** Their roles in the resolution of architectural problems.

IV: Practical exercises related to the theory of architectural composition

1 **Monumentality.**
Study from examples: Egypt; antique Greece; the Quattrocento.
Independent compositions: a) Solution on a planar surface, b) solution in volume; c) solution of the ensemble (a facade, a decorative wall), the architecture of monuments, town squares, streets and towns.
2 **Harmony.**
Study from examples: Greece, Cinquecento.
Independent compositions: Three exercises.
3 **Picturesque expression.**
Study from examples: Italian Baroque; European drawings; rococo.
Independent compositions: three exercises.
4 **Horizontal rhythm.**
Study from examples: Venice; Neo-Classicism; Ledoux.
5 **Horizontal and vertical rhythm.**
Study from examples: Chaldean architecture; Gothic architecture; Modern architecture.
Independent composition: three exercises.

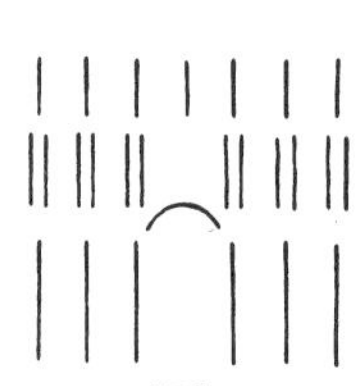
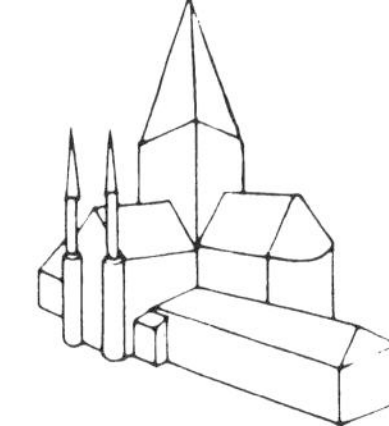
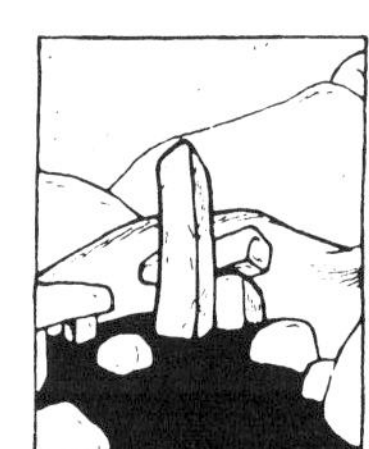

Sketches by Ginzburg 'to illustrate relevant features of the monuments concerned', from his Rhythm in Architecture, *1923. He apologises that current exigencies prevent him using photographs.*

Doc. 27

ACADEMIC CONFERENCES IN THE VKHUTEMAS

SA 1926, 5-6, pp.135-7

'In November each faculty in the Vkhutemas had a conference and set itself the following aims:

1 to establish direct links between the school and its main 'consumers', ie the state economic organisations and soviet society;
2 to sort out the faculty's own programme;
3 to take note of practical shortcomings in their training of specialists and to discuss proposals for correcting the teaching programme appropriately, and to look at the ideological make-up of their curriculum.

The conference in the Architecture Faculty took place on Thursday 18 November.

The first session attracted 70 percent of those invited. Vkhutemas Rector P.I. Novitsky was elected chairman and spoke on the change taking place in the social context of our lives, with its requirement that we give form to the new way of life and solve architectural tasks of a vast scale in the fields of **social, industrial and housing construction.**

Dean of the Architecture Faculty I.V. Rylsky then reported on the academic life of the faculty and on the structure of the curriculum. He noted that of the 70 students who have left the school in the three graduation classes completing their whole course since the Revolution, only one has remained on the unemployment list at the Labour Exchange – which shows that architects emerging from here really are being trained to meet today's practical requirements.

Academician **A.V. Shchusev** spoke in his lecture of the opposing views current with us today about the architect's proper role. The first view holds, he said, that the architect must be an engineer, since the economic condition of the country does not permit us luxuries, and so any elements of decoration or 'beauty' must be regarded as superfluous to the tasks of construction.

The second maintains that the architect's role is precisely to embellish the constructive scheme worked out by the engineer, but this requires supplementary means which at present time we do not have.

Both these opinions, he said, are unfounded, as the correct view is that an architect's work must always correspond to the economic solution of the task. In organising space, which is the main task of the architect, it is necessary to have the capacity to think spatially, and that is what permits the architect at all times to be become the organiser of construction. A good solution is also a beautiful solution, since beauty is inseparable from the right spatial and volumetric solution of the task. Also inalienably beautiful is our conception of the joy of life to which humanity is aspiring, and it must always be one of the fundamental tasks of architecture to satisfy this aesthetic sensibility of humanity.

The second speaker was Professor **N.V. Dokuchaev**, who spoke about the organisation of courses in the theory of architecture, and of the research institute. Points were made during the discussions by the representatives of **AKhRR** [Association of Artists of Revolutionary Russia, a doctrinaire socialist-realist organisation, CC], of **Asnova** and **OSA**.

Architect **Sukhanov**, speaking in the name of **AKhRR**, concentrated his criticism on the ideological line of **Vkhutemas** architecture, being convinced of the necessity to return to the classic traditional models.

The **Asnova** representative, architect **Lamtsov** said that architecture has a right of existence since it is not something that costs a lot of money. Architects Burov and Kornfeld gave greetings to Vkhutemas from **OSA** and the journal ***SA***, noting the vast revolutionary role of **Vkhutemas** in creating a new understanding of architecture.

The second day was devoted to work of two sections, on academic aspects of both artistic and technical sides of the curriculum, hearing lectures and preparing resolutions on them. The technical section examined the curriculum in detail, and found it in general to correspond to the faculty's requirements. It noted the necessity for strengthening the use of seminar and laboratory sessions in a number of subjects.

The sections did not support the view of comrade **Bekker**, the representative of **Glavprofobr** [Chief Committee for Professional and Technical Training], who in the first plenum had proposed a significant reinforcement of the faculty's technical curriculum.

The contemporary condition of technology forces the technologist to pursue the path of a broader scientific differentiation, advancing both the organisational methods and the practical work.

The second plenum adopted all proposals of the scientific and technical sections without discussion, including the resolutions on the lectures of professors **Rylsky** and **Lakhtin** in the first plenum and of Professor **Ladovsky** on tasks of research institute being established in the faculty. Also accepted without discussion were the arguments of Professor **A.A. Vesnin**'s lecture on the programme for teaching freehand drawing and sketching (*risovanie*) in the faculty. This posed in a new way the problem of an all-round development of spatial thinking in the students and of mastering the methods of perception and communicating volume, surface, colour, form. It offered a means of studying the particularly important question of the connections between internal arrangements of objects and the forms expressing this structure externally. In a teaching structure of the kind he proposed, this sort of drawing becomes an inseparable part of architectural education.

Also accepted without discussion were resolutions on the lecture of Prof **L.A. Vesnin**, on methods of systematically linking tasks set in the faculty with real problems being addressed by various state economic organs. The work already done up to now on such tasks convinces us of the realism and appropriateness of this method of working, which ought to be applied more widely. In the second plenum as in the first, discussion also focussed on questions of the ideology of contemporary architecture, in this case in relation to the lecture of professors **Krinsky** and **Dokuchaev** on methods of teaching on the 1st and 2nd years, in the Faculty's Basic Course, and of linking the programmes of these years to the work of students in the 3rd year. At the present time the teaching on the first two years is conducted by architects who are members of **Asnova**. Their teaching method is based on studying form from the point of view of its independent existence and perception. The result of this is to isolate form from the functional aims of the object being designed and from its constructive and technical essence. In reality the study of 'foundation disciplines' of volume, space, colour, mass, weight, scale etc, leads to complete abstraction and is perceived by the students as canons of a new metaphysical understanding of space quite removed from real life.

OSA members who spoke in the discussion contrasted this method of abstract formal study to the method of building up a design organically on materialist principles, i.e. the method of functional thinking, which establishes elements of the form in response to specific concrete preconditions.

Only under these conditions can we eliminate that gulf of which the lecturers were speaking, between the first two years' courses and the later ones.

Ia. A. Kornfeld

CONFERENCE IN THE FACULTY OF WOOD- AND METAL-WORKING

This faculty's conference was devoted to rethinking its aims in the light of the fact it constitutes an entirely new phenomenon in Soviet technical and artistic education. It has no past. Here everything has had to be built up from first principles. The problems of rationalisation and materialisation of artistic work find their practical realisation here. On the one hand the faculty must train artist-constructors (*khudozhniki-konstruktory*), the shapers of objects for our new public and personal lives, and on the other hand, it has simultaneously to train a new kind of engineer specialised in the equipment (*armatura*) of everyday life, who fundamentally understands the organisation and rationalisation of production.

This conference decisively dissociated itself from the old traditions of the Stroganov College, manifested in the advocacy of hand labour of the old, artisan, applied-art kind.

RESOLUTIONS

The First Academic Conference of the Faculty for Wood and Metal-Working, having heard lectures by the Dean, the Academic Secretary of the Faculty, by professors and teachers, affirms:

1. The correctness of the faculty's aspiration to give artistic and technological form to concrete requirements of everyday life, in:

a the organisation and equipping of the dwelling and of buildings for public and community purposes;

b the organisation of public places (streets, squares, public gardens);

c the organisation and equipping of accommodation serving transport, and also the means of transport and other objects of material culture.

2. The correctness of the posing of research tasks in the cross-section of the faculty's aspirations.

3. The correctness of the curriculum plan and the methodological structure of the faculty's work.

4. The significant difficulties encountered by students in getting through and mastering the curriculum, as a result of the inadequacy of materials and equipment available to both students and the faculty.

5. The unplanned and inappropriate composition of the student body that enters the faculty.

6. Their progress in the constructive part of the curriculum is adequate, but as far as the technical part is concerned it is not fully satisfactory as a result of:

a the constant changes caused to the academic life of the faculty by Glavprofobr;

b the erroneous time-budgeting done by Glavprofobr and the inadequate time allowed in that for technical disciplines;

c the qualititative and quantitative inadequacy of the old-dated equipment in the workshops;

d the inadequacy of the summer period of practical experience as training in mastery of industrial processes;

e the lack of laboratories and class rooms. Also the lack of the necessary basic equipment and supplies.

НА ФАКУЛЬТЕТЕ ОБРАБОТКИ ДЕРЕВА И МЕТАЛЛА

КОНФЕРЕНЦИЯ ВО ВХУТЕМАСЕ

Doc. 28

Lightweight lamp, Anton Lavinsky, *before 1925;*
Folding chair, Boris Zemlianitsyn *in Lissitzky's studio. 1927-8.*

CONSTRUCTIVISM IN THE EQUIPMENT OF DAILY LIFE
SA, 1926, no.2, inside cover

КОНСТРУКТИВИЗМ В АРМАТУРЕ ПОВСЕДНЕВНОГО БЫТА

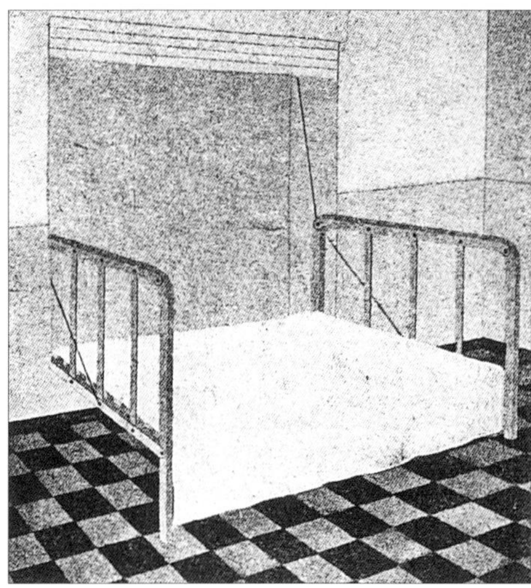

Folding bed, by Constructivist Sobolev, Vkhutemas.

A metal bed. Besides the basic framework of the bed, the design has a wire net to carry the mattress which is attached to the end springs of the metal frame. These springs can be tightened up with a special key in one of the end frames.

The bed closes up with the help of a weight on a wire passing over a pulley of small radius, which means it can be lifted with the minimum effort, to fold away into the thickness of the wall, in the wall-niche. The depth of this niche is forty centimetres. The bed itself and the bedclothes are ventilated through ventilation channels within the niche. During the day the niche is covered over with venetian blinds.

The convenience of such a bed lies in the fact that:
1) it occupies no space in the room during the day,
2) is easily folded away and
3) it consists of extremely simple structural elements.

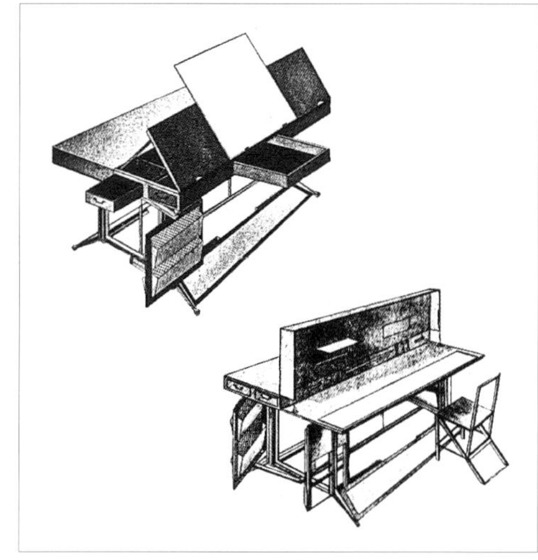

Multi-purpose table, by Constructivist Morozov, Vkhutemas.

A table for writing, technical drawing and eating. Four folding chairs store in the lower part, alongside folding pockets for storage of magazines, papers etc. One half of the table-top lifts up, along with its end elements. When vertical, it exposes the eating surface on which there is a movable table runner in slots (table cloth). In the raised vertical board are folding shelves; below that are hooks and straps to hold dinner plates or tea-service. When the upper surface is lowered again it covers the dining table without touching the dishes, and its upper surface can be used for working on. The second half of the table-top lifts about a hinge along the front edge and can be used at any slope for drawing. The table has a series of drawers for storing drawings, working materials and general possessions. The table legs are on balls and the whole table can be easily moved and entirely dismantled.

Doc. 29

GEORGI KRUTIKOV
THE ARCHITECTURAL RESEARCH LABORATORY IN THE ARCHITECTURE FACULTY OF THE VKHUTEMAS-VKHUTEIN

Report on its first two years by Ladovsky's assistant in the Lab's operation. Stroitel'naia promyshlennost', 1928, no.5, pp.372-5

Psychotechnics, having established methods for the professional selection of workers for physical and mental work, is conquering ever new fields of application. America, where psychotechnics was born and developed, uses it widely to establish the so-called 'psychological profile' of talents at entry to University. Experience has shown the accuracy and relevance of these experiments. In the USSR, psychotechnics has penetrated into diverse fields, amongst them the academic life of certain Higher Education establishments (VUZi), having established a scientific method for selection and for assessment of progress.

Up till now we have felt very acutely the absence of any sort of scientific approach in the determining of aptitude for those entering architectural higher education. The existing view, which holds that capacities in drawing define capacity for art, and hence also for architecture, has to be regarded as entirely without foundation. The capacity to organise spatial forms is absolutely not connected directly with capacities to depict in a fine-art manner on a plane. Suffice it to recall, that the majority of sculptors are not very good at drawing. The strangeness of this view has its roots, certainly, in the false view of what architectural education should consist of, which was current in our recent past. If a correct definition of the concept 'architect' could be established it would naturally be reflected in the quality of production of the individual – and hence on the architecture.

The Architecture Faculty of Vkhutein, having organised a laboratory for scientific investigation of questions of architecture, has set off on the path that was long ago identified and its first results in this field are to be welcomed.

The architectural Research Laboratory with its attached Architectural *kabinet* began work in the last year. Both undertakings, being on the one hand supplementary academic research units in the Institute, also have an importance as independent scientific institutions.

The fundamental task of the Vkhutein Architectural Laboratory is the creation of a scientifically-founded and experimentally-proven basis for architectural questions that could supplement the existing methods which depend on individual intuition.

The programme of the laboratory falls into three groups of questions. To characterise these I quote some of the most interesting questions they tackle.

GROUP 1: Questions of the analysis of elements of architecture:

a) study of the effect of elements of architecture (form, colour, volume, space etc) on the psyche;

b) the influence of the mutual interactions of the elements of architecture (for example, form and colour; colour and space and so on);

c) multi-faceted working out and experimental verification of spatial disciplines.

GROUP 2: Questions establishing the links between architecture and the social factors of the way of life, as well as technical and economic factors:

a) architectural sociology, architectural form and its surroundings, architecture and the new way of life, etc;

b) the functional method of thinking in architecture and evaluation of it;

c) the interactions of ideas of progressive architecture and progressive technology;

d) criticism of the technical norms operating on the architect;

e) architectural standards;

f) N.O.T. in the creative work of the architect and the techniques of architectural designing.

GROUP 3: Questions of pedagogy and psychotechnics

a) psychotechnics of the architect;

b) working out of rational methods of teaching architectural design in contemporary architectural schools.

As a consequence of its location in the Institute the Laboratory has concentrated its attention first of all on questions that are closely involved with the life of the architecture school. This means above all questions of psychotechnics and the architect, the explanation and evaluation of his professional capacity (Group 3).

The photographs reproduced here show a group of devices constructed by Professor Ladovsky for measuring the capacity to estimate dimensions by sight [*izmerenie glazomera – mer* = measure; *glaz* = eye, CC].

As an example of how these devices work let us examine one of the methods of analysing and measuring architectural capacities.

The simplest of the devices in this group is the ***Liglazometr*** [literally linear sight measure, CC] a device for measuring the visual capacity to measure distance as a linear dimension. This consists of a smooth flat baton, freely suspended in space (Fig.1). With the help of a slide which moves along this ruler, the person being investigated divides the given length. The reverse side of the baton being like a ruler with a scale, it indicates to the researcher what the error in linear dimension was in centimetres. As a result the percentage error is

Figs.1 & 2: Liglazometr, Ploglazometr. Fig.3: Oglazometr. Figs.4-5: Uglazometr. Fig.6: Prostrometr.

determined.

The ***Ploglazometr*** [lit: plane sight measure, from *ploskost'*, plane], is a device for measuring visual capacity in relation to planar dimensions, and the ***Oglasometr*** [from *ob"em*, volume] is a device for measuring visual capacity in relation to volumetric quantities. These give the possibility to determine the degree of error of the eye in division or comparison of planar and volumetric quantities, as embodied in diverse forms like a square, a circle a sphere or a cone.

In the *Ploglazometr* (fig.2) the moving element is a piece of glass with lines on it. In moving the glass around, these lines cut off a certain portion of a planar figure located under the glass. The scales are then folded back to indicate the degree of precision [in estimating how much was cut off].

The moving element of the *Oglazometr* (fig 3) is the surface of water filling this or that given volume. The water is poured from a graded cylindrical vessel which thus forms a kind of scale, measuring cubic centimetres, and giving the possibility to determine the degree of precision in this case. The pouring and control is conducted by means of a system of rubber hoses and taps.

The last device in this group is the ***Uglazometr*** [from *ugol*, corner or angle, CC], in figs 4-5, which measures the accuracy of the eye in its capacity to estimate angles, and also the verticality and horizontality of lines.

'The main parts of the device are a circle which rotates in the vertical plane on which is marked a straight line, and a hanging arrow line a plumb line on the back side. Rotation of the circle makes it possible to set up a line at any chosen inclination, with the hanging arrow and the reverse side of the circle, which has a scale with graded divisions, give the possibility to determine the degree of error.

The work with the devices which I have described, measuring the visual capacities, gives an example of the sort of measurements of spatial quantities that can be made, these being far from the only examples. I will mention also a means of measuring and making a quantitative comparison of positive and negative solutions, applied by the Laboratory for measuring the feeling for spatial imagination and the feeling for relationships.

In investigating any of these more complex capacities, they need to be broken down in advance into a series of simpler component elements, that are susceptible to quantitative measurement. In this direction we are conducting investigations into the feelings for architectural composition.

The first step is to set up a method for measuring capacity for spatial combinations, as one of the basic elements of architectural composition. In this process the psychotechnical method is preceded by application of special formulae operating on the basis of the theory of unions [*teoria soedinenii*].

Without dwelling on the details of this latter work, which would require the space of another article, I just mention one of the questions which arise in connection with it, namely the possibility for establishing the links between the selection of architectural elements or compositions, and public emotional concerns.

Everything that I have mentioned in the line of methods and means of breaking down and measuring the professional capacities of the architect has been discovered by the laboratory, and is being developed further in its present practical application towards creating systems of psychotechnical selection of students entering the architecture faculty of Vkhutein.

But apart from this, they can also serve to establish systems for rational development of the architect's professional capacities, by working out training exercises for those areas where he is backward.

Finally, by studying the psychotechnics of the architect, by measuring his capacity, we we also find ourselves unwittingly moving along the path to also assessing actual designs from the point of view of their architectural qualities.

'Thus from questions of evaluating architectural capacities we move on to assessment of architectural projects and actual buildings, to questions of perception and to questions of public psychology, i.e. to working out questions in the first and second groups of our programme.

In this direction very little has so far been done, and the work has a somewhat disparate character. However we must also note a series of successes on this path. By means of a survey and special questionnaire, i.e. by the psychoanalytic method, a study is being conducted of the architectural viewer, or more precisely, of the architectural consumer, in a series of different levels of soviet society, eg. workers, students in workers' preparatory faculties (*rabfaks*)of higher education, ordinary students in HE, local administrators etc.

The Laboratory is also conducting experimental verification of the spatial disciplines that are taught in the Basic Course of the Architecture Faculty at Vkhutein. Figure 6 shows another device constructed by Professor Ladovsky, the ***Prostrometr*** [*prostranstvo* = space, CC]. Its purpose is to make possible a wide range of experiments, aimed at manifesting the laws of perception of spatial relationships. Built on the principle of contrasts, the device consists of systems of hanging and inclined planes, intersecting each other and able to be set at angles, two of them having the capacity to hang vertical like plumb-lines. All this taken together gives the possibility to locate formal objects in diverse positions in space, and to experiment with them widely. A special apparatus of binoculars controls the angles and areas of vision of the person being tested.

Doc. 30

NIKOLAI KRASILNIKOV PROBLEMS OF CONTEMPORARY ARCHITECTURE

Final diploma project in Alexander Vesnin's studio in Vkhutein, 1928 SA, 1928, no.6, pp.170-6

'In order to really know an object, it is necessary to comprehend, to study all sides of it, all its internal and external connectivities.' *Lenin*

It is necessary for every specialist field to pursue and elaborate the implications of this proposition.

My initial premises:

1 The environment in which an organic body exists has an influence upon its form. [NOTE: The published text here does not actually say *formo-obrazovanie*, 'form', but *farmo-obrazovanie*, which would be a slightly idiosyncratic word for 'chemical composition'. The first seems more likely to have been intended, although either would have meaning here, and in *SA* misprints are very rare. CC].

2 The forms of the various parts of the organic body are determined by their functions. Thus in a tree the forms of the root, the trunk, and the leaves are determined by the purposes they serve.

3 To put it mathematically, the form of every body is a complex function of many variables (and the concept of form embraces the internal structure of the body matter).

4 A scientific theory of the design of form can be developed through the dialectical method of thinking, with the application of mathematical methods of analysis; analysis, that is, which uses the infinitesimal quantities of analytical geometry and the differential and integral calculus, and the theory of probability and mathematical statistics.

5 A theory of the design of architectural form must be based on the physical, mechanical, chemical, and biological laws of nature.

6 Socialist construction is unthinkable without solution of economic aspects of the problem such as would yield the maximum economic effect in the very broadest sense. So the constructional economics of a building for human work or habitation must be measured in terms of:

1 the material resources expended in erecting and running it;

2 wear (amortisation) and repair of the building;

3 the time expended by people on all forms of movement in and around it;

4 impairment of the health of individuals, which depends on the extent to which the sanitary-technical norms and the laws on safety at work and leisure are observed; and

5 the working conditions which would promote an improvement in the productivity of labour in general and mental work in particular, or in the conditions for leisure.

In present Soviet circumstances, the achievement of maximum constructional economics is also a vital necessity for the successful realisation of socialism.

Architects are atavistically following the work methods of a thousand and more years ago.

To us, the creative process of the designer appears an inscrutable business, full of mysterious and intensely individualistic characteristics.

Contemporary architecture is a blind alley, because it is not based upon a precise, scientific method.

Within the limited compass of the present article I am trying, through mathematical analysis, through use of the theories of limits and mathematical statistics, and mathematical maxima and minima, to draw some conclusions about the laws and conditions to which architectural form is subject.

This is a question as yet hardly broached by scientific thought. The postulates which I list below, and the mathematical derivation of architectural form which I am putting forward, represent no more than a statement of the problem.

Buildings for any site must be so arranged as to observe certain conditions, namely:

1 normal day-lighting and sun penetration;

2 normal wind-exposure of the walls and through ventilation ol buildings in the whole town;

3 convenient links between individual buildings and with the periphery. The buildings must be so grouped in one organic whole that they achieve maximum density for the given area of the site. In arranging the buildings in space (on any given site), their form must be sketched out in accordance with the functions and capacities of the buildings, and standards must be established by which to operate in grouping the buildings. The form of each building must be solved for:

1 convenience of internal connections;

2 lighting of the internal accommodation;

3 ventilation of the accommodation and streamlining of the walls;

4 thermal insulation: here it is always necessary that the volume of building, the quantity of materials expended, and the surface area of the building, be as small as possible. On the other hand, the norms for lighting, ventilation, and relative positioning of the accommodation will vary with the building's purpose.

Through plotting maxima and minima in relation to each of these factors, we should arrive at that building form which diverges least from them (recalling that we have to find the building arrangement which gives the town the maximum built volume on its site area). In practice it will be necessary to find the maximum built volume in relation to each of these factors individually, taking into account specific features of the building and its proposed use.

The technical possibilities, that is the structural form, the building materials, the condition and quality of the ground, all the preliminary, technical and economic investigations of the town etc, must be examined with a view to minimising the aggregate costs of constructing and using the building. In the end we shall arrive at the solution which is most economic overall, diverging as little as possible from the optimum for each factor, and this will then be the solution which is most rational for that particular case.

The problem that the designer will have to face first is that of arranging the units of accommodation so that their inter-connections and links with the street will be as convenient as possible; that is to say, so that the amount of time expended in all forms of movement will be minimal.

As an example through which to investigate this problem let us take a building with one central entrance and find conditions under which the time wasted on operations of this kind will be minimum (but the method would be the same for a building which had several entrances).

In any building of a certain size, people will circulate both vertically, in lifts, and horizontally, in corridors. Taking various plans, and establishing the functional relationships between the total amount of time spent by people on movement and the distances covered by them in that time, we shall find the most favourable plan with mathematical precision.

We examine first a cylindrical building, taking as variables:

S – the total amount of time taken to distribute people to their work places,

N – the number of floors,

R – the radius of the base of the cylinder, and as constants:

m – the number of people,

a – the number of occupants per square metre of the building,

d – the height of the floors in metres,

K_I – the speed of movement of the lifts in metres per second,

K_2 the speed of movement of a person, horizontally.

For the cylindrical plan we get:

$$S=\frac{md}{2\ k_1}+\frac{6dm^2}{2a\ K_1\ \Pi R\,(R+6)}+\frac{12\ m}{AK_2\ \ (R+6)}\left[\frac{R^2}{18}+\right.$$

$$\left.+\frac{R}{2}+1\right],\ \text{где}\ R=-3+\sqrt{9+6_m\sqrt{a\,\Pi N}}$$

min получен графическим путем.

Для планов —, ⊥, +,

$$S=\frac{md}{2\ k,}(N+1)+\frac{m}{2\ k_2}\left(\frac{m}{NDa}+1\right);\ \text{min будет при}$$

$$N=\sqrt{\frac{mk.}{adDK_2}}$$

для плана +++

$$S=\frac{md}{2\ k_1}(N+1)+\frac{m}{2\ k_2}\left(\frac{m}{NDa}+1\right)+\frac{6m^2}{aD^2K_2N};\ \text{min будет}$$

$$\left(N=\sqrt{\frac{m\,K_1\,D+12mK_1}{adD^2K_2}}\right)$$

Let us take a building whose volume is one million cubic metres. Putting on the abscissa the number of floors, and on the ordinate axis the number of seconds expended by a person on movement then by differentiating the equations we build up curves for each plan individually. [In his plot, reproduced below, these are the five curves rising to the top right, CC.]

From the diagram it is clear that the cylinder will be the most rational solution, followed by **+++**, **+**, and finally, the rectangle [for which there seem to be two curves, CC]. However, the lighting and ventilation requirements of a building of institutional type and of this volume make the cylinder an inappropriate solution in practice.

Obviously the **+++** plan will give the best solution from the point of view of the flow diagram.

Thus we map out very schematically the plan of a building of this volume (were it smaller, a less complex form would be required). As the plan is further developed to take account of the institution's particular needs, this basic form will go through certain transformations.

In order to check the calculation on the minimum surface area of the building, I constructed appropriate curves upon those diagrams [the lower pair, CC]. As variables I took:

C – the total surface of the building,

Z – the height of the building, and as constants:

V – the volume of the building,

a – the depth of the building.

For the cylinder we have:

$$\text{Для цилиндра будем иметь: } C=\sqrt{V\Pi Z}+\frac{V}{Z}=$$

$$\frac{dc}{dz}=\text{o при } Z=\frac{\sqrt[3]{v}}{\sqrt[3]{\Pi}}$$

$$\text{для } —,\ +,\ +++,\ C=\frac{2v}{a}+2az+\frac{v}{z}=$$

$$\frac{dc}{dz}=\text{o при } Z=\sqrt{\frac{V}{2a}}$$

On the basis of these curves we can also state that:

1 the minimum amount of time required for movement and the minimum area of building surface occurs for the same heights of the buildings;

2 for a given height and volume of building, the minimum surface area of all the rectangular forms is the same, since all the curves coincide.

As has already been mentioned, there is another aspect of the project to be provided for, besides these two factors and the sanitary-engineering aspects which we have studied in solving the first task we posed. That is the constructional aspect.

The question of constructional economics is no less important than the question of convenience; indeed under our state of economic backwardness it is perhaps even more important.

Up till now, all economic calculations relating to building have been performed by imprecise and rule-of-thumb methods; by certain categories of specialists they have even been ignored.

Today, when rationalisation and a strict regime of economy are the most pressing tasks facing the building industry, a more scientific approach to these tasks is urgently required.

To my mind, the importance of applying mathematical analysis in architecture is incontestable. Through calculations such as those I have already outlined it can perform an enormous service.

What we are doing is to replace the habitual intuitive-graphic method of designing, which operates without any form of mathematical analysis or calculation, by the mathematical-graphic, on the basis of the dialectical method of thinking. Intuition is not eliminated

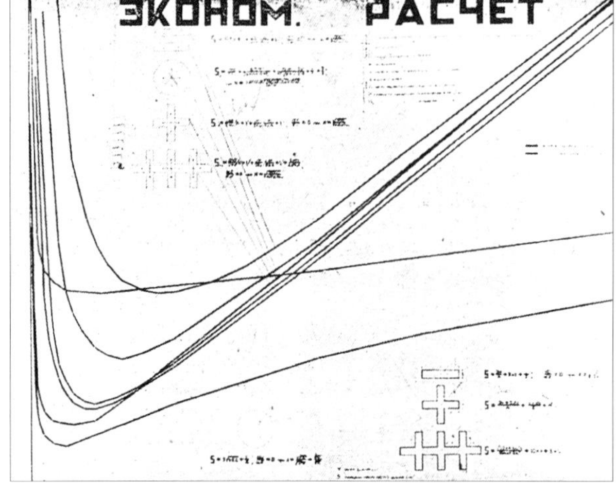

Figure 1: 'The economic calculation'.

*The upper bundle of curves represents the plotting of evacuation time **S** (on the vertical) against number of floors, **n**. The four plan-forms he considers are just visible under the letters KO, top left: from the top, they are **–**, **o**, **+**, **+++**.*

*In the lower pair, external area of building surface **C** (on the vertical) is plotted against building height, **z**, assuming constant total built volume. The upper curve represents the three plan forms **–**, **+** and **+++**, the lower one, the building of circular plan, **o**.*

thereby; it merely comes to occupy its proper place.

Calculations such as this aim to consider design questions in the light of science, to make them accessible to public discussion, and to harness the collective efforts of all specialists to working out their theoretical bases.

It has to be recognised that the business of building is the most backward of all branches of knowledge. There is no science behind the existing building norms; they are wholly empirical. When it comes to assessing architectural projects, the subjective approach holds sway; there exist absolutely no criteria for establishing the merits of one over another.

To illustrate a practical (if partial) application of this new method of designing, I will quote (in shortened form) my Vkhutemas diploma project for a socialist town as an administrative and trade centre and for a trades-union headquarters.

The socialist revolution that is impending in a whole series of countries has to create new economic and industrial planning organs to consolidate its revolutionary conquests. The new technical apparatus will have to be moulded to the socialist system of administration: that means large areas whose administration will have to be concentrated geographically in order to function properly, thus creating the 'socialist business centre'.

This new scientific and materialist system for organising human life not only gives a new form to the administrative apparatus, but demands in turn the appropriate equipment and set-up with which to operate; and these material requirements must in their turn be reflected in the architecture of buildings and in the plans of the towns.

Quite obviously, the whole look of a town that forms such a politico-economic centre and seedbed for socialist culture will differ significantly from that of the contemporary town which was generated and shaped by capitalism and its anarchically unplanned handling of the economy. The arguments of commercial speculation determined the plan and form of its buildings.

The towns that were centres of bourgeois culture are gradually losing their relevance for the new forms of life.

Either they must be turned into ancient monuments, or they must fully or partially replan themselves to take account of the economic, geographical and other conditions in which they now find themselves. There are a whole number of conditions which will require that there will be even more building of new towns in future than replanning of existing ones.

We have to look ahead to this, and to prepare for it. There will be both small settlements and large towns to be created. How to approach this problem?

It is certainly impossible to produce more or less precise plans for new socialist towns or settlements in the absence of a well defined brief. In the USSR we have only just embarked upon the building of socialism, while other countries have not yet turned that way. We have as yet no more than the rudiments of a prototype socialist economy, and even less of a culture.

But to us socialism is not a utopia; it is a reality towards which we are moving. The basic characteristics of a socialist economy and culture are clear, and can be specified in advance.

When bourgeois specialists draw or describe 'a town of the future' they become sunk in utopianism, eclecticism, and unreality, for they have no reliable materialistic base or starting point from which to work; if their intuitive guesses at the form of the future town ever prove at all accurate, it is only by chance. Their lack of any corresponding ideological aspirations wholly prevents them making realistic projects. ...

In conclusion I must say that the mathematicisation of architectural projects (in which this work does not pretend to any degree of finality), must be based on a mass of scientific research into such factors as the psycho-physical effect on the human organism of light, heat energy, the quality of air, of colour, space and form, amongst many other factors.

The successes of the last decade in mathematical statistics and analysis must herald their even further development in the future, and all such progress will greatly assist the solution of our architectural tasks.

Programme

The town is the centre of economic and administrative life for a large number of countries. The site set aside for it has a diameter of 2 km, and covers 314 hectares.

The permanent administrative work-force is 500,000, but at any one time there may be up to 150,000 delegates and visitors coming to attend congresses, conferences, and meetings of all kinds.

The town must provide the accommodation for these in the form of rooms and halls of various capacities and all the necessary auxiliary facilities. (The figures quoted here are nominal, since their accuracy does not affect the principles which I have developed in this work.)

ПРОБЛЕМЫ
СОВРЕМЕННОЙ АРХИТЕКТУРЫ

For reasons of space the full account of the design of the city, other drawings and the bulk of the mathematics have been omitted here. For enthusiasts the complete paper may be found in English translation in: C. Cooke 'Nikolai Krasil'nikov's quantitative approach to architectural design: an early example', Environment and Planning B, *1975, vol.2, pp.3-20.*

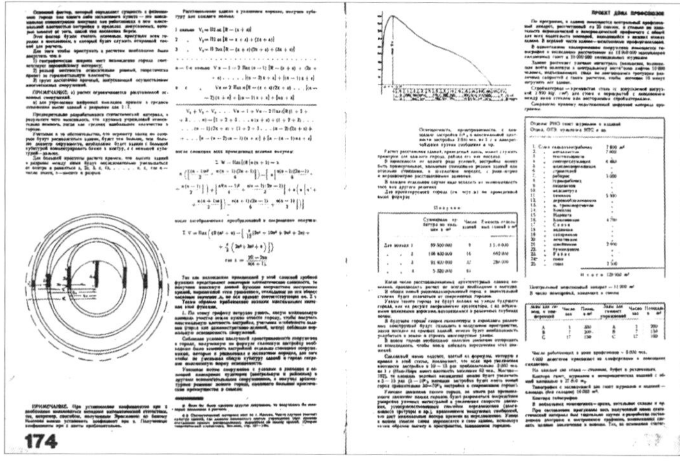

Two pages from publication of Krasilnikov's paper in SA *(1928, no.6). Left, p.174, with the plan and section of his new city, Figure 2.* Right, *p.175 with his graph, Figure 3, indicating the slight error in his calculations of total built volume against number of rings of building in his city.*

In Figure 2, the plan and cross-section of his town on p.174, Krasilnikov assumes that the total volume of building in the town will be distributed, as shown here, in continuous annular rings. He then calculates the number of rings, n, which will give him the maximal total volume of building, $\sum V$, on a site of given radius, R, and given the height and spacing constraints he chooses to adopt (this is the graph in Figure 3). Though the maximum volume appears to be achieved at about 15 rings, he takes the simpler case of 4 rings for his example. 'To provide the best possible ventilation of the town' he then breaks down the 'continuous rings' of building into 'freestanding structures', whose plan forms are based upon the lessons of his calculations on the efficiency of internal circulation and other factors in Figure 1. In the interests of day-lighting he arranges these buildings 'in a chequerboard manner'. Figure 4, right, then shows his Trades Union Headquarters standing astride one of the two inner ring roads.

Figure 3, the graph on p.175 above, is Krasilnikov's plot of $\sum V$, in millions of cubic metres, against n, the number of rings of building.

An independent derivation of the formula for $\sum V$ indicates that his algebra is correct. The unlikely-looking dip in his curve results from an error in his arithmetic. A recalculation of $\sum V$ suggests that the maximum in fact occurs not at 15 rings, but at around 10, and that the strange change of sign of the gradient around $n = 70$ is indeed fallacious, having been produced by Krasilnikov's excessively high value of $\sum V$ for $n = 90$.

This does not affect the originality of the work, but as I have commented on p.176, it is strange that neither he nor his more mathematical teachers in Vkhutein such as Professor Lakhtin were not also alerted to some discrepancy by this visual anomaly, either in the studio, or certainly before they published it.

The fact that they did not is a reminder that despite his references to Lakhtin's textbook on Distribution Curves, *and one Vikhlaev's* Outline of Theoretical Statistics, *Krasilnikov and his colleagues were operating very close to the limits of their mathematical knowledge.*

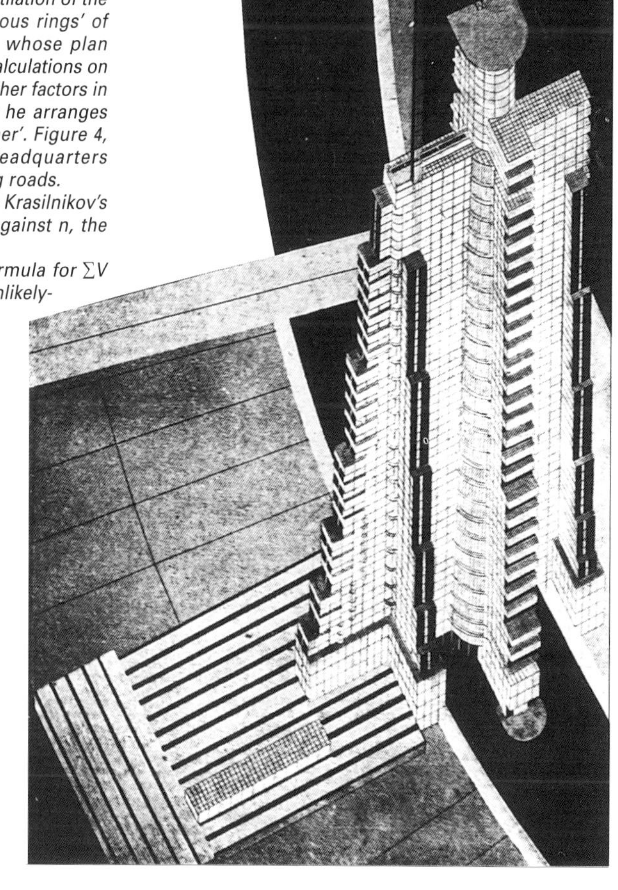

11: STATIC FORM OR DYNAMIC SYSTEM? RATIONALIST AND CONSTRUCTIVIST APPROACHES TO THE CITY

Modernism in architecture and urbanism is inseparably connected to its wider context of societal modernisation, and in this respect the situation of early twentieth-century Russia was very different from that of Europe.

At the turn of the century and throughout the 1920s, Russia was still in large measure a pre-modern society. Not until 1861, with the abolition of serfdom, had the vast majority of the population secured the possibility of free citizenship under the law, and only during the later years of that decade, almost a century after England, for example, had started on the same path, did industrialisation seriously take hold in Russia. The late arrival of the industrial revolution meant that its elements were not the organic products of an indigenous and widely permeating culture, but islands of imported modern technology in a broad ocean of genuinely medieval agriculture, transportation and building. Whilst industrial production was expanding faster in Russia during the 1890s than in any other country, arbitrary transport tariffs had still further exaggerated the irrationality of its distribution in relation to free-market principles, and its impact, in both negative and positive aspects, was extremely localised.

The relationship between industry and the overall pattern of urbanisation was equally different from the general pattern in Europe. The economic base of a great number of the largest towns was entirely agricultural, whilst the need for proximity to sources of raw material meant that most large-scale industry operated on isolated sites, surrounded only by hutted 'factory villages'. Middle-rank towns functioned on a mainly administrative base. Well laid out in the eighteenth century to Classical standard plans by the tsarist government, these were seen by early planners of the Russian Garden Cities movement as most advantageously spatious compared to their European equivalents.[1]

Between these provincial towns and the two alternate capitals of St Petersburg and Moscow, was a small group of provincial cities such as Riga, Odessa, or Kiev that were industrial, trading and cultural centres as well as nodes of government. All had populations of about half-a-million by 1914, but Moscow and St Petersburg were four times their size.

Seen in relation to the distribution of population and economic activity that was normal for Europe at that date, or at that level of industrialisation, these Russian patterns were severely skewed. An even more powerfully distorting factor was the Imperial Russian system of strict social ranks and censorship, which massively retarded the development of that free-ranging, free-experimenting bourgeoisie that was the main motor of societal modernisation elsewhere.

On the other hand, an indigenous class of great industrial millionaire dynasties had developed by the First World War, despite the fact that industrial capital had initially been largely foreign. When they fled after the 1917 Revolution, the industrial plants they left behind were amongst the best items of material infrastructure inherited by the Soviet government. But four years of civil war reduced most of that infrastructure to ruins. For the post-Revolutionary generation, therefore, 'industrialisation', was a mere dream, though one which their government swore to realise as the embodiment of its promise 'catch up and outstrip capitalism'. But modernisation of the urban fabric had even further to go to 'catch up'.

Before the war, Moscow and Petersburg had held all European records for their lack of sewage systems and piped water, and for the overcrowded living conditions of their working populations. When building activity resumed after 'ten years asleep' in the early 1920s,[2] Revolution, the Civil War and economic collapse had left most of the housing stock with no glass in its windows, dripping with moisture, and stripped of its floorboards for firewood, and public buildings were little better. Berthold Lubetkin lived through it and has left vivid descriptions of how:

> *'since the floor boards had been used for firewood we slept, wrapped in old newspapers, across the bare joists ... Water from the taps in the yard was fetched in an up-ended umbrella because there was no bucket. The heating system involved fetching a hot flat-iron from the House Committee in the basement and pouring water over it to produce steam [which had the added result of] steaming off the wallpaper.'* [3]

Coming from a wealthy and travelled pre-Revolutionary family, Lubetkin was entirely untypical of the young profession of the early Twenties. Amongst the avant-garde architects who represent Modernism in Russia, the Soviet-educated young, who formed the majority of the architectural avant-garde, had never seen 'a modern city' at first hand, and only very scantily in pictures. Direct experience of such an environment was confined to those who had travelled abroad before the Revolution, and in general only their teachers were old enough to have had that chance. Even fewer of these had been trained in analysis of the modern city. Only on the eve of the War had courses in 'town building' been launched in the Academy School of Architecture in Petersburg and in Kiev.[4] There was not even a consistent name for the activity which integrated social and technical concerns of 'public utilities engineering' – literally the 'arrangements for well-being' (*blagoustroistvo*) – with the formal or aesthetic concerns on which historical towns had developed as compositional 'ensembles'. Only slowly did the eventual term *gradostroitelstvo*, literally 'town-building' become standard vocabulary. Some European treatises had been imported: Baumeister, Stübben and Unwin were well known among specialists,[5] but these mainly served as tools for the radical activists who formed the 'urban movement' rather than as handbooks for any integrated profession. Thus 'the city' was a highly conflictual territory, and the profession of town planning as Europe or North America already understood it was so under-developed when tsarism collapsed that the young Soviet Union inherited hardly more than a handful of specialists capable of looking at urban form as a whole.

When the new Soviet government nationalised 'the land and all immovable property' on 26 October 1917, within days of taking power, it laid the foundations for a whole new conception of the built environment and of its coordinated management. Its 'Decree on land' declared 'the right to private ownership of land is abolished forever ... without any compensation'; 'land is no longer saleable, buyable, to be rented either by mortgage or any other form of alienation.' The same applied to property on that land: 'Land holdings and estates, as well as all crown, monastic and church lands with all their live and fixed inventory, buildings, and property attached to them' would now pass into hands of local political organs 'and become the property of the whole people'. Likewise: 'All mineral wealth in the land' such as 'ore, oil, coal, salt etc, and also timber and water resources having national significance, shall pass into the exclusive use of the state', smaller resources being 'handed over to local organs of government'. Control of land use was transferred to the state in its various local guises. 'All land', urban and rural, now became:

> *'part of a national land fund ... its distribution amongst workers to be conducted by local and central government bodies, ranging from the democratically organised and non-class-based [*bezsoslovnye*] village and city communes, up to central bodies of regional [*oblastnye*] government.'*[6]

The basis on which such distribution was to take place was another, and naturally more complex matter.

Under the influence of pre-war pioneers like Vladimir Semionov and Grigori Dubelir the new administration made laudable moves to establish planning offices and some basic norms for a more habitable urban environment.[7] However, with economic devastation and the chronic shortage of trained manpower, even these small-scale efforts at development control were doomed to be ineffective. More significantly for the future, it was no one's specialism or professional task to address the larger strategic issue of what the 'correct' city form should be for the new socialist form of society.

In this context the ideas of those middle-generation architects who led the avant-garde were naive, but they served at least to keep open this larger theoretical issue which had started to be debated in Russia in the later 1900s, not least under the impact of Ebenezer Howard and other theoreticians of the Garden City. By the time industrial reconstruction and economic management practice had reached a level where the Soviet government could start centralised planning, in the late Twenties, each of the two main avant-garde groups had pursued their own rather one-dimensional logic to the point of having a 'theory' for the Soviet city, and between these two, the conflictual situation of ten years earlier had become precisely replicated. Thus the Rationalists were preoccupied with the city as an object of the individual human-being's perception, to be read for its 'messages' about the larger social structure and appreciated for its aesthetic satisfactions. The Constructivists by contrast saw the city as a dynamic social and technological organism in which change must be embraced, but steered and harnessed to a larger social benefit than merely economic output.

In the Twenties that economic imperative of 'output' was state-driven. Before 1917 it was driven by an equally compelling ideology of entrepreneurial freedom. The effect on living conditions for the non-affluent and on the aesthetic coherence of urban form was equally devastating in both cases, and professional reactions amongst architects were polarised in the same way before the Revolution as they were by the end of the Twenties.

Central Moscow traffic c.1910. Typical scene by City Duma, just off Red Square: horse-drawn carts, taxis and a tram, which advertises Moscow's Scottish department store Muir & Mirrielees.

Red Square, if the industrial and building boom continued, from the series of popular postcards 'Moscow of the Future' published in 1913. View north towards Historical Museum (cf. p.205.

Pre-Revolutionary foundations

Before the Revolution, the 'aesthetic' view was represented most prominently by an influential Petersburg pressure group that was outraged by the desecration which bourgeois mercantile capital was wreaking on the Imperial classical city which they considered the heart and supreme embodiment of Russian high culture. The protagonists were members and colleagues of the courtly architectural dynasty of the Benois. Alexander Benois and his colleague the architectural historian and critic Georgi Lukomsky led the attack on this 'vandalism', in their own journals, the public press and at the Fourth Congress of Russian Architects in 1911. Elder brother Leonti Benois collaborated with engineers to demonstrate that there was a defence, in a 'Scheme for the replanning of St Petersburg'[8] This sought to accommodate commercial growth and increased traffic whilst preserving, even restoring, the propriety and hierarchy of scale of the classical city, whose focussed spatial structure embodied the Imperial order and 'infused the people with patriotic feelings and a love of their native town'.

The European planning texts which Benois' engineer collaborator Fedor Enakiev commended to his Congress audience are a significant selection. Thus his list of the 'extensive literature on the transformation of contemporary towns' that 'has emerged in Western Europe in recent years' comprised Raymond Unwin's *Town Planning in Practice*, Eugène Hénard's *Transformation de Paris*, but most significantly Emile Man's *L'Estetique des Villes* and Camillo Sitte's *Der Städtebau nach seinen künstlerischen Grundsätzen*. All these, said Enakiev, 'recognise the necessity to adapt our cities to the cultural conditions of today and its rapid changes', but with the same aim defined by Aristotle, that 'the city must be so designed that the citizen is happy and lives in safety.' With 'the aesthetics of cities' and 'city planning according to artistic principles' representing half the literature, the design priorities intended were clear.

This pressure group was professionally and socially influential, but numerically it was very small. The number of people seriously addressing the deeper structural and social problems of modernising Russia's cities was only slightly larger, but they were politically far more radical. They too had studied European developments attentively, but their reference points were more technical and more socially aware: Stübben and Baumeister in the first category, and Ebenezer Howard most prominently in the second. The most important architect-planner among the lawyers, doctors and economists on this front was Vladimir Semionov, not just for the breadth and balance of his pre-Revolutionary writing, but because by the mid-1920s he had become the USSR's most senior city-planner and remained so throughout the Stalin era. Indeed he led the work on Moscow's 1935 Plan which sought to integrate precisely these two dimensions of urbanism, technical modernisation and aesthetic composition, in response to the new and yet more powerful ideological pressures.

Semionov's pioneering book of 1912 provided Russia with her first indigenous town planning text, and the word in its title which English renders as 'town planning' was characteristically the socially and technically rooted term *blagoustroistvo*. Semionov's *The Planning of Towns* was published on his return to Russia after several years travelling around from a base in England, and provided the first systematic presentation of European technical experience and ideas in the Russian language. At the same time, however, it issued a firm warning that would be equally important when Russian 'national peculiarities' became Soviet 'differences from the West' a few years later. 'We are too different in natural conditions and in character to repeat European models without modification', wrote Semionov. 'We must work out a type for the Russian town, appropriate to our severe climate, to the spaciousness of our terrain, and to our national peculiarities.'[9]

Members of the socially-concerned planning movement like Semionov were already discussing the relative merits of dispersion versus concentration and their implications for future urban development. Many were persuaded that the future would see an 'inevitable' trend towards dispersion as a result of new technologies being applied to transportation, and Emile Vandervelde's book, *L'Exode Rurale et le Retour aux Champs*, which had a Russian edition in 1901, was commonly quoted in support of this argument. However the general conclusion for the more immediate future was that voiced by another Russian, M.A.Kurchinsky in his *Municipal Socialism and the Development of Urban Life* of 1907: 'Towns do not perhaps represent the last word in human culture; but the mass of people must, very probably, pass through the crucible of urban existence in order to be prepared for the better life.'[10]

Questions of the proper form of that 'urban existence' and its built environment were not seriously addressed at a public level until after the Revolution of 1917, although the building boom which seized Moscow just before the War did provoke attempts to imagine what 'modernity' might mean for them if the pace of growth should continue unchecked. A well known and remarkable example was the series of postcards widely distributed by one of the sugar conglomerates in 1913, showing Marinettian images of a 'Moscow of the Future' awash with modern transport on the ground, in the air and on various structures in between. Visually this was perhaps the most dramatic of such speculations. But Marx's insistence that 'Russia must not be deprived of the finest chance which history ever offered to a nation to avoid the misadventures experienced by capitalist regimes'[11] locked the country into a love-hate relationship with that Futurist technological dream.

The post-Revolutionary avant-garde was soon haunted by questions of whether that dream was appropriate for Soviet Russia. If it was, should it be embraced at the level of its forms and what they symbolised, or through analysis of its inner imperatives?

First steps towards a 'modern' scale for the inherited city

Against this historical background, the relative scarcity of urbanistic projects in avant-garde Russian work is readily explicable. The under-developed state of the USSR's urban fabric was another dimension to that technological backwardness which helps explain why 'the machine' was not just invoked philosophically as 'the spirit of the age', but was psychologically depended upon to effect miraculous transformations. It was reasonable enough to see mechanisation as the only means of effecting the vast physical modernisation which Russia required, let alone for delivering the promises of a socialist revolution. As Chapter 5 showed, it was that unique social and philosophical role which led the Constructivists, as the most analytical avant-garde group, to see its spatial logic as the historically 'correct' model for their approach to revolutionary building design.

The first avant-garde projects for urban intervention were in varying degrees unbuildable, but nevertheless were important steps in reevaluating the inherited capitalist prototypes. Amongst the earliest concepts was one from Alexander Rodchenko, as a member of the emerging group of Constructivist artists, in 1920.

Man's buildings had evolved from a generally pyramidal form to the cubic box, said Rodchenko, and in the present stage the pyramid should be inverted as a means to clear ground-space in the city whilst increasing the intensity of activity on a given ground area. Thus existing buildings would become the bases for a new species of architectural forms in the airspace above. 'All kinds of walkways and cantilevered roofs, light as bridges, all transparent and highly interesting from the aesthetic point of view', would create a new 'upper zone' for the city, with aerial transport providing for circulation.[12] The continuity with those postcard images of 'Moscow of the Future' is strikingly direct.

Amongst the emerging group of Rationalists, as the Constructivists' rivals, Semionov's injunction to treat capitalist models with caution seemed forgotten. To them in 1923 'modernity' meant only one thing: the form and drama of the skyscraper. No functional arguments were advanced, only such civic design factors as 'its role for orientation ... its effect in giving tone and form to a featureless square', legitimated by the formal precedent of towers in traditional Russian urbanism.[13]

It was to these Rationalists that the itinerant El Lissitzky allied himself, and his well known *Wolkenbügel* or Skyhook project for Moscow of 1923, later published in their journal, can be seen as combining elements of Rodchenko's concept with their vision of the skyscraper as formal orientation point for the citizen. The technical realism of the project reflected the fact that he designed it whilst in Germany, with help from a Zurich engineer, Emil Root. But at the same time those elements of Western experience that were useful had been sifted out from those inappropriate to Russia's social or technological circumstances. Hence the project is especially significant as representing an attempt to devise 'a Russian type'.

America, said Lissitzky, had turned 'the European horizontal corridor into a vertical lift-shaft', and he was now turning it back again by developing the upper floors of activity horizontally. By varying colour and form he developed his ring of six towers as a system of orientation points for the new Moscow citizen. (His full description is translated in Document 31). In the proletarian worker's name the Soviets had wrested ownership of the inner city core from those who had previously excluded him. This new openness would be manifested by a bold system of orientation points that empowered him to circulate in and around it with appropriate confidence. Over and above that, Lissitzky's towers were conceived as a re-scaling and restructuring device for the whole city in circumstances where 'our needs are no longer satisfied by the towns created before our day, but we cannot demolish and rebuild them overnight'. He explained that by locating these towers at street intersections around the Boulevard Ring: 'I have sought to give a new scale to the city: the individual today does not measure it by the cubit of his own arm, but by hundreds of metres'. At the same time, his thinking was focused on the inner pace of activity levels within the city and how these are spatially distributed. Economically, he said, 'the city consists of atrophying old areas and growing new ones'. Amongst the symbolically most important of the new ones were those associated with the new Soviet institutions of government and social administration such as he proposed should occupy the skyhooks. In implanting these nodes of intensive activity 'at critical locations', he explained, 'I want to deepen this contrast' between the old and the new social orders.[14]

As Lissitzky moved between Berlin and Moscow, between Rationalism, Suprematism and Constructivism, that same notion of 'misfit' between historic city and the new society's needs had been stressed the previous year within Russia itself, and not just as part of one design project, but as a highly politicised element in the new Constructivist theoretical programme. In his overtly and aggressively Marxist manifesto of 1922 entitled simply *Constructivism*, discussed already in Chapters 4 and 5, Alexei Gan identified the inherited urban fabric as an active impediment to the spread of the new ideology. 'As the material and technological organs of society,' he declared, 'the capitalist towns which we inherited are staunch allies of counter revolution ... By their small and awkward buildings, ... their cramped streets and squares ... they stubbornly obstruct even the most timid measures of revolutionary re-organisation.' Thus 'the planned reworking of the whole urban territory' was unavoidably to be 'one of the basic tasks of Constructivism'. But at the same time, he insisted, 'we must establish a scientific foundation for our approach'.[15]

As Chapters 5 and 6 have shown, it was in responding to this ideological insistence on 'a scientific foundation for our approach' that the Constructivist architects looked to the machine as an organisational model, both for the object being designed and for the design process itself. In relation to this specific issue of the city, just as for their development of the machine analogy, Moisei Ginzburg's *Style and Epoch* of 1924, their first architectural manifesto, moved them a little way beyond Le Corbusier's *Vers une Architecture*, but not very far. As a result of student years in Italy, Ginzburg was one of the select few in his generation who had known European cities in detail. He now described it as their collective task 'to formulate an adequate expression' for that 'sonorous ensemble of contemporary life' of which Marinetti had been shouting when Ginzburg himself was a student in Milan, which their colleague the poet Mayakovsky would shortly experience in America and report as current reality. Thus wrote Ginzburg:

'To feel the significance, the meaningfulness, of the sonorous ensemble of contemporary life, to be embraced by its joys and fears, its rhythm, its landscapes, its sky riddled with wires and hovering aeroplanes; to understand distance as it is broken down into fragments by the movement of the machine;

the street cut about with sharp silhouettes, a bridge and the minute specks of the pedestrians scattered upon it – to feel all this and to formulate an adequate expression of it, is the task of our contemporary creativity.' [16]

The romanticism of this passage is unusual in Ginzburg's writing, and can perhaps be read as the attempt precisely to communicate this experiential quality of the modern city to Russian colleagues who never experienced it for themselves. The etching by Edgar Norvert which he uses in the book to evoke 'a modern city' is a little heavy: Mayakovsky's description of standing 'On Brooklyn Bridge' the next year, 1925, came closer to his description in its depictions of 'rhythms' and a 'sky riddled with wires.'[17] If this image was stolid, the visual element of *Style and Epoch* as a whole, associating architecture with delicate French and Italian biplanes and triplanes, the racing circuit on the Fiat factory roof-top, steel bridges and trainsheds – even one battleship – must have come as an even greater shock to Ginzburg's Moscow audience than Corbusier's use of those images ever did in France.

Towards analysis

Looking for a means 'to build a bridge' between all this and revolutionary new buildings, as Chapter 5 has shown, Ginzburg presented the machine and the modern flow-line factory as prototypes for functional analysis and formal organisation in architecture, and potentially in urbanism.[18] A few years later, this analysis of the machine in terms of 'flow' and 'event' would serve the Constructivists equally well as a tool for restructuring the city. But early issues of their journal *SA* show that in 1926 they were still feeling their way towards such as analytical approach.

From the start they showed a scepticism towards skyscrapers that was unusual, given the hold which 'Americanism' had in some avant-garde circles. Perhaps this reflected influence from the commonsense attitude of their pre-Revolutionary professional forebears. William Brumfield has documented the equivocal attitudes of the pre-Revolutionary profession to American building's preoccupation with the 'colossal' and the 'fast'.[19] The scepticism of skyscrapers through fear of fire is an interesting reflection of this historic identification of fire hazards and density (see Chapter 7). It was however Corbusier whom the Constructivists thanked specifically for having shown them that the merit of Manhattan's form in accommodating 'the American tempo of life' in the vertical was matched only by the grotesque impediment it represented in the horizontal. Beyond that particular issue, the review of Le Corbusier's *Urbanisme* in *SA*'s very first issue, in 1926, explains their growing sympathy and admiration for him as the person who taught them to be critical analysts.

'In Vers une Architecture *... he opened our eyes to truths already existing but unrecognised. In* L'Art Decoratif *he showed us how machines ... have been gradually teaching us a new way-of-life entirely different from that of previous decades ... In* Urbanisme *however we see modernity as something already built, as a finished system. [We see how] our cities have got left behind by life; how the mechanisation of all forms of movement and public utilities has so changed the tempo of urban life that we can no longer fit ourselves into our streets.'* [20]

The reviewer was Boris Korshunov, one of Ginzburg's older teaching colleagues at MVTU (see Chapter 10). His conclusions echo the awareness of cultural and environmental differences that we observed before the Revolution. 'The whole book is full of crisp paradoxes and sparkling, very French ideas,' he says. However:

'For us, standing on the eve of a stormy period of growth in our towns and cities, this book has a very special importance. We too shall not cope without surgery in our large centres: our economic advantage is that we have only one-third the density of building that they have in European capitals.'

That same first issue of *SA* contained a review by Ginzburg himself of Erich Mendelsohn's photographic album *Amerika.*[21] Understandably, in view of his personal exposure to Western urbanity and its imagery, Ginzburg was able to take the material in his stride. Later, however, and most unusually, a second review of the book appeared by one of the younger Constructivists, Alexander Pasternak. Unusually for one so young, he too had had the opportunity to travel abroad. His father Leonid was a famous pre-Revolutionary portraitist, long-time professor at MUZhVZ, and Alexander with his brother Boris Pasternak, the writer, had accompanied their painter-father to Germany in the early 1920s.

Despite the absence of text, said Pasternak, the dramatically angled and therefore richly three-dimensional images in Mendelsohn's book enable us 'to draw conclusions for ourselves. Here the problem of the modern city thrusts itself forward at us.'

'In a simple collation of photographs you are suddenly hit by the realisation of an idea that was formerly only vaguely coalescing in your mind. In certain photographs in particular, the idea of the urbanistic city turns from

ИЗВѢСТІЯ
Центральнаго Исполнительнаго Комитета
и Петроградскаго Совѣта
Рабочихъ и Солдатскихъ Депутатовъ.
ДЕКРЕТЪ О ЗЕМЛѢ

'Dekret o zemle': *Decree on land, 26 October 1917, nationalising all land and real estate.*

Rodchenko, project for the 'upper zone' of the future city, 1920.

New York: illustration to Ginzburg's review of Mendelsohn's Amerika *in* SA*, 1926, no.1.*

Headline and illustration from Korshunov's review of Corbusier's Urbanisme, SA, *1926, 1.*

an abstract concept into a reinforced-concrete reality. And whereas the architecture of Ferris and others showed us individual skyscrapers, here the photographed results of the New York City Planning Commission's "Regional Plan" confirm the possibility of the urbanised city.' [22]

For many of the younger Constructivists this was plainly their first exposure to notions of the future city as a form of urbanism which had by-passed that *ville européenne de pierre* to which Le Corbusier was applying his surgery.

Back in the first issue of *SA*, Pasternak had already been trying to deduce something about the proper future shape of Soviet cities from a simple analysis of the forces creating the capitalist city, and perhaps it was he himself who insisted that *Amerika* should be reviewed a second time, in a more analytical fashion. Certainly his article is the first genuinely structural rethinking of city form we come across in the avant-garde literature. Though still essentially sculptural, it is the first example of observed relationships between politico-economic structure and urban form being reworked with new content at city scale.

We can only speculate as to whether Pasternak was familiar with gravity-model concepts as they had developed from Von Thünen, but it is an argument along these lines that he applies.

'We may draw an analogy between the physical magnet and the town, which is also a magnetic field and this gives it its characteristic distribution of forces. The magnetic poles of the city are its trading and administrative part, and the part given over to housing. Its natural development has proceeded in such a way as to make the former the heart, the core, and to spread housing quarters around the periphery through which the city connects to the countryside.

'The area of the centre is always small, but in cross-section it is the highest part. This is well understood in the West, but it is erroneous to consider, as their main theorists like Bruno Taut, Möhring and Berg do, that only this central area may contain high buildings. In fact they may happen wherever conditions are right in relation to the new principles of city planning, in the periphery as well as the centre.' [23]

It was already the nature of the Soviet 'Plan' that all aspects of life, political, administrative and social, should be broken down to operate within local 'cells' or neighbourhoods, maximising contacts and minimising travel distances. Pasternak saw this new organisational structure as 'the central force for the new physical structure of the city ... In rebuilding housing areas we have to see that the central catalyst or nucleus of each district cannot be dispersed, but must stand in one place: it will be a skyscraper.' Then he combined this functional analysis with a classically Russian conception of the urban settlement as a three-dimensional object in the landscape to be sculpturally composed in its own right.

'The town is the maximal concept of architectural spatial forms, where all subordinates and is subordinated, and the result is not an aggregate but an organism ... This is not observed in the towns of the New World – the Americans make a mistake here. The silhouette is a city's physiognomy ... The task of the architect and planner consists in finding those qualitative and quantitative relationships between the high buildings and the low ones, which will be functional in relation to the live development of the city; in other words, to find the limits to possible urbanisation.

'Thus in the housing periphery, where high buildings are the accents amongst lower structures, the architect must find the percentage concentrations in relation to the rhythmic strokes of the skyscrapers. In this game of oscillations he must uncover and manifest the particular character of the town being planned.' [24]

All this was intended not as a solution but as an approach. 'We are not trying to delineate an ideal type of town, or an abstract theory', he insisted, 'we are merely trying to outline a direction of thinking.' But how was it to be moved further?

We return here to the themes of Chapter 5. In following the development of the Constructivists' 'functional method' we saw how Ginzburg had already focused in *Style and Epoch* upon the dynamic organisation of forces and material in the machine as a potential model for spatial organisation in the new architecture. Chapter 6 and its Documents have shown how during this year, 1926, they returned to the supremely modern machine, the aeroplane, as an object-lesson in taking the approach further (and further than Le Corbusier did). 'Architects! Do not imitate the forms of technology, but learn the method of the engineering designer, the *konstruktor*'. And what was that method? As the engineer Akashev's article alongside demonstrated [Document 10], it was a mathematical analysis of the dynamic forces operating in and around the object. Another bold slogan in the middle of his paper declared 'This is the way to understand the materialistic foundations of the aesthetic of Constructivism.'[25]

It is significant to the eventual fate of their ideas that even as these first injunctions to study the machine were being formulated by the Constructivist leaders, the very man who had initially been the avant-garde's greatest patron after the Revolution was already declaring the machine to be politically unacceptable as a source of inspiration. In mid-1926, Commissar of Enlightenment Lunacharsky was declaring to the State Academy of Artistic Sciences Gakhn, successor to Rakhn, that:

'It is being said that this is a new stage in human history; that the proletariat is entering the stage of urbanisation; that the machine is poetic; that the factory is the most powerful thing that can be seen on earth; that any form of literary tale is a mere mirage compared to the poetic situation in which science brings about a new factory.

'I do not in any way deny that the proletariat may find original and attractive colouration for its life in poems of productivity ... But it has to be said that ... only futurism and the artists of LEF, that seedbed of Constructivism, who are the avant-garde of a leftist Euro-American urban culture, can become wholly immersed in this element ...

'We [Bolsheviks] have not entered the world in order to make the machine the mistress of our lives, as time-and-motion study advocates like Gastev are advocating through their socio-political literature. We came in order to liberate the individual from under the power of the machine. Certainly mechanised urbanism is one source of images for proletarian poetry, but it cannot serve our needs since it can only drive the proletariat towards its own lack of humanity and personality, and that we absolutely do not want.' [26]

Just as Constructivists and other Modernists were launching their battles against all forms of traditionalism in earnest, Lunacharsky was already declaring that 'the more nourishing environment for proletarian arts is that mass of vernacular, peasant work ... which evolved over the course of centuries, ... because of its multivalued character, and because of the collective nature of the basic principles underlying the products themselves.'[27]

In fact the Constructivists were far from rejecting Lunarcharsky's view that the vernacular could be 'almost irreproachable in the inner rigour and order of its crystallisation of form', in settlement patterns as in individual buildings [cf. p.51]. But they regarded them as structures to be understood 'in relation to the climatic, technological and economic conditions of each area', not as forms to be imitated.[28] Such analysis was inevitably too subtle for increasingly tense times.

From objects to processes

After Pasternak's initial discussion of overall urban form in *SA*, the Constructivists concentrated for several years on reformulating what he had called 'the elementary architectural masses' which comprised it. Some of this work on housing was mentioned in Chapter 5, and numerous other building types are illustrated on pages 42-59. During the next few years they ventured into quasi-planning questions only as far as they were thrown up by debates on housing.

Obsessed as they were with the spatial economics of 'flow', with routes and expenditures of time, these parameters of the housing district were the main subject of their mathematical battle with the increasingly powerful advocates of so-called 'extensive' urban development through cottage housing. These people were in general the legatees of the pre-Revolutionary Garden City movement. This was nominally re-established in the early twenties, and made new contacts with European Garden City Associations that it could not sustain.[29] But in the person of Nikolai Markovnikov, whose work has been mentioned in Chapters 4 and 7, the new Housing Cooperative movement was advancing again some of the old arguments about the undesirability of extreme urban concentration. In 1927, the young Constructivist Mikhail Barshch had something of a set-piece battle with Markovnikov on the pages of *SA* and the official journal *The Building Industry*, over the issue summed up by the question 'Extensive or Intensive development?' Markovnikov argued the economics of the 'extensive' model, for which the new Sokol garden suburb on the North edge of Moscow, planned by Shchusev with houses designed by himself, served as a 'socialist' demonstration [p.86]. Markovnikov claimed to show that a low density of '60 person per hectare is economically more justified than 200 persons a hectare'. Barshch declared such housing 'a disastrous influence on cultural development'. It went 'absolutely contrary to the need to maximally free workers from household labour and thereby raise the cultural level of the whole country', but was also 'paradoxical' mathematically.

Having meticulously calculated comparative maintenance and snow clearing costs, heat-loss surfaces, pipe lengths and travel distances between a site developed like that, and one with the same accommodation 'intensively' developed with compact, collectivised 'blocks' of several stories, the Constructivists' conclusions were unequivocal:

> *'If you want a healthy and civilised dwelling under today's conditions, today, now; if you want to free the woman worker from the domestic burdens she is currently having to carry, then you are obliged to reconcile yourself to the small disadvantages of intensive development.'* [30]

This argument laid the foundation of all their housing work in the mid 1920s, and the whole 'communal house' concept demonstrated in their complex for the People's Commissariat of Finance, Narkomfin (Chapters 5 and 7) and other housing schemes. Methodologically however this statement was important for its conditionality. It represented a particular and important demonstration of the principle that, in Ginzburg's words, 'Form is a function, x, that has always to be evaluated anew by the architect ... in accordance with the changing conditions of the form-making situation'.[31] As was consistent with their principles, therefore, Barshch's assertion was accompanied by the rider that 'certainly intensification [i.e. compact urban development] is not a dogma. It is not a universal or eternal truth. But today's economics dictate it to us mercilessly.'[32]

In the USSR of the 1920s today's economics became tomorrow's very quickly. In autumn 1927, in an *SA* editorial to mark the tenth anniversary of the Revolution, Ginzburg was deploring the failure of state building to exploit the town planning possibilities created by land nationalisation.[33] By the next year, however, with the launching of the first Five Year Plan, the Soviet Government's political priorities were changing and technological possibilities were expanding. Industry was now deemed to have got outputs back to the 1913 levels which were the economists' historic datum and hence the target of the whole so-called 'restoration' period of the middle Twenties. The first Five Year Plan which officially started in the budget year 1928/9 then launched the historic new stage of 'socialist reconstruction'. Responding to this new perspective, the Constructivists resolved at their conference of April 1928 'to consider the planning of the town', as they already considered the design of buildings, 'only in relation to all the factors having an influence upon its character, and its role in the socialist reconstruction of the country.' Their resolution went on to assert that 'The functions of the city must henceforth be studied not in their static condition, but in terms of their change, dialectically, looking as far as it is possible to see into their future development.'[34]

What then was the 'process' that interested their rivals the Rationalists at this urban scale? As before, a different one: the process of perception.

In mid-1926, contemporaneous with publication of Lissitzky and Krinsky's skyscraper projects in the sole issue of Asnova's *Izvestiia* and with the first issues of *SA*, and just before Lunacharsky's anti-machine speech, the Rationalist Nikolai Dokuchaev published a position paper on 'Architecture and the planning of towns' in a journal where he often wrote, *Soviet Art*. Dokuchaev was the third of Asnova's founder-leaders, with Ladovsky and Krinsky, but he was closer to professional practice than them and was regularly the author of their position papers or their attacks on others.

Dokuchaev also addressed the models offered by Europe and America.

'There is now a whole literature [and] a new science on town planning (he is firmly using the now well-established term *gradostroitel'stvo*) and on urban improvement (*gorodskoe blagoustroistvo*) or what is known as "urbanism", a literature thrown up by the urgency and importance' of the practical crises of 'traffic, fresh air and so on'. 'The French architect Corbusier-Saugnier' he says, 'has lately made a charming proposal for solving this, which is the very latest novelty in the West.', and Dokuchaev showed some pictures. 'But even this has the same fatal shortcoming of all such concentrations on technical issues, that it only partially touches on questions of the architectural treatment, and even then regards them as incidental.'

This 'underestimating of the role of architecture in the practice of town planning produces results that are merely palliatives' declared Dokuchaev. People assume that architecture 'should simply come in after the street network has been laid out and the plots for development have been defined.'

'Here we see merely the narrow understanding of the task of architecture to which the broad mass of the population subscribes. As they will usually say, architecture is about rich facades, decoration, beautiful forms. Hence they conclude: Architecture is not for us, especially under the current "regime of economy". What we need is technology with its advanced methods, economic efficiency, practicality and relevance. However a somewhat more careful look shows that this supposedly pure "technology" can never manage without application in some degree or other of the form-making resources of art in order to produce its products. ... since form, the image of the form, with its organisation and coordination, has enormous importance in the process of invention.' [35]

This is even more true in the city, where 'Architecture must not only solve practical technical and constructional tasks; it must also solve formal tasks, that are of equally practical necessity.' The practical purpose of these formal tasks is quite explicit. It is:

'to manifest all [the building's] qualities, its constructive and rational characteristics in such a way that their meaningful perception by the viewer can be accomplished easily, without mistakes, with the minimal expenditure of energy and time. In solving the problem of space, architecture, by manifesting the mutual relationships and hierarchies of things, serves as one of our organic necessities for orienting ourselves and moving around in real space.'

Historical models of great cities like Rome show that this is nothing new, says Dokuchaev, in terms that echo the arguments of Benois' group before the Revolution. 'Architecture has always given formal organisation to the way of life, giving it order, powerfully acting on the individual, determining his mood, arousing him to activity or contemplation and serving as a real factor in his cultural development.' City planning like architecture will thus be a 'synthesis'. What matters is that:

'The plan of the town or replanning of its parts must be drawn up around a specific idea, a concept, that fully answers to the cultural, social and state significance of the town, conforms with the organisation of its parts as much in its formal and spatial orientation as in technical and utilitarian respects.'

He discussed how relationships between some major Moscow landmarks, like the Cathedral of the Saviour and the Ivan Bell Tower, demonstrated 'formal factors which influence the extent of expressiveness of architectural structures and of whole urban ensembles ... all of which remain applicable to questions of town planning today.'[36]

This whole approach and set of assertions followed very naturally from the line which Asnova had adopted at its formation in the very early Twenties, discussed in Chapter 4 above. Two years after this paper, in autumn 1928, Asnova split over the issue of how to approach town planning. Like OSA their thoughts were increasingly focussed onto this scale of work by the start of massive building programmes outlined in the First Five Year Plan. Whilst OSA were increasingly moving towards analysis of dynamics of technology, Ladovsky created a breakaway group called ARU, the Association of Architect-Urbanists, leaving Krinsky and Dokuchaev to head Asnova, while he set out to pursue a more purely formal approach.

Dynamics of form or system?

Ladovsky was preoccupied with the 'evolution of the urban dynamic' as 'the tempo of socialist construction and economic development impacts ever more upon our cities'. But he wanted in a more abstract and theoretical way than the others, to study 'the planning and architectural formation of towns as a socio-psychological factor in the cultural and educational development (*vospitanie*) of the masses.' He believed this perceptual approach could offer the Soviet planner a uniquely powerful tool where at present there was inertia. As ARU's founding statement declared:

'In a series of its edicts, the state has outlined the path of a planned regulation of town planning. Examples are the Central Committee decree of 4.X.1926, and the Commissariat of Interior's Instructions etc. Meanwhile our architectural community has so far devoted almost no effort to pursuing any organised solution of the whole group of questions concerned with townplanning.'

On the other hand:

'The fundamental characteristics of a city in a socialist system, which distinguish it in particular from theoretical and practical models in the West, are its aspiration to fully eliminate the social inequalities amongst the population, its aim of simplifying and eventually banishing any class structure in society, its nationalisation of land and elimination of all alienation of land or speculation in it, all of which open up a broad path to a rational replanning and development of our existing towns.

'These circumstances give the Soviet architect the possibility to solve the questions of urbanism by methods that are inaccessible to the Western planner ...

'The soviet state, which has put the principle of planning and control at the cornerstone of all its activity, should also utilise architecture as a powerful means for organising the psychology of the masses. However, unfortunately, the objective levels of development of the humanitarian sciences, the completely inadequate development of the science of art, and the insignificant results that have emerged from modern psychology, do not give us the possibility fully to appreciate that psycho-organisational role which the spatial arts can have in life. Therefore the architect has not so far been able to

occupy the position in town planning which by rights belongs to him. ...

'The architectural structures of the city directly influence the feelings of the "consumer" of architecture, producing a certain world-view by its forms and appearances. ... Architecture, understood as a unified spatial whole, should solve the task of grouping buildings into a unified spatial system.'

'Such a definition of town planning', ARU insisted, 'offers the unique basis for solving architectural tasks as a system of psychologically and ideologically powerful forces acting on the social whole of the city'. To apply this to 'the mass of towns of the USSR, a far higher level of organisation of specialist workforce is necessary', they declared, which must be recognised 'by an initiative of state and society'.[37]

The reference here to 'the insignificant results emerging from modern psychology' conveys the impression that it was disappointing results from his laboratory which were pushing Ladovsky back to more empirical applications of formal dynamics. Planning projects done in competitions and by his students showed precisely the attempt to deal dynamically with 'the grouping of buildings into a unified spatial system' [p33]. The most manifestly 'dynamic' of all was his own proposal for replanning Moscow, in 1930, which dramatically split the congested circular plan into a parabola that could embrace 'the dynamic of growth'.

Meanwhile OSA were moving yet further from dynamic forms, to study implications of the dynamic of underlying technological and social processes. The result was a proposal in which cities as a 'form' dissolved entirely.

At the centre of their attention were the changing technologies of energy and communications. The national electrification progamme under the Goelro plan was already eliminating the need to locate new developments near fuel sources. Through the government's contracts with Ford, 'automobilisation' promised to flood the Soviet Union with cars, tractors and other 'automobiles'. The political traumas of the late 1920s had also brought to the top of the political agenda the old Marxist ideal of eliminating the differences between urban and rural living standards.

In these circumstances, asked an article by Mikhail Okhitovich in *SA* in 1929, is it still true 'that the crowded city is the inevitable result of the technological and economic possibilities available to us? That other solutions are impossible?' No longer. Re-examining the 'flow' aspects through the prism of their 'method' they reached dramatic conclusions that overturned all the decisions about 'intensive' development patterns which they had reached in the mid-Twenties. As Okhitovich declared:

'The revolution in transport represented by automobilisation reverses all the old arguments about the inevitability of congestion and the crowding together of activities and buildings ... Energy transmission and the new communications possibilities have eliminated the need for territorial contiguity. Space is now measured by time.'

What now becomes the logical form for the Soviet city?

'If we talk about the essence, then this new complex will not be called a point, a place or a city, but a process, and this process will be called "disurbanisation". It is the process of centrifugal force and repulsion, and is based on just such a centrifugal tendency in the new technology. Proximity is henceforth a function of distance.'[38]

In this situation the compact 'communal house' would be replaced by a scattered 'community of houses'. Cities would disappear as industrial and agricultural populations were resettled alongside each other in identical prefabricated (and stylistically rather Corbusian) cottages, with identical access to collective facilities. A linear, a-nodal community would stretch out in ribbons across the whole Soviet continent. The Corbusian aspiration of *espace, soleil, verdure* for all would be achieved, liberated from pipework by digestive systems of sewage disposal, and liberated from crowding by the automobile.

Thanks to the accuracy of the underlying observation here, congruent as it was with Western trends already observed before the Revolution, this so-called Disurbanist idea was taken seriously enough to become highly controversial. As the whole existence of Constructivism drew to a close, these proposals led to an important exchange of views between Le Corbusier, as representative of the West on the one hand, and the Constructivists as spokesmen for the Revolution on the other.

Le Corbusier saw the design projects based on this idea when he visited Moscow at the turn of 1929/30 in connection with his Tsentrosoiuz building. He wrote a letter to Ginzburg during the journey home, and his reactions were simple. 'Dispersion makes no sense', he insisted, because 'human intelligence is the fruit of concentration', and tiresome though the consequences may be, 'man aspires to urbanisation'. Ginzburg replied in the politest terms that Corbusier had missed the point:

'You are the finest surgeon of the modern city, you want to cure its ills at whatever cost ... But this is because you are trying to keep the city in essentially the form that capitalism made it. We in the USSR are in a more favourable position: we are not tied by the past.'

Liberated by the Revolution, said Ginzburg, 'We prefer to destroy this mortally sick organism, the city, and to begin work on devising a new form of human settlement that will be free of internal contradictions and can genuinely be called socialist.'[39]

When the Communist Party issued their judgment on the Disurbanist proposals they were most unusually respectful of their authors' seriousness,

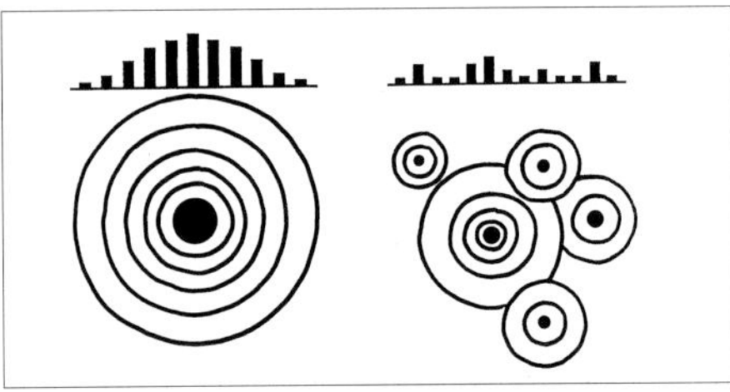

Pasternak: 'magnetic' principle underlying over-centralised capitalist city and 'districtised' soviet one [Diagram, CC].

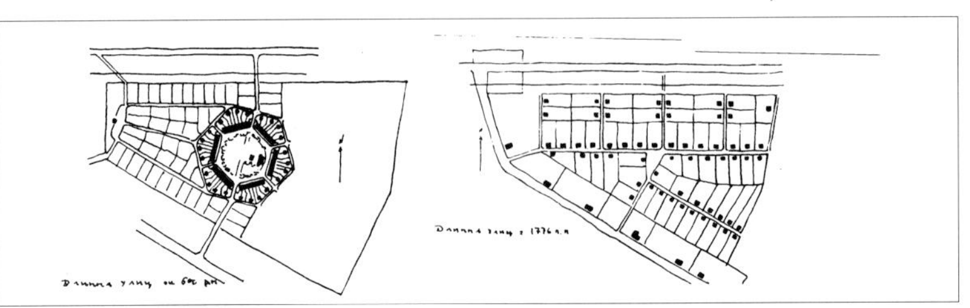

Barshch's illustrations of 'intensive' and 'extensive' development, i.e. large compact housing blocks or dispersed cottages, from his debate with Markovnikov in *SA*, 1927, no.3.

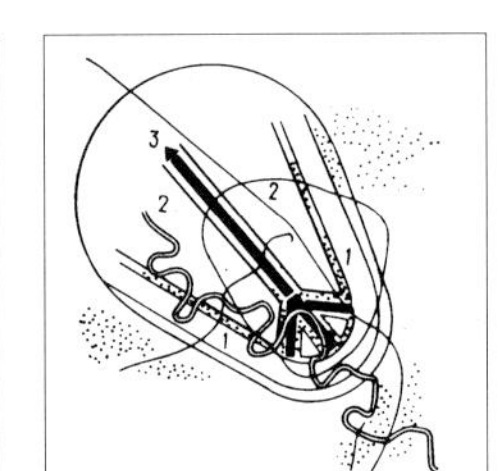

Ladovsky: 'parabolic' concept for growth of Moscow, 1930.

but could not at first separate the forms from their conventional content. 'You have only to travel in Holland from Amsterdam to Rotterdam to see such "socialism" realised,' said the Party spokesman Chernia. 'These individual structures, "maximally distant from each other", are the very ideal of the petit-bourgeoisie.' Then, rather remarkably, he conceded 'We are not arguing with these comrades about the future.' Such systems might indeed represent 'the socialist ideal' when the technologies for them really were available in the USSR. The decisive factor was political.

'Not for a moment can one forget that the petit-bourgeois mentality still prevails in this country. Not for a moment must we forget that we are surrounded externally by a desirous and powerful enemy – the capitalist world. The concentration of the proletariat IN A CONFINED SPACE, the rallying of the concentrated forces of the proletariat, is VITAL in these conditions ... Any suggestion that one can introduce completely new structures of human contacts and attitudes in one step is utterly utopian; THE PARTY OF THE PROLETARIAT CANNOT PERMIT ITSELF THAT LUXURY.' [40]

The stylistic aspirations of the Constructivist architects would die with the Palace of Soviets competition in 1931-2, but their planning aspirations, and with them their methodological aspirations, died here with their Disurbanist thesis in early 1930.

Recalling Kurchinsky's view in 1907, we see that Pre-Revolutionary and Soviet socialists thus shared the conviction that the psyche of most individuals within the mass was not yet ready for the preservation of cultural discipline 'at a distance'. Both expressed the view, found also in Western socialists' thinking of the time, that physical contiguity was the only generator of a collective will; that *Stadtluft macht frei* remained the only psychologically appropriate slogan. By the 1990s electronic technology is beginning to make the alternative a reality in the West. So far are these media from the communications technologies of the USSR in the late Twenties that one has to conclude the Party decision was sound. They must also be given credit for their rider, after all, that 'comrade Okhitovich might be right about the future'.

In a paper of 1929, written soon after he returned to Moscow, and published in Vienna the next year, Lissitzky had described the Socialist architect's battle to the West as one of 'raising the instinctual into consciousness'.[41] In part this was an echo of the Constructivist notion of the building as 'social catalyst', but intentionally or not, it contained even more forcefully the notion of an artist's role as it was being seen by the enemies of Modernism as they formulated Socialist Realism. Where the avant-gardist, as Lunacharsky had deplored in his Gakhn speech of 1926, is irretrievably 'secluded in his personal sphere of life', the Socialist Realist artist and professional's role was to remain inside the collective, leading it forward at a pace the mass can manage, rather than setting up distant flags to which they may one day learn to run. The Party's rebuttal of the Disurbanist idea was effectively another assertion of just that principle.

■

1 For example: G.D. Dubelir, Introduction to G.P. Kovalevskii, *Bol'shoi gorod i goroda sady* (The Large City and Garden Cities), Kiev, 1916 **2** I.B. Shub, 'Stroitel'stvo v gody vosstanovitel'nogo protsessa 1923/4-1926/7', *Plannovoe khoziaistvo*, 1926, no.10, pp.43-56 **3** B. Lubetkin, 'The Revolution of 1917', part 2 of a lecture given Cambridge, 1969, London 1971, published in P. Coe & M. Reading, *Lubetkin and Tecton: Architecture and Social Commitment*, London 1981, p.196. The full passage contains much other more colourful detail. **4** The first course was launched at the Academy in 1910 by Leonti Benois's assistant Marian Peretiatkovich and it was replicated in the following year in Kiev by Dubelir. **5** R. Baumeister, *Stadterweiterungen in technischern, baupolizeilicher und wirtschaftlicher Beziehung*, Berlin, 1876. J. Stübben, *Der Städtebau*, Darmstadt, 1890. R. Unwin, *Town Planning in Practice*, London, 1909. **6** 'Dekret o zemle' (Decree on Land), approved by Congress of Workers and Soldiers' Deputies, 26 Oct 1917, publ. *Izvestiia* of their Central Executive Committee (TsIK), 28 Oct 1917, p.1; from facsimile in E. Teumin, ed., *Lenin (V. I. Ul'ianov)*, memorial volume, OGIZ-GIPL (State Publishers of Political Literature), Moscow, 1939 **7** For early planning documents see V. Khazanova, comp., *Iz istorii sovetskoi arkhitektury 1917-25. Dokumenty i materialy*, Moscow, 1970, pp.13-25. For a broader discussion see C. Cooke, 'The Town of Socialism: the origins and development of Soviet townplanning', PhD thesis, University of Cambridge, 1974. **8** F.E. Enakiev, 'Osnovy razvitiia sovremennykh gorodov' (Fundamentals of the development of contemporary cities), and 'Plan preobrazovaniia goroda S. Peterburga', *Trudy IV s"ezda russkikh zodchikh, 5-12 ianv. 1911* (Proceedings of the 4th Congress of Russian architects, 5-12 Jan 1911), St Petersburg, 1911, pp.607-25 and plates **9** V.N. Semionov, *Blagoustroistvo gorodov*, Moscow, 1912, p.2. **10** M. A. Kurchinsky, *Munitsipal'nyi sotsializm i razvitie gorodskoi zhizni*, St Petersburg, 1907, p 29. Vandervelde's book published in Russian in Moscow in 1901. **11** K. Marx, 'Letter to the editor of *Otechestvennie zapiski*', 1877. **12** Quoted from archival materials in S.O. Khan-Magomedov, *Rodchenko: The Complete Works*, London, 1986 **13** 'Neboskreb na Liubianskoi ploshchadi: proekt V F Krinskogo' (V.F Krinsky's project for a skyscraper in Liubianka Square) *Izvestiia ASNOVA*, 1926, no.1, p.5, and V.Lavrov, 'Neboskreby SSSR i Ameriki' (Skyscrapers of the USSR and America), ibid, pp.1 and 4. **14** 'Seriia neboskrebov dlia Moskvy. Proekt El Lisitskogo' (A Series of Skyscrapers for Moscow: El Lissitzky's Project), *Izvestiia ASNOVA*, 1926, No 1, pp.2-3. See Document following this chapter. **15** A. Gan, *Konstruktivizm*, Tver, 1922, pp.53, 63, 64. **16** M. Ginzburg, *Stil' i epokha*, Moscow, 1924, p.128. An English translation by A. Senkevitch was published by MIT Press, 1982. **17** 'Bruklinskii most' (Brooklyn Bridge), 1925. Poem appears in most Mayakovsky collections. **18** Ginzburg, *Stil' i epokha*, pp.93, 121, 128 **19** W.C. Brumfield, 'Russian perceptions of American architecture, 1870-1917', in W. Brumfield, ed., *Reshaping Russian Architecture: Western technology, utopian dreams*, Cambridge, 1990, pp.43-66 **20** B. Korshunov, 'Urbanisme', *SA*, 1926, no.1, pp.37-8. **21** M. Ginzburg, 'Amerika', *SA*, 1926, no.1, p.38 **22** A. Pasternak, 'Amerika', *SA*, 1926, no.4, pp.92-4 **23** A. Pasternak, 'Urbanizm', *SA*, 1926, no.1, pp.4-8 **24** ibid **25** *SA*, 1926, No 3, pp.63 and 65-6. See also Chapter 6 above. **26** A. Lunacharsky, lecture to Gakhn, Oct 1926, in: G.A. Belaia, ed., *Iz istorii sovetskoi esteticheskoi mysli 1917-32* (From the history of Soviet aesthetic thought 1917-32), Moscow, 1980, pp.85-7 **27** ibid **28** 'Rezoliutsiia po dokladam ideologicheskoi sektsii OSA' (Resolutions on speeches of OSA's Ideological Section at its First Conference, April 1928), *SA*, 1928, no.3, p.78 **29** For background see C. Cooke, 'Russian responses to the Garden City idea', *Architectural Review*, 1978, June, pp.353-63 **30** M. Barshch, 'Ekstensivnaia ili intensivnaia zastroika?' (Extensive or Intensive Development?), *SA*, 1927, no.3, pp.90-95; no.6, p.184 **31** M. Ginzburg, 'Konstruktivizm kak metod laboratornoi i pedagogicheskoi raboty' (Constructivism as a method of laboratory and teaching work), *SA*, 1927, no.6, pp.160-6 **32** Barshch, 'Ekstensivnaia', p.90 **33** 'Desiatiletiu oktiabr'ia' (For the 10th anniversary of the Revolution), *SA*, 1927, no.4-5, p.111 **34** 'Rezoliutsii' (Resolutions of the Housing and Planning Section of OSA's First Conference, April 1928), in *SA*, 1928, no.4, p.123. **35** N. Dokuchaev, 'Arkhitektura i planirovka gorodov' (Architecture and the planning of towns), *Sovetskoe iskusstvo*, 1926, no.6, pp.8-17 **36** ibid **37** 'Pervaia deklaratsiia ARU' (ARU's first Declaration), in V. Khazanova, comp., *Iz istorii sovetskoi arkhitektury 1926-32, dokumenty i materialy* (From the history of Soviet architecture 1926-32: documents and materials), Moscow, 1972, p.125 **38** M Okhitovich, 'K probleme goroda' (On the problem of the city), *SA*, 1929, no.4, pp.130-134. On Okhitovich's personal fate after these proposals see H. Hudson, *Blueprints and Blood. The Stalinisation of Soviet Architecture 1917-1937*, Princeton, 1994, pp.147-65 **39** Letters, Le Corbusier to Ginzburg and Ginzburg to Le Corbusier, *SA*, 1930, no.1-2, pp.61-62. In English: A Kopp, *Town and Revolution*, London, 1970, pp.252-4. **40** I. Chernia, 'Na zemliu!' (On to the land!), *Revoliutsiia i kul'tura* (Revolution and Culture), 1930, VII, pp.35-45. **41** El Lissitzky, 'Russland – Rekonstruktion der Arkhitektur in der Sowjetunion', *Neues Bauen in der Welt*, 1, Vienna, 1930, p.38

Doc. 31

EL LISSITZKY
A SERIES OF SKYSCRAPERS FOR MOSCOW: WOLKENBUGEL 1 (1923-25)
Izvestiia ASNOVA, no.1, 1926

The new type of building proposed here can be considered as a form of skyscraper. It is intended not for housing, but as accommodation for central institutions.

America created a particular type of high building by transforming the European horizontal corridor into a vertical lift shaft, and threading tiers of floors around it. The spread of this type took place entirely anarchicly, without any concern at all for the larger organisation of the city as a whole. The sole concern of each one was to outdo its neighbours in height and luxuriance.

In devising our type we have proceeded from entirely opposite preconditions:

1: We consider that the part is subordinate to the whole and that the system of the city determines the character of its structures;

2: We say 'structures' (*sooruzheniia*) and not buildings (*doma*) because we consider that the new city should overcome and replace the concept of the individual building.

3: We consider that so long as no means of entirely free soaring flight has been invented, it remains our natural human characteristic to move horizontally and not vertically.

Therefore if there is not enough space on a given site for horizontal planning at ground level, we shall raise the required usable area up on stilts and these will serve as the communication between the horizontal pavements of the street and the horizontal corridors of the building. The aim is maximum usable area for minimum structural support. The consequence will be a clear articulation of functions.

But is there a real necessity to build in the air?

'In general', there is not. There is still plenty of space left on the ground.

But 'in a specific case'?

We live in cities that grew up before our time. They do not satisfy the needs and the pace of our age. We cannot demolish them overnight and build them again 'correctly'. It is not possible to change their structure or type immediately. By its plan Moscow belongs to the medieval, concentric type, akin to Paris or Vienna. Its structure is as follows: a centre, which is the Kremlin; ring 'A', ring 'B' and radial streets. Its critical points are those places of intersection where the main radial streets, like the Tverskaia, Miasnitskaia etc meet the encircling ones, the boulevards. Here urban spaces [literally 'squares' in Russian] have grown up which need to be utilised without the impediment of traffic movement which is especially dense at these places: see plan. These are also the locations of the central institutions. This is where the idea for the present proposals arose.

To achieve a stable condition in a freely balanced body, three points of support are necessary and sufficient. (One leg of a four-legged table hangs in the air.) Therefore we have limited ourselves to three uprights with open channels of lifts and paternosters, and with glazed channels for staircase shafts between them. The supports operate with a system of rollers and ribs in the foundations. (This is the principle applied in elastic bridge and girder constructions.) One support goes down into the ground amongst the lines of the metro system and serves as one of its stations. Each of the other two forms a tramstop at street level. The structure of the upper working parts (offices, institutions) is a skeletal central tube, open from floor to the light above, which carries the balconies of the corridors. Thus on coming out of the lift at the first floor it is possible to read the numbers on doors of the accommodation on the second and third floors. From this central framework the horizontal floor areas are held up by brackets. The whole body is like a railway wagon placed on a column.

The skeleton is made of new types of non-rusting and high tensile steels (from Krupp). Materials used for the internal walls and floors would be light and highly insulating in both thermal respects, and to sound transmission. The glass is chemically processed to permit transmission of light but obstruct heat rays.

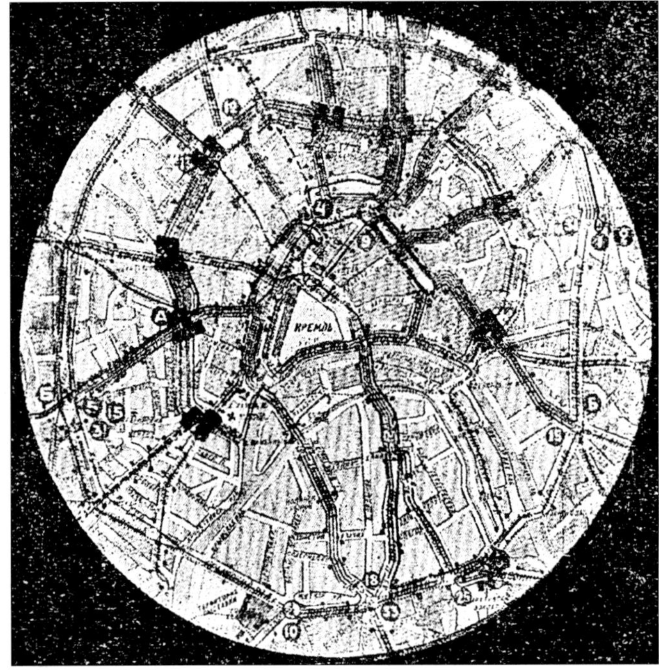

This project (Wolkenbugel) was shown for the first time at the Novembergruppe exhibition in Berlin, then at the International Exhibition of Contemporary Architecture in Mannheim.

In working out and calculating this construction I was helped by Emil Root of Zurich, to whom I am grateful and here express my indebtedness.

In the next series, WB2, an entirely different form of construction will be demonstrated.

All elements of the framework conform to standard norms, and therefore to the extent that there is a requirement to build further area on the line of ring-roads 'A' or 'B', it remains only to assemble ready-made components. The assembly process can be executed WITHOUT SCAFFOLDING: up to the stage of mounting the upper forms, the support structures are held in place with wire cables. Thus construction can take place without interrupting the traffic movement in the square below. At the same time it has the property that almost nothing of the pre-existing building stock needs to be demolished. By comparison with the American tower type of skyscrapers there are also enormous advantages in access to light and air.

1: In the three-dimensional design of this structure I have considered construction only as one of the several primary elements in achieving the required useful action (mechanical effect). As far as I am concerned one could take any other construction that could satisfy all the utilitarian requirements with the same logical consistency, if one wanted to achieve a different aesthetic effect.

2: I consider that the force of the aesthetic effect is basically determined by quality and not by quantity: it is a condition, a temperature.

3: I have proceeded from an equilibrium between two pairs of contrasts:

a) The city consists of atrophying old parts and growing, live new ones. We want to deepen this contrast.

b) The actual building derives its spatial equilibrium from contrasting vertical and horizontal tensions.

4: To give a new scale to the city, in which the individual person today does not measure distances with his own elbow, but by hundreds of metres.

5: To make a building of clearly organised elements: with ribs, planes and volumes, penetrating each other, transparent and solid, together comprising a coherent uniform spatial system.

6: From all the six basic viewpoints the given building is uniformly characterised thus:

Top: Lissitzky's plan of central Moscow with skyscrapers placed around 'ring A' (The Boulevard) at intersections with main radial roads Tversksia, Miasnitskaia etc.
Above: Typical perspective view along the Boulevard.

Diagram of the building form from different viewpoints:
1. From above **2.** From below **3.** Towards the Kremlin **4.** Looking away from the Kremlin **5.** Along the Boulevard **6.** In the opposite direction

This characteristic gives an absolutely clear orientation in the city by means of these buildings. With the whole series in place, the introduction of colour to identify each of the skyscrapers will serve to strengthen their orientational characteristics.

Doc. 32

MIKHAIL OKHITOVICH ON THE PROBLEM OF THE CITY

Extracts from SA, 1929, no.4, pp.130-4

It is necessary to reassess the nature of the possible in accordance with the requirements of the epoch.

Under present conditions, with public servicing and utilities whose cost is proportional to the width of the plot, the dwelling has had to be built upwards and backwards, and it must be constructed of strong and durable materials on solid foundations.

Does it emerge that the crowded town is the inevitable result of the technical and economic possibilities? Does it emerge that all other solutions to the problem are technically or economically impossible?

The city is a specific socially, not territorially, determined human entity ... It is an economic and cultural complex.

The question to be elucidated is now, must the different functions of the 'city' exist in one body; will they become fatally estranged by separation, as the parts of a living organism would be? In other words, is the growth of huge crowding, including 'socialist' crowding, of people, buildings and so forth on one spot inevitable, or not?

The planning of an industrial enterprise can now reflect the possibilities of conveyor belt production on the scale of the whole national economy, and eventually of the whole world economy.

The exceptional growth in the strength, quality, qantity and speed of the means of mechanical transport now permits separation from centres: space is here measured by time. And this time is itself beginning to be shortened.

The revolution in transportation, the automobilisation of the territory, reverses all the usual arguments about the inevitability of congestion and the crowding together of buildings and apartments.

We ask ourselves, where will we resettle all the urban population and enterprises? Answer: not according to the principle of crowding, but according to the principle of maximum freedom, ease and speed of communications possibilities.

All these linked functions make up a single organisational complex. But the city was also a complex. Having destroyed one form of city, will we not be creating a new city? If you like a quarrel about terminology, let this complex be a city.

Let us call it, shall we say, the Red city of the planet of communism.

If one talks about the essence, then this new complex will be called not a point, a place or a city, but a process, and this process will be called disurbanisation.

Disurbanisation is the process of centrifugal force and repulsion. It is based on just such a centrifugal tendency in technology ... which reverses all the former assumptions. Proximity is here a function of distance; community is now a function of separateness.

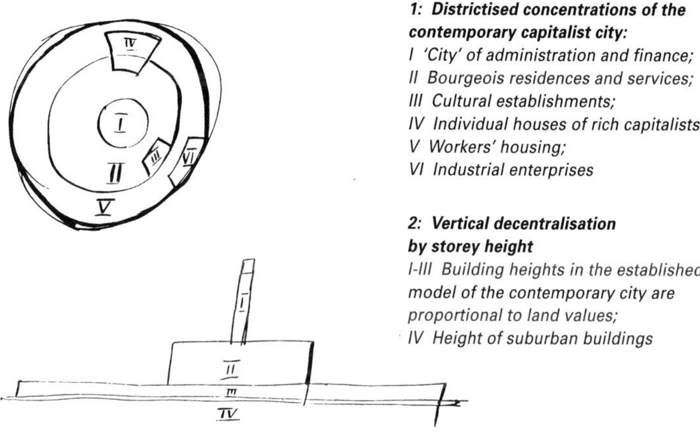

1: Districtised concentrations of the contemporary capitalist city:
I 'City' of administration and finance;
II Bourgeois residences and services;
III Cultural establishments;
IV Individual houses of rich capitalists;
V Workers' housing;
VI Industrial enterprises

2: Vertical decentralisation by storey height
I-III Building heights in the established model of the contemporary city are proportional to land values;
IV Height of suburban buildings

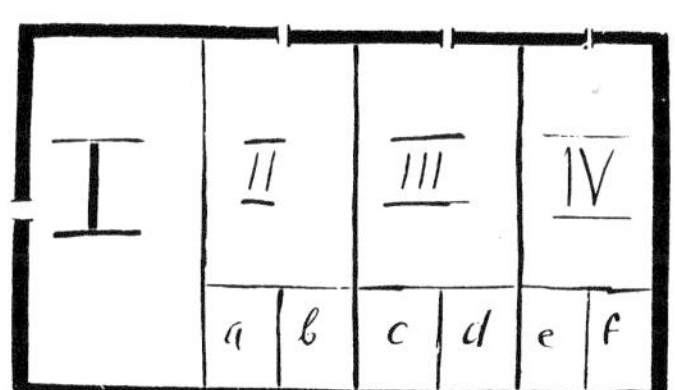

3: The normal city building in contemporary capitalism
[This is a Russian model, where the capitalist owner has his own grand residence within the block of apartments he rents out, CC]
I The building owner (capitalist);
II-IV Apartments rented to bourgeoisie;
a-f Rooms rented to proletariat or for domestic staff.

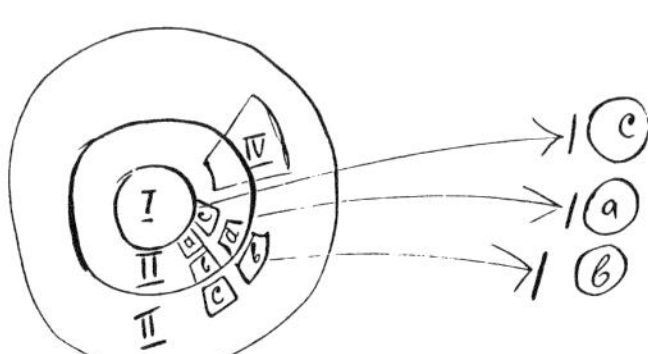

4: Specialised quarters become decentralised outside of the city for functional reasons
(a) Medical establishments;
(b) Cultural amenities;
(c) Sports and recreational facilities

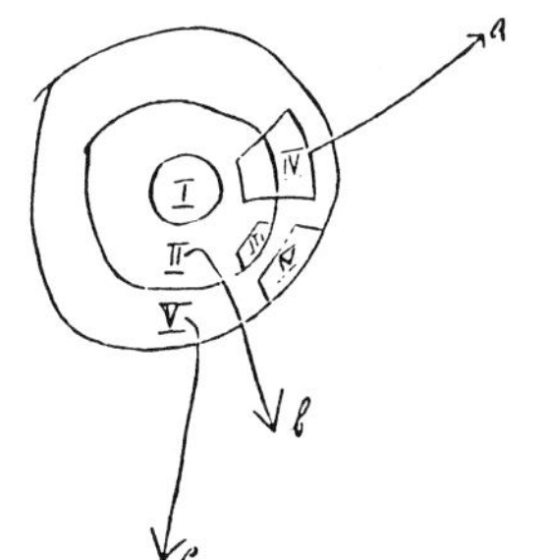

5: Decentralisation of residential accommodation
IV – a Private houses move out to become villas;
II-V – b + c Apartments become cottages.

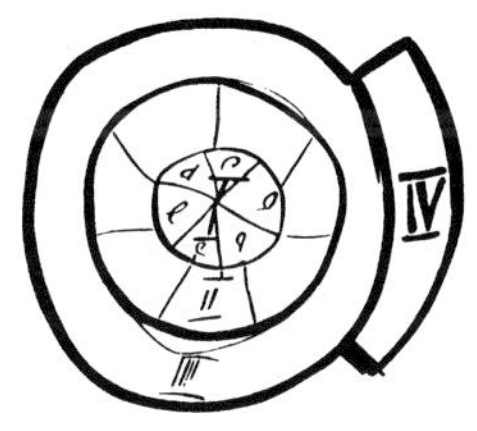

6: Concentric planning around large industrial enterprises
I The industrial enterprise; II Districts serving the enterprise, alternating with workers' housing; III Collective farms serving the population dependent on the enterprise; IV Spontaneous shanty-type growth.

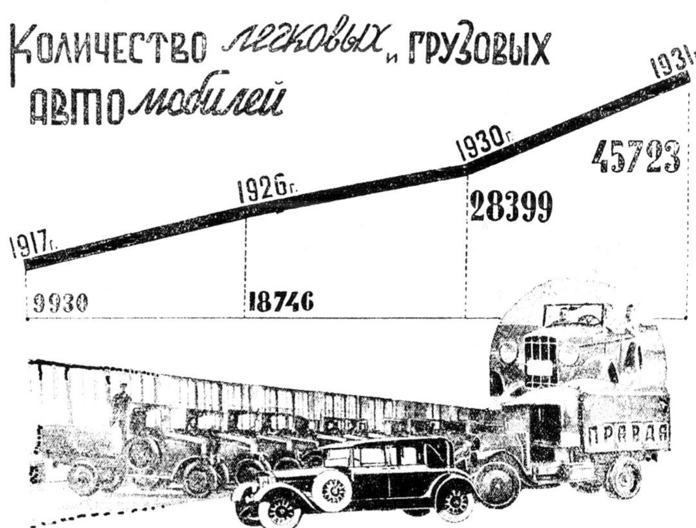

Soviet outputs 'of light automobiles and lorries', from Our Achievements*, No.1, 1932*

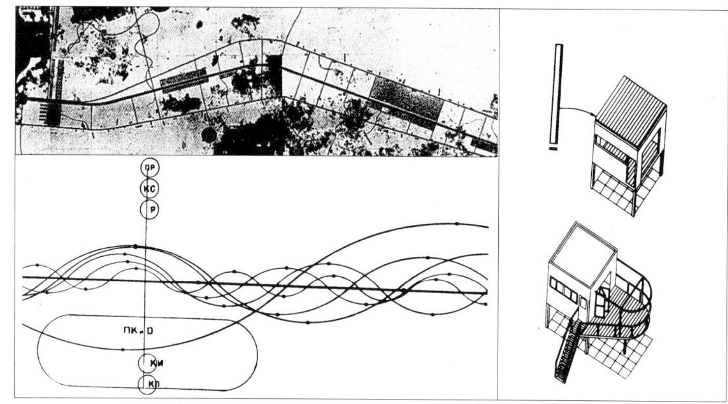

Above: Disurbanist ribbon of settlement crosses the landscape, Socialist Settlement Group under Ginzburg, 1930. Below: 'Rhythmic' distribution of all facilities along such a Disurbanist ribbon. Right: The Group's one-person housing type, prefabricated and assembled on site.

12: CONSTRUCTIVISM, SUPREMATISM AND HISTORICISM: LEONIDOV'S URBANISM AND NARKOMTIAZHPROM

In the last chapter we saw how debates about the proper pattern of settlement for the future Soviet society during late 1929 and early 1930 showed the Constructivists' design methodology to be incompatible with the priorities and politics of the Party in the Five Year Plan era. The Soviet government's long-drawn out architectural competition for a vast Palace of Soviets in central Moscow during 1931-33 is conventionally regarded, and quite rightly, as effecting a similar closure of avant-garde debate about the proper principles on which to generate a Soviet socialist architecture. That competition has now been well documented in Western literature.[1] More interesting here is thus the next question, of how the avant-garde managed to cope with the new design priorities which emerged from that competition as the principles which the Party now decreed must be followed. The medium through which this was demonstrated was another competition, far smaller in its number of entrants and of lower public profile, which took place in 1934 for an even more prominent and central site at the other end of the Kremlin, running right along one side of Red Square. This building would house the Commissariat of Heavy Industry, Narkomtiazhprom.

Two dimensions of this design task were particularly demanding. Firstly, the site involved urban design on a scale not hitherto conceived even in the Soviet Union (though such vast ensemble-making would become increasingly common as megalomania swept through the later Thirties and the years after the Second World War). Secondly, the injunctions which emerged from the Palace of Soviets decisions involved a subtle and as yet entirely undefined 'method' that demanded a wholly new kind of contextualism. The challenge of each project was now to produce a synthesis of those elements of heritage and historical context that were still politically or culturally relevant, with the most advanced technology available. Through this competition we see the incapacity of the design methods of the leading Modernists (or indeed of semi-traditionalists like Fomin) to handle either an urban design of this scale and contextual complexity, or the specific injunctions to achieving this 'critical' architectural synthesis of old and new.

Only one scheme, amongst either traditionalists or the avant-garde, produced anything that could be said to represent such a genuinely new synthesis. This was by the young Constructivist Ivan Leonidov who had already distinguished himself, as we saw in Chapter 10, by a somewhat different approach. He solved the urban design aspects through the tools of spatial composition at this scale which set him apart in the Twenties and were drawn from Suprematism. Architecturally, he achieved a synthesis of advanced technology with an extraordinarily subtle contextual analysis – this latter undoubtedly fed by his peasant origins and innate feeling for the deeper elements of medieval Russian compositional systems. The scheme was naturally not lauded for any such achievements in its time. Looked at it in a longer perspective, however, it seems to me to represent a uniquely sophisticated model, then or later, of what this new synthesis demanded of Soviet architecture could be. It can now be better understood amidst present concern to remake historic cities with precisely this synthesis of innovation and continuity.

Legacies of the Palace competition

The Soviet professional environment changed radically for all the arts during the years 1931-33 while the government was deliberating over the Palace of Soviets. All the independent literary and artistic organisations of the Twenties were dissolved by a government decree of 23 April 1932 and soon after that architectural groups were replaced by one single official Union of Soviet Architects.[2] Leading names of the Twenties were appointed to its Board alongside many who were intensely hostile to them.[3]

The competition itself had been an invitation for all trends to display themselves through an absurd design task. Auditoria for six and fifteen thousand workers' delegates were to be the core of a building that would 'show our friends and foes' what Stalin and the Party considered their status in the world. Ton's memorial cathedral to the defeat of Napoleon [p.7], which had barely been finished forty years, was summarily demolished. All Modernists who attempted to solve the brief as a practical design task were in different ways defeated by it. Of the Western entries, Corbusier's was the most innovative and hence the most vilified. Soviet architects – Rationalists, Constructivists and others – hardly produced more than diagrams. Inevitably the diagrams which were clad in some grammar of 'architecture' looked more sophisticated than those with bare walls of unspecific 'modern' materials. As the stages of elimination proceeded, all pretence at functional critique gave way to aesthetic critique. 'Bits scattered around', as Modernists tended to do, and anything looking 'like an accidental agglomeration' or 'industrial' was deemed 'on principle' unable to communicate either 'an impression of plannedness' or 'unity of ideological expression'.[4] Under Lunacharsky's aesthetic guidance, the Palace Construction Committee declared the building must be 'ideologically active' in 'characterising the epoch and embodying the workers' aspiration towards communism'. If this was indeed the main purpose, it was reasonable for them to specify that:

'The functional method of design must be supplemented by a corrective: an artistic treatment of the form. All the spatial arts must be employed: architecture, which gives proportionality to the parts; painting, which uses colour; sculpture, for its richness of light and dark, in combination with lighting technology and the art of the theatrical producer.' [5]

Notions of a 'union of the arts' here were closer to those of Shekhtel than Tatlin, but the message and audience were no longer individual. With the ruthlessness that would only be fully manifest a few years later, they were the messages of the Second Five Year Plan, Collectivisation and the Purges.

No one knew what this synthesis would mean for architecture till they saw it. Guiding principles did exist, however, in those Marxist conceptions of cultural continuity discussed in relation to the early political festivals in Chapter 3. As the competition entered its 'open' stage in summer 1931, Moscow Party Secretary Lazar Kaganovich had very publicly deplored 'the lack of serious Marxist-theoretical bases for our practice' in architecture and city planning. As they embarked on devising the 1935 Stalin Plan for making Moscow 'the model socialist city', he challenged the profession 'to devise an architectural formulation of the city that will give it the necessary beauty'.[6] In terms of style, the principle of continuity was in fact spelt out in relatively unprejudiced terms when the Construction Committee decreed that:

'Without any specific prejudgements on style, design explorations must be directed towards utilisation of both the new and the best models of traditional architecture, simultaneously operating with all the achievements of contemporary architectural and constructional technology.' [7]

Out of this insistence on 'using the best models of traditional architecture' came the crucial concept of 'critical assimilation of the heritage' which defined the filter through which 'continuity' would operate to make the new Realism 'Socialist'. To draw on the heritage 'critically' meant to select those structures, paradigmatic features, symbolic elements – or in literature and art, those myths, narratives and heroes – which embodied some ideal integral to the Party's vision of socialism, and used it aspirationally.[8] A discussion of architecture in the Party paper *Izvestiia* in 1932 made it clear that 'assimilation does not mean copying: it is a creative activity of upward march from the peaks of former culture towards new achievements.[9] Even more open-endedly, in conditions of cultural diversity and constant technological advance, the result of that injunction would clearly never be a unitary set of stylistic motifs. As Lunacharsky put it in 1933:

'Although the word "style" does not have any fully exact, established definition, one must object strongly against any identification of the term "Socialist Realist" with any specific style, since Socialist Realism presumes a diversity of styles, indeed it requires a diversity of styles.' [10]

In the oft-repeated phrase, Socialist Realism was thus 'not a style but a method'. This much it had in common with movements of the Twenties like Constructivism. As the Committee's talk of 'the functional method of design' has already shown, the opposition had picked up their concepts and jargon.

Amid the generalisations, four approaches to what this 'critical assimilation' of historical sources might mean for a specific building design did emerge, in 1932. According to this classification, 'critical assimilation' could be achieved firstly, by using particular compositional and spatial features of the old architecture in the new context. Secondly, it could be done by replicating the spaces and volumes of historical architecture but modernising them to fit new functions and materials. Thirdly, it could mean a more or less mechanical application of decorative and formal details. The fourth option was revival of old forms in their entirety, transposing whole 'buildings' or compositional schema to new contexts and scales.[11] Leonidov's Commissariat used the first and most powerful of these approaches.

The Narkomtiazhprom

After the complexities and relatively sophisticated discussions opened up by the Palace of Soviets project at the other end of the Kremlin, the brief for this next great Soviet competition was strangely myopic.[12] The task was manifestly one of urban design, but the brief was almost entirely concerned with internal office requirements. It made no mention of the extraordinary uniqueness of the site, though this was more central, more complex and of infinitely greater symbolic potency than that surrounding the Palace.

In medieval Russia the centralisation and rigid hierarchies of autocracy had been written on the ground in every town plan just as solidly as the

Melnikov, Narkomtiazhprom, 1934: view through bearing-like portico up one of the escalators leading from Red Square.

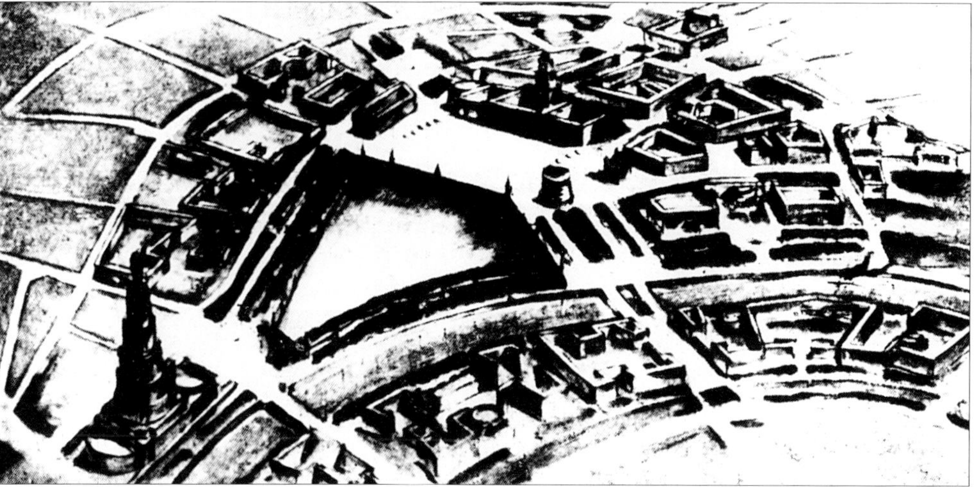

Korshunov & Zubin, perspective showing, from lower left to top right: Palace of Soviets, Kremlin, Red Square, their own Narkomtiazhprom scheme, and beyond it a schematicised Kitaigorod, which was the central business district of Tsarist Moscow.

structure of orthodox communities was symbolised in their church forms. In Moscow the radial-concentric plan which focused on the Kremlin, as simultaneously fortress, palace, seat of government and seat of spiritual authority, had made this the unitary heart of Empire in a manner not paralleled in any Western capital. Even during the two centuries while government and court were based in St Petersburg, Tsars returned to be crowned at the seat of their legitimacy in the Moscow Kremlin.

Alongside this heart of state power, the market place of Red Square, and the walled Kitaigorod area beyond it were almost equally long-established as the heart of Russian commerce. With the rise of capitalism in the later nineteenth century, this had become the central business district. Its medieval alley-ways were transformed into a dense matrix of four-six storeyed banks, corporate offices, headquarters and warehousing of the most powerful business dynasties and industrial conglomerates. Though it was never spelt out in the published literature, there was thus deep symbolism in choice of that area as headquarters of central planning for Soviet heavy industry, that *tiazhelaia promyshlennost'*, which was to spearhead the drive of the world's first socialist state 'to catch up and outstrip capitalism'.

Circulation problems generated in the surrounding area were also largely ignored in the brief. It was generally accepted however (and became an element of Moscow's 1935 Plan) that Red Square was too small for the new mass parades. These aggressively political events had long ago expanded beyond the scale of the early street festivals. The inherited Red Square was too cramped for its role as the central assembly space of the socialist world. Only the appropriate extent of enlargement was at issue.

Masterpieces which were themselves of great symbolic importance in their own times surrounded the site. They ranged from the wildest medieval polychrome of the sixteenth century victory-cathedral of St Basil's, through the cool Neo-Classicism of the Bolshoi Theatre and its elegant square, the old Gostinyi Dvor trading centre, and the Kremlin's Senate, to idiosyncratic historicism of the 1870s in the Historical Museum of crimson brick.

Russian space

In trying to work with this heritage, one crucial underlying dilemma, not clearly recognised until the early Fifties, was uncertainty about the specific nature of Russian tradition amidst all those 'national traditions' of other Soviet republics which Socialist Realism was so determined to recognise. In the resurgence of national consciousness after the Second World War, a work from the Academy of Architecture pointed out that that 'in theoretical works on Soviet architecture' there was 'extensive research on the traditions of a whole series of other Soviet republics like Georgia, Armenia, Azerbaidzhan 'but 'hardly any analysis of the national forms of architecture created in Moscow, Leningrad and the other towns of Russia.'[13]

In this context there was a relevant pointer in the most scholarly examination of Russian historical architecture of the immediate pre-Revolutionary years 1909 -12. Writing in that period when they had again studied the facts of their own tradition after its post-Petrine eclipse, the famous Igor Grabar, colleague of Benois and young Fomin, had hinted in this direction:

> *'Breadth of scope, love of freedom and spaciousness, aspiration to simplicity, these are the qualities that have constantly attended all the best Russian architects. Is it not in these features – however much they may seem undemonstrative and rather indefinite – that the future historian, equipped with data of a precision we currently still lack, will discover the national particularity of the architectural treasures created by Russia?'* [14]

These observations on 'spaciousness' and 'the aspiration to simplicity' are apposite here in relation to Leonidov's solution.

Around this site and the Palace, the obsessive creation of 'spaciousness' was intuitive and megalomaniac. More thoughtful 'opening up' would soon become one of the key aims of Moscow's 1935 Plan, sanctified by quotation from Kaganovich but coinciding with social-hygiene aspirations retained by its planners from their pre-Revolutionary practice [see Chapter 11].[15]

Legitimated by this mix of politics and principle, most Narkomtiazhprom schemes demolished large areas of the surrounding architecture. As if to eliminate the problem of contextualism they eliminated the context. Thus Fomin, Ginzburg and the Vesnins were among those who demolished the Historical Museum to the north of Red Square so that Red Square, Revolution and Theatre Squares become one vast undifferentiated terrain, and the Kremlin, Bolshoi Theatre and the entire surroundings become distant scaleless trivia. Urban composition on this scale seemed to defeat them. To the Party's horror Ginzburg even proposed demolishing 'the historically

Leonidov, competition project for the Sovkino film studios complex outside Moscow, 1927: his abstracted plan from SA, *1928, no.1, reflecting the Suprematist basis of his planning.*

Leonidov, Diploma project for a Lenin Institute of Librarianship, Alexander Vesnin's studio, Vkhutemas, 1927: the model [see also pp.174-5].

valuable Gostinyi Dvor by Quarengi.'[16] Fomin had got rid of St Basil's.

But they also demonstrated, by what they put into this void, their lack of design tools for tying the city together again at this new scale. What they put in the hole were lumps with no scalar or formal relationship to Moscow's lively historic skyline of churches and slender towers which even the Palace had sought to embellish. From Ginzburg and the Vesnins came a whole series of 'variants' of differing numbers of office blocks on a podium. They had applied a functional method to a functional brief which specified every aspect of central heating and lift capacity for a mammoth office block, and were plainly stuck in a rut with it. As urban compositions the schemes were unrelated to specifics of site or the aesthetic policy now demanded. As the official commentator Aranovich put it, they had showed yet again 'that there is almost no common ground between the solution of a building's function and the aesthetic and ideological content of architecture as an art', and they manifested 'the deficiencies of Constructivism's theory of architectural composition' in this respect.[17]

This failure at the level of urban design was the main thrust of Aranovich's official criticism on the whole competition. It was only Lissitzky, in the other official published commentary, who saw that 'Leonidov is the only one who, as his drawing sequence shows, has tried to find a unity in the whole complex created by the Kremlin, St Basil's and the new building.'[18]

In his critique of Leonidov's diploma project for the Lenin Institute back in 1927, Moisei Ginzburg had recognised the potential of the Constructivist 'unity of method' to produce 'stereotyped stylistic templates'. Leonidov's scheme, on the other hand,

> *'whilst remaining in principle a work of our philosophy, results in a purely space-oriented architecture which leads away from the traditional conception of building and towards a reorganisation of the very concept of the public space and the city in which such a building might stand.'* [19]

In that sense, as he had recognised then, 'Leonidov's work constitutes a landmark and reference point for our future work.'

Seven years later the Heavy Industry Commissariat offers a rare example of Leonidov tackling the same brief as Ginzburg and the Vesnins, and thus makes the contrast forcefully. It also refutes Anatole Kopp's judgment, as a pioneering champion of Leonidov's work, that this countrybred son of a peasant 'was an architect with nothing in his past to tie him to a cultural tradition.'[20] In this tradition undoubtedly lay the reason why Malevich's Suprematism offered not just a *tabula rasa*, but soul-food, to so many of the younger post-Revolutionary avant-garde. Each made his own disciplines from it: Rodchenko in one direction, Chernikhov in another; Leonidov in yet another, and spatially the most powerful. In projects for his 'new type' of workers' club, in particular, Leonidov had gone beyond the Lenin Institute in exploding elements of an organism across space and setting up extraordinary tensions, using his prismatic 'units of energy' just as Suprematism did, to make new connections across the voids. The composition of Sovkino film studio complex of later 1927 stood between these and the Institute.[21]

We see here that the older architects of essentially urban sensibility, to whom Rome, London, Paris had been the pilgrimage sites of their youth, and Manhattan their later dream, were in fact tuned to a wave-length of spatial density and scale that had never been characteristically Russian. The divide was never clearer than in this competition, between the peasant-born Leonidov of the wide open spaces and his teachers in mainstream Constructivism, whose origins were in the urban middle classes.

Leonidov's synthesis

As the diagram on page 205 shows, Leonidov's scheme for Narkomtiazhprom retained everything around the site. He also made it explicitly his task to tie them all into a new ensemble. 'As the focal space of the entire proletarian collective, Red Square must not be cut off from access by this proletariat, and therefore the low parts of the building must be so treated that they enter into the great ideological idea of the Square', as he explained, forming tribunes for viewing the parades. All round the site, 'low parts of my building ... are related in height to the surrounding architecture and are assembled in a composition of lesser contrasts' to form new public spaces of pleasantly human scale. On the larger context of the city, said Leonidov, 'It is natural that the role of some buildings within the ensemble of this central Moscow complex will change with the construction of a colossal new building on Red Square.' In response to the new era's values, it was now Narkomtiazhprom, not 'the Kremlin and St Basil's which must occupy the central place'. Into this 'delicate and majestic piece of music', he insisted, 'an instrument so strong

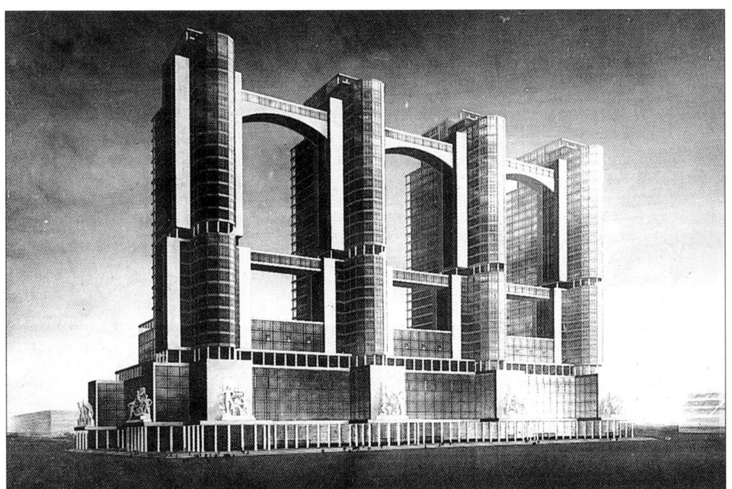

Alexander & Viktor Vesnin with Ginzburg as consultant, 1934: one of numerous variants of their Narkomtiazhprom design viewed from the north west with Red Square in the foreground.

Fomin, Narkomtiazhprom, 1934: screen facing northwards from the central courtyard on to Theatre Square and the Bolshoi Theatre.

in its sound ... can only be introduced on the condition that the new instrument will lead the orchestra, and will excel over all the others in its architectural quality.' In phrases redolent of Grabar, the means for doing this lay 'not in splendour or in the florid trumpery of details and forms, but in simplicity, severity, harmonious dynamism' and 'a clear structure of composition.'[22]

He does not explain the devices, but they seem to me clear.

The first one is certainly the triad of verticals which characterised the so-called *pogost* as the spiritual and commercial heart of the old Russian village, combining church and bell-tower with storehouse of the village's produce. The focal role of the *pogost* as symbol and locational node in the flat Russian landscape resulted from its asymmetry. From every direction the profile was different, the three elements separating and coalescing as the viewer moved. By comparison the single vertical of the Palace was entirely static. As Leonidov's montage of the Moscow River frontage shows, his building was intended as compositional replacement for the Ivan Bell-tower of the Kremlin, whose single white vertical was historically the city's visual and symbolic focus. But the *pogost* model has split the tower into three. The Ivan Bell-tower's faceted form is reinterpreted in Leonidov's triad as one circular tower and one of concave faceted form. The third, square one echoes the square lower tower adjoining Ivan's with an image of conventional modernity whose slender pinnacles on the top address those of the Historical Museum. The circular tower makes another very potent reference for Russians, to the Rostral Columns by their other former nest of capitalism, St Petersburg Stock Exchange. The Classical Gostinyi Dvor to the south, like the Bolshoi Theatre and its square to the north, provide starting points for the carefully scaled stairs and courtyard with which the ends of his complex re-engage with the old city fabric. In purely Suprematist mode a new link is also thrown from the Classical theatre to the medieval St Basil's, riotous in its polychrome, by the polychrome drum, abstract, organic, in red, white, dark green and gold, of the Commissariat workers' club. The formal source of that, consciously or not, must surely be the rural stooks of wheat.

Leonidov's perspective looking towards the Bolshoi [opposite] is surely among the most satisfying and subtle images produced by the Twenties' avant-garde, precisely because of this combination of those Russian characteristics identified by Grabar: spaciousness with such undemonstrative simplicity and deep roots in the collective cultural memory.

'Leading' not avant-garde

If this project was such a subtle demonstration of the new aesthetic 'method', and used such popularly understood reference points, why was it not acclaimed at the time? With the Palace of Soviets under construction nearby, Leonidov's work could no longer be dismissed as 'unbuildable'. Melnikov's scheme, exposing sixteen underground floors and defiant with heroic and mechanical images, was very different, but also a more subtle essay in the new rules than the Palace. In the official judgement, however, they were indistinguishable, as 'reminding us of that period in our architecture when such utopianism was considered a form of compulsory virtue, and when the creation of architectural abstractions was considered to display "progressive" architectural thinking.' Today, 'they look like an accidental anachronism' and 'make us feel vexed disappointment toward the authors who have misused their talents for artistic and spatial invention.'[23]

Both schemes were confronting the familiar situation of a public with a less developed grasp of the possibilities of a certain aesthetic rule-set than the architect. Whilst this competition was in progress, however, the ideological 'incorrectness' of this literally 'out-front', avant-garde position, and the nature of its proper socialist replacement, were clearly spelt out by Maxim Gorky in his keynote speech to the First Congress of Soviet Writers. The avant-garde position was 'leaderism'. Its artists and authors were 'full of effete self-importance and impoverished individualism'. The new artist's task was 'leadership'. His role was a 'leading' one, *vedushchyi*, leading the mass forward from a position within the popular awareness, not charting distant horizons.[24] In this model the arts must not lose contact with the sensibilities of their public, and notions of an autonomous 'condition of architecture' ceded their defining role to 'the state of awareness of the client'. After ten years of consistent statements by Lunacharsky, and a political autocracy of unsophisticated, peasant origin, it can be no surprise that the popular aesthetic values prevailed. Despite metropolitan veneers, the battle has ultimately been similar in the West.

■

1 A. Samonà, *Il Palazzo dei Soviet*, Rome, 1976; A. Cunliffe, 'The competition for the Palace of Soviets', *A.A. Quarterly*, 1979, no.2, pp.36-48; C. Cooke & I. Kazus, *Soviet Architectural Competitions*, London, 1992, pp.58-83; P. Lizon, *The Palace of the Soviets*, Colorado Springs, 1992 **2** 'Postanovlenie TsIK o perestroike literaturno-khudozhestvennykh organizatsii', 23 April 1932 (On reconstruction of literary and artistic organisations), Russian in, V. Khazanova, ed., *Iz istorii sovetskoi arkhitektury, 1926-32*, Moscow, 1970, p.163; English in C. Vaughan-James, *Soviet Socialist Realism*, London, 1973, p120 **3** On creation of Union, 18 July 1932, Khazanova, *Iz istorii*, pp.163-4 **4** M. Kriukov, ed., *Biuleten' upravleniia stroitel'stvom Dvortsa sovetov* (Bulletin of the Palace of Soviets Construction Administration), 1931, no.2-3, pp.var. **5** ibid, p.1 **6** L.N. Kaganovich, 'O gorodskom khoziaistve Moskvy' (On the urban economy of Moscow), speech to June Plenum of TsK, *Pravda*, 4 July 1931, pp.3-4 **7** 'Postanovlenie Soveta stroitel'stva dvortsa sovetov' (Statement of Palace of Soviets Construction Council), Moscow, 1931 **8** Maxim Gorky, 'Soviet literature', speech to the First Congress of Soviet Writers, 1934, in H.G. Scott, ed., *Soviet Writers' Congress*, London 1935 & 1977, pp.27-69 **9** A.N. Tolstoi, 'Poiski monumental'nosti' (Searches for monumentality), *Izvestiia*, 27 Feb 1932 **10** A.V. Lunačharsky, 'Vmesto zakliuchitel'nogo slova' (In place of a concluding word), *Literaturnyi kritik*, 1933, no.14 **11** I. Voblyi, 'Dvorets sovetov i arkhitekturnoe nasledstvo' (The Palace of Soviets and the architectural heritage), *Brigada khudozhnikov* (Brigade of Artists), 1932, no.3, pp.23-30 **12** NKTP brief, see D. Aranovich, 'Arkhitekturnaia rekonstruktsiia Moskvy' (The architectural reconstruction of Moscow), *Stroitel'stvo Moskvy*, 1934, no.10, pp.20-9 **13** Iu. Savitsky, *Russkoe classicheskoe nasledie i sovetskaia arkhitektura* (The Russian classical heritage and Soviet architecture), Moscow, 1953, p.8 **14** I. Grabar, *Istoriia russkogo iskusstva*, Moscow, 1909, vol.II, p.472 **15** *General'nyi plan rekonstruktsii g. Moskvy* (General Plan for the Reconstruction of Moscow), vol.1, Moscow, 1936 **16** Aranovich, 'Arkhitekturnaia'. **17** ibid **18** L. Lisitsky, 'Forum sotsialisticheskoi Moskvy' (The forum of socialist Moscow), *Arkhitektura SSSR*, 1934, no.10, p.5 **19** M. Ginzburg, 'Itogi i perspektivy' (Achievements and prospects), *SA*, 1927, no.4-5, p.116 **20** A. Kopp, *Ville et Revolution*, Paris, 1967, p.200 **21** On his 'Club of new social type' etc, see A. Gozak & A. Leonidov, *Ivan Leonidov*, London, 1988, pp.60 ff; on Sovkino, ibid, pp.50-2 **22** *Arkhitektura SSSR*, 1934, no.10, pp.14-15; full text in English in Gozak & Leonidov, *Leonidov*, pp.115-6. All extant drawings, incl. colour, in ibid pp.105-16 **23** Editorial, *Arkhitektura SSSR*, 1934, no.10, p.4 **24** Gorky, 'Soviet

Leonidov's Narkomtiazhprom, 1934, in its urban and architectural context.

Clockwise from right:

Ivan Leonidov, Narkomtiazhprom, 1934: perspective looking northwards up the east side of Red Square, with the Bolshoi Theatre just visible in the distance, far left.

One of the two Rostral Columns (de Tomon, 1810) outside the Stock Exchange on the tip of Vasilevsky Island, St Petersburg.

Most famous extant example of the timber pogost*, at Kizhi, north Russia: a view where the three vertical elements are separated.*

Leonidov's montage on an old print of the Kremlin river front, showing the towers of his Narkomtiazhprom in relation to the Ivan Bell-tower (1505-8) just right of centre.

Boris Iofan with Shchuko and Gelfreikh, final approved version of the Palace of Soviets as under construction: perspective of 1933.

Historical Museum (Shervud, 1874-83), which closes the north end of Red Square; a view of about 1900, Kremlin wall and gate tower just visible extreme left.

Vignette: Bolshoi Theatre (Bove, 1820s; Kavos, 1850s).

Sketch, centre, by author.

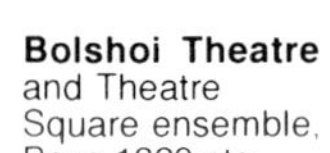

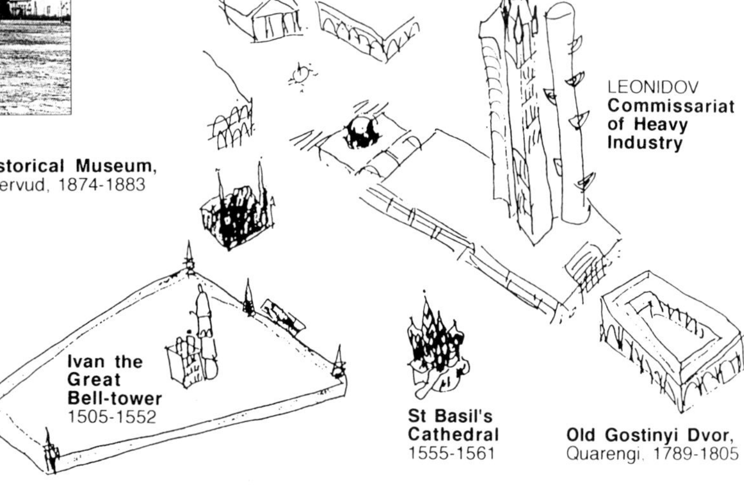

Palace of Soviets
by Iofan,
Shchuko &
Gelfreikh
under construction

INDEX OF NAMES

Wagner, Otto, 10
Walcot, William (Viliam Frantsevich), 13
Williams-Ellis, Clough, 145
Wölfflin, Heinrich, 89, 108
Women's Polytechnic, Moscow, 13
Wright, Frank Lloyd, 112, 145

Yalovkin, see Ialovkin

Zakharov, Adrian .Dmitrievich (1761-1811), archt. 6-7, 22
Zalesskaia, Liubov Sergeevna (1906-79), archt. 32
Zemlianitsyn, Boris Petrovich (1897-?), designer, 184
Zhirov, Mikhail Stepanovich (1898-1977), archt. 175
Zhivskulptarkh (Zhivopis, skulptura i arkhitektura: Group for Painting, Sculpture & Architecture), Moscow, 29-30, 161
Zholtovsky, Ivan Vladislavovich (1867-1959), archt. 26-7, 29, 51, 78, 94-5, 107, 110, 123, 160-3, 181.

INDEX OF DOCUMENTS

Abbreviations:
SA: *Sovremennaia arkhitektura* (Contemporary Architecture), Moscow, journal of the Constructivist architects' group OSA, published Moscow, 1926-30
TsGALI: Tsentral'nye gosudarstvennye arkhivy literatury i iskusstva (Central State Archives of Literature and Art), Moscow
Barkhin, *Mastera*: M. G. Barkhin, editor, *Mastera sovetskoi arkhitektury ob arkhitekture* (Masters of Soviet Architecture on Architecture), vols. 1 & 2, Moscow, 1975

Sources:
All texts translated from the original Russian except Doc. 26, translated via French. All texts complete or only very slightly edited unless indicated as 'extracts'.

1: Vasili Kandinsky p.16
Extracts from Russian original of *On the Spiritual in Art* (*O dukhovnom v iskusstve*), completed 1909, publ., 1911 **From:** V. Kandinsky, *O dukhovnom v iskusstve*, Moscow, 1992, pp.49-50, 84-5 (Colour and form); pp.97-8 (Theory).

2: Vladimir Tatlin, p.97
with Tevel Shapiro, Iosif Meerzon, Pavel Vinogradov
'The work ahead of us' (*Nasha predstoishchaia rabota*), 31 December 1920. **From:** *VIII s"ezd sovetov: ezhednevnyi biulleten' s"ezda* (*8th Congress of Soviets: daily congress bulletin*), Moscow, no.13, 1 Jan 1921, p.11

3: Nikolai Ladovsky p.97
'On the programme of the Working Group of Architects in Inkhuk' (*O programme rabochei gruppy arkhitektorov INKhUKa*), from protocols of their meetings, Moscow 26-27 March 1921 et al. **From:** unspecified archives, Moscow, published in Barkhin, *Mastera*, vol.1, pp.345-6

4: Alexander Vesnin p.98
'Credo' (*Kredo*), manuscript notes of a personal position statement to Inkhuk, April 1922. **From:** private archive, Moscow, published in Barkhin, *Mastera*, vol.2, p.14. Facsimile reproduction of ms. itself appears in S. O. Khan-Magomedov, *Inkhuk i rannii konstruktivizm* (*Inkhuk and early Constructivism*), Moscow, 1944, pp.226-7

5: Nikolai Ladovsky p.98
'The psychotechnical laboratory of architecture: a posing of the question' (*Psikho-tekhnicheskaia laboratoriia arkhitektury: v poriadke postanovki voprosa*), 29 March 1926. **From:** *Izvestiia ASNOVA* (*Asnova News*), no.1, 1926, p.7

6: Moisei Ginzburg p.120
The development of the Constructivists' Functional method through ideas in Ginzburg's theoretical writings, 1923-4 to 1927. **Diagrammatic resumé from:** *Style and epoch* (*Stil' i epokha*), Moscow, 1924; .'New methods of architectural thought' (*Novye metody arkhitekturnogo myshleniia*), *SA*, 1926, no.1, pp.1-4; 'The functional method and form' (*Funktsional'nyi metod i forma*), *SA*, 1926, no.4, pp.89-92; 'Aims in contemporary architecture' (*Tselevaia ustanovka v sovremennoi arkhitektury*), *SA*, 1927, no.1, pp.4-10; 'Constructivism as a method of laboratory and teaching work' (*Konstruktivizm kak metod laboratornoi i pedagogicheskoi raboty*), *SA*, 1927, no.6, pp.160-6.

7: Moisei Ginzburg p.120
'The housing complex for employees of Narkomfin, Moscow' (*Dom sotrudnikov Narkomfina*) **Extracts from:** *SA*, 1929, no.5, pp.161-2

8: Moisei Ginzburg p.121
'Constructivism as a method of laboratory and teaching work' (*Konstruktivizm kak metod laboratornoi i pedagogicheskoi raboty*) **Diagrammatic resumé of:** *SA*, 1927, no.6, pp.160-6

9: Moisei Ginzburg pp.129-30
'New methods of architectural thought' (*Novye metody arkhitekturnogo myshleniia*), **From:** *SA*, 1926, no.1, p.1-4

10: Engr. K. Akashev p.131
'The form of the aeroplane and the methods of designing it' (*Forma samoleta i metody ego proektirovaniia*). **From:** *SA*, 1926, no.3, pp.65-6

11: Konstantin Melnikov p.138
Manuscript notes on the construction of his house, 7 August 1927. **From:** family archives, Moscow, published in: I.V. Kokkinaki & A.A Strigalev, eds., *Konstantin Stepanovich Mel'nikov*, Moscow, 1985, p.198

12: Nikolai Lukhmanov p.139
'The cylindrical house' (*Tsilindricheskii dom*). **From:** *Stroitel'stvo Moskvy* (*The Construction of Moscow*), 1929, no.4, pp.16-22

13: Konstantin Melnikov p.153
Manuscript notes dated 11 December 1923 (*sic*: error on p.153 gives 1933) on his Makhorka Tobacco Trust pavilion, All-Russian Agricultural and Handicraft exhibition, Moscow 1923: the design principles (*Dlia vystavochnogo pavil'ona "Makhorka". Osnovy postroeniia form*). **From:** family archives, Moscow, published in: Kokkinaki & Strigalev, *Mel'nikov*, pp.155-6

14: Konstantin Melnikov p.153
'The plastic expression of form' (*Plasticheskaia vyrazhenie formy*), on his Soviet Pavilion for the Exposition des Arts Decoratifs et Industriels, Paris, 1925: part of a lecture to the Architecture Faculty, Academy of Military Engineers, Moscow, November 1933. Extracts from: manuscript notes, private archive Moscow, published in: Kokkinaki & Strigalev, *Mel'nikov*, pp.115-7

15: Unovis Group, Vitebsk: p.158
M. Kunin, Lazar Khidekel, Ilia Chashnik
'Partiinost [the nature of Party] in Art' (*Partiinost' v iskusstve*), 'Unovis in the studios' (*Unovis v mastersk-ikh*), 'The architectural and technical faculty' (*Arkhitektu-rno-tekhnicheskii fakul'tet*). **From:** *Unovis Almanac No.2*, hand lithographed 16 pp. pamphlet, Jan. 1921, pp.3-15

16: Kazimir Malevich p.159
Diagnosis and prescription of the student painter's 'health': texts of pedagogical panels nos.17-21, and other extracts, prepared in Ginkhuk, taken to Bauhaus and Poland May-June 1927, now in MOMA-New York and Stedelijk Museum Amsterdam. **From:** Original panels in exhibition and Russian texts in W. Beeren & J. Joosten, eds., *Malevich*, Amsterdam-Leningrad, 1988.
Full set illustrated & translated in Beeren, and Cooke 'Malevich: from theory to teaching', as footnote 4, p.157.

17: Alexei Gan p.159
Extracts from 'Notes on Kazimir Malevich' (*Spravka o Kazimire Maleviche*). **From:** *SA*, 1927, no.3, pp.104-6

18: Nikolai Ladovsky pp.178-9
'Foundations for building a theory of architecture (under the banner of rationalist aesthetics)' (*Osnovy postroeniia teorii Arkhitektury (pod znakom ratsionalisticheskoi estetiki*), dated 20 & 30 October 1920. **From:** *Izvestiia ASNOVA* (*Asnova News*), no.1, 1926, pp.3-6

19: Ilia Golosov p.179
Lecture notes for a programme of architectural education (*Dokladnaia zapiska k programmnoi skheme arkhitekturnogo obucheniia*), ms. notes dated 8 April 1921. **From:** TsGALI, f.1979, cat.1, doc.66, published in Barkhin, *Mastera*, vol.1, pp.406-9.

20: Ilia Golosov pp.179-80
'The concepts of form and mass in architectural composition' (*Poniatie massy i formy v protsesse arkhitekturnoi kompozitsii*), early 1920s. **Extracts from:** TsGALI, (catalogue details not given), in S.O. Khan-Magomedov, *Ilia Golosov*, Moscow, 1988, pp.210-28

21: Konstantin Melnikov & Ilia Golosov p.181
Slogans of their Vkhutemas studio 'The New Academy' (*Lozungi masterskoi "Novaia akademiia"*), 10-15 Nov. 1923. **From:** manuscript in TsGALI, Moscow, published in Kokkinaki & Strigalev, *Mel'nikov*, pp.92-3.

22: Konstantin Melnikov & Ilia Golosov p.181
'Instructions for architectural study in The New Academy' studio' (*Nakaz arkhitekturnogo obucheniia po programme masterskikh 'Novaia Akademiia'*), Nov. 1923. **Extracts from:** manuscript in private archives, Moscow, published in Kokkinaki & Strigalev, *Mel'nikov*, p.93.

23: Konstantin Melnikov p.181
'Architecture': from a lecture to the Technical College for Cinematography (*Arkhitektura: lektsii v tekhnikume kinematografii*), Moscow, 16 Nov. 1926. **From:** manuscript in private archives, Moscow, published in Kokkinaki & Strigalev, *Mel'nikov*, pp.98-9.

24: A. M. pp.181-2
'Life in the Schools' (*Zhizn vuzov*): 'The architecture students' society in Vkhutemas (*Arkhitekturnyi kruzhok Vkhutemasa*); 'The architecture students' society in MVTU' (*Arkhitekturnyi kruzhok MVTU*). **From:** *SA*, 1926, no.1, pp.23-4

25: MVTU Student Research Society p.182
'The student research society of the Industrial Building Department, Faculty of Constructional Engineering, MVTU' (*Nauchno-tekhnicheskii kruzhov fabrichno-zavodskikh stroitelei pri inzhenerno-stroitel'nom fakul'tete MVTU, Moskva*). **From:** *SA*, 1926, no.5-6, p.141

26: Moisei Ginzburg p.182
'Programme for his course on "Theory of Architectural Composition", Vkhutemas, 1926'. **From:** TsGALI , f.681, cat.2, doc.14, p.29, in French in S.O. Khan-Magomedov, *Vhutemas Moscou 1920-30*, Paris, 1990 vol.2, pp.612-3.

27: Iakov Kornfeld et al p.183
'Academic conferences in Vkhutemas, Nov. 1926' (*Konferentsiia vo Vkhutemase*): Architecture (*Arkhitektura*); Faculty of Wood- and Metal-working (*Na fakul'tete obrabotki dereva i metala*). **From:** *SA*, 1926, no.5-6, pp.135-7

28: Unsigned p.184
'Constructivism in the equipment of daily life' (*Konstruktivizm v armature povsednevnogo byta*). **From:** *SA*, 1926, no.2, inside of front cover.

29: Georgi Krutikov pp.184-5
'The architectural research laboratory in the Architecture Faculty of Vkhutemas-Vkhutein' (*Arkhitekturnaia nauchno-issledovatel'skaia laboratoriia pri arkhitekturnom fakul-'tete Moskovskogo Vkhuteina*). **From:** *Stroitel'naia promyshlennost'* (*The Building Industry*), 1928, no.5, pp.372-5

30: Nikolai Krasilnikov pp.185-7
'Problems of contemporary architecture' (*Problemy sovremennoi arkhitektury*), final diploma project in Alexander Vesnin's studio, Vkhutein. **Extracts from:** *SA*, 1928, no.6, pp.170-6

31: El Lissitzky p.198
'A series of skyscrapers for Moscow: Wolkenbugel 1, 1923-25' (*Seriia neboskrebov dlia Moskvy. WB1. 1923-5*). **From:** *Izvestiia ASNOVA*, no.1, 1926, pp.2-3

32: Mikhail Okhitovich p.199
'On the problem of the city' (*K probleme goroda*). **Extracts from**: *SA*, 1929, no.4, pp.130-4.